AUTODESK® ARCHITECTURAL DESKTOP 2006
A Comprehensive Tutorial

H. Edward Goldberg

Taken From:

Autodesk® Architectural Desktop 2006: A Comprehensive Tutorial
by H. Edward Goldberg

Taken from:

Autodesk® Architectural Desktop 2006: A Comprehensive Tutorial
by H. Edward Goldberg
Copyright © 2006 by Prentice-Hall, Inc.
A Pearson Education Company
Upper Saddle River, New Jersey 07458

This special edition published in cooperation with Pearson Custom Publishing.

Printed in the United States of America

10 9 8 7 6 5 4 3 2

ISBN 0-536-12046-3

2005200330

EM

Please visit our web site at *www.pearsoncustom.com*

PEARSON CUSTOM PUBLISHING
75 Arlington Street, Suite 300, Boston, MA 02116
A Pearson Education Company

*Many thanks to Robert Conn of the Newburgh, Indiana campus,
ITT Technical Institute, for his editorial review and selection of this textbook.*

Acknowledgments

I want to sincerely thank John E. Herridge, AIA, ADT Certified Expert and Technical Services Manager of AEC CADCON, Inc., for his help in checking this book, and for his suggestions. John is a Registered Architect, and understands the productivity that Autodesk Architectural Desktop brings to our profession.

Thanks go to Norb Howell, CEO of AEC CADCON, Inc., for his assistance in having my book checked.

I also want to acknowledge all the wonderful and dedicated people at the Building Systems Division of Autodesk in Manchester, New Hampshire, for their professional assistance, their excellent and creative work, and for their friendship. Special thanks go to Julian Gonzalez, Bill Glennie, and Dennis McNeal.

Once again, I want to acknowledge Sara Ferris and Lara Sheridan at *CADALYST* magazine for being so wonderful to work with, and to Sara for giving me the opportunity to express my opinions in print.

Lastly, I again want to thank Art Liddle, past editor of *CADALYST*, who introduced me to this excellent program and gave me my first opportunity to write for *CADALYST* magazine.

How to Use This Book

This book has been organized into two main parts: "Sections," typically made up of several tutorial exercises that illustrate commands, and "Putting It All Together," which uses the knowledge gleaned from the sections to create a building.

The exercises in this book have been designed as tutorials for most of the major commands and routines used in operating Autodesk Architectural Desktop 2006. Rather than require the student to read a great deal of verbiage and theory, this book was designed to use the "hands-on" method of learning, with each exercise guiding the student through the typical use of the commands for a subject. It is suggested that the student perform the exercises first before attempting to use the program to design a building. It is also suggested that the student perform the sections in the order presented, as they often add information for later exercises. Even if a student understands a particular command, he or she should complete that exercise either to gain new insight or to compare operator strategy. This book assumes a general knowledge of standard AutoCAD or AutoCAD LT up to Release 2004. Students without knowledge of Paperspace and Modelspace will be at a very great disadvantage. It is also important that the student have a good understanding of the Windows operating system and be able to quickly navigate the various navigation trees in that system.

Because buildings are so complex, and the variations are so numerous, 3D Computer-Aided Architectural Design (CAAD) programs such as Autodesk Architectural Desktop are not inherently easy to use. In my opinion, Autodesk Architectural Desktop has never been a program for the computer or CAD novice. Because of its complexity, one can become very frustrated when first approaching its multitude of commands, even though the programmers have gone to great effort to make this software user-friendly.

This author believes that the sign of a good operator depends on several fundamental working values.

- Use the least number of keystrokes for a particular operation. Do not use the full typed name of a command if the command can be performed with a letter alias.
- Use the Space bar on the keyboard while operating the program instead of the Enter key, except when inserting text.
- Use a strategy of operating this program as one would play a game of chess, thinking several moves ahead, and never moving backwards unless absolutely necessary.

Online Instructor's Manual

An online Instructor's Manual is available to qualified instructors for downloading. To access supplementary materials online, instructors need to request an instructor access code. Go to *www.prenhall.com*, click the **Instructor Resource Center** link, and then click **Register Today** for an instructor access code. Within 48 hours after registering, you will receive a confirming e-mail, including an instructor access code. Once you have received your code, go to the site and log on for full instructions on downloading the materials you wish to use.

Autodesk Learning License

Through a recent agreement with Autodesk Architectural Desktop publisher, Autodesk®, Prentice Hall now offers the option of purchasing *Autodesk® Architectural Desktop 2006: A Comprehensive Tutorial* with either a 180-day or a 1-year student software license agreement. This provides adequate time for a student to complete all the activities in this book. The software is functionally identical to the professional license, but it is intended **for student or faculty personal use only**. It is not for professional use. For more information about this book and the Autodesk Learning License, contact your local Pearson Prentice Hall sales representative, or contact our National Marketing Manager, Jimmy Stephens, at 1-800-228-7854 x3725 or at *Jimmy_Stephens@prenhall.com*. For the name and number of your sales rep, please contact Prentice Hall Faculty Services at 1-800-526-0485.

Walk-through

Autodesk® Architectural Desktop 2006
A Comprehensive Tutorial

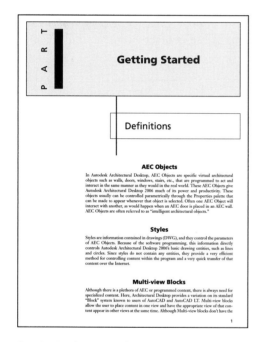

Part I—Getting Started sections provide essential information, preparing users for the guided tutorial on Autodesk Architectural Desktop 2006, including Definitions, Concepts, Abbreviations, and more.

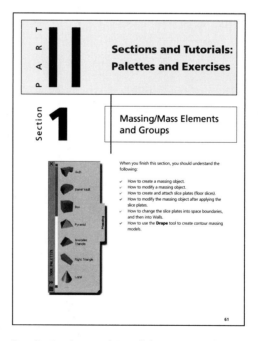

Part II—Sections and Tutorials presents Tool Palettes in the order in which they are commonly used.

514 Part II Sections and Tutorials: Palettes and Exercises

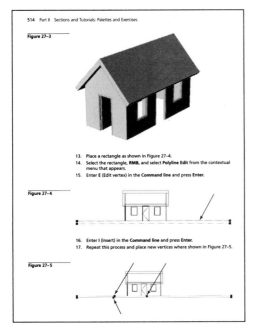

Figure 27–3

13. Place a rectangle as shown in Figure 27–4.
14. Select the rectangle, **RMB**, and select **Polyline Edit** from the contextual menu that appears.
15. Enter **E** (Edit vertex) in the **Command line** and press **Enter**.

Figure 27–4

16. Enter **I** (Insert) in the **Command line** and press **Enter**.
17. Repeat this process and place new vertices where shown in Figure 27–5.

Figure 27–5

Numerous walk-throughs and hands-on activities teach commands and routines in relation to the production of architectural drawings.

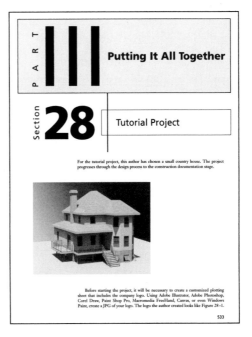

PART III Putting It All Together

Section 28 Tutorial Project

For the tutorial project, this author has chosen a small country house. The project progresses through the design process to the construction documentation stage.

Before starting the project, it will be necessary to create a customized plotting sheet that includes the company logo. Using Adobe Illustrator, Adobe Photoshop, Corel Draw, Paint Shop Pro, Macromedia FreeHand, Canvas, or even Windows Paint, create a JPG of your logo. The logo the author created looks like Figure 28–1.

533

Part III—Putting It All Together uses the knowledge gleaned from the Sections and Tutorials to create a building.

Contents

PART II   Sections and Tutorials: Palettes and Exercises   61

Section 1

Section 2

Section 3

Section 13

Section 14

Section 15

Section 16

Section 17

Section 18

Section 23

Section 24

Section 25

Section 26

Section 27

Getting Started

Definitions

AEC Objects

In Autodesk Architectural Desktop, AEC Objects are specific virtual architectural objects such as walls, doors, windows, stairs, etc., that are programmed to act and interact in the same manner as they would in the real world. These AEC Objects give Autodesk Architectural Desktop 2006 much of its power and productivity. These objects usually can be controlled parametrically through the Properties palette that can be made to appear whenever that object is selected. Often one AEC Object will interact with another, as would happen when an AEC door is placed in an AEC wall. AEC Objects are often referred to as "intelligent architectural objects."

Styles

Styles are information contained in drawings (DWG), and they control the parameters of AEC Objects. Because of the software programming, this information directly controls Autodesk Architectural Desktop 2006's basic drawing entities, such as lines and circles. Since styles do not contain any entities, they provide a very efficient method for controlling content within the program and a very quick transfer of that content over the Internet.

Multi-view Blocks

Although there is a plethora of AEC or programmed content, there is always need for specialized content. Here, Architectural Desktop provides a variation on its standard "Block" system known to users of AutoCAD and AutoCAD LT. Multi-view blocks allow the user to place content in one view and have the appropriate view of that content appear in other views at the same time. Although Multi-view blocks don't have the

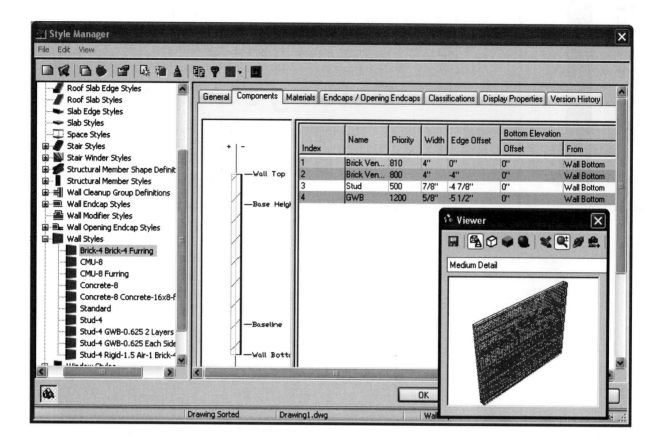

intelligence, they can increase productivity greatly. Architectural Desktop 2006 includes many routines that depend on Multi-view blocks. An exercise in the creation of Multi-view blocks is given in this book.

Tool Palettes

Common to Autodesk 2004, 2005, and now version 2006, these palettes can be sized, renamed, modified, and moved. Most of the major architectural routines are represented as icons or pictures, and they can be implemented by either dragging into or clicking in the Drawing Editor from these palettes. The developers of the program have replaced most of the standard toolbars and icons with this method in order to optimize the drawing environment for maximum productivity.

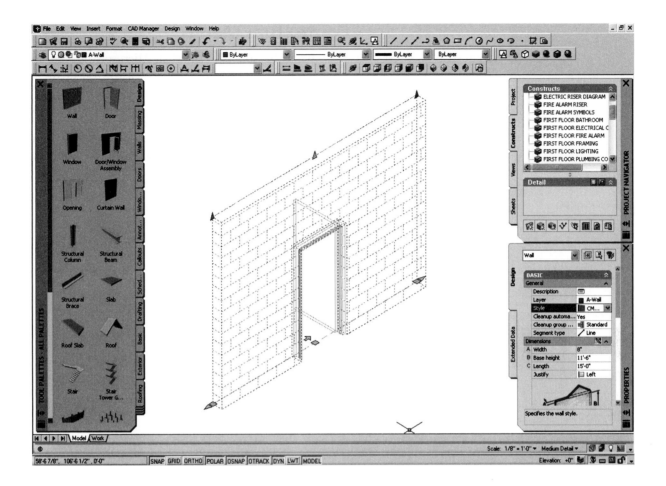

Check Boxes

Check boxes indicate the on or off state of available options. If they are in a group, several check boxes can be selected at the same time.

```
┌─ Object Snap modes ─
│  ☐  ☑ Endpoint
│  △  ☐ Midpoint
│  ○  ☐ Center
```

Radio Buttons

Radio buttons (the name comes from the button selectors on car radios) indicate the on or off state of available options. Only one button in a group of buttons can be chosen.

```
┌─ Object Snap Tracking Settings ──────
│  ○ Track orthogonally only
│  ◉ Track using all polar angle settings
```

Contextual Menus

Contextual (Context–Sensitive) menus became popular when Microsoft introduced Windows 95. Autodesk Architectural Desktop 2006 makes extensive use of these menus to control options and subcommands of various components. Contextual menus typically are summoned by clicking the right mouse button on a specific object, entity, or spot in the interface. Through programming, the appropriate menu or "context" will appear for that object at that point in its command structure. As an example, clicking the right mouse button on a door within a wall will provide all the commands available for the door and its relationship to the wall.

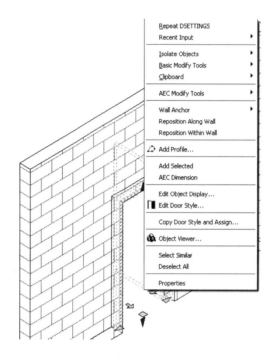

Dynamic Input

Dynamic Input is new for AutoCAD and Architectural Desktop 2006. It offers a group of features that allow to user to view the Command line at the cursor.

Pointer input: Allows you to key commands "into the pointer," which displays a small "pop-up" replacing the cursor until the command entry is finished. This allows keyboard commands previously entered on the command line to be entered "on the fly." If you type L for line entering, it will cause "L" to display in a pop-up, and as soon as you press **Enter,** the Line command will begin.

Dimension input: Allows direct entry of dimensions at the cursor or on dynamic object dimensions during grip editing. The value entered is displayed and can be edited in a pop-up at the cursor location.

Dynamic prompts: Messages that display at the cursor location to lead you through command sequences. One of the first things any Architectural Desktop user learns is *Read the command line prompts.* Along with prompts, the command line often presents a range of options for each stage in a given command. The default option is presented as a dynamic prompt, and pressing the keyboard "Down arrow" will present a pick list of all the other appropriate options.

Drafting Settings

Snap and Grid | Polar Tracking | Object Snap | Dynamic Input

☑ Enable Pointer Input   ☑ Enable Dimension Input where possible

Pointer Input

[black preview box with crosshairs]
15.1643   22.0669

Settings...

Dimension Input

[black preview box with crosshairs and dimension]

Settings...

Dynamic Prompts

[black preview box with crosshairs]
Specify first point:

☑ Show command prompting and command input near the crosshairs

💡 In a dynamic prompt, press the Down Arrow key to access options.

Drafting Tooltip Appearance...

Options...   OK   Cancel   Help

Tooltip Appearance

Model Preview	Layout Preview
2.34 < 4.65	2.34 < 4.65

Color

Model Color   Layout color

Size

0   [slider]

Transparency

0%   [slider]

Apply to:

○ Override OS settings for all drafting tooltips

⊙ Use settings only for Dynamic Input tooltips

OK   Cancel   Help

Concepts

As with previous versions of Autodesk Architectural Desktop, this new release uses three different concepts for eventually creating documentation. These concepts are the mass model concept, the space planning concept, and the virtual building concept. Of course, you can always operate Autodesk Architectural Desktop 2006 as a typical 2D electronic CAD drafting program, but that really negates the benefits of the virtual building features and eliminates much of the intrinsic volumetric information endemic to the virtual building.

The Mass Model

The mass model concept is based on a modeling tradition called "massing model" used by many architects. In that system, the architect or designer makes a cardboard, wood, or clay "study model" of the building. These small models often show the relationship between parts of the structure while also indicating scale and the effect of light and shadow on the facades. Typically the architect would create more sophisticated models later while creating the construction documents.

In Architectural Desktop 2006, you can make very sophisticated virtual massing models. These massing models can then be sliced into "floorplates" or horizontal sections from which walls can be generated automatically. These walls are the connection point between the massing model and the construction documentation in Architectural Desktop 2006.

Space Planning

The space-planning concept is one that has been used by architects and designers for years. In this concept, rectangles and circles represent building program areas. The designer then places these forms in relationship to each other to create "flow diagrams." After the relationships have been established, they are then used to help create the form of the structure. In Autodesk Architectural Desktop 2006, the developers took this one step farther by combining a 3D component to the relationships. Every space planning object also contains information about floor-to-ceiling heights, and floor-to-floor heights. After the space planning has been completed, the space plan can be converted automatically into three-dimensional walls into which doors, windows, and so on can be added. These three-dimensional walls, etc. can then form the basis for construction documents. Besides being the basis for construction documents, the space plan can be culled for space information that can be transferred to data base programs.

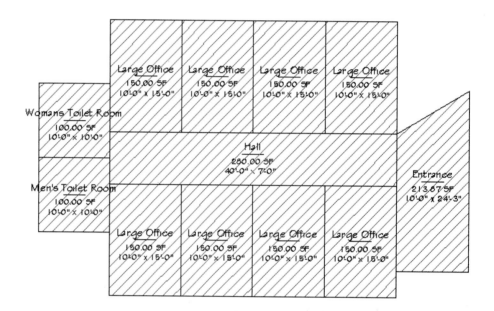

The Virtual Building Model

The virtual or 3D model differs from standard electronic drafting with the concept of placing components of a building much as one would place objects in the real world. Instead of drawing lines and circles, one places doors, windows, walls, roofs, and so on, which can be controlled or modified parametrically and relate to each other as they would in the real world. To this end Architectural Desktop 2006 has a myriad of parametric tools. The virtual building concept has been greatly discussed by architects and designers and is generally accepted as the direction that CAAD is progressing. Autodesk Architectural Desktop 2006 and its previous releases have always been considered leaders in this trend.

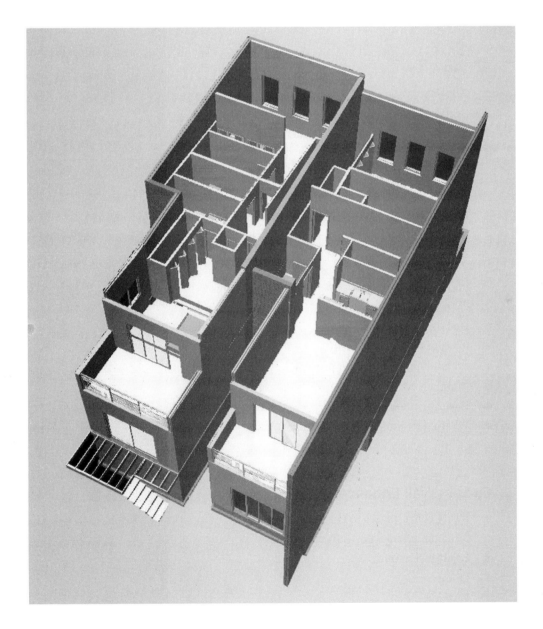

New Architectural Desktop Features for 2006

Details and Keynoting

- More detail components
- Masonry anchors
- Control joints
- Roof copings
- Add Component Wizard
- Easily add new detail components—Details Database Editing
- Make custom content accessible via Detail Component Manager

Edit-In-View

- Allows work on specific portions of your design in any view
- Section
- Elevation
- Plan
- Streamlines existing view creation methods
- Reduces dialogs and steps
- Easily change UCS
- Select Linework or Face

Object Conversions

- Reduce rework
- Change objects on-the-fly
- Streamline modification process
- Maintain consistency
- Layering Standards
- Width, Height, Vertical alignment

Curtain Wall Enhancements

- Easily convert faces to curtain walls
- Streamlined In-Place Edit functionality
- Easily assign infills
- Doors
- Windows
- Assemblies

New Tools for Ease of Use

- Schedule Tag Wizard
- Eases creation of custom tag content
- Break Mark Tools
- Streamlined creation
- New dual break ability
- Material Tools
- Drag and drop materials from VIZ Render into Architectural Desktop

Display Themes

- Graphically analyze and present design intent
- 2D or 3D
- Assign Display Themes based on specific values or value ranges
- Create Display Legends

Data Connectivity

- Easily manage project design data
- Perform queries and create reports
- Link external data to designs

Project Standards and Tool Palettes

- Establish and maintain project standards
- Style definitions
- Display settings
- Synchronize project standards
- Maintain consistency across drawing files

3D DWF

- Share design intent
- Property Set Definition support
- Material support
- Navigate 3D models
- Orbit
- Zoom
- Pan
- Control visibility of objects
- Isolate
- Hide
- Transparent

AutoCAD 2006 Command Updates

Because Architectural Desktop is based on AutoCAD, it provides a multitude of commands that enable you to draw and edit geometry of any shape and size. In Architectural Desktop 2006, common AutoCAD editing commands have been updated to provide more consistent and efficient command interaction.

The **COPY** command includes an Undo option, enabling you to undo multiple copied objects within a single COPY operation.

The **COPY, MOVE,** and **STRETCH** commands maintain the most recent displacement value throughout the current editing session.

The **STRETCH** command provides more flexible and consistent object-selection options. You can use standard object selection methods such as picking on the object, and AutoCAD automatically treats those objects with a MOVE operation. In addition, you can apply multiple crossing selections within a single STRETCH operation to simultaneously stretch objects from varying selection sets.

The **ROTATE** and **SCALE** commands include Copy options, which enable you to create a copy while you rotate or scale an object. The most recent rotation angle or scale value remains persistent throughout the current editing session, and using enhanced Reference functionality, you can pick any two points to specify a new angle or scale. You are no longer limited to the basepoint as one of the reference points.

The **OFFSET** command enables you to offset an object multiple times without exiting the command. Additional options within the command enable you to Undo, automatically erase the source object, and specify whether the new object is created on the current layer or on the same layer as the source object.

The **CHAMFER** and **FILLET** commands include an Undo option enabling you to undo chamfer or fillet operations within each command. Additional functionality enables you to quickly create a zero distance chamfer or a zero radius fillet using the Shift key to select the two lines.

The **TRIM** and **EXTEND** commands provide easy access to additional object selection options. A default Select All option enables you to quickly select all visible geometry as cutting or boundary edges and the Fence and Crossing options are now available when selecting objects to trim or extend. When using the Crossing option, the initial pickpoint of your crossing window determines how the selected objects are trimmed or extended.

The **RECTANGLE** command provides new Area and Rotation options. Using the Area option, you can create a rectangle by specifying its area and the length of one of its sides.

The **Rotation** option enables you to rotate the rectangle during the creation process by entering a rotation angle or picking two points.

Questions and Answers about Autodesk Architectural Desktop 2006

The following information was gleaned from Autodesk Press releases. The author has selected this information to answer questions that might be in readers' minds.

? Has the user interface changed for Autodesk Architectural Desktop?

Not really; the user interface for Architectural Desktop 2006 continues the improvements seen in Architectural Desktop 2004 and 2005 and it will be quite familiar to users of those products. The streamlined user interface first introduced with Autodesk Architectural Desktop 2004 improves on traditional CAD design software and earlier versions of Architectural Desktop in terms of look and feel and overall functionality. Highly visual, simpler, and more intuitive, the interface helps you increase productivity using process-focused tools that make the software easier to use. With less focus on dialog boxes and more emphasis on designing directly in the workspace, the design tools in the software are easily accessible. Furthermore, enhanced tool palettes, the Properties palette, and the new Content Browser complement this redesigned workspace to help you work more efficiently.

? Are Autodesk Architectural Desktop and Autodesk® Revit® files interoperable?

Yes. You can exchange drawing information (2D DWG files) between Autodesk Architectural Desktop and the Autodesk Revit software through their respective Export to AutoCAD features.

? Which versions of AutoCAD do Autodesk Architectural Desktop software's Export to AutoCAD feature support?

This release supports Export to AutoCAD 2004, AutoCAD 2005, AutoCAD 2006, and AutoCAD 2000 DWG and DXF™ formats, as well as Release 12 DXF. This makes it possible for users of AutoCAD 2000, AutoCAD 2000i, AutoCAD 2002, AutoCAD 2004, AutoCAD 2005, and AutoCAD 2006 to open Autodesk Architectural Desktop 2006 files without using object enablers.

? Can I export more than one Architectural Desktop file at a time?

Yes. With Architectural Desktop 2006, you can export multiple Architectural Desktop files.

Enhanced e-transmit functionality allows users to transmit multiple entire projects, sheet sets, and specific DWGs.

? What is the Autodesk AEC Object Enabler?

The Autodesk AEC Object Enabler is a free downloadable and distributable utility that gives AutoCAD users functionality and design flexibility through the power of Autodesk Architectural Desktop objects. With the proper version of the AEC Object Enabler, any AutoCAD 2000, AutoCAD 2000i, AutoCAD 2002, AutoCAD 2004, AutoCAD 2005, or AutoCAD 2006 user can have full compatibility with Autodesk Architectural Desktop objects. The AEC Object Enabler is included with AutoCAD

2005. For more information and to download the AEC Object Enabler, go to **http://www.autodesk.com/aecobjecten.**

? Will Autodesk continue to develop Autodesk Architectural Desktop?

Yes. With well over 300,000 Autodesk Architectural Desktop licenses worldwide, Architectural Desktop clearly continues to be a powerful AutoCAD-based solution for Autodesk architectural customers.

? How does VIZ Render differ from Autodesk VIZ?

VIZ Render, Autodesk Architectural Desktop's native visualization tool, uses some of the core technology developed in Autodesk VIZ. Much of the photometric lighting and rendering technology from (Discreet®) 3ds max® software has been included in VIZ Render. However, VIZ Render has been optimized to accept the data organization from Autodesk Architectural Desktop in a much more efficient way, and the entire user interface has been revised and simplified to make the process of creating high-quality visualization more accessible to Architectural Desktop users. The guiding principle in using VIZ Render is that Architectural Desktop is the model authoring application. You organize and build the model exclusively in Architectural Desktop and then seamlessly link to VIZ Render for rendering.

? Can I export VIZ Render files to Autodesk VIZ?

Yes. VIZ Render files (DRF) can be exported to Autodesk VIZ or 3ds max software, and VIZ Render can also import files (MAX) from both Autodesk VIZ and 3ds max.

? Is a network version of Autodesk Architectural Desktop available?

Yes. Autodesk Architectural Desktop software uses standard Autodesk network license management. For more information, see "Platforms, System Requirements, and Network" later in this section.

? What is building information modeling, and how does it apply to Autodesk Architectural Desktop?

Building Information Modeling (BIM) is an innovative approach to building design, construction, and management introduced by Autodesk in 2002. BIM delivers high-quality information about project design scope, schedule, and cost when you need it and how you need it, dramatically helping reduce inefficiencies and risk throughout the building process. The ability to keep this information up to date and accessible in an integrated digital environment gives architects, engineers, builders, and owners a clear overall vision of their projects. It also contributes to the ability to make better decisions faster, helping raise the quality and increase the profitability of projects. Although building information modeling is not itself a technology, it does require suitable technology to be implemented effectively. Examples of some of these technologies, in increasing order of effectiveness, include

- CAD
- Object CAD
- Parametric Building Modeling

With a high level of effort, CAD-based software can be used to achieve some of the benefits of BIM. With some effort, so can object CAD-based software. Parametric Building Modeling (PBM) software offers the highest level of effectiveness with the least effort, but it also requires a full commitment to building information modeling (a new way of working). There is no other way to use PBM to support a traditional drafting workflow.

Autodesk Architectural Desktop is built on object CAD technology, adding intelligent architectural and engineering objects to the familiar AutoCAD platform. It can be used to deliver BIM benefits with significantly less effort than CAD technology. Since it is built on AutoCAD, however, it can also be used very productively for design and documentation in a traditional drafting or CAD-based workflow unrelated to BIM. For more information about BIM and Autodesk's strategy for the application of information technology to the building industry, please see Autodesk's white paper on the subject at **http://www.autodesk.com/bim**.

What are intelligent architectural objects?

The ObjectARX® technology used in Autodesk Architectural Desktop enables you to create intelligent architectural objects that know their form, fit, and function and behave according to their real-world properties. This technology improves software performance, ease of use, and flexibility in design. Intelligent architectural objects respond directly to standard AutoCAD editing commands in the same way that common AutoCAD drawing objects (such as lines, arcs, and circles) do. Yet they also have the ability to display according to context and to interact with other architectural objects. Object-based technology transforms ordinary geometry into intelligent architectural objects whose behavior models that of physical objects.

What is the significance of door, wall, window, and other architectural objects?

These intelligent objects improve design productivity and efficiency because they behave according to the specific properties or rules that pertain to them in the real world.

Architectural objects thus have a relationship to one another and interact with each other intelligently. For example, a window has a relationship to the wall that contains it. If you move or delete the wall, the window reacts appropriately. In addition, intelligent architectural objects maintain dynamic links with construction documents and specifications, resulting in more accurate and valuable project deliverables that can be used to manage a building throughout its lifecycle. When someone deletes or modifies a door, for example, the door schedule is updated automatically.

Will Autodesk Architectural Desktop and Autodesk Revit be combined into a single product in the future?

No. Autodesk Architectural Desktop is based on the AutoCAD platform. Autodesk Revit is based on an entirely different technology and principle of operation. Thus, the products cannot be combined, and Autodesk has no plans to do so.

What is the significance of 3D in Autodesk Architectural Desktop?

Because the objects in Autodesk Architectural Desktop describe real-world building components, both 2D and 3D representations can be created automatically, and either one can be used to view or edit the model. This conveniently and smoothly integrates 2D and 3D functionality and allows exploration of design ideas within CAD in a fashion similar to the way architects and designers envision their designs. For example, you can quickly and easily create 3D massing studies in the initial phases of the design process to explore multiple design scenarios. Or you can develop a floor plan in 2D and then immediately see a perspective view of it in 3D. You can even use 3D to visually check for any type of interference in your design.

Additionally, Autodesk Architectural Desktop 2005 has introduced many features that allow you to work in 3D easily. 3D also provides you with exportable geometric information that can be used for other applications to perform functions like energy analysis.

? **Has 2D functionality been enhanced in Autodesk Architectural Desktop 2006?**

Yes. Although recent releases of Autodesk Architectural Desktop offer many new 3D features, the software's intelligent objects and architectural tools provide important benefits for 2D design development and construction documentation. You have all the functionality of AutoCAD plus powerful architectural design and drafting tools, including a detailing toolkit that vastly accelerates the production of construction details. Therefore, you can create key project deliverables more efficiently and accurately.

? **Is Autodesk Architectural Desktop interoperable with other Autodesk products?**

Yes. AutoCAD is the foundation for an interoperable family of Autodesk products, including Autodesk Architectural Desktop. Sharing the same database framework component—ObjectDBX™ for reading and writing drawing files—helps to ensure that each generation of Autodesk products is interoperable with Autodesk Architectural Desktop. These include industry-specific products such as Autodesk Building Systems, Autodesk Revit, Autodesk Map™, AutoCAD® Mechanical, Autodesk Mechanical Desktop®, and Autodesk Land Desktop®, as well as software that addresses many industries such as Volo® View, Autodesk Express Viewer, Autodesk Raster Design, and Autodesk OnSite View. Because there has been no file format change between the Autodesk 2004, 2005, and 2006 generations of products, Architectural Desktop is interoperable with the majority of applications in both of these release cycles.

? **Is Autodesk Architectural Desktop 2006 compatible with earlier releases of Autodesk Architectural Desktop?**

Earlier versions of Architectural Desktop are forwards-compatible with the current release; i.e., designs created in earlier versions of Autodesk Architectural Desktop easily migrate to the current release of Architectural Desktop. Autodesk Architectural Desktop 2006 is backwards compatible with Architectural Desktop 2004 and 2005 at the object level (AEC objects used in Architectural Desktop). Architectural Desktop 2006, 2005 and Architectural Desktop 2004 are *not* backwards compatible at the object level with earlier releases of Architectural Desktop, but files created in these versions of the software can be saved as DWG files to be read by versions of Autodesk Architectural Desktop based on AutoCAD 2000, AutoCAD 2000i, and 2002 platforms.

? **Will my third-party applications work with the current release of Autodesk Architectural Desktop software?**

Your existing third-party applications may or may not be compatible with the current release of Autodesk Architectural Desktop. Contact your independent software supplier for details. For more information about the availability of third-party applications compatible with the current release of AutoCAD and Architectural Desktop, visit **http://www.autodesk.com/partnerproducts**.

? **Is Architectural Desktop compatible with Industry Foundation Classes (IFCs)?**

Yes. IAI-certified support for IFCs is currently provided in Autodesk Architectural Desktop through G.E.M. Team Solutions GbR. A trial version of the IFC-Utility2x for Architectural Desktop can be downloaded at **http://www.inopso.com**, the web site of Inopso GmbH, a partner of G.E.M. Team Solutions which distributes the plug-in.

? **Autodesk Architectural Desktop 2006 has AutoCAD 2006 as its foundation. Has the AutoCAD 2006 drawing file format (DWG) changed from the AutoCAD 2005 products, as it did between AutoCAD 2000 and AutoCAD 2004?**

No. The AutoCAD 2006 DWG file format is the same as the AutoCAD 2005 and 2004 formats. The AutoCAD 2004 file format was updated and is different from the AutoCAD 2000, AutoCAD 2000i, and AutoCAD 2002 DWG file format. This new format was necessary to provide performance enhancements, smaller file sizes, presentation graphics, and drawing security.

? Can I run Autodesk Architectural Desktop side by side with other AutoCAD platform-based applications?

Yes. You can install the current release of Autodesk Architectural Desktop side by side with any other AutoCAD 2000i–, AutoCAD 2002–, AutoCAD 2004–, AutoCAD 2005–, or AutoCAD 2006–based product. These products include Autodesk Architectural Desktop, Autodesk Building Systems, Autodesk Mechanical Desktop, AutoCAD Mechanical, Autodesk Land Desktop, Autodesk Map, and AutoCAD LT® software.

? How can I find technical support information for Autodesk Architectural Desktop 2006?

You can learn about all support options from your local Autodesk Authorized Reseller or Distributor. Visit **http://www.autodesk.com/archdesktop-support** and find a knowledge base of commonly asked support questions. Also, you can ask questions and read information about the use of Autodesk products in the peer-to-peer discussion groups on **http://www.autodesk.com/discussion**. Autodesk hosts topical discussion groups about specific products, including Autodesk Architectural Desktop, and about general topics, such as drafting techniques and customization. Alternatively, Autodesk software manuals and documentation are a great source of answers to your support questions.

? How do I obtain direct technical support?

Autodesk® Subscription is the best way to keep your design tools and learning up to date. In the United States and Canada, for an annual fee you get the latest versions of your licensed Autodesk software, web support direct from Autodesk, self-paced training options, and a broad range of other technology and business benefits. You must purchase a subscription at the time you purchase or upgrade an Autodesk product. For more information, contact your Autodesk Authorized Reseller or visit **http://www.autodesk.com/subscription**.

Autodesk Systems Centers (ASCs) and Autodesk Authorized Resellers also provide support services for Autodesk Architectural Desktop software and all other Autodesk products. In the United States and Canada, call 800-964-6432 to locate an ASC or reseller near you, or visit **htpp://www.autodesk.com/reseller**. You can find a complete list of support options from Autodesk at **http://www.autodesk.com/archdesktop-support**.

? Can I rely on my AutoCAD knowledge to use Autodesk Architectural Desktop? How quickly can I learn the new features in Autodesk Architectural Desktop?

Autodesk Architectural Desktop builds on the speed, performance, and familiarity of AutoCAD, so AutoCAD users have a strong foundation from which to learn Autodesk Architectural Desktop.

? Where do I find training courses for Autodesk Architectural Desktop 2006?

Training courses are available from Autodesk Professional Services as well as at Autodesk Authorized Training Center (ATC®) locations and Autodesk Authorized Resellers. Training courses are available through Autodesk Professional Services, and include Autodesk Virtual Classroom Training (online, instructor-led), custom training to match your organization's specific needs, as well as Autodesk Classroom Training. To obtain more information about Autodesk's training services, visit **http://www.autodesk.com/archdesktop-training**.

Other helpful training resources include the online discussion groups you can access through the Autodesk Architectural Desktop Communication Center. The Communication Center also features industry specific news, tips and tricks, product updates, and Autodesk Architectural Desktop software manuals and online documentation.

? **Should I get training with this release?**

Although Autodesk Architectural Desktop takes advantage of your existing knowledge of AutoCAD software, some training is recommended. Training improves productivity, increases return on investment, and enhances your Autodesk Architectural Desktop knowledge.

? **What consulting services are available for Autodesk Architectural Desktop 2006?**

Autodesk Professional Services provides customer consulting offerings for project assessments, process audits, implementation services, networking setup, application porting, and other custom services to help you get the best possible return on your investment in Autodesk technology. For more information on Autodesk Professional Services, contact your Autodesk Account Executive or your local Autodesk Authorized Reseller; or visit **http://www.autodesk.com/professionalservices.**

Platforms, System Requirements, and Network

? **Do I need to buy new hardware to run Autodesk Architectural Desktop 2006?**

Following are the minimum hardware and operating system requirements for running Autodesk Architectural Desktop.

Description Minimum Requirement

Operating system

- Microsoft® Windows 2000 Professional, SP3, or later
- Windows XP Professional, SP1, or later
- Windows XP Home Edition, SP1, or later
- Windows XP, Tablet PC Edition

Windows 95, 98, and NT are no longer supported.

CPU
Intel® Pentium® 4 or AMD K7 with 1.4-GHz processor

RAM
512 MB (1 GB recommended)

Hard Disk Space
650 MB free and 75 MB swap space

Display Resolution
1024 × 768 with True Color

? **Why was the hardware requirement raised from pre-2004 releases of Architectural Desktop?**

The hardware requirements are defined in order to ensure that customers have expected performance when fully using the product. With Autodesk Architectural Desktop 2004, these requirements were raised accordingly. Not only did Autodesk Architectural Desktop 2004 contain a new and robust visualization tool, VIZ Render, that really benefits from robust systems, but this release also supports the Materials feature which provide, surface and section hatching as well as texture mapping in shaded views.

? **I'm upgrading from Autodesk Architectural Desktop 3.3, but my hardware does not meet the minimum requirements for this release; can I still use the current release of Autodesk Architectural Desktop effectively?**

Yes—if you are using Architectural Desktop strictly for drafting and design. On hardware that does not meet the minimum system requirements however, you should avoid using certain features that may cause below optimal performance. These features include VIZ Render and Materials with surface hatching enabled.

? **Are there any changes to the licensing for stand-alone seats?**

Yes. SafeCast is now the stand-alone licensing technology used in Autodesk products worldwide. For customers in the United States and Canada, this is a change in the stand-alone licensing.

Why change SafeCast? CD-Secure and SafeCast store licensing information on the user's hard drive, typically on the hard disk. Examining re-authorization statistics, it became clear that a number of technical issues with storing information on the hard drive could be resolved by implementing a new feature of SafeCast.

What will this feature do instead? This feature will store a duplicate set of licensing information in the computers registry. For the types of errors that render the hard-drive storage ineffective, there will now be a fallback location in the registry, which will allow the licensing system to continue without error.

? **Where can I purchase Autodesk Architectural Desktop?**

Autodesk Architectural Desktop is available worldwide. Contact your local Autodesk Authorized Reseller or Distributor for more information. To locate one near you, visit **http://www.autodesk.com/reseller.**

Autodesk Architectural Desktop is also available through the Autodesk online store at **http://www.autodesk.com/estore.**

? **Is Autodesk Architectural Desktop being released as an English-only product?**

No. This product will be released worldwide. Versions of this product will be available in a wide of range of languages and with localized content in many countries. For information on product availability contact your local Autodesk Authorized Reseller or Autodesk Systems Center (ASC).

? **Is subscription available for Autodesk Architectural Desktop?**

Yes. Subscription is available in most countries around the world for many of Autodesk's products including Autodesk Architectural Desktop. Autodesk Subscription is the best way to keep your design tools and learning up to date. In the United States and Canada, for an annual fee you get the latest versions of your licensed Autodesk software, web support direct from Autodesk, self-paced training options, and a broad range of other technology and business benefits. You must purchase a subscription at the time you purchase or upgrade an Autodesk product. For more information, contact your Autodesk Authorized Reseller or visit **http://www.autodesk.com/subscription.**

Installing Autodesk Architectural Desktop 2006

Autodesk Architectural Desktop 2006 ships with three CDs labeled 1 of 3, 2 of 3, and 3 of 3.

Installing Autodesk Architectural Desktop 2006 is relatively easy; follow these directions.

1. Insert the disk labeled 1 of 3 in your CD drive and close the CD tray.

2. If your Windows Operating system is set for **Autorun,** the CD will begin to self-load.

3. If the CD does not self-load, go to the next step.

4. In the Microsoft Windows Desktop, select the **Start** button, and pick the Run icon to bring up the Windows **Run** dialog box.

5. In the Windows **Run** dialog box, press the **Browse** button, and select the CD drive letter (labeled ADT 2006-1).

6. In the ADT 2006-1 directory on the CD drive, select **Setup,** and press the **OK** open button to return to the **Run** dialog box.

7. In the **Run** dialog box, press the **OK** button to start the installation process.

Be prepared to wait for several seconds until the main Autodesk Architectural Desktop 2006 screen appears (see the figure below).

In the main Autodesk Architectural Desktop 2006 installation screen, you can choose from several sources of information. It is a good idea to select each of these sources in order to make sure that you have met the correct hardware and operating system requirements for the program. If everything is OK, do the following.

8. Select the underlined word **Install** in, and wait several seconds until the **Autodesk Architectural Desktop 2006 Setup** dialog box appears (see the figures below).

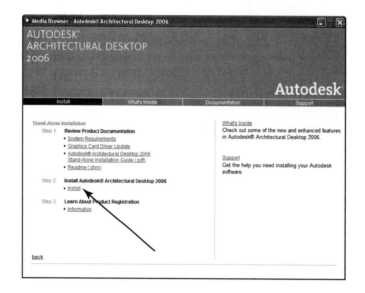

9. In the **Autodesk Architectural Desktop 2006 Setup** dialog box, press the **OK** button to install the support components.

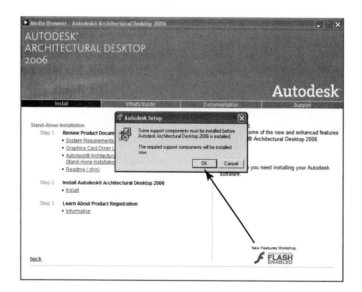

10. The **Installation Wizard** will now appear; press the **Next** button to bring up the Autodesk Software License Agreement.

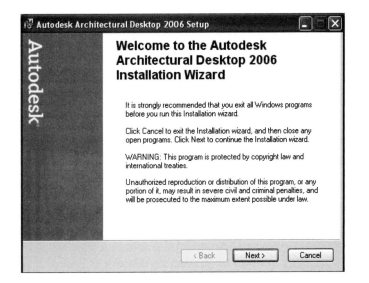

10.   If you accept the agreement, select the **I accept** radio button, and press the **Next** button to bring up the **Serial Number** data field (see the figure below).

11.   In the **Serial Number** data field, enter the serial number that comes with your copy of the program (see the figure below), and press the **Next** button to bring up the **User Information** data field.

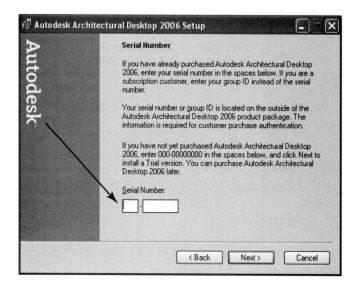

12. After entering your personal information, press the **Next** button to bring up the **Remote Content Installation** screen (see the figure below).

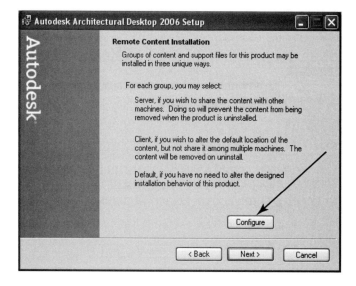

13. Press the **Configure** button to bring up the **Remote Content and Support File Settings**. Unless you want to put the content on a Client or server for others to access, press the **Default** radio button, and then press the **OK** button to return to the **Remote Content Installation** screen (see the figure below).

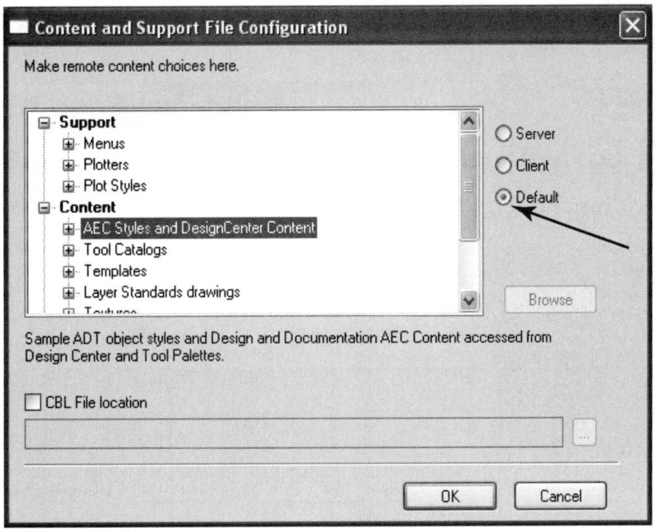

14. In the **Remote Content Installation** screen, press the **Next** button to bring up the **Select Installation Type** screen. This author prefers the **Custom** radio button. The following information illustrates that use; if you prefer, you can select the **Typical, Compact** or **Full** installation options (see the figure below).

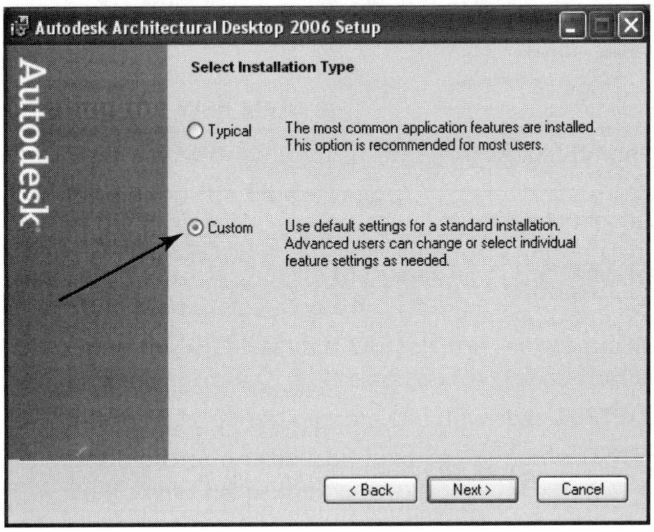

15. In the **Select Installation** type screen, select the **Custom** radio button, and press the **Next** button.

16. After selecting the **Custom** radio button and pressing the **Next** button, the **Feature** dialog box will appear (see the figure below). For each feature that you want to install, activate the **Will be installed on local hard drive** field. Activate to install on the local hard drive the **Imperial** content, **VIZ render,** and **Program Files.** When finished selecting, press the **Next** button to bring up the **Destination Folder** dialog box.

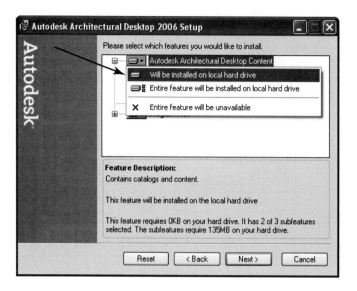

17. In the **Destination Folder** dialog box, accept the destination location (**c:\program files\Autodesk Architectural Desktop 2006** by default) or change the location to suit your computer (see the figure below).

! **Note:** Regardless of where you place the Autodesk Architectural Desktop 2006 program, it will always create a folder for keeping your project files on the **C** drive in the **My Documents** folder.

18. Press the **Next** button to bring up the **Choose a default text editor for editing text files** dialog box—accept the default text editor location or browse to the location in which it exists, and check the **Display the Autodesk Architectural desktop 2006 shortcut on my desktop** checkbox (see the figure below).

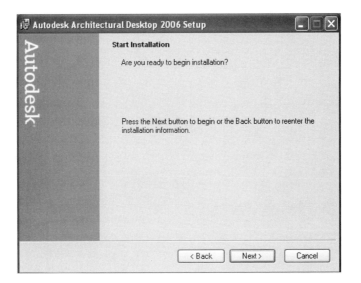

19. Press the **Next** button to bring up the **Are you ready to begin installation?** (just a last check) dialog box (see the figure below).

20. Press the **Next** button to start the installation.
21. Insert the other CDs when requested on screen.

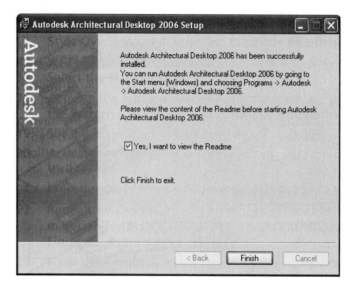

Tip

After you have saved an Autodesk Architectural Desktop drawing, you can also start the program by dragging and dropping that drawing icon onto the Architectural Desktop icon. This will automatically start Architectural Desktop 2006 and bring up that drawing.

Abbreviations

In order to make this book easier to understand, shortcut abbreviations are often used. The following list codifies those abbreviations.

Please Read Before Proceeding

Activate a field   Refers to selecting a selection made up of a sentence.

Activate a viewport   Refers to clicking in a viewport to make it the active viewport.

ADT or ADT 2006   Refers to Autodesk Architectural Desktop 2006.

AEC Objects   Refers to any Autodesk Architectural Desktop 2006 intelligent object such as walls, stairs, schedules, etc.

Ancillary   Refers to space between the ceiling and the floor above.

Browse   Refers to searching through the file folders and files.

Contextual menu   Refers to any menu that appears when an object or entity is selected with a **Right Mouse Button (RMB).**

Dialog box   Refers to any menu containing parameters or input fields.

Display tree   Refers to Microsoft Windows folder listing consisting of + and − signs. If a + sign appears, then the listing is compressed with more folders available.

Drawing editor   Refers to the drawing area where drawings are created.

Drop-down list   Refers to the typical Windows operating system list with arrow. When selected, a series of options appear in a vertical list.

DWG   Refers to an Architectural Desktop Drawing.

Elevation View   Refers to **Front, Back, Right** or **Left Views,** perpendicular to the ground plane.

Layouts   Refers to drawing areas. All layouts except the **Model Layout** can be broken down into **Paper Space** viewports. More layouts can be added.

Plan View   Refers to looking at a building from the **Top View.**

Press the Enter button   Refers to any **Enter** button in any dialog box on the screen.

Press the Enter key   Refers to the keyboard **Enter** key (the **space bar** will usually act as the **Enter** key, except when entering dimensions, text, or numerals).

Press the OK button   Refers to any **OK** button in any dialog box on the screen.

RMB   Refers to clicking using the **Right Mouse Button.** This is most often used to bring up contextual menus.

Tooltips   Refers to the information that appears when the cursor is held momentarily over an icon.

Viewports   Refers to **Paper Space** viewports.

The Autodesk Architectural Desktop 2006 Interface

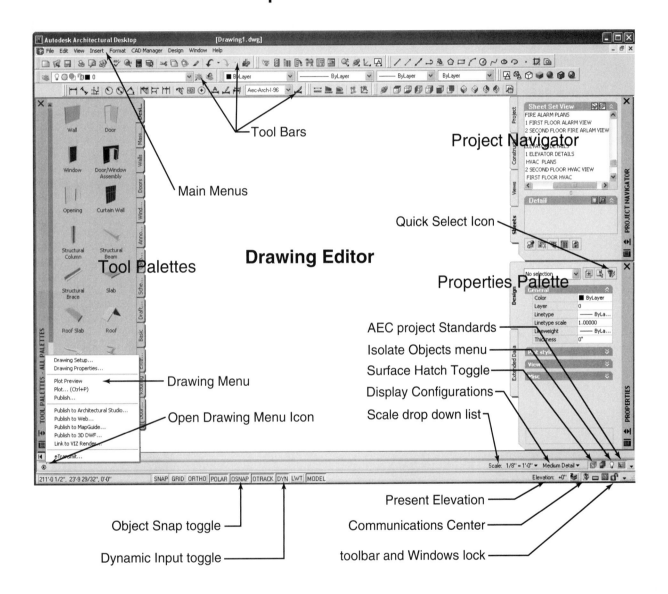

Tool Bars

Project Navigator

Main Menus

Quick Select Icon

Tool Palettes

Drawing Editor

Properties Palette

AEC project Standards
Isolate Objects menu
Surface Hatch Toggle
Display Configurations
Scale drop down list

Drawing Menu

Open Drawing Menu Icon

Present Elevation

Communications Center

toolbar and Windows lock

Object Snap toggle

Dynamic Input toggle

Tool Palettes

Autodesk Architectural Desktop 2006 ships with seven default tool palettes and the **Properties** palette in place. These can be easily modified or deleted, or new palettes can be added.

Bringing Up the Tool Palettes

The tool palettes can be brought up by three methods:

a. Typing **toolpalettes** in the **Command line.**
b. Pressing **Ctrl + 3** on the keyboard.
c. Selecting the **Tool Palettes** icon.

Resizing the Palette

You can resize the tool palettes by moving your cursor to the cut corner at the bottom of the palettes. Your cursor will change to a "double arrow." Click, hold, and drag vertically and horizontally to resize, as shown in the figure below.

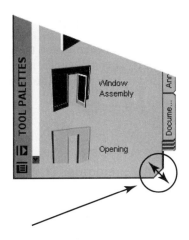

If you have more tool palettes than are showing, a "stair step" icon will appear at the bottom of the last tab name. (See the figure below.)

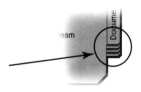

If you click on the "stair step" icon, a menu will appear that you can use to select all the tool palettes, as shown in the figure below.

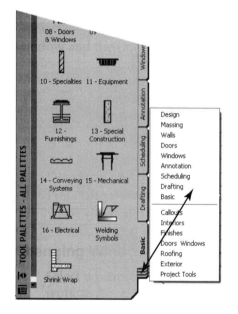

Auto-hide

Because the palettes cover some of the Drawing Editor, there is a control called **Auto-hide** that opens and closes the palette when the cursor is moved over its surface. The following figures show the icon used to turn **Auto-hide** on or off.

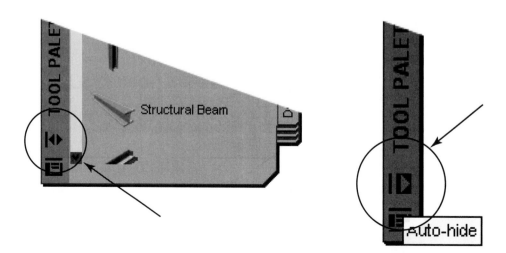

Tool Palettes Properties

The Tool Palettes Properties give access to options necessary to control the size, location, and appearance of the palettes. **Tool Palettes Properties** also allow for creation and renaming of palettes. (See the figures below.)

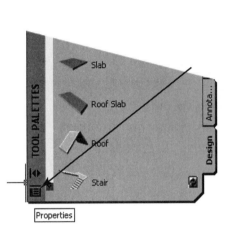

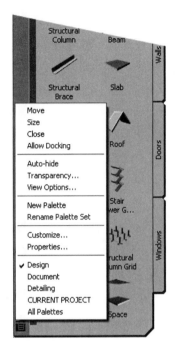

Allow Docking

Allows the palette to attach to the sides of the Drawing Editor.

Transparency

Makes the palette transparent, allowing entities on the Drawing Editor to be seen.

View Options

Changes the sizes of the **Tool Palette** icons, as shown in the figure below.

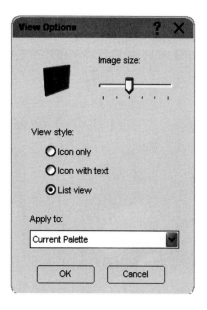

New Palette

Creates new palettes.

Rename Palette Set

Renames the entire set of palettes.

Customize

Groups, adds, deletes and renames tool palettes.

1. Select the **Customize** option from the **Tool Palette** contextual menu to bring up the **Customize** dialog box.
2. In the **Customize** dialog box, select the **Tool Palettes** tab.
3. **RMB** in the **Tool Palettes** list to bring up the contextual menu for creating, renaming, and deleting tool palettes.
4. **RMB** in the **Palette Groups** list to bring up the contextual menu for creating or deleting tool palette groups.
5. Select a palette group, **RMB** to bring up the contextual menu for creating, renaming, deleting, and making a tool palette group current.
6. Drag and drop selections from **Tool Palettes** into **Palette Groups.**

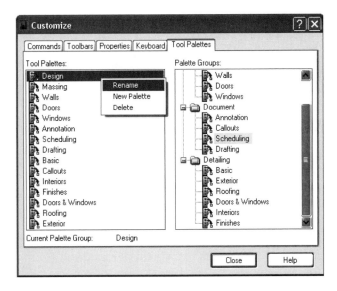

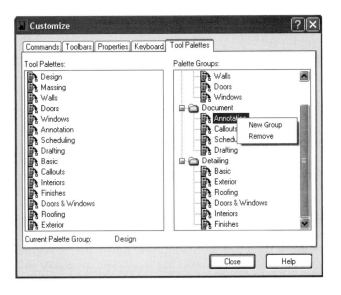

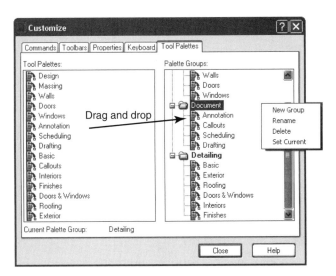

The Properties Palette

The **Properties** palette changes depending on the AEC Object or entity that is selected. All the properties of the selected object can be changed in this palette. The palette also contains the **Quick Select Icon;** this is very useful in selecting objects, especially when several objects are located together.

Bringing Up the Properties Palettes

The Properties palettes can be brought up by three methods:

a.   Typing properties in the **Command line.**

b.   Pressing **Ctrl + 1** on the keyboard.

c.   Double-clicking any AEC Object or entity (see the figure below).

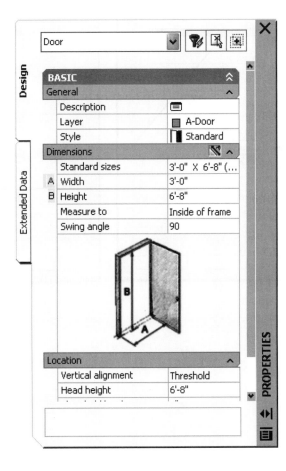

Quick Select

The Quick Select toggle icon allows you to filter and select from any of the AEC objects or entities presently in the Drawing Editor. To use this filter, select the **Quick Select** icon at the top right of the Properties Palette to bring up the **Quick Select** dialog box

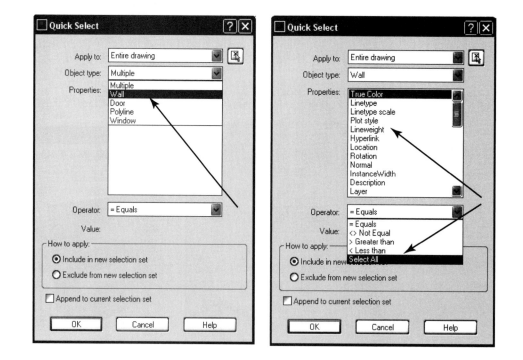

PICKADD Toggle

The **PICKADD** toggle turns the PICKADD system variable on and off. When PICKADD is on, each object selected, either individually or by windowing, is added to the current selection set. When PICKADD is off, selected objects replace the current selection set.

SELECT

Click to deselect a selection.

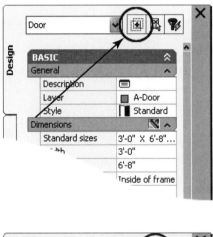

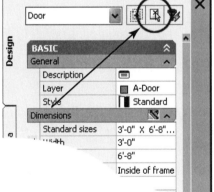

The Content Browser

The Content Browser locates all your AEC tools such as walls, windows, and doors. You drag your tools into your tool palettes using Autodesk's idrop technology. You can also drag AEC content back into your tool palettes to create new tools. After creating a new tool palette, it is a good idea to drag a copy of the tool palette back into the **My Tool Catalog** folder in the Content Browser to save a copy of the palette.

Bringing Up the Content Browser

The Content Browser can be brought up by three methods:

a. Typing **aeccontentbrowser** in the **Command line.**
b. Pressing **Ctrl + 4** on the keyboard.
c. Selecting the **Content Browser** icon (see the figure below).

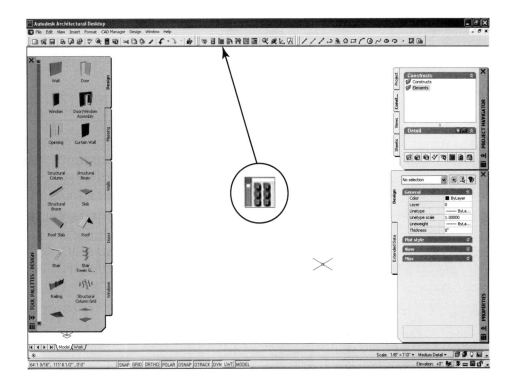

The Content Browser starts off with the Catalog Library, which contains several catalogs (see the figure below).

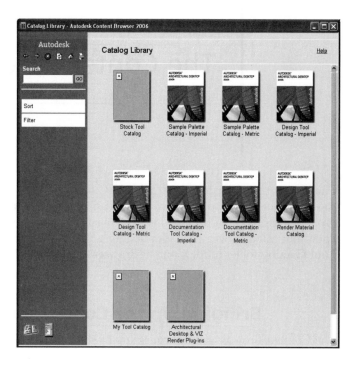

Click the **Modify Library View Options** icon to open the **Content Browser Preferences** dialog box. Here you can set the number of Catalog rows and new Catalog types.

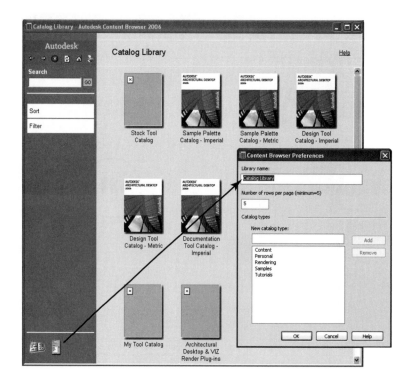

Click the **Add or Create a Catalog** icon to open the **Add Catalog** dialog box. Here you can create a new **Catalog** or add an existing **Catalog** from a location such as a **website.**

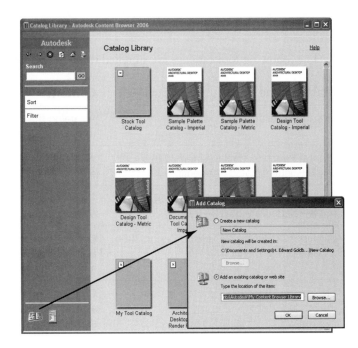

You drag content from the Catalog folders into your tool palettes, as shown in the figure below. (Make sure **Auto-hide** is turned off when you do this.)

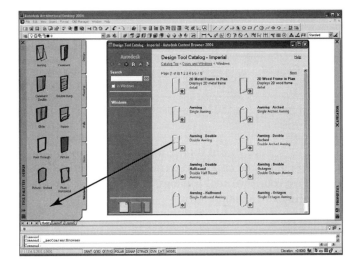

You can also create a tool by just by dropping an ADT Object from the drawing to a tool palette, a style from **Style Manager** to a tool palette, or a piece of AEC Content from the **Custom** tab in the **DesignCenter.**

Note: Some objects use fixed images like the Schedule Tool, AEC Dimension Tool, and the Layout Object Tools.

The following tool catalogs are supplied with the program:

Catalog Name	Contents
Stock Tool Catalog	A catalog that contains the standard, stock tools in Autodesk Architectural Desktop
Autodesk® Architectural Desktop 2006 Sample Palette Catalog—Imperial	A sampling of tools in imperial units for objects such as doors, walls, and windows.
Autodesk® Architectural Desktop 2006 Sample Palette Catalog—Metric	A sampling of tools in metric units for objects such as doors, walls, and windows
Autodesk® Architectural Desktop Design 2006 Tool Catalog—Imperial	Content tools in imperial units for design and documentation of multiview blocks and symbols
Autodesk® Architectural Desktop Design Tool Catalog—Metric	Content tools in metric units for design and documentation of multiview blocks and symbols.
Autodesk® Architectural Desktop 2006 Documentation Tool Catalog—Imperial	Content tools in imperial units for annotation and documentation
Autodesk® Architectural Desktop 2006 Documentation Tool Catalog—Metric	Content tools in metric units for annotation and documentation
Autodesk® Architectural Desktop 2006 Render Material Catalog	Architectural render materials for use with Autodesk Architectural Desktop and Autodesk VIZ Render.
My Tool Catalog	An empty tool catalog provided so that you can create your own tool set.
Architectural Desktop and VIZ Render Plug-ins	Links to third-party plug-ins for Autodesk Architectural Desktop and VIZ Render

You cannot add or remove items from the Autodesk-supplied tool catalogs, but you can create your own tool catalogs. You can also copy other tool catalogs and website links into your catalog library.

The Open Drawing Menu

The **Open Drawing Menu** icon is located at the bottom left of the Autodesk Architectural Desktop 2006 interface (see the figure below).

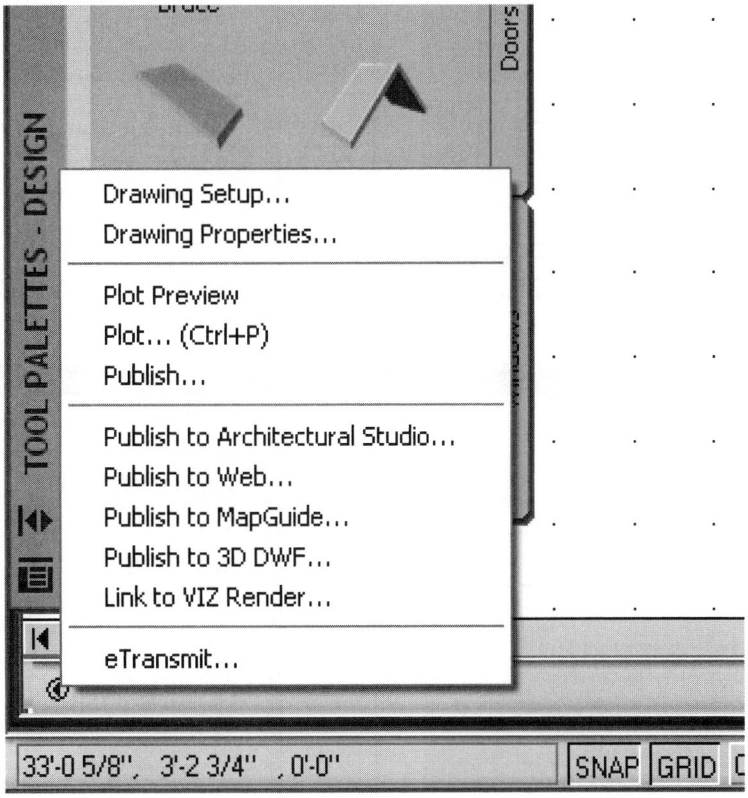

Drawing Setup

Selecting **Drawing Setup** brings up the **Drawing Setup** dialog box with tabs to set drawing units, scale, layers, and display. The **Drawing Setup** dialog box can also be accessed from the **Format** menu in the **Main** toolbar (see the figures below).

Publish—DWF Publisher

Selecting **Publish** brings up the **Publish** dialog box (see the figure below). In this dialog box, press the **Publish Options** button to select the publish options for the DWFs (see the figure below).

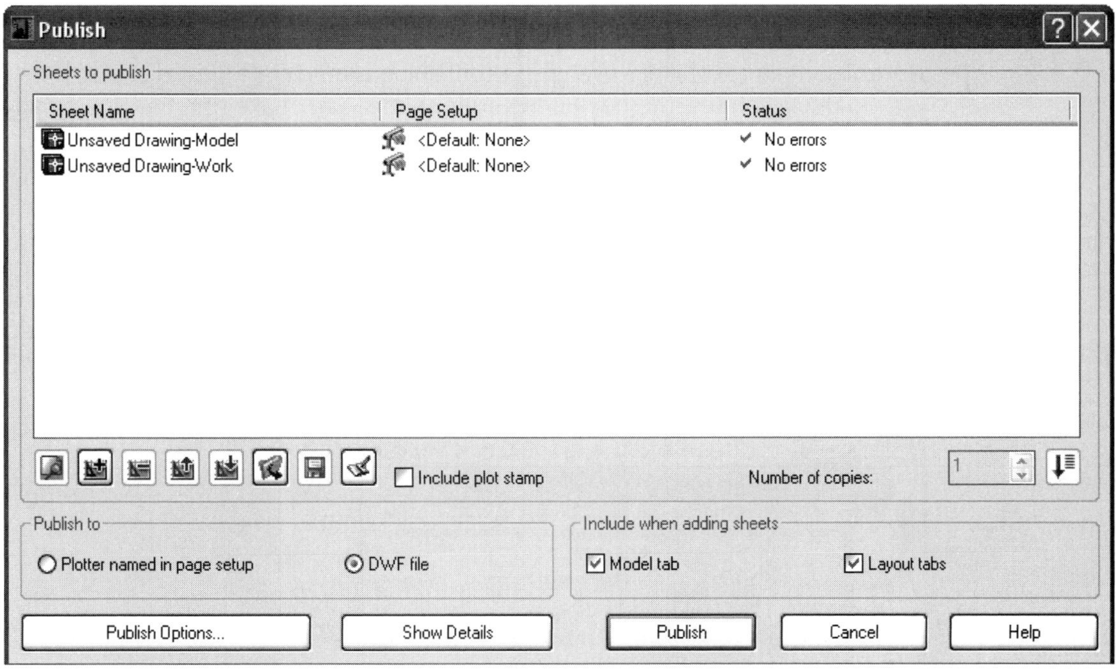

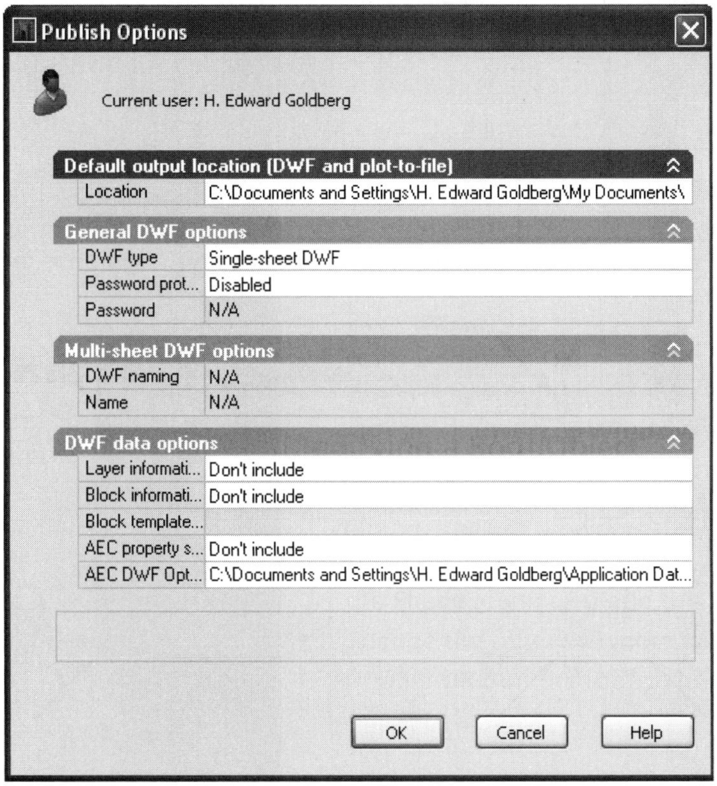

Publish to Architectural Studio

If you have Autodesk Architectural Studio, and it is running, you can send your 2D and 3D information to that program.

Publish to Web

! **Note:** This feature creates a Web page containing examples of drawings that you wish to display on the Internet. Before using this feature, make sure that you display your building in the drawing as you wish to have it shown. If you have zoomed in and saved your drawing, it will display as zoomed in. Also, either create a new named layout, or rename the Model layout to the name that you wish to have displayed on the Web page (this will not be necessary if you want to publish sheets).

Selecting **Publish to Web** from the Open Drawing Menu opens the **Publish to Web** wizard to create a Web page with i-drop capability. For this tutorial, select the **Create New Web Page** radio button and press the **Next** button.

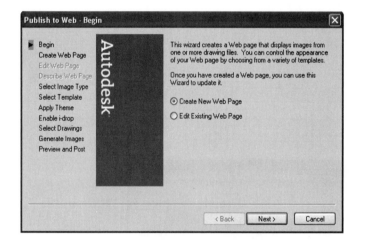

You will probably get the following message telling you that only a saved drawing can be published. If you want to publish your current drawing, save it and press the **OK** button.

The **Publish to Web** drawing selection dialog box will now appear. Browse to select a drawing that you wish to have on the Web page. After selecting a file from the **Publish to Web** dialog box, press the **Open** button to move to the next dialog box (**Create Web page**).

In the top field of the **Create Web Page** dialog box, enter a unique name for the web page. In the next field browse to a location on your computer and create a new file folder and location for the web page. Press the **Next** button to move to the **Select Image Type** dialog box.

In the **Select Image Type** dialog box, select JPG (the most popular picture format). If you want people to be able to download DWFs, choose **DWF** from the drop-down list. Select a size for the images from the Image size drop-down list, and press the **Next** button to move to the **Select Template** dialog box.

In the **Select Template** dialog box, select one of the four templates listed (this author chose the **List plus Summary** template). Press the **Next** button to move to the **Apply Theme** dialog box.

In the **Apply Theme** dialog box, select a color theme from the drop-down list (this author chose **Autumn Fields**). Press the **Next** button to move to the **Enable I-drop** dialog box.

In the **Enable i-drop** dialog box, check the **Enable i-drop** check box if you wish to add DWF i-drop drag-and-drop capability to your Web page. This will allow users to drag DWFs directly into their copy of AutoCAD or Architectural Desktop. Press the **Next** button to move to the **Select Drawings** dialog box.

In the top drop-down list of the **Select Drawings** dialog box, browse to the location of your project on your computer, and choose another drawing to publish on your page from the **Publish to Web** dialog box that appears. After choosing a file, press the **Open** button to return to the **Select Drawings** dialog box. Select a layout from the **Layout** drop-down list, and press the **Add** button to add the drawing to the **Image list.** Repeat until you have several drawings listed, and then press the **Next** button to move to the **Generate Images** dialog box.

In the **Generate Images** dialog box, select the Regenerate images for drawings that have changed radio button, and then press the **Next** button to move to the **Preview and Post** dialog box. (This may take a few moments while the drawings are brought up and regenerated.)

In the **Preview and Post** dialog box, press the **Preview** button to see the Web page in your Web browser. After viewing, close the Web page, press the **Post Now** button and find a location for the files. Upload the files to your own website.

Publish to MapGuide

If you have MapGuide installed, you can deploy MapGuide GIS and digital design data applications on the Internet, on your intranet, or in the field.

Publish to 3D DWF

Selecting **Publish to 3D DWF** from the Open Drawing Menu opens the **AEC 3D DWF Publishing Options** dialog box. Browse in the top field, and create the name and place your 3D DWF. Select the **Includes Properties from AEC DWF** Options check box, and press the **Edit Aec DWF Options** button to bring up the **AEC DWF Publishing Options** dialog box.

In the **AEC DWF Publishing Options** dialog box, select the Browse button and select the **Published Properties List** you wish to use for this DWF. Select the **Property Sets** you desire, and press the **Add** button to bring up the **Add Property Sets** dialog box. Press the **OK** button.

In the **Add Property Sets** dialog box, **Browse** to find the drawing containing the **Property Set Definitions** you want to include. Check the Styles you wish to add from the list shown, and press the **OK** buttons to close all the dialog boxes. After the last dialog box has closed, select the objects in the Drawing Editor that you wish to show in the 3D DWF. After selecting the object, press the **Enter** key on the keyboard to publish and view the 3D DWF.

In the 3D DWF Viewer, under **Navigation**, select the **Model** or **Bookmarks** tab.

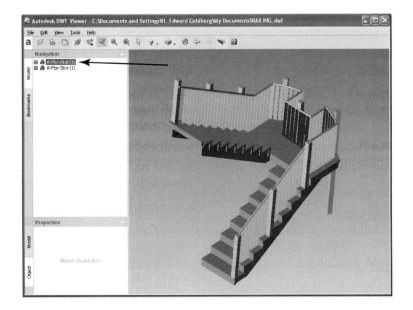

Selecting **Right** from the **Bookmark** tab will show the object in the **Right** view.

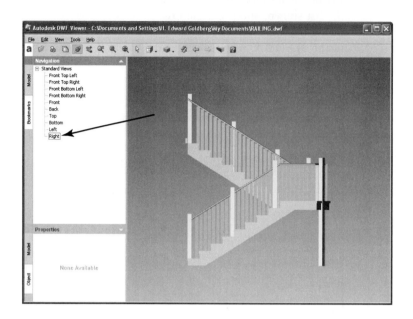

Link to Autodesk VIZ Render

The VIZ Render will give you access to photorealistic rendering plus animation. The process is described in the Viz Render section of this book.

eTransmit

Selecting **eTransit** creates a compressed email package of your drawings with all necessary files. It also includes a transmittal (see the figure below).

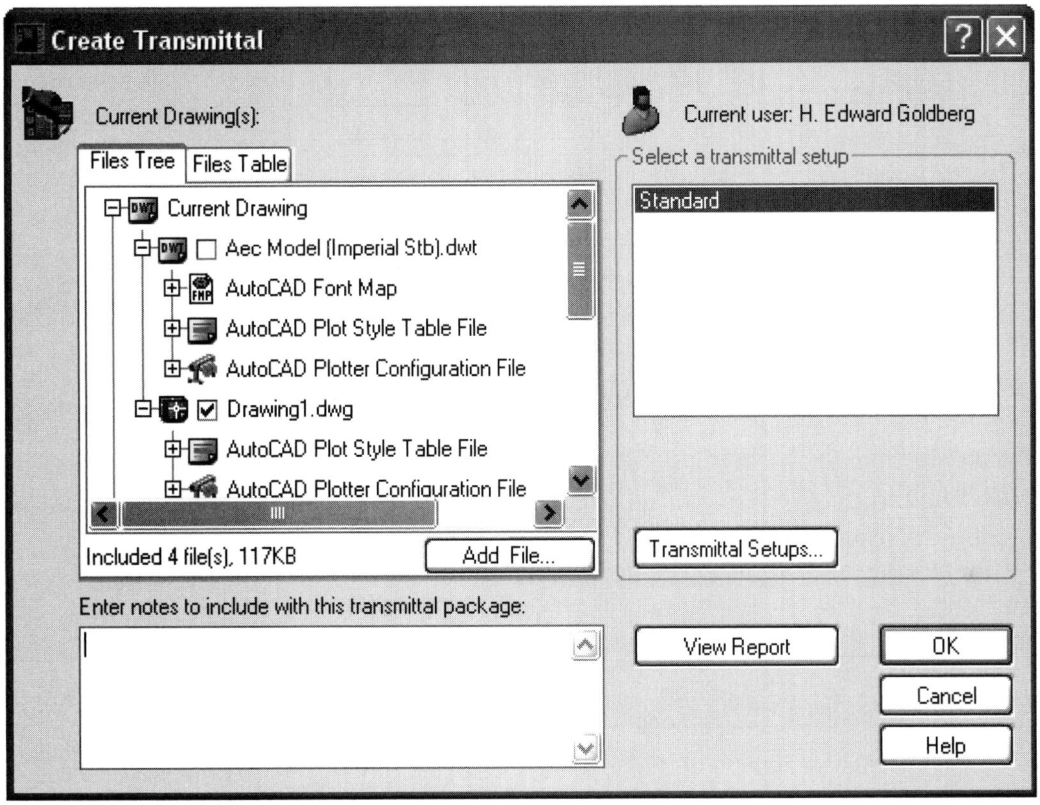

Sections and Tutorials:
Palettes and Exercises

1

Massing/Mass Elements
and Groups

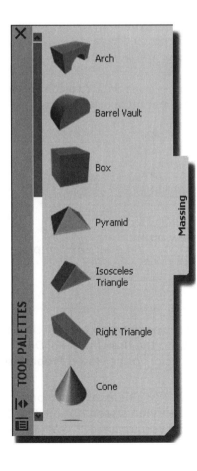

When you finish this section, you should understand the following:

- ✔ How to create a massing object.
- ✔ How to modify a massing object.
- ✔ How to create and attach slice plates (floor slices).
- ✔ How to modify the massing object after applying the slice plates.
- ✔ How to change the slice plates into space boundaries, and then into Walls.
- ✔ How to use the **Drape** tool to create contour massing models.

Massing objects can be dragged or inserted either from the **Design Tool palette,** or by typing **MassElementAdd** on the **Command line**.

Massing and Mass Modeling

Mass modeling is unique to Autodesk Architectural Desktop 2006. It replicates the system frequently used by architects on large buildings. The initial design studies for large buildings are often modeled in clay or wood first. These small models generally show the relationship between parts of the building while indicating scale as well as how light and shadow react with the facades. Mass modeling is meant to be a quick process, akin to the building blocks we all played with as children.

With massing, Autodesk Architectural Desktop 2006 takes the concept of mass modeling one step farther. Not only can you model the concept, but also within the program, you can take that model through to the document creation stage automatically.

The **Massing** tool palette comes with 16 preconfigured primitives (3D shapes). The primitives can be dragged or inserted into your drawing from the tool palette. The size of the primitive can be preset or can be modified when inserting. This can be determined by selecting yes or no from the **Specify on Screen** drop-down list in the **Properties** tool palette when inserting the primitive. Selecting and pulling on grips or changing parameters in the **Properties** tool palette associated with massing can easily modify each primitive's size and shape.

After a massing model has been created, floor slices can be created from the model. These floor slices can be used as a basis for area and space studies, or for eventually generating walls. It is this method that allows you to quickly model a building and electronically convert that model into construction documents.

The following exercises are designed to give you a hands-on feel for using the **Massing** feature of the program. After doing these exercises, I recommend that you explore all the primitives, and try making new ones using the **Extrusion and Revolution** feature as well as the **Convert to Mass Element** tool that converts solid models and AEC Objects into mass elements.

Hands-On

Creating a Massing Object

1. Start a new drawing using the Aec Model (Imperial Stb) template.
2. Change to the Work Layout.
3. Change to the NE Isometric View.
4. Select the **Massing** tool palette.
5. Drag the **Box Primitive** massing icon to the drawing area or click once on the Box icon and move your cursor to the drawing area. *Don't click in the drawing area yet!* Move your cursor to the closed **Properties** toolbar to open it (see Figure 1–1).
6. When the **Properties** toolbar opens, notice a blue asterisk icon (settable option upon insertion) next to the **Specify on screen** option. Select No from the drop-down list (this will allow you to preset the **Width, Depth,**

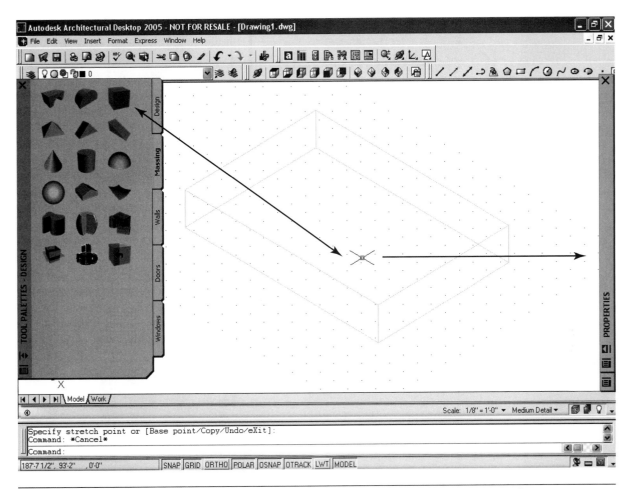

Figure 1–1

and **Height** of the box). Set the Width to **60′**, Depth to **260′,** and Height to **60′** (see Figure 1–2).

7. Once the size properties have been set, click to locate the **BOX** primitive, and then press **Enter** twice to accept the default rotation and close the command. Save this file.

Hands-On

Modifying a Massing Object

1. Select the primitive to activate its grips, and then select **Free Form** from the **Shape** drop-down list to make the massing box editable (see Figure 1–3).

Note: Before the massing primitive has been changed to a free form, it can be adjusted in the standard ADT 2006 manner by activating grips and entering dimensions, or pulling on the grips.

Figure 1–2

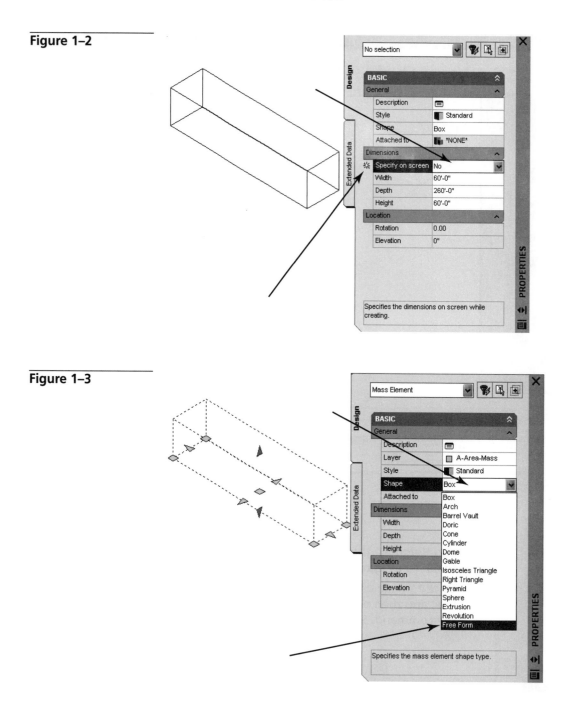

Figure 1–3

2. Select the free form, and move your cursor over the "dot," right-mouse-click, and select **Split Face** from the contextual menu (see Figure 1–4).

You can recognize an editable free form shape because its grips will be changed to dots. Selecting the dots will select the faces of the free form massing object (see Figure 1–5).

3. Set your **OSNAP** settings to **Endpoint** and **Perpendicular**.

4. Enter **fro** in the **Command line** and click on the upper right corner of the face.

Figure 1–4

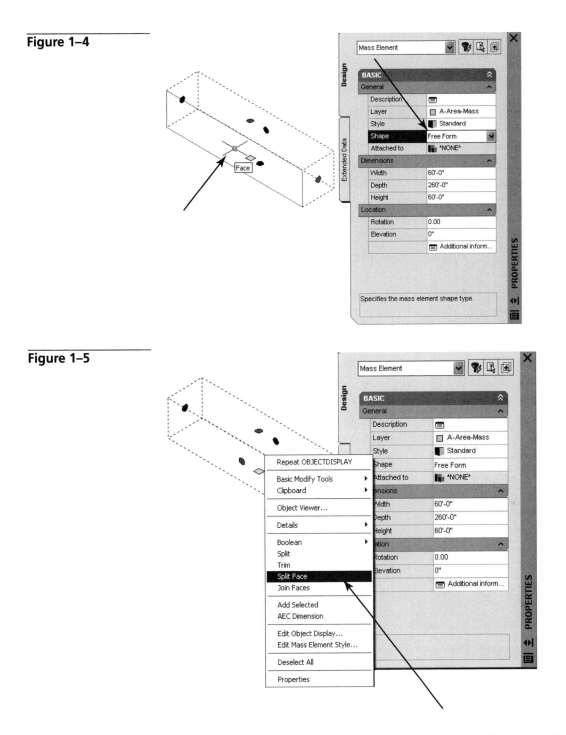

Figure 1–5

5. Move the cursor to the left along the top of the face, and then enter **80′** in the **Command line** and press **Enter.**

6. Finally, move your cursor down to the lower edge of the face until the **Perpendicular Osnap** icon appears, and then click to split the face. Press the **Esc** key to complete the command (see Figure 1–6).

Select the control dot on the new face to see your FACE options. Grab the control dot and drag the face. There are six adjustments that can be made to the faces. These are selected by pressing the **Ctrl key** on the keyboard as you drag (see Figure 1–7).

Figure 1–6

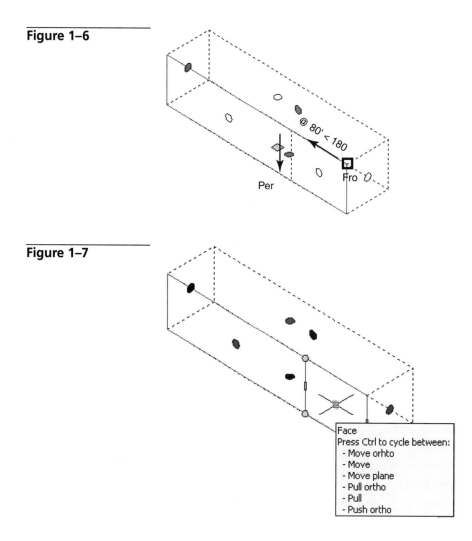

Figure 1–7

Face
Press Ctrl to cycle between:
- Move orhto
- Move
- Move plane
- Pull ortho
- Pull
- Push ortho

Figure 1–8 shows illustrations of different variations. It also illustrates moving edges. Pushing or pulling on the vertical tabs that appear at the edges can move these edges.

By using various primitives and adjusting them by splitting, pushing, pulling, and moving their faces, you can quickly create a mass model of your proposed building.

Now continue on to the next step in the hands-on tutorial.

7. Pull on the dot and press the **Ctrl** key on your keyboard until the face pulls forward.

8. Enter **60′** in the **Command line** and press **Enter** (see Figure 1–9).

9. Drag another box massing object into the drawing area.

10. This time, similar to Step 6, select **YES** from the drop-down list next to the **Specify on screen** option on the **Properties** tool palette. (This will now allow you to adjust your massing object while placing it.)

11. Make sure your **End Point Osnap** is active.

12. Place a box massing object on top of the massing object that has been modified previously.

Figure 1–8

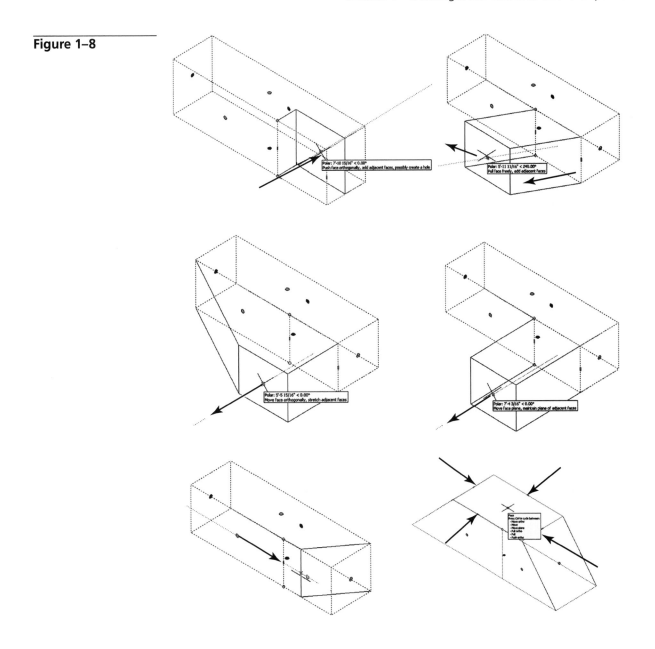

Polar: 7'-10 15/16" < 0.00°
Push face orthogonally, add adjacent faces, possibly create a hole

Polar: 5'-11 11/16" < 240.00°
Pull face freely, add adjacent faces

Polar: 5'-5 15/16" < 0.00°
Move face orthogonally, stretch adjacent faces

Polar: 7'-4 3/16" < 0.00°
Move face plane, maintain plane of adjacent faces

13.   With the new box massing object selected, right-mouse-click and select **Boolean** > **Union** from the contextual menu (see Figure 1–10).

You have now created a modified massing object made from two massing objects (see Figure 1–11).

Figure 1–9

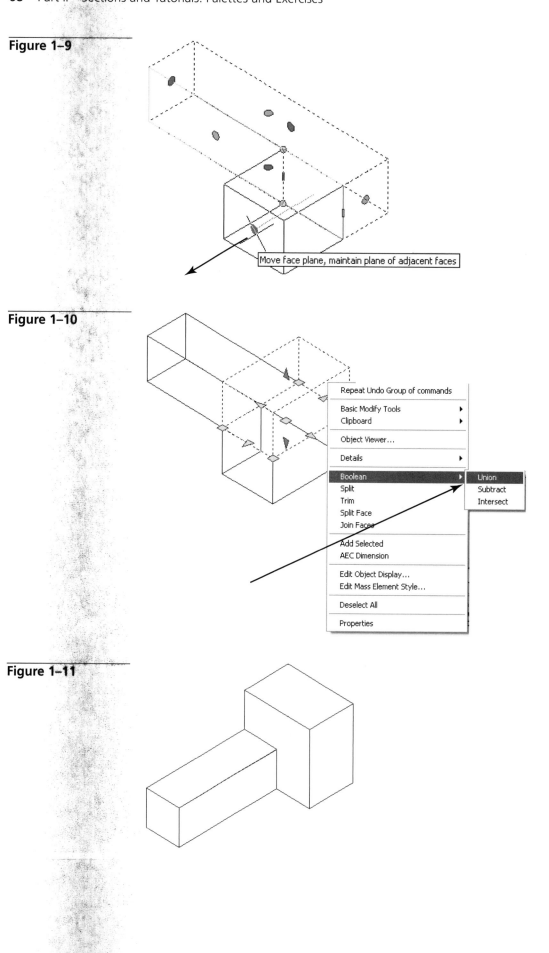

Move face plane, maintain plane of adjacent faces

Figure 1–10

Repeat Undo Group of commands

Basic Modify Tools
Clipboard

Object Viewer...

Details

Boolean   Union
Split   Subtract
Trim   Intersect
Split Face
Join Faces

Add Selected
AEC Dimension

Edit Object Display...
Edit Mass Element Style...

Deselect All

Properties

Figure 1–11

Hands-On

Creating and Attaching Slice Plates (Floor Slices)

1. Select the **Massing** tool palette, and select the **Slice** icon (see Figure 1–12).
2. Click in the Top viewport.
3. Enter 11 in the **Command line** and press **Enter.**
4. Select a spot near the massing model, and then place a second to create a rectangle. (**Note:** This rectangle is just a marker; make it big enough to be comfortable for you to see.)
5. Accept the default **Rotation (0.00),** accept **Starting height (0"),** and set the distance between slices to 10'-0". Then press the **Enter** key to complete the command.
6. Select all the markers with a window crossing, **RMB,** and select **Attach Objects** from the contextual menu that appears.
7. Select the massing object that you created in the previous section and press **Enter.**

You have now created 11 slice plates (floor slices) in your massing object (see Figure 1–13).

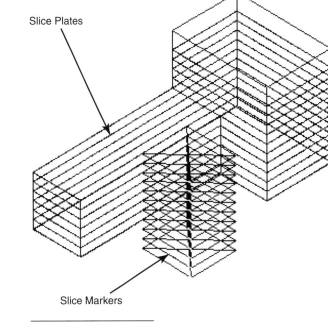

Slice Plates

Slice Markers

Figure 1–12

Figure 1–13

8. Change to the **NW Isometric View** and select the topmost slice marker.
9. **RMB** and select **Set Elevation** from the contextual menu.
10. Enter **115'** in the **Command-line** and press **Enter** (note that the topmost slice plate moves downward). Save this file.

 Note: Slice plates can also be adjusted by selecting the Front View and moving the slice markers in the Y direction.

Hiding the Slice Markers

1. Select one of the slice markers, **RMB,** and select **Edit Object Display** from the contextual menu that appears to bring up the **Object Display** dialog box.

2. Double-click on the word **General** to bring up the Display Properties dialog box.

3. Turn the **Cut Plane** and **Outline** visibility off, and then press the **OK** buttons on the dialog boxes to complete the command and return to the Drawing Editor.

Hands-On

Modifying the Massing Object After Applying the Slice Plates

1. Select another box massing object from the **Massing** tool palette, and give it a 30′ width, 60′ depth, and 60′ height.

2. Place the new object as shown in Figure 1–14.

3. Select the original massing object, **RMB,** select **Boolean > Subtraction** from the contextual menu, and select the new massing object.

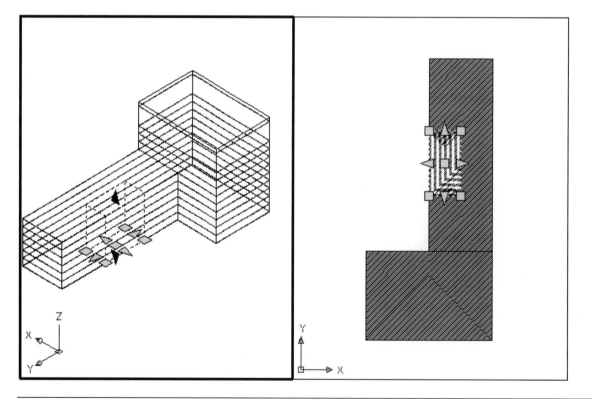

Figure 1–14

Note: If you have trouble selecting the massing objects because you keep selecting the slice plates instead, you can temporarily turn off the visibility of their layer.

4. Enter **Y** (Yes) in the **Command line** to erase the layout geometry.

Notice that the slice plates follow the new outline created by the Boolean subtraction (see Figure 1–15).

5. Using the massing object modification techniques, modify the massing object.

Figure 1–15

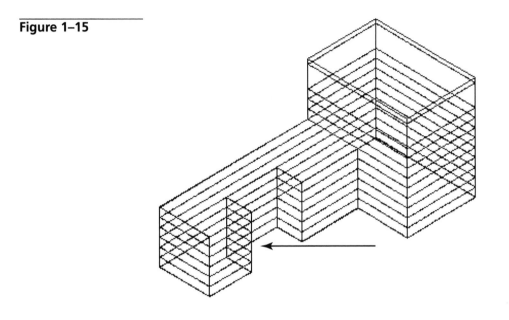

6. Create new massing objects and Boolean them to the original object.

The slice plates will always follow the modified massing object (massing model) (see Figure 1–16).

7. **RMB** in an empty space in the Drawing Editor, select Object Viewer from the contextual menu, and select the massing object.

8. Turn on **Perspective** and **Flat Shaded** to see the model (see Figures 1–17 and 1–18). Save the file.

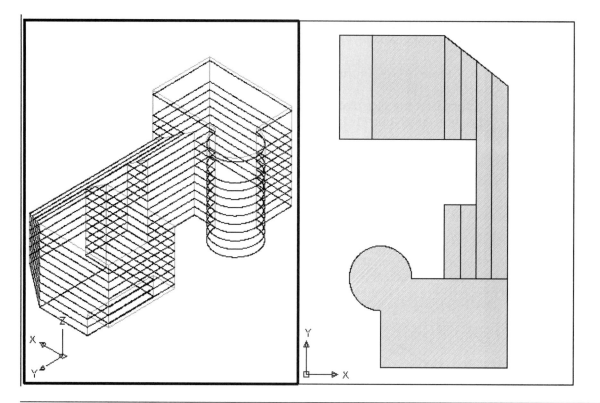

Figure 1–16

Figure 1–17

Figure 1–18

Hands-On

Changing the Slice Plates into Space Boundaries and Walls

1. Use the previous exercise's file.
2. Change to the **Model Layout.**
3. Change to SW **Isometric View.**
4. Select the **Content Browser** icon from the **Main** toolbar to bring up the Content Browser.
5. Select the **Autodesk Architectural Desktop Stock Tool Catalog > Architectural Object Tools > Page 2,** and drag the **Space Boundary** tool into your tool palette.
6. **RMB** on the **Space Boundary** tool and select **Apply Tool Properties > Slice** from the contextual menu that appears.
7. Select all the slices and press **Enter.**
8. Select each space boundary, open the Properties palette, and change the **Base Height** to **10'-0".**
9. Select any other slice and change its particular height to match your needs.
10. Select each space boundary, **RMB,** and select **Generate Walls** from the contextual menu that appears.

The slices have now been converted to wall objects.

Hands-On

Using the Drape Tool to Create Contour Massing Models

1. Start a new drawing using the Aec Model (Imperial Stb) template.
2. Change to the **Model Layout.**
3. Change to the **Top View.**
4. Using the **Rectangle** tool from the **Draw** menu, draw and modify until you get a drawing similar to that in Figure 1–19.

Figure 1–19

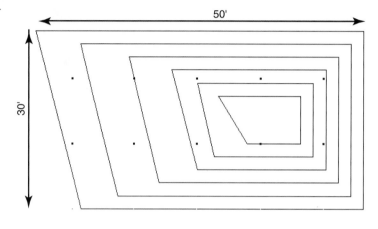

5. Select each modify rectangle, **RMB,** and change the elevation of each to 2'-0" increments with the smallest rectangle having an elevation of 12'-0".
6. Change to **SW Isometric View** (see Figure 1–20).
7. Select the **Drape Tool** from the **Massing** tool palette, select all the contours, and press **Enter.**
8. Select two opposite corners of the bottommost modified rectangle, and press **Enter.**

Figure 1–20

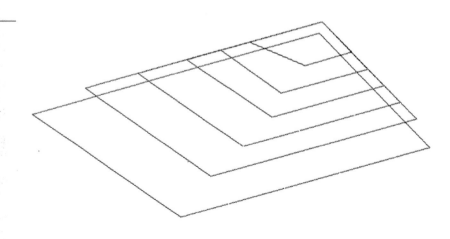

9. Accept the mesh size of 30, and press **Enter.**

10. Enter **2'-0"** in the **Command line** for the base thickness and press Enter to complete the command.

11. Erase the modified rectangles.

12. Press the **Gouraud** icon in the **Shading** toolbar to shade the contour massing model (see Figure 1–21).

Figure 1–21

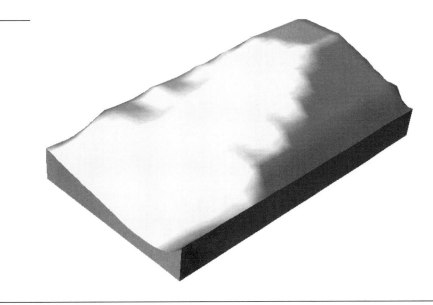

Space and Space Boundary Objects

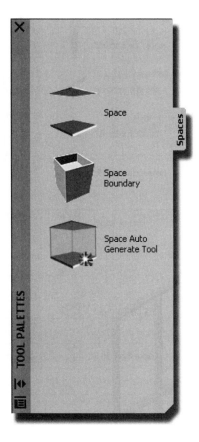

When you finish this section, you should understand the following:

- ✔ How to create a spaces tool palette.
- ✔ How to create a space object.
- ✔ How to create a simple space plan with space objects.
- ✔ How to apply space boundaries.
- ✔ How to use the **Space Auto Generate** tool.
- ✔ How to use the **AEC Modify Trim** option.
- ✔ How to use the **AEC Modify Divide** option.
- ✔ How to use the **AEC Modify Merge** option.
- ✔ How to use the **AEC Modify Crop** option.
- ✔ How to use the space object grip features.

Space objects and space boundary objects create a sophisticated but easy-to-use space-planning system.

Space objects can contain Property Set Data that can be retrieved automatically and read in AEC schedules. They can also represent ceilings and floors in cut sections.

The space object represents contained 3D space. It includes floor and ceiling thickness, floor-to-ceiling heights, elevation, and ancillary space heights. All the aforementioned attributes can be modified easily. The space object does not contain wall information.

The space boundary object represents the area that contains space. It includes wall thickness and height, which can be modified through the **Properties** tool palette. The space object does not contain floor or ceiling information.

Space boundary objects can Manage the space objects that they contain.

Space Objects Properties Tool Palette

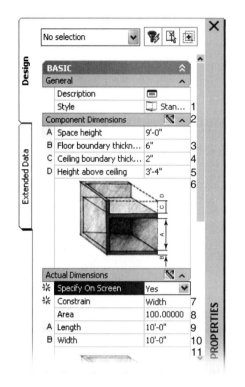

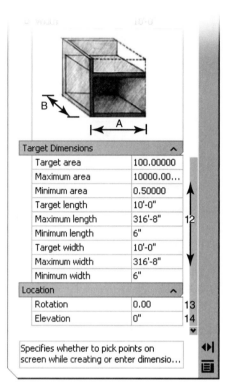

Number	Name	Purpose
1	Style	Select from available space styles
2	Create Type	Insert, Rectangle, or Polygon shapes
3	Space height	Floor-to-ceiling height
4	Floor boundary thickness	Floor thickness
5	Ceiling boundary thickness	Ceiling thickness
6	Height above ceiling	Distance above top of ceiling to top of wall (when space boundary or wall is generated)
7	Specify on screen	Change length and width by dragging on screen
8	Constrain	Constrain dragging of object to only Area, Length, Width, or None
9	Area	Preset area value of space object
10	Length	Preset length value of space object
11	Width	Preset width value of space object
12	Target dimensions	Preset space object style values
13	Rotation	Preset rotation angle of space object
14	Elevation	Preset elevation of space object

Hands-On

Creating a Spaces Tool Palette

1. Click on the tool palettes **Properties** icon at the bottom left of the tool palette to pop up the **Tool Palette** contextual menu.

2. Select **New Palette** and name it **Spaces** (see Figure 2–1).

3. Select the **Contact Browser** icon from the **Main** toolbar to bring up the Content Browser.

4. Select the **Autodesk Architectural Desktop Stock Tool Catalog** to open the next page.

5. At the next page, select **Architectural Object Tools** to open the next page.

6. Click on **Next** in the bottom right corner of the page to bring up **Page 2.**

7. Click on the **iDrop** icon and drag space, space boundary, and **Space Auto Generate** tool onto your new **Spaces** tool palette.

8. Repeat this process selecting the **Architectural Desktop Documentation Tool Catalog-Imperial > Schedule Tags > Room & Finish Tags** and dragging the **Space Tag** into the **Spaces** tool palette (see Figure 2–2).

You have now created and populated your own **Spaces** tool palette.

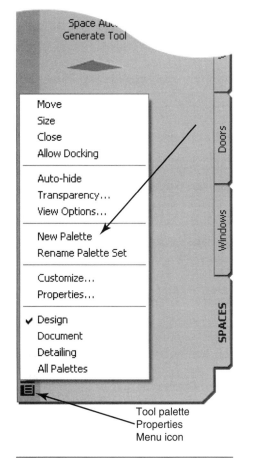

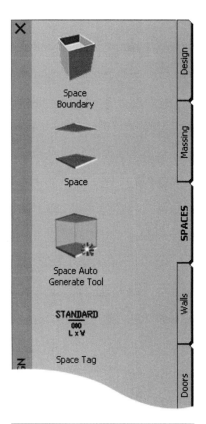

Figure 2–1   **Figure 2–2**

Hands-On

Creating a Space Object and Labeling It with a Space Tag

1. Start a new drawing using the Aec Model (Imperial Stb) template.
2. Change to the **Model Layout.**
3. Change to the **Top View.**
4. From the **Main menu,** select **Format > Style Manager** to bring up the **Style Manager** dialog box.
5. Select the **Architectural Objects** folder and double-click on **Space Styles. RMB** and select **New** from the contextual menu.
6. Create several new space styles and call them **Hall, Small Office, Large Office, Men's Toilet Room, Women's Toilet Room,** and **Entrance.** Press the **OK** button to close this dialog box.
7. Click on the **Space** icon on the **Spaces** tool palette, and move your cursor over the **Properties** tool palette to open it.
8. Set the following:

    a. Style = **Hall**
    b. Space height = **7'-0"**
    c. Ceiling boundary thickness = **2"**
    d. Floor boundary thickness = **4"**
    e. Height above ceiling = **1'-6"**
    f. Specify on screen = **Yes**
    g. Constrain = ***NONE***

9. Click in the Drawing Editor and press **Enter** three times to complete the command.

You have now placed a space object called Hall.

10. Click on the **Space Tag** icon on the **Spaces** tool palette and select the space object you just placed.
11. Press **Enter** to center the tag on the object and bring up the **Edit Property Set Data** dialog box.
12. Select the **Add Property Sets** icon (Figure 2–3) to bring up the **Add Property Sets** dialog box (Figure 2–4).

! ● **Note:** The **Edit Property Set Data** dialog box is where you enter information to be stored in the space object.

The **Add Property Sets** dialog box contains check boxes to determine if you wish to include room finish and/or room object information in the space object.

13. In the **Add Property Sets** dialog box check the **RoomFinishObjects** and **RoomObjects** check boxes and press **Enter** to return to the **Edit Property Set Data** dialog box.
14. Stretch the **Edit Property Set Data** dialog box to its full extent.

Edit Property Set Data ✕

Edit the property set data for the object:

GeoObjects	⌃
Data source	H:\ARCHITECT 4\SPA…
Building	--
Department	--
Description	--
Division	

[Add property sets]

[OK] [Cancel] [Help]

Figure 2–3

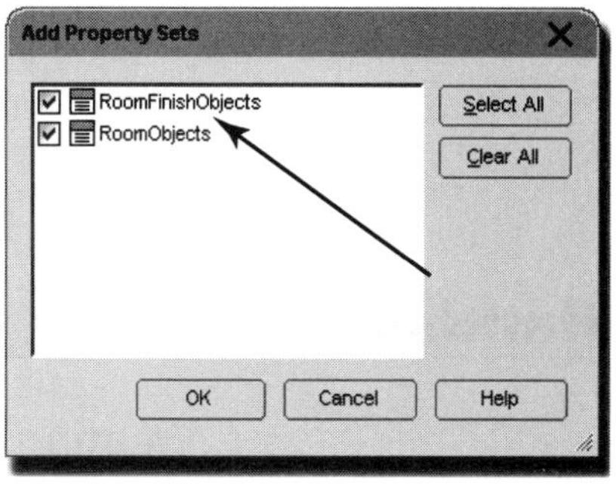

Add Property Sets ✕

| ☑ 🗒 RoomFinishObjects | Select All |
| ☑ 🗒 RoomObjects | Clear All |

[OK] [Cancel] [Help]

Figure 2–4

15.   In the **Edit Property Set Data** dialog box enter the data shown in Figure 2–5.

! **Note:** The yellow lightning bolts in the **Edit Property Set Data** dialog box signify information that already exists in the space object (see Figure 2–5).

16.   Press **OK** to complete the command and return to the Drawing Editor.

You now have a tagged space object (see Figure 2–6). Save this drawing.

Figure 2–5

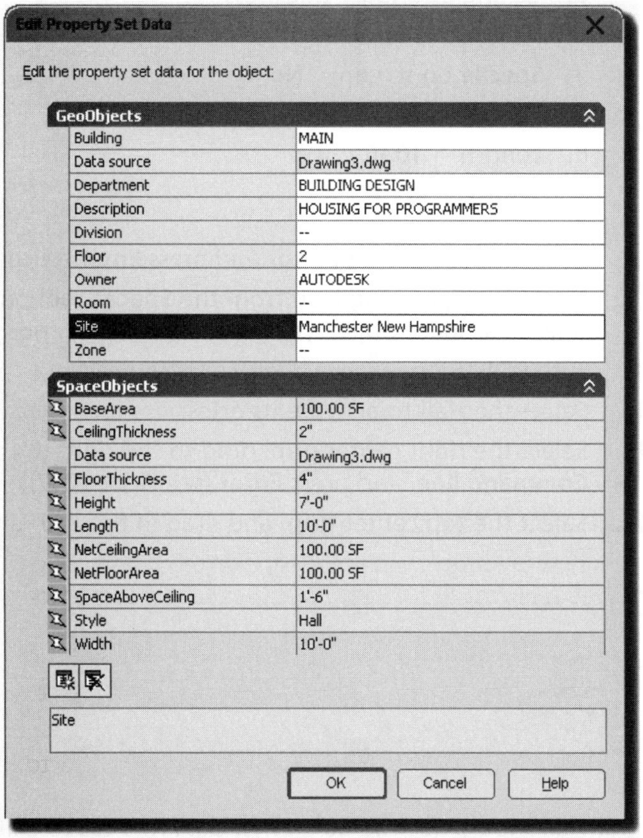

Edit Property Set Data ✕

Edit the property set data for the object:

GeoObjects	⌃
Building	MAIN
Data source	Drawing3.dwg
Department	BUILDING DESIGN
Description	HOUSING FOR PROGRAMMERS
Division	--
Floor	2
Owner	AUTODESK
Room	--
Site	Manchester New Hampshire
Zone	--

SpaceObjects		⌃
⚡	BaseArea	100.00 SF
⚡	CeilingThickness	2"
	Data source	Drawing3.dwg
⚡	FloorThickness	4"
⚡	Height	7'-0"
⚡	Length	10'-0"
⚡	NetCeilingArea	100.00 SF
⚡	NetFloorArea	100.00 SF
⚡	SpaceAboveCeiling	1'-6"
⚡	Style	Hall
⚡	Width	10'-0"

Site

[OK] [Cancel] [Help]

Figure 2–6

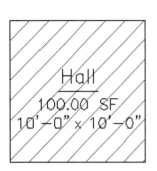

Hands-On

Creating a Simple Space Plan with Space Objects

1. Use the previous exercise.
2. Change to the **Model Layout.**
3. Change to the **Top View.**
4. Select the **Space** icon from the **Spaces** tool palette you created.
5. Move your cursor over the **Properties** palette to open it.
6. Set the following:

   a. Style = **Hall**
   b. Space height = **9′-0″**
   c. Floor boundary thickness = **12″**
   d. Ceiling boundary thickness = **2″**
   e. Height above ceiling = **0″**
   f. Specify on screen = **No**
   g. Constrain = ***NONE***
   h. Length = **10′-0″**
   i. Width = **10′-0″**

7. Click in the **Drawing Editor** and press **Enter** twice.
8. Select the **Space Tag** icon from the **Spaces** tool palette you created, select the space object you placed in Step 7, and press **Enter** twice.
9. Turn **POLAR** on.
10. Select the Hall to activate its grips.
11. Select the right center grip, drag to the right (0°), enter **30′-0″** in the **Command line,** and press **Enter** (see Figure 2–7).
12. Select the top center grip, and drag in the 270° direction 3′-0″.

Figure 2–7

Your Hall should now be 40′ × 7′ wide. Press **Esc** to exit the command.

13. Again select the **Space** icon from the **Spaces** tool palette you created.

14. In the **Properties** palette set the following:

    a. Style = **Entrance**

    b. Space height = **12'-0"**

    c. Floor boundary thickness = **12"**

    d. Ceiling boundary thickness = **2"**

    e. Height above ceiling = **0"**

    f. Specify on screen = **No**

    g. Constrain = ***NONE***

    h. Length = **10'-0"**

    i. Width = **30'-0"**

15. Place the **Entrance** space as shown in Figure 2–8.

16. Select the **Entrance** space, **RMB,** and select **AEC Modify Tools;** then select **Divide** from the contextual menu that appears.

Figure 2–8

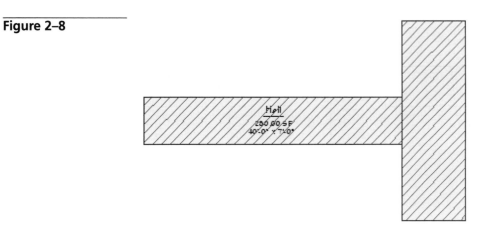

17. Drag a line across the Entrance space to create two spaces as shown in Figure 2–9.

Figure 2–9

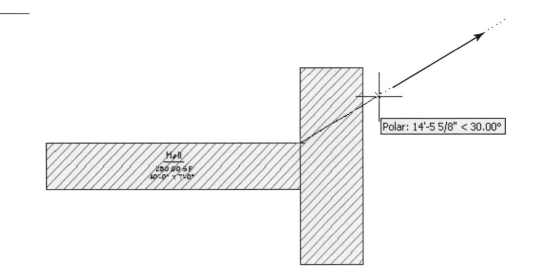

18. Again select the **Space** icon from the **Spaces** tool palette you created.

19. In the **Properties** palette set the following:

  a. Style = **Large Office**

  b. Space height = **7'-0"**

  c. Floor boundary thickness = **12"**

  d. Ceiling boundary thickness = **2"**

  e. Height above ceiling = **0"**

  f. Specify on screen = **No**

  g. Constrain = ***NONE***

  h. Length = **10'-0"**

  i. Width = **15'-0"**

20. Enter **D** in the **Command line** and press **Enter** until the insertion point of the Large Office space object is at the upper left of the object.

21. Snap the Large Office space object, the Hall, as shown in Figure 2–10.

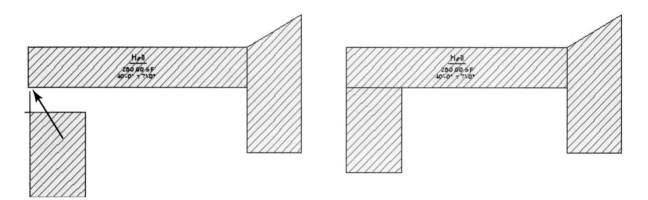

Figure 2–10

22. Array the Large Office four columns to the right, and mirror it as shown in Figure 2–11.

23. Complete the space plan by adding the toilet rooms.

24. Select the **Space Tag** icon from the **Spaces** tool palette, select each space, and press **Enter** to continue placing each tag until all the space are labeled (Figure 2–12).

Figure 2–11

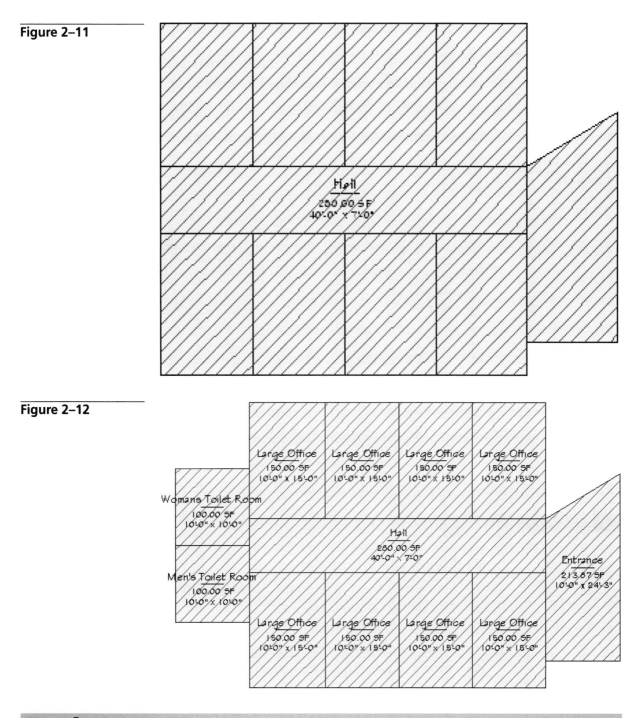

Figure 2–12

Hands-On

Applying Space Boundaries

1. Use the previous exercise. Review Steps 6–9 on page 73 before you do steps 2–5.

2. RMB on the **Space Boundary** icon and select **Apply tool properties to > Space** from the contextual menu that appears.

3. Move your cursor over the **Properties** palette to open it.

4. Select the **Quick Select** icon; select **Space Boundary** from the **Object Type** drop-down list.

5. Choose **Select All** from the **Operator** drop-down list, and press the **OK** button.

6. Again move your cursor over the **Properties** palette to open it.

7. Select **Solid** from the **Boundary** type drop-down list.

8. Press the **Esc** key twice to complete the command.

Space boundaries have been placed around the spaces (see Figure 2–13).

Figure 2–13

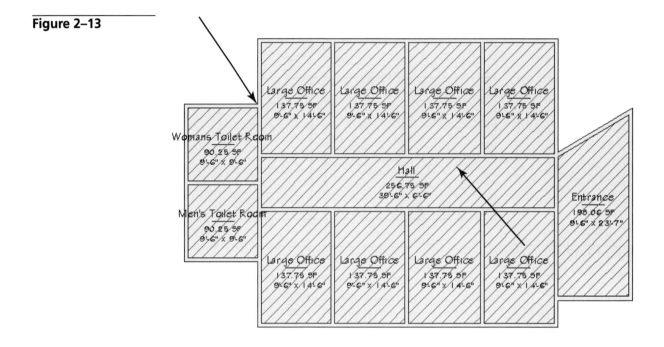

Hands-On

Modifying Space Boundaries

1. Start a new drawing using the Aec Model (Imperial Stb) template.

2. Change to the **Model Layout.**

3. Change to the **Top View.**

4. Select the **Space** icon from the **Spaces** tool palette you created.

5. Insert a space in the Drawing Editor with the following properties:

   a. Style = **Standard**

   b. Space height = **8'-0"**

   c. Floor boundary thickness = **12"**

   d. Ceiling boundary thickness = **2"**

   e. Height above ceiling = **2"**

   f. Specify on screen = **No**

   g. Constrain = ***NONE***

   h. Length = **30'**

   i. Width = **30'**

6. From the **Design** Palette, **Pick** the **Space Boundary** icon. **RMB.** Select **Apply Tool Properties to > Spaces,** and select the space.

7. Using **Quick Select,** find and change the space boundary to Solid boundary type, with a width of 12".

8. Change to the **SW Isometric View.**

9. Double-click the space boundary to open its **Properties** palette.

10. Select **Ceiling stops at boundary** from the **Ceiling condition** drop-down list. The upper wall will appear in a boundary condition.

11. Enter **3'-0"** in the **Upper extension** data field and press **Enter.**

12. Press the **Esc** key twice to clear the space boundary's grips (see Figure 2–14).

Figure 2–14

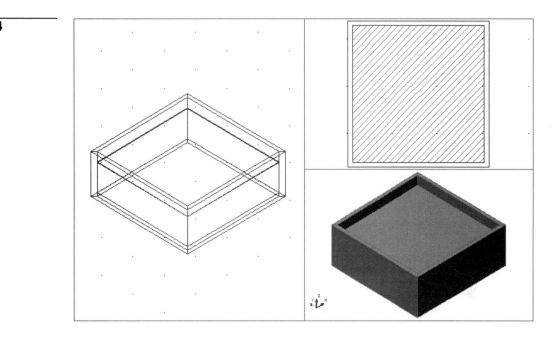

13. Select the space boundary again, and **RMB** anywhere in the Drawing Editor to bring up the contextual menu.

14. Select **Edit Edges** from the contextual menu.

> **!** *Note:* **Edit Edges** and **Add Edges** are the options Architectural Desktop uses to edit any segment of a space boundary.

15. Select the space boundary again, and **RMB** anywhere in the Drawing Editor to bring up the contextual menu.

16. Select **Edit Edges** from the contextual menu.

17. Select the edge shown in Figure 2–15, and press **Enter** to bring up the **Boundary Edge Properties** dialog box.

18. Select the **Dimensions** tab.

This tab contains controls for the type, width, and justification of space boundaries.

19. Select the **Design Rules** tab.

Figure 2–15

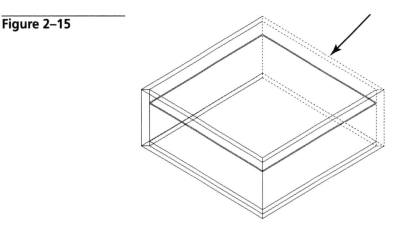

This tab contains controls for the space boundary conditions at the ceiling and floors in relation to spaces.

20.   Uncheck the **Automatically Determine from Spaces** check box.

This will disconnect the relationship of the chosen space boundary segment from the adjacent space.

21.   In the **B-Upper Extension** data box, enter 8′-0″.
22.   Select the **Ceiling Stops at Wall** radio button, and press **Enter.**

The top of the space boundary segment is now **8′-0″** above the ceiling of the adjacent space (Figure 2–16).

Figure 2–16

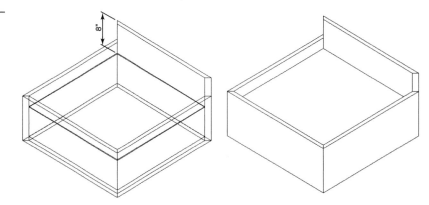

23.   Change to the **Top View.**
24.   Select the space boundary, **RMB,** and select **Insert Joint** from the contextual menu that appears.
25.   Select the midpoint of the leftmost space boundary segment.

Nothing will appear to happen, but a joint has been added. (If you change to **SW Isometric View,** you can see the joint.)

26.   Select the space boundary again and notice that two more grips appear on the leftmost segment.
27.   Click and drag one of the new grips to the left (180°) **10′-0″** and press **Enter.**

Notice that the Space Object fills the space. This is because the **Manage spaces** check box is checked (Figure 2–17).

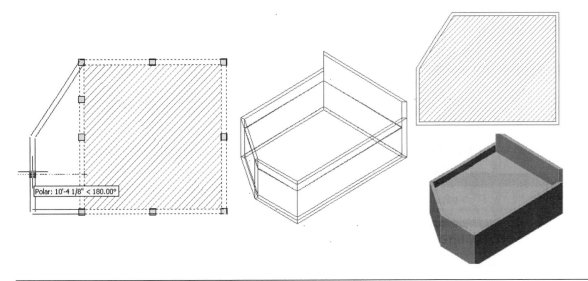

Figure 2–17

28. Undo the command, and return to Step 27 of this exercise.
29. Repeat Step 27, but hold down the **Ctrl** button while dragging the grip.
30. Again enter **10'-0"** in the **Command line** and press **Enter.**
31. Double-click the space boundary again to open its **Properties** palette.

Notice that the space boundary drags a rectangular space out from the segment (Figure 2–18). To accomplish the movement shown in Figure 2–18, grab the grip and move it; then hold down the **CTRL** key.
   Repeat this process inserting joints and pulling on different grips (see Figure 2–19).

Figure 2–18

Figure 2–19

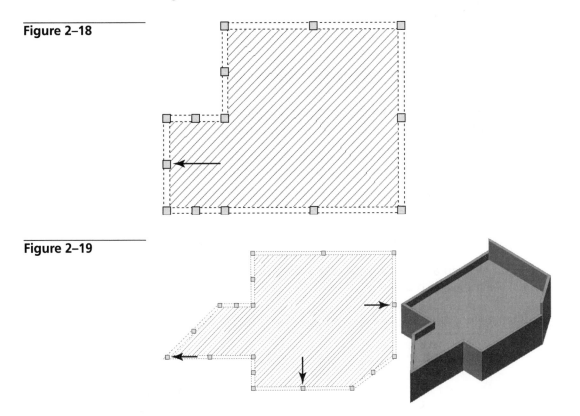

32. Double-click on the space boundary again to bring up its **Properties** palette.
33. Change the selection in the **Manage contained spaces** drop-down list to **No.**

This disconnects the intelligent linkage between the space boundary and the adjacent space object.

34. **RMB** anywhere in the Drawing Editor to bring up the contextual menu.
35. Select **Remove Edges** from the contextual menu.
36. Select the segment shown in Figure 2–20, and press **Enter** to complete the command.
37. Change to the **Top View.**

Figure 2–20

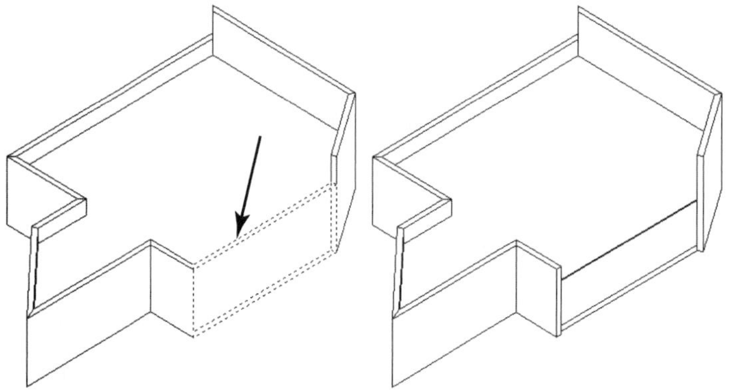

38. Double-click on the space boundary again to bring up its **Properties** palette.
39. Change the **Manage contained spaces** drop-down list back to **Yes** to reconnect electronically the space boundary and the space object.
40. Again **RMB** anywhere in the Drawing Editor to bring up the contextual menu.
41. Select **Add Edges** from the contextual menu.
42. Move your cursor over the **Properties** palette to open it.
43. Set **Width** to **18".**
44. Turn the **Near** and **Perpendicular** snaps on.
45. Near snap to the right-hand space boundary segment, and add three 109-00 segments returning perpendicular to the starting segment as shown in Figure 2–21. These new segments are now part of the original space boundary.

To add a Space object to the **Added Edges**, use the **Space Auto Generate** tool, which is demonstrated in the following exercise.

Figure 2–21

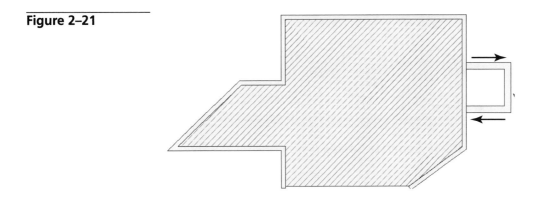

Hands-On

Using the Space Auto Generate Tool

1. Start a new drawing using the Aec Model (Imperial Stb) template.
2. Change to the **Model Layout.**
3. Change to the **Top View.**
4. Select **Format** > **Style Manager** from the **Main** toolbar to bring up the **Style Manager** dialog box.
5. Create five new space styles and call them **A, B, C, D,** and **E,** respectively, and then press the **OK** button.
6. Using lines, polylines, and a circle, create the 2D drawing shown in Figure 2–22.
7. Select the **Space Auto Generate** tool from the **Spaces** tool palette to bring up the **Generate Spaces** dialog box (see Figure 2–23).

Figure 2–22

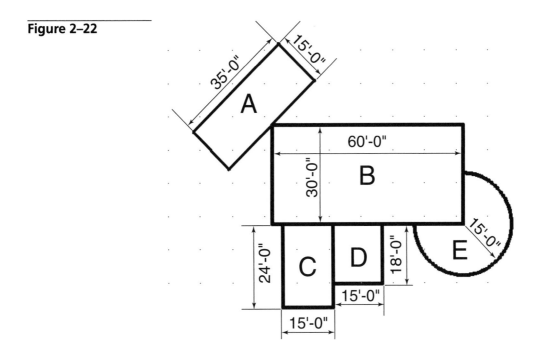

Figure 2–23

8.   In the **Generate Spaces** dialog box set the following

   a.   Style = **A**
   b.   Name = **Room A**
   c.   Increment = **1** (this will record how many spaces have been placed)
   d.   Select the **Automatic** radio button
   e.   Filter = **All Linework**

9.   Press the **Tag Settings** button to bring up the **Tag Settings** dialog box.

10. Check the **Add Tag to New Spaces** check box to open the **Tag Settings** dialog box. Select **Aec3_Room_Tag** from the **Tag Definition** drop-down list, check the **Auto-Increment Numerical Properties** check box, check the **Add Properties Set to New Spaces** check box, check the **Auto-Increment Numerical Properties** check box and set **Increment** to **1** (this will set the tag to increment the space 1 number each time a space is placed).

11. Press the **OK** button to close the **Tag Settings** dialog box, and click inside the A enclosure. Don't close the **Generate Spaces** dialog box.

12. In the **Generate Spaces** dialog box, change the **Style** to **B,** and **Name** to **Room B** and then click in the B enclosure. Repeat this process changing the **Style** and **Name** until all the spaces have been created with all the space styles.

13. Apply a space boundary to the spaces. To do this, **RMB** on the **Space Boundary** palette icon, select the **Apply Tools Properties to Space,** and select all the spaces.

14. Change the space boundary to **Solid** boundary. To do this, double-click on the space boundary to bring up the **Properties** palette. In the **Properties** palette, select **Solid** from the **Boundary Type** drop-down list. (see Figure 2–24).

Figure 2–24

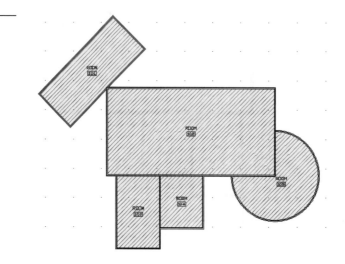

15. Enter space on the **Command line** and press **Enter.**
16. Enter **Q** (Query) on the **Command line** and press **Enter.**
17. The **Space Information** dialog box will appear.
18. Select the **Space Info Total** tab.

Here you will see the quantities and areas of each space (Figure 2–25).

19. Press the **Create MDB** button and save the file for use in a database program such as Microsoft Access.

Figure 2–26 shows a shaded perspective of the space plan created using the **Space Auto Generate** tool.

Figure 2–25

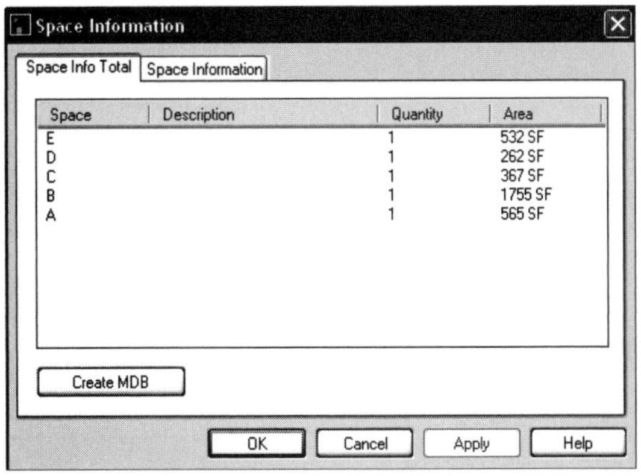

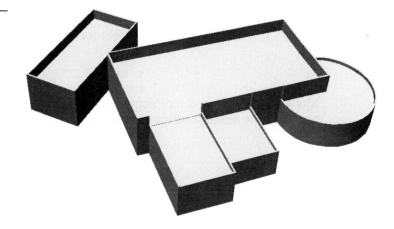

Figure 2–26

Hands-On

Using the AEC MODIFY Tool To Modify Spaces

Using the Trim Option

1. Start a new drawing using the Aec Model (Imperial Stb) template.
2. Change to the **Model Layout**
3. Change to the **Top View.**
4. Select the **Space** object icon from the **Design** tool palette, and place a 10′ × 10′ Standard style space object in the Drawing Editor.

5. Select the space object you just placed to activate its grips.

6. Drag the space object to 30' × 30', and press the **Esc** key to deselect the grips.

7. **RMB** in the Drawing Editor and select **AEC Modify Tools > Trim** from the contextual menu that appears (see Figure 2–27).

8. Select the space object and press **Enter.**

9. Select a point to the left of the space object, drag your cursor as shown in Figure 2–28, and click your mouse button. This creates your **Trim** line.

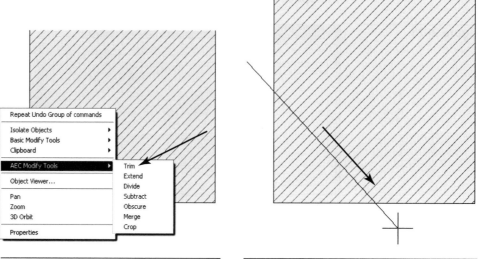

Figure 2–27

Figure 2–28

10. Move your cursor in the direction that you wish to trim, left of the line, and click the mouse button to trim the space object (see Figure 2–29).

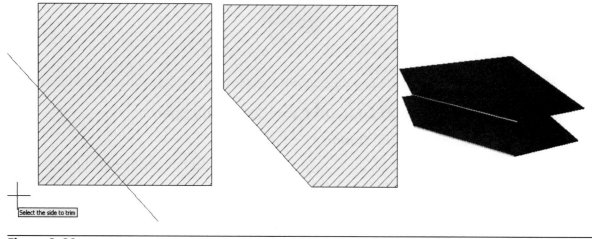

Figure 2–29

Using the Divide Option

11. With the space object *not selected,* **RMB** in the Drawing Editor and select **AEC Modify Tools > Divide** from the contextual menu that appears.

12. Select the space object and then press **Enter.**

13. Select two points in a similar manner as in the **Trim** exercise.

14. Move one division to the right (see Figure 2–30).

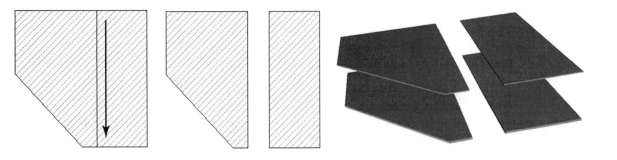

Figure 2–30

Using the Subtract Option

15. From the **Draw** toolbar, place two rectangles and a circle as shown in Figure 2–31.

16. With the space object *not selected,* **RMB** in the Drawing Editor and select **AEC Modify Tools > Subtract** from the contextual menu that appears.

17. Select the right object division and press **Enter.**

18. Select the rectangles and the circle and then press **Enter.**

19. Enter **Y** (Yes) in the **Command line** and press **Enter** (see Figure 2–32).

Figure 2–31

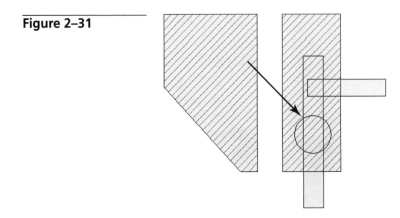

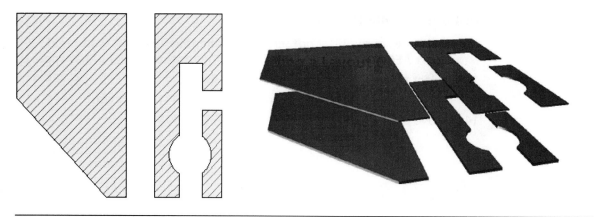

Figure 2–32

Using the Merge Option

20. From the **Draw** toolbar, place two rectangles and a circle as shown in Figure 2–33.

21. With the space object *not selected,* **RMB** in the Drawing Editor and select **AEC Modify Tools > Merge** from the contextual menu that appears.

22. Select the right object division and press **Enter.**

23. Select the rectangles and the circle and then press **Enter.**

24. Enter **Y** (Yes) in the **Command line** and press **Enter** (see Figure 2–34).

Figure 2–33

Figure 2–34

Using the Crop Option

25. From the Draw toolbar, place a rectangle and circle as shown in Figure 2–35.

26. With the space object *not selected,* **RMB** in the Drawing Editor and select **AEC Modify Tools > Crop** from the contextual menu that appears.

27. Select the space object division and press **Enter.**

28. Select the rectangle and the circle and then press **Enter.**

29. Enter **Y** (Yes) in the **Command line** and press **Enter** (see Figure 2–36)

Figure 2–35

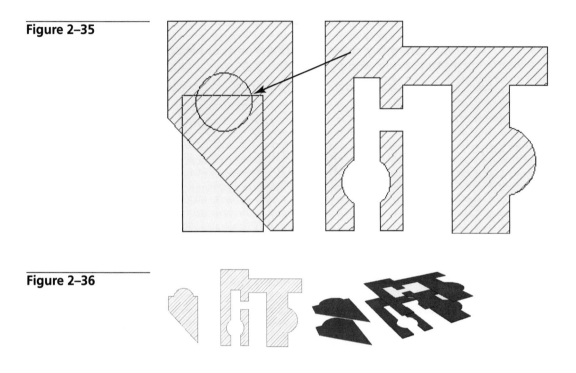

Figure 2–36

Hands-On

Using the Space Object Grip Features

Adding and Removing a Vertex

1. Start a new drawing using the Aec Model (Imperial Stb) template.

2. Change to the **Model Layout.**

3. Change to the **Top View.**

4. Select the **Space** object icon from the **Design** tool palette, and place a 10′ × 10′ Standard-style space object in the Drawing editor.

5. Select the space object to activate its grips.

6. Move your cursor over the right **Edge** grip to show the grip's "tool tip" (see Figure 2–37).

7. Select the right **Edge** grip, and drag to the right (see Figure 2–38).

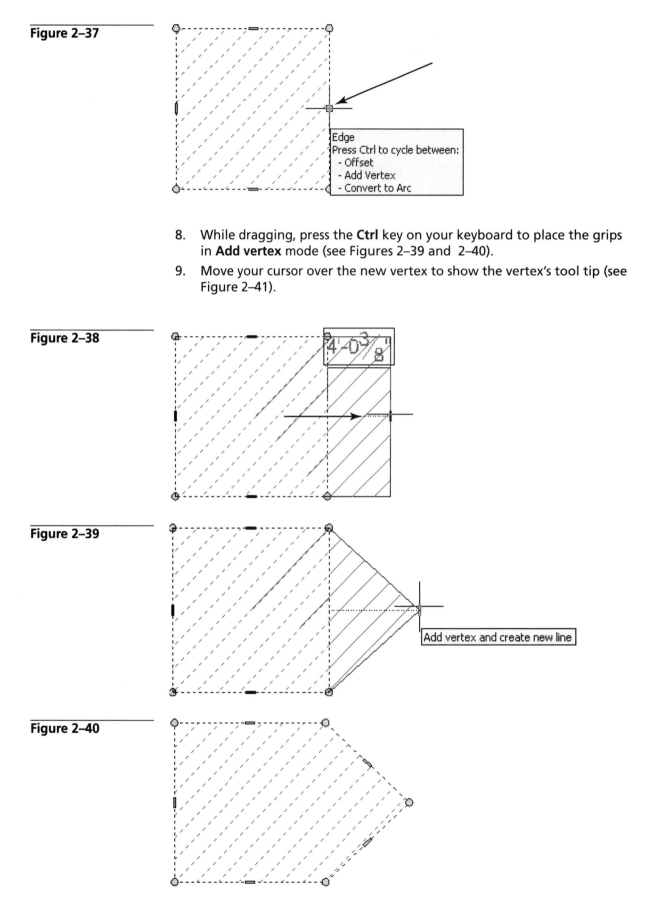

Figure 2–37

8. While dragging, press the **Ctrl** key on your keyboard to place the grips in **Add vertex** mode (see Figures 2–39 and 2–40).

9. Move your cursor over the new vertex to show the vertex's tool tip (see Figure 2–41).

Figure 2–38

Figure 2–39

Figure 2–40

Figure 2–41

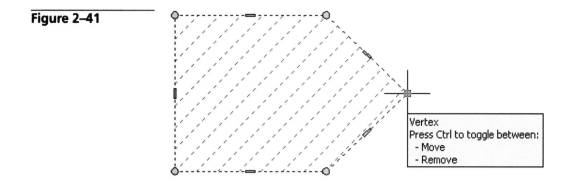

10. Select the new vertex, press the **Ctrl** key on your keyboard, and click the mouse button to remove or move the vertex.

11. Remove the vertex.

12. Click the right **Edge** grip again and drag it to the right. While dragging, press the **Ctrl** key on your keyboard twice and then click to create an arc (see Figure 2–42).

Figure 2–42

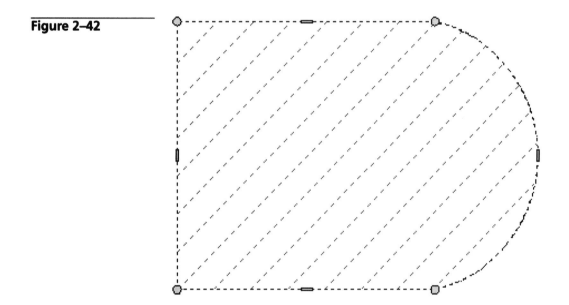

Walls

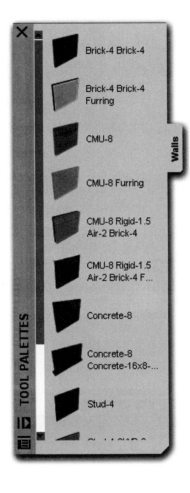

TOOL PALETTES

Brick-4 Brick-4

Brick-4 Brick-4 Furring

CMU-8

CMU-8 Furring

CMU-8 Rigid-1.5 Air-2 Brick-4

CMU-8 Rigid-1.5 Air-2 Brick-4 F...

Concrete-8

Concrete-8 Concrete-16x8-...

Stud-4

Walls

When you finish this section, you should understand the following:

✔ How to place a wall object.
✔ How to change walls by dynamically pulling on grips.
✔ How to create **wall sweeps.**
✔ How to create wall endcaps using **Calculate Automatically.**
✔ How to use **plan modifiers.**
✔ How to use **body modifiers.**
✔ How to use the **Roof/Floor** line option.
✔ How to use **interference conditions.**
✔ How to use **Cleanups—Applying 'T' Cleanup** and **Wall Merge.**
✔ How to edit wall styles.

Wall objects can be dragged or inserted either from the **Design** tool palette, or by typing **walladd** in the **Command line.**

WALLS

Wall objects are the basis of all buildings; they enclose space and give the building its character. Because buildings require a vast variety of wall types and configurations, these objects have become very sophisticated in Autodesk Architectural Desktop 2006. In order to understand how to use ADT 2006's wall objects, we must first understand some basic ADT 2006 wall object conventions. Among these conventions are **Base Height, Baseline, Roofline Offset from Base Height, Floor Line Offset from Baseline,** and **Justification** (see Figure 3–1).

Figure 3–1

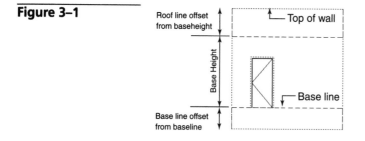

Wall Objects Properties Tool Palette

ADT 2006 contains controls and routines for modifying the shape of the wall itself. These include **Wall Sweeps, Wall Endcaps and Opening Endcaps, Plan Modifiers, Body Modifiers, Modifications to the Roof/Floor lines, and Interference Conditions.**

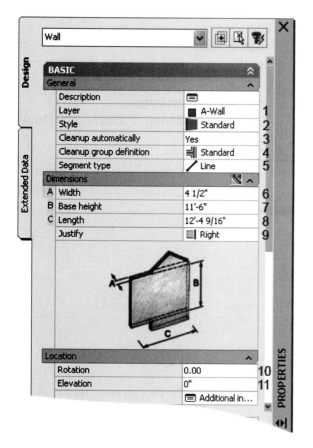

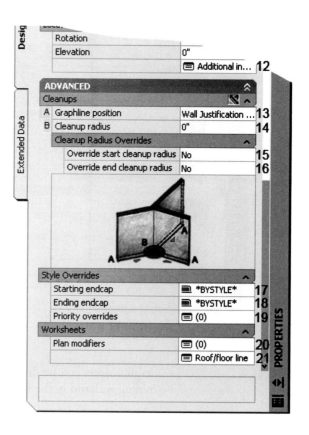

Number	Name	Purpose
1	Layer	Change this to place the wall on another layer
2	Style	Change this to change to another style such as 12″ brick and block, etc.
3	Cleanup automatically	Change to Yes or No if you want the wall to join with similar components of intersecting walls

4	Cleanup group definition	Change to Style allowing Wall Cleanup between host and XREF drawings and/or allowing objects anchored to walls in other cleanup groups to be moved or copied to walls in this cleanup group
5	Segment type	Change to either Line or Arc to create linear or curved walls
6	Width	Set the width for nonpreset walls
7	Base Height	Set a new base height
8	Length	Set a new wall length
9	Justify	Change whether the wall is placed and references from the left, center, right, or baseline of the wall
10	Rotation	Rotation angle for the wall
11	Elevation	Elevation of the Base Line of the wall
12	Additional information	Launches the Additional Information Worksheet with more wall location information
13	Graphline position	Specifies the graphline position—either at Justification line or center line of wall
14	Cleanup radius	Specifies the radial distance from a wall endpoint within which other walls will be connected
15	Override start cleanup radius	Overrides the cleanup radius at a wall start point—(No or Yes). Yes will bring up radius field
16	Override end cleanup radius	Overrides the cleanup radius at a wall end point—(No or Yes). Yes will bring up radius field
17	Starting Endcap	Drop-down list for wall start endcap profile
18	Ending Endcap	Drop-down list for wall end endcap profile
19	Priority overides	Displays the wall component priority override dialog box
20	Plan modifiers	Displays the wall Plan modifier dialog box, which controls the location of plan modifiers.
21	Roof/floorline	Displays the Roof/Floorline dialog box, which allows for wall vertex editing.

Hands-On

Placing a Wall Object

1. Start a new drawing using the Aec Model (Imperial Stb) template.
2. Change to the **Model Layout.**
3. Change to the **Top View.**
4. Select the **Wall** icon from the **Design** tool palette and drag your cursor over the **Properties** palette to open the palette.

Note: The blue asterisks are called "Add" icons, and they represent properties that are available only when adding an object.

Here you will find all the size parameters that you can change upon insertion of a wall.

5. Set the following in the **Properties** palette:

   a. Style = **Standard**
   b. Width = **6″**
   c. Base Height = **8′-0″**
   d. Justify = **Left**
   e. Roof line offset from base height = **4′-0″**
   f. Floor line offset from base line = **-3′-0″**

6. Click in the drawing area and drag a 10′-0″-long wall, and click a second time to complete the command.

7. Change to **SW Isometric View** (see Figure 3–2).

Figure 3–2

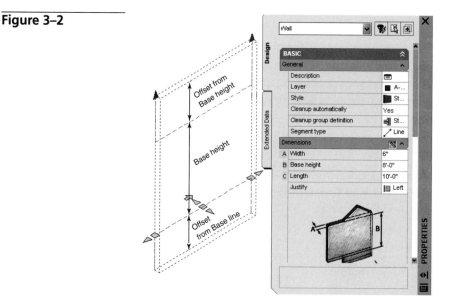

Hands-On

Changing Walls by Dynamically Pulling on Grips

Example: Dynamically changing the roof offset

1. Select the wall to activate its grips
2. Move your cursor over the leftmost top grip, and notice the tool tip.
3. Select the grip and move your cursor upward.
4. Tab to change the magenta-colored dimension selection.
5. Enter **8′-0″** for the "overall dimension of the roof offset, and press the **Enter** key to complete the command (see Figure 3–3).

Figure 3–3

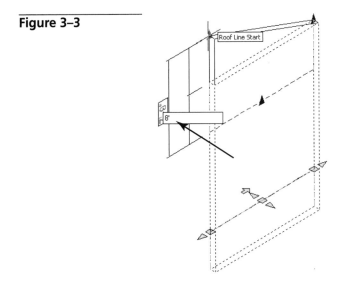

Hands-On

Creating Wall Sweeps

1. Create a new drawing, and change to **Top View.**
2. Select the **CMU-8 Furring** icon from the **Walls** tool palette, and drag your cursor over the **Properties** palette to open the palette.
3. Place a new wall with the following properties:

   a. Style = **CMU-8 Furring**
   b. Width = **9-1/2"**
   c. Base Height = **10'-0"**
   d. Justify = **Left**
   e. Roof line offset from base height = **0**
   f. Floor line offset from base line = **0**

4. Change to **NW Isometric View.**
5. Select the wall, **RMB,** and select **Sweeps > Add** from the contextual menu that appears to bring up the **Add Wall Sweep** dialog box.
6. In the **Add Wall Sweep** dialog box enter the following:

   a. Wall Component = **CMU**
   b. Profile Definition = **Start from scratch**
   c. New Profile Name = **TEST SWEEP PROFILE**

7. Press the **OK** button. Select a location on the wall for editing, and a blue field with grips will appear (see Figure 3–4).
8. Grab the lower grip of the blue field, drag it in the direction of 180 degrees, enter 2'-0" in the **Command line,** and press **Enter** (see Figure 3–5).

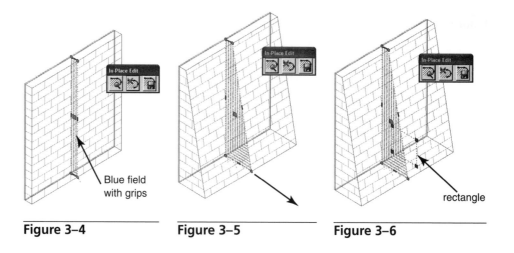

Figure 3–4   **Figure 3–5**   **Figure 3–6**

9. Select the **Rectangle** icon from the **Draw** menu and place a rectangle as shown in Figure 3–6.

10. Select the blue field, **RMB,** and select **Add Ring** from the contextual menu that appears.

11. Select the rectangle, enter **Y** (Yes) in the **Command line,** and press **Enter.**

12. Accept **Join** in the Command line and press Enter.

13. Press the **Save All Changes** icon in the **In-Place Edit** dialog box to complete the command and create the new wall sweep (see Figure 3–7).

14. Select the wall again, **RMB,** and again select **Sweeps > Edit Profile In Place** from the contextual menu that appears.

15. Select a place on the wall to bring up the blue **Edit Profile In Place** field.

16. Select the edge grip of the **Edit Profile In Place** field as shown in Figure 3–8.

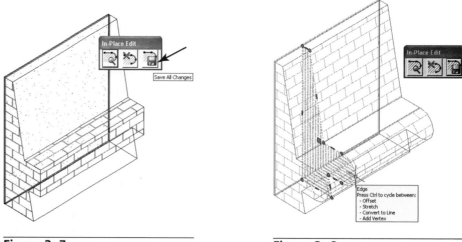

Figure 3–7   **Figure 3–8**

17. Drag the grip to the right, and press the **Ctrl** key on your keyboard twice to convert the edge to an arc.

18. Click the mouse button to complete the command.
19. **RMB** on the blue **Edit Profile In Place** field, and select **Save As New Profile** from the contextual menu that appears to bring up the **New Profile** dialog box.
20. Enter a new name for the new wall sweep profile, and press the **OK** button.

You have now created a new wall sweep (see Figure 3–9).

Figure 3–9

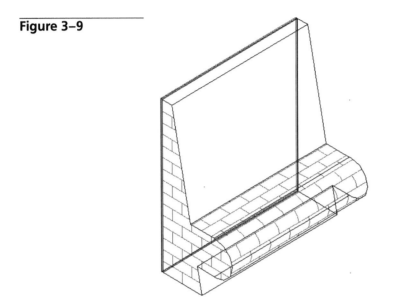

Hands-On

Creating Wall Endcaps Using Calculate Automatically

1. Create a new drawing.
2. Change to **Top View.**
3. Select the **CMU-8 Rigid-1.5 Air-2 brick 4 Furring 2** icon from the **Walls** tool palette and drag your cursor over the **Properties** palette to open the palette.
4. Place a new wall with the following properties:

   a. Style = **CMU-8 Rigid-1.5 Air-2 brick 4 Furring 2**
   b. Width = **1'-5"**
   c. Base Height = **10'-0"**
   d. Justify = **Left**
   e. Roof line offset from base height = **0**
   f. Floor line offset from base line = **0**

5. Zoom close to the left end of the wall (see Figure 3–10).

This will allow you to draw a new wall endcap on top of the existing wall.

Figure 3–10

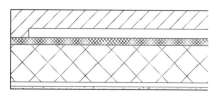

6. Select **Format > Style Manager** from the **Main** menu to bring up the **Style Manager.**

7. In the **Style Manager,** left panel, expand the **Architectural Objects** folder.

8. In the **Architectural Objects** folder, expand the **Wall Endcap Styles.**

9. Click on the **CMU-8 Rigid-1.5 Air-2 brick 4 Furring 2** style to open it.

This endcap style will be in your **Style Manager** because you placed a CMU-8 Rigid-1.5 Air-2 brick 4 Furring 2 wall that uses this endcap style. For your own information, compare the endcap style in the **Style Manager** with the end of the wall you placed (see Figure 3–11); then close the **Style Manager** dialog box.

10. Select the **Polyline** icon from the **Draw** menu, and trace in a counterclockwise direction a new polyline for the end of each component in the wall.

This author has moved the wall away and moved each polyline to illustrate how they were created (see Figure 3–12).

Figure 3–11

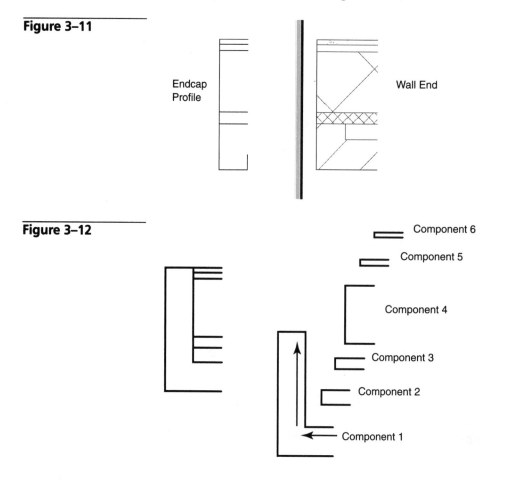

Endcap Profile

Wall End

Figure 3–12

Component 6

Component 5

Component 4

Component 3

Component 2

Component 1

11. Place a line that crosses all your new polylines as shown in Figure 3–13, and trim all ends of the polylines so that they are even.

!   ***Note:*** If the ends are not even, the new endcap will be twisted!

Figure 3–13

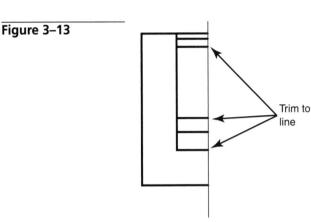

Trim to line

12. Erase the trim line.
13. Move the original wall near the new polylines (see Figure 3–14).
14. Select the wall, **RMB,** and select **End Caps >Calculate Automatically** from the contextual menu that appears.
15. Select all your new polylines with a window crossing and press **Enter.**

Figure 3–14

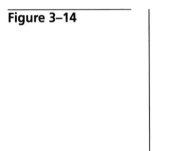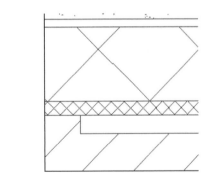

16. Enter **Y** (Yes) in the **Command line** to erase the polylines and press **Enter.**
17. In response to **Modify Current Endcap Style** Enter **N** (No) in the **Command line** and press **Enter.**
18. In response to **Apply the new wall endcap style to this end as,** enter **O** (Override) in the **Command line** and press **Enter** to bring up the **New Endcap Style** dialog box.
19. In the **New Endcap Style** dialog box, enter **ENDCAP TEST** and press the **OK** button.

Your wall will now have your new endcap, and the new endcap style will appear in the **Style Manager** (see Figure 3–15).

To change your endcap back to the original or to place your new endcap on the other end of the wall, do the following:

Figure 3–15

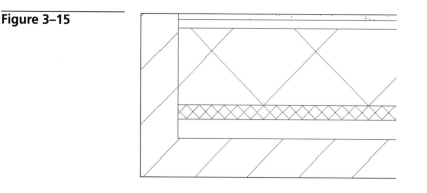

20. Select the wall, **RMB**, and select **Endcaps > Override Endcap Style** from the contextual menu that appears.

21. Select a point on the end of the wall to bring up the **Select an Endcap Style** dialog box.

22. Select the endcap style you wish to replace and press the **OK** button.

Hands-On

Using Plan Modifiers

1. Create a new drawing.

2. Change to the **Work Layout.**

3. Select the **CMU-8 Rigid-1.5 Air-2 brick 4** icon from the **Walls** tool palette, and drag your cursor over the **Properties** palette to open the palette.

4. Place a new 10'-long wall in the **Top View** with the following properties:

   a. Style = **CMU-8 Furring**
   b. Width = **1'-3-1/2"**
   c. Base Height = **10'-0"**
   d. Justify = **Left**
   e. Roof line offset from base height = **0**
   f. Floor line offset from base line = **0**

5. Place an open polyline as shown in Figure 3–16.

6. Select the wall, **RMB**, and select **Plan Modifiers > Convert Polyline to wall Modifier** from the contextual menu that appears.

7. Select the polyline, enter **Y** (Yes) in the **Command line**, and enter **TEST WALL MODIFIER** in the **New Wall Modifier Style Name** dialog box that appears.

8. The **Add Wall Modifier** dialog box now appears. Press the **OK** button to end the command and add the wall modifier (see Figure 3–17).

9. To modify the modifier, double-click the wall to bring up the **Properties** palette.

Figure 3–16

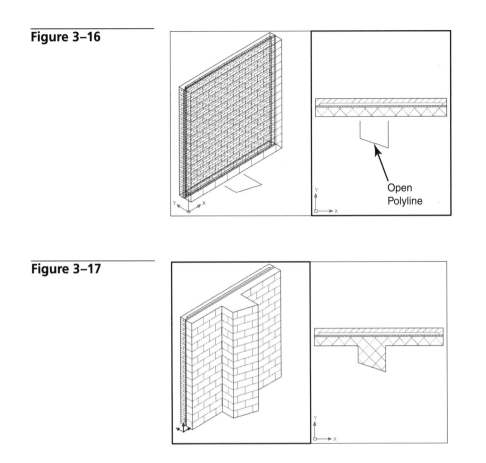

Open
Polyline

Figure 3–17

10. Scroll down to the bottom of the **Properties** palette, and click on **Plan Modifiers** to bring up the **Wall Modifiers** dialog box (see Figure 3–18).

Figure 3–18

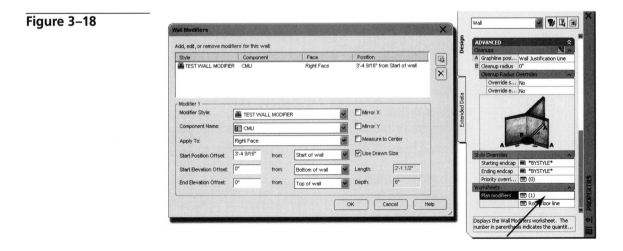

11. Place the dimensions shown in Figure 3–19.
12. Press **OK** and see the result (see Figure 3–20).

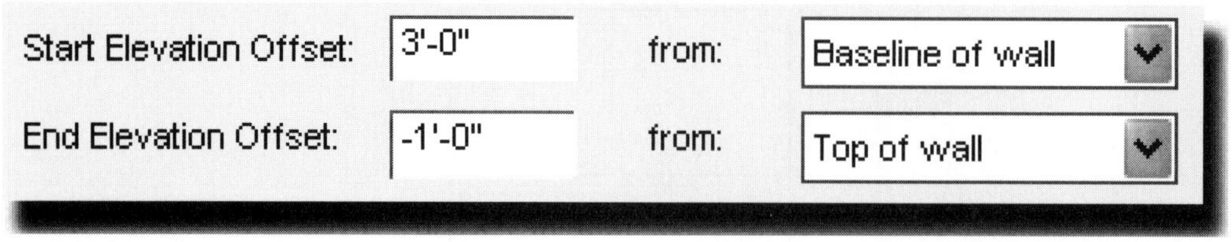

Start Elevation Offset:
3'-0"
from:
Baseline of wall
End Elevation Offset:
-1'-0"
from:
Top of wall

Figure 3–19

Figure 3–20

End Elevation Offset -1' 0"
Start Elevation Offset 3' 0"
Y
X

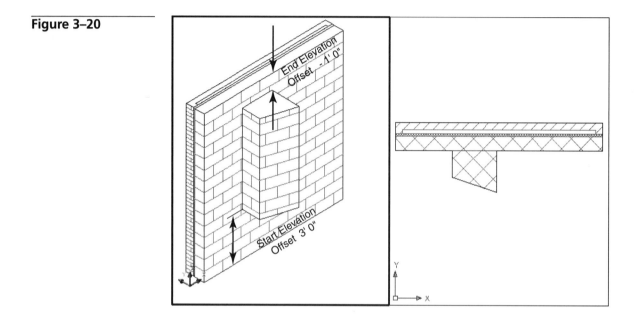

Hands-On

Using Body Modifiers

1. Clear the previous exercise.
2. Change to the **Work Layout.**
3. Select the **Wall** icon from the **Design** tool palette, and drag your cursor over the **Properties** palette to open the palette.
4. Place a new 10′-long wall in the **Top View** with the following properties:

   a. Style = **Standard**
   b. Width = **12**
   c. Base Height = **10′-0″**
   d. Justify = **Left**
   e. Roof line offset from base height = **0**
   f. Floor line offset from base line = **0**

5. Select the **Arch Massing** object from the **Massing** tool palette, and drag your cursor over the **Properties** palette to open the palette.

6. Place the **Massing** object with the following properties:

    a. Style = **Standard**
    b. Width = **5'-6"**
    c. Depth = **3'-0"**
    d. Height = **3'-0"**
    e. Radius = **2'-0"**
    f. Elevation = **2'-0"**

7. Place it as shown in Figure 3–21.

Figure 3–21

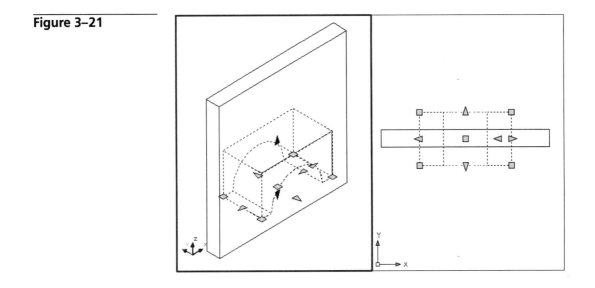

8. Select the wall, **RMB,** and select **Body Modifiers > Add** from the contextual menu that appears.
9. Select the massing object and press **Enter** to bring up the **Add Body Modifier** dialog box.
10. Select **Subtractive** from the **Operation** drop-down list, and check the **Erase Selected Object(s)** check box (see Figure 3–22).
11. Finally, press the **OK** button to complete the command and add the body modifier (see Figure 3–23).

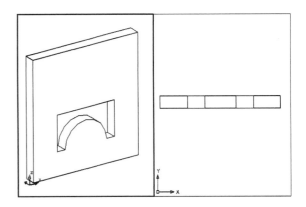

Figure 3–22

Figure 3–23

If you now wish to change the component you added or adjust the Operation, do the following:

1. Double-click the wall to activate the **Properties** palette.
2. Click on the **Body modifiers** field under Worksheets near the bottom of the palette to open the **Body Modifiers** worksheet.
3. In the Body Modifiers worksheet, select a new operation or Component from the **Component** or **Operation** drop-down lists (see Figure 3–24).

Figure 3–24

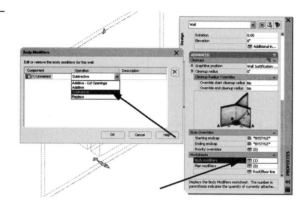

Hands-On

Using Roof/Floor Line Option

1. Clear the previous exercise.
2. Select the **Wall** icon from the **Design** tool palette, and drag your cursor over the **Properties** palette to open the palette.
3. Place a new 10'-long wall in the **Top View** with the following properties:

   a. Style = **Standard**
   b. Width = **6**
   c. Base Height = **10'-0"**
   d. Justify = **Left**
   e. Roof line offset from base height = **0**
   f. Floor line offset from base line = **0**

4. Select the **NE Isometric** icon from the **Views** toolbar to change to the **NE Isometric** view.
5. Select the wall, **RMB**, and select **Roof/Floor Line > Edit in Place** from the contextual menu that appears to apply a blue editing field on the wall (see Figure 3–25).
6. Select the blue field, **RMB**, and select **Add Gable** from the contextual menu that appears.
7. Select the roof line—the wall adds a gable (see Figure 3–26).
8. Select the wall so the blue field reappears, **RMB**, and select **Add Step** from the contextual menu that appears. The wall adds a step (see Figure 3–27).

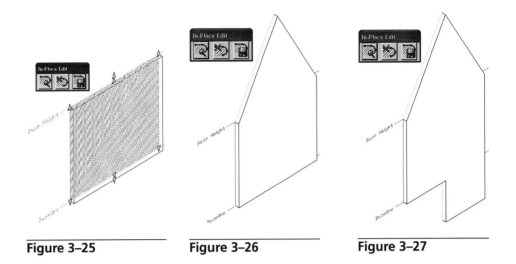

Figure 3–25   **Figure 3–26**   **Figure 3–27**

9. Select the wall so the blue field reappears, **RMB,** and select **Add Vertex** from the contextual menu that appears.

10. With the near Object Snap set, click on a point on the gable, and press **Enter.**

11. Select the wall again so the blue field reappears, and an additional vertex will appear where you clicked.

12. Drag on the vertex to change the wall and click to change the shape of the wall (see Figure 3–28).

13. Select the blue field, **RMB,** and select **Remove** from the contextual menu that appears.

14. Click on the gable to remove it.

15. Change to the **Front View.**

16. Place a polyline as shown in Figure 3–29. The polyline does not have to be on the same plane as the wall, only parallel to the plane of the wall.

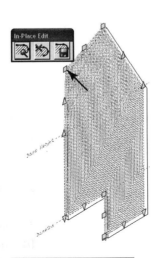

Figure 3–28

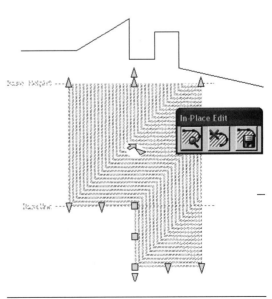

Figure 3–29

17.   **RMB** on the blue field and select **Project to Polyline** from the contextual menu.

18.   Select the top of the wall, then select the polyline.

19.   Enter **N** (No) in the Command line, and press the **Enter** key on your keyboard.

20.   Press the **Save All Changes** icon in the **In-Place Edit** toolbar to complete the command.

21.   Change to the **SW Isometric View,** and press the **Hidden** icon in the **Shading** toolbar (see Figure 3–30).

Figure 3–30

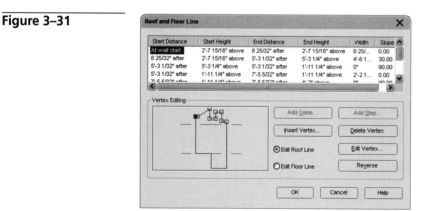

22.   Double-click the wall you just edited to bring up its **Properties** palette.

23.   Scroll down to the last field on the palette called **Roof/floor line.**

24.   Click on the **Roof/floor line** field to bring up the **Roof and Floor Line** dialog box (see Figure 3–31).

Figure 3–31

Start Distance	Start Height	End Distance	End Height	Width	Slope
At wall start	2'-7 15/16" above	8 25/32" after	2'-7 15/16" above	8 25/...	0.00
8 25/32" after	2'-7 15/16" above	5'-3 1/32" after	5'-3 1/4" above	4'-6 1...	30.00
5'-3 1/32" after	5'-3 1/4" above	5'-3 1/32" after	1'-11 1/4" above	0"	90.00
5'-3 1/32" after	1'-11 1/4" above	7'-5 5/32" after	1'-11 1/4" above	2'-2 1...	0.00

Vertex Editing

Add Gable...   Add Step...

Insert Vertex...   Delete Vertex

● Edit Roof Line   Edit Vertex...

○ Edit Floor Line   Reverse

OK   Cancel   Help

25.   Select the **Edit Floor Line** radio button, and select the vertex shown in Figure 3–32.

Figure 3–32

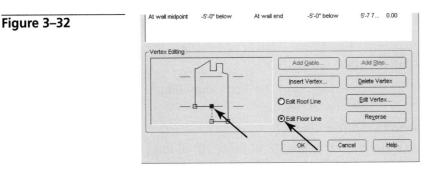

26. In the **Roof and Floor Line** dialog box, press the **Edit Vertex** button to bring up the **Wall Roof/Floor Line Vertex** dialog box (see Figure 3–33).

Figure 3–33

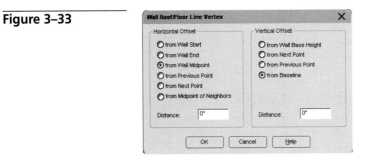

27. Enter **3'-0"** in the **Vertical Offset > Distance** data field.
28. Select the from **Baseline** radio button, and press **OK** to return to the **Roof and Floor Line** dialog box. Then press the **OK** to return to the Drawing editor.

You have now modified the wall floor line through the Roof/Floor dialog boxes (see Figure 3–34).

Figure 3–34

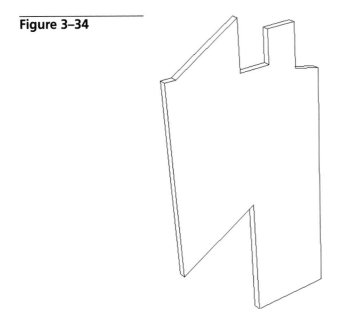

Hands-On

Using Interference Condition

1. Start a new drawing using the Aec Model (Imperial Stb) template.
2. Change to the **Model Layout.**
3. Change to the **Top View.**
4. Place a Standard 6"-wide 10'-0"-high, 10'-0"-long wall. Baseline = 0, roofline = 0, floorline = 0
5. From the **Design** tool palette select the **Stair** icon, and place a Standard, Straight 3'-0"-wide stair with a height of 10'-0" (see Figure 3–35).

Figure 3–35

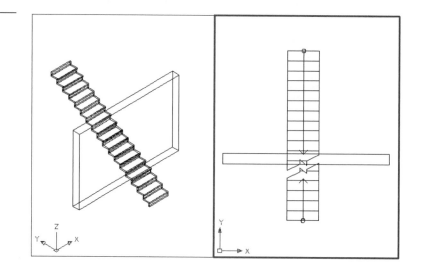

If you don't understand how to place stairs, see Section 8, Stairs, for exercises on placing and modifying stair objects.

6. Select the wall, **RMB,** and select **Interference Condition > Add** from the contextual menu that appears.
7. Select the stair you placed and press **Enter.**
8. Enter **S** (Subtractive) in the **Command line** and press **Enter.**

The interference area located above the stair and set in the stair **Properties** palette is removed from the wall (see Figure 3–36).

9. Double-click the stair to bring up its **Properties** palette.
10. Scroll down to **Interference > Headroom height.**
11. Change the headroom height to **4',** and notice the change in the interference condition in the wall (see Figure 3–37).

Wall interference conditions will work in concert with any intelligent ADT AEC object.

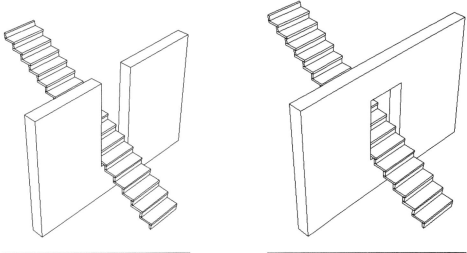

Figure 3–36   **Figure 3–37**

Hands-On

Cleanups—Apply 'T' Cleanup, and Wall Merge

1. Start a new drawing using the Aec Model (Imperial - Stb) template.
2. Change to the **Model Layout.**
3. Change to the **Top View.**
4. Place a Standard 6″-wide 10′-0″-high, 10′-0″-long wall.
5. Select the walls, **RMB,** and select **Add Selected** from the contextual menu that appears.
6. Place another wall perpendicular to the first as shown in Figure 3–38.

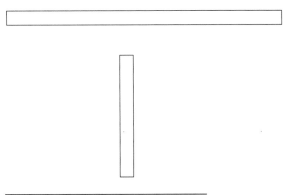

Figure 3–38

7. Select the vertical wall segment, **RMB,** and select **Cleanups > Apply 'T' Cleanup** from the contextual menu that appears.
8. Select the horizontal wall to create the 'T' cleanup (see Figure 3–39).
9. Add another vertical wall adjacent to the vertical wall; make the adjacent wall 24″ and overlapping it (see Figure 3–40).

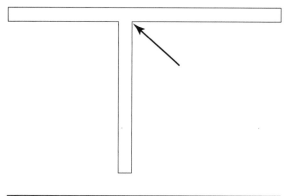

Figure 3–39

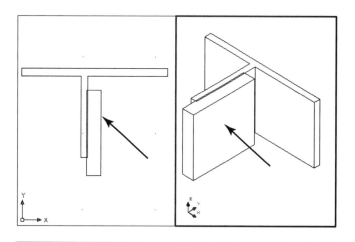

Figure 3–40

10. Select the new wall segment, **RMB,** and select **Cleanups > Add Wall Merge Condition** from the contextual menu that appears.

11. Select the first walls and press **Enter.**

The wall is now merged into one wall, but the new segment can still be adjusted and moved separately (see Figure 3–41).

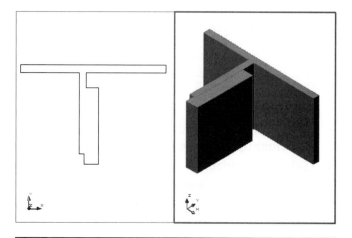

Figure 3–41

Hands-On

Editing Wall Styles

Base Height, Baseline, Edge, and Floor line concepts (see Figure 3–42)

In this exercise, you learn how to create a wall and foundation using the components shown in Figure 3–43.

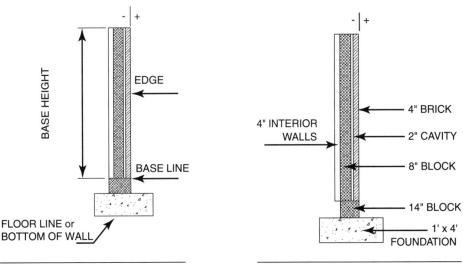

Figure 3–42   **Figure 3–43**

Creating the wall style

1. Start a new drawing using the Aec Model (Imperial Stb) template.
2. Change to the **Model Layout.**
3. Change to the **Top View.**
4. Select **Format > Style Manager** from the **Main** toolbar to bring up the **Style Manager** dialog box.
5. Open the **Architectural Objects** tree, select the **Wall Styles** icon, **RMB,** and select **New** from the contextual menu that appears.
6. In the right panel, rename the new style **TESTWALL** and deselect it.
7. Double-click on the icon next to the name **TESTWALL** to bring up the **Wall Styles Properties** dialog box.
8. Select the **Components** tab, and open the floating **Viewer** (see Figure 3–44).

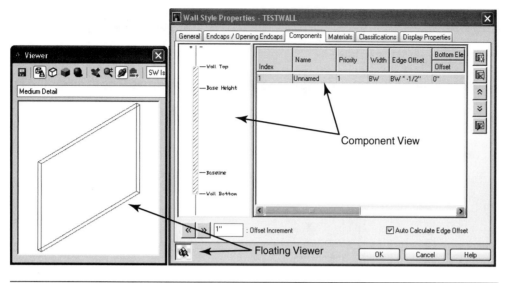

Figure 3–44

Adding and Modifying Wall Components

On the **Component** tab, notice that the **Edge Offset** drop-down list reads BW* -1/2". This means that the edge offset is set to be half the width of the **Base Width** (BW). (BW refers to any wall having a parametric or user-enterable width.) The author normally sets the edge offset to the outer edge of the total wall (see Figure 3–45).

Figure 3–45

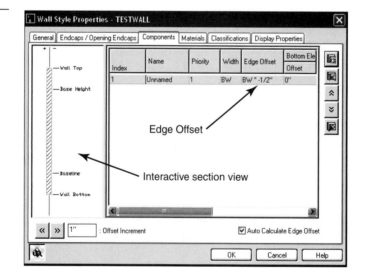

9. In the **Wall Style Properties** dialog box, click on the **Add Component** icon at the top right side of the **Components** tab, and add five components called **BRICK, CAVITY, BLOCK WALL, 14″ BLOCK, FRAMING,** and **FOOTING.**

10. Set the settings for the components as shown in Figure 3–46.

Wall Style Properties - TESTWALL

General | Endcaps / Opening Endcaps | Components | Materials | Classifications | Display Properties

Index	Name	Priority	Width	Edge Offset	Bottom Elevation		Top Elevation	
					Offset	From	Offset	From
1	BRICK	1	4"	-6"	1'-8"	Wall Bottom	0"	Wall Top
2	CAVTY	1	2"	-2"	1'-8"	Wall Bottom	0"	Wall Top
3	BLOCK	1	8"	0"	1'-8"	Wall Bottom	0"	Wall Top
4	14" BLOCK	1	1'-2"	-6"	1'-0"	Wall Bottom	1'-8"	Wall Bottom
5	FRAMING	1	4"	8"	1'-8"	Wall Bottom	0"	Wall Top
6	FOOTING	1	4'-0"	-2'-0"	0"	Wall Bottom	1'-0"	Wall Bottom

—Wall To

—Base H

—Baselin

—Wall Bc

« » 1" : Offset Increment

☑ Auto Calculate Edge Offset

OK   Cancel   Help

Figure 3–46

! **Note:** Set the settings one component at a time and observe the result in the inter-active viewer.

11. Change to the **Materials** tab.

12. Select the **Add New Material** icon to bring up the **New Material** dialog box.

13. Enter the name **BRICK SECTION,** and press the **OK** button to return to the **Materials** tab.

14. Activate the **BRICK** component, and select **BRICK SECTION** from the **Material Definition** drop-down list.

15. With the **BRICK** component still active, press the **Edit Material** icon to bring up the **Material Definition Properties** dialog box and select its **Display Properties** tab. (see Figure 3–47).

Figure 3–47

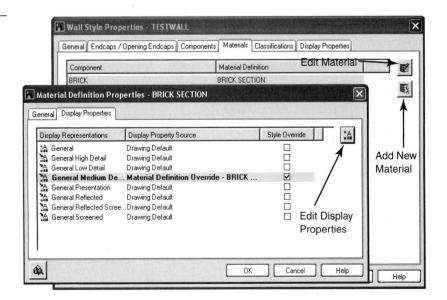

16. Activate the **General Medium Detail** display representation, check its **Style Override** check box, and press the **Edit Display Properties** icon to bring up the **Display Properties** dialog box.

17. Select the **Hatching** tab.

18. Activate the **Surface Hatch** display component, select the **Hatch** icon in the **Pattern** column, and select **AR-BR-816C** pattern (predefined type).

19. Set the Scale/Spacing to 1″ and Angle to 0.00.

20. Activate the **Layer/Color/Linetype** tab and turn the **Surface Hatch** to **Visible**.

21. Press the **OK** buttons to return to the **Wall Style Properties** dialog box.

22. Repeat the process for all the other components creating the following materials for **BLOCK, FRAMING,** and **FOOTING,** respectively (see Figures 3–48 through 3–50).

23. From the **Design** palette, select the **Wall** icon. Drag the cursor across to the **Properties** palette. In the **Properties** palette, pick the **Style** drop-down list and select the new **Test Wall** style. Return to the drawing editor to place the wall. Place a wall with this new style (see Figure 3–51).

Figure 3–48

Figure 3–49

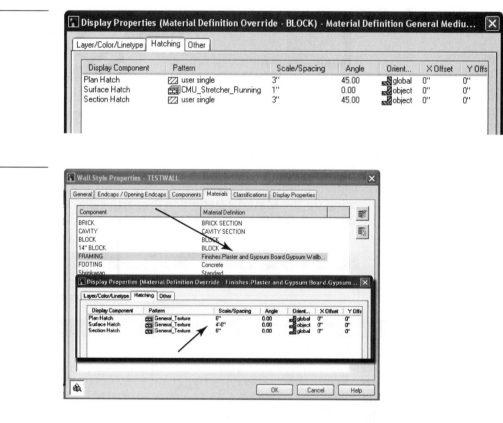

Figure 3–50

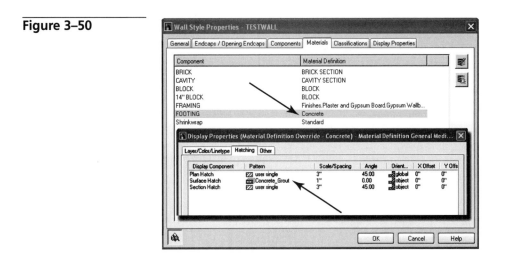

Figure 3–51

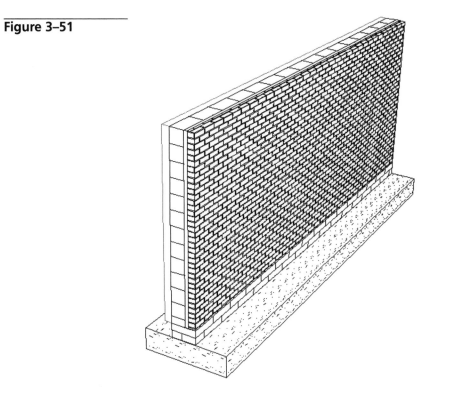

Windows

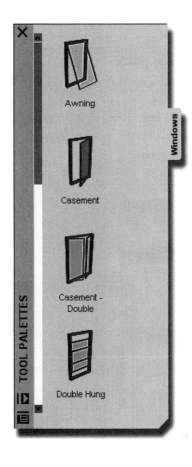

When you finish this section, you should understand the following:

- ✔ How to place a Window object using **Reference.**
- ✔ How to place a Window object using **Offset/Center.**
- ✔ How to change Window Sizes with Grips.
- ✔ How to add a Profile (change window shape).
- ✔ How to move the window vertically, within the wall, and along the wall.
- ✔ How to edit Window Styles.

Window objects can be dragged or inserted either from the **Design** tool palette, by clicking **RMB** on a wall, or by typing **window add** on the **Command line.**

Windows can be placed directly into walls by right-clicking on the wall and selecting **Insert > Window** from the contextual menu, or by selecting from the **Windows** or **Design** tool palettes and pressing **Enter.**

Number	Name	Purpose
1	Style	Change this to change to another style such as Casement, etc.
2	Standard sizes	Select from a list of preset sizes.
3	Width	Change width of window.
4	Height	Change height of window.

127

5	Measure to	Set width and height to inside or outside of window frame.
6	Opening percent	Set amount that window is open in model and elevation view.
7	Position along wall	Set to **Offset/Center** or **Unconstrained;** Offset/Center automatically offsets a set distance from the wall ends, or inserts at center of wall.
8	Automatic offset	Set to amount of offset when position along wall is set to **Unconstrained.**
9	Vertical alignment	Set to **Head** or **Sill;** this will govern on insert.
10	Head height	Set elevation for top of window if **Vertical alignment** is set to **Head.**
11	Sill height	Set elevation for bottom of window if **Vertical alignment** is set to **Sill.**

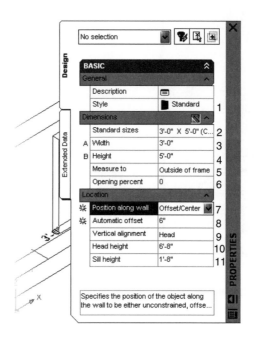

Hands-On

Placing a Window Object Using Reference

1. Sart a new drawing using the Aec Model (Imperial Stb) template.
2. Change to the **Model Layout.**
3. Set the **Object Snap** to **End Point.**
4. Change to the **Top View.**
5. Place a standard wall 10'-0" long, 10'-0" high, and 6" thick. (See Section 3, "Walls," for information on how to place walls.)
6. Select the **Double Hung** icon from the **Windows** tool palette and drag your cursor over the **Properties** palette to open it.

7. Enter the following data:

   a. Style = **Double Hung**
   b. Width = **3'-0"**
   c. Height = **5'-0"**
   d. Measure to = **Outside of Frame**
   e. Position along wall = **Unconstrained**
   f. Vertical alignment = **Head**
   g. Head height = **6'-8"**

8. Select the wall and enter **RE** (Reference point) in the **Command line.**

9. Select the left corner of the wall, move the cursor to the right (0°), and enter **3'** on the keyboard. Then press **Enter** to place the window 3'-0" from the left wall corner (Figure 4–1).

Figure 4–1

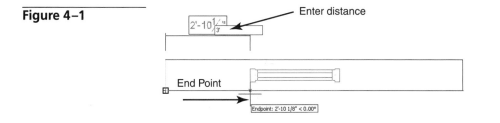

Hands-On

Placing a Window Object Using Offset/Center

1. Erase the window in the previous exercise.
2. Turn off all Object Snaps.
3. Select the **Double Hung** icon from the **Windows** tool palette and drag your cursor over the **Properties** palette to open it.
4. Enter the following data:

   a. Style = **Double Hung**
   b. Width = **3'-0"**
   c. Height = **5'-0"**
   d. Measure to = **Outside of Frame**
   e. Position along wall = **Offset/Center**
   f. Automatic Offset = **6"**
   g. Vertical alignment = **Head**
   h. Head height = **6'-8"**

5. Select the wall near the left end of the wall, click the mouse, and press **Enter** to complete the command and place the window.

The Window will be placed 6" from the left end of the wall (see Figure 4–2).

Note: By pressing the tab key you can cycle the 6" dimension and enter an overriding dimension.

Figure 4–2

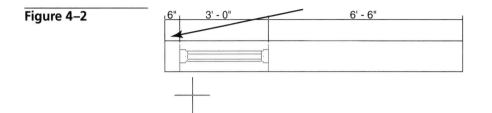

6. Again, select the **Double Hung** icon from the **Windows** tool palette and drag your cursor over the **Properties** palette to open it.

7. Select the wall near the center of the distance left between the previous window placement and the right-hand wall end. Click the mouse, and press **Enter** to complete the command and place the window.

The Window will be placed at the center of the distance between the second window and the right end of the wall (see Figure 4–3).

Figure 4–3

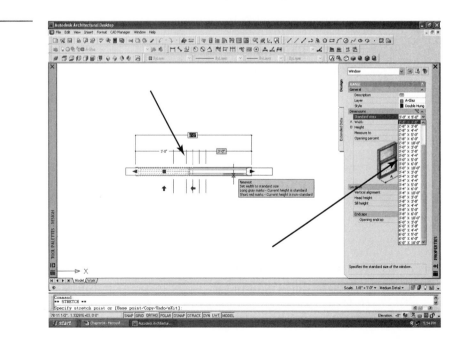

Hands-On

Changing Window Size with Grips

1. Select a window to activate its grips, and drag to the right (0°). If the window has sizes listed in its **Window Styles Properties > Standard Sizes,** it will snap at gray lines in plan. These are sizes listed in the aforementioned **Properties** (see Figure 4–4).

Figure 4–4

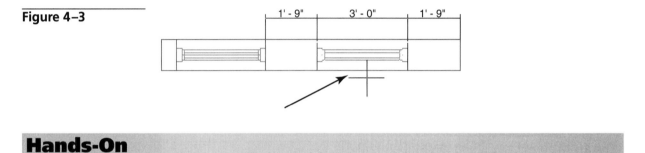

Hands-On

Adding a Profile

1. Erase the previous exercise.
2. Place a Standard wall 15'-0" long, 10'-0" high, and 6" thick.
3. Select the **Pivot Horizontal** icon from the **Windows** tool palette and drag your cursor over the **Properties** palette to open it.
4. Enter the following data:

   a. Style = **Pivot Horizontal**
   b. Width = **5'-0"**
   c. Height = **4'-0"**
   d. Measure to = **Outside of Frame**
   e. Position along wall = **Unconstrained**
   f. Vertical alignment = **Head**
   g. Head height = **6'-8"**

5. Place the window 2'-0" from the left edge of the wall.
6. Change to the **Front View.**
7. Place a closed Polyline as shown in Figure 4–5.

Figure 4–5

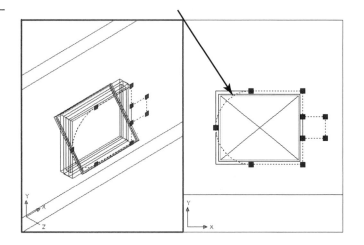

8. Select the window, **RMB,** and select **Add Profile** from the contextual menu that appears to bring up the **Add Window Profile** dialog box.
9. Select **Start from scratch** from the **Profile Definition** drop-down list, enter **TEST PIVOT WINDOW** in the **New Profile Name** data field, and press **Enter.**

A blue hatch field will appear on the window.

10. **RMB** on the blue hatch field and select **Replace Ring** from the conceptual menu that appears.
11. Select the closed polyline that you created in Step 7 of this exercise.
12. Enter **Y** (Yes) in the **Command line,** and press **Enter** to complete the command.

13. **RMB** on the blue hatch field and select **Save Changes** from the conceptual menu that appears (see Figure 4–6).

14. Mirror the window in the **Front View** (see Figure 4–7).

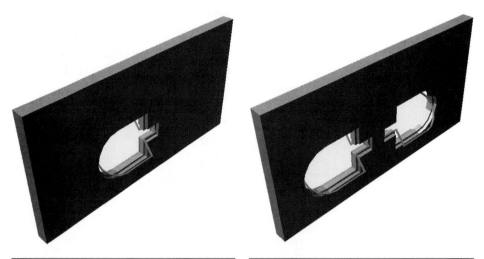

Figure 4–6　　　　　　　　　　　　　　**Figure 4–7**

15. Delete the windows you just created.

16. Select the **Double Hung** icon window from the **Windows** tool palette, and place a 5'-high by 3'-wide window constrained to the center of the wall (see Figure 4–8).

Figure 4–8

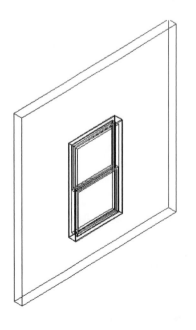

17. Select the window, **RMB,** and select **Add Profile** from the contextual menu that appears to bring up the **Add Window Profile** dialog box.

18. At the **Add Window** dialog box, select **Start from scratch** from the **Profile Definition** drop-down list, enter **Curved Top window** in the **New Profile Name** data field, and press the **Enter** key.

As with the editing of the previous window, a blue hatch field will appear on the window.

19. Click on the top **Edge** grip, and drag upwards (see Figure 4–9).
20. Press the **Ctrl** key on your keyboard twice, and click the mouse key.

Figure 4–9

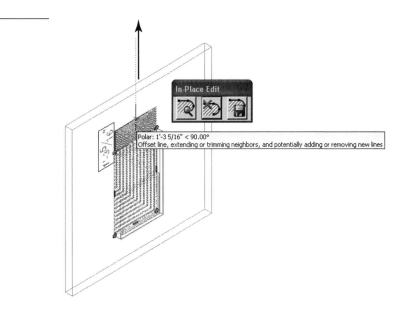

21. Press the **Save All Changes** icon in the on-screen **In-Place Edit** dialog box.

You have now created a double hung window with a curved top (see Figure 4–10).

Figure 4–10

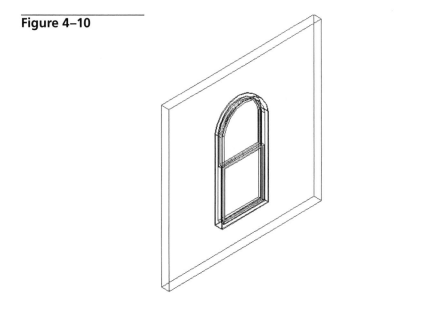

22. Select **Format** > **Style Manager** from the **Main** menu.
23. Expand the multipurpose Objects folder.
24. Expand Profiles.

25. Double-click on **Curved Top window** to bring up the **Profile Definitions Properties** dialog box (see Figure 4–11).

Notice that the window profile you created in place is now in your Style Manager.

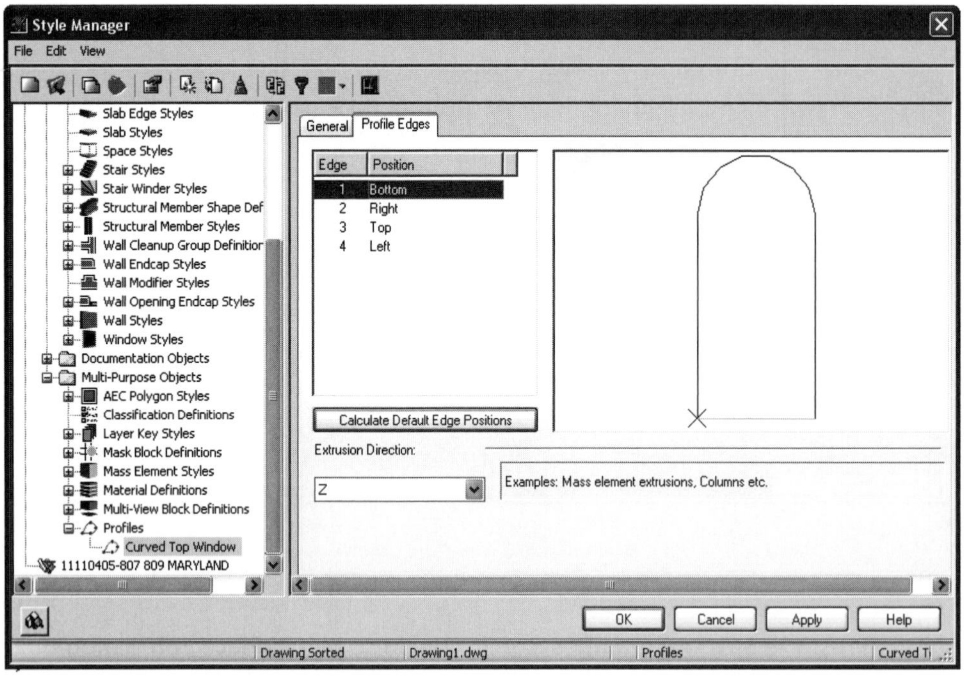

Figure 4–11

Hands-On

Modifying Window Height

1. Use the previous exercise.
2. Change to the **Front View.**
3. Select the window to activate its grips.
4. Pick and move the square grip at the bottom of the window; a yellow dialog field appears (see Figure 4–12).

Figure 4–12

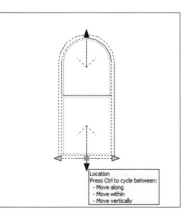

5. Press the **Ctrl** key until the dialog field reads **Move Vertically.**
6. Press the **Tab** key until the data field turns magenta in color.
7. Enter **3'-0"** in the **Command line** and press **Enter.**

The window will move vertically and be 3'-6" above the wall baseline.

8. Activate the square grip at the bottom of the window again.
9. Press the **Ctrl** key until the dialog field reads **Move Along.**
10. Enter **3'-0"** in the **Command line** and press **Enter.**

The window will move horizontally 3'-0" in the direction that the grip was moved.

11. Change to the **Top View.**
12. Activate the square grip at the center of the window.
13. Press the **Ctrl** key until the dialog field reads **Move Within.**
14. Move the grip vertically.
15. Enter **2"** in the **Command line** and press **Enter.**

The window will move vertically within the wall 2" in the direction the grip was moved. Save this file.

Hands-On

Editing Window Styles

1. Use the previous exercise.
2. Change to the **Front View.**
3. Select the window, **RMB,** and select **Edit Window Style** from the contextual menu that appears to bring up the **Window Style Properties** dialog box.
4. Select the **Dimensions** tab.

This is where you set the **Frame Width** and **Depth.** Check the **Auto-Adjust** check box if you want the frame depth to match the wall in which it has been inserted.

The **Sash Width** and **Depth** plus the **Glass Thickness** are also located in the **Dimensions** tab.

5. Select the **Floating Viewer** icon at the lower left corner of the **Window Style Properties** dialog box to bring up the **Viewer.**
6. In the **Viewer,** select the **Gouraud Shaded** icon in the top **Viewer** toolbar (see Figure 4–13).
7. Enter the following data in the entry fields:

    a. Frame Width = **1"**
    b. Frame Depth = **12"**
    c. Sash Width = **4"**
    d. Sash Depth = **4"**

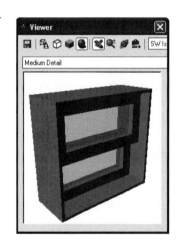

Figure 4–13

Press **Enter** after entering the last data field, and note the change in window in the **Viewer** (see Figure 4–14).

8. Reset the data fields to the following:

    a. Frame Width = **2"**
    b. Frame Depth = **5"**
    c. Sash Width = **1"**
    d. Sash Depth = **2"**

Figure 4–14

9. Select the **Design Rules** tab.
10. Select the **Predefined** radio button; select **Round** from the **Predefined** drop-down list, and **Awning-Transom** from the **Window Type** drop-down list.

Note the change in window in the **Viewer** (see Figure 4–15).

11. Select the **Use Profile** radio button, and select **TEST PIVOT WINDOW** from its drop-down list (**TEST PIVOT WINDOW** was the profile created in Step 9 of "Adding a Profile" in this section).

Note the change in window in the **Viewer** (see Figure 4–16).

12.   Change to the **Standard Sizes** tab.

The **Standard Sizes** tab is where standardized windows are entered. These sizes allow you to change windows interactively as shown in the following exercise.

Figure 4–15

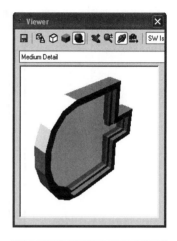

Figure 4–16

13.   Press **OK** to close the **Window Style Properties** dialog box.
14.   Change to the **Top View.**
15.   Double-click on the window to bring up its **Properties** palette.
16.   Set the style to **Double Hung,** and allow the palette to close.
17.   Select the window's right arrow grip, and drag it to the right.

You will see a yellow dialog field explaining the gray and red marks that appear above the window. These marks are "snap" points corresponding to the preset width sizes set in the **Standard Sizes** tab of the **Window Style Properties** dialog box (see Figure 4–17).

Figure 4–17

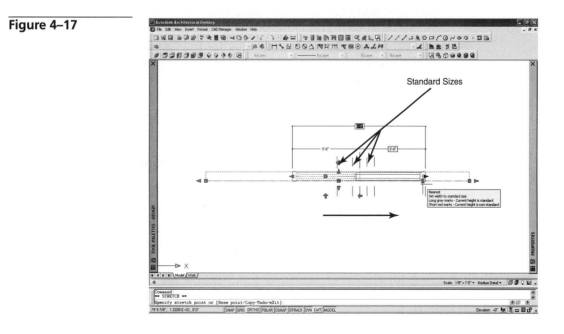

18. **RMB** on the window again and select **Edit Window Style** from the contextual menu that appears.

19. Change to the **Materials** tab.

20. Activate the **Frame** field, and click on the **Material Definition** drop-down list (see Figure 4–18).

Figure 4–18

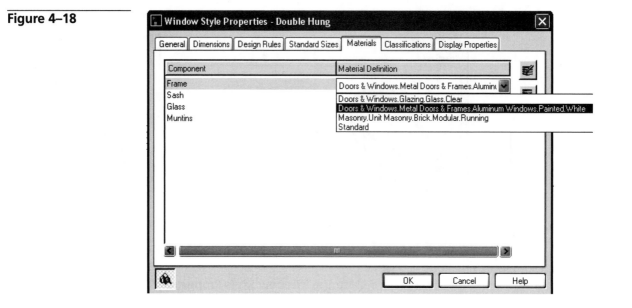

Four preset materials are shipped with the program. If you need more materials, you need to add and edit a new material.

21. To add and edit new material, press the **Add New Material** icon at the right side of the materials tab.

22. Enter a new name for the new material in the **New Material** data field that appears, and press **OK.**

23. Activate the **New Material** field in the **Material Definition** column, and select the **Edit Material** icon above the **Add Material** icon to bring up the **Material Definition Properties** dialog box.

24. Check the **Style Override** check box for the **General Medium Detail** display representation to open the **Display Properties** dialog box.

25. Select the **Other** tab (see Figure 4–19).

In the **Other** tab you can control the placement of hatches on surfaces, and Browse for materials made in the VIZ Render module (see Figure 4–20).

26. Press the **OK** buttons until you return to the **Window Style Properties** dialog box.

27. Change to the **Display Properties** tab.

28. Select the **Elevation** field.

Figure 4–19

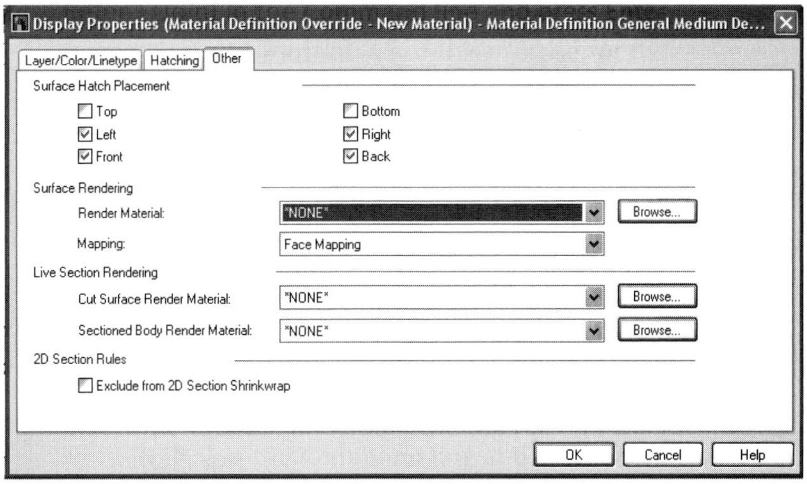

Display Properties (Material Definition Override - New Material) - Material Definition General Medium De... ☒

Layer/Color/Linetype | Hatching | Other

Surface Hatch Placement
☐ Top   ☐ Bottom
☑ Left   ☑ Right
☑ Front   ☑ Back

Surface Rendering
Render Material: "NONE"   ▼   Browse...
Mapping: Face Mapping   ▼

Live Section Rendering
Cut Surface Render Material: "NONE"   ▼   Browse...
Sectioned Body Render Material: "NONE"   ▼   Browse...

2D Section Rules
☐ Exclude from 2D Section Shrinkwrap

OK   Cancel   Help

Figure 4–20

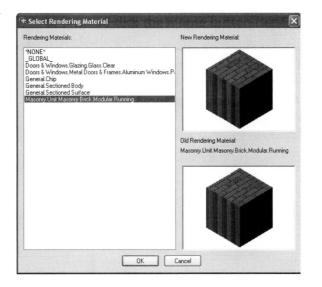

Select Rendering Material   ☒

Rendering Materials: New Rendering Material:
"NONE"
GLOBAL
Doors & Windows.Glazing.Glass.Clear
Doors & Windows.Metal Doors & Frames.Aluminum Windows.P-
General.Chip
General.Sectioned Body
General.Sectioned Surface
Masonry.Unit Masonry.Brick.Modular.Running

Old Rendering Material:
Masonry.Unit Masonry.Brick.Modular.Running

OK   Cancel

29.   Press the **Edit Display** icon at the upper right side of the **Display Proper-ties** tab to bring up the **Display Properties** dialog box.

30.   Select the **Muntins** tab.

31.   Press the **Add** button to bring up the **Muntins Block** dialog box.

32.   Select the **Prairie - 12 Lights** from the **Pattern** drop-down list, check the **Clean Up Joints** and **Convert to body** check boxes, and then press the OK buttons to close the command and view the window (see Figures 4–21 and 4–22).

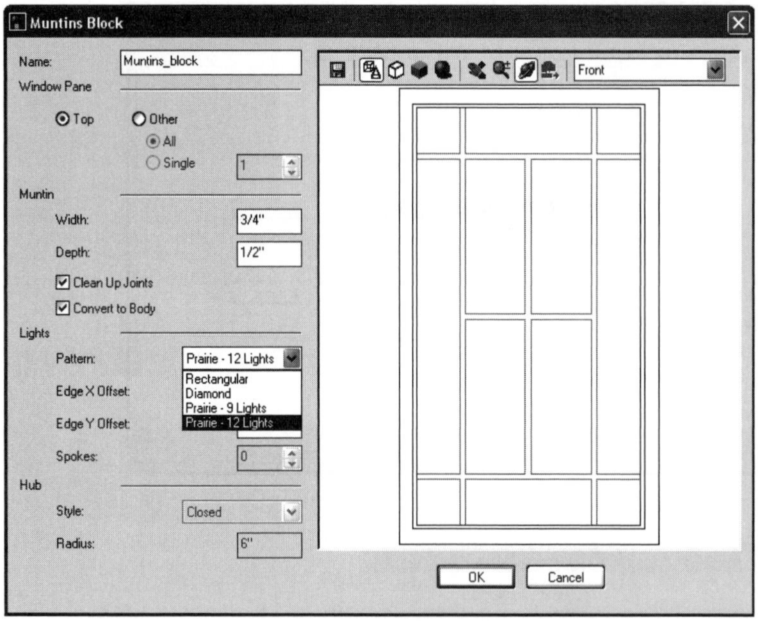

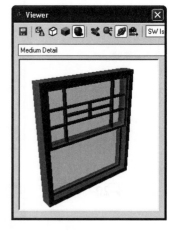

Figure 4–21

Figure 4–22

Doors

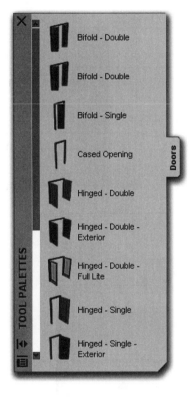

When you finish this section, you should understand the following:

- ✔ How to place a door object using **Reference.**
- ✔ How to place a door object using **Offset/Center.**
- ✔ How to change door size and swing location with **Grips.**
- ✔ How to control the door swing angle.
- ✔ How to add a profile (change door panel shape).
- ✔ How to add a door knob.
- ✔ How to move the door within the wall and along the wall.
- ✔ How to edit door styles.
- ✔ How to use the **Materials** tab.

Wall objects can be dragged or inserted either from the **Design** tool palette, or by typing **dooradd** in the **Command line.**

Doors

In Autodesk Architectural Desktop 2006, door objects are totally customizable. All is possible in this program—from customizing the size and shape of the door or the size and shape of the jamb to including side lights, mullions, and/or a sill. As with other features of this program, a premade library of door styles greatly enhances productivity.

It is hoped that manufacturers will jump on the ADT bandwagon and place their door styles on the Web. If they do this, you will be able to quickly **idrop** or update your catalogs with premade doors and door accessories. If this happens and the manufacturer makes changes, you will be able to update your catalogs and drawings automatically directly from the Internet.

Number	Name	Purpose
1	Style	Change this to change to another style, such as **Double Doors.**
2	Standard sizes	Select from a list of preset sizes in the **door style** dialog box.
3	Width	Set custom width.
4	Height	Set custom height.
5	Measure to	Set width and height to measure inside of frame or outside of frame.
6	Swing angle	Set door swing opening 0° to 90°.
7	Position along	**Unconstrained** (any placement); **Offset/Center** (set offset from ends of wall or midpoint of wall).
8	Automatic Offset	Set distance for offset from wall end if **Position along** set to **Offset/Center.**
9	Vertical alignment	Set to head height or threshold governs.
10	Head height	Head height above wall baseline if **Vertical Alignment** set to **Head.**
11	Threshold height	Head height above wall baseline if **Vertical Alignment** set to **Threshold.**

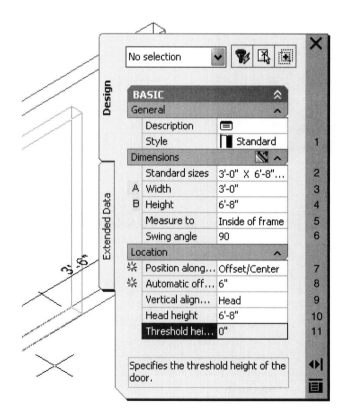

Doors can be placed directly into walls by right-clicking on the wall and selecting **Insert > Door** from the contextual menu or by selecting from the **Doors** or **Design** tool palettes and pressing **Enter.**

Hands-On

Placing a Door Object Using Reference

1. Start a new drawing using the Aec Model (Imperial Stb) template.
2. Change to the **Model Layout.**
3. Change to the **Top View.**
4. Set the Object snap to **End Point.**
5. Place a Standard 10'-long, 10'-high wall.
6. Select any door from the **Doors** tool palette and drag your cursor over the **Properties** palette to open the palette.
7. Enter the following data:

   a. Style = **Standard**
   b. Width = **3'-0"**
   c. Height = **6'-8"**
   d. Measure to = **Outside of Frame**
   e. Swing angle = **90**
   f. Position along wall = **Unconstrained**
   g. Vertical alignment = **Head**
   h. Head height = **6'-8"**
   i. Threshold height = **0"**

8. Select the wall and enter **RE** (Reference point) in the **Command line.**
9. Select the left corner of the wall, move the cursor to the right (0°), and enter **5'** on the keyboard. Press **Enter** to place the door 5'-0" from the left wall corner (see Figure 5–1).

Figure 5–1

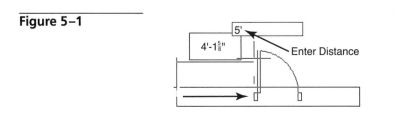

Hands-On

Placing a Door Object Using Offset/Center

1. Erase the door in the previous exercise.
2. Turn off all Object Snaps.
3. Select any door icon in the **Doors** tool palette and drag your cursor over the **Properties** palette to open it.
4. Enter the following data:

   a. Style = **Standard**
   b. Width = **3'-0"**

    c. Height = **6'-8"**

    d. Measure to = **Outside of Frame**

    e. Position along wall = **Offset/Center**

    f. Automatic Offset = **6"**

    g. Vertical alignment = **Head**

    h. Head height = **6'-8"**

    i. Threshold = **0**

5. Select the wall near the left end of the wall, click the mouse, and press **Enter** to complete the command and place the door.

The door will be placed 6" from the left end of the wall (see Figure 5–2).

> *!* ***Note:*** By pressing the **Tab** key, you can cycle the 6" dimension and enter an overriding dimension.

Figure 5–2

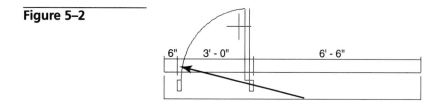

Hands-On

Changing Door Size and Swing Location with Grips

1. Select the door to activate its grips and drag the green arrow on the right door edge to the right (0°). If the door has sizes listed in its **Door Styles Properties > Standard Sizes,** it will snap at gray lines in plan.

2. To add doors to the **Standard Sizes** menu, **RMB** on the door and select **Edit Door Style** from the contextual menu that appears to bring up the **Door Style Properties** dialog box.

3. Select the **Standard Sizes** tab.

4. Press the **Add** button to bring up the **Add Standard Size** dialog box (see Figure 5–3).

5. Add the four doors shown in Figure 5–4 to the **Standard Sizes** tab, and close the **Door Style Properties** dialog box by pressing the **OK** button.

6. Again, select the door to activate its grips and drag to the right (0°). The door will now snap to the sizes you added in the **Standard Sizes** tab (see Figure 5–5).

7. Select the arrow grip shown in Figure 5–6 to flip the door swing in different directions. Save this file.

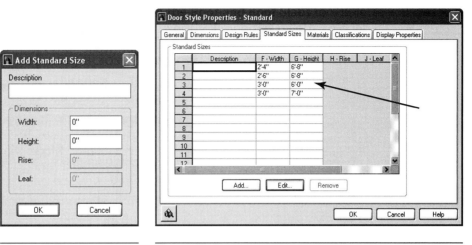

Figure 5–3

Figure 5–4

Figure 5–5

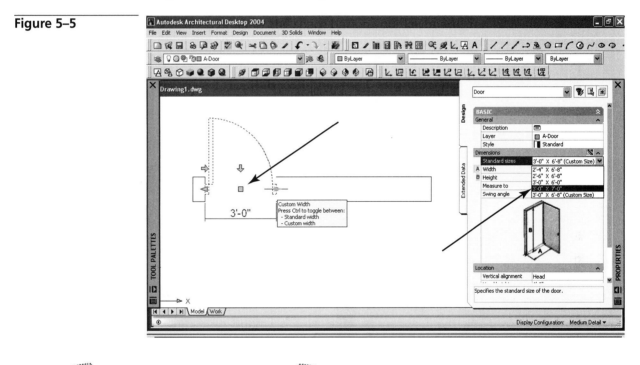

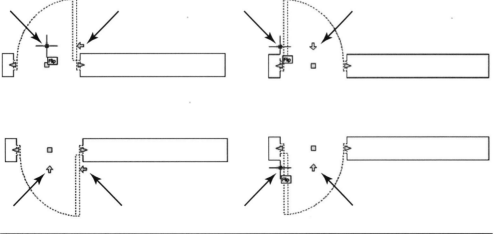

Figure 5–6

Hands-On

Controlling the Door Swing Angle

1. Using the previous exercise, change to **SW Isometric view.**

Notice that although the swing shows open in **Top View** (Plan), the door swing is closed in the **SW Isometric (Model View).** Architectural Desktop ships from the developer with the doors closed in **Model View** (see Figure 5–7).

Figure 5–7

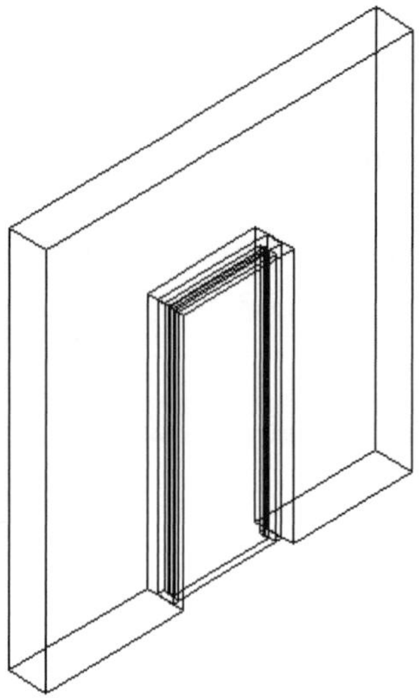

2. Double-click the door to bring up its **Properties** palette.
3. Notice that the swing angle is 90.
4. Change the swing angle to **45,** and press **Enter.** Note that nothing happens in the isometric or model view (the plan view will show a change).

Nothing happens because there is a model override set at **0,** which prevents the door's **Properties** palette from controlling the door swing angle. To allow control from the **Properties** palette do the following:

5. Select the door, **RMB,** and select **Edit Door Style** from the contextual menu that appears to bring up the **Door Style Properties** dialog box.
6. Select the **Display Properties** tab.
7. Double-click the **Model** field (don't check the style **Override** check box because that would only control the door selected, and not all the doors) to bring up the **Display Properties** dialog box.
8. Select the **Other** tab.
9. *Clear* the **Override Open Percent** check box, and press the **OK** buttons until you return to the Drawing Editor (see Figure 5–8).

The **Override Open Percent** check box overrides the **Properties** palette. You can also change the door swing to a straight swing in the **Other** tab.

Figure 5–8

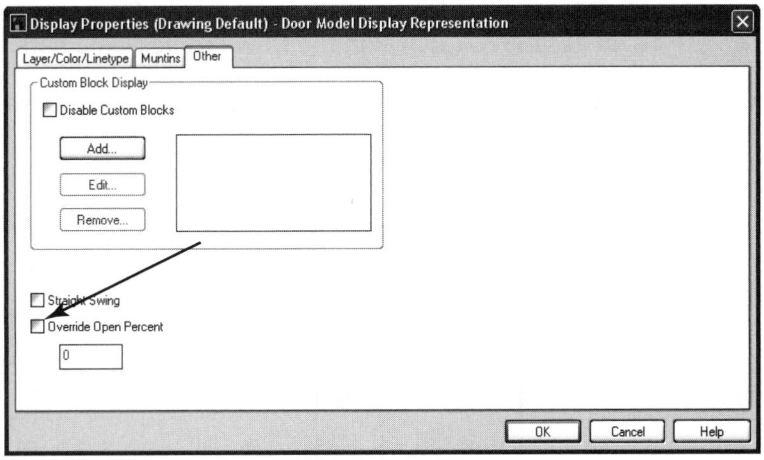

Display Properties (Drawing Default) - Door Model Display Representation

Layer/Color/Linetype | Muntins | Other

Custom Block Display

☐ Disable Custom Blocks

Add...

Edit...

Remove...

☐ Straight Swing

☐ Override Open Percent

0

OK   Cancel   Help

10. In the Drawing Editor, double-click the door again to bring up its **Properties** palette.

11. Change the swing angle to **90** and press **Enter.**

The door swing is open (see Figure 5–9).

Figure 5–9

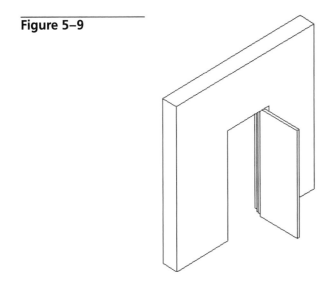

Hands-On

Adding a Profile

1. Use the previous exercise.
2. Change to **Front View.**
3. Place the closed polylines shown in Figure 5–10 over the door.
4. Select the door, **RMB,** and select **Add Profile** from the contextual menu that appears to bring up the **Add Door Profile** dialog box.

5. Select **Start from scratch** from the **Profile Definition** drop-down list, enter **TEST PIVOT DOOR** in the **New Profile Name** data field, and press **Enter.**

A blue hatch field will appear on the door (see Figure 5–11).

Figure 5–10

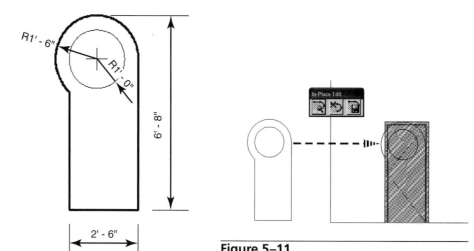

Figure 5–11

6. **RMB** on the blue hatch field and select **Replace ring** from the conceptual menu that appears.

7. Select the closed polyline that you created in Step 3 of this exercise.

8. Enter **Y** (Yes) in the **Command line** and press **Enter.**

9. **RMB** again on the blue hatch field and select **Add ring** from the contextual menu that appears.

10. Select the 1'-0" circle that you created with the polyline in Step 3 of this exercise.

11. Again enter **Y** (Yes) in the **Command line,** and press **Enter** to complete the command.

12. Change to the **NE Isometric view** and select the **Hidden** icon from the **Shading** toolbar.

13. **RMB** on the blue hatch field and select **Save Changes** from the conceptual menu that appears (see Figure 5–12).

Save this exercise.

Figure 5–12

Hands-On

Adding a Doorknob

1. Use the previous exercise.
2. Draw the closed polyline shown in Figure 5–13.
3. Select **Door** > **Pulldowns** > **3D Solids Pulldown** from the **Main** toolbar to place the **3D Solids** menu group on the **Main** toolbar.
4. Now, select **3D Solids** > **Revolve** from the **Main** toolbar and revolve 360° (see Figure 5–14).
5. Select **Mirror** to mirror the knob (see Figure 5–15).

Figure 5–13

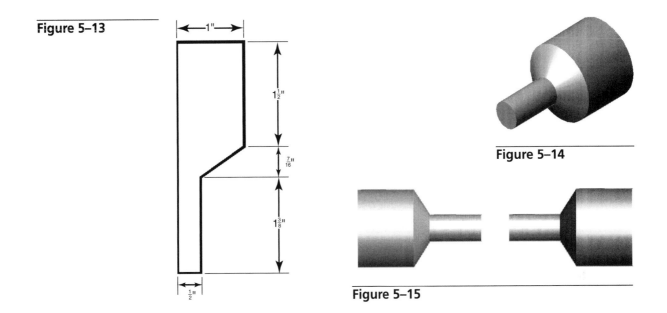

Figure 5–14

Figure 5–15

6. Select **Format** > **Blocks** > **Block Definition** from the **Main** toolbar to bring up the **Block Definition** dialog box.
7. Create two blocks named **KNOB1** and **KNOB2.**
8. Select the door you created in the previous exercise, **RMB,** and select **Edit Door Style** from the contextual menu that appears to bring up the **Door Style Properties** dialog box.
9. Select the **Display Properties** tab.
10. Double-click on the **Elevation** field to bring up the next **Display Properties** dialog box.
11. Select the **Other** tab.
12. Press the **Add** button to bring up the **Custom Block** dialog box (see Figure 5–16).
13. Select the **Select Block** button to bring up the **Select A Block** dialog box.
14. Select **KNOB1** and press the **OK** button.

Figure 5–16

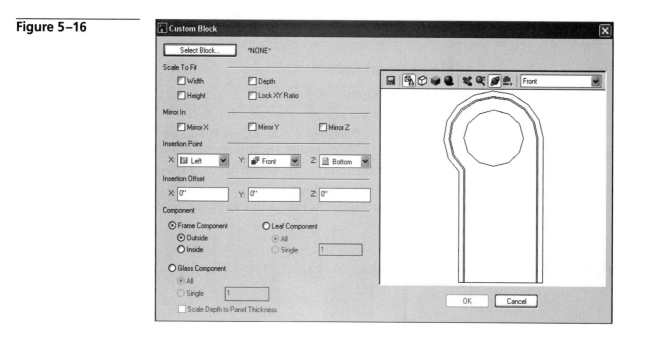

15. Use the settings shown in Figure 5–17 to move KNOB1 into position in the **Front View,** and then press the **OK** button to return to the **Display Properties** dialog box > **Other** tab.

16. Select the **Add** button to again bring up the **Custom Block** dialog box.

17. Press the **Select Block** button, this time select **KNOB 2,** and press **OK** to return to the **Custom Block** dialog box.

18. Use the same settings for KNOB2 that you used for KNOB1, and press the **OK** buttons until you return to the Drawing Editor (see Figure 5–18).

Save this file.

Figure 5–17

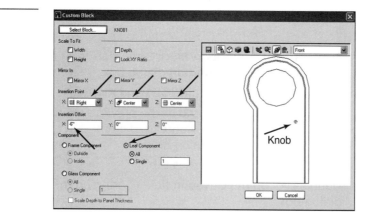

Figure 5–18

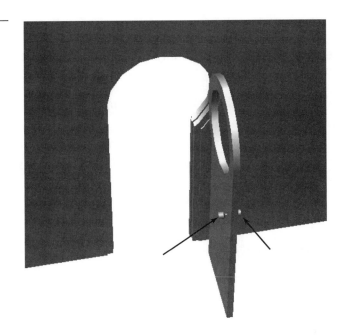

Hands-On

Moving the Door Vertically, within the Wall, and along the Wall

1. Use the previous exercise.
2. Change to the **Front View.**
3. Select the door to activate its grips.
4. Activate the square grip at the bottom of the door—a yellow dialog field appears (see Figure 5–19).
5. Activate the square grip at the bottom of the door.
6. Drag the grip to the right until the yellow dialog field appears.

Figure 5–19

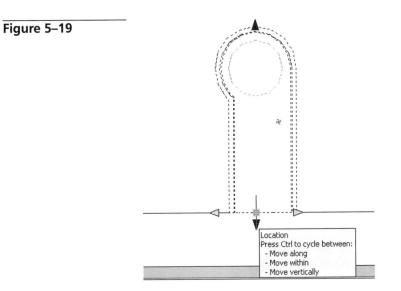

Location
Press Ctrl to cycle between:
- Move along
- Move within
- Move vertically

7.   Enter **3'-0"** in the **Command line** and press **Enter.**

The door will move horizontally 3'-0" in the direction that the grip was moved.

8.   Enter **3'-0"** in the **Command line** and press **Enter.**
9.   Change to the **Top View.**
10. Activate the square grip at the center of the door.
11. Press the **Ctrl** key once until the dialog field reads **Perpendicular move within width.**
12. Move the grip vertically.
13. Enter **2"** in the **Command line** and press **Enter.**

The door will move vertically within the wall 2" in the direction that the grip was moved.
Save this file.

Hands-On

Editing Door Styles

1.   Use the previous exercise.
2.   Change to the **Front View.**
3.   Select the door, **RMB,** and select **Edit Door Style** from the contextual menu that appears to bring up the **Door Style Properties** dialog box.
4.   Select the **Dimensions** tab.

This is where you set the **Frame Width** and **Depth.** Please note the **Auto-Adjust** check box; check this if you want the frame depth to match the wall in which the door has been inserted.

The **Stop Width** and **Depth** plus the **Door Thickness** and **Glass Thickness** are also located in the **Dimensions** tab.

5.   Select the **Floating Viewer** icon at the lower left corner of the **Door Style Properties** dialog box to bring up the **Viewer.**
6.   Select the **Hidden Shaded** icon in the top **Viewer** toolbar (see Figure 5–20).
7.   Enter the following data in the entry fields:

   a.   Frame Width = **3"**
   b.   Frame Depth = **6"**
   c.   Stop Width = **1"**
   d.   Stop Depth = **1"**

Press **Enter** after entering the last data field, and notice the change in door in the Viewer (see Figure 5–21).

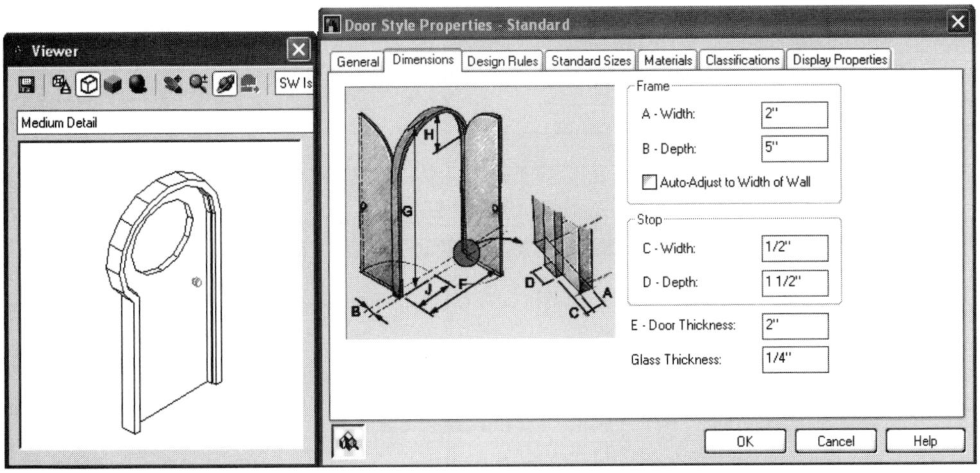

Figure 5–20

Figure 5–21

Hands-On

Using the Materials Tab

1. Select the door in the previous exercise, **RMB,** and select Edit Door Style from the contextual menu that appears to bring up the **Door Style Properties** dialog box.

2. In the **Door Style Properties** dialog box, change to the **Materials** tab.

3. In the **Materials** tab, activate the **Frame** field and click on the **Material Definition** drop-down list (see Figure 5–22).

There are four preset materials that are shipped with the program. If you need more materials, you need to add and edit a new material.

4. To add and edit a new material, press the **Add New Material** icon at the right side of the **Materials** tab.

5. Enter a new name for the new material in the **New Material** data field that appears and press the **OK** button.

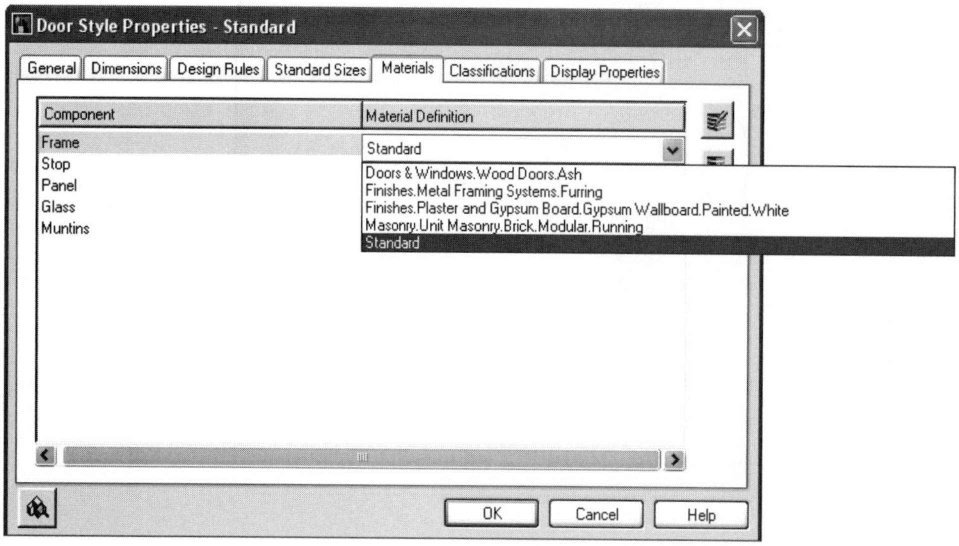

Figure 5–22

6. Activate the **New Material** field in the **Material Definition** column, and select the **Edit Material** icon above the **Add Material** icon to bring up the **Material Definition Properties** dialog box.

7. Check the **Style Override** check box for the **General Medium Detail** display representation to open the **Display Properties** dialog box.

8. Select the **Other** tab (see Figure 5–23).

Note: In the **Other** tab, you can control the placement of hatches on surfaces, and browse for materials made in the VIZ Render module (see Figure 5–24).

9. In the **Display Properties** dialog box, press the **OK** buttons until you return to the **Door Style Properties** dialog box.

10. Change to the **Display Properties** tab.

11. Select the **Elevation** field.

12. Press the **Edit Display** icon at the upper right side of the **Display Properties** tab to bring up the **Display Properties** dialog box.

Figure 5–23

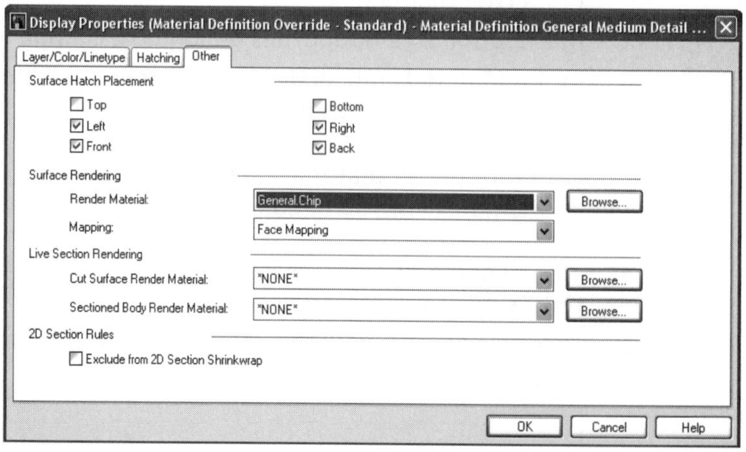

Figure 5–24

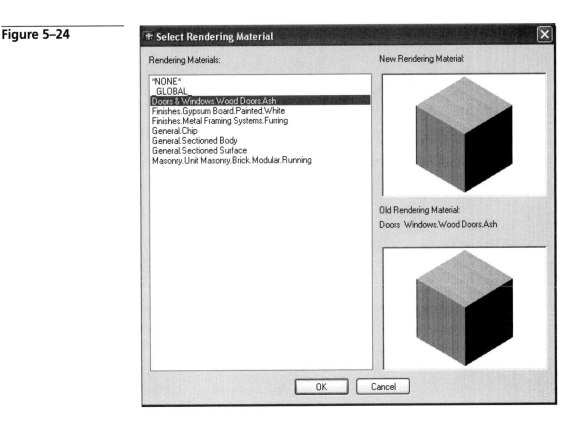

13. Select the **Muntins** tab.
14. Press the **Add** button to bring up the **Muntins Block** dialog box.
15. Select the **Prairie – 12 Lights** from the **Pattern** drop-down list, check the **Clean Up Joints** and **Convert to body** check boxes, and then press the **OK** buttons to close the command and view the door (see Figures 5–25 and 5–26).

Figure 5–25

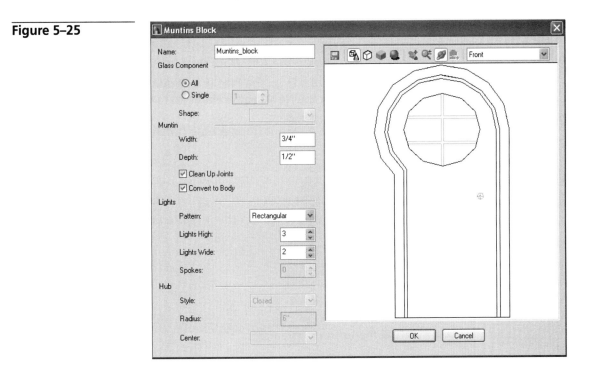

Figure 5–26

Hands-On

Using In-Place Edit

1. Start a new drawing using the Aec Model (Imperial Stb) template.
2. Change to the **Model Layout.**
3. Change to **Top View.**
4. Place a Standard 10'-long, 10'-high wall.
5. Place a Standard 3'-wide × 7'-high door constrained to the center of the wall.
6. Change to the **NW Isometric View.**
7. Select the door, **RMB,** and select **Add Profile** from the contextual menu that appears to bring up the **Add Door Profile** dialog box.
8. Select **Start from scratch** from the **Profile Definition** drop-down list, enter **CURVED TOP door** in the **New Profile Name** data field, and press **Enter.**

As with the editing of the previous door, a blue hatch field will appear on the door.

9. Click on the top **Edge** grip and drag upward (see Figure 5–27).
10. Press the **Ctrl** key on your keyboard twice and click the mouse key.
11. Press the **Save All Changes** icon in the **In-Place Edit** dialog box.

You have now created a double-hung door with a curved top (see Figure 5–28).

12. Change to the **Front View.**
13. Select the door, **RMB,** and again select **Edit Profile In Place** from the contextual menu that appears.

Figure 5–27

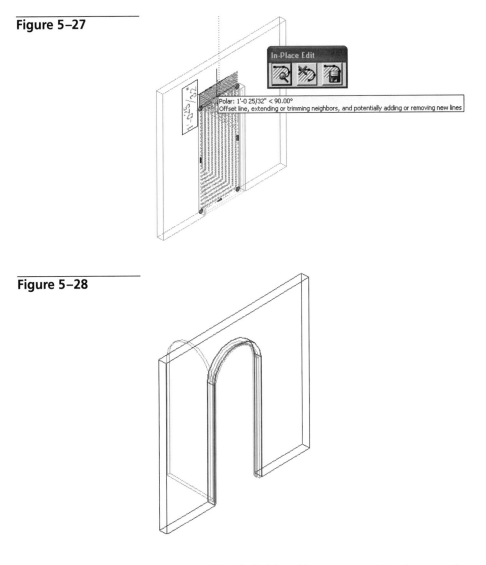

Figure 5–28

The blue hatch fields will appear on the door again.

14. Click on the left hand edge grip, and press the **Ctrl** key to change to **Add vertex** mode.

15. Move vertically downward and click the mouse button to add a new edge grip and vertex (see Figure 5–29).

16. Select the new edge grip, drag to the right, and click the mouse button (see Figure 5–30).

17. Press the **Save All Changes** icon in the **In-Place Edit** dialog box.

18. Select **Format > Style Manager** from the **Main** menu.

19. Expand the multipurpose **Objects** folder.

20. Expand **Profiles.**

21. Double-click on **CURVED TOP DOOR** to bring up the **Profile Definitions Properties** dialog box.

Notice that the door profile you created in place is now in your Style Manager (see Figure 5–31).

Figure 5–29

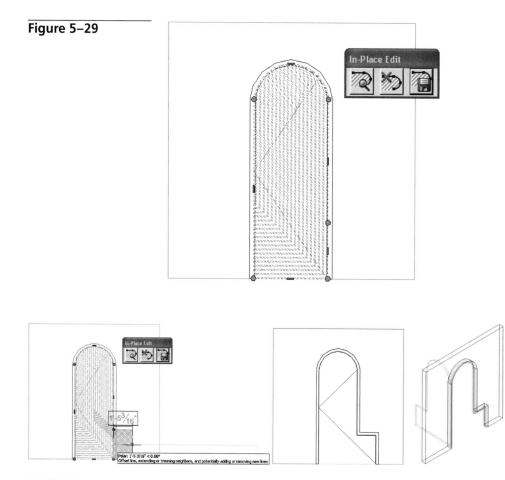

Figure 5–30

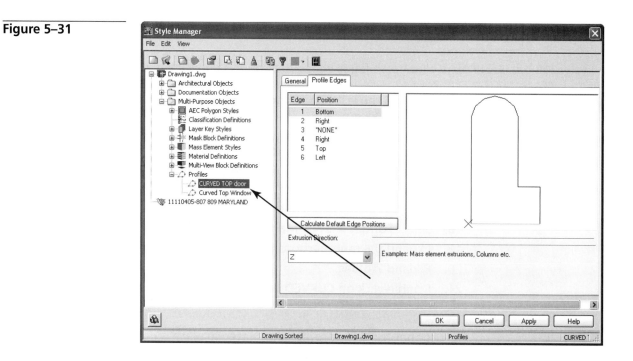

Figure 5–31

6

Curtain Walls

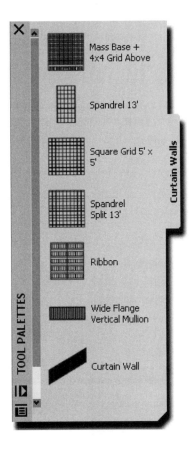

When you finish this section, you should understand the following:

- ✔ How to create a **Curtain Walls** tool palette.
- ✔ How to place a curtain wall.
- ✔ How to set miter angles.
- ✔ How to use the **Roof Line/Floor Line** command.
- ✔ How to apply tool properties to a layout grid.
- ✔ How to apply tool properties to an elevation sketch.
- ✔ How to edit a grid in place.
- ✔ How to edit curtain wall styles.
- ✔ How to apply Curtain Walls to faces.
- ✔ How to add Doors to Curtain Walls

Curtain Wall objects can be dragged or inserted from the Design tool palette or by typing **curtainwall add** in the **Command line.**

Curtain Wall objects can serve many purposes in Autodesk Architectural Desktop 2006. Originally created to represent storefront and nonbearing perimeter walls, curtain wall objects can be easily modified to represent many different kinds of walls. Their unique feature is their modifiable grid that can contain 3D solids, AEC polygons, and door and window assemblies. Curtain wall objects can even be modified to represent roof and floor trusses, with the curtain wall's parametrically changeable frames representing the truss members.

Besides being created from direct numerical input, **Curtain Wall objects** can be generated from **layout grids** and elevation **sketches.**

Once created, the resultant curtain wall styles can be applied to existing walls (the curtain wall object will replace the wall) or applied to a **reference base curve** (the curtain wall will use a curve on the ground plane as a basis for its shape in **Plan View**).

Number	Name	Purpose
1	Style	Select from available curtain wall styles.
2	Segment type	Choose Line or Arc for a linear or curved wall, respectively.
3	Base height	Get height of curtain wall.
4	Length	Present length value of curtain wall object.
5	Start miter	Miter of curtain wall frame at corner, at start of wall (in degrees).
6	End miter	Miter of curtain wall frame at corner, at start of wall (in degrees).
7	Roof line offset from base height	Any part of the curtain wall above the Base height such as parapet, gable end, etc.
8	Floor line offset from baseline	Any part of the curtain wall below the floor line.
9	Rotation	Elevation of curtain wall base.
10	Elevation	Height above level.
11	Roof/floor line	Vertex modifications for roof or floor line.

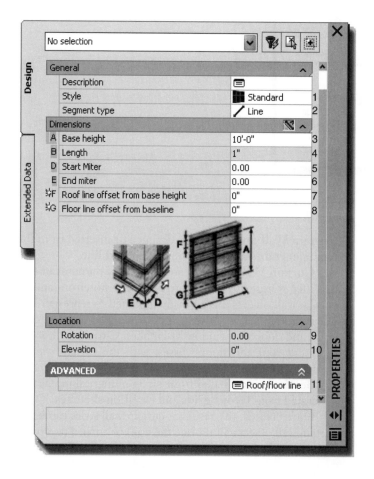

Hands-On

Creating a Curtain Walls Tool Palette

1. Select the **Content Browser** icon from the **Navigation** toolbar to bring up the Catalog Library in the Content Browser (see Figure 6–1).
2. In the Catalog Library, double-click the **Design Tool Catalog - Imperial** catalog to open it (see Figure 6–2).
3. Double-click on the area shown in Figure 6–3 to open the pages with all the tool folders.
4. Change to **Page 2,** select the **Curtain wall** folder, open it, and drag all the curtain walls to a new tool palette labeled **Curtain Walls.**

Figure 6–1

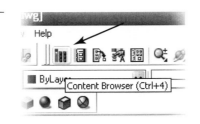

Figure 6–2

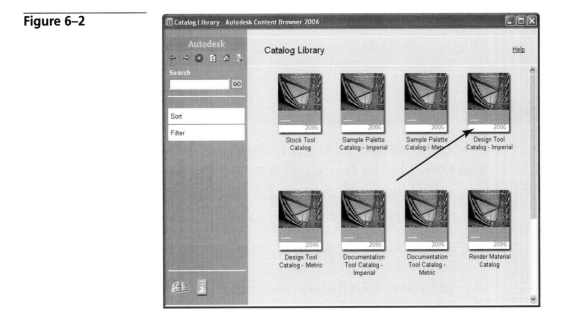

Figure 6–3

Hands-On

Placing a Curtain Wall

1. Start a new drawing using the Aec Model (Imperial Stb) template.
2. Change to the **Model Layout.**
3. Change to the **Top View.**
4. Turn the **ORTHO** button on.
5. Click on the **Curtain Wall** icon on the **Design** tool palette and move your cursor over the **Properties** tool palette to open it.
6. Set the following parameters:

   a. Style = **Standard**
   b. Segment type = **Line**
   c. Base height = **10'-0"**

7. Click to set the curtain wall start point, drag your cursor to the right, enter **10'-0"** in the **Command line**, and press **Enter.**
8. Move your cursor vertically and again enter **10'-0"** in the **Command line.**
9. Press **Enter** twice to finish the command.

You have now created two joined sections of curtain wall.

Hands-On

Setting Miter Angles in the Contextual Menu and the Start and End Miters in the Curtain Wall Properties Toolbar

1. Press the **SE Isometric View** icon on the **Views** toolbar.
2. Press the **Flat Shaded** icon on the **Shading** toolbar to shade the curtain walls.
3. Select one of the segments of curtain wall and **RMB** to bring up the **Curtain Wall** contextual menu.
4. Select **Edit Object Display** to bring up the **Object Display** dialog box.
5. Select the **Display Properties** tab, and then select the **Model** display representation, and click the **Edit Display Properties** icon to bring up the **Display Properties** dialog box (see Figure 6–4).
6. Open the **Layer/Color/Linetype** tab, and turn the **Default Infill** light off. Press all the **OK** buttons in the dialog boxes to return to the Drawing Editor.

Notice that your curtain walls now have no glass (infill) showing.

7. Zoom close to the top corner joint between the two sections of curtain wall (see Figure 6–5).

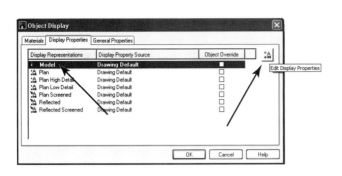

Figure 6–4

Figure 6–5

8. Select a section of curtain wall, **RMB,** select **Set Miter Angles** from the **Curtain Wall** contextual menu, and then select the other section of curtain wall (see Figure 6–6).

You have now mitered the corners of the curtain wall's frame.

Figure 6–6

If you select one of the curtain wall sections to bring up its **Properties** tool palette, you will see that its **Start Miter** or **End Miter** has been set. The vertical part of the frame can also be mitered, as we will see later.

9. Click each section of curtain wall separately to bring up its **Properties** tool palettes and check the **End Miter** for the left section, and the **Start Miter** for the right section.

The **End Miter** for the left section should now read **45,** and the right section of curtain wall should read **315.**

10. Erase everything in the Drawing Editor.
11. Again, click on the **Curtain Wall** icon on the new **Curtain Walls** tool palette and move your cursor over the **Properties** tool palette to open it. This time, enter the **Start** and **End** miter values you got in the previous exercise.
12. Click to set the curtain wall start point, drag your cursor to the right, enter **10'-0"** in the **Command line,** and press **Enter.**
13. Move your cursor vertically, and again enter **10'-0"** in the **Command line.**

14. Enter **OR** (ORTHO) in the **Command line** and press **Enter.**

15. Drag your cursor to the left and click in response to the **Command line** "Point on wall in direction of close."

You have now created a four-wall enclosure with mitered corners (see Figure 6–7). Save this file.

Figure 6–7

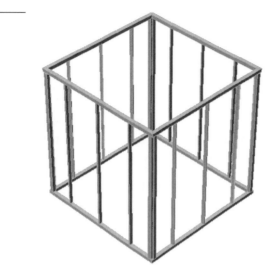

Hands-On

Using the Roof Line/Floor Line Selections in the Contextual Menu

1. Using the walls from the previous exercise, select a wall, **RMB,** and select **Roof Line/Floor Line > Edit In Place** from the contextual menu that appears (see Figure 6–8).

When editing a curtain wall in place, an **In-Place Edit** toolbar will appear in the Drawing Editor, and blue shading will appear over the wall. This shading shape can be modified and saved back to the curtain wall (see Figure 6–9).

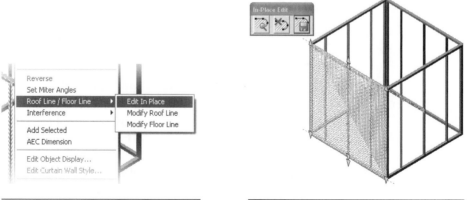

Figure 6–8

Figure 6–9

2. Select the blue shading, **RMB,** and select **Add Step** from the contextual menu that appears.

3. Select the floor line of the curtain wall. **The curtain wall steps** (see Figure 6–10). Repeat Step 2, this time picking **Add Gable** (see Figure 6–11).

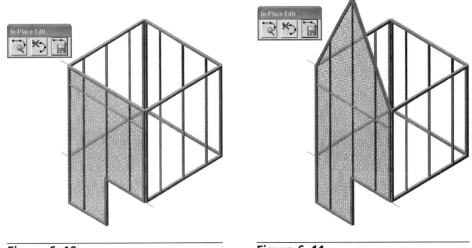

Figure 6–10   **Figure 6–11**

4. Select the blue shading again, **RMB,** and select **Reverse** from the contextual menu that appears.

5. Select the floor line of the curtain wall.

The curtain wall step will reverse (see Figure 6–12).

Figure 6–12

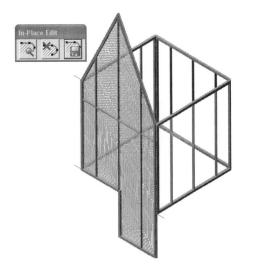

6. Select the **Left View** icon from the **Views** toolbar to change to the **Left View.**

7. Select the **Polyline** icon from the **Shapes** toolbar, and draw a polyline as shown in Figure 6–13. The polyline does not have to be in the same plane or touch the curtain wall.

8. Select the blue shading again, **RMB,** and select **Project to Polyline** from the contextual menu that appears.

9. Select the polyline that you just drew, enter **Y** for Yes in the **Command line,** and press **Enter.**

The curtain wall changes shape to match the polyline (see Figure 6–14).

10. Press the **Save All Changes** icon in the **In-Place Edit** toolbar to save the changes.

Save this file.

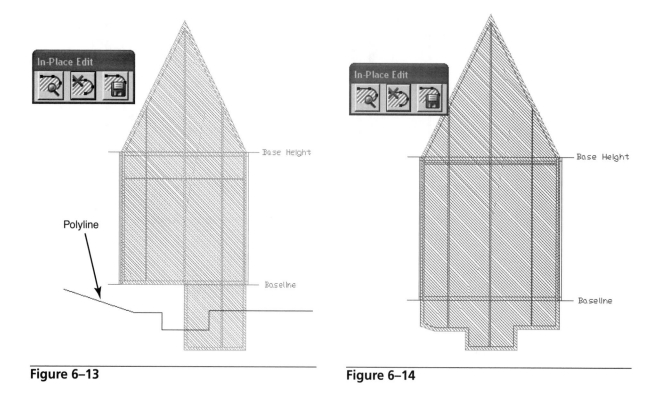

Figure 6–13

Figure 6–14

Hands-On

Applying Tool Properties to a Layout Grid

1. Start a new drawing using the Aec Model (Imperial Stb) template.
2. Change to the **Model Layout.**
3. Create two viewports, one showing **Top** view and the other showing the **NW Isometric** view.
4. Press the **Content Browser** icon in the **Main** toolbar or enter **Ctrl + 4** on the keyboard to bring up the Content Browser.
5. In the Content Browser, select the **Stock Tool Catalog** to open it.
6. Open the **Parametric Layout & Anchoring** folder.
7. Drag the **Layout Grid 2D** icon into the **Curtain Walls** tool palette you created, and then close the **Stock Tool Catalog.**
8. Select the **Layout Grid 2D** icon, and move your cursor over the **Properties** palette to open the palette.

9. Enter the following:

    a. Shape = **Rectangular**
    b. Boundary = ***NONE***
    c. Specify on screen = **No**
    d. X-Width = **30'-0'**
    e. Y-Depth = **15'-0"**
    f. (For X axis) Layout type = **Space evenly**
    g. Number of bays = **6**
    h. (For Y axis) Layout type = **Space evenly**
    i. Number of bays = **3**

10. Place the grid in the **Top View** viewport, and press the **Enter** key twice to complete the command (see Figure 6–15).

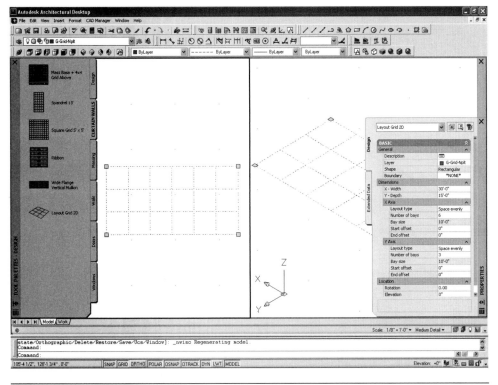

Figure 6–15

11. Select the layout grid, **RMB,** and select **X-Axis** > **Layout Mode** from the contextual menu that appears.
12. Enter **M** (Manual) in the **Command line,** and press **Enter.**
13. Select the layout grid again, and move some of the grips in the X direction to change the layout (see Figure 6–16).
14. **RMB** on the **Layout Square Grid 5'× 5'** icon and select **Apply Tool Properties to** > **Layout Grid** from the contextual menu that appears.
15. Select the layout grid, enter **Y** (Yes) in the **Command line**, and press **Enter.**

Figure 6–16

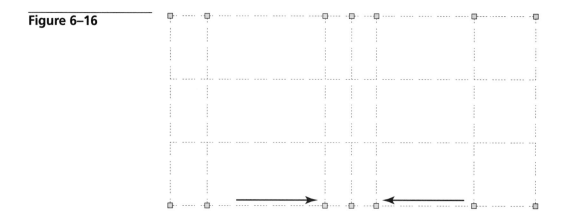

16. Enter **V** (Vertical) in the **Command line** (to make the verticals one piece and the horizontals segments) and press **Enter.**

17. Give the curtain wall a new name in the **Curtain Wall Style Name** dialog box that appears and press **Enter** to create the new curtain wall (see Figure 6–17).

Save this exercise.

Figure 6–17

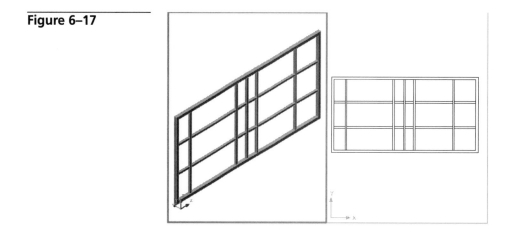

Hands-On

Applying Tool Properties to an Elevation Sketch

1. Start a new drawing using the Aec Model (Imperial Stb) template.
2. Change to the **Work Layout.**
3. Select the **Front View** and create the line drawing shown in Figure 6–18.
4. **RMB** on the **Square Grid 5′ × 5′ Curtain Wall** icon from the **Curtain Walls** tool palette you created to bring up its contextual menu.
5. Select **Apply Tool Properties to > Elevation Sketch** from the contextual menu.
6. Select the line drawing you made in Step 3 of this exercise, and press **Enter** twice.

Figure 6–18

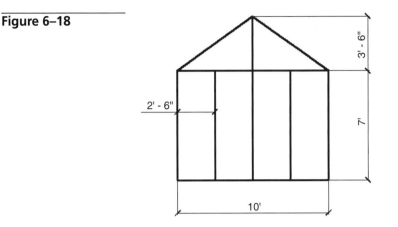

7. Enter **Y** (Yes) in the **Command** line when asked to "Erase the Geometry," and press **Enter** to create the curtain wall.

Your line work will now create a curtain (see Figure 6–19).

8. Select the new curtain wall, **RMB**, and select **Infill > Show Markers** from the contextual menu that appears.

The cell markers will now become visible (see Figure 6–20).

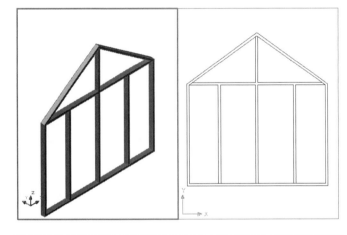

Figure 6–19   **Figure 6–20**

9. Select the new curtain wall again, **RMB,** and select **Infill > Merge** from the contextual menu that appears.
10. When the **Command line** reads, "Select cell A," select the leftmost cell marker, and press **Enter.**
11. When the **Command line** reads, "Select cell B," select the next cell marker, and press **Enter.**

The two curtain wall divisions merge into one cell.

12. Repeat Steps 8, 9, and 10 to merge the upper cell (see Figure 6–21).
13. Select the curtain wall again, **RMB,** and select **Infill > Override Assignment** from the contextual menu that appears.

14. Select the leftmost marker and press **Enter** to bring up the Infill **Assignment Override** dialog box.

15. Check the **Bottom** check box and press **OK** to remove the bottom frame (see Figure 6–22).

> **Note:** For clarity, the author has removed the display of the window (infill) itself in these illustrations.

16. Select the curtain wall again, and select **Infill > Hide Markers** from the contextual menu that appears.

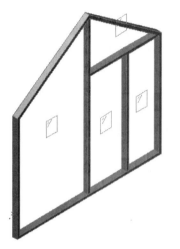

Figure 6–21

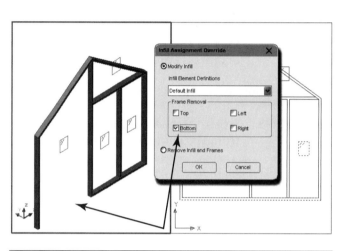

Figure 6–22

Hands-On

Editing a Grid in Place

1. Start a new drawing using the Aec Model (Imperial Stb) template.
2. Change to the **Model Layout.**
3. Change to the **Top View.**
4. Place a Square Grid 5′ × 5′ curtain wall 10′ high and 15′ long.
5. Change to the **Front View.**
6. Click on the curtain wall to activate its grips.
7. Click on the **Edit Grid** grip (see Figure 6–23).
8. **RMB** and select **Division in place** from the contextual menu that appears.
9. Move your cursor over to the left edge of the grid making sure that a red hatch appears in the entire grid, and click (see Figure 6–24).

The grid will now be in Auto Grid Bay Spacing mode (you can see this if you move your cursor over the left middle edge arrow.

10. **RMB** on the grid to bring up the contextual menu that appears, and select **Convert To Manual** (see Figure 6–25).

Figure 6–23

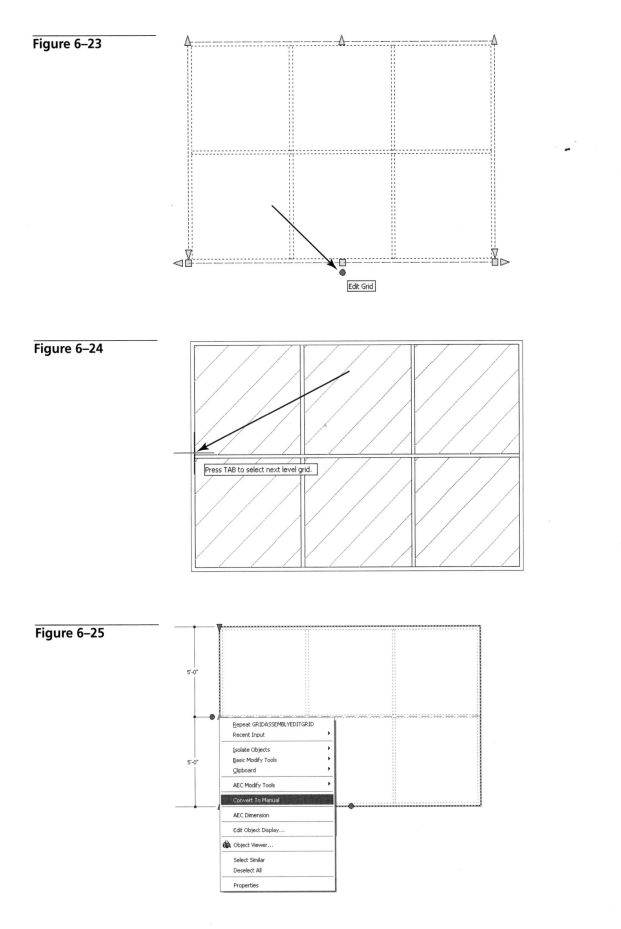

Figure 6–24

Press TAB to select next level grid.

Figure 6–25

5'-0"

5'-0"

Repeat GRIDASSEMBLYEDITGRID
Recent Input
Isolate Objects
Basic Modify Tools
Clipboard
AEC Modify Tools
Convert To Manual
AEC Dimension
Edit Object Display...
Object Viewer...
Select Similar
Deselect All
Properties

Edit Grid

Figure 6–26

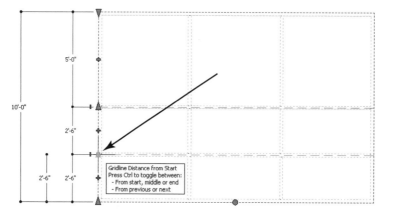

Figure 6–27

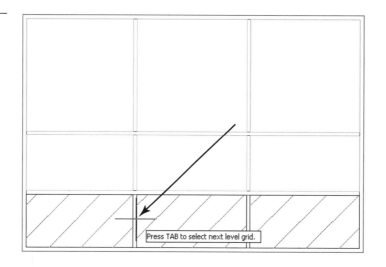

When you select **Convert To Manual,** + and − icons appear.

11.   Select the + icon to add a horizontal mullion (see Figure 6–26).

12.   Select the **Exit Editing Grid** icon to bring up the **Save Changes** dialog box, press the **New** button to bring up the **New Division Override** dialog box, enter **New Horizontal Mullion** in the **New Name** data field, and press **OK** to complete the command.

13.   Repeat Steps 7–11, picking a vertical mullion and creating a **New Vertical Mullion** (see Figures 6–27 and 6–28).

14.   Change the view to **SW Isometric View** and select the **Gouraud** icon in the **Shading** toolbar (see Figure 6–29).

Save this file.

Figure 6–28

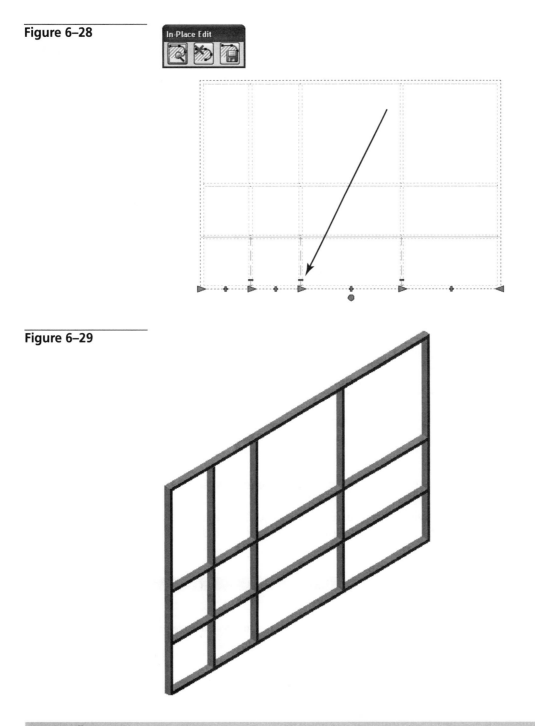

Figure 6–29

Hands-On

Editing Curtain Wall Styles

1. Use the previous exercise.
2. Select the curtain wall, **RMB,** and select **Edit Curtain Wall Style** from the contextual menu that appears to bring up the **Curtain Wall Style Properties** dialog box.

3.   Select the **Design Rules** tab.

4.   Select the **Floating Viewer** icon at the bottom left of the **Curtain Wall Style Properties** dialog box, and size it so that both the **Viewer** and the dialog box are open at the same time. Be sure to set the viewer in SW Isometric (see Figure 6–30).

Figure 6–30

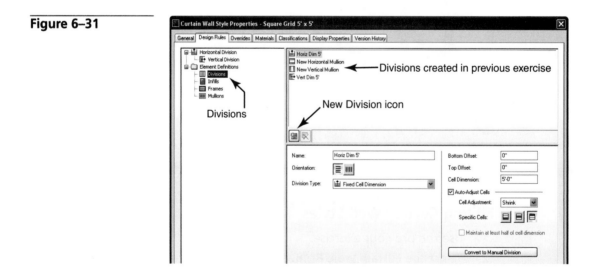

5.   Select the **Divisions** icon in the **Element Definitions** tree (see Figure 6–31).

Note the divisions made and saved in the previous exercise and the **New Division** icon for creating divisions in this dialog box.

Figure 6–31

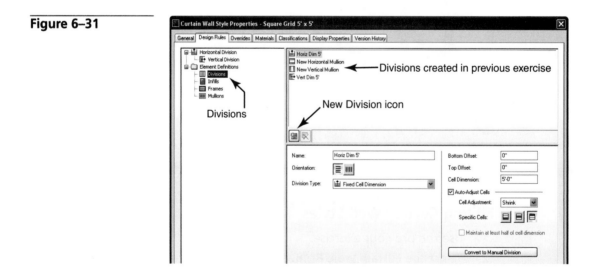

6.   Select the **Horizontal Division** in the tree and select **New Horizontal Mullion** from the **Division Assignment** drop-down list shown in Figure 6–32.

Figure 6–32

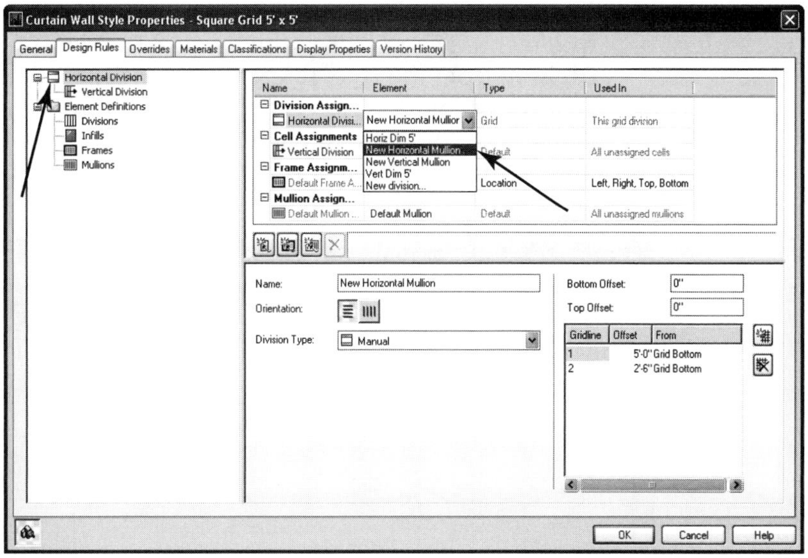

7. Select **Vertical Division** from the tree and select **New Vertical Mullion** from its **Division Assignment** drop-down list.

We will need a **Pivot - Horizontal** window for this next part of the exercise so use the **Content Browser** to drag a pivot window style into your drawing. To do this: Exit the **Style** dialog box, select the **Content Browser,** and then select the **Design Tool Catalog- Imperial.** In this catalog select **Doors and Windows** and then the **Windows** folder. From the Windows folder, drag the **Pivot - Horizontal** window onto your **Windows** tool palette. Place a **Pivot-Horizontal** window in the drawing editor or a spare wall so that the style and properties will be available in the **Properties** palette.

8. Select **Infills** from the tree, select the **New Infill** icon, name the new infill **Pivot Window,** select **Style** from the **Infill Type** drop-down list, and pick the **Pivot - Horizontal** style from the **Style** list (see Figure 6–33).

Figure 6–33

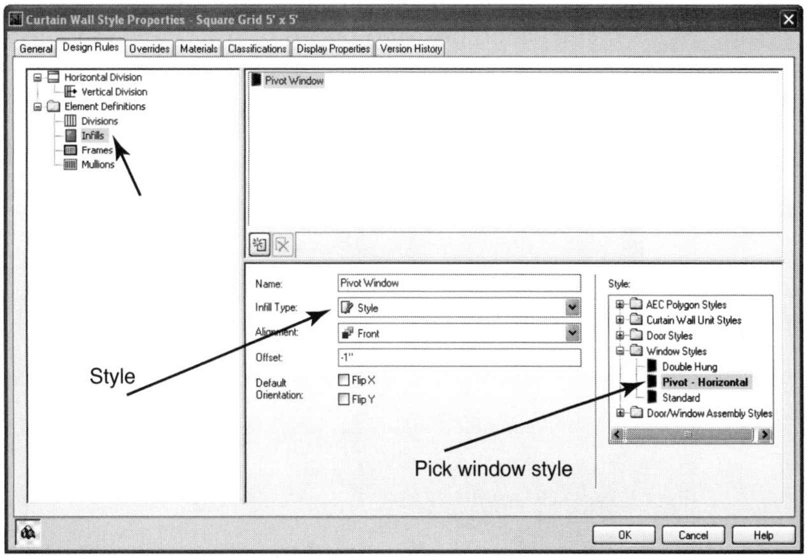

9. Select the "boxed +" symbol; next to the Horizontal Divisions in the tree menu. This will drop the Vertical Division tree. Select **Vertical Division** from the tree, select the **New Cell Assignment** icon to create a new cell assignment, select **Pivot Window** from the **New Cell Assignment Element** drop-down list, and select **End** from the **Used In** drop-down list (see Figure 6–34).

Figure 6–34

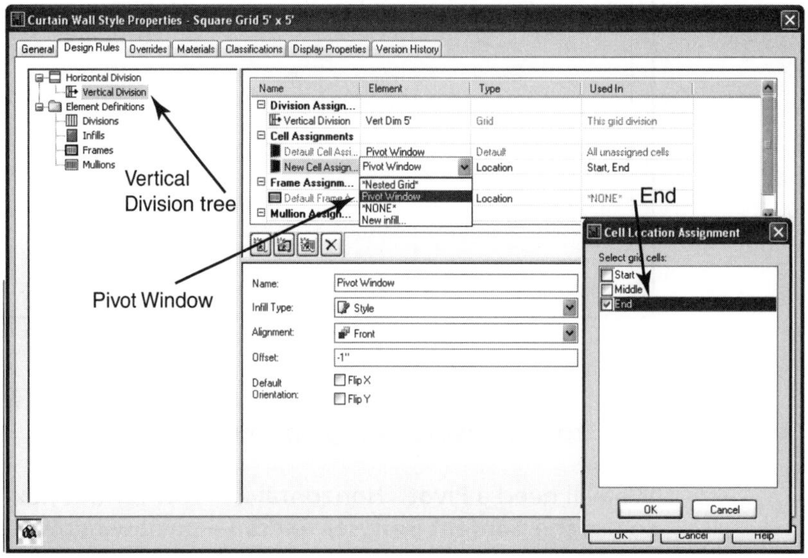

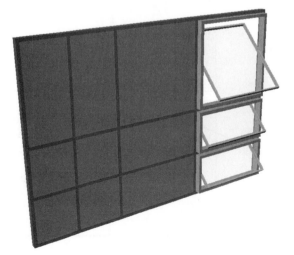

10. Press the **OK** buttons to complete the command and return to the Drawing Editor.

11. Select a pivot window that you just installed in the curtain wall, **RMB,** and select **Edit Object Display** from the contextual menu that appears to bring up the **Object Display** dialog box.

12. Make sure the **Model** field is selected, select the **Display Properties** tab, and press the **Edit Display Properties** icon at the upper right to bring up the **Display properties** dialog box.

13. Select the **Other** tab.

14. Set the **Override Open Percent** to **30,** and press the **OK** buttons in all the dialog boxes to return to the Drawing Editor (see Figure 6–35).

Figure 6–35

Applying Curtain Walls to Faces

1. Start a new drawing using the Aec Model (Imperial Stb) template.
2. Select the **Box** tool from the **Massing** tool palette, and place a **6'-0"**-wide, **4'-0"**-deep, and **7'-0"**-high mass element in the Drawing Editor.
3. Change to the **SW Isometric** view.
4. Double-click the mass element to open the **Properties** palette, and select **Free Form** from the **Shape** drop-down list.
5. With the mass element in **Free Form** mode, select the element, **RMB,** and select **Split by Plane** from the contextual menu that appears.
6. Enter **3** (3points) in the **Command** line, and press the **Enter** key on your keyboard.
7. With the endpoint and nearest Osnaps set, select the points shown in Figure 6–36 in the order shown to create a split plane.
8. Select the top mass form and delete it. You have now created the mass element for placing faces in this exercise (see Figure 6–37).
9. Select the **Curtain Wall** tool in the **Design** tool palette, **RMB,** and select **Apply Tool Properties to > Faces** from the contextual menu that appears.
10. Move your cursor over the front face of the mass element until a red hatch appears on that face; then click the cursor to bring up the **Convert to Curtain Walls** dialog box.

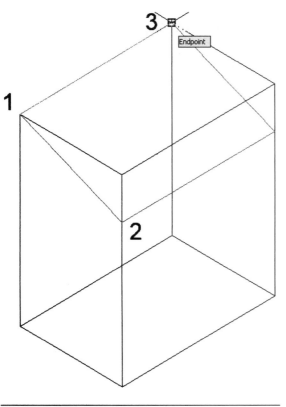

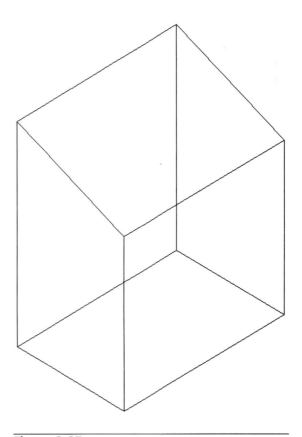

Figure 6–36   **Figure 6–37**

11. In the **Convert to Curtain Walls** dialog box, select **Standard,** and press the **OK** button to place the curtain wall on the front face (see Figures 6–38 and 6–39).

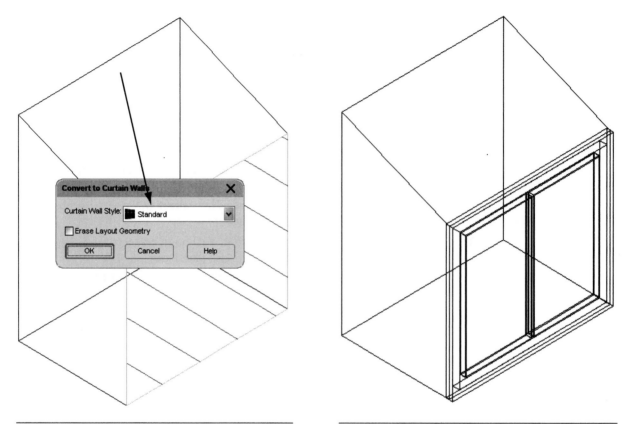

Figure 6–38   **Figure 6–39**

12. Zoom in and observe that the midpoint of the curtain wall frame extrusion has been placed on the face of the mass element, and that there is an extra inner frame (see Figure 6–40).

Figure 6–40

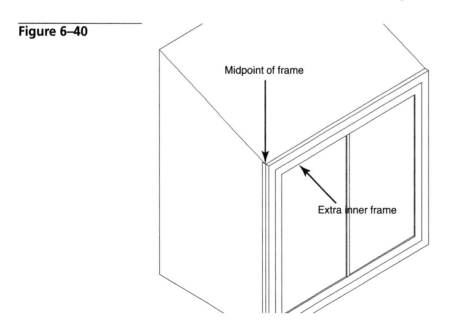

To correct this, do the following:

13. Select the curtain wall you just placed, **RMB,** and select **Design Rules** > **Save to Style** from the contextual menu that appears to bring up the **Save Changes** dialog box.

14. In the **Save Changes** dialog box, press the **New** button to bring up the **New Curtain Wall Style** dialog box.

15. In the **New Curtain Wall Style** dialog box, enter **FRONT,** and press the **OK** buttons to close all the dialog boxes and return to the Drawing editor (see Figure 6–41).

Figure 6–41

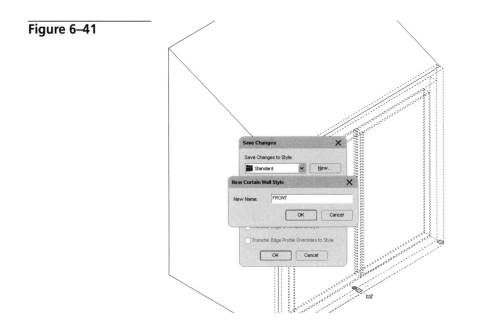

16. Now that you have changed the curtain wall you placed to **FRONT,** select it, **RMB,** and select **Edit Curtain Wall Style** from the contextual menu that appears to open the **Curtain Wall Style Properties** dialog box for this style.

17. In the **Curtain Wall Style Properties** dialog box, select the **Design Rules** tab.

18. In the **Design Rules** tab, in the left pane, click Unnamed at the top of the tree, and expand the **Frame Assignments** in the right pane.

19. Under **Frame Assignments** select the **Default Frame Assignment** field, click to the right of (**Left, Right, Top, Bottom**) in the **Used In** column and select the button that appears to bring up the **Frame Location Assignment** dialog box.

20. In the **Frame Location Assignment** dialog box, *uncheck* all the check boxes, and press the OK button to return to the **Curtain Wall Style Properties** dialog box (see Figure 6–42). **This will remove the extra inner frame.**

21. In the **Curtain Wall Style Properties** dialog box, in the right pane, set the Default Frame **Width** to **2"** and depth to **5"**. Finally, set the **"Y" Offset** to **2-1/2"**. **This will move the 5"-deep frame forward from the point.** Press the **OK** button to close the dialog box and return to the Drawing editor (see Figure 6–43).

Figure 6–42

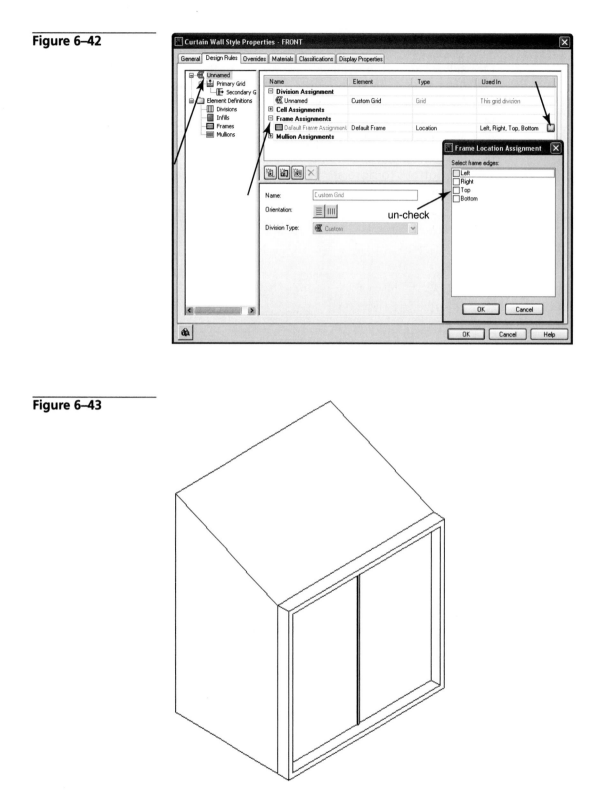

Figure 6–43

22. Repeat Steps 9–21 for the left, right, and top faces using **Design Rules >**
    Save to Style to save them as **LEFT, RIGHT,** and **TOP.** (For the LEFT style
    you will have to set the **"Y" Offset** to – **2-1/2".**) See Figure 6–44.

Figure 6–44

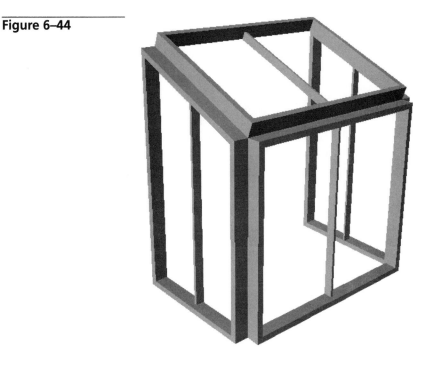

Hands-On

Adding Doors to Curtain Walls

1. Start a new drawing using the Aec Model (Imperial Stb) template.
2. Change to the **Top** view.
3. Select the **Curtain wall** tool from the **design** tool palette, and move your cursor over the **Properties** palette to open it.
4. In the **Properties** palette set the **Style** to **Standard,** and **Base height** to **10′** and place a curtain wall 8′ long in the Drawing Editor.
5. Change to the **Front** view.
6. Using the techniques shown in the **Edit in Place** exercise in this section, edit the curtain wall to resemble that shown in Figure 6–45.
7. Select the **Hinged–Single–Full Lite** door from the **Doors** tool palette, and select the curtain wall—the cell markers will appear.
8. Move your cursor over the center cell till a red hatch appears, and click to bring up the **Add Infill** dialog box.
9. In the **Add Infill** dialog box, select the Add as Cell Override radio button, select the New Infill radio button, enter TEST DOOR in the New Infill field, and check the Bottom check box in the Override Frame Removal (to remove the frame below the door). Press the OK button to complete the command and place the door (see Figures 6–46, 6–47, and 6–48).

This same process can be done for doors, windows, and door and window assemblies.

Figure 6–45

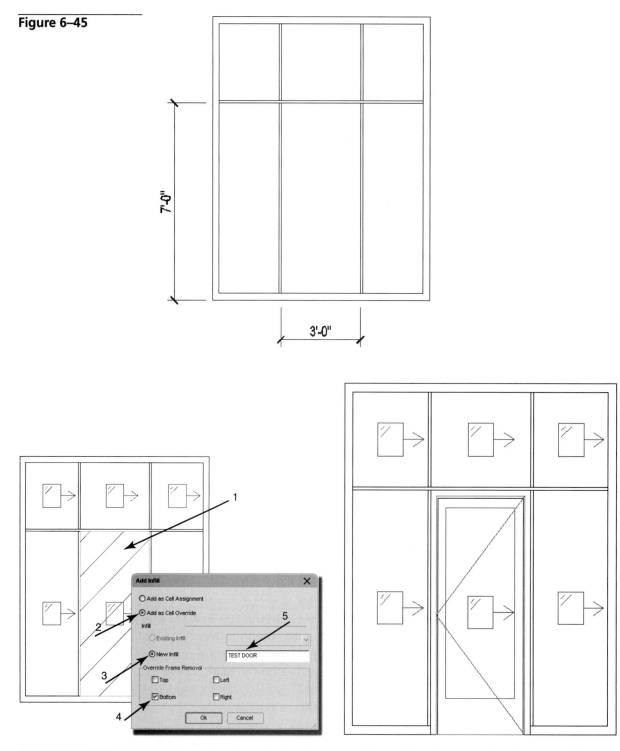

Figure 6–46

Figure 6–47

Figure 6–48

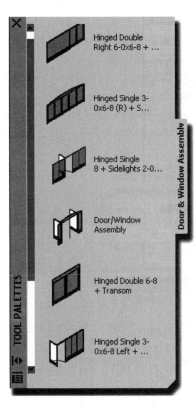

Door and Window Assemblies

When you finish this section, you should understand the following:

✔ How to create a **Primary Grid** for a **Door/Window Assembly.**

✔ How to create a door style for double doors.

✔ How to assign doors to a **Door/Window Assembly** infill.

✔ How to test the partially complete **Door/Window Assembly.**

✔ How to add sidelites.

✔ How to size the frame of a **Door/Window Assembly.**

✔ How to remove the sill of a **Door/Window Assembly.**

✔ How to use a **Door/Window Assembly.**

Door/window assemblies provide a grid or framework for the insertion of windows or doors that are commonly used in the design of storefront Windows. With this framework, you can create complex window or door assemblies for insertion in a wall or as repetitive elements of the curtain wall.

Window assemblies insert like doors and windows, and they are customized by using the same methods used to create curtain walls.

Hands-On

Creating a Primary Grid

1. Start a new drawing using the Aec Model (Imperial Stb) template.
2. Change to the **Model Layout.**
3. Select **Format > Style Manager** from the **Main** menu to bring up the **Style Manager.**
4. Select **Architectural Objects > Door/Window Assembly Styles.**
5. Select the **Door/Window Assembly Styles** icon, **RMB,** and select **New** from the contextual menu that appears.
6. Name the new style **TEST DRWIN ASSEM STYLE.**
7. Double-click on the **TEST DRWIN ASSEM STYLE** icon to bring up the **Door/Window Assembly Style Properties** dialog box.
8. Select the **Floating Viewer** icon and place the **Viewer** adjacent to the **Door/Window Assembly Style Properties** dialog box on the screen (see Figure 7–1).

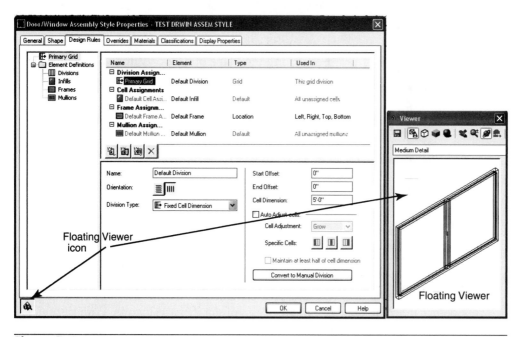

Figure 7–1

9. Change to the **Design Rules** tab.
10. Select the **Divisions** icon and follow the directions in Figure 7–2.
11. Select the **Primary Grid** icon, and change its **Element** to the **DOUBLE DOORS DIVISION** that you just created (see Figure 7–3).

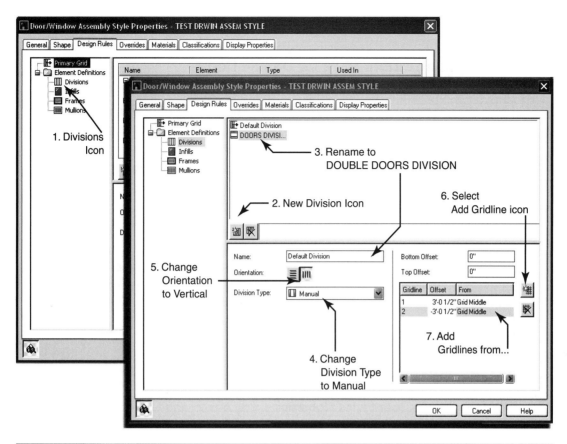

Figure 7–2

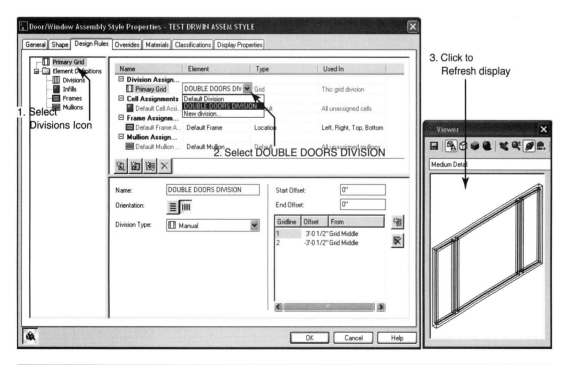

Figure 7–3

Hands-On

Creating a Door Style for Double Doors

1. Select the **Content Browser** icon to bring up the **Content Browser.**
2. Locate the **Design Tool Catalog – Imperial > Doors and Windows > Doors > Page 3** folder.
3. In the **Page 3** folder, locate the **Hinged-Single** door.
4. Drag the **Hinged-Single** door onto your **Design** toolbar.

Now you need a Double Door style using this door.

5. Select **Format > Style Manager** from the **Main** menu to bring up the **Style Manager.**
6. Locate the **Architectural Objects > Door Styles > Hinged-Single** icon.
7. Double-click on the **Hinged-Single** icon to bring up the **Door Styles Properties** dialog box.
8. Change to the **Dimensions** tab.
9. Set the **Frame A- Width** to 0".

This makes the door frameless.

10. In the **Door Styles Properties** dialog box, change to the **Design Rules** tab.
11. Select **Double** from the **Door Type** list, and press **OK** to return to the **Style Manager.**
12. Rename the door **DOUBLE HINGED SINGLE**, and then press the **Apply** and **OK** buttons to return to the Drawing Editor.

Hands-On

Assigning Doors to a Door/Window Assembly Infill

1. Select the **Infills** icon and follow the directions in Figure 7–4.
2. After creating the **DOUBLE DOORS** infill, press the **Primary Grid** icon again, and follow the directions in Figure 7–5.
3. Click on the **New Nested Grid** icon below the **Primary Grid** icon and follow the directions in Figure 7–6.
4. Press **OK** to return to the Drawing Editor.

Figure 7–4

Figure 7–5

Figure 7–6

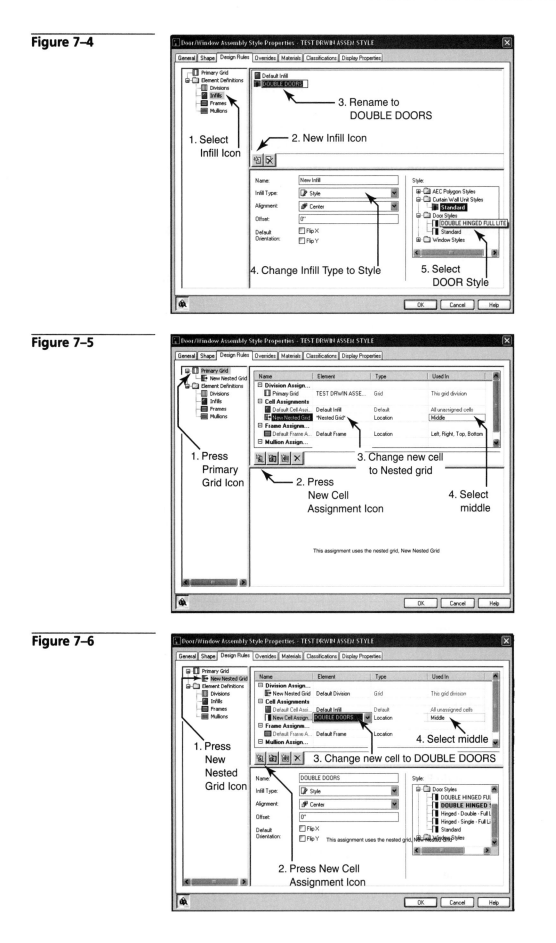

Hands-On

Testing the Partially Complete Door/Window Assembly

1. Select the **Door/Window Assembly** icon from the **Design** menu, and move your cursor over the **Properties** palette to open it.
2. Select **TEST DRWIN ASSEM STYLE** from the **Style** drop-down list.
3. In the **Top View,** press **Enter,** and place the door/window assembly.
4. Change to **SW Isometric View** (see Figure 7–7).

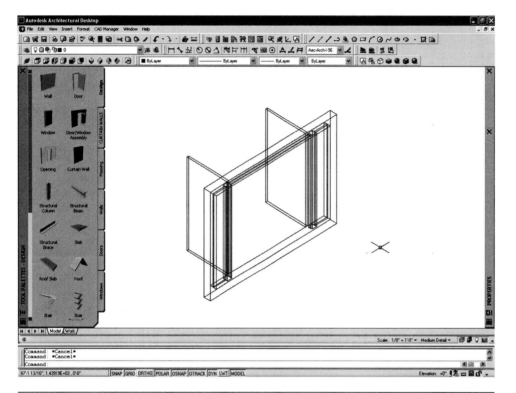

Figure 7–7

Hands-On

Adding Sidelites

1. Select the door/window assembly frame you just placed in the Drawing Editor, **RMB,** and select **Edit Door/Window Assembly Style** from the contextual menu that appears to bring up the **Door/Window Assembly Style Properties** dialog box.
2. Select the **Design Rules** tab again.
3. Select the **Primary Grid** icon and follow the directions in Figure 7–8.
4. Select the **SIDELITE GRID** icon below the **Primary Grid** icon and follow the directions in Figure 7–9.
5. Select the **Infill** icon and create another infill called **BASE** with a panel thickness of 1'-0" (see Figure 7–10).

Figure 7–8

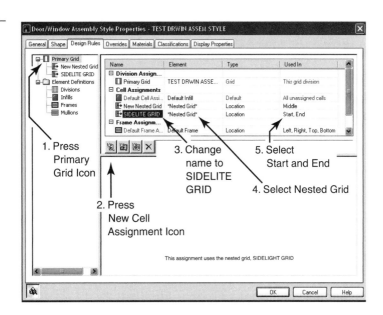

1. Press Primary Grid Icon

2. Press New Cell Assignment Icon

3. Change name to SIDELITE GRID

4. Select Nested Grid

5. Select Start and End

This assignment uses the nested grid, SIDELIGHT GRID

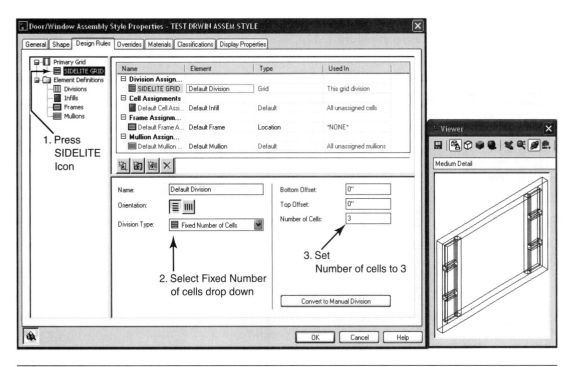

1. Press SIDELITE Icon

2. Select Fixed Number of cells drop down

3. Set Number of cells to 3

Medium Detail

Figure 7–9

Figure 7–10

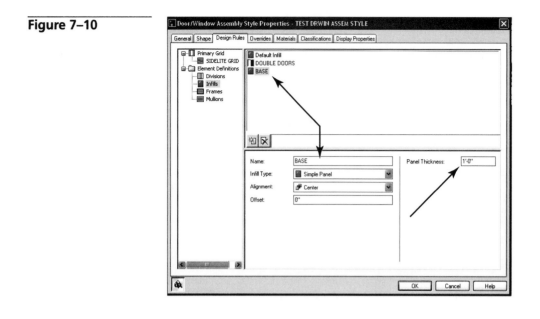

6. Select the **SIDELITE GRID** icon below the **Primary Grid** and follow the directions in Figure 7–11.

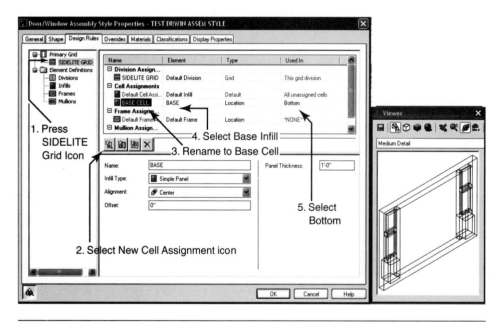

Figure 7–11

Hands-On

Sizing the Frame of a Door/Window Assembly

1. Click on the **Frames** icon, change the **Width** to 2″ and the **Depth** to 6″, and press **OK** to return to the Drawing Editor (see Figure 7–12).

Figure 7–12

Hands-On

Removing the Sill of a Door/Window Assembly and Changing the Sidelite

1. Select the door/window assembly frame, **RMB,** and select **Infill > Show Markers** from the contextual menu that appears (see Figure 7–13).
2. Select the frame again, **RMB,** and select **Infill > Override Assignment** from the contextual menu that appears.

Figure 7–13

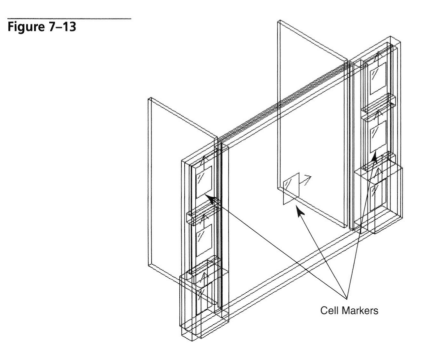

Cell Markers

3. Select the cell marker in the center of the door opening, and press **Enter** to bring up the **Infill Assignment Override** dialog box.

4. Check the **Frame Removal - Bottom** check box (see Figure 7–14).

Figure 7–14

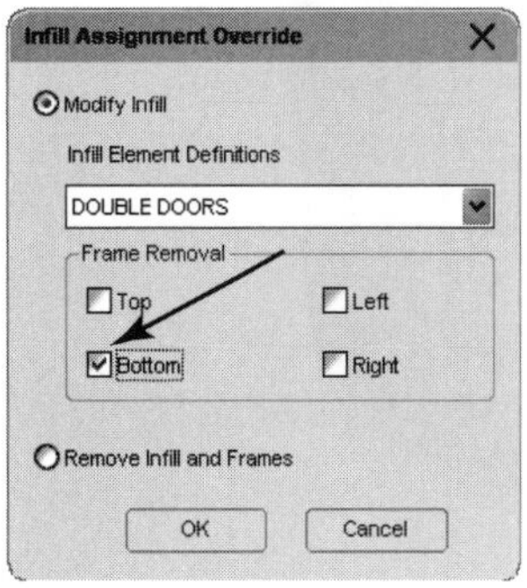

5. Press **OK** to remove the sill and return to the Drawing Editor.

6. Select the frame again, **RMB,** and select **Infill > Merge** from the contextual menu that appears.

7. Select the top two cells in each sidelite to merge the top cells.

8. Select the frame again, **RMB,** and select **Infill > Hide Markers** from the contextual menu that appears.

You now have created a new custom door/window assembly. Save this file.

Hands-On

Using the New Custom Door/Window Assembly

1. Use the previous file.

2. Change to the **Top View.**

3. Select the **Wall** icon from the **Design** tool palette, and place a 20′-0″-long Standard wall 8″ thick and 10′-0″ high.

4. Select the **Door/Window Assembly icon** from the **Design** tool palette.

5. Move your cursor over the **Properties** palette to open it.

6. Select the following:

    a. Style = **TEST DRWIN ASSEM STYLE**

    b. Position along the wall = **Offset/Center**

    c. Vertical alignment = **Sill**

    d. Sill Height = **0″**

7. Click on the wall to place the assembly (see Figure 7–15).

Figure 7–15

Stairs

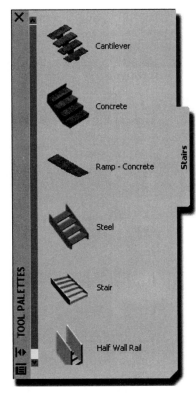

When you finish this section, you should understand the following:

- ✔ How to set **AEC Object Settings.**
- ✔ How to make a **Stairs** tool palette.
- ✔ How to place a **Stair** object.
- ✔ How to modify a stair with stair grips.
- ✔ How to change an **AEC Stair** object style.
- ✔ How add a **Stair Rail** object.
- ✔ How to edit a **Stair Style.**
- ✔ How to place a multilanding stair.
- ✔ **Interference Conditions** for stairs.
- ✔ How to anchor a second stair to an existing landing.
- ✔ How to project a stair edge to a polyline.
- ✔ How to project a stair edge to a wall or AEC object.
- ✔ How to generate a polyline from a stair object.
- ✔ How to create a **Stair Tower.**

Stair objects can be dragged or inserted either from the **Design** tool palette or by typing **stair add** in the **Command line.**

Stairs are an important part of almost every project, and it is here that designers often make mistakes. Autodesk Architectural Desktop 2006's stair and railing systems aid in the productivity and accuracy of these objects. Because of the complexity and variance of stairs, there is a multitude of settings. Once these settings are understood and preset, placing and modifying stairs is quite easy.

Stair styles are controlled by three factors: style, shape, and turn type. The Content Browser contains eight different preset styles. They are standard, Cantilever, Concrete, Steel, Half Wall Rail, Ramp Concrete, Ramp Concrete-Curb, and Ramp-Steel. As with the other styles in this program, there are many controls available for the styles in the **Stair Styles** dialog box. By creating your own styles, you can place stairs into a project quickly and efficiently.

PROPERTIES PALETTE

Number	Name	Purpose
1	Style	Select from available stair styles
2	Shape	U-shaped, Multi-landing, Spiral, Straight
3	Turn type	½ landing, ½ turn, ¼ landing, ¼ turn
4	Horizontal Orientation	Specifies the horizontal direction in which the stair turns for spiral or u-shaped: counterclockwise or clockwise
5	Vertical Orientation	Specifies whether the stair goes up or down when its height is changed.
6	Width	Width of stair.
7	Height	Height of stair vertically
8	Justify	Right, Center, or Left insertion points
9	Terminate with	Terminate with Riser, Tread, or Landing
10	Calculation rules	Brings up **Calculation Rules** dialog box

11	Straight length	Length of stair set by **Calculation Rules** dialog box
12	Riser count	Amount of risers calculated by stair-calculation rules
13	Riser	Riser height calculated by stair-calculation rules
14	Tread	Length of tread set by **Calculation Rules** dialog box
15	Rise/tread calculation	Calculation formula used by stair-calculation rules
16	Rotation	Rotation of stair
17	Elevation	Starting elevation of stair
18	Alignment type	Alignment between stairs at landings
19	Alignment offset	Offset at alignment between stairs at landings
20	Extend alignment	Extend alignment on Upper or Lower stair flight
21	Uneven tread on	Uneven tread on Upper or Lower flight
22	Top offset	Floor-surface depth above top riser or top treads, depending on their setting
23	Top depth	Floor surface support depth above top riser or top treads depending on their setting
24	Bottom offset	Floor-surface depth below first riser
25	Bottom depth	Floor-surface support depth below first riser
26	Minimum Limit type	Riser or flight height minimums
27	Maximum Limit type	Riser or flight height maximums
28	Headroom height	Used to control interference above the stair
29	Side clearance	Used to control interference at the sides of the stair
30	Components	Information on tread and riser thickness, nosing length, etc.
31	Landing extensions	Information on landings

Before beginning to use the stair object, AEC Object Settings must be set for the stairs.

Hands-On

Setting the AEC Object Settings for Stairs

1. Select **Format > Options** from the **Main** toolbar to bring up the **Options** dialog box.

2. Select the **AEC Object Settings** tab (see Figure 8–1).

3. In the **Stair Settings** area select **Flight & Landing Corners** from the **Node Osnap** drop-down list and **Finished Floor to Floor** from the **Measure Stair Height** drop-down list (see Figure 8–2).

Figure 8–1

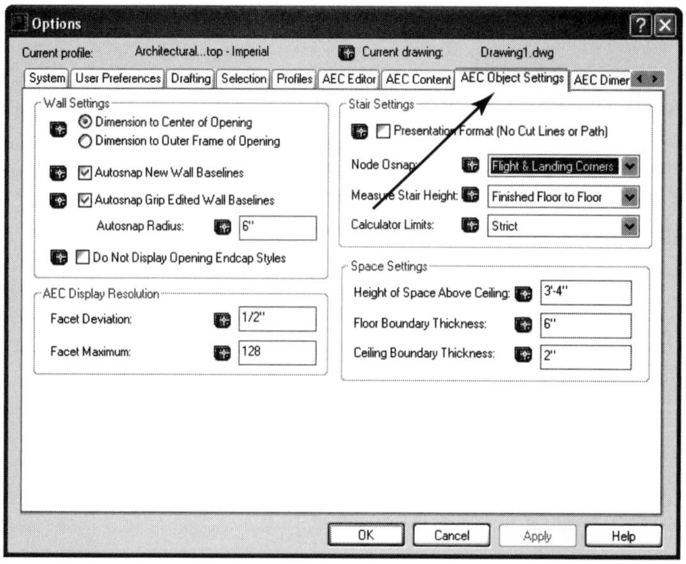

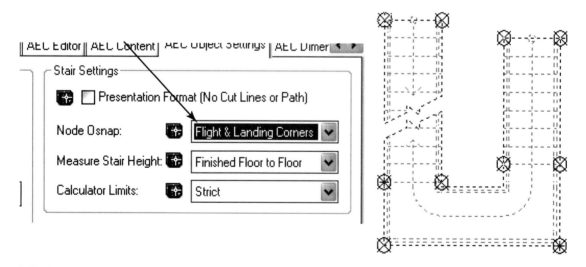

Figure 8–2

Hands-On

Making a New Stairs Tool Palette

1. Create a new tool palette, and name it **Stairs**.
2. Select the **Content Browser** icon from the **Main** toolbar to launch the Content Browser.
3. In the **Design Tool Catalog - Imperial,** locate the **Stairs** folder in the **Stairs and Railings** folder.
4. Drag all the stairs into the new tool palette you created.

Hands-On

Placing a Stair

1. Start a new drawing using the Aec Model (Imperial Stb) template.
2. Change to the **Model Layout.**
3. Change to **Top View.**
4. Select the **Stair** icon in the **Stairs** tool palette you created and drag your cursor over the **Properties** palette to open it.
5. Set the following:

   a. Shape = **U-shaped**
   b. Turn type = **1/2 landing**
   c. Horizontal Orientation = **Clockwise**
   d. Vertical Orientation = **Up**
   e. Width = **3'-0"**
   f. Height = **10"**
   g. Top offset = **0"**
   h. Top depth = **10"**
   i. Bottom offset = **0"**
   j. Bottom depth = **10"**
   k. Headroom height = **7'-0"**
   l. Side clearance = **0**

6. Click in the viewport and drag the stair to the right, enter 10' in the command line and press **Enter** twice to complete the command and create the stair (see Figure 8–3).

Figure 8–3

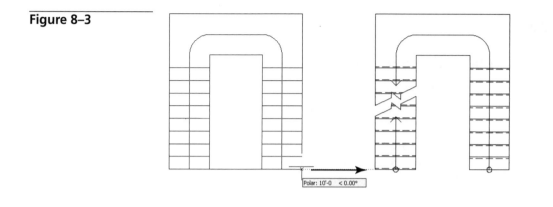

Hands-On

Modifying the Stair with the Stair Grips

1.   Select the stair object to activate the stair. Select the **Edit Edges** button to activate the stair grips. Place and modify six stairs using Figures 8–4 through 8–9 as examples. After placing each stair, change to **SW Isometric View** to examine your stair. Save this DWG as STAIR.

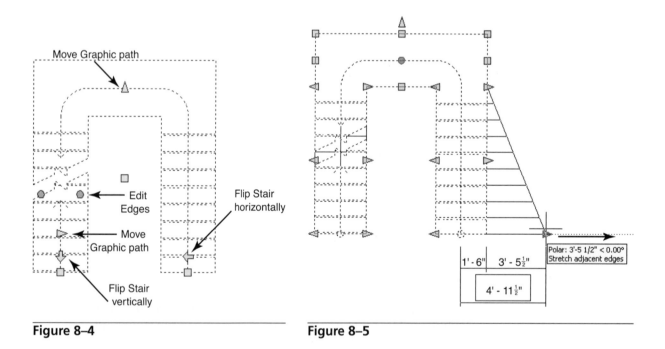

Figure 8–4

Figure 8–5

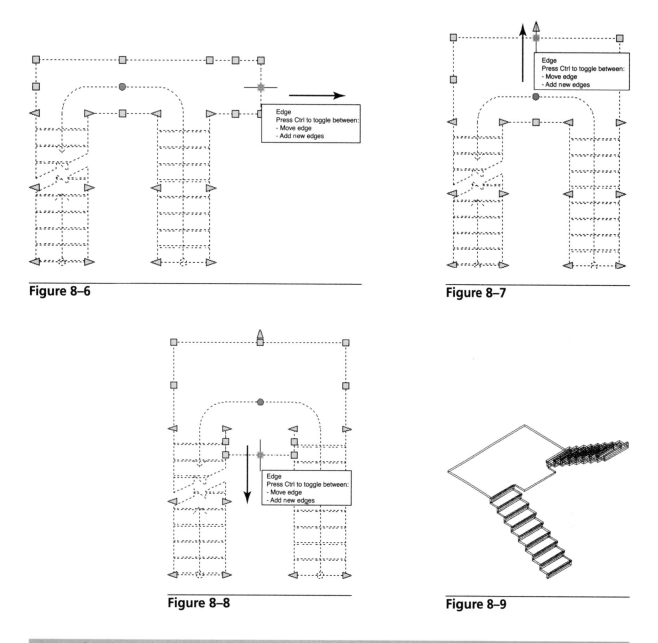

Figure 8–6

Figure 8–7

Figure 8–8

Figure 8–9

Hands-On

Changing Stair Styles

1. Change to **SW Isometric View.**
2. In your new **Stairs** tool palette, **RMB** on the **Half Wall Rail** icon and select **Apply Tool Properties to Stair** from the contextual menu that appears.
3. Select your stair, and press **Enter** to complete the command.
4. **RMB** in an empty space in the Drawing Editor, and select **Object Viewer** from the contextual menu that appears.
5. Select the stair, and press **Enter** to open the **Object Viewer** with the stair.

6. Expand the **Object Viewer,** and select the **Perspective** and **Flat Shaded** icons to display the stair in perspective and color (see Figure 8–10).

7. Close the **Object Viewer** to return to the Drawing Editor.

8. Repeat this process with all the other stair styles in your Stairs tool palette. Save the file.

Figure 8–10

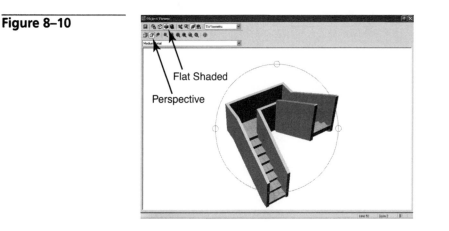

Flat Shaded

Perspective

Hands-On

Adding a Stair Rail

Modifying railings is explained in Section 9, "Railings."

1. Change your stair back to the Stair style by **RMB** and applying that style to your stair.

2. Select the stair, **RMB,** and select **Add Railing** from the contextual menu that appears.

3. Move your cursor over the closed **Properties** palette to open it.

4. Click on the *** Attached to** drop-down list, and select **Stair** flight (see Figure 8–11).

5. Select the lower corners of the lower stair flight to place a rail (see Figure 8–12).

/ *Note:* If you have difficulty placing the rails in 3D or if the rails don't appear, change to **Top View,** and place the rails in that view.

6. Remove the stair rails and repeat this using the **Stair** and **NONE** options in the **Properties** palette.

/ *Note:* The **NONE** option is for custom placing of a rail. This railing option is explained in Section 9, "Railings."

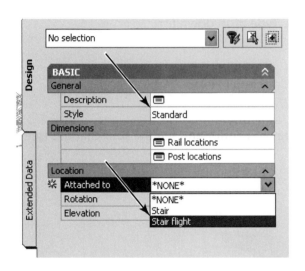

Figure 8–11

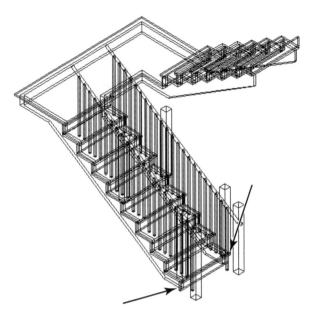

Figure 8–12

Hands-On

Editing a Stair Style

This can also be done through the Style Manager.

1. Select your stair, **RMB,** and select **Edit Stair Style** from the contextual menu that appears to bring up the **Stair Styles** dialog box.
2. Select the **Design Rules** tab. This is where the **Riser Heights**, **Tread Depth,** and the stair calculator are located (see Figure 8–13).
3. Change to the Stringers tab. This is where the stair stringers are added, removed, and modified.

Figure 8–13

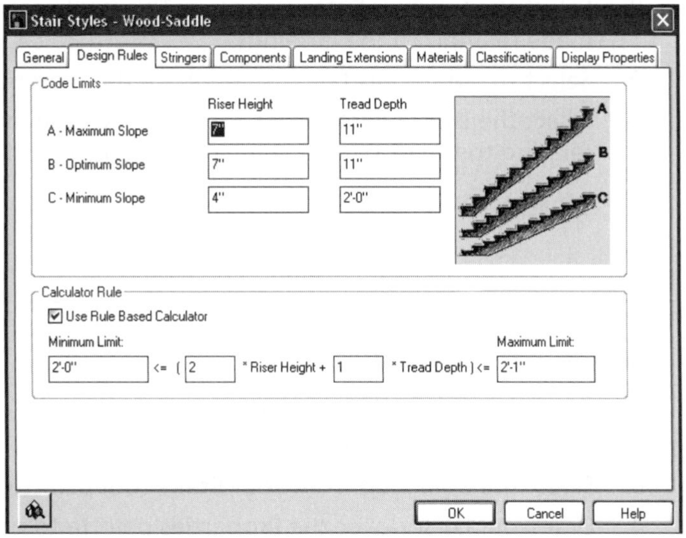

4. In the **Stringers** tab, press the **Add** button and create a left stringer with the following settings:

   a. **Housed** option from the **Type** drop-down list
   b. D - Total = **12″**
   c. F - Total = **12″**
   d. E - Waist = **6″**
   e. F - Total = **12″**

5. Press **OK** to return to the Drawing Editor and see the stair changes (see Figure 8–14).

Figure 8–14

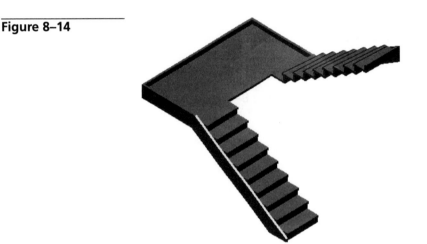

6. Select the stair, **RMB** and open the **Stair Styles** dialog box again.
7. Select the **Components** tab. This is where modifications to the tread, riser, and landing thicknesses are controlled. This is also where tread nosing length and straight or sloping risers are controlled. (Sloping risers are typically used on steel and concrete stairs.)
8. Select the **Landing Extensions** tab. This is where modifications are made relating to the landings.
9. Select the **Materials** tab. This is where the materials for the stair are set.
10. Select the **Display Properties** tab. This is where modifications are made relating to the display of stair components in different views.

Hands-On

Placing a Multilanding Stair

1. Erase the stair in the previous exercise.
2. Change to the **Top View**.
3. Select the **Stair icon** from your **Stairs** tool palette.
4. Drag your cursor over the **Properties** palette to open it.

5. Set the following:

   a. Shape = **Multi-landing**
   b. Turn type = **1/2 landing**
   c. Vertical Orientation = **Up**
   d. Width = **3'-0"**
   e. Height = **10"**
   f. Top offset = **0"**
   g. Top depth = **10"**
   h. Bottom offset = **0"**
   i. Bottom depth = **10"**
   j. Headroom height = **7'-0"**
   k. Side clearance = **0**

6. Click in the viewport and drag the stair vertically (90°) until 7/18 appears to the left of the stair, and click again; this starts the landing.

7. Continue to move the cursor in the direction of 90°, enter **5'** in the **Command line**, and press **Enter**; this establishes the end of the landing.

8. Drag the cursor to the right (0°) until 18/18 appears above the stair, and click the mouse to complete the stair.

9. Change to **SW Isometric View** and press the **Flat Shaded** icon in the **Shading** toolbar (see Figure 8–15). Save this file.

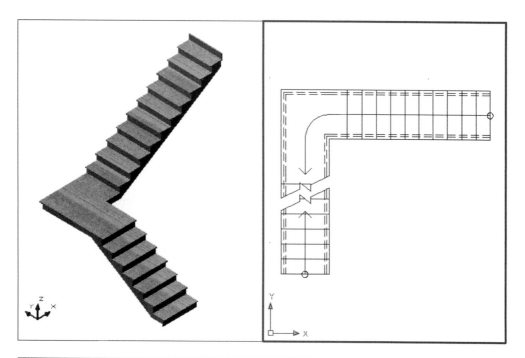

Figure 8–15

Hands-On

Interference Conditions

1. Using the stair from the previous exercise, change to the **Top View.**
2. Place a 20'-high wall as shown in Figure 8–16.

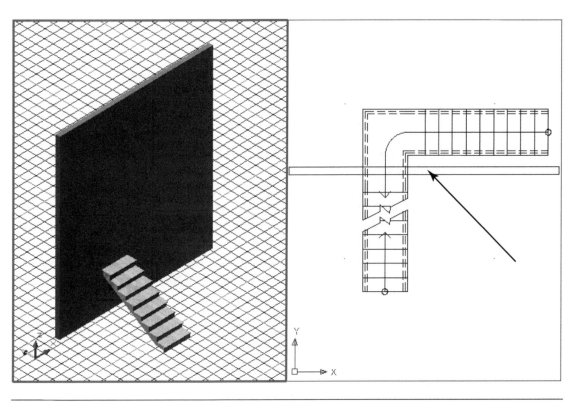

Figure 8–16

3. Select the wall, **RMB,** and select **Interference Condition > Add** from the contextual menu that appears.
4. Select the lower stair flight, and press **Enter.**
5. Enter **S** (Subtractive) in the **Command line** and press **Enter** to complete the command.

The wall is cut by the stair (see Figure 8–17), and the interference distance above the stair is set in the stair properties under **Interference Headroom height** (see Figure 8–18).

Note: Stair interference conditions are also available for slabs.

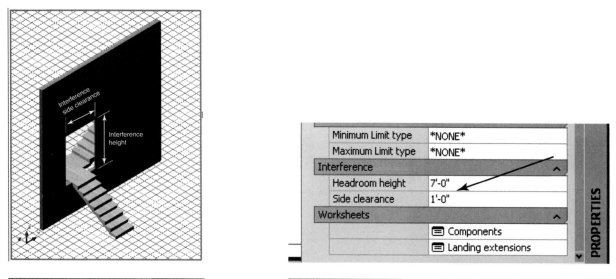

Figure 8–17

Figure 8–18

Hands-On

Anchoring a Second Stair to an Existing Landing

1. Use the stair created in "Placing a Multilanding Stair" Hands-on exercise.
2. Change to the **Work Layout.**
3. Change to the **Top View.**
4. Create a new straight Standard stair with **Vertical Orientation** set to **Up** (see Figure 8–19).
5. Select the original stair, **RMB,** and select **Stair landing Anchor > Anchor to Landing** from the contextual menu that appears.

Figure 8–19

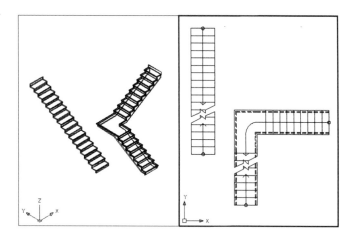

6. Select the second stair.
7. Select the first stair's landing to attach the second stair to the landing.

! **Note:** once anchored, the new stair might not be in the right location. If you drag the new stair around the landing, it will stop at different locations, similar to a door or window that is anchored to a wall.

8. Once it is attached, you can change to the **Top View** and move the second stair into a desired location (see Figure 8-20).

Figure 8–20

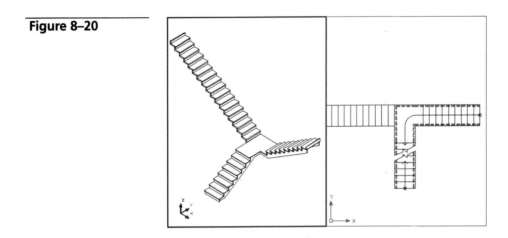

Hands-On

Projecting a Stair Edge to a Polyline

1. Start a new drawing using the Aec Model (Imperial Stb) template.
2. Change to the **Model Layout.**
3. Change to **Top View.**
4. Select the **Polyline** icon from the **Draw** toolbar and draw the shape shown in Figure 8–21.

Figure 8–21

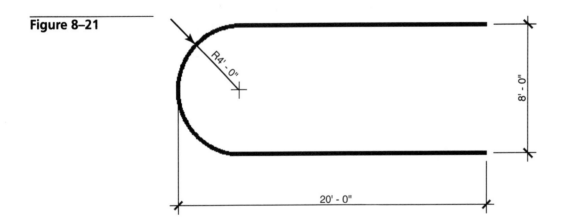

5. Select the **Stair** icon from the **Stairs** tool palette and add a U-shaped stair 8' high inside the polyline as shown in Figure 8–22.
6. Select the stair, **RMB,** and select **Customize Edge > Project** from the contextual menu that appears.
7. In the **Top View** select the front of the stair landing, select the curved part of the polyline, and then press **Enter** to project the landing (see Figure 8–23).

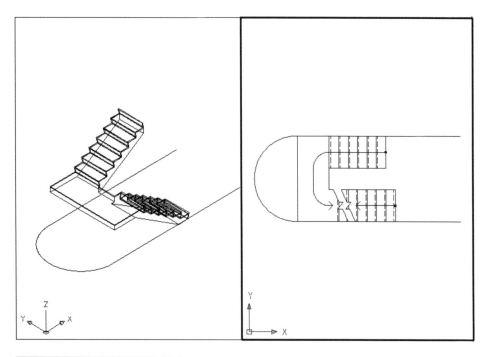

Figure 8–22

Figure 8–23

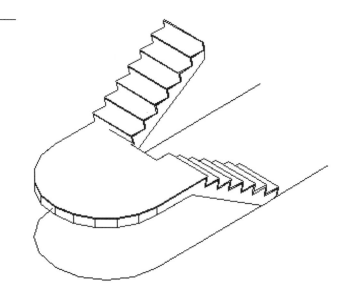

Hands-On

Projecting a Stair Edge to a Wall or AEC Object

1. Using the previous exercise, select the polyline to activate its grips.
2. Select an end grip, and modify the polyline as shown in Figure 8–24.
3. Select the **Wall** icon from the **Design** tool palette, **RMB,** and select **Apply Tool properties to > Linework.**
4. Select the polyline and press **Enter.**
5. Enter **Y** (Yes) in the **Command line,** and press **Enter** to create the wall.

Figure 8–24

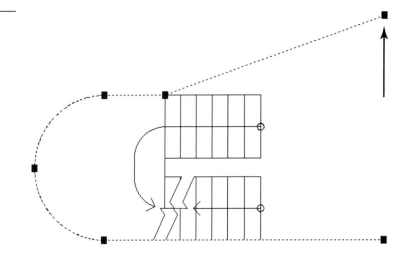

6. While the wall is still selected, move your cursor over the **Properties** palette to open it.

7. Set the following:

    a. Style = **CMU-8 Rigid-1.5 Air-2 Brick-4**
    b. Base height = **8"-0'**
    c. Justify = **Left**

! *Note:* If you don't have the **CMU-8 Rigid-1.5 Air-2 Brick-4** style in your **Walls** tool palette, you can find it in the **Architectural Desktop Design Tool Catalog-Imperial > Walls > CMU > Page 4.**

You now have a stair within a masonry enclosure (see Figure 8–25).

8. Select the stair, **RMB,** and select **Customize Edge > Project** from the contextual menu.

9. Select the right-hand edge of the stair run, select the wall opposite it, and then press **Enter** to complete the command.

The stair run projects itself to the wall (see Figure 8–26).

Figure 8–25

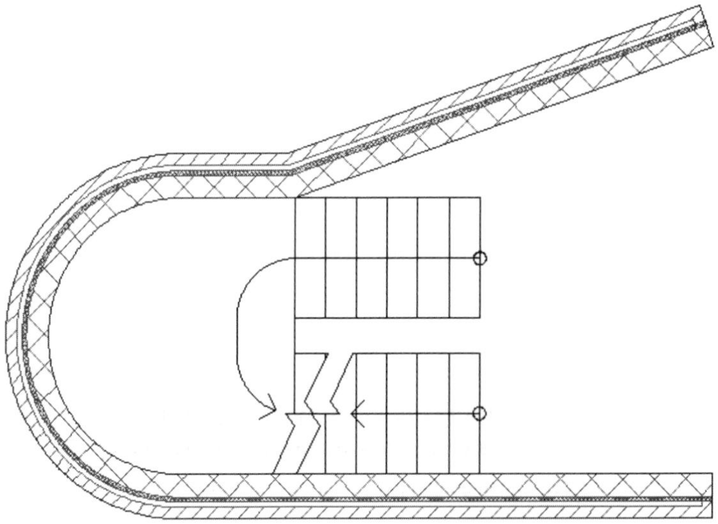

Figure 8–26

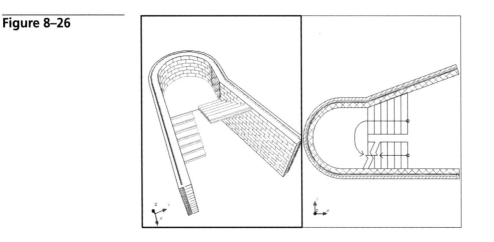

Hands-On

Generating a Polyline from a Stair Object

The **Generate Polyline** command is very useful when you have created a stair, and need a polyline to create walls, or to create an opening in a slab.

1. Use the previous exercise.
2. Erase the walls leaving just the stair.
3. Select the **Slab** icon from the **Design tool** palette, and place a Standard 6″, Direct-mode, top-justified slab underneath the stair as shown in Figure 8–27.

Figure 8–27

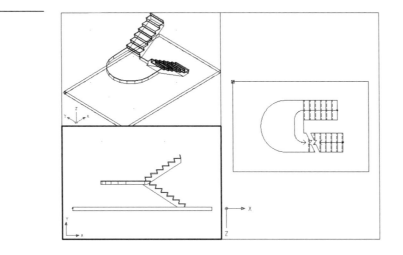

4. Select the stair, **RMB,** and select **Customize Edge > Generate Polyline** from the contextual menu that appears.
5. Select the outer edge of the stair, repeat Step 4, and touch the inside of the lower stair run. Press **Enter** to complete the command, and then place a line at the inner edge of the stair run (see Figure 8–28).
6. Select the **Layers** icon from the **Object Properties** toolbar and **Freeze** the **Stair** layer (A-Flor-Strs) to hide the stair.
7. Using **Extend** and **Trim,** clean up the polylines created by the **Generate Polyline** option of **Customize Edges** in Steps 4 and 5.

Figure 8–28

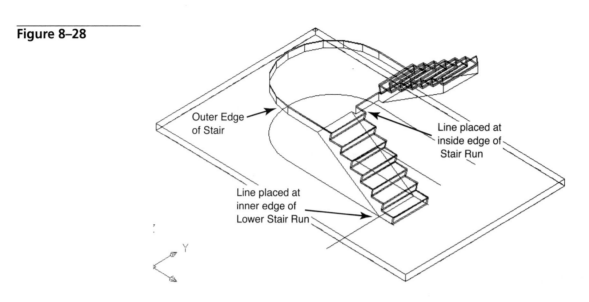

8. Type **Pedit** in the **Command line** and create two polylines as shown in Figure 8–29.

9. Select the slab object, **RMB,** and select **Hole > Add** from the contextual menu that appears.

10. Select the closed polyline, and press **Enter.**

11. Enter **Y** (Yes) in the **Command line** and press **Enter** to create the hole in the slab.

You have now made a hole in the slab exactly matching the stair through the use of the **Generate poly** option of the **Customizing Edge** command.

Figure 8–29

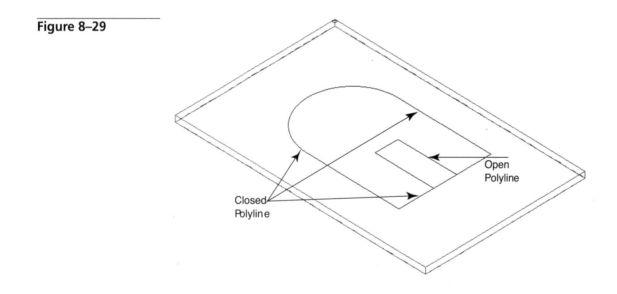

Finishing the Stairway

12. Unfreeze the stair layer to unhide the stair.

13. Select the **Wall** icon from the **Design** tool palette, **RMB,** and select **Apply Tool Properties to > Linework** from the contextual menu that appears.

14. Select the open polyline, enter **Y** (Yes) in the **Command line**, and press **Enter** to create a wall.

15. While the wall is still selected, move your cursor over the **Properties** palette to open it.

16. Set the following:

    a. Style = **Standard**
    b. Width = **6"**
    c. Base height = **8'-0"**
    d. Justify = **Left**

You have now created a stair, a slab, and walls (see Figure 8–30).

17. Select the **Railing** icon from the **Design** tool palette, and move your cursor over the **Properties** palette to open it.

18. Select the following:

    a. Style = **Standard**
    b. Attached to = **Stair**
    c. Side offset = **2"**
    d. Automatic placement = **Yes**

19. Select the stair to create the railing; then press **Enter** to complete the command.

Figure 8–30

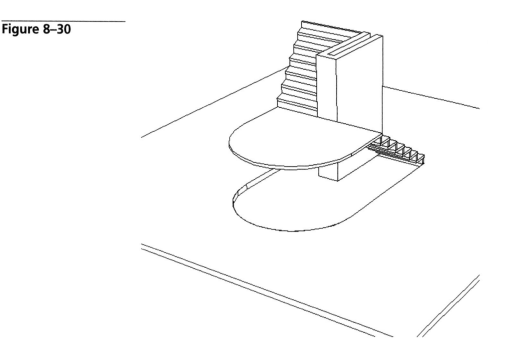

Hands-On

Creating a Stair Tower

You create a stair tower from one stair, which is replicated on selected levels in the building. You can create a stair tower with all stair shapes except spiral. The floor-to-floor height and starting elevation of each stair are adjusted to match those for each selected level. The X, Y coordinates for each stair start point are fixed.

Note: To create a stair tower, the stair must be in a construct with multiple levels.

1. Select **File > Project Browser** from the **Main** menu to bring up the **Project Browser** dialog box.
2. Select the **New Project** icon at the bottom left of the dialog box, and create a new project. Name the new project **STAIR TOWER TEST,** and press the **OK** button.
3. Press the **Close** button in the **Project Browser** dialog box to bring up the **Project Navigator** dialog box.
4. Select the **Edit Levels** icon in the **Levels** icon to bring up the **Levels** dialog box.
5. Press the **Add Level** icon five times to create five levels. Set the **Floor Elevations** and **Floor to Floor Heights** as shown in Figure 8–31, and press the **OK** button to return to the Drawing Editor.

Figure 8–31

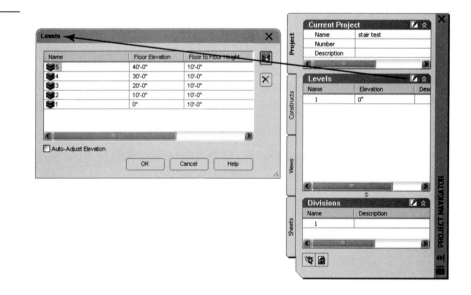

6. In the **Project Navigator,** select the **Constructs** tab, **RMB** on the **Constructs** icon, and select **New > Construct** from the contextual menu that appears to bring up the **Add Construct** dialog box.
7. Enter **STAIR TOWER** in the **Name** field.
8. Check all check boxes in the **Division** column and press the **OK** button (see Figure 8–32).

Figure 8–32

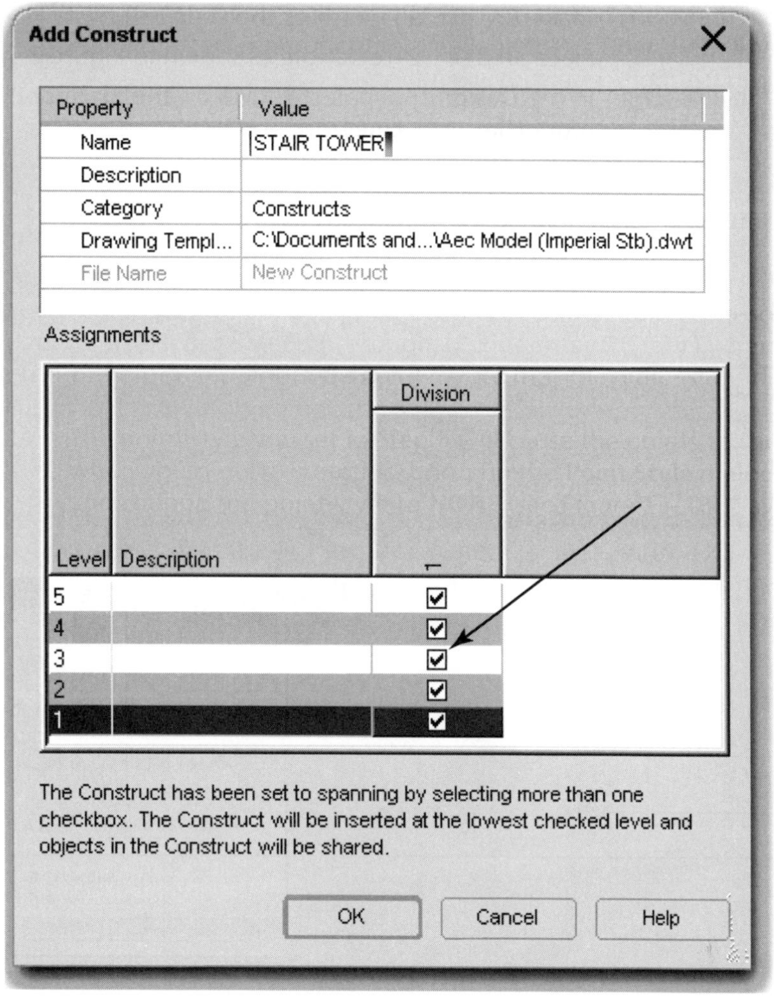

Add Construct   ✕

Property	Value
Name	|STAIR TOWER▌
Description	
Category	Constructs
Drawing Templ...	C:\Documents and...\Aec Model (Imperial Stb).dwt
File Name	New Construct

Assignments

		Division	
Level	**Description**	**⌐**	
5		☑	
4		☑	
3		☑	
2		☑	
1		☑	

The Construct has been set to spanning by selecting more than one checkbox. The Construct will be inserted at the lowest checked level and objects in the Construct will be shared.

OK   Cancel   Help

9. In the **Project Navigator,** select the **Constructs** tab and double-click on the **STAIR TOWER** construct you just created to open it in the Drawing Editor.

10. Place a Standard U-shaped stair with the following property settings:

    a. Shape = **U-shaped**

    b. Turn type = **1/2 landing**

    c. Horizontal Orientation = **Clockwise**

    d. Vertical Orientation = **Up**

    e. Width = **3'-0"**

    f. Height = **10"**

    g. Justify = **Outside**

    h. Top offset = **0"**

    i. Top depth = **10"**

    j. Bottom offset = **0"**

    k. Bottom depth = **10"**

    l. Headroom height = **7'-0"**

    m. Side clearance = **0"**

11. Make the overall width of the stair **7'-0"**.

12. Place an 8' × 12' rectangle as shown in Figure 8-33.

13. In the **Design** tool palette, **RMB** on the **Slab** tool, and select **Apply tool properties to > Linework and Walls**.

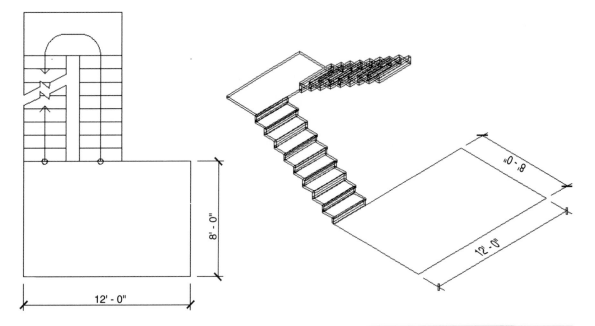

Figure 8–33

14. Select the rectangle you just created and press **Enter**.

15. Enter **Y** (Yes) in the **Command line** and press **Enter**.

16. Enter **P** (Protected) in the **Command line** and press **Enter**.

17. Enter **10'** in the **Command line** and press **Enter**.

18. Enter **T** (Top) in the **Command line** and press **Enter**.

You have you how placed a slab at the top of the stair (see Figure 8–34).

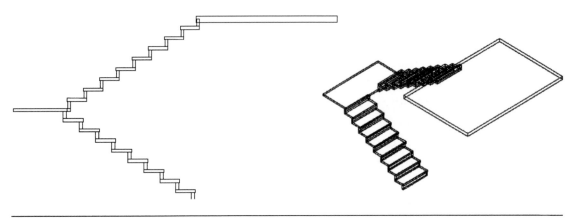

Figure 8–34

19. Change to the **SW Isometric View.**
20. In the **Design** tool palette, select the **Stair Tower Generate** tool, select the stair and then the slab you just created, and press **Enter** to bring up the **Select Levels** dialog box (see Figure 8–35).
21. Press the **OK** button in the **Select Levels** dialog box to generate the stair tower (see Figure 8–36).

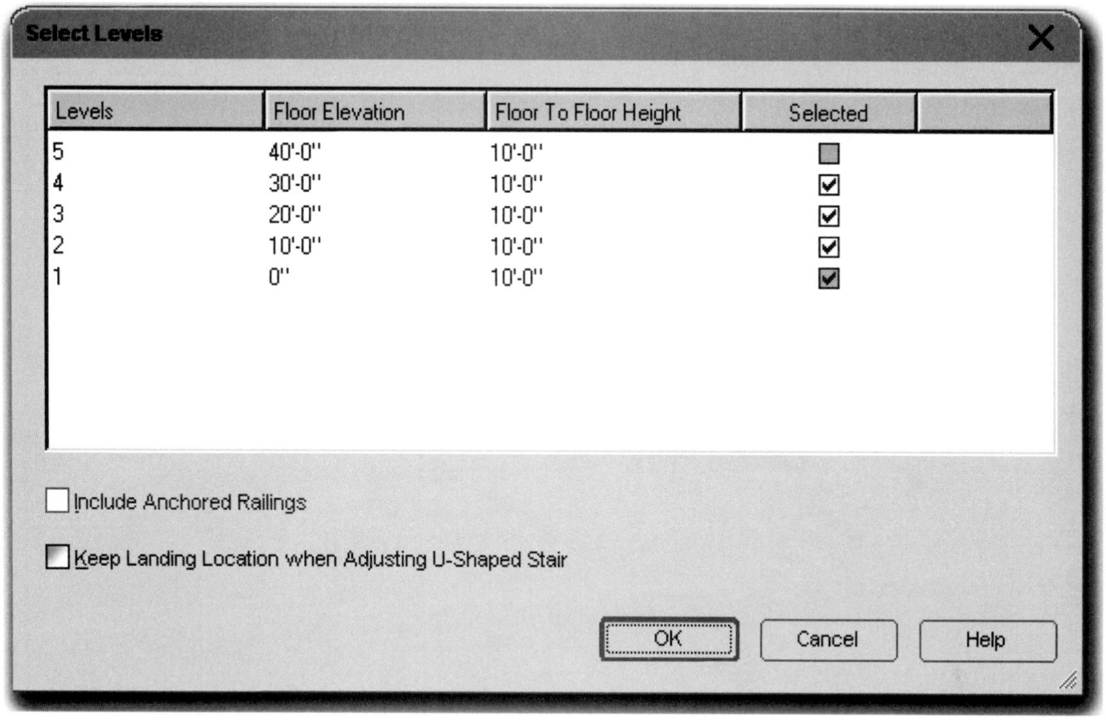

Select Levels   ✕

Levels	Floor Elevation	Floor To Floor Height	Selected	
5	40'-0"	10'-0"	☐	
4	30'-0"	10'-0"	☑	
3	20'-0"	10'-0"	☑	
2	10'-0"	10'-0"	☑	
1	0"	10'-0"	☑	

☐ Include Anchored Railings

☐ Keep Landing Location when Adjusting U-Shaped Stair

[OK]   [Cancel]   [Help]

Figure 8–35

Figure 8–36

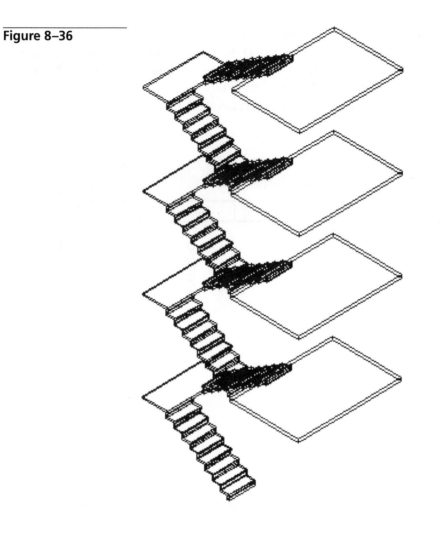

Railings

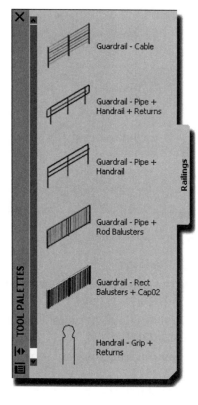

When you finish this section, you should understand the following:

✔ How to make a **Railing** tool palette.
✔ How to place a **Railing.**
✔ How to edit a **Railing Style.**
✔ How to modify balusters.
✔ How to add a railing to a stair and stair flight.
✔ How to add a railing to a landing.
✔ How to add a railing and landing support—**Anchor to Object.**
✔ How to create a railing using a polyline.
✔ How to edit a **Railing Profile** in place.

Number	Name	Purpose
1	Style	Select from available railing styles.
2	Rail locations	Set locations of rails fixed by Style.
3	Post locations	Set locations of posts fixed by Style.
4	Attached to	Set None, Stair, or Stair Flight.
5	Rotation	Set rotation of railing.
6	Elevation	Set elevation of railing from level.

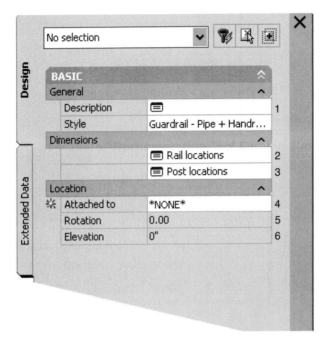

Hands-On

Making a New Railing Tool Palette

1. Create a new tool palette, and name it **Railings**.
2. Select the **Content Browser** icon from the **Main** toolbar to launch the Content Browser.
3. In the **Architectural Desktop Design Tool Catalog - Imperial,** locate the **Stairs** folder in the **Stairs and Railings** folder.
4. From the **Railings** folder, drag all the railings into the new tool palette you created.
5. Click and hold on the tab of your new tool palette and drag a copy to **My Tool Catalog** in the Content Browser.

Hands-On

Placing a Railing

1. Start a new drawing using the Aec Model (Imperial Stb) template.
2. Change to the **Model Layout.**
3. Change to **Top View.**
4. Select any **Railing** icon in the **Railings** tool palette you created and drag your cursor over the **Properties** palette to open it.
5. In the **Properties** palette select **Standard** from the **Style** drop-down list and ***NONE*** from the **Attached to** drop-down list.

6. Click in the Drawing Editor, drag your cursor to the right (0°), enter **10′** in the **Command line**, and press **Enter** three times to complete the command.

You have now placed a 10′-0″-long Standard railing.

> **Note:** When you select ***NONE***, you can use your railing as a fence, porch rail, and so on.

Hands-On

Editing a Railing Style

1. Select the railing you placed in the previous exercise, **RMB,** and select **Edit Railing Style** from the contextual menu that appears to bring up the **Railing Styles** dialog box.
2. Press the **Floating Viewer** icon to bring up the **Viewer.**
3. Resize the **Viewer** so that both **Viewer** and **Railing Styles** dialog box are side by side, and open at the same time. In the **Viewer**, set the drop-down list to **SW Isometric View**, and press the **Flat Shading** icon (see Figure 9–1).

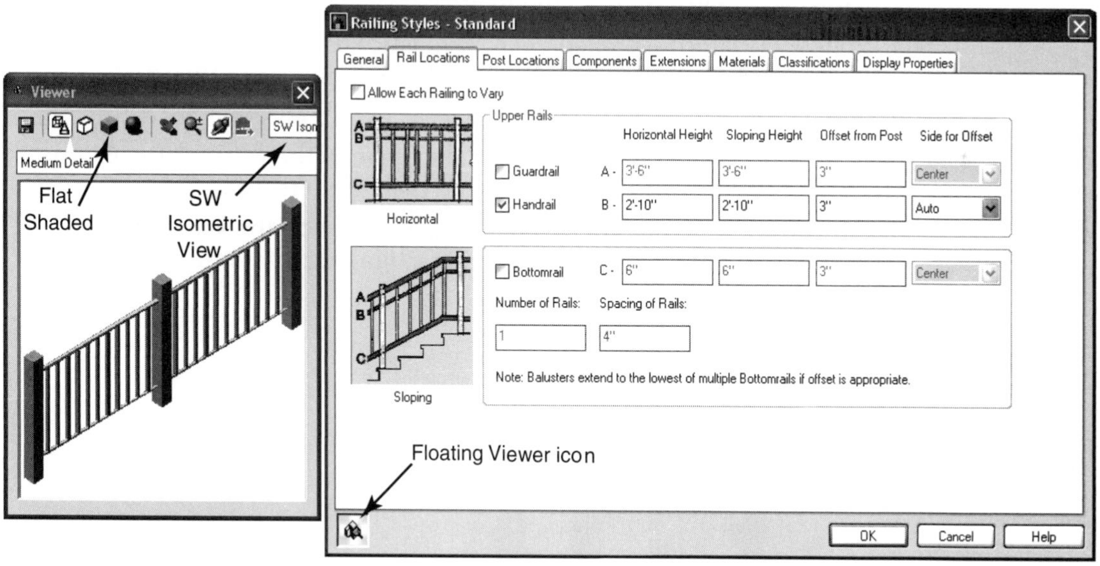

Figure 9–1

4. In the **Railing Styles** dialog box, select the **Rail Locations** tab.
5. Check and uncheck **Guardrail, Handrail,** and **Bottomrail** check boxes and view the changes in the **Viewer.**
6. Change the **Side for Offset** by clicking on the **Side for Offset** drop-down lists and view the changes in the **Viewer.**

7.   Enter **8** in the **Number of Rails** value entry field, and **4″** in the **Spacing of Rails** value entry field. Press **Enter**, and view the changes in the **Viewer** (see Figure 9–2).

Figure 9–2

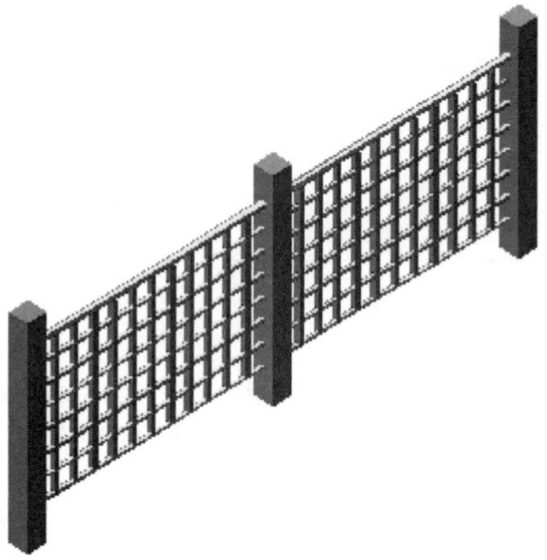

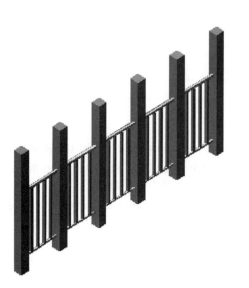

8.   Reset to all the original settings.
9.   Change to the **Post Locations** tab.
10. Check and uncheck **Guardrail, Handrail,** and **Bottomrail** check boxes and view the changes in the **Viewer.**
11. Check and uncheck **Fixed Posts, Dynamic Posts,** and **Balusters** check boxes and value entry fields. View the changes in the **Viewer.**
12. Change to the **Post Locations** tab.
13. Check the **Fixed Posts** check box, and change the value in the **Extension of ALL Posts from Top Railing** value entry field to **18″.**
14. Check the **Dynamic Posts** check box, and change the value in the **Maximum Center to Center Spacing** value entry field to **2′-0″**. View the changes in the **Viewer** (see Figure 9–3).
15. Reset to all the original settings.
16. Change to the **Components** tab.

Figure 9–3

17. Select the **D - Fixed Post** field.

18. Select ***circular*** from the drop-down list under **Profile Name,** and press **Enter.** Set its width to **1'-0",** and again press **Enter.**

19. View the changes in the **Viewer** (see Figure 9–4).

20. Reset to all the original settings.

21. Change to the **Extensions** tab.

The settings in this tab are used to set the extensions to the railings when the rails are connected to stairs. These extension dimensions are usually governed by the building codes (see Figure 9–5).

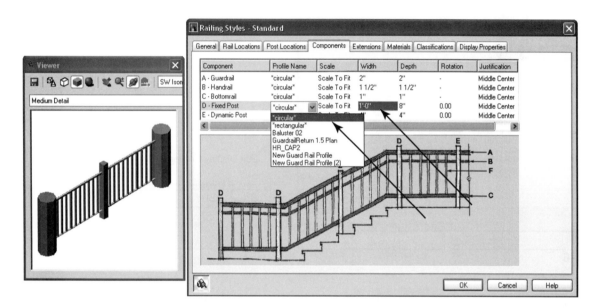

Figure 9–4

Figure 9–5

22. Change to the **Materials** tab.

23. Select the **Fixed Post** field and press the **Edit Material** icon to bring up the **Material Definition Properties** dialog box. Press the **Edit Display Properties** icon to bring up the **Display Properties** dialog box (see Figure 9–6).

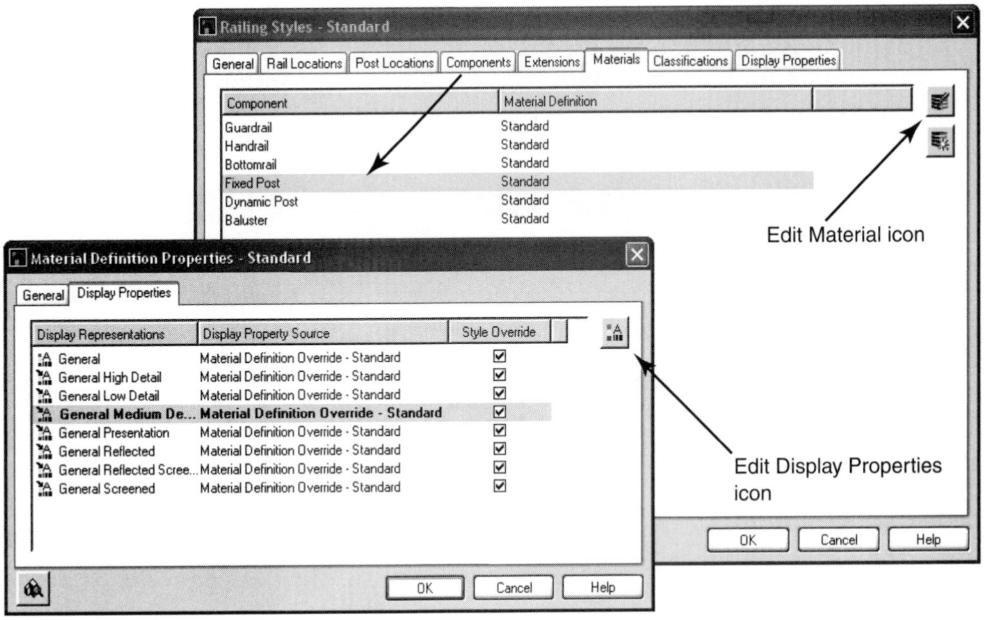

Figure 9–6

24. Select the **Other** tab. Select **Woods & Plastics > Architectural Woodwork > Wood Stairs and Railings > Ash** from the **Surface Rendering - Rendering Material** drop-down list (see Figure 9–7).

Figure 9–7

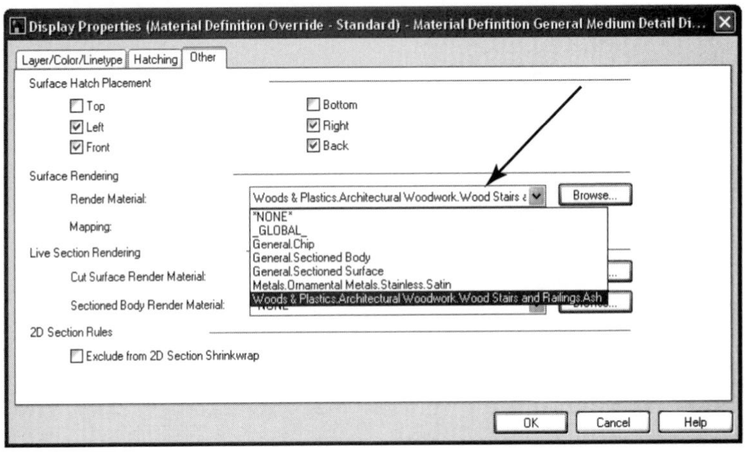

25. Press the **OK** buttons in the **Display Properties** and **Material Definition Properties** dialog boxes to return to the **Railing Styles** dialog box. View the material changes in the **Viewer** (see Figure 9–8).

Figure 9–8

Hands-On

Modifying Balusters

1. Return to the Drawing Editor.
2. **RMB** on the **Guardrail - Wood Balusters 02** icon in the **Railings** tool palette you created, and select **Apply Tool Properties to** > **Railing** from the contextual menu that appears. (If this railing style is not available in the tool palette, get it from the **Design Tool Catalog - Imperial.**
3. Select the railing that you placed in "Placing a Railing" in this section, and press **Enter.**

The railing changes to the new railing style.

4. Select the railing again, **RMB,** and select **Edit Railing Style** from the contextual menu that appears to bring up the **Railing Styles** dialog box.
5. Press the **Floating Viewer** icon to bring up the **Viewer.**
6. Again resize the **Viewer** so that the **Viewer** and **Railing Styles** dialog box are side by side, and open at the same time. In the **Viewer,** set the drop-down list to **SW Isometric View,** and press the **Flat Shading** icon.
7. View the railing (see Figure 9–9).

Figure 9–9

8. In the **Railing Styles** dialog box select the **Display Properties** tab and press the **Edit Display Properties** icon to bring up **Display Properties** dialog box. Select the **Other** tab (see Figure 9–10).

9. Press the **Remove** button to remove the Baluster 02 block.
10. Press **OK** and view the railing in the **Viewer** again. This time the balusters are the default balusters (see Figure 9–11).

Figure 9–11

If you press the **Edit** button in the **Display Properties** dialog box, you can add your own balusters made from 3D solid model or surface model blocks.

Hands-On

Adding a Railing to a Stair and Stair Flight

1. Start a new drawing using the Model (Imperial Stb) template.
2. Change to the **Work Layout.**
3. Change to **Top View.**
4. Place a Standard-style U-shaped stair with 3′-0″-wide stair flights, a total of 9′-0″ overall in width, and 10′ height.
5. Select the **Guardrail** icon in the **Railings** tool palette you created and move your cursor over the **Properties** palette to open it.
6. Select **Stair** from the **Attached to** drop-down list.
7. Select the outside side of the stair and inside side of the stair to place the rail (see Figure 9–12).

Figure 9–12

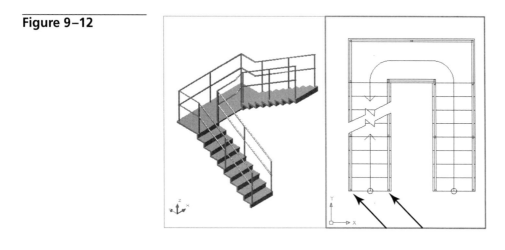

Note: You can add a railing to a stair in the **3D View**, but it is easier in the **Top View**.

8. Erase the railing, and repeat this process using the **Stair flight** option from the Attached to drop-down area of the **Properties** palette (see Figure 9–13).

Figure 9–13

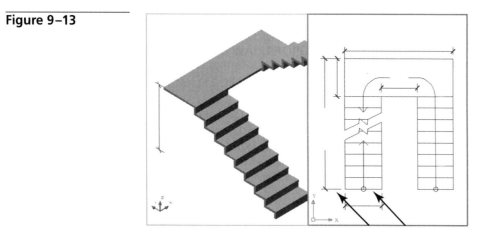

Hands-On

Adding a Railing to a Landing

1. Erase the previous railing.

2. Activate the **SW Isometric View.**

3. Type **UCS** in the command line and press **Enter** twice to make sure the **SW Isometric View** is in the World UCS.

4. Measure the railing landing. Type **ID** in the command line, press **Enter,** and snap to any top corner of the landing. Read the Z dimension (5'-0" for my landing). See Figure 9–14.

Figure 9–14

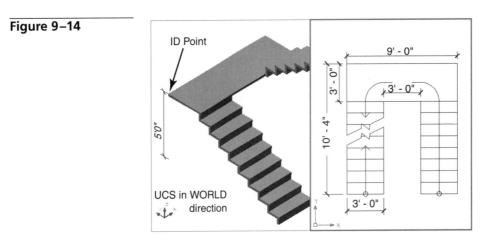

5. Activate the **Top View.**

6. Turn the **End Point Osnap** on.

7. Select the **Guardrail** icon in the **Railings** tool palette you created and move your cursor over the **Properties** palette to open it.

8. Select ***NONE*** from the **Attached to** drop-down list.

9. Start at the corner, and place a rail as shown in Figure 9–15.

10. Double-click on the railing to bring up the **Properties** palette for the railing.

Figure 9–15

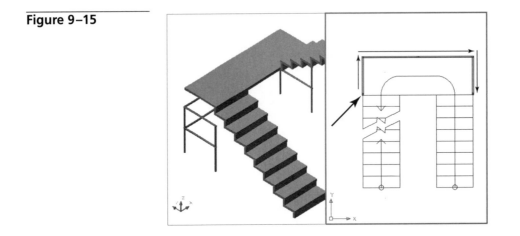

11. Enter 5′ in the **Elevation** data entry field—the railing will move to the top of the landing (see Figure 9–16). Save the file.

Figure 9–16

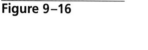

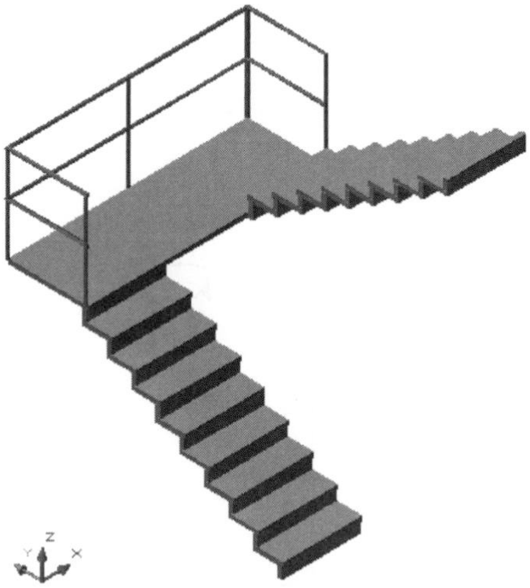

You can return to the Top View and use the Stretch command to adjust the railing lengths.

Hands-On

Adding a Railing and Landing Support—Anchor to Object

1. Undo the previous exercise to Step 9.
2. Select the railing, **RMB,** and select **Railing Anchor** > **Anchor to Object** from the contextual menu that appears.
3. Select the landing and press **Enter.**
4. Enter **Y** (Yes) in the command line and press **Enter.**
5. Enter **F** (Follow surface) in the command line and press **Enter.** Save the file.

The railing moves to the top of the landing, but the posts extend to the ground (see Figure 9–17).

Figure 9–17

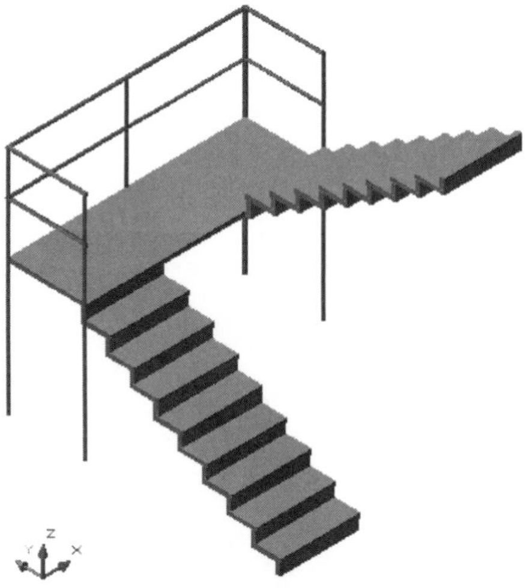

Hands-On

Creating a Railing Using a Polyline

1. Clear the Drawing Editor.
2. Using the **Polyline** tool, create the shape shown in **Figure 9–18**.

Figure 9–18

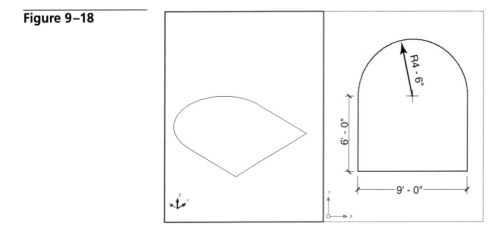

3. **RMB** on the **Guardrail - Cable** icon in your **Railings** palette and select **Apply Tool Properties to > Polyline** from the contextual menu that appears.
4. Select the polyline and press **Enter.**
5. Enter **Y** (Yes) in the **Command line** to erase the layout geometry and press **Enter** to create the railing (see Figure 9–19).

Figure 9–19

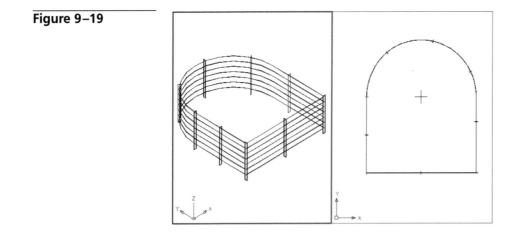

6. Select the railing, **RMB,** and select **Edit Railing Style** from the contextual menu that appears to bring up the **Railing Styles** dialog box.

7. Select the **Post Locations** tab.

8. Check the **Dynamic Posts** check box and enter **1'-0"** in the **Maximum Center to Center Spacing** data entry field.

Your railing changes to include more posts (see Figure 9–20).

Figure 9–20

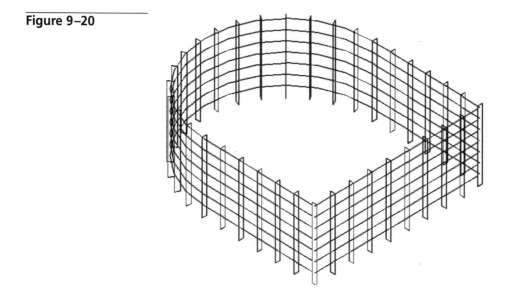

Hands-On

Editing a Railing Profile in Place

1. Clear the Drawing Editor.

2. Change to the **Model Layout.**

3. Change to **Top View.**

4. Select the **Guardrail - Wood balusters 01 Railing** icon in the Railings tool palette you created and drag your cursor over the Properties palette to open the palette.

5. Select **Standard** from the **Style** drop-down list and ***NONE*** from the Attached to drop-down list.

6. Click in the Drawing Editor, drag your cursor to the right (0?), enter **12'** in the **Command line,** and press **Enter** three times to complete the command.

7. Change to the **Right View.**

8. In the **Right View,** select the railing, **RMB,** and select **Edit Profile In-Place** from the contextual menu that appears.

9. Select the top rail of the railing. You will get an AutoCAD message that the profile shape must be converted. Press the **Yes** button.

10. The top rail end will turn light blue with magenta grips (see Figure 9–21).

You can drag on the grips to edit the profile, or do the following:

11. Draw a circle and a rectangle similar to that shown in Figure 9–22.

Figure 9–21

Figure 9–22

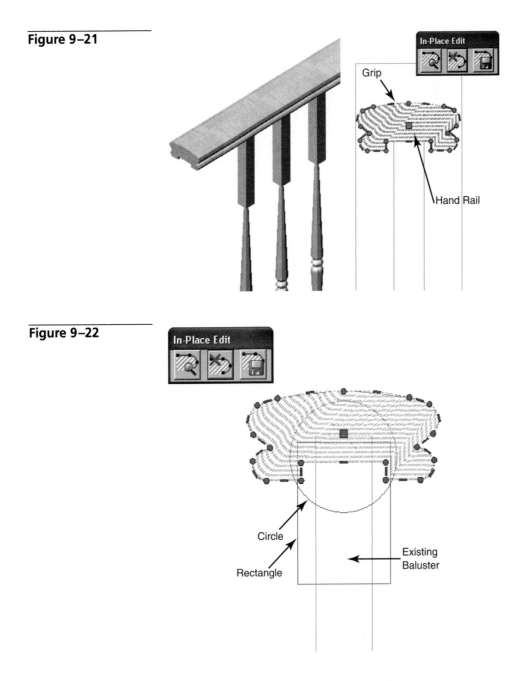

12. Select the blue-shaded top rail, **RMB,** and select **Add Ring** from the contextual menu that appears.
13. Select the circle you drew in Step 10, enter **Y** (Yes) in the **Command line,** and press **Enter.**

14. Enter **J** (Join) in the **Command line** and press **Enter.**
15. Repeat Steps 11 through 13 of this exercise for the rectangle.
16. Select the blue-shaded top rail again, **RMB,** and select **Save As New Profile** from the contextual menu that appears to bring up the **New Profile** dialog box.
17. In the **New Profile** dialog box, type the name **TEST RAIL PROFILE,** and press the **OK** button.

You have now edited the top rail in place (see Figure 9–23).

18. Select the top rail you just created, **RMB,** and again select **Edit Profile In-Place** from the contextual menu that appears.
19. Select the top rail, and again the top rail end will turn light blue with magenta grips.
20. Grab the lower right **Edge** grip, drag to the right and press the **Ctrl** button on your keyboard until the tool tip message reads **Convert line to arc,** and click the mouse button (see Figure 9–24).

Figure 9–23

Figure 9–24

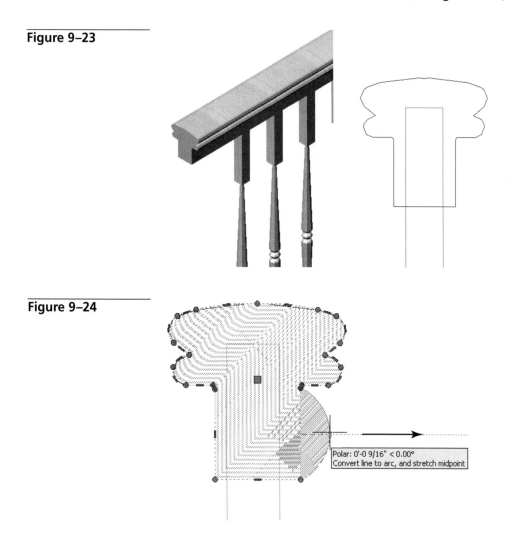

Polar: 0'-0 9/16" < 0.00°
Convert line to arc, and stretch midpoint

21. Repeat the process for the lower left **Edge** grip.

22. **RMB** in the blue field and select **Save As New Profile** from the contextual menu that appears to bring up the **New Profile** dialog box.

23. In the **New Profile** dialog box, type the name **TEST RAIL PROFILE 2**, and press the **OK** button to create the new profile (see Figure 9–25).

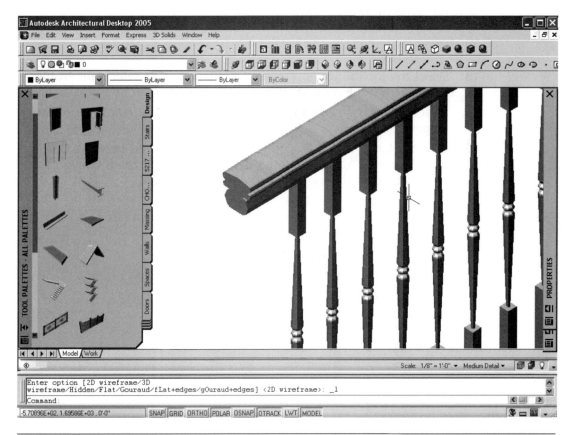

Figure 9–25

10

Roofs and Roof Slab Objects

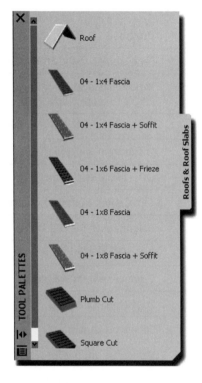

When you finish this section, you should understand the following:

- ✔ How to make a **Roof** and **Roof Slabs** tool palette.
- ✔ How to place a **Roof** object.
- ✔ How to modify a **Roof** object.
- ✔ How to edit a roof edge.
- ✔ How to **Convert to Roof** and changing Segments (smoothing round roofs).
- ✔ How to use the **Convert to Roof Slabs** command.
- ✔ How to use the **roofslabmodifyedges** command.
- ✔ How to use **Apply Tool Properties.**
- ✔ How to cut a hole in a roof slab.
- ✔ How to add edge profiles in place.
- ✔ How to create a **Roof Dormer.**

ROOFS

Number	Name	Purpose
1	Thickness	Thickness of the roof structure
2	Edge cut	**Square** (perpendicular to the roof) or **Plumb** (parallel to the walls)
3	Shape	**Single slope, Double slope, or Gable**
4	Overhang	Distance beyond roof edge
5	Lower Slope—Plate height	Height above elevation
6	Lower Slope—Rise	Vertical rise per foot dimension

7	Lower Slope—Run	Horizontal dimension
8	Slope	Angle in degrees of slope
9	Rotation	Rotation of roof
10	Elevation	Elevation

ROOF SLABS

Number	Name	Purpose
1	Style	Style created in the Style Manager
2	Mode	Projected (elevated) or Direct (at 0 elevation)
3	Thickness	Thickness of the roof structure
4	Vertical offset	Offset from wall top
5	Horizontal offset	Offset from wall edge
6	Justify	Top, Center, Bottom, Slopeline
7	Base height	Height above 0 elevation
8	Direction	Direction of slope
9	Overhang	Distance beyond wall edge
10	Baseline edge	Edge type at baseline
11	Perimeter edge	Edge type at perimeter
12	Slope—Rise	Vertical height per foot dimension
13	Slope—Run	Horizontal run per foot dimension
14	Slope	Slope angle in degrees
15	Rotation	Rotation of roof slab
16	Elevation	Elevation of roof slab from level

ROOFS

No selection				
BASIC				⌃
General				^
	Description	🖹		
Dimensions				^
	Thickness	10"		1
	Edge cut	Square		2
Next Edge				^
	Shape	Single slope		3
	Overhang	1'-0"		4
	Lower Slope			^
		Plate height	8'-0"	5
		Rise	1'-0"	6
		Run	12	7
		Slope	45.00	8
Location				^
	Rotation	0.00		9
	Elevation	0"		10

Design · Extended Data · PROPERTIES

ROOF SLABS

No selection			
BASIC			⌃
General			^
	Description	🖹	
	Style	Standard	1
✳	Mode	Projected	2
Dimensions			^
A	Thickness	1'-0"	3
B	Vertical offset	0"	4
C	Horizontal offset	0"	5
✳	Justify	Slopeline	6
✳	Base height	8'-0"	7
✳	Direction	Left	8
✳	Overhang	1'-4"	9
✳	Baseline edge	1x4 Fascia	10
✳	Perimeter edge	*NONE*	11
Slope			^
	Rise	7'-2 3/32"	12
	Run	1'-0"	13
	Slope	82.07	14

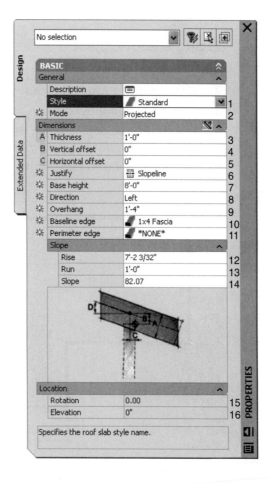

Location			^
	Rotation	0.00	15
	Elevation	0"	16

Specifies the roof slab style name.

Design · Extended Data · PROPERTIES

Hands-On

Making a New Roof and Roof Slabs Tool Palette

1. Create a new tool palette, and name it **Roof & Roof Slabs.**
2. Select the **Content Browser** icon from the **Main** toolbar to launch the Content Browser.
3. In the **Desktop Stock Tool Catalog** locate the **Roof in Architectural Object Tools.**
4. Drag all the roof objects into the new tool palette you created.
5. In the **Design Tool Catalog - Imperial,** locate the **Roof Slabs** folder in the **Roof and Roof Slabs** folder.
6. Drag all the roof slabs into the new tool palette you created.
7. Click and hold on the tab of your new tool palette and drag a copy to **My Tool Catalog** in the Content Browser.

Roofs are intelligent AEC Objects. There are several ways to place them and many controls to modify them. It is probably easiest to place a roof and then modify it rather than set the roof controls before placement.

Do the following lesson to experience how to add, convert, and modify roof objects.

Hands-On

Placing a Roof Object

1. Start a new drawing using the Aec Model (Imperial Stb) template.
2. Change to the **Model Layout.**
3. Change to **Top View.**
4. Using the wall object, place the floor plan shown in Figure 10–1. Make the walls **Standard** style **6"** wide and **9'-0"** high.
5. Set Object Snap to **End Point.**

Figure 10–1

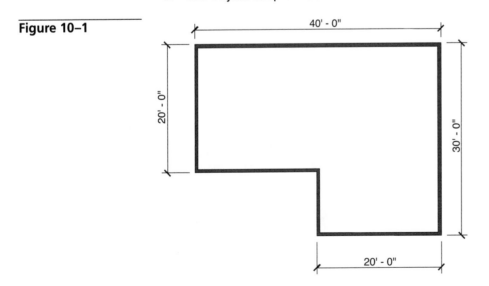

6. Select the **Roof** icon in the **Roof and Roof Slabs** tool palette you created and drag your cursor over the **Properties** palette to open it.

7. Set the following:

   a. Thickness = **10"**
   b. Edge cut = **Square**
   c. Shape = **Single slope**
   d. Overhang = **1'**
   e. Plate height = **9'-0"**
   f. Rise = **1'-0"**
   g. Run = **12**
   h. Slope = **45.00**

8. Starting at the top left outside corner shown in Figure 10–2, move clockwise until you get back to the last point shown in the figure. Then press **Enter** or the space bar on your keyboard. You have now placed a roof object.

Figure 10–2

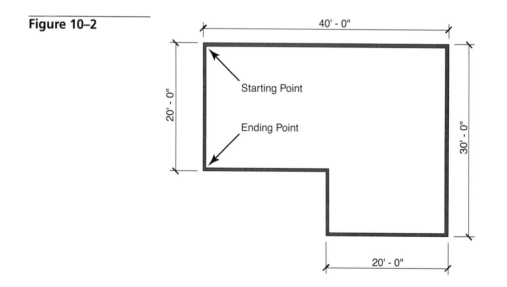

Hands-On

Modifying a Roof Object

1. Change to the **Work Layout,** and zoom extents in both viewports. Change the left viewport to **SW Isometric View.**
2. In the **SW Isometric View,** select the **Flat Shaded, Edges On** icon from the **Shade** menu to shade the **SW Isometric View.**
3. Change the other viewport to **Front View** (see Figure 10–3).
4. Double-click on the roof to bring up its **Properties** palette.

Figure 10–3

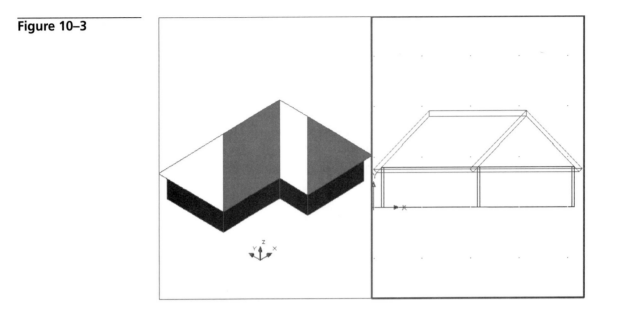

5. In the **Properties** palette, change the **Shape to Double,** and the **Upper slope's Upper height** to **12',** and **Slope** to **55.00.** Notice the change to the roof (see Figure 10–4).

Figure 10–4

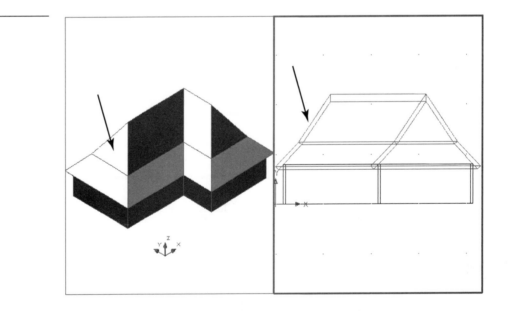

6. In the **Front View** viewport, zoom close to the edge of the roof.
7. Again, double-click on the roof to bring up its **Properties** palette.
8. Change the **Edge cut to Plumb,** and notice the change (see Figure 10–5).

Figure 10–5

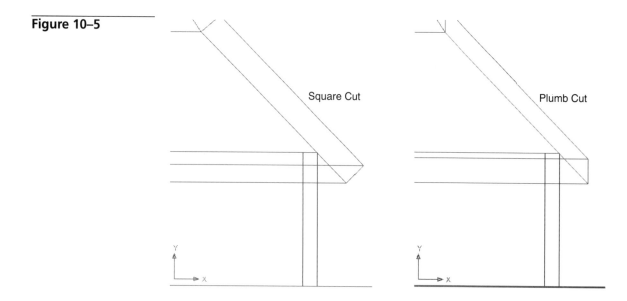

Hands-On

Editing a Roof Edge

1. Double-click and reset the roof object to single slope in the **Properties** palette.

2. Select the roof, **RMB,** and select **Edit Edges/Faces** from the menu that appears.

3. Select a roof edge and press **Enter** to bring up the **Roof Edges and Faces** dialog box (see Figure 10–6).

Figure 10–6

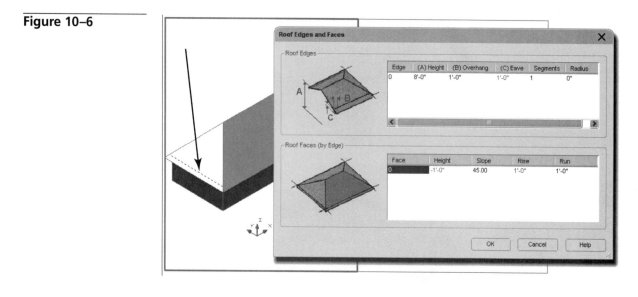

4. Set Slope to **90,** and press **OK** to return to the Drawing Editor.

The roof now has a gable end, but there is no infill between the top of the lower end wall and the underside of the roof (see Figure 10–7).

Figure 10–7

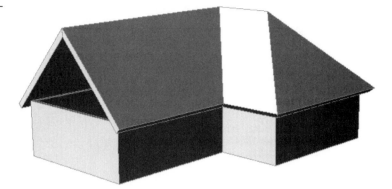

5. Select the end wall, **RMB,** and select **Modify Roof line** from the contextual menu that appears.
6. Enter **A** (Auto project) in the command line and press **Enter.**
7. Select the wall again and press **Enter.**
8. Select the **Roof** object and press **Enter** twice to end the command. The wall now meets and closes the gable end (see Figure 10–8).

This same process can be done with a curtain wall (see Figure 10–9). To get this image you must select the **Design** tool palette, and select the **Curtain Wall** icon. **RMB** the icon, and select **Apply tool property to > Walls.** Select the appropriate wall, accept **Baseline** for the **Curtain wall baseline alignment,** and enter **Y** (Yes) to erase layout geometry, and press the **Enter** key to complete the command.

Figure 10–8

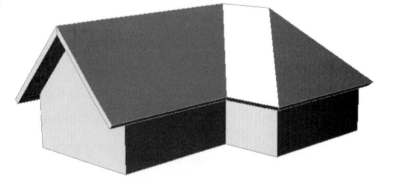

Figure 10–9

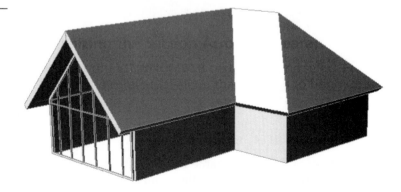

9.   Change to the **Work Layout.**

10.   In the **Top View** viewport, select the roof and pull on the vertex shown in Figure 10–10.

You have now created a simple roof and roof overhang. Save this file.

Figure 10–10

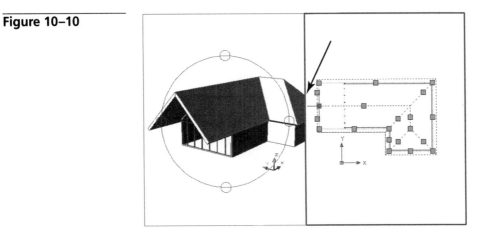

Hands-On

Changing Facets

Another way to create a roof is to use **Apply Tool Properties to.** In the following exercise **Apply Tool Properties to** was used because of the curved walls.

1.   Create a new drawing.

2.   Activate the **Top View** viewport.

3.   Create the floor plan with 6″ -wide walls 9′ high as shown in Figure 10–11.

4.   Select the **Roof** icon from the **Roof and Roof Slabs** tool palette you created previously, **RMB,** and select **Apply Tool Properties to** from the contextual menu that appears.

Figure 10–11

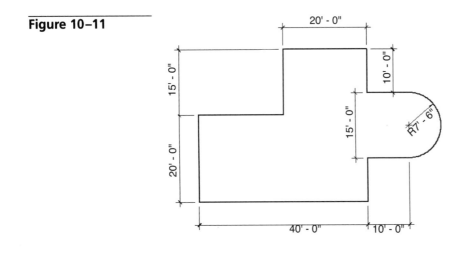

5.   Select all the walls.

6.   At the **Command line** question "Erase layout geometry?" type **N** (No) and press **Enter** to create a roof.

7.   While the new roof is still lit (grips showing), move your cursor over the **Properties** palette to open it.

8.   Change the **Edge Cut to Plumb,** and **Elevation** to **9'-0"** (see Figure 10–12).

Figure 10–12

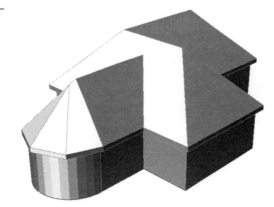

9.   Select the roof again, and move your cursor over the **Properties** palette to open it.

10.   In the Properties palette, press the **Edges/Faces** button to open the **Roof Edges and Faces** dialog box.

11.   In the **Roof Edges and Faces** dialog box, you will see 6 in **the segments column.** Change this to **24,** and the curved section of the roof will become smoother.

Figure 10–13 shows the effects of increasing the **Segments** to **24.**

Figure 10–13

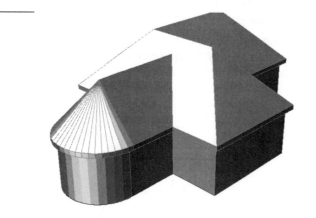

Hands-On

Converting to Roof Slabs

!   ***Note:*** Roofs can also be created by adding roof slab objects. This system is identical to that for creating slabs (see the next section, "Slabs and Slab Objects," for exercises on creating, modifying, and editing slabs).

Converting roofs to slabs allows you the flexibility to adjust one slab or cut holes inherent in slabs. For pitched roofs it is often best to start with a standard roof object, and then convert it to roof slabs.

1.   Use the previous exercise.
2.   Select the roof, **RMB,** and select **Convert to Roof Slabs** from the contextual menu that appears.
3.   Type **Y** (Yes) at the **Command line** question "Erase layout geometry" and press **Enter.** Accept the Standard roof, and again press **Enter** to complete the command.

The roof color should now change, because the roof will now be made of roof slab objects and is now on the A-Roof-Slab layer.

Hands-On

roofslabmodifyedges

Although not documented in the manual, **roofslabmodifyedges** allows you to adjust all the roof slab edges at one time.

1.   Use the previous exercise.
2.   Type **Slabmodifyedges** in the **Command line** and press **Enter.**
3.   Type **All** at the **Command line** request to select slabs to modify, and press **Enter.**
4.   Select the **Baseline** option in the **Command line** and press **Enter.**
5.   Enter **OV** (Overhang) in the **Command line** and press **Enter.**
6.   Enter **3'-0"** in the **Command line,** and press **Enter.**

You have now adjusted the overhang for all the roof slab objects (see Figure 10–14).

Figure 10–14

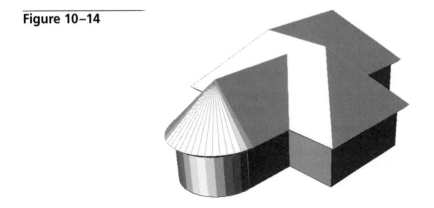

Hands-On

Applying Tool Properties to a Roof Slab

1. Select the roof slabs (this can be done by selecting the **Quick Select** icon at the top of the **Properties** palette to bring up the **Quick Select** dialog box and selecting **Roof Slab** from the **Object type** drop-down list).

2. **RMB** on any **Roof Slab** icon in the **Roof and Roof Slabs** toolbar that you created.

3. Select **Apply Tool properties to > Roof Slab** from the contextual menu that appears and press **Enter**. Press the **Gouraud** icon in the **Shading** toolbar. Save this file.

The roof slabs change to the new applied roof slabs style, and the roof slab material is displayed (see Figure 10–15).

Figure 10–15

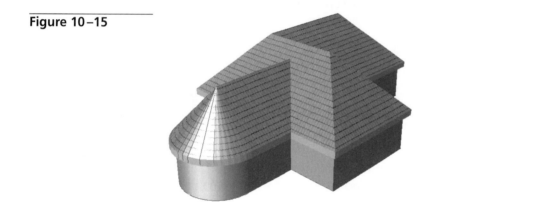

Hands-On

Cutting a Hole in a Roof Slab

1. Zoom close to a roof slab in which you wish to place a hole.
2. Select the **Object UCS** icon from the **UCS** toolbar.
3. Select the roof slab in which you wish to place a hole.

The UCS now matches the surface of the roof slab.

4. Select the **Rectangle** icon in the **Draw** toolbar and place a rectangle on, over, or under the roof slab (see Figure 10–16).
5. Select the roof slab in which you wish to place a hole, **RMB,** and select **Hole > Add** from the contextual menu that appears.
6. Select the rectangle created in Step 4 of this exercise, and press **Enter.**
7. Enter **Y** (Yes) in the **Command line** and press **Enter** to complete the command.

You have now created a hole in the roof slab (see Figure 10–17).

Figure 10–16

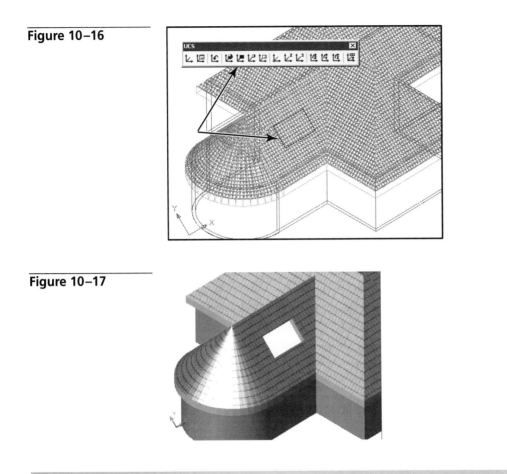

Figure 10–17

Hands-On

Adding Edge Profiles in Place

1. Select **Format > Style Manager** from the Main toolbar to bring up the **Style Manager** dialog box.

2. Expand the **Architectural Objects** tree, select **Slab Edge Styles, RMB,** and select **New** from the contextual menu that appears.

3. Rename the new style to **SLAB EDGE TEST,** and press **OK** to return to the Drawing Editor.

4. Select a roof slab, **RMB** and select **Add Edge Profiles** from the contextual menu that appears.

5. Select an edge of the roof slab, and a dialog box will appear (see Figure 10–18).

! **Note:** This dialog box may not appear, and you will immediately go to the **Edit Roof Slab Edges** dialog box shown in (Figure 10–19).

Figure 10–18

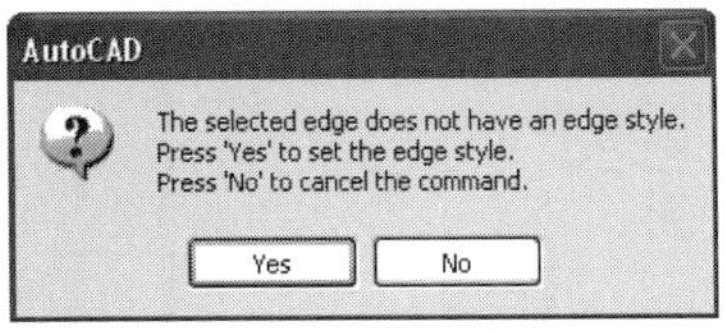

AutoCAD

The selected edge does not have an edge style.
Press 'Yes' to set the edge style.
Press 'No' to cancel the command.

[Yes]   [No]

6. Press the **Yes** button to bring up the **Edit Roof Slab Edges** dialog box.

7. Select **Standard** for the **Edge Style** and press **OK** (see Figure 10–19).

Figure 10–19

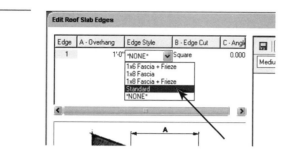

8. The **Add Fascia/Soffit Profiles** dialog appears.

9. Check the **Fascia Profile** check box, select **Start** from scratch from the drop-down list, enter the name **FASCIA PROFILE TEST** as the **New Profile Name,** and press **OK** to enter the **In-Place Edit** mode (see Figure 10–20).

10. Change to the **Right View,** and zoom close to the blue shading that signifies the **In-Place Edit** area.

11. Create a gutter from a closed polyline as shown in Figure 10–21.

Figure 10–20

Figure 10–21

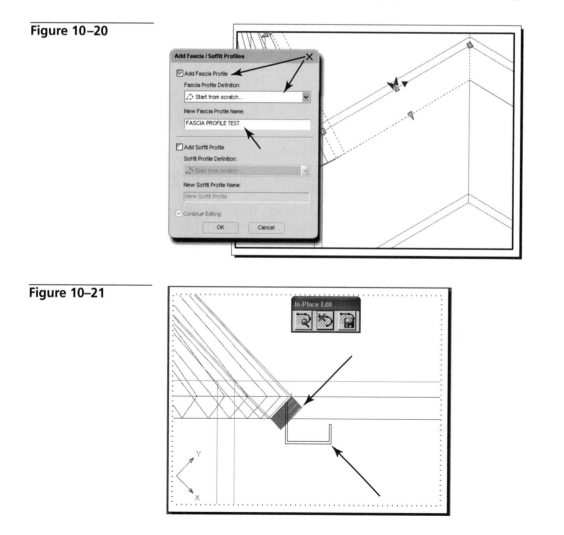

12. Select the blue area and grips will appear.

13. **RMB** on the blue area and select **Replace ring** from the contextual menu that appears.

14. Select the gutter drawn in Step 11 of this exercise, enter **Y** (Yes) in the command line, and press **Enter**.

The blue hatch will be replaced by the gutter in blue hatch.

15. Select the blue gutter, **RMB,** and select **Save Profile** from the contextual menu that appears.

The **FASCIA PROFILE TEST** is now the gutter.

Hands-On

Creating a Roof Dormer

Dormers are in vogue today, and ADT 2005 has a command that aids in the creation of these objects.

1. Start a new drawing using the Aec Model (Imperial Stb) template.

2. Change to the **Model Layout.**

3. Change to the **Top View.**

4. Select the **Wall** icon from the **Design** tool palette, and create a 43'-0" × 31'-wide structure 8'-0" high with 6"-wide Standard walls.

5. Add a 15' × 8' enclosure 14'-0" high with 6"-wide Standard walls.

6. Add a **Gable** roof to the 43' × 31' enclosure with a 30° slope (see Figure 10–22).

Figure 10–22

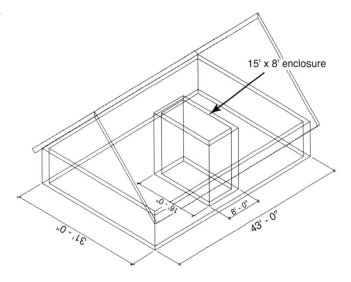

7. Select the **Roof Slab** icon from the **Design** menu, **RMB,** and select **Apply Tool Properties to > Linework, Walls, and Roof** from the contextual menu.

8. Select the left wall of the 15' × 8' enclosure and press **Enter.**

9. Enter **N** (No) in the **Command line** and press **Enter.**

10. Enter **B** (Bottom) in the **Command line** and press **Enter.**

11. Enter **R** (Right) in the **Command line** and press **Enter.**

12. Enter **L** (Left) in the **Command line** and press **Enter** to create the first roof slab of the dormer (see Figure 10–23).

! **Note:** Steps 11 and 12 may be reversed depending on which direction the walls were drawn.

Figure 10–23

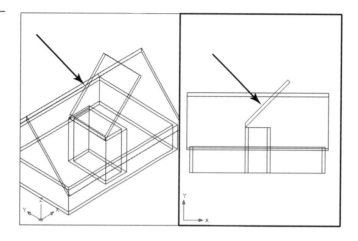

13. Again, select the **Roof Slab** icon from the **Design** menu, **RMB,** and select **Apply Tool Properties to > Linework, Walls, and Roof** from the contextual menu.

14. Select the right wall of the 15' × 8' enclosure and press **Enter.**

15. Enter **N** (No) in the **Command line** and press **Enter.**

16. Enter **B** (Bottom) in the **Command line** and press **Enter.**

17. Enter **L** (Left) in the **Command line** and press **Enter.**

18. Enter **R** (Right) in the **Command line** and press **Enter** to create the first roof slab of the dormer.

! **Note:** If your roof slab doesn't follow the above rules, reverse the wall direction and repeat (see Figure 10–24).

Figure 10–24

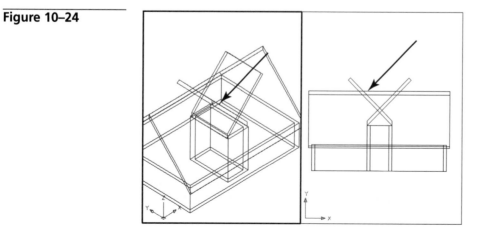

19. Select both new roof slabs, and move your cursor over the **Properties** palette to open it.

20. Change the **Slope** to **25** (25°).

21. Select one of the roof slabs, **RMB,** and select **Miter** from the contextual menu.

22. Accept the default <**Intersection**> in the **Command line** and press **Enter.**

23. Select the lower part of the slab at the intersection of the two slabs, and then select the lower part of the other slab.

The two roof slabs will now miter, forming the roof of the dormer. This could also have been done with the roof object, making it a gable roof.

24. Change to the **Top View** and drag each roof slab 2'-0" (see Figure 10–25).

Figure 10–25

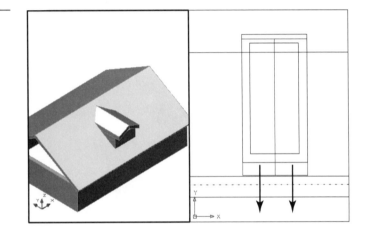

25. Select the main gable roof over the 43' × 31' enclosure, **RMB,** and select **Convert to Roof Slabs** from the contextual menu.

26. Enter **N** (No) in the **Command line,** and press **Enter** twice to change the roof object into roof slabs.

27. Press the **ESC** key to deselect the slabs.

28. Select the roof slab shown in Figure 10–26, **RMB,** and select **Roof Dormer** from the contextual menu.

29. Select the 15' × 8' enclosure and its roof slabs and then press **Enter.**

30. Enter **Y** (Yes) in the **Command line,** and press **Enter** to form the dormer.

31. Erase any unneeded walls (see Figure 10–27).

Figure 10–26

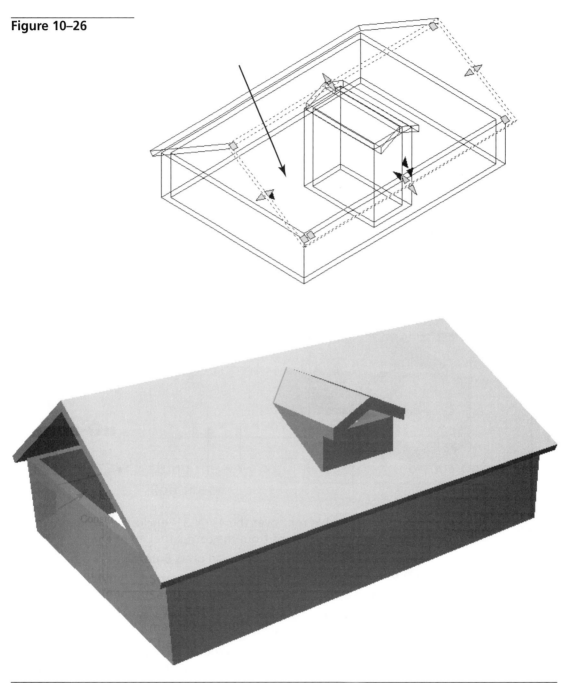

Figure 10–27

11

Slabs and Slab Objects

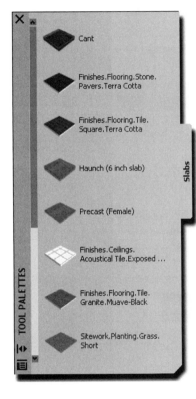

When you finish this section, you should understand the following:

✔ How to use the new Architectural Desktop 2006 **Convert Space Object to slab** option.
✔ How to make a **Slabs** tool palette.
✔ How to use **Direct Mode** and **Direction.**
✔ How to use **Projected** mode.
✔ How to apply tool properties to slabs.
✔ How to cut slabs.
✔ How to modify a slab object.
✔ How to make a new edge from a Profile.
✔ How to change a slab edge profile.

Number	Name	Purpose
1	Style	Select from available slab styles
2	Mode	Specifies whether the slab is created in **Direct** or **Projected** modes
3	Thickness	Specifies the thickness of the slab
4	Vertical offset	Specifies the vertical offset of the slab
5	Horizontal offset	Specifies the horizontal offset of the slab while Picking points
6	Justify	Specifies the slab justification—**Top, Bottom, Center,** or **Slopeline**

7	Direction	Specifies the **Left** or **Right** direction for the slab
8	Overhang	Distance of overhang; specifies the overhang depth for the slab
9	Perimeter edge	Specifies the edge style along the perimeter of the slab
10	Rotation	Rotation reference angle for the slab
11	Elevation	Elevation of the slab

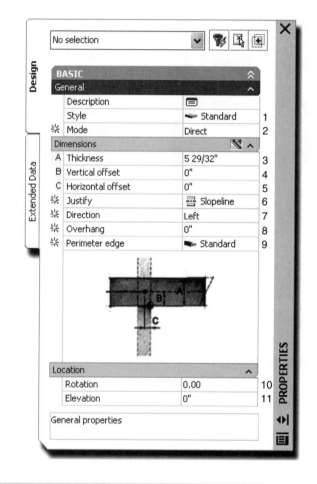

Hands-On

Creating a New Slab Tool Palette

1. Create a new tool palette, and name it **Slab.**
2. Select the **Content Browser** icon from the **Main** tool bar to launch the Content Browser.
3. In the **Design Tool Catalog - Imperial,** locate the **Slabs** folder in the **Roof Slabs and Slabs** folder.
4. From the **Slabs** folder, drag all the slabs into the new tool palette you created.
5. Click and hold on the tab of your new tool palette and drag a copy to **My Tool Catalog** in the Content Browser.

New for Architectural Desktop 2006

Using the New ADT 2006 Convert Space Object to Slab Option to Create a Slab

Hands-On

1. Select File > New, and start a new drawing using the Aec Model (Imperial Stb) template.
2. Change to the Top or Plan view.
3. Select the **Wall** tool from the Design toolbar, and using a standard 10'-high, 6"-wide wall, create the enclosure shown in Figure 11–1.
4. Select the **Space Auto Generate** tool from the **Design** tool palette, and move over one of the subenclosures of the enclosures you just created. The **Generate Spaces** dialog box will appear (Figure 11–2).

Figure 11–1

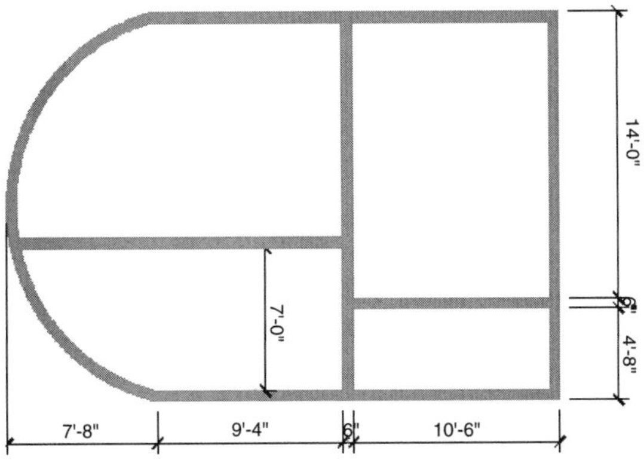

Figure 11–2

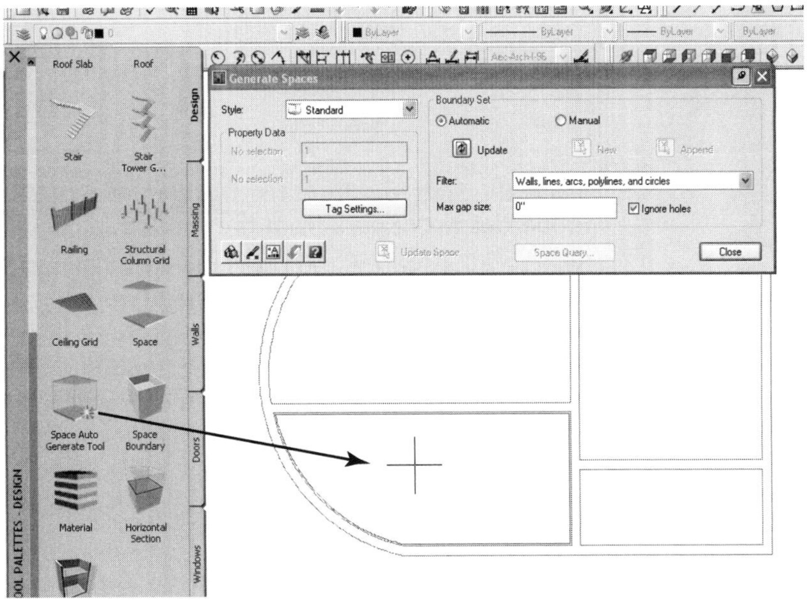

5. Click in each of the subenclosures of the enclosure, and then press the **Close** button in the **Generate Spaces** dialog box to return to the Drawing Editor. You have now created space objects in all the enclosures.

6. Change to the **SW Isometric** view.

7. Select one of the walls, **RMB,** and choose **Select Similar** from the contextual menu that appears to select all the walls.

8. With all the walls selected, click on the **Isolate Objects** icon (lightbulb) at the lower right of the Drawing Editor, and select **Hide Objects** from the contextual menu that appears. The walls will now be hidden, showing only the space objects.

9. Select each space object individually, and move your cursor over the **Properties** palette to open the palette.

10. In the **Properties** palette, change the **Space height, Floor boundary thickness,** and **Ceiling boundary thickness** for every space (see Figure 11–3).

Figure 11–3

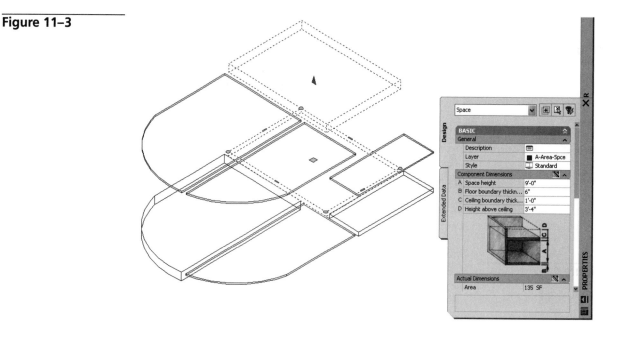

11. Select the **Slab** tool from the **Design** menu, **RMB,** and select **Apply Tool Properties to > Space** from the contextual menu that appears.

12. Select all the spaces, and press the **Enter** key on the keyboard to bring up the **Convert Space To Slab** dialog box.

13. In the **Convert Space To Slab** dialog, Check the **Convert Ceiling to Slab, Convert to Slab,** and **Erase Layout Geometry** check boxes, and then Press the **OK** button to return to the Drawing Editor (see Figure 11–4).

14. These slabs can now be treated as standard slab objects. They can be cut, have their elevations changed, have holes created in them, and be stretched and edited with vertices (see Figure 11–5).

Figure 11–4

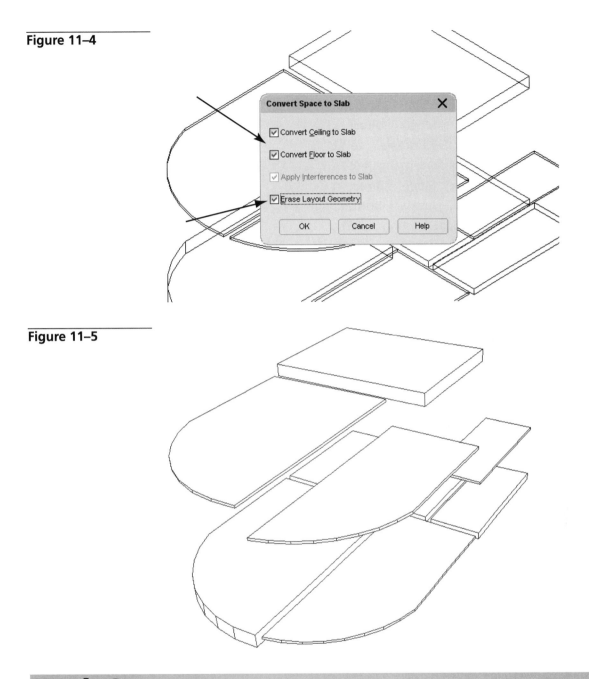

Figure 11–5

Hands-On

Using Direct Mode and Direction

Slabs can be either **Direct** or **Projected** modes. **Direct** mode allows you to place a Flat slab, **Projected** mode allows you to place a slab at a location in space with a given slope. **Direction** is used when using **Ortho Close.**

The first point establishes slab origin and pivot point. The first line establishes the base line.

1. Start a new drawing using the Aec Model (Imperial Stb) template.
2. Change to the **Model Layout.**
3. Change to **Top View.**

4.   Select the **Slab** icon from the **Design** toolbar.

5.   Move your cursor over the **Properties** palette to open it.

6.   Set the following parameters:

   a.   Style = **Standard**
   b.   Mode = **Direct**
   c.   Thickness = **to 12″**
   d.   Overhang = **0″**
   e.   Mode = **Direct**
   f.   Justify = **Bottom**
   g.   Direction = **Left**

7.   Set the first point of your slab.

8.   Moving clockwise, set the second point at **10′** to the right.

9.   Enter **O** (Ortho close) in the **Command line,** and press **Enter.**

10.   Repeat Steps 5, 6, 7, 8 and 9 slightly below the first slab in the **Top** viewport, but change the direction arrow to the **Right** direction arrow.

11.   Select each slab, and change the slope of each slab to **45** (45 degrees)

Ortho Close works differently for slabs than for walls. For slabs, only one line is drawn, so the direction arrow dictates in which direction the slab is cast (see Figures 11–6 and 11–7).

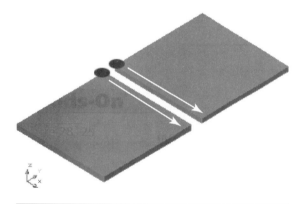

Figure 11–6

Figure 11–7

Hands-On

Projected Model

1.   Create a new drawing.

2.   Again select the **Slab** icon from the **Design** tool palette.

3.   Move your cursor over the **Properties** palette to open it.

4.   Set the following parameters:

   a.   Style = **Standard**
   b.   Mode = **Projected**

c. Thickness = **to 12″**

d. Justify = **Bottom**

e. Base height = **0**

f. Direction = **Right**

g. Overhang = **0″**

Notice that selecting the **Projected** mode causes the **Slope** option to now be available in the **Properties** palette.

5. In the **Properties** palette under **Slope,** set **Rise** to **6** and, **Run** to **12.**

6. Set a point, and moving clockwise, set the second point at **10′** to the right.

Notice that the **Pivot** symbol is at your starting point. Also notice that selecting the **Projected** mode causes the **Slope** option to be available.

7. Enter **O** (Ortho close) in the **Command line,** and press the **Enter** key.

8. Repeat Steps 5, 6, and 7, but change the **Direction** to **Left** (see Figure 11–8).

You only change the **Rise** numbers. Leave **Run** at **12.000,** and the **Angle** will automatically calculate.

Figure 11–8

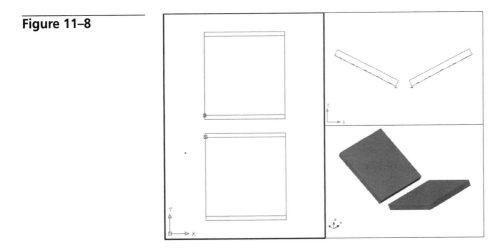

Hands-On

Applying Tool Properties to Slabs

Convert to Slab uses closed polylines or walls as a basis for creating slabs. You don't need closed walls to use **Convert to Slab;** one wall will work just fine. The default location for slabs created by **Convert to Slab** using walls is at the top of the wall.

1. Start a new drawing using the Aec Model (Imperial Stb) template.

2. Change to the **Model Layout.**

3. Make the left viewport Top view, and the right viewport SW Isometric view.

4.   Change to **Top View.**

5.   Select the **Wall** icon from the **Design** tool palette.

6.   Starting at the bottom left and moving clockwise, place a 8′ × 8′ enclosure 8′-0″ high (see Figure 11–9).

Figure 11–9

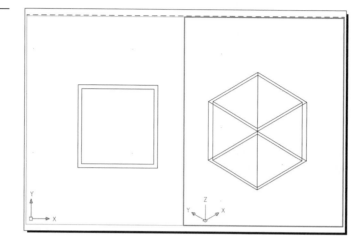

7.   Select the **Slab** icon from the **Design** tool palette, **RMB,** and select **Apply Tool properties to > Linework and Walls** from the contextual menu that appears.

8.   In the **Top View,** select all the walls of the 8′ × 8′ enclosure starting at the bottom wall and moving counterclockwise.

!   ***Note:*** The first wall you pick becomes the pivot wall.

9.   In the **Command line,** accept **N** to leave the **Walls** in place.

10.   For **Slab Justification,** select **Bottom;** for **Wall Justification** select **Left;** for **Slope Direction,** select **Right** or **Left** (either is OK); and accept the **Standard** slab style by pressing the **Enter** key on the keyboard.

11.   While the new slab is still selected, open the Properties palette and change the slab's thickness to 24″.

You have now placed a Standard 24″-thick slab object at the top of the wall enclosure (see Figure 11–10).

Figure 11–10

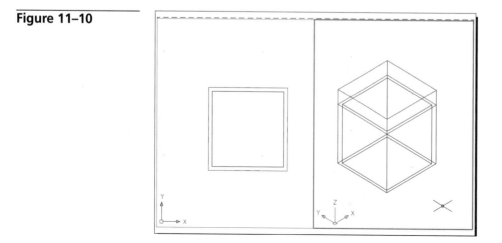

12. Repeat the above exercises, changing the **Wall Justification, Slab Justification,** and **Slope Direction** until you feel comfortable with the controls.

13. Double-click the slab to open the **Properties** palette.

14. Set the Slope **Rise** to **12** (12″) (see Figure 11–11).

15. Select the slab, **RMB,** and select **Edit Slab Edges** from the **contextual menu** to bring up the **Slab Edges** dialog box.

16. In the Slab Edges dialog box, change the **Edge Cut** to **Plumb** (see Figures 11–12 and 11–13).

Figure 11–11

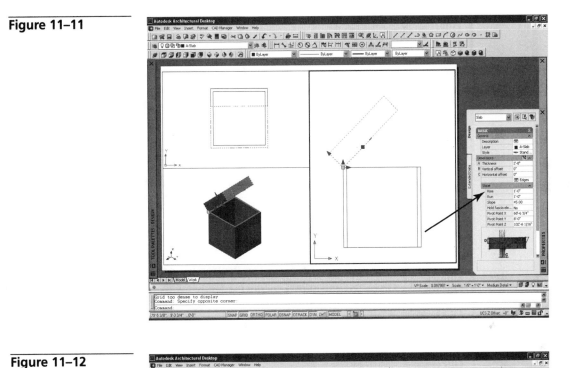

Figure 11–12

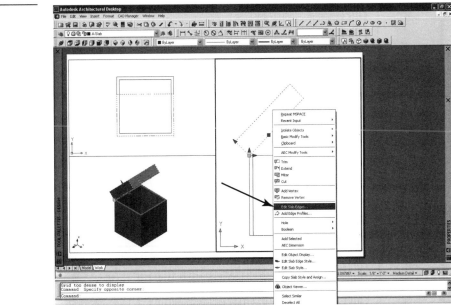

Figure 11–13

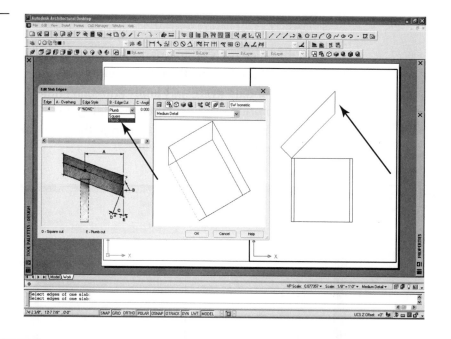

Hands-On

Cutting Slabs

1. Use the previous exercise.
2. Double-click the slab to open the **Properties** palette.
3. Set the Slope **Rise** to **0** (0") to return the slab to a flat position (the changed edge is still plumb).
4. In the **Top View,** place and **Offset** several polylines as shown in Figure 11–14.

Figure 11–14

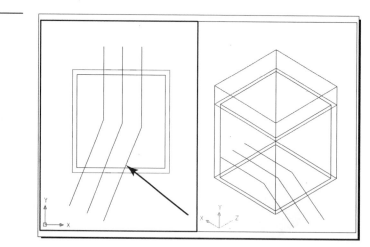

We are going to cut the slab with the polylines, even though the polylines are at 0" elevation, and the slab is at 8'-0" elevation.

5. Select the slab, **RMB,** and select **Cut** from the contextual menu that appears.
6. Select one of the polylines, and press **Enter.**

7. Enter **Y** (Yes) in the **Command line,** and press **Enter.**
8. Repeat Steps 5 through 7 for the other polylines.

You should now have three slab sections.

9. Select each slab section, and move your cursor over the **Properties** palette to open it.
10. Set the thickness for each section 8″ higher than the previous one (see Figure 11–15). Save this file.

Figure 11–15

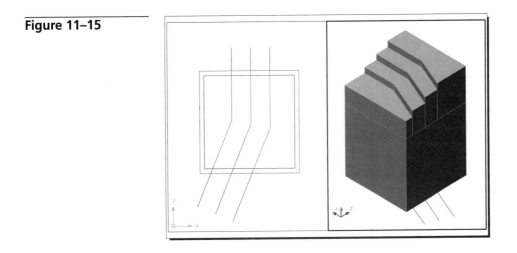

Hands-On

Making a New Edge from a Profile

1. Erase the slabs created in the previous exercise, and place a new 12″ slab starting at the upper left corner and moving clockwise.
2. Create a profile polyline shape by drawing the polyline shown in Figure 11–16.
3. Select the polyline, **RMB,** and select **Convert to > Profile Definition** from the contextual menu that appears.

Figure 11–16

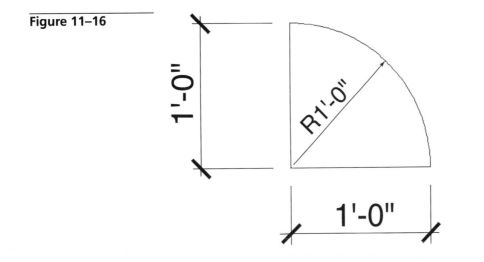

4. Select the upper left corner of the polyline you just created.

5. Press **Enter** to bring up the **Profile Definition** dialog box.

6. Enter **CURVED EDGE PROFILE,** and press the **OK** button.

7. Select **Format > Style Manager** to bring up the **Style Manager.**

8. Select **Architectural > Slab Edge Styles, RMB,** and select **New** from the contextual menu that appears.

9. Rename the new style **CURVED EDGE STYLE.**

10. Double-click on the **CURVED EDGE STYLE** icon you just created to bring up the **Slab Edge Styles** dialog box.

11. In the **Slab Edge Styles** dialog box select the **Design rules** tab.

12. Check the **Fascia** check box, select **CURVED EDGE PROFILE** from the **Fascia Profile** drop-down list, and press the **OK** and **Apply** buttons to return to the Drawing Editor (see Figure 11–17).

Figure 11–17

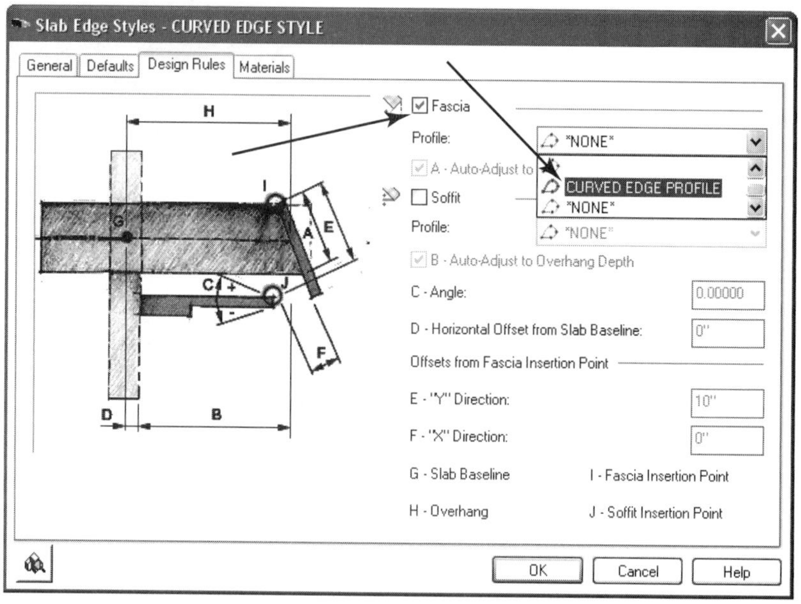

13. Double-click the slab to bring up the **Properties** palette.

14. Select **Edges** to bring up the **Slab Edges** dialog box.

15. Select all the edges, select **CURVED EDGE STYLE** from the **Edge Style** drop-down list, and then press the **OK** button.

You have now placed a new curved edge on all the slab edges (see Figure 11–18).

Figure 11–18

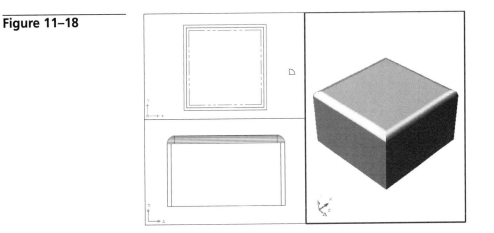

Hands-On

Changing the New Slab Edge Profile

1. Return to the profile you created in the last exercise.
2. Add a rectangle as shown in (see Figure 11–19).
3. **RMB** on an empty place in the Drawing Editor, and select **AEC Modify Tools > Merge** from the contextual menu that appears.
4. Select the rectangle and press **Enter.**
5. Select the original profile and press **Enter.**
6. Enter **Y** (Yes) in the **Command line** and press **Enter** (see Figure 11–20).
7. Select the changed profile, **RMB,** and select **Convert To > Profile Definition** from the contextual menu that appears.

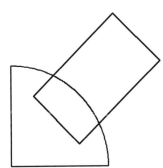

Figure 11–19

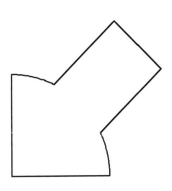

Figure 11–20

8. Select the lower left corner of the profile and press **Enter.**
9. Enter **E** (Existing) in the **Command line,** and press **Enter** to bring up the **Profile Definitions** dialog box.
10. Select **CURVED EDGE PROFILE** (the one you created in the last exercise), and press **OK.**

The slab edge now reflects the changed profile (see Figure 11–21).

Figure 11–21

Structural Members, Column Grids, Grids, and Anchors

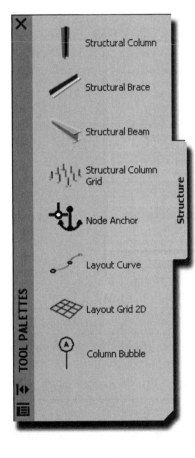

When you finish this section, you should understand the following:

- ✔ How to make a **Structure** palette.
- ✔ How to place a column and **Structural Column Grid.**
- ✔ How to modify a **Structural Column Grid.**
- ✔ How to create a **Structural Column Grid** from linework.
- ✔ How to place **Structural Beams on Structural Column Grids.**
- ✔ How to use the **Structural Beam "fill and array" options.**
- ✔ How to modify structural members.
- ✔ How to create a round composite concrete and steel column.
- ✔ How to add bar joists.
- ✔ How to label a grid.
- ✔ How to add and label a layout grid (2D).
- ✔ How to create and use a **Layout Curve.**
- ✔ How to use a wall as a **Layout Curve.**
- ✔ How to use the **trim planes.**
- ✔ How to **frame** floors and roofs Slabs and Structural Members.
- ✔ Creating a Custom Structural Member from linework, and applying a **Miter.**

All buildings have a structural system. In the design of commercial buildings, the understanding and documentation of the structural system is of utmost importance. In Autodesk Architectural Desktop 2006, structural members give control over this phase of construction.

Structural members can be used as columns, beams, and braces, and can be configured in many ways not originally intended by the developers of the program. In reality, columns, beams, and braces are the same AEC object used in different work planes. When understood, structural members can be some of the most important AEC objects in your portfolio of tools.

Column grids are a variant on grids; they can be planar (flat) or volumetric (three-dimensional). Columns can be attached to any grid, but column grids can have columns attached upon input of the grid.

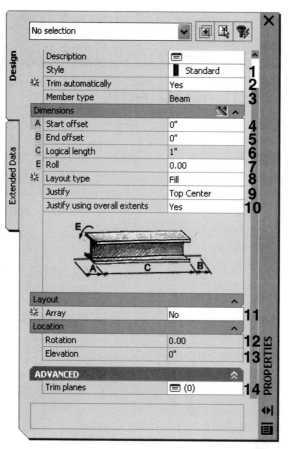

Number	Name	Purpose
1	Style	Select from available structural member styles
2	Trim Automatically	Specifies whether to trim member ends against existing members
3	Member type	**Column, Beam,** or **Brace**
4	Start offset	Distance offset from the start end of member
5	End offset	Distance offset from the end of member
6	Logical length	Actual length of structural member
7	Roll	Roll angle around the main axis through member
8	Layout type—Fill or Edge	Specifies whether to create new members along the hovered object's edges or within the area of the hovered object.
9	Justify	Insertion node location
10	Justify using overall extents	
11	Array—Yes or No	Specifies whether to add multiple members as you drag
12	Rotation	Rotation of the structural member
13	Elevation	Elevation of the structural member
14	Trim planes	Planes used to modify end conditions of the structural member

Hands-On

Making a New Structure Tool Palette

1. Create a new tool palette named **Structure**.
2. Select the **Content Browser** icon from the **Main** toolbar to launch the **Content Browser**.
3. In the **Stock Tool Catalog** locate the **Structural Beam, Structural Brace, Structural Column,** and **Structural Grid Object** in the **Architectural Object Tools** folder.
4. From the **Architectural Object Tools** folder, drag the objects into the new tool palette you created.
5. In the **Stock Tool Catalog** locate the **Cell Anchor, Node Anchor, Layout Curve** and **Layout Grid (2D)** tools in the **Parametric Layout & Anchoring** folder, and drag these tools to the **Structure** palette you created.
6. Click and hold on the tab of your new tool palette and drag a copy to **My Tool Catalog** in the Content Browser.
7. In the **Sample Palette Catalog - Imperial**, locate the **Column Bubble** tool in the **Annotation** folder, and drag these tools to the **Structure** palette you created.

Hands-On

Placing a Column and Grid

1. Start a new drawing using the Aec Model (Imperial Stb) template.
2. Change to the **Work Layout.**
3. Erase the existing viewports.
4. Select **View > Viewports > 3 Viewports** from the **Main** menu.
5. Set the left viewport to **Top View,** the upper right to **Front View** and the lower right to **SW Isometric.**
6. Activate the **Top View.**
7. Select **Structural Column Grid** from the **Structure** tool palette you created and drag your cursor over the **Properties** palette to open it.
8. Enter the following data:

    a. Shape = **Rectangular**
    b. Boundary = ***NONE***
    c. Specify on screen = **No**
    d. X - Width = **60'**
    e. Y - Depth = **40'**
    f. XAXIS Layout type = **Repeat**
    g. Bay size = **20'-0"**
    h. YAXIS Layout Type = **Repeat**

    i. Bay size = **20'-0"**

    j. Column Style = **Standard**

    k. Column Logical Length = **10'-0"**

    l. Justify = **Middle Center**

9. Click in the Drawing Editor in the Top View to place the grid and columns, and press **Enter** twice to complete the command (see Figure 12–1).

Save this file.

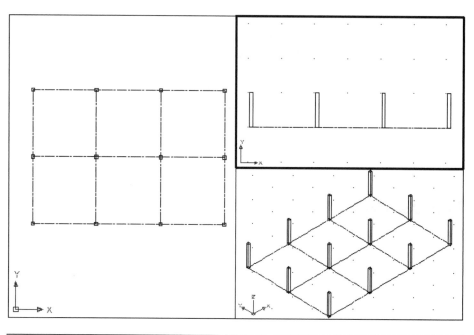

Figure 12–1

Hands-On

Modifying a Column Grid

1. Using the previous exercise, select the column grid and move your cursor over the **Properties** palette to open it.

2. In the **Properties** palette change the **X Axis** and **Y Axis Layout** type to **Manual**. This will allow you to drag the grid lines with your cursor and will also enable you to manually add guide lines (see Figure 12–2).

Figure 12–2

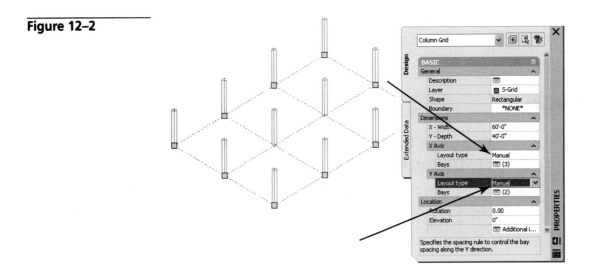

3. In the **Top View,** select the grid, and drag the middle left node **10'** in the **270** degree direction (see Figure 12–3).

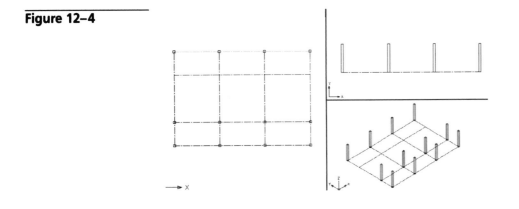

Before   After

Figure 12–3

4. Again, select the grid, **RGB,** and select **Y Axis > Add Grid line** from the contextual menu that appears.

5. Enter **30'** in the **Command** line, and press the **Enter** key. This will add a new grid line **30'** from the lowest grid line (see Figure 12–4).

Figure 12–4

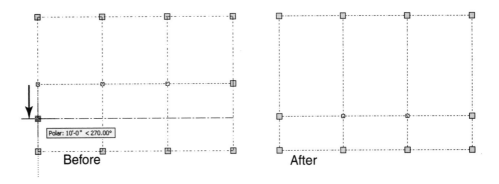

6. Select **Structural** column from the **Design** tool palette, and place columns at the new grid nodes created by the new grid line. Save this file.

Hands-On

Creating a Column Grid from Linework and Placement of Structural Columns

1. Start a new drawing using the Aec Model (Imperial Stb) template.
2. Using the Line and Arc commands, create the line drawing shown in Figure 12–5.

Figure 12–5

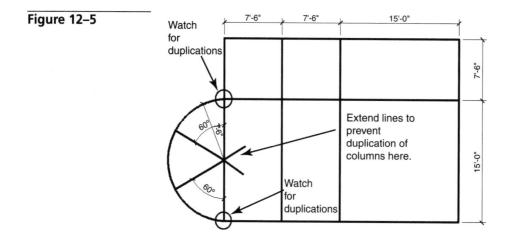

Watch for duplications

7'-6"   7'-6"   15'-0"

60°   6'   60°

Extend lines to prevent duplication of columns here.

Watch for duplications

7'-6"   15'-0"

3. Select the **Structural Column Grid** tool from the **Design** tool palette, **RMB**, and select **Apply Tool Properties to > Linework**.
4. Select all the linework you created in Step 2 of this exercise, and press the **Enter** key on your keyboard.
5. Enter **Y** (Yes) in the Command line to erase the selected linework, and press the **Enter** key on your keyboard.

The linework changes into a Structural Column Grid with nodes (see Figure 12–6).

Figure 12–6

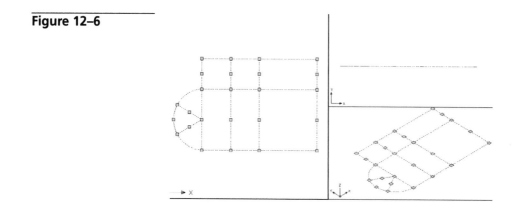

Placing all the Structural Columns at one time (new Architectural Desktop 2006 feature)

6.   Select the **Structural Column** tool from the **Design** tool palette.

7.   Click on the column grid, and release the mouse button until you see the tool tip.

8.   Press the **Ctrl** key on the keyboard until you see small red circles at the node points. When they appear, click the left mouse button again to place columns at all the grid nodes.

9.   Press the **Esc** key on the keyboard to end the command (see Figure 12–7).

Figure 12–7

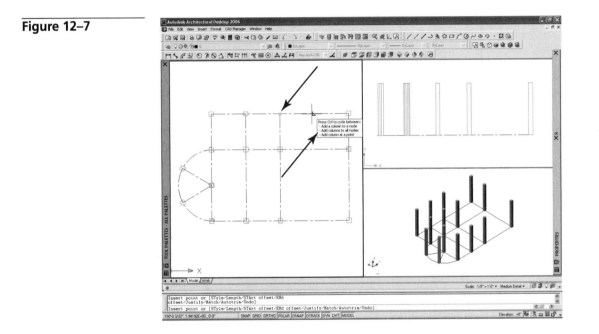

> ! **Note:** The placing of all the Structural Columns at one time can be used with all the creation methods for Structural Column Grids. **Be sure to turn OSNAP off to see the Ctrl tool tips for Structural member placement.** Save this file.

Hands-On

Placing Beams on Structural Column Grids (New Automated Feature for Architectural Desktop 2006)

> ! **Note:** This feature will only work with Structural Column grids and not with any other type of grid.

1.   Open the drawing for the first exercise in this chapter.

2.   Activate the **Top** View.

3.   Select the **Structural Beam** tool from the **Design** tool palette.

4. Move your cursor over the **Properties** palette to open it.
5. In the **Properties** palette, select **Yes** from the **Trim Automatically** drop-down list and **Edge** from the **Layout Type** drop-down list.
6. Move your cursor over the Structural Column Grid (not at a column or node), and press the **Ctrl** key twice.

You will see that the beam expands to fill the entire grid line (see Figure 12–8).

Figure 12–8

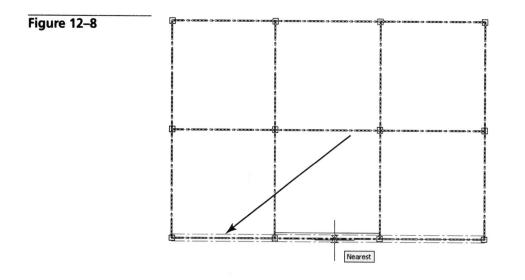

7. Move your cursor over the Structural Column Grid (not at a column or node), and press the **Ctrl** key twice more.

You will see that the beam expands to fill all the grid lines.

8. Click the left mouse button to place the beams (see Figure 12–9).

Figure 12–9

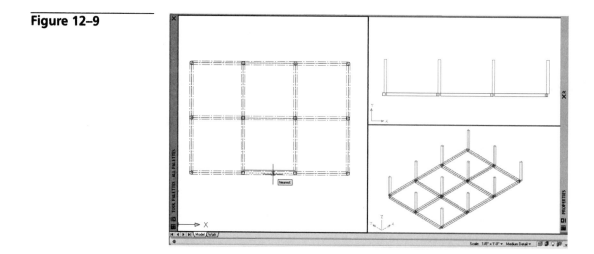

The default Structural Column that you placed on the structural column grid is 12'-0".

9. Erase all the beams you placed.

10. Select the new (for 2006) **Replace Z value with current elevation** icon at the bottom right of the Drawing Editor. This must be set before starting a placement command (see Figure 12–10).

Figure 12–10

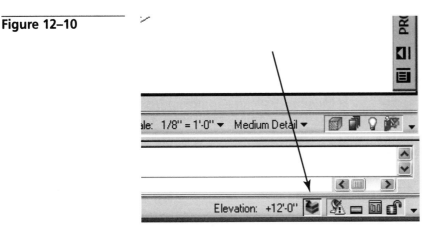

11. Select the +**0** to the left of the **Replace Z value with current elevation** icon you selected in Step 9 to bring up the **Elevation Offset** dialog box.

12. In the **Elevation Offset** dialog box, enter **12'-0"**, and press the **OK** button to return to the Drawing Editor.

13. Select the **Structural Beam** tool from the **Design** tool palette.

14. Move your cursor over the **Properties** palette to open it.

15. In the **Properties** palette, select **Yes** from the **Trim Automatically** drop-down list and **Edge** from the **Layout Type** drop-down list.

16. Repeat Steps 6–8 of this exercise to place beams at the top of the columns (see Figure 12–11).

Save this file.

Figure 12–11

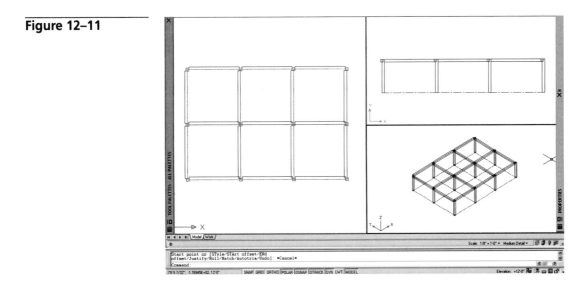

Hands-On

Using the New Structural Beam "Fill and Array" Options (New for Architectural Desktop 2006)

1. Use the drawing file from the previous exercise previous.
2. Select Format > Structural members > Catalog from the **Main** menu to bring up the **Structural Member Catalog** dialog box.
3. In the **Structural Member Catalog** dialog box, in the left pane, expand **Imperial**, then expand **Timber**, and finally expand **Nominal Lumber.**
4. In the **Structural Member Catalog** dialog box, in the right pane, double-click on **2 × 4** to bring up the **Structural Member Style** dialog box.
5. In the **Structural Member Style** dialog box, press the **OK** button, and then close the **Structural Member Style** dialog box to return to the Drawing Editor (see Figure 12–12).
6. Select the **Structural Beam** tool from the **Design** tool palette.
7. Move your cursor over the **Properties** palette to open it.

Figure 12–12

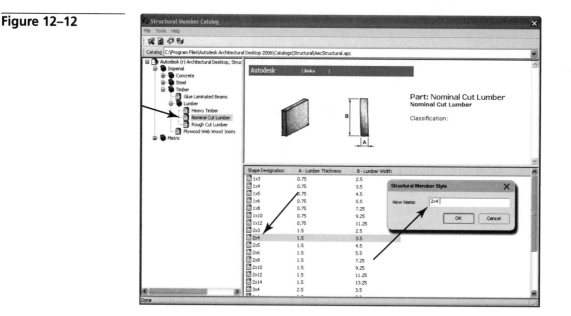

8. In the **Properties** palette, select **Yes** from the **Trim Automatically** drop-down list, **Fill** from the **Layout Type, Yes** from the **Array** drop-down list, **Space evenly** from the **Layout method** drop-down list, and insert **5** in the **Number of bays** field (see Figure 12–13).

Figure 12–13

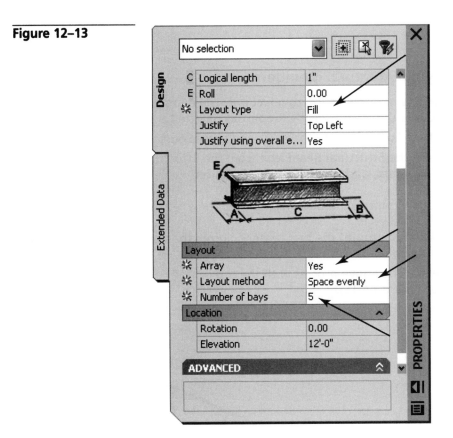

9. Move your cursor over the structural column grid (not at a node or column), click the **Ctrl** key on your keyboard twice, and then click the left mouse button to place the beams as shown in (Figure 12–14).

Figure 12–14

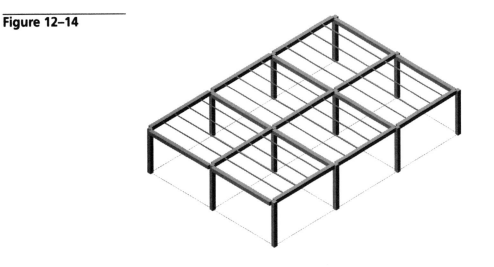

Hands-On

Modifying Structural Members

1.   Use a window selection to select only the middle row of columns, and move your cursor over the **Properties** palette to open it.
2.   Set the **Logical length** to 14'-0", and press **Enter.**
3.   Select the **Structural Beam** icon from the **Structure** toolbar, set the **Style** to **Standard,** and **Justify** to **Bottom Center.**

!   *Note:* Bottom center is the location of the grips now set for the beam.

4.   Click at the top of the first center column, then at the top of the second center column.
5.   Repeat the above process with the top center nodes of the columns (see Figure 12–15).
6.   Repeat the process for the other columns to create the frame illustrated in Figure 12–16.

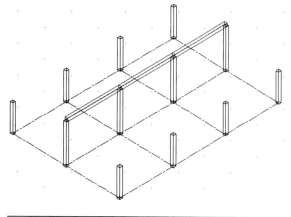

Figure 12–15

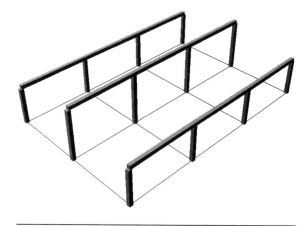

Figure 12–16

7.   Select the end beams on the left side and right sides, and move your cursor over the **Properties** palette to open it.
8.   Set the **Start offset** to −2'-0" (see Figure 12–17).

Figure 12–17

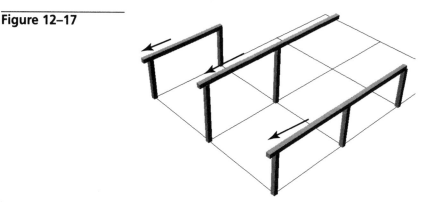

9. Repeat this process on the beams at the opposite end. Use +2'-0" for **End offset.**

10. Select **Format** > **Structural Member Catalog** from the **Main** toolbar.

11. Select **Imperial I Steel I AISC I Channels I MC, Miscellaneous Channels.**

12. Double-click the **MC12 × 10.6** channel.

13. When the **Structural Member Style** dialog box appears, accept the default **MC12 × 10.6** name (see Figure 12–18).

Figure 12–18

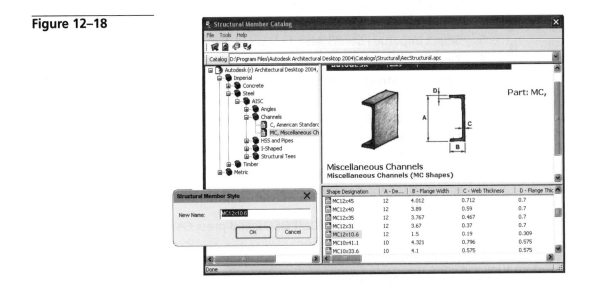

14. Select all the outer beams, **RMB,** and select **Properties** from the **contextual** menu. In the structural **Properties** dialog box, select the **Style** tab and change the style to **MC12 × 10.6** (see Figure 12–19).

15. Repeat the above process for the beams on the other side. This time also change **Roll** to **180** and **Justification** to **Top Center.** This will cause the other channels to rotate 180° with the grip on the bottom.

Figure 12–19

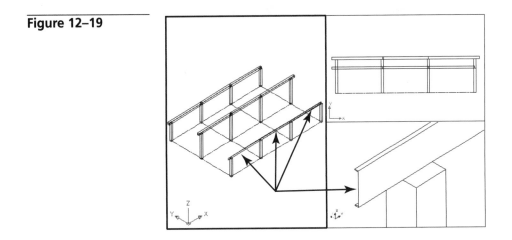

Creating a Round Composite Concrete and Steel Column

1. Select **Format** > **Structural Members** > **Catalog** from the **Main** toolbar.
2. Select **Imperial** > **Concrete** > **Cast - in place** > **Circular Columns.**
3. Double-click the 14″ diameter.
4. When the **Structural Member Style** dialog box appears, enter **14 DIA COL** and then press **OK.**
5. Select **Imperial l Steel l AISC l I Shaped, Wn Wide-Flange Shapes.**
6. Double-click **W6 × 25.**
7. When the **Structural Member Style** dialog box appears, accept **W6 × 25** and then press **OK.**
8. Close the **Structural Member Catalog.**
9. Select **Format** > **Style Manager** to bring up the **Style Manager** dialog box.
10. **RMB** on the **Structural Member Styles** icon in the **Architectural Objects** folder in the display tree and select **New** from the contextual menu that appears.
11. Rename the new style **COMPOSITE** and press **OK.**
12. Double-click on the icon adjacent to the new **COMPOSITE** style to bring up the **COMPOSITE** dialog box.
13. Select the **Design Rules** tab.
14. Press the **Edit Style** icon.
15. Name the **unnamed** component **CONC.**
16. Under **Start Shape Name,** select **14″-Diameter** from the drop-down list.
17. Press the **Add** button, and rename the next component **W6 × 25.**
18. Select **W6 × 25** under **Start Shape Name,** and press **OK** (see Figure 12–20).

Figure 12–20

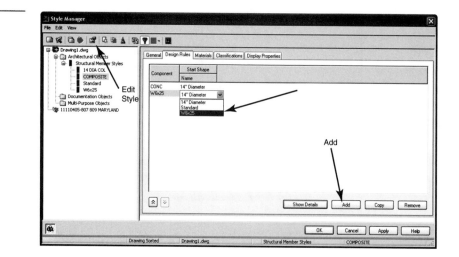

You have now created the composite round concrete column with steel shape inside.

19. Select all the columns in the Drawing Editor, and move your cursor over the **Properties** palette to open it.
20. Select **COMPOSITE COL Structural Beam** from the **Style** drop-down list. All the columns change to composite columns (see Figure 12–21).

Figure 12–21

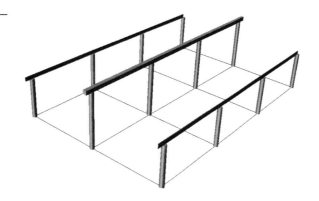

Hands-On

Adding Bar Joists

1. Select the **Content Browser** icon from the **Main** toolbar to launch the **Content Browser.**
2. In the **Design Tool Catalog - Imperial** locate the **Bar Joists** in the **Structural** folder.
3. From the **Bar Joists** folder, drag the **Steel Joist 24** into the **Structure** tool palette you created, and close the Content Browser.
4. Select **Line** from the **Draw** toolbar, and place a line from the middle beam to the top outside edge of the channel (see Figure 12–22).

Figure 12–22

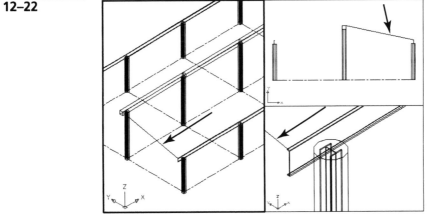

5. Select the **Steel Joist 24** icon from the **Structure** palette you created, **RMB,** and select **Apply Tool Properties to > Linework** from the contextual menu that appears.

6. Select the line you placed in Step 4 of this exercise and press **Enter.**

7. Enter **Y** (Yes) in the **Command line** and press **Enter.**

The line changes to a 24″ steel bar joist. If it is on its side, change the **Roll** to **0** in the **Properties** palette while it is still selected (see Figure 12–23).

Figure 12–23

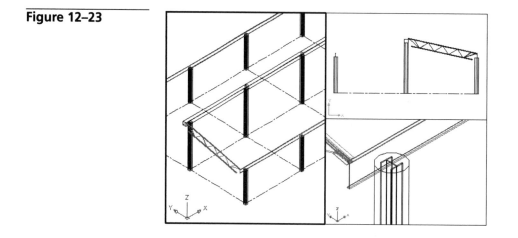

8. Change to the **Model Layout.**

9. Change to the **Left View,** and zoom window around the location of the joist seat and the channel (see Figure 12–24).

Figure 12–24

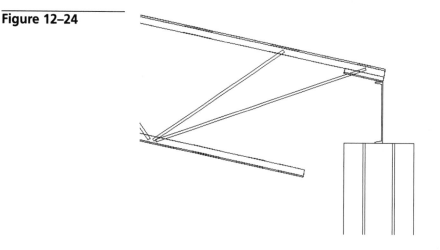

10. Select the bar joist, **RMB,** and select **Edit Member Style** from the contextual menu that appears to bring up the **Structural Member Style** dialog box.

11. Select the **Design Rules** tab. This is where you control the components of the bar joist.

12. Press the Show details button at the bottom of the dialog box to expand the truss details.

13. Set the settings shown for the **TopChord** and **JoistSeat-End** and press **OK** (see Figure 12–25).

Figure 12–25

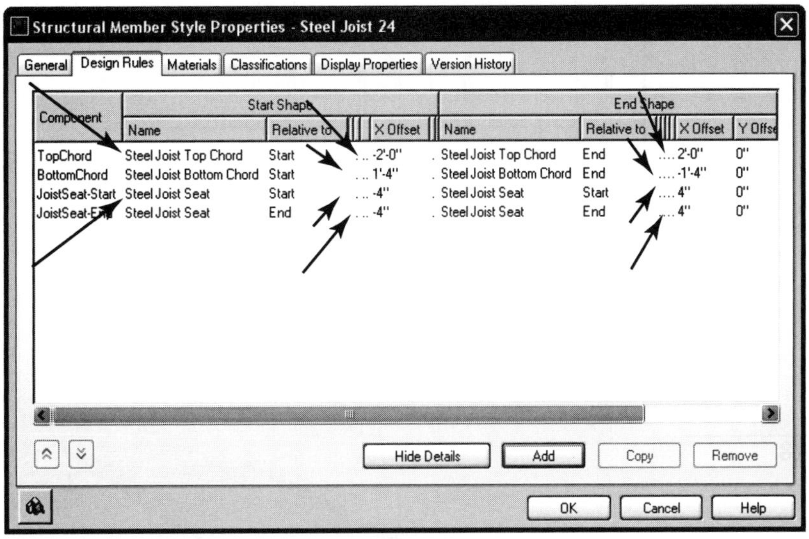

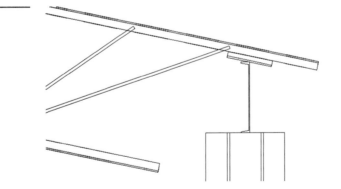

> **Note:** The author adjusted the titles in the details columns to the left so some columns such as Mirror, Rotate, Y and Z offsets are not illustrated.

The bar joist top chord and joist seat change (see Figure 12–26).

Figure 12–26

14. Change to the Top view.
15. Select the bar joist, **RMB,** and select **AEC Modify Tools > Array** from the contextual menu that appears.
16. Select the front edge of the bar joist as an edge, drag to the right, and enter **2'-0"** in the dynamic input field.
17. When you reach the last set of columns, click the left mouse again to complete the command (see Figure 12–27).
18. Mirror the bar joists to the other side of the structure, and you are finished (see Figure 12–28). Save this exercise.

Figure 12–27

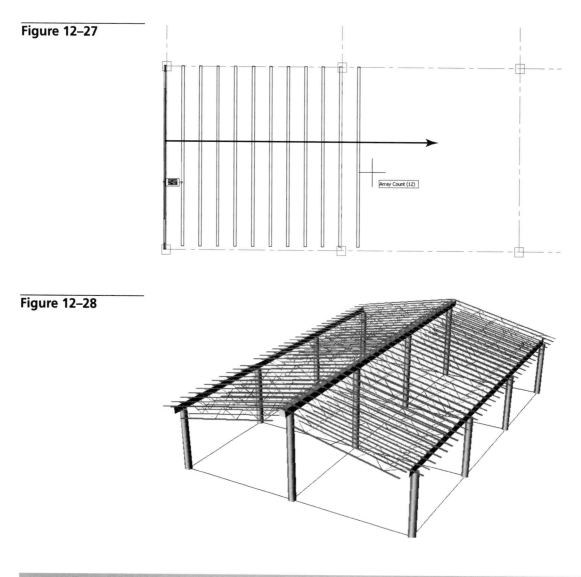

Figure 12–28

Hands-On

Labeling a Column Grid

1. Use the previous exercise.
2. Change to the **Top View.**
3. Select the **Layer Manager** icon from the **Layer Properties** toolbar to bring up the **Layer Manager.**
4. Turn the **S-Beam** and the **S-Cols** layers off, and press **OK** to return to the Drawing Editor.

The column grid will now be exposed.

5. Select the column grid, **RMB,** and select **Label** from the contextual menu that appears to bring up the **Column Grid Labeling** dialog box.
6. Select the **X-Labeling** tab.
7. In the **Number** list enter the letter **A** and press **Enter** to fill the other letters automatically.

8. Also do the following on the same tab:

    a. Check the **Automatically Calculate Values** for **Labels** check box.
    b. Select the **Ascending** radio button.
    c. Check the **Bottom** check box for **Bubble Parameters.**
    d. Enter **4′-0″** for **Extension** under **Bubble Parameters.**
    e. Check the **Generate New Bubbles On Exit** check box.

9. Change to the **Y - Labeling** tab.
10. In the **Number** list enter the number **1** and press **Enter** to fill the other numbers automatically.
11. Also do the following in the same tab:

    a. Check the **Automatically Calculate Values** for **Labels** check box.
    b. Select the **Ascending** radio button.
    c. Check the **Right** check box for **Bubble Parameters.**
    d. Enter **4′-0″** for **Extension** under the **Bubble Parameters.**
    e. Check the **Generate New Bubbles On Exit** check box.

12. Press **OK** to return to the Drawing Editor (see Figure 12–29).
13. Select the bubble containing the letter **A** to activate its grips.
14. Drag the grip above the bubble to the right; the leader will follow (see Figure 12–30).

Figure 12–29

Figure 12–30

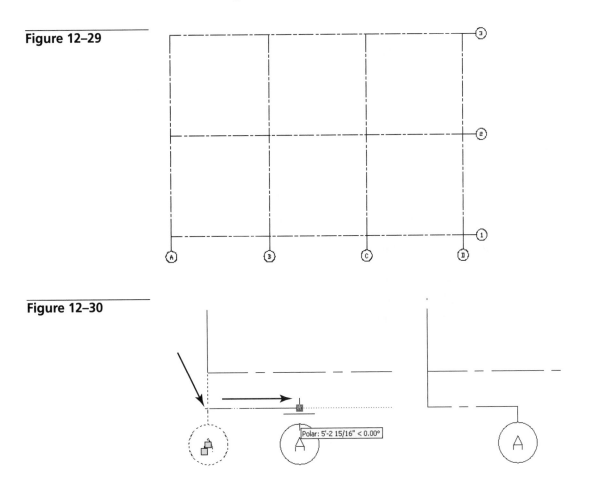

Hands-On

Adding and Labeling a Layout Grid (2D)

1. Start a new drawing using the Aec Model (Imperial Stb) template.
2. Activate the **Top View.**
3. With various tools from the **Draw** menu, create the plan shown in Figure 12–31.

Figure 12–31

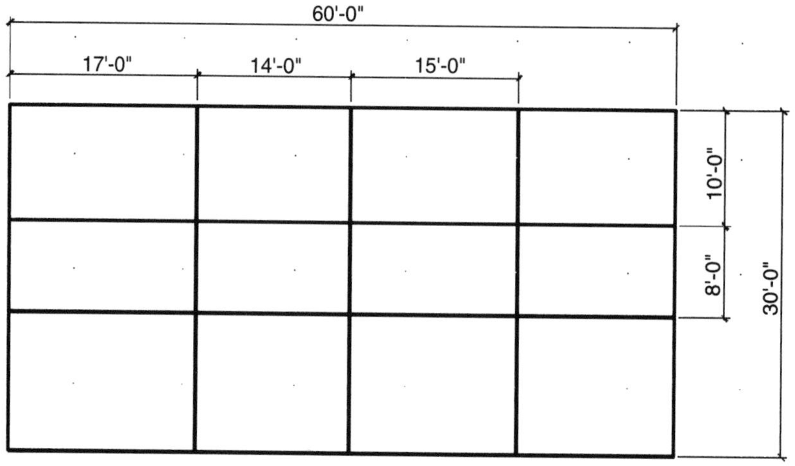

4. Select the **Layout Grid 2D** icon from the **Structure** palette that you created, **RMB,** and select **Apply Tool Properties > Linework** from the contextual menu that appears.
5. Select the plan you created in Step 4 of this exercise and press **Enter.**
6. Enter **Y** (Yes) in the **Command line,** and press **Enter.**
7. Select the **Column Bubble** from the **Structure** tool palette, and click the bottom left node of the plan to bring up the **Create Grid Bubble** dialog box.
8. Enter **A1** in the **Label** data field, **4'-0"** in the **Extension** data field, uncheck the **Apply at both ends of gridline** check box, and press the **OK** button.
9. Repeat for the following right-hand nodes (see Figure 12–32).

If a column bubble is misplaced or at an angle, do the following:

10. Select the column bubble, **RMB,** and select **Leader Anchor > Set Direction** from the contextual menu that appears.
11. For this example, enter **270°** and press **Enter** (see Figure 12–33).

Figure 12–32

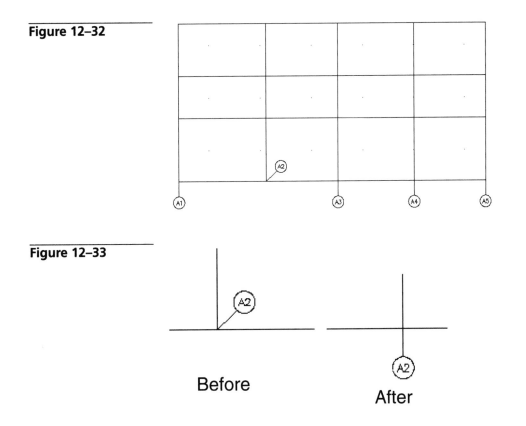

Figure 12–33

Before

After

Layout Curves

Layout curves are not necessarily curves. Straight lines and many AEC objects such as walls, stairs, and doors can also be used as layout curves. If a line were placed on a wall, changed to a layout curve, and then moved vertically 24″ up the wall, attached content would move with the layout curve. If the wall had been used as a layout curve, the nodes would be at its base.

Use a layout curve to anchor objects along a path. You can define the following objects as layout curves:

■ Walls
■ Curtain walls
■ Window assemblies
■ Spaces
■ Mass elements
■ Roofs
■ Lines
■ Arcs
■ Circles
■ Ellipses
■ Polygons
■ Polylines
■ Splines

Hands-On

Creating and Using a Layout Curve

1. Start a new drawing using the Aec Model (Imperial Stb) template.
2. Select **Spline** from the **Draw** menu, and place a spline.
3. Select the **Layout Curve** icon from the **Structure** palette.
4. Select the spline, enter **S** (Space evenly) in the **Command line,** and press **Enter.**
5. Enter **5** in the **Command line** for the **Number of** nodes and press **Enter.**
6. Enter **0"** for **Start** and **End** offsets.
7. Change to the **SW Isometric View.**
8. Turn on the **Node** Object Snap.
9. Select **Structural Column** from the **Structure** tool palette, select one of the nodes on the spline, and click the mouse to place it.
10. Select **Node Anchor** from the **Structure** tool palette.
11. Enter **C** (Copy to each node) in the **Command line,** and press **Enter** as the object to be copied.
12. Select the column you placed and press **Enter.**
13. Select any other node on the spline and press **Enter.**
14. Enter **Y** (Yes) in the **Command line** and press **Enter.**

All the nodes on the spline now have columns (see Figure 12–34).

Figure 12–34

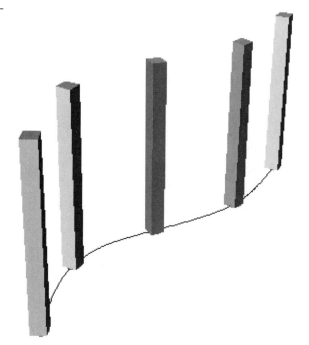

Hands-On

Using a Wall as a Layout Curve

1. Use the previous drawing.
2. Select the **Wall** icon from the **Design** menu and place a **Standard** 15'-0"-long 10'-high, 6"-wide wall.
3. Select the **Layout Curve** icon from the **Structure** palette, and select the wall you just created.
4. Enter **S** (Space evenly) in the **Command line,** and press **Enter.**
5. Enter **24"** for the **Start offset** and press **Enter.**
6. Enter **24"** for the **End offset** and press **Enter.**
7. Accept **3** as the **Number of nodes,** and press **Enter** to place the nodes.
8. Select the **Content Bowser** icon from the **Main** toolbar and select and drag into the drawing the **Regular** drinking fountain from the **Design Tool Catalog - Imperial** > **Mechanical** > **Plumbing Fixtures** > **Fountain** folder (see Figure 12–35).

Figure 12–35

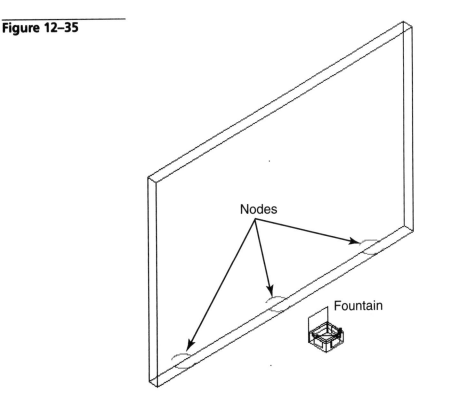

Nodes

Fountain

9. Select the **Node Anchor** icon from the **Structure** palette.
10. Enter **C** (Copy to each node) in the **Command line** and press **Enter.**
11. Select the drinking fountain, and then select one of the nodes anchored to the wall.

The fountains are now anchored to the wall as the layout tools.

12. Select all the fountains and move your cursor over the **Properties** palette to open it.
13. Select the **Anchor** field to bring up the **Anchor** dialog box.
14. Change the **Insertion Offset Z** to **3'-0"**, the **Rotation Z** to **270,** and press **OK** to return to the Drawing Editor.

All the fountains move vertically up the wall 3'-0" (see Figure 12–36).

Figure 12–36

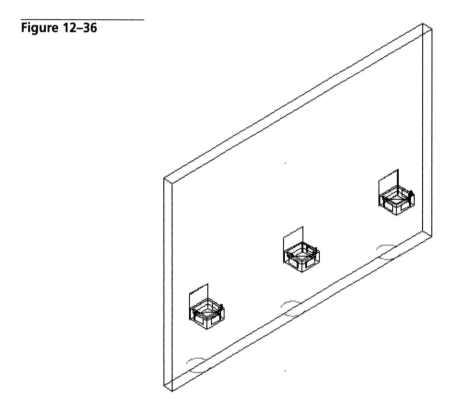

Hands-On

Layout Grid (2D)

1. Start a new drawing using the Aec Model (Imperial Stb) template.
2. Change to the **Model Layout.**
3. Change to the **Top View.**
4. Create a 40'-long × 30'-wide building with a 6"-rise roof.
5. Select the **Roof Slab** icon from the **Design** tool palette, **RMB,** and select **Apply Tool Properties to > Linework, Walls, and Roof** from the contextual menu that appears.
6. Select the roof object, Enter **N** (No) in the **Command line,** and press **Enter** to change the roof object to roof slabs.
7. Select the **Object UCS** from the **UCS** toolbar, and select the front roof slab. Make sure the **ucsicon OR option** is on (see Figure 12–37).

8. Select the **Layout Grid (2D)** icon from the **Structure** tool palette.
9. Center a 15′ × 10′ grid on the front roof slab with three divisions in the X direction and two divisions in the Y direction. The grid will lie parallel to the roof because the UCS was set parallel to the roof in Step 7 (see Figure 12–38).
10. Place a 5′-0″-high × 1′-0″-radius mass element cylinder in a convenient place in your drawing.
11. Select the **Cell Anchor** icon from the **Structure** tool palette.
12. Type **C** at the **Command line** to copy to each cell, and press **Enter**.
13. Select the mass object, and then select the layout grid on the roof slab (see Figures 12–39 and 12–40).

Note in Figures 12-25 and 12-26 that the mass elements in the cells of the layout grid match the size of the grid.

14. Select the grid, and move your cursor over the **Properties** palette to open it.
15. Change the grid size to **5′-0″** in the **X-Width** and **5′-0″** in the **Y-Depth**.

Note that the mass elements in the cells automatically change size (see Figures 12–41 and 12–42).

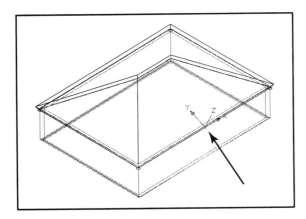

Figure 12–37

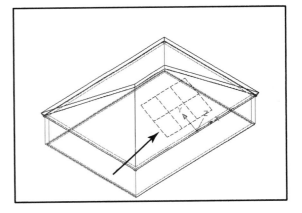

Figure 12–38

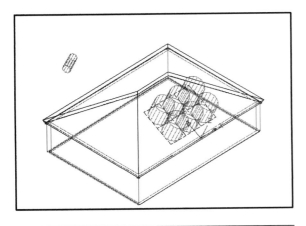

Figure 12–39

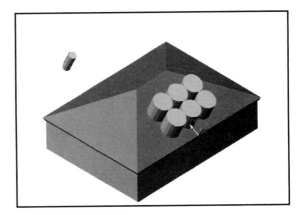

Figure 12–40

16. Place another grid on the roof; 9′ × 6′ will fit.
17. Select the **Node Anchor** icon from the **Structure** tool palette.
18. Enter **C** (Copy to each node) in the **Command line** and press **Enter**.
19. Select the mass element, and then select the layout grid (see Figure 12–43).

Note that the mass elements attached to the nodes of the layout grid. Moving or modifying the grid will then move the anchored objects.

The layout volume grid (3D) works and is modified in a similar manner to the 2D layout grid.

Experiment with all the different settings, and try anchoring and rotating different kinds of content to AEC objects and AutoCAD entities. Don't forget that you can use the layout grid to put a series of skylights or windows on a roof or wall. **Save this file.**

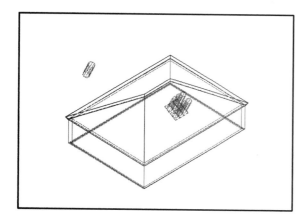

Figure 12–41

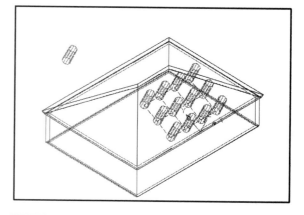

Figure 12–43

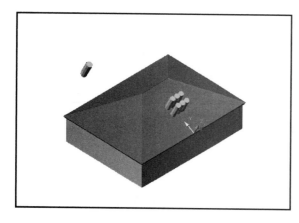

Figure 12–42

Hands-On

Using the New Trim Planes

1. Start a new drawing using the Aec Model (Imperial Stb) template.
2. Select **Format > Structural members > Catalog** from the **Main** menu to bring up the **Structural Member Catalog** dialog box.

3. In the **Structural Member Catalog** dialog box, expand **Timber** and then expand **Nominal Cut Lumber.**

4. In the right pane of the **Structural Member Catalog** dialog box, double-click on **2 × 6** to bring up the **Structural Member Style dialog box.**

5. Press the **OK** button to return to the right pane of the **Structural Member Catalog** dialog box. Close the **Structural Member Catalog.**

6. Change to the **Top** view.

7. Select the **Structural Beam** tool from the **Design** menu, and move your cursor over the **Properties** palette to open it.

8. In the **Properties** palette, select **2 × 6** from the **Style** drop-down list, and **Top Left** from the **Justify** drop-down list.

9. Place a 4'-long beam in the **Top** viewport.

10. Change to the **Front** view.

11. Select the beam, **RMB,** and select **Trim Planes > Edit Trim Planes** from the contextual menu that appears.

12. Notice the + signs that appear at the top ends of the beam, this signifies that you are ready to add an **Edit** trim plane.

13. Select the left-hand **+sign** to add the plane, and the + changes to − meaning that you have now added the **Edit** Trim plane, and are ready to make the edit. Grip the node, make the changes shown in (Figure 12–44), and then press the **Esc** key on your keyboard to complete the command.

Figure 12– 44

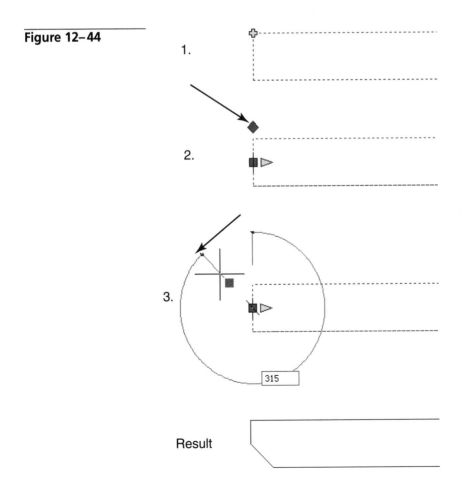

Result

14. Select the beam again, **RMB,** and again and this time move your cursor over the **Properties** palette to open it.

15. At the very bottom of the **Properties** palette, under **ADVANCED,** click on **(1)** in the trim planes field to open the **Beam Trim Planes** dialog box.

16. In the **Beam Trim Planes** dialog box, enter 6″ in the X column, and press the **OK** button.

The trim plane can be controlled directly from the beam or through the **Beam Trim Planes** dialog box (see Figure 12–45).

Figure 12–45

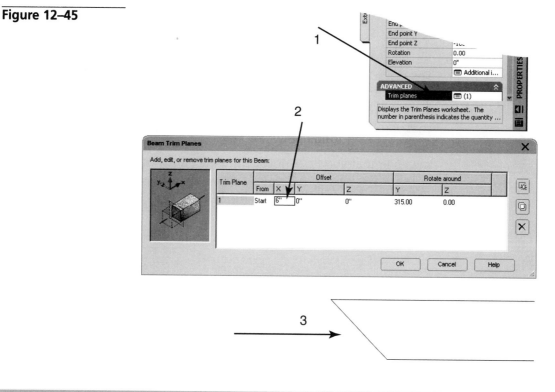

Hands-On

Framing Floors and Roofs Using Slabs and Structural Members

1. Start a new drawing using the Aec Model (Imperial Stb) template.

2. Select **Format > Structural members > Catalog** from the **Main** menu to bring up the **Structural Member Catalog** dialog box.

3. In the **Structural Member Catalog** dialog box, expand **Timber** and then expand **Plywood Web Wood Joists.**

4. In the right pane of the **Structural Member Catalog** dialog box, double-click on **10in Plywood Web Wood Joist** to bring up the **Structural Member Style dialog box.**

5. Press the **OK** button to return to the right pane of the **Structural Member Catalog** dialog box. Close the **Structural Member Catalog.**

6. Change to the **Top** view, select the **Wall** tool from the **Design** tool palette, and using a **9′-0″** high **Standard** wall; place a **10′ × 20′** enclosure.

Creating the floor and floor framing

7. Select the **Space Auto Generate Tool** from the **Design** tool palette, and place a **Standard** space in the enclosure.

8. Double-click the space you just created to open the **Properties** palette.

9. In the **Properties** palette, set the **Space height** to **10-1/4"**, **Floor boundary thickness** to **1/2"**, **Ceiling boundary thickness** to **3/4"**, and **Elevation to 1/2"**.

10. Select the **Slab** tool from the **Design** tool palette, **RMB**, and select **Apply Tool Properties to > Space** from the contextual menu that appears.

11. Click on the space object you just created and adjusted, and press the **Enter** key on your keyboard to bring up the **Convert Space to Slab** dialog box.

12. In the **Convert Space to Slab** dialog box, check all the check boxes, and press the **OK** button to return to the Drawing Editor. The space object has been changed to slabs.

13. Change to the **SW Isometric** view to see the slabs you created.

14. Select the **Structural Beam** tool from the **Design** tool palette, and move your cursor over the **Properties** palette to open it.

15. In the **Properties** palette, set **Style** to **10in Plywood Web Wood Joist**, **Layout Type** to **Edge**, and **Justify** to **Top Left.**

16. Select the top slab that you created on the left edge, and then on the right edge (see Figure 12–46).

Figure 12–46

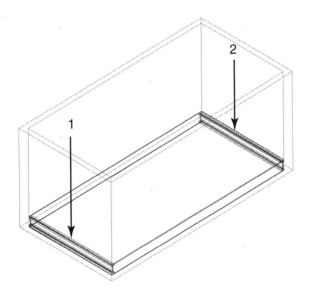

17. After placing the two end joists, again move your cursor over the **Properties** palette to open it.

18. In the **Properties** palette, set **Layout type** to **Fill**, **Array** to **Yes**, **Layout method** to **Repeat**, and **Bay side** to **2'-0".**

19. Click on the side edge of the top floor slab you created to place the remaining joists (see Figure 12–47).

Figure 12–47

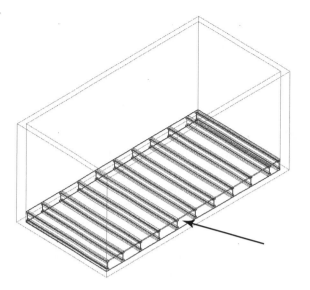

Creating the roof and roof framing

20.   Select the **Roof** tool from the **Design** tool palette, **RMB,** and select **Apply Tool Properties to > Linework and Walls** from the contextual menu that appears.

21.   Select all the walls; press the **Enter** key on your keyboard.

22.   Press the **Enter** key on your keyboard again to not erase layout geometry.

A room appears on the enclosure. Press the **Esc** key to complete the command, and deselect the new roof (see Figure 12–48).

Figure 12–48

23.   Change to the **Top** view.

24.   Move the vertices as shown in (Figure 12–49) to create the roof shown in (Figure 12–50).

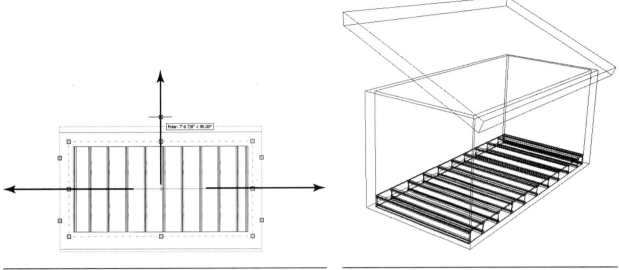

Figure 12–49

Figure 12–50

25. Select the three walls shown in Figure 12–51, **RMB,** and select **Roof/Floor Line** > **Modify Roof Line** from the contextual menus that appear.

26. Enter **A** (Auto project) in the **Command line,** and press the **Enter** key twice.

27. Select the roof slab, and press the **Enter** key.

The walls now project to the underside of the slab (Figure 12–52).

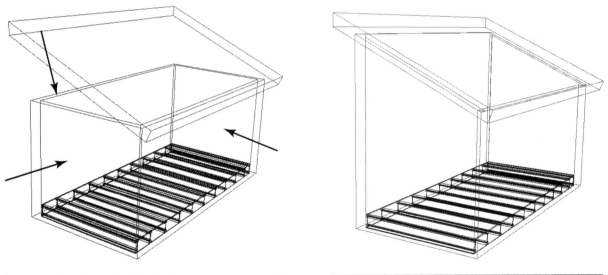

Figure 12–51

Figure 12–52

28. Select the roof, **RMB,** and select **Convert to Roof Slabs** from the contextual menu that appears.

29. The **Convert to Roof Slabs** dialog box will appear, check the **Erase Layout Geometry** check box, and then press the **OK** button to return to the Drawing Editor.

30. With the new roof slab still selected, move your cursor over the **Properties** palette to open it.

31. In the **Properties** palette, set **Thickness** to **3/4″** and **Elevation** to **9′-11″**.

32. Select the **Face UCS** from the **UCS** toolbar, and move your cursor over the roof slab until a red hatch appears (Figure 12–53).

Figure 12–53

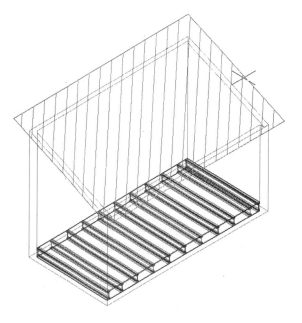

33. Click the lower-right corner of the slab as the UCS origin, and press the **Enter** key to complete the command.

You have now set the UCS so that the roof trusses will be perpendicular to the roof slab you created.

34. Again, select the **Structural Beam** tool from the **Design** tool palette, and move your cursor over the **Properties** palette to open it.

35. In the **Properties** palette, set **Layout type** to **Fill, Array** to **Yes, Layout method** to **Repeat**, and **Bay side** to **2′-0″**.

36. Click on the left edge of the roof slab to place the joists, and then press the **Esc** key to complete the command (Figure 12–54).

Figure 12–54

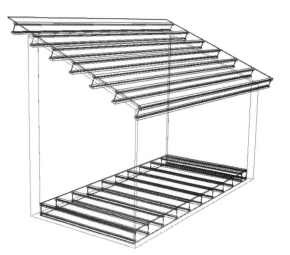

Hands-On

Creating a Custom Structural Member from Linework, and Applying a Miter

1. Start a new drawing using the Aec Model (Imperial Stb) template.
2. Select **Format > Structural members > Catalog** from the **Main** menu to bring up the **Structural Member Catalog** dialog box.
3. In the **Structural Member Catalog** dialog box, expand **Steel,** expand **AISC,** expand **I Shaped** and, then, **HP Bearing Piles.**
4. In the right pane of the **Structural Member Catalog** dialog box, double-click on **HP14 × 117** to bring up the **Structural Member Style dialog box.**
5. Press the **OK** button to return to the right pane of the **Structural Member Catalog** dialog box.
6. Select the line command from the **Draw** menu and create the drawing shown in (Figure 12–55).

Figure 12–55

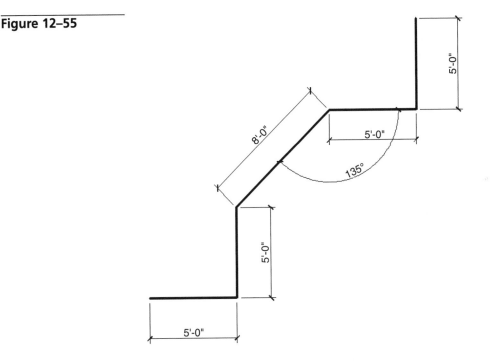

7. Select the **Structural Column tool** from the **Design** tool palette, **RMB,** and select **Apply Tool Properties to** from the contextual menu that appears.
8. The **Convert to Column** dialog box appears; check the **Erase Layout Geometry** check box, and press the **OK** button. The line drawing turns into structural members.
9. Select all the structural members, and move your cursor over the **Properties** palette to open it.
10. In the **Properties** palette, set the **Style** to **HP14 × 117** (see Figure 12–56).

Figure 12–56

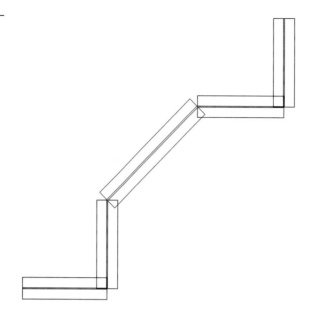

11. Select the top member, **RMB,** and select **Miter** from the contextual menu that appears.

12. Select the next member to miter the first to the second.

13. Press the **Enter** key on your keyboard to repeat the **Miter** command, and select the next member.

14. Continue pressing the **Enter** key and selecting members until you have converted all the linework.

15. Change to the **SW Isometric** view, and press the **Flat Shaded, Edges On** icon in the **Shading** menu (see Figure 12–57).

! ***Note:*** The Miter will not work with arc lines that have been converted to structural members.

Figure 12–57

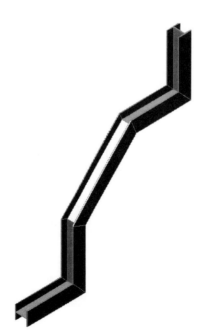

13

AEC Dimensions

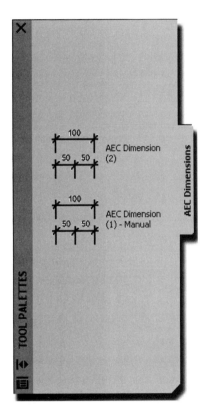

When you finish this section, you should understand the following:

- ✔ How to set the text style.
- ✔ How to create a **Dimension Style.**
- ✔ How to create an **AEC Dimension Style.**
- ✔ How to use and modify an **AEC Dimension Style.**
- ✔ How to dimension doors and windows with **AEC Dimension Styles.**
- ✔ How to add a manual AEC Dimension.
- ✔ How to detach objects from AEC Dimensions.
- ✔ **AEC Dimension Chains.**
- ✔ **The Dimension Wizard**

AEC Dimensions

AEC dimensions are automatic dimensions based on styles. Because there are so many variables in the dimension system, there are many dialog boxes. To make it easier, the developers have also added a Wizard to aid in variable setup.

Standard AutoCAD dimensions can be converted into AEC dimensions, and AEC dimensions can be mixed with the manual AEC and standard AutoCAD dimensioning systems.

AEC dimensions can dimension only AEC objects such as walls, windows, stairs, structural members, and so on. If you add non-AEC objects to AEC objects, you have to add manual dimension points to the automatic AEC dimension or create manual AEC or standard AutoCAD dimensions.

The following table describes the difference between the three available dimensioning systems.

AutoCAD Dimensions	Manual AEC Dimensions	AutoCAD dimension style
Logical dimension points taken from object	Manual dimension points taken from drawing	Manual dimension points taken from drawing
Dimension AEC objects	Dimension picked points in drawing	Dimension picked points in drawing
Associative toward building elements	Associative or nonassociative toward points, depending on user settings	Associative toward points
Dimension groups	Dimension groups	Single dimensions
Support superscripting, variable-extension line length	Support superscripting, variable-extension line length	Supports no superscripting, variable-extension line length
Dimension texts cannot be edited	Dimension texts cannot be edited	Dimension texts can be edited
Defined by AEC dimension style and AutoCAD dimension style	Defined by AEC dimension style and Auto CAD dimension style	Defined by AutoCAD dimension style

Tip

Because the AEC dimensions are based on AutoCAD's standard dimensioning variables, it is imperative that you have a good understanding of that system and its operation. This includes an understanding of the relationship between dimensioning and Model - Paperspace. This book assumes that understanding.

Hands-On

Setting the Text Style

Before setting the dimension styles, change the **Standard** text style.

1. Start a new drawing using the Aec Model (Imperial Stb) template.
2. Select **Format > Text Style** from the **Main** toolbar to bring up the **Text Style** dialog box.
3. Select the **New** button and create a new style name called **NEW Text.**
4. Set the **NEW Text** font to **Stylus BT** in the **Font Name** drop-down list, apply, and close (see Figure 13–1).

You have now created a Text style that you can use with AutoCAD Dimensions and Architectural Desktop AEC dimensions. Save this file.

Figure 13–1

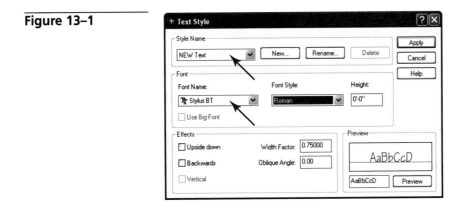

Hands-On

Creating a Dimension Style

1. Select **Format** > **Dimension Style** from the **Main** toolbar to bring up the **Dimension Style Manager** dialog box.
2. Press the **New** button to bring up the **Create New Dimension Style** dialog box.
3. Set the following:

   a. New Style Name = **(Put your name here)**
   b. Start With = **Standard**
   c. Use for = **All dimensions**

4. Press the **Continue** button to bring up the **New Dimension Style** dialog box.
5. Select the **Text** tab.
6. Set the following:

   a. Text style = **NEW Text**
   b. Text height = **1/8″**
   c. Text Placement Vertical = **Above**
   d. Text Placement Horizontal = **Centered**
   e. Text Alignment = **Aligned with dimension line**

7. Change to the **Lines** tab.
8. Set the following:

   a. Extend beyond dim lines = **1/16″**
   b. Offset from origin = **1/16″**

9. Change to the **Symbols and Arrows** tab, and set the following:

   a. Arrowheads 1st = **Architectural tick**
   b. Arrowheads 2nd = **Architectural tick**
   c. Leader = **Closed filled**
   d. Arrow size = **1/16″**

10. Change to the **Fit** tab, and set **Use overall scale of:** to **48.0.**
11. Change to the **Primary Units** tab, and set the **Unit** format to **Architectural.**
12. Press **Set Current,** and then press **OK** to close the dialog boxes and return to the Drawing Editor.

You have now set the AutoCAD dimension style for **NEW DIMENSION STYLE** dimensions.

Hands-On

Creating an AEC Dimension Style

1. Select **Format > AEC Dimension Styles** from the **Main** toolbar.
2. At the **Style Manager** dialog box, select the **New Style** icon in the top toolbar, and rename the new style **(STUDENT's Name)** (see Figure 13–2).

Figure 13–2

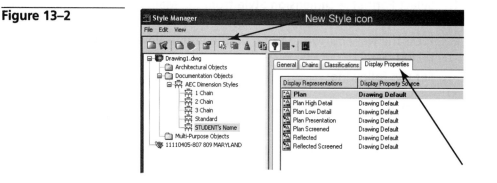

3. Select **(STUDENT's Name),** and select the **Display Properties** tab.
4. Double-click on **Plan** in the **Display Representations** column to bring up the **Display Properties** dialog box.
5. Select the **Contents** tab.
6. Select **Wall** from **Apply to,** check the **Length of Wall** check box, check the **Chain 1** check box, and select **Wall Length** from the **Length of Wall** drop-down list (see Figure 13–3).

Figure 13–3

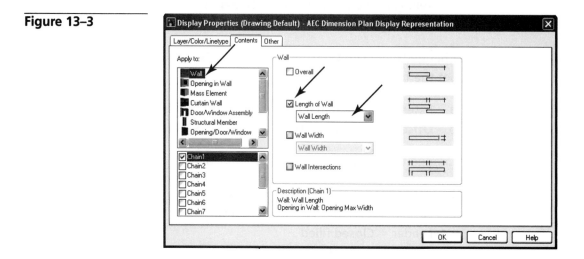

7. Select the **Other** tab, and select **(STUDENT's Name)**, at the **Dimension Style** drop-down list. Make sure the check boxes are unchecked, and then press the **OK** buttons to return to the Drawing Editor.

You have now created an AEC dimension style called **(STUDENT's Name).** Save this file.

Hands-On

Using and Modifying an AEC Dimension Style

1. Use the previous exercise.
2. Change to the **Work Layout.**
3. Clear the viewports and create one viewport.
4. Change to the **Top View.**
5. Change to **Paper space,** select the viewport frame, and move your cursor over the **Properties** palette to open it.
6. Set the following:

   a. Standard scale = **1/4" = 1'-0"**

7. Change to **Model** space.
8. Select the **Wall** icon from the **Design** tool palette, and move your cursor over the **Properties** palette to open it.
9. Set the following settings:

   a. Style = **Standard**
   b. Width = **6"**
   c. Justify = **Left**

10. Create the walls shown in Figure 13–4. Don't include the dimensions shown.

Figure 13–4

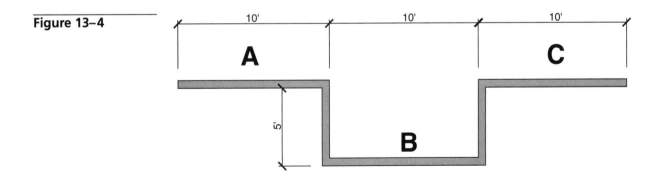

11. Select all wall segments, **RMB,** and select **AEC Dimension** from the contextual menu that appears.
12. Move your cursor over the **Properties** palette to open it.
13. Set the **Style** to **(STUDENT's Name)** from the **Style** drop-down list.

14. Drag your cursor above the walls, and click to place dimensions for the walls.

15. Select the dimension string you just placed, **RMB,** and select **Remove Dimension Points** from the contextual menu that appears.

16. Select the dimension extension lines that you want removed, and they will turn red (see Figure 13–5).

Figure 13–5

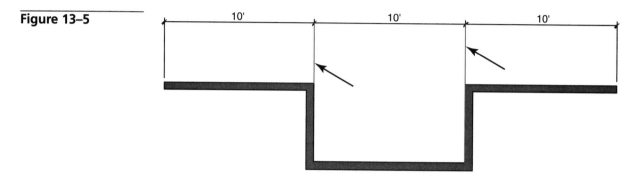

17. Press **Enter.** The extension lines will disappear, and the dimension string will show the total width between walls (see Figure 13–6).

Figure 13–6

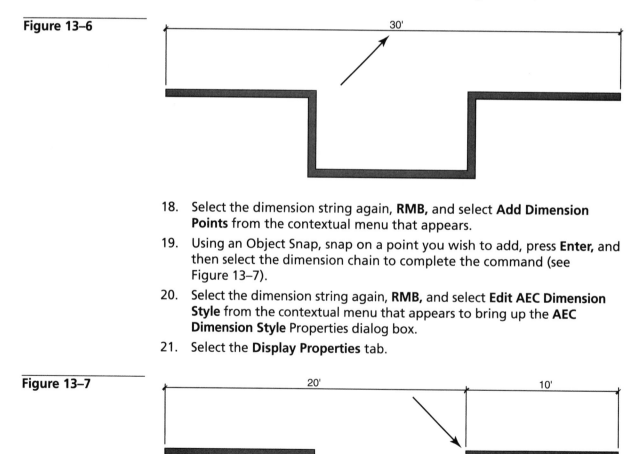

18. Select the dimension string again, **RMB,** and select **Add Dimension Points** from the contextual menu that appears.

19. Using an Object Snap, snap on a point you wish to add, press **Enter,** and then select the dimension chain to complete the command (see Figure 13–7).

20. Select the dimension string again, **RMB,** and select **Edit AEC Dimension Style** from the contextual menu that appears to bring up the **AEC Dimension Style** Properties dialog box.

21. Select the **Display Properties** tab.

Figure 13–7

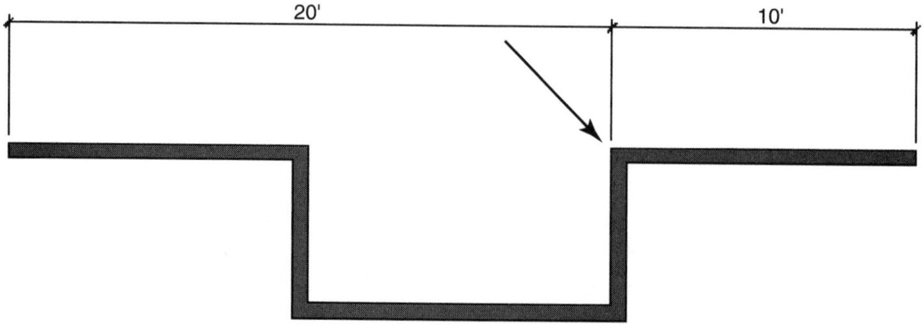

22. Double-click on **Plan** in the **Display Representations** column to bring up the **Display Properties** dialog box, and select the **Contents** tab.
23. Check the **Wall Intersections** check box, and press the **OK** buttons to close the dialog boxes and return to the Drawing Editor.

The AEC dimension string now shows the wall intersections (see Figure 13–8). Save this file.

Figure 13–8

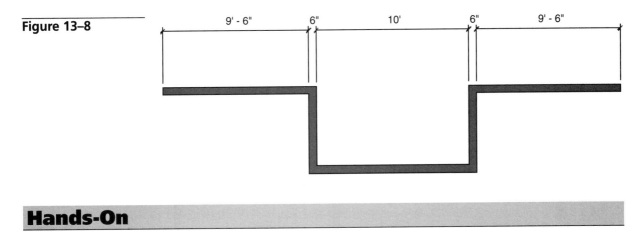

Hands-On

Dimensioning Doors and Windows with AEC Dimension Styles

1. Start a new drawing using the Aec Model (Imperial Stb) template.
2. Select **Format > AEC Dimension Styles** from the **Main** toolbar again to bring up the **Style Manager.**
3. Double-click on **(STUDENT's Name)** to bring up the **AEC Dimension Style Properties** dialog box.
4. Select the **Display Properties** tab.
5. Double-click on **Plan** in the **Display Representations** column to bring up the **Display Properties** dialog box.
6. Select the **Contents** tab, and select **Opening/Door/Window** from the **Apply to** list.
7. Check the **Center** check box, and clear the other check boxes (see Figure 13–9).

Figure 13–9

Display Properties (Drawing Default) - AEC Dimension Plan Presentation Display Representation

Layer/Color/Linetype | Contents | Other

Apply to:

Opening in Wall
Mass Element
Curtain Wall
Door/Window Assembly
Structural Member
Opening/Door/Window
Grid

Opening/Door/Window

☐ Overall

☐ Bounding Box

☐ Edges
All Edges

☑ Center

☑ Chain1
☐ Chain2
☐ Chain3
☐ Chain4
☐ Chain5
☐ Chain6
☐ Chain7

Description (Chain 1)
Wall: Wall Length + Wall Intersections
Opening in Wall: Opening Max Width

OK   Cancel   Help

8. Select **Opening in Wall** from the **Apply to** list.

9. Check the **Center** check box, and clear the other check boxes.

10. Select the wall, **RMB,** and select **Insert > Window** from the contextual menu that appears.

11. In the **Properties** tool palette make sure to check the **Automatic Offset/Center** check box, and insert a Standard 3'-wide, 5'-high window in the center of the wall.

12. Select all the walls, **RMB,** and select **AEC Dimension** from the contextual menu that appears.

13. Drag your cursor vertically above the horizontal walls, and click the mouse to place the dimension string.

The window will now be dimensioned by its center (see Figure 13–10).

Figure 13–10

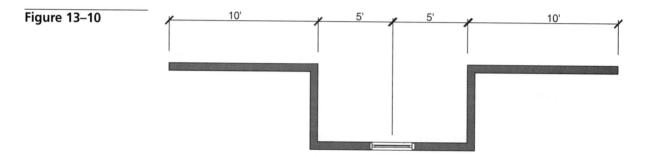

14. Select the dimension string again, **RMB,** and select **Edit AEC Dimension Style** from the contextual menu that appears to bring up the **AEC Dimensional Style Properties** dialog box.

15. Select the **Display Properties** tab.

16. Double-click on **Plan** in the **Display Representations** column to bring up the **Display Properties** dialog box.

17. Select the **Contents** tab, and select **Opening/Door/Window** from the **Apply to** list

18. Check the **Center** check box, and clear the other check boxes (see Figure 13–11).

Figure 13–11

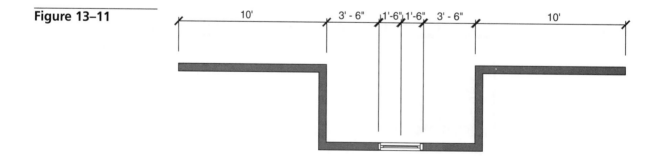

If there is some problem where dimension text overlaps, or if you want to modify the location of the text, you must do the following:

You can display and move the **Edit in Place** grips of an AEC dimension text only if the underlying AutoCAD dimension style has the correct text placement settings. To do this, select the AEC dimension string, **RMB,** and select **Edit AEC Dimension Style** from the contextual menu that appears. Then, select the display representation where you want the changes to appear, and check the **Style Override** check box to bring up the **Display Properties** dialog box. Click **Edit,** and in the **Dimension Style Manager,** click **Modify.** Click the **Fit** tab, and select **Over the dimension line, without a leader** for **Text Placement** (see Figure 13–12).

Figure 13–12

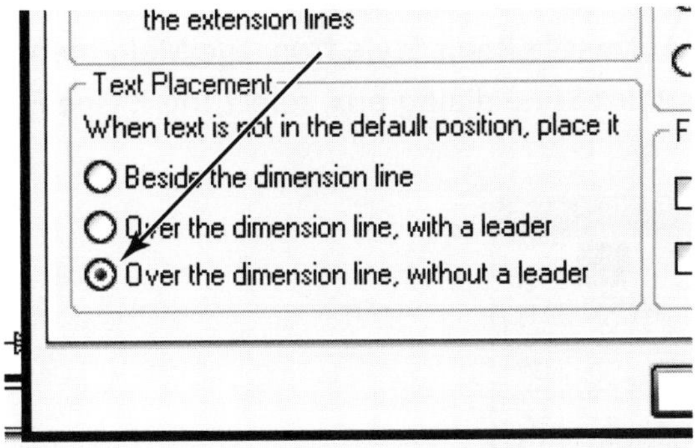

the extension lines

Text Placement
When text is not in the default position, place it
○ Beside the dimension line
○ Over the dimension line, with a leader
◉ Over the dimension line, without a leader

Now when you select the **Edit in Place** button for the AEC dimensions, a grip will appear on the dimension itself. You can grab that grip and move the dimension text anywhere you wish.

19. Move the window **24'-0"** to the left. (Use the move command, or activate the window's grips.)

Note that the AEC dimensions move with the window.

20. Select wall **B, RMB,** and again select **Insert > Window** from the contextual menu that appears.
21. Move your cursor over the **Properties** palette to open it.
22. Set the **Automatic Offset/Center** to **18",** and pick a spot near the right side of wall B.

You should now have two windows centered in wall B, and the AEC dimensions should show the dimensions for the new window (see Figure 13–13).
Explore the other Display Props for dimension styles. Save this exercise. Sometimes you will want to create an AEC dimension manually. Perhaps you will want to dimension somewhere else than the built-in logical points.
Save this file.

Figure 13–13

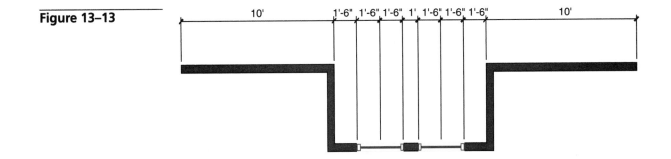

Hands-On

Adding a Manual AEC Dimension

1. Use the previous exercise.
2. Lock your viewport.
3. Be sure the **MODEL** space button is activated.
4. Zoom in close to the two windows inserted in the B wall.
5. Select **Format > Point Style** from the **Main** menu.
6. In the **Point Style** dialog box, select the **X** (see Figure 13–14).

Figure 13–14

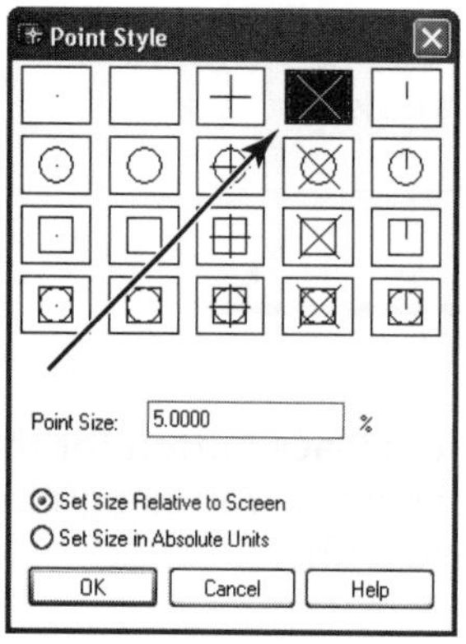

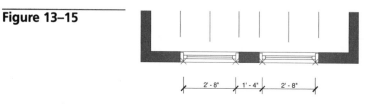

7. Type **dimpointmode** in the **Command line,** and press the space bar or **Enter.**
8. Type **T** in the **Command line,** and press the space bar or **Enter.**

This sets the dimension points to transformable. Transformable dimension points move and are updated with the object; static points stay in place.

9. Set the **Intersection** Object Snap.
10. Select the **AEC Dimension (1)-Manual** icon from the **Annotation** tool palette.
11. Pick the two corners of the two window jambs, and press the space bar or **Enter.**
12. Pick a point to place the dimension string, and then pick a second point to complete the command (see Figure 13–15).

Figure 13–15

2' - 8"   1' - 4"   2' - 8"

13. Select the **Move** icon from the **Modify** toolbar, and select the left window with a window marquee (see Figure 13–16), and move it to the left 1'-0". Repeat with the right window (see Figure 13–17).

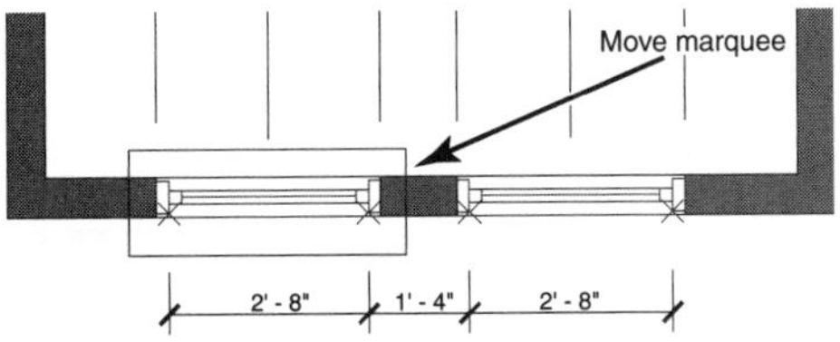

Figure 13–16

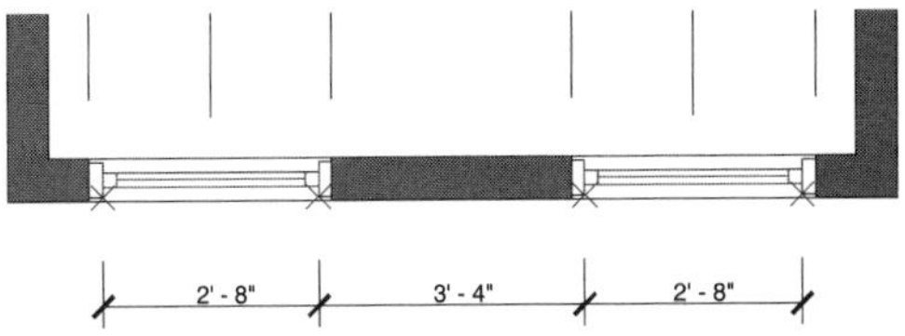

Figure 13–17

You must move the points with the window to maintain the associative dimensions. Repeat Steps 7 through 12, but enter **S** (Static) when prompted for dimpointmode points. Note that the dimensions don't move.

14. The point style you set in Step 6 will cause the points to show as X when you plot. To stop this, bring up the **Point Style** dialog box again, and change the point style to **NONE** (see Figure 13–18). Save this file.

Figure 13–18

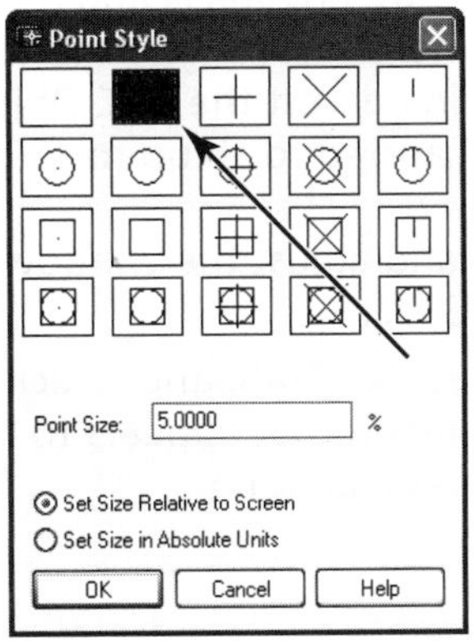

Hands-On

Detaching Objects from AEC Dimensions

1. Use the previous exercise.
2. Zoom Extents (because the viewport is locked, the **Paperspace View** will zoom extents).
3. Select the AEC dimension string, **RMB,** and select **Detach Objects** icon from the contextual menu that appears.
4. Select the top AEC dimension group (dimension string), and press the space bar or **Enter.**
5. Select the left window object, and press the space bar or **Enter** (see Figure 13–19).

You have now detached the left window from the top AEC Dimension Group. Save this file.

Figure 13–19

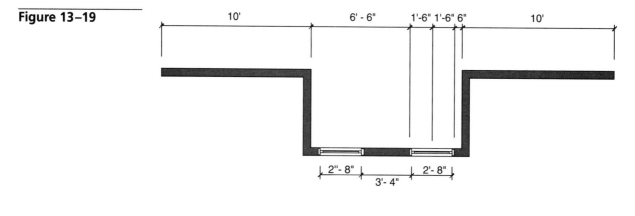

Hands-On

AEC Dimension Chains

In order to clarify dimension strings, architects and architectural drafts-people often add additional dimension strings. Architectural Desktop 2006 calls these *chains.* The chain nearest the AEC Object is called "Chain1," the next is "Chain2," and so forth up to 10 chains.

1. Use the previous exercise, and adjust the windows and AEC dimension settings to match Figure 13–20.

2. Select the AEC dimension string, **RMB,** and select **Edit AEC Dimension Style** from the contextual menu that appears to bring up the **AEC Dimensional Style Properties** dialog box.

Figure 13–20

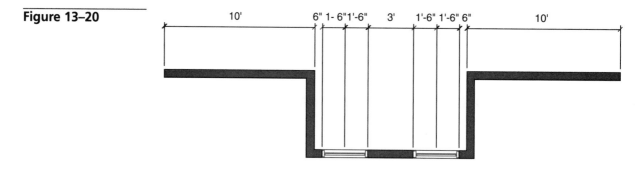

3. Select the **Chains** tab.
4. Change the **Number of Chains** to **2.**
5. Change to the **Display Properties** tab.
6. Double-click on **Plan** in the **Display Representations** column to bring up the **Display Properties** dialog box.
7. Select the **Contents** tab.

Notice that two **Chain** check boxes now appear at the lower right of the **Contents** tab (see Figure 13–21).

8. Activate the **Chain1** field, select the **Wall** icon in the **Apply to** field, and clear all the **Wall** check boxes.

Figure 13–21

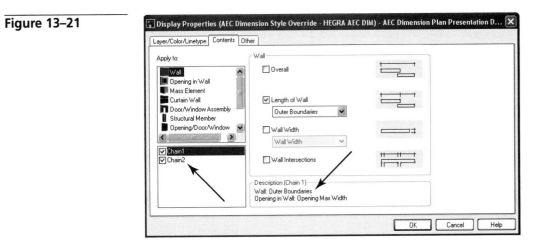

9. Select the **Opening/Door/Window** icon in the **Apply to** field, and check the **Opening/Door/Window Center** check box.

10. Activate the **Chain2** field, select the **Wall** icon in the **Apply to** field, and check the **Length of Wall** check box.

11. Press the **OK** buttons to return to the Drawing Editor (see Figure 13–22).

Figure 13–22

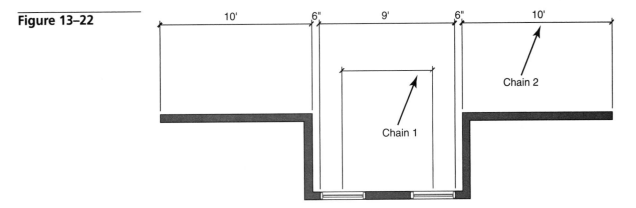

12. Select the AEC dimension string, **RMB,** and select **Add Dimension Points** and add a point to locate the windows.

13. Repeat Step 12, selecting **Remove Dimension points,** and remove the two **Chain2** dimension extension lines to create the image shown in Figure 13–23.

Figure 13–23

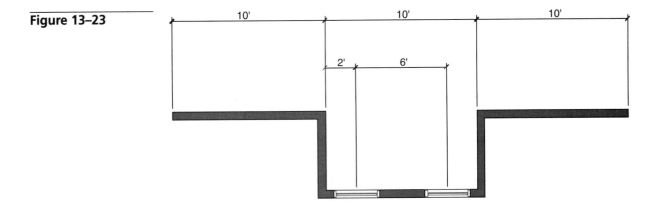

Hands-On

The AEC Dimension Wizard

Although you can set the AEC Dimension display manually as shown at the beginning of this section, Autodesk Architectural Desktop 2006 has provided a Wizard to aid you in setting the display.

Selecting the **Format** > **AEC Dimension Style Wizard** from the **Main** toolbar activates the dialog boxes shown in Figures 13–24 through 13–27.

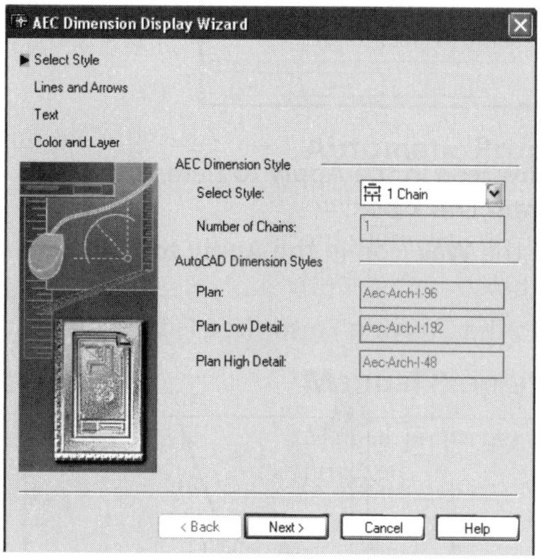

Figure 13–24

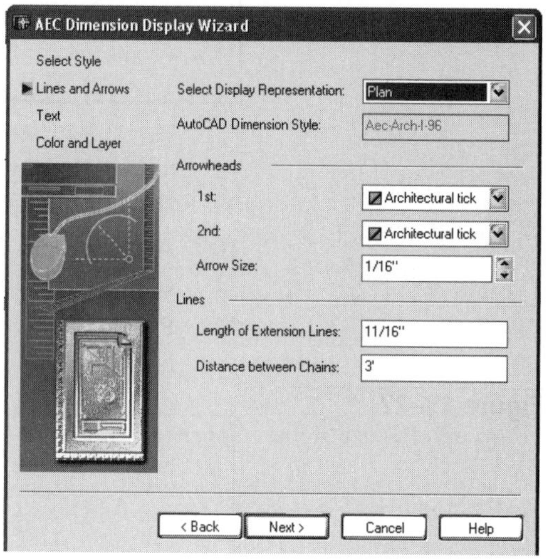

Figure 13–25

Figure 13–26

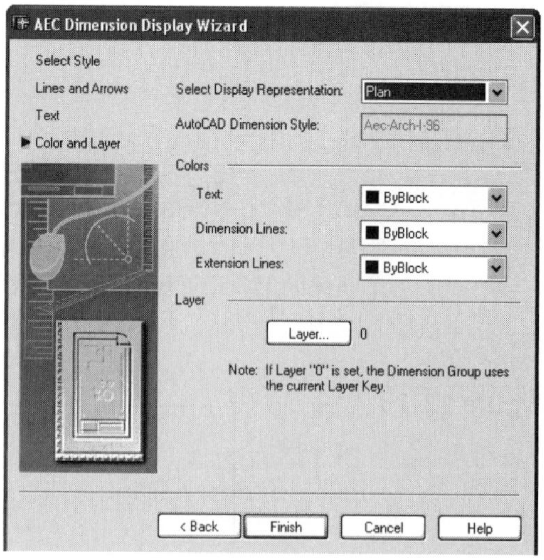

Figure 13–27

Section

14

Elevations

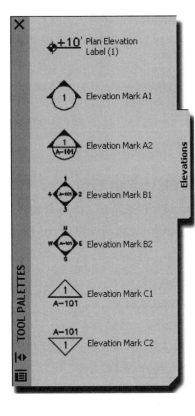

When you finish this section, you should understand the following:

- ✔ How to make a new **Elevations** tool palette.
- ✔ How to create a simple building.
- ✔ How to make an **Elevation.**
- ✔ How to modify and update a **2D Elevation.**
- ✔ How to understand elevation subdivisions work.
- ✔ How to work with **Material Boundaries.**

Hands-On

Making a New Elevation Tool Palette

1.   Create a new tool palette and name it **Elevations.**
2.   Select the **Content Browser** icon from the **Main** toolbar to launch the Content Browser.
3.   Locate the **Documentation Tool Catalog - Imperial.**
4.   Locate the **Callouts > Elevation Marks** folder.
5.   Drag all the elevation marks into the new tool palette you created.
6.   Click and hold on the tab of your new tool palette and drag a copy to **My Tool Catalog** in the Content Browser.

For the following exploration of elevations, first create a simple three-story building.

Hands-On

Creating a Sample Building for the Elevation Exercises

1.   Start a new drawing using the Aec Model (Imperial Stb) template.
2.   Change to **Top View,** and create the outline shown in Figure 14–1.

Figure 14–1

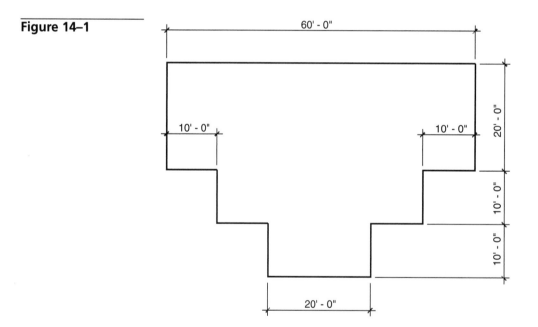

3.   Select the **Wall** icon from the **Design** tool palette, **RMB,** and select **Apply Tool properties to > Linework** from the contextual menu that appears.
4.   Select the outline you created.
5.   Enter **Y** (Yes) in the command line to erase the geometry, and press **Enter** to create walls from the outline.
6.   While the walls are still selected, move your cursor over the **Properties** palette to open it.

7. Set the following:

    a. Style = **Standard**
    b. Wall Width = **8″**
    c. Base Height = **10′-0″**
    d. Justify = **Baseline**

8. Save the drawing as **Floor 1.**
9. Save the drawing two more times as **Floor 2** and **Floor 3.**
10. Open **Floor 3,** select the **Roof** icon from the **Design** tool palette, **RMB,** and select **Apply Tool Properties to** > **Linework and Walls** from the contextual menu that appears.
11. Select all the walls in the **Floor 3** drawing.
12. Enter **N** (No) in the **Command line,** and press **Enter** to create the roof.
13. While the roof is still selected, move your cursor over the **Properties** palette to open it.
14. Set the roof to the following:

    a. Thickness = **10″**
    b. Edge cut = **Square**
    c. Shape = **SingleSlope**
    d. Plate height = **10′-0″**
    e. Rise = **6″**

15. Save **Floor 3.**
16. Start a new drawing and save it as **Composite.**
17. Using **Insert** > **Xref Manager** from the **Main** toolbar, **Attach** the three floors at Z elevation of 0′ for Floor 1, 10′ for Floor 2, and 20′ for Floor 3 in the Composite drawing.

You have now created the building in Figure 14–2.

Figure 14–2

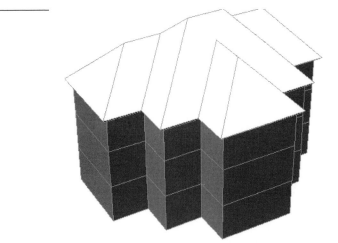

18. Select **Floor 1** in the **Composite** drawing, **RMB,** and select **Edit Xref in place** from the contextual menu that appears to bring up the **Reference Edit** dialog box.

19. Press **OK** to return to the Drawing Editor.

20. Select different walls in the floor, **RMB,** and insert windows and a door.

21. Press the **Save back changes to reference** icon in the **Refedit** dialog box, and press the **OK** button that appears.

22. Repeat for each floor until you have a building similar to that shown in Figure 14–3. Save this exercise.

Figure 14–3

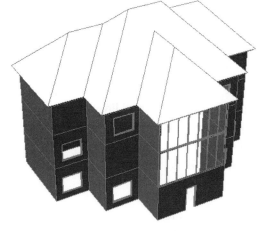

Hands-On

Making an Elevation

Using the previous exercise, select the Composite drawing.

1. Select the **Model Layout**, activate the **Top View,** and then pan the building to the left until it takes up a little less than half the page. Change the scale to **1/8″ = 1′-0″** in the **Scale** pop-up list (see Figure 14–4).

Figure 14–4

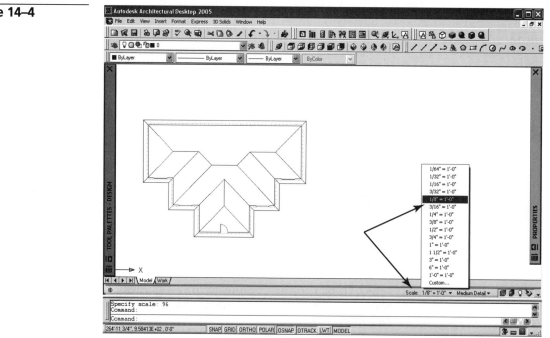

2. Select the **Elevation Mark A1** from the **Elevations** tool palette, and click and place an elevation line starting at the lower center in front of the building. Drag your cursor as shown in Figure 14–5.

3. Click your mouse again to bring up the **Place Callout** dialog box.

4. Check the **Generate Section/Elevation** check box. Make sure the scale is set to the same scale you set in the **Scale** pop-up list, and press the **Current Drawing** icon (see Figure 14–6).

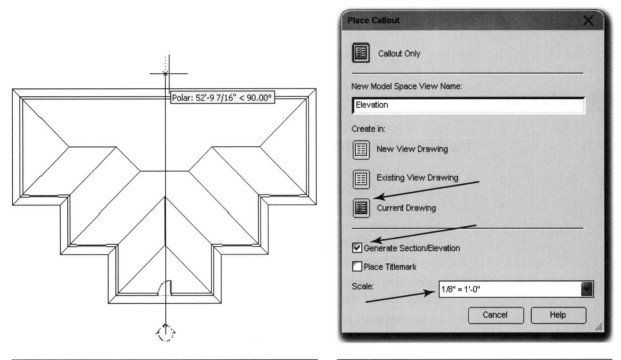

Figure 14–5   **Figure 14–6**

5. Select the region of the elevation you wish to generate (see Figure 14–7).

6. Move your cursor to an insertion point for your generated elevation, and click the mouse button. Your elevation will now appear (see Figure 14–8). Save this exercise.

Figure 14–7

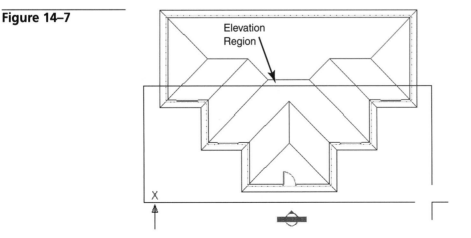

Figure 14–8

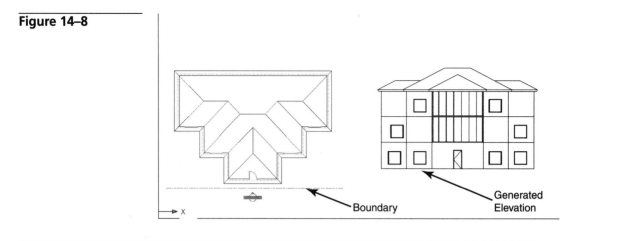

Boundary

Generated
Elevation

Hands-On

Modifying and Updating the 2D Elevation

1. Open the **Composite** drawing from the previous exercise.
2. Change to the **SW Isometric View.**
3. Select the first floor in the Composite drawing, **RMB,** and select **Edit Xref in place** from the contextual menu that appears to bring up the **Reference Edit** dialog box.
4. Press **OK** to return to the Drawing Editor.
5. Select the front wall of the first floor, **RMB,** and insert windows on either side of the front door.
6. In the **Refedit** dialog box, press the **Save back changes to reference** icon button, and press **OK** at the AutoCAD message.
7. Change back to the **Top View,** and select the 2D elevation that you created.
8. **RMB** the 2D elevation, and select **Refresh** from the contextual menu that appears.

The 2D elevation now reflects the changes made in the 3D model (see Figure 14–9). Save this exercise.

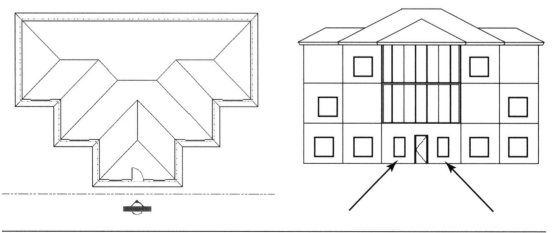

Figure 14–9

Hands-On

Understanding Subdivisions

1. Using the previous exercise, select the elevation line object to open the **Properties** palette.
2. Click in the **Subdivisions** field to open the **Subdivisions** dialog box.
3. Press the **Add** button, add a 10'-0" subdivision, and press **OK** to return to the Drawing Editor.

You have now created Subdivision 1 (see Figure 14–10).

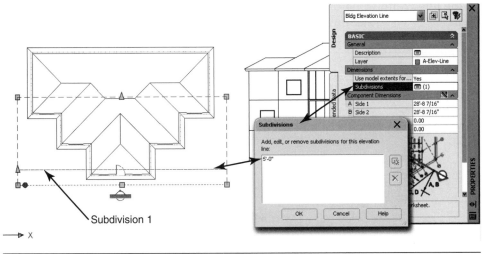

Subdivision 1

Figure 14–10

> **Note:** Once you have a subdivision, you can select the elevation and move the subdivision with grips.

4. Move the Subdivision 1 line so that the front extension of the building is within the first subdivision (see Figure 14–11).

Figure 14–11

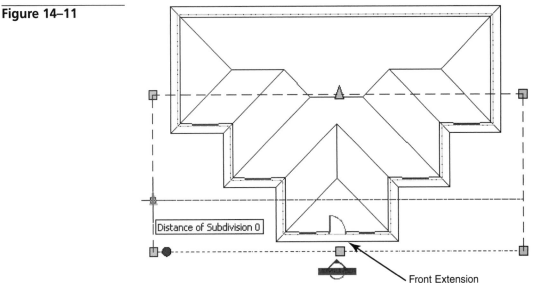

Distance of Subdivision 0

Front Extension

5.   Select the 2D elevation, **RMB,** and select **Edit Object Display** from the contextual menu that appears to bring up the **Object Display** dialog box.

6.   Select the **Display Properties** tab, and check the **Override** check box to bring up the **Display Properties** dialog box.

7.   Select the **Layer/Color/Linetype** tab.

8.   Change the Subdivision 1 **Color** to **blue,** select **OK,** and close all the dialog boxes.

9.   Select the elevation, **RMB,** and select **Refresh** from the contextual menu.

You have now changed Subdivision 1 to a blue color. Anything between the defining line and Subdivision 1 will be blue in the elevation. You can also set the line width to be different in a subdivision (see Figure 14–12).

Figure 14–12

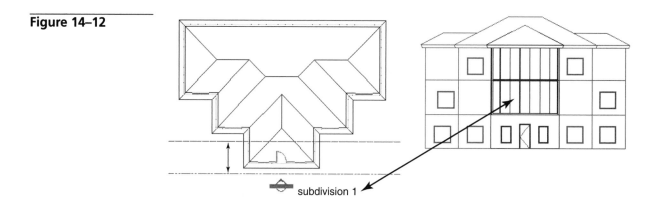

subdivision 1

10.   Select the elevation line object, **RMB,** and add two more subdivisions.

11.   In the **Top View,** move the topmost boundary to the back of the building.

12.   Select the elevation, **RMB,** and again select **Edit 2D Section/Elevation Style** from the contextual menu that appears.

13.   Change the Subdivision 2 **Color** to **green,** and Subdivision 3 **Color** to **black** (black will say "white" in the dialog box). Change the **Lineweight** of Subdivision 3 to **.30 mm,** select **OK,** close all the dialog boxes, and return to the Drawing Editor (see Figure 14–13).

14.   Select the elevation line to activate it, and using the grips (be sure your Object Snap is turned off) move the subdivisions to look like Figure 14–14.

15.   Select the elevation, **RMB,** and select **Refresh** from the contextual menu that appears. Make sure the **LTW** button at the bottom of the screen is active (to visually show lineweights in the drawing).

Display Properties (2D Section/Elevation Override) - 2D Section/Elevation General Display Representation

Layer/Color/Linetype | Hatching | Other

Display Com...	Visible	By Ma...	Layer	Color	Linetype	Linewei...	Lt Scale	Plot Style
Defining Line			0	9	ByBlock	ByBlock	1.0000	ByBlock
Outer Shrinkwrap			0	9	ByBlock	ByBlock	1.0000	ByBlock
Inner Shrinkwrap			0	9	ByBlock	ByBlock	1.0000	ByBlock
Shrinkwrap Hatch			0	9	ByBlock	ByBlock	1.0000	ByBlock
Surface Hatch Lir			0	9	ByBlock	ByBlock	1.0000	ByBlock
Section Hatch Lin			0	9	ByBlock	ByBlock	1.0000	ByBlock
Hidden			A-Sect-Hide	9	ByLayer	ByLayer	1.0000	ByLayer
Erased			G-Anno-Nplt	9	ByBlock	0.18 mm	1.0000	Normal
Unknown Compor			G-Anno-Nplt	9	ByBlock	0.18 mm	1.0000	Normal
Subdivision 1			A-Sect-Thin	blue	ByLayer	ByLayer	1.0000	ByLayer
Subdivision 2			A-Sect-Fine	green	ByLayer	ByLayer	1.0000	ByLayer
Subdivision 3			A-Sect-Fine	white	ByLayer	0.30 mm	1.0000	ByLayer
Subdivision 4			A-Sect-Fine	9	ByLayer	ByLayer	1.0000	ByLayer
Subdivision 5			A-Sect-Fine	9	ByLayer	ByLayer	1.0000	ByLayer
Subdivision 6			A-Sect-Fine	9	ByLayer	ByLayer	1.0000	ByLayer
Subdivision 7			A-Sect-Fine	9	ByLayer	ByLayer	1.0000	ByLayer
Subdivision 8			A-Sect-Fine	9	ByLayer	ByLayer	1.0000	ByLayer
Subdivision 9			A-Sect-Fine	9	ByLayer	ByLayer	1.0000	ByLayer
Subdivision 10			A-Sect-Fine	9	ByLayer	ByLayer	1.0000	ByLayer

OK | Cancel | Help

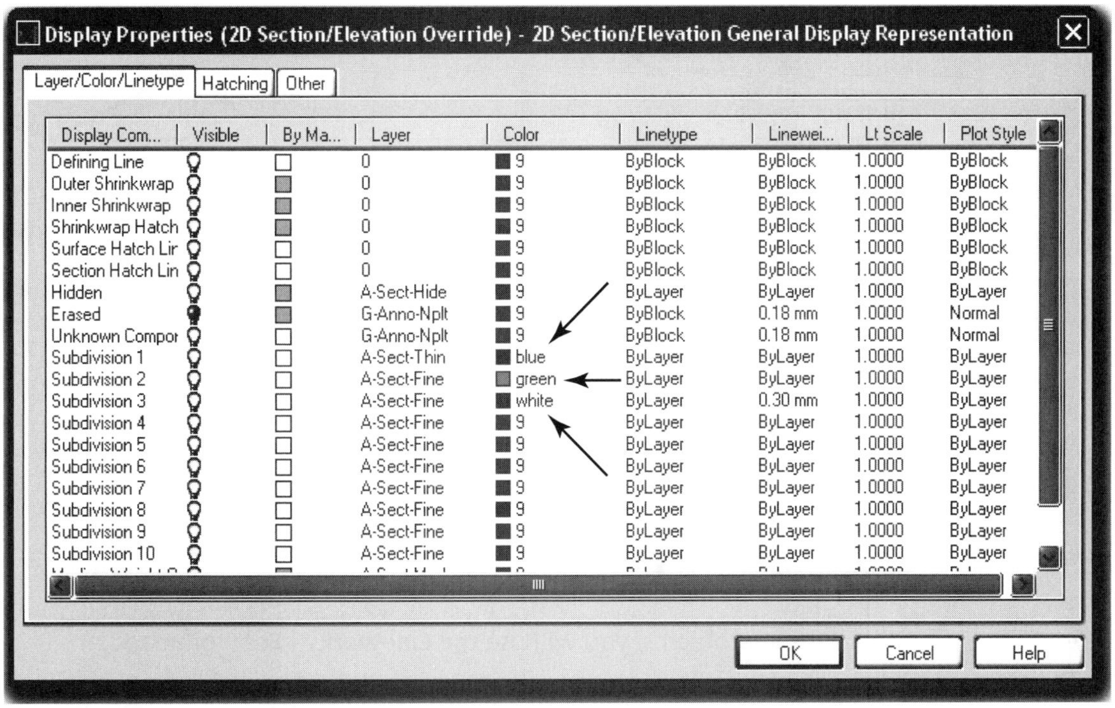

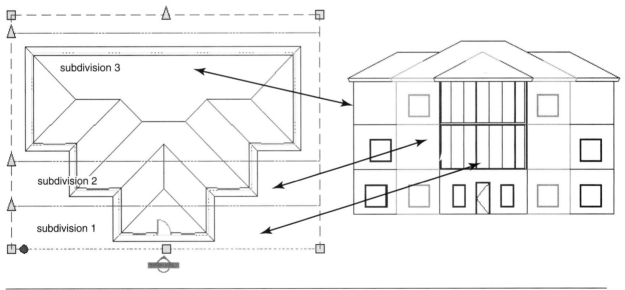

Figure 14–13

Figure 14–14

Notice that the back outline of the building is black with a .30-mm outline. This is because everything between Subdivision 2 and 3 will have the attributes of Subdivision 3. Notice that there is a problem at the roof. Because the roof is pitched, it crosses both Subdivision 2 and 3. You might also want the roof pitch between Subdivision 1 and 2 to be all one color (see Figure 14–15).

Figure 14–15

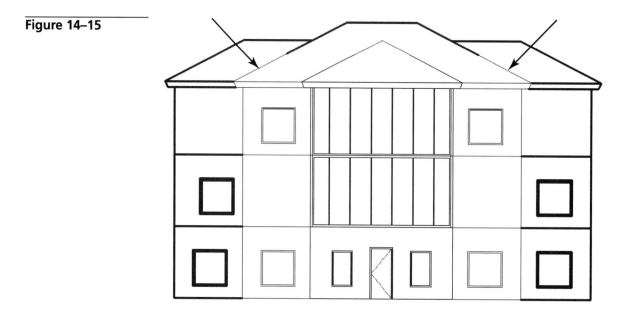

To fix these problems, you will use the **Linework > Edit** command.

1. Select the 2D elevation, **RMB**, and select **Linework > Edit** from the contextual menu that appears (see Figure 14–16).

Figure 14–16

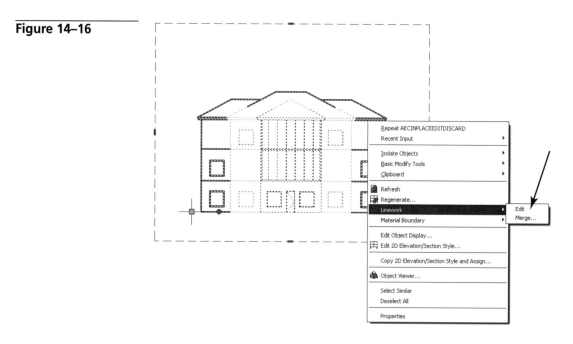

2. Select the segment of lines that you wish to edit, and erase them.
3. Using the **Line** command, replace the line with new lines (see Figure 14–17).
4. After placing the new lines, press the **Save All Changes** icon in the **In-Place Edit** dialog box shown in Figure 14–17.
5. Select the elevation again, **RMB,** and select **Linework > Merge** from the contextual menu that appears.
6. Select the two lines you just placed and press **Enter.**

Figure 14–17

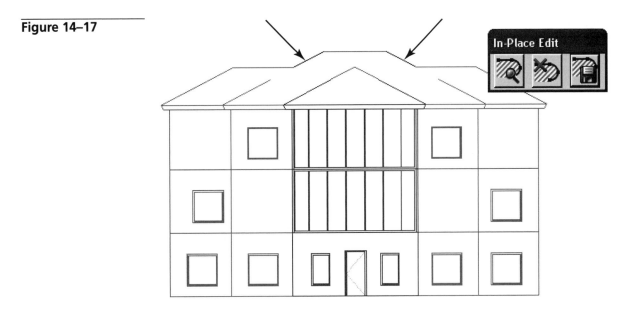

7. The **Select Linework Component** dialog box will now appear.
8. Select **Subdivision 3** from the **Linework Component** drop-down list, and press the **OK** button (Figure 14–18).

Figure 14–18

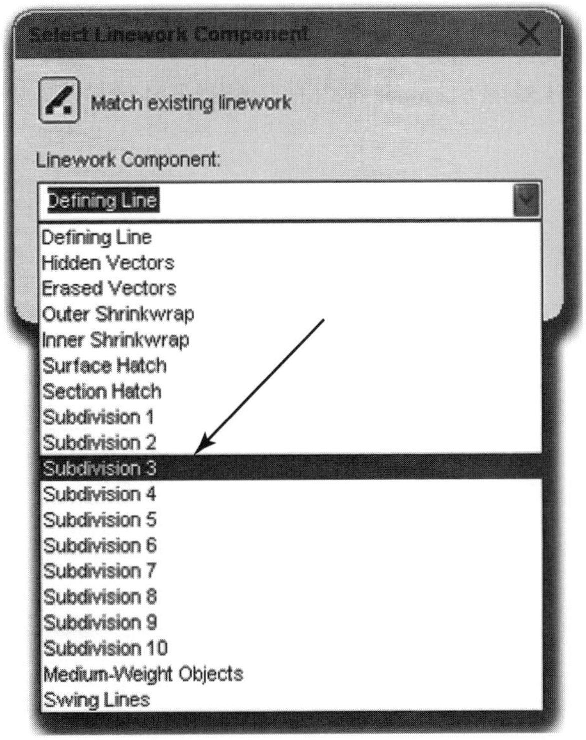

The lines will merge with the subdivision lines and have the same lineweight (see Figure 14–19).

To fix the roof pitch between Subdivision 1 and 2 do the following:

9. Select the elevation again, **RMB,** and select **Linework > Edit** from the contextual menu that appears.

Figure 14–19

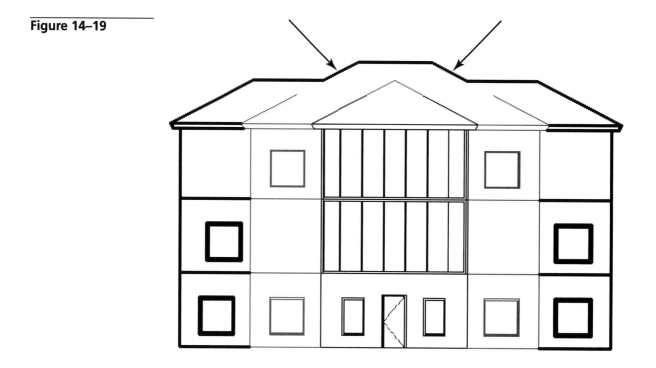

10. Select the two lines at the top of the front roof pitch, **RMB,** and select **Modify Component** from the contextual menu that appears (see Figure 14–20).

11. The **Select Linework Component** dialog box will appear again.

Figure 14–20

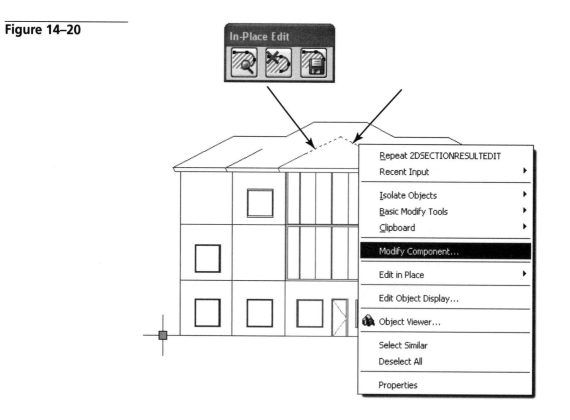

12. Select **Subdivision 1** from the **Linework Component** drop-down list, and press the **OK** button. The lines will now turn blue to match Subdivision 1.

Add the remaining lines, select **Linework > Edit,** and complete the elevation. Save this file.

Hands-On

Working with Material Boundaries

1. Close the Composite drawing.
2. Reopen the drawings for Floors 1, 2, and 3.
3. In each drawing, select all the walls, **RMB** on the **Brick4 Brick 4** icon in the **Walls** tool palette and select **Wall** from the option that appears. The walls will turn into brick walls.
4. Save all the drawings you just changed, and reopen the Composite drawing. All the walls in the building model are now brick.
5. Select the generated elevation, **RMB,** and select **Refresh** from the contextual menu that appears. The elevation now contains brick walls (see Figure 14–21).
6. Zoom in close to the generated elevation, and using the polyline command, create the closed polyline shown in Figure 14–22.

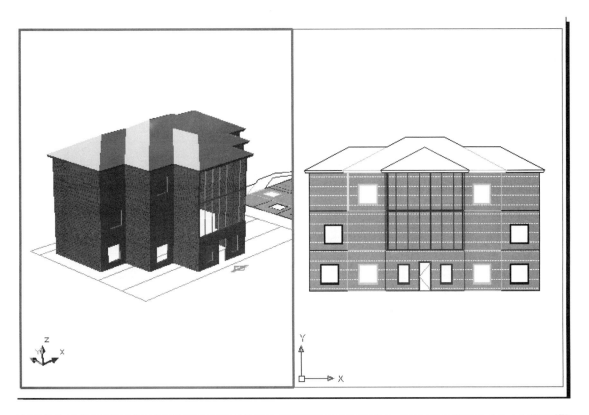

Figure 14–21

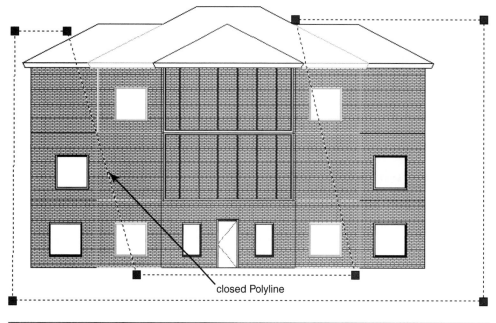

closed Polyline

Figure 14–22

7. Select the generated elevation, **RMB,** and select **Material Boundary >**
    Add from the contextual menu that appears.

8. Select the closed polyline, enter **Y** (Yes) in the **Command line,** and press
    Enter to bring up the **2D Section/Elevation Material Boundary** dialog box.

9. Select **Limit** from the **Purpose** drop-down list, and Surface **Hatching**
    Only from the **Apply to:** drop-down list.

10. Press the **OK** button to create the material boundary (see Figure 14–23).

Figure 14–23

Hands-On

Showing Common Materials as One Surface and Showing Objects Hidden Behind Other Objects in Generated Elevations

1. Start a new drawing using the Aec Model (Imperial Stb) template.
2. Change to the **Top View.**
3. Select the **Concrete-8** icon from the **Walls** tool palette and create a 10′ × 10′ enclosure 8′ high.
4. Select the **Slab** icon from the **Design** tool palette, **RMB,** and select **Linework and Walls** from the contextual menu that appears.
5. Select all the walls of the enclosure you just created and press **Enter.**
6. Enter **N** (No) in the **Command line** and press **Enter.**
7. Enter **B** (Bottom) in the **Command line** and press **Enter.**
8. Enter **R** (Right) in the **Command line** and press **Enter.**
9. Enter **L** (Left) in the **Command line** and press **Enter.**
10. Select the slab you have just created, move your cursor over the **Properties** palette to open it, and set the **Thickness** to **8″,** and **Elevation** to **0.**
11. Change to the **Front View** and using the **Array** command, array your enclosure and slab three rows high (see Figure 14–24).
12. Change to the **Top View** and, using the **Elevation Mark A1,** generate an elevation in the current drawing. Notice the floor division lines (see Figure 14–25).

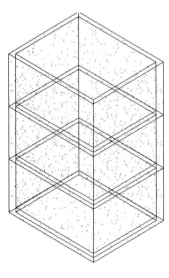

Figure 14–24

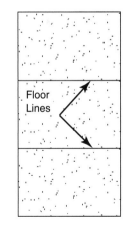

Floor Lines

Figure 14–25

13. Select **Format > Material Definitions** from the **Main** menu to bring up the **Style Manager.**
14. Double-click on **Concrete.Cast-in-place.Flat** to bring up the **Material Definition Properties** dialog box.

15. Double-click on **General Medium Detail** to open the **Display Properties** dialog box.

16. Change to the **Other** tab.

17. Check the **Merge Common Materials** check box, press the **OK** button, and close all the dialog boxes (see Figure 14–26).

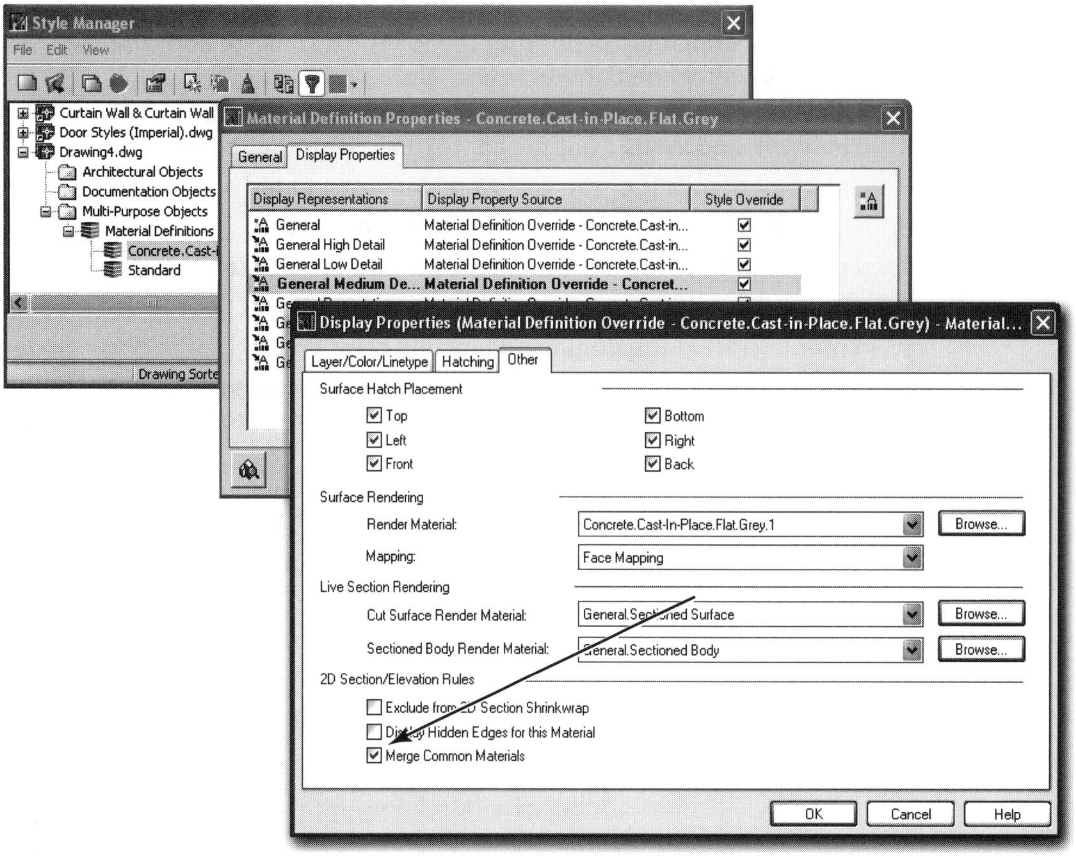

Figure 14–26

18. Select the generated elevation, **RMB,** and select **Refresh** from the contextual menu that appears. The floor lines disappear (see Figure 14–27).

19. Repeat Steps 13 through 17, this time checking the **Display Hidden Edges for this Material** check box in the **Display Properties** dialog box.

20. Again, select the generated elevation, **RMB,** and select **Refresh** from the contextual menu that appears. The hidden wall lines appear (see Figure 14–28).

21. Because the slabs are using standard material, repeat Steps 13 through 17, selecting the standard material and checking the **Display Hidden Edges for this Material** check box in the **Display Properties** dialog box.

22. Again, select the generated elevation, **RMB,** and select **Refresh** from the contextual menu that appears. The hidden slab lines appear (see Figure 14–29).

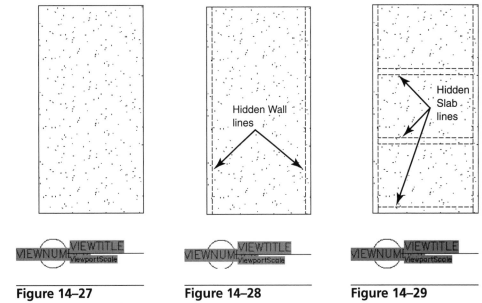

Figure 14–27   **Figure 14–28**   **Figure 14–29**

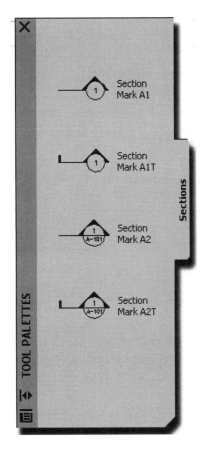

When you finish this section, you should understand the following:

- ✔ How to make a new **Section** tool palette.
- ✔ How to create a simple building.
- ✔ How to place a **Section Object.**
- ✔ How to **Generate a Section.**
- ✔ How to change the section arrow appearance.
- ✔ **Live Section definitions.**
- ✔ Creating a sample building for a live section.
- ✔ How to create a **Live Section.**
- ✔ How to modify a **Live Section.**

Sections

There are two different types of sections you can create in Architectural Desktop: Standard sections and Live sections.

Live sections cut only in Model Views and are limited to the following AEC Objects only:

- ■ Walls
- ■ Doors, windows, and door and window assemblies
- ■ Mass elements and mass groups
- ■ Stairs and railings
- ■ Roofs and roof slabs

- Spaces and space boundaries
- Curtain wall layouts and units
- Structural members

Hands-On

Making a New Section Tool Palette

1. Create a new tool palette, and name it **Section.**
2. Select the **Content Browser** icon from the **Main** tool bar to launch the Content Browser.
3. Locate **Documentation Tool Catalog - Imperial.**
4. Locate the **Callouts > Section Marks** folder.
5. Drag all the section marks into the new tool palette you created.
6. Click and hold on the tab of your new tool palette and drag a copy to **My Tool Catalog** in the Content Browser.

For the following exercise create a sample residence.

Hands-On

Creating a Sample Building

1. Start a new drawing using the Aec Model (Imperial Stb) template.
2. Change to the **Model Layout.**
3. Change to **Top View,** select the **Wall** icon from the **Design** tool palette, and move your cursor over the **Properties** palette to open it.
4. Set the following:

   a. Style = **Standard**
   b. Wall Width = **8″**
   c. Base Height = **8′-0″**
   d. Justify = **Baseline**

5. Place the walls as shown in Figure 15–1.
6. Select the **Roof** icon from the **Design** tool palette, **RMB,** and select **Apply Tool Properties to > Linework and Walls** from the contextual menu that appears.
7. Select all the walls in your drawing.
8. Enter **N** (No) in the command line, and press **Enter** to create the roof.
9. While the roof is still selected, move your cursor over the **Properties** palette to open it.
10. Set the roof to the following:

    a. Thickness = **10″**
    b. Edge cut = **Square**

Figure 15–1

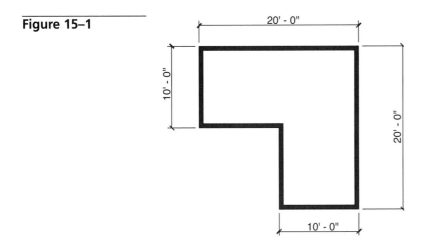

c. Shape = **SingleSlope**

d. Plate height = **8′-0″**

e. Rise = **12″**

11. Select the **Slab** icon from the **Design** tool palette, **RMB,** and select **Apply Tool Properties to > Linework and Walls** from the contextual menu that appears.

12. Again, select all the walls in your drawing, and press **Enter.**

13. Enter **N** (No) in the command line and press **Enter.**

14. Enter **T** (Top) in the command line and press **Enter.**

15. Enter **R** (Right) in the command line and press **Enter** twice to place the slab.

16. While the slab is still selected, move your cursor over the **Properties** palette to open it.

17. Set the following:

a. Style = **Standard**

b. Thickness = **4″**

c. Elevation = **0″**

18. Select the **Quick Select** icon in the **Properties** palette, select all the walls, and press **OK**.

19. With the walls selected, **RMB** anywhere in the Drawing Editor, and select **Insert > Window** from the contextual menu that appears.

20. Place 2′ × 4″-high Standard windows on each wall as shown in Figure 15–2.

21. With the walls still selected, **RMB** anywhere in the Drawing Editor, and select **Insert > Door** from the contextual menu that appears.

22. Place a 3′-0″ × 6′-8″-high Standard door as shown in Figure 15–2.

Figure 15–2

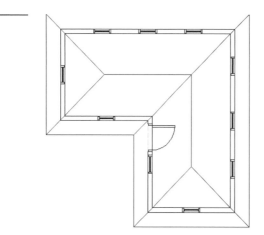

Hands-On

Placing the Standard Section Object

1. Select the **Section Mark A1** from the **Section** tool palette, click and drag through a window, and then click again through another window.

2. Press **Enter,** move your cursor in the view direction you wish to cut the section, and click the mouse button to bring up the **Place Callout** dialog box.

3. Name the view, check the **Generate Section/Elevation** check box, set the **Scale** to **1/8″ = 1′-0″**, and press the **Current Drawing** icon.

4. Move your cursor to an insertion point for the generated section, and click the mouse button to create the generated section.

   Note: If you want to show the section object constantly in the Drawing Editor, do the following:

   a. Select the section line, **RMB,** and select **Edit Object Display** from the contextual menu that appears to bring up the **Object Display** dialog box.

   b. Check the **Object Override** check box for the **Plan** display representation to bring up the **Display Properties** dialog box.

   c. Turn on the visibility of the boundary, press **OK,** and close all the dialog boxes to return to the Drawing Editor (see Figure 15–3).

Hands-On

Reversing the Section Direction

1. Select the section line, **RMB,** and select **Reverse** from the contextual menu that appears.

2. Using the **Mirror** command, select the direction arrow and view number and reverse them.

3. Select the generated section, **RMB,** and select **Refresh** from the contextual menu that appears (see Figure 15–4).

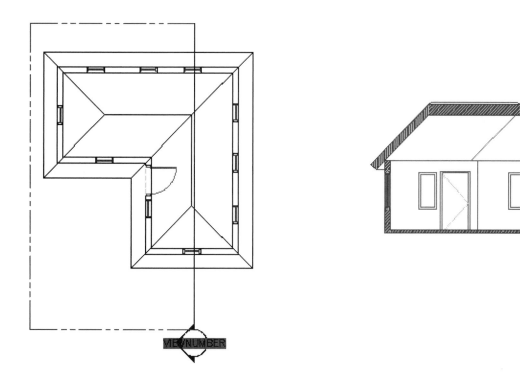

Figure 15–3

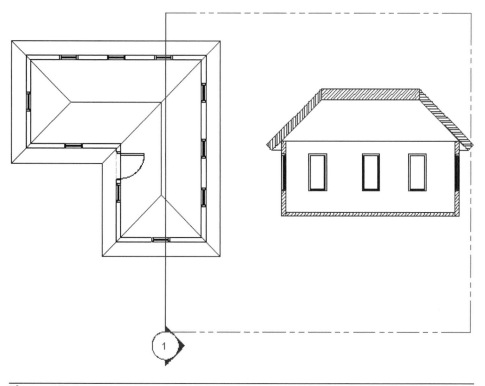

Figure 15–4

Modifying the Section

1. Reverse the section again.
2. Double-click the roof to open the **Properties** palette.
3. Change the **Rise** to **4"**.
4. Select the generated section, **RMB,** and select **Refresh** from the contextual menu that appears. Notice that anything you change in the building model will change in the generated section when you refresh it (see Figure 15–5).

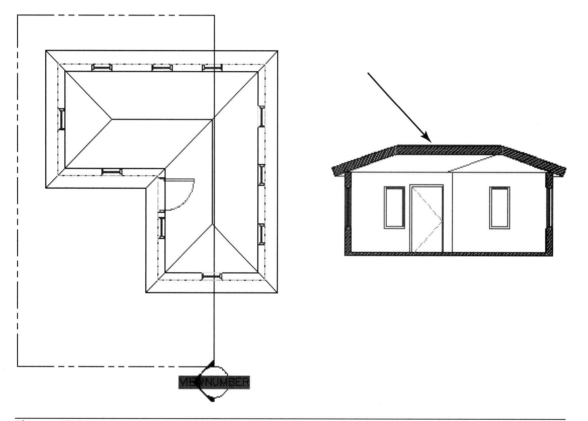

Figure 15–5

Customizing the Section Arrow Appearance

1. Select the **VIEWNUMBER** text, **RMB,** and select **Edit Block in-place** from the contextual menu that appears to bring up the **Reference Edit** dialog box.
2. Press **OK** to return to the Drawing Editor.
3. Erase the circle and add a rectangle (see Figure 15–6).
4. Press the **Save back changes to reference** icon in the **Refedit** dialog box that appeared near the arrow.

5. Select the direction arrow, **RMB** and select **Edit Block in-place** from the contextual menu that appears to bring up the **Reference Edit** dialog box.

6. Press **OK** to return to the Drawing Editor.

7. Erase the existing arrow and add a new arrow. You could even add your company logo. You now have a custom section line object arrow (see Figure 15–7).

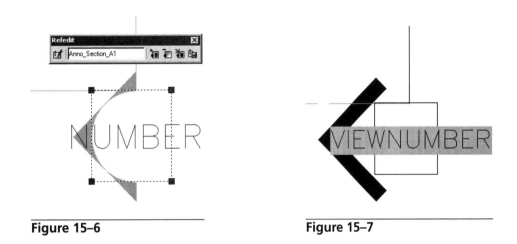

Figure 15–6   **Figure 15–7**

Live Sections

Unlike generated sections, Live sections retain the original objects after sectioning, can set display properties for all objects in a section, and can set hatching for section boundaries.

Note: Each new Live section is displayed in a separate display configuration created specifically for that section. See the explanation of display configurations in this book.

Live section AEC objects consist of six components (see Figure 15–8).

- **Cutting boundary:** Outside limit of the section (section line)
- **Hatch:** Graphic indication of area inside the cutting boundary
- **Inside cutting boundary:** Remaining object cut by cutting boundary *inside* cutting boundary
- **Outside cutting boundary:** Remaining object cut by cutting boundary *outside* cutting boundary
- **Inside full body:** Object completely *inside* section
- **Outside full body:** Object completely *outside* section

Before a live section or any section can be created, a section mark or section line must be placed in your drawing to identify where the section is to take place.

Creating a Sample Building for a Live Section

1. Start a new drawing using the Aec Model (Imperial Stb) template.
2. Change to **Top View.**
3. Select the **CMU-8 Rigid-1.5 Air-2 Brick-4 Furring Wall** icon from the **Walls** tool palette in the **Autodesk Architectural Desktop Sample Palette Catalog - Imperial,** and create a 10'-0" × 10'-0" enclosure.

Figure 15–8

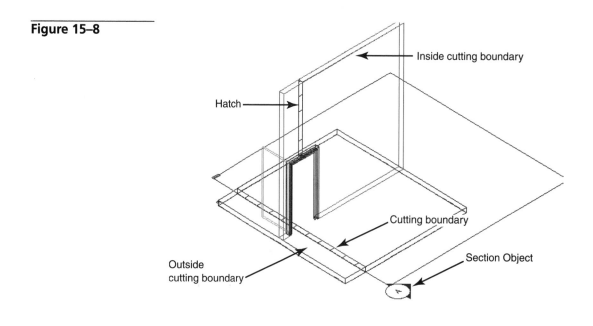

4. Select the left wall, **RMB,** and select **Insert Door** from the contextual menu.
5. Place a 3'-0" Standard door centered in the left wall, swinging inward (see Figure 15–9).
6. Select **Sections Mark A1** from the **Section** tool palette.
7. Place the start point at the left of the door, place the second point to the right of the right wall, and press **Enter.** Move your cursor in the

Figure 15–9

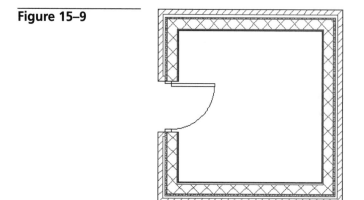

view direction you wish to cut the section, and click the mouse button to bring up the **Place Callout** dialog box.

8. Name the view, check the **Generate Section/Elevation** check box, set the **Scale** to **1/8″ = 1′-0″,** and press the **Current Drawing** icon.

9. Move your cursor to an insertion point for the generated section, and click the mouse button to create a generated section (see Figure 15–10).

It is a good idea to show the section object constantly in the Drawing Editor (follow the directions mentioned in the earlier section, "Placing the Standard Section Object").

Figure 15–10

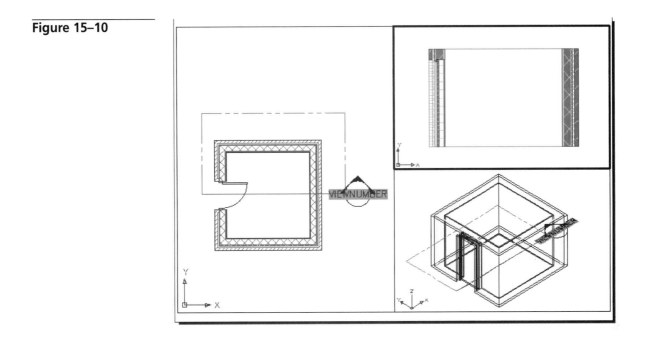

Hands-On

Creating a Live Section

1. Use the previous exercise.
2. Change to the **Work Layout.**
3. Select the section object (the cutting plane), **RMB,** and select **Enable Live Section** from the contextual menu that appears.

A 3D sectioned model of the enclosure appears in the Isometric view (see Figure 15–11).

4. Place one viewport of the enclosure in **Top View** and the other in **Front View.**
5. Change to the **Front View.**
6. Select the **Hidden** icon in the **Shading** toolbar to display the Live section in hidden display.

Figure 15–11

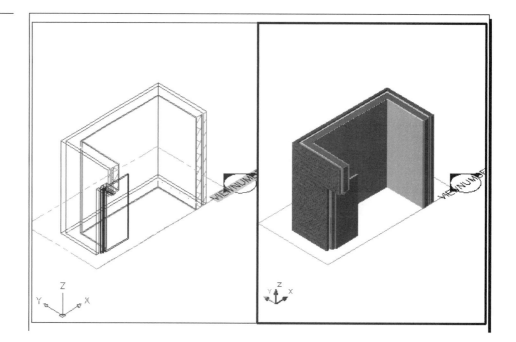

7.   Notice that the sectioned view displays symbols of all the materials set for the wall components (see Figure 15–12).

8.   Double-click on the front wall to open its **Properties** palette.

9.   Change the **Style** to **Standard.**

Figure 15–12

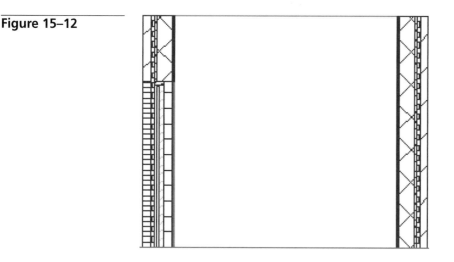

10.   Return to the Drawing Editor, and notice that the front wall in the **Top View (Plan View)** has changed (see Figure 15–13).

11.   Open the Content Browser (by pressing **Ctrl + 4).**

12.   Add the **Bow Window Set** from the **Design Tool Catalog** to your tool palette.

13.   Click the **Bow Window Set** icon in your tool palette, and select the wall illustrated in Figure 15–14.

Figure 15–13

Figure 15–14

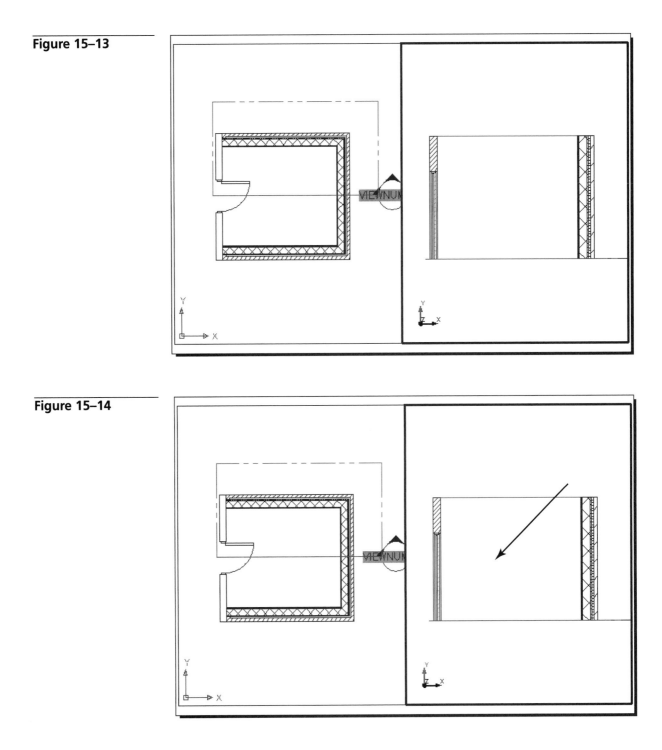

14.   Insert the **Bow Window Set** into the live section in the **Front View.** Notice that the window now also appears in the **Top View** (see Figure 15–15).

All the AEC components in a live section such as door size, hatching, etc., can be changed in the section and will reflect in the 2D plan drawing.

Figure 15–15

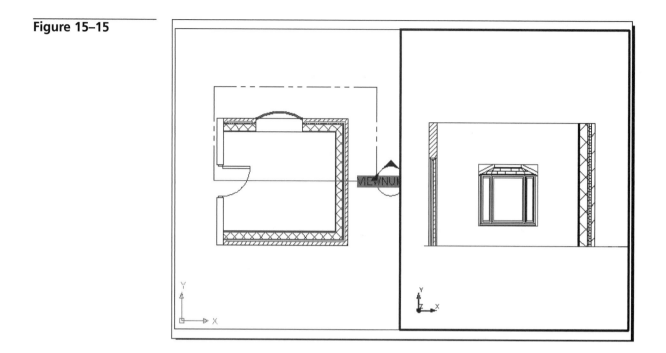

Hands-On

Modifying a Live Section

1. Select the section line object and move it so that it does not pass through the door. See that the Live section changes (see Figure 15–16).

Figure 15–16

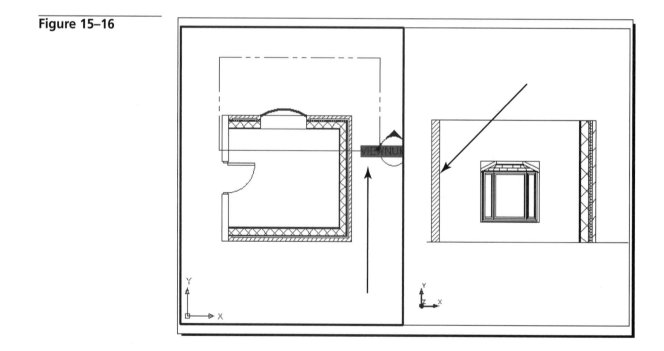

2. Select the section line object and rotate it. See that the Live section changes (see Figure 15–17).

Using the Live section concept, you can adjust your sections automatically, even in another drawing, by changing the plan or changing the Live section.

Figure 15–17

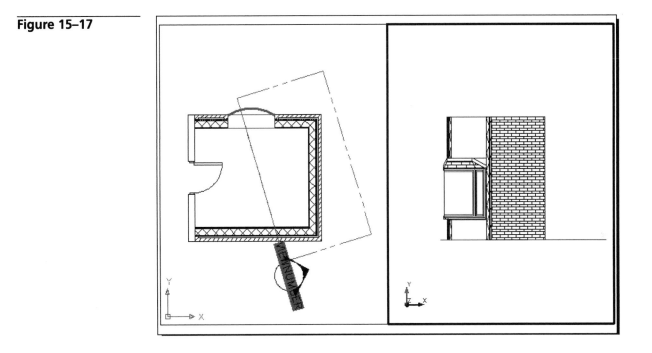

16

Drawing Management

When you finish this section, you should understand the following:

- ✔ The Drawing Management concept.
- ✔ How to use the **Project Browser.**
- ✔ How to create constructs and elements in the **Project Navigator.**
- ✔ How to work with constructs and elements in the **Project Navigator.**
- ✔ How to assign constructs and elements in the **Project Navigator.**
- ✔ How to create views in the **Project Navigator.**
- ✔ How to create plotting sheets in the **Project Navigator.**

Autodesk Architectural Desktop 2006's Drawing Management feature automates the building design and document process. With this feature, all your project document files are codified in a central location from which you can call up and modify any drawing. This feature allows you to manage projects, automatically control levels, and create views and sheets. See Figure 16–1.

Figure 16–1

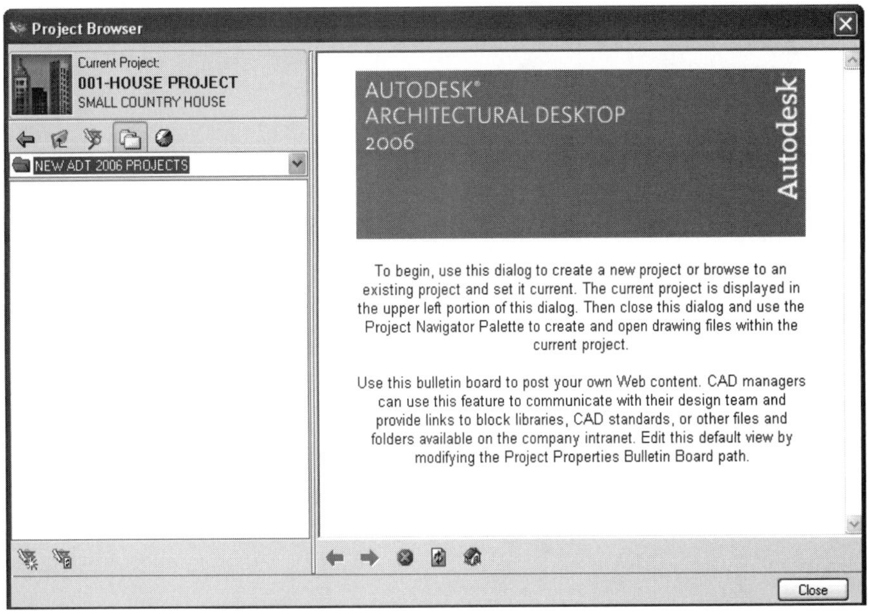

In reality, the new Drawing Management feature is an advanced form of external referencing (XREF), which has been a feature of AutoCAD and Architectural Desktop for many releases. Using XML programming in conjunction with XREF, the programmers have created a very comprehensive system for automating this process.

Because the Drawing Management system is so closely related to the XREF system, those who understand how to use the conventional XREF will find the learning curve for this advanced feature easily comprehendible. For those who are totally new to AutoCAD or Architectural Desktop, this author suggests that you first read the online help on XREF before going on to the Drawing Management system.

The Drawing Management Concept

The Drawing Management system is based on a hierarchy starting with the project, which is made of constructs, elements, views, and plot sheets. Through sophisticated automated XREF commands, elements are XREFed into constructs, which are XREFed into views and then XREFed into plot sheets. See Figure 16–2.

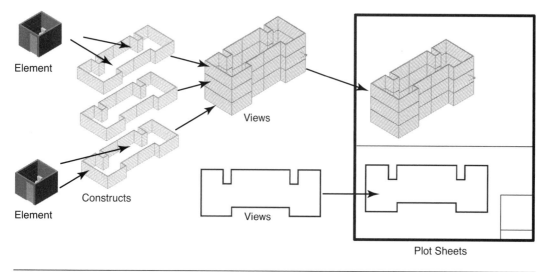

Figure 16–2

Hands-On

Using the Project Browser

1. In **Windows Explorer,** create a Microsoft Windows file directory and name it **NEW ADT 2006 PROJECTS.**

2. Start **Autodesk Architectural Desktop 2006.**

3. Start a new drawing using the Aec Model (Imperial Stb) template.

4. Select **File > Project Browser** from the **Main** menu to bring up the **Project Browser** dialog box.

5. Locate the **NEW ADT 2006 PROJECTS** directory from the drop-down list. (see Figure 16–3).

Figure 16–3

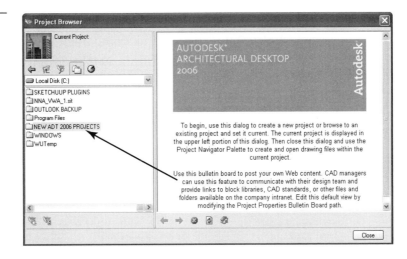

6. Press the **Add Project** icon to bring up the **Add Project** dialog box.

7. In the **Add Project** dialog box, enter the following information:

    a. Number = **100**
    b. Name = **TEST PROJECT**
    c. Description: **3 Story Building**
    d. Check the **Create from template project** check box, and accept the default file.

8. After entering the information, press the OK button to return to the **Project Browser** dialog box.

9. In the **Project Browser** dialog box, **RMB** on **TEST PROJECT** you just created, and select **Project Properties** from the contextual menu to bring up the **Modify Project** dialog box.

10. In the **Modify Project** dialog box, enter the following additional information as shown in (Figure 16–4).

    a. Bulletin Board = (Any Intranet or leave Default directory).
    b. Project Image = (Any small GIF image or leave Default directory).
    c. Prefix Filenames with project Number = **Yes** (from drop-down list).
    d. Use Relative Xref Paths = **Yes**
    e. Tool Palette File Location = Accept the default
    f. Tool Palette Storage Type = Accept the default
    g. Tool Content Root Path = Accept the default
    h. Tool Catalog Library = Accept the default
    i. Default Construction Template = (accept default—Aec Model (Imperial Stb).
    j. Default Element Template = (accept default—Aec Model (Imperial Stb).
    k. Default Model View Template = (accept default—Aec Model (Imperial Stb).
    l. Default Section/Elevation View Template = (accept default—Aec Model (Imperial Stb).

m.   Default View Template = (accept default—Aec Model (Imperial Stb).

n.   Display Only Project Detail Component Databases = **No**

o.   Display Only Project Keynote Databases = **No**

Figure 16–4

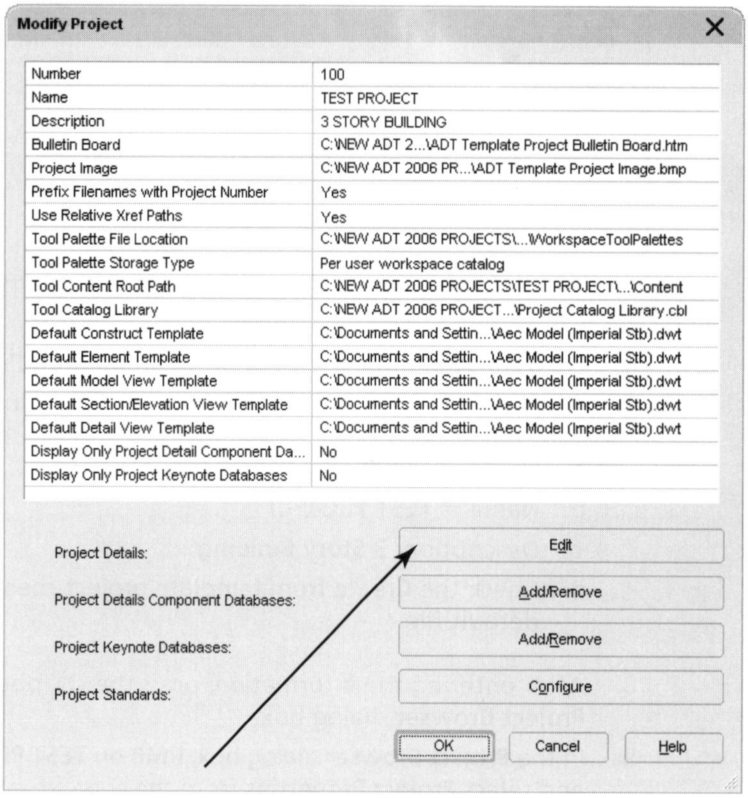

11.   Press Edit to bring up the **Project Details** dialog box. Here you can add information such as telephone numbers, billing addresses, and owner's representative (see Figure 16–5).

Figure 16–5

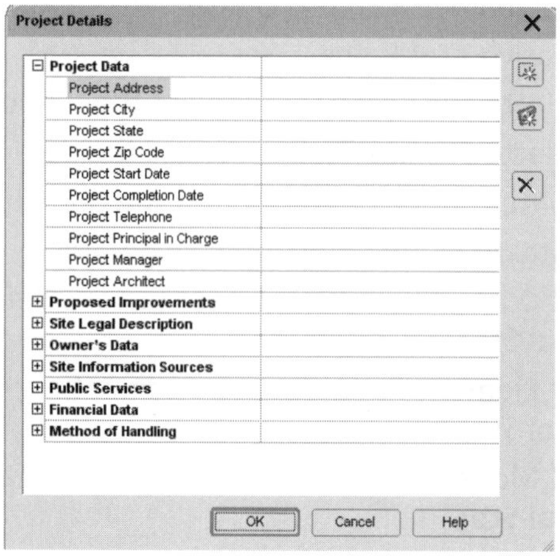

12. Press the **OK** buttons to return to the **Project Browser.**
13. **RMB** on **TEST PROJECT** in the list and select **Set Project Current** from the contextual menu that appears.

The project will now appear in the Project Browser's header (see Figure 16–6).

!   ***Note:*** If **Set Project Current** is grayed out, than you have already set this project as current. After you create more projects, you will be able to change from project to project by setting different projects current.

14. Press the **Close** button in the **Project Browser** to return to the Drawing Editor, and automatically bring the **Project Navigator** palette into the Drawing Editor if it is not already there. The **Project Navigator** palette will now contain the TEST PROJECT (see Figure 16–7).

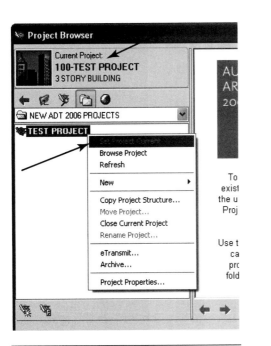

Figure 16–6

Figure 16–7

!   ***Note:*** New for Architectural Desktop 2006, when you create a new project, a new emptyTool Palette will also be automatically created with the name of that project. You can drag all the tools you need from the Content Browser, and whenever you set that Project Current, the tool palette associated with that particular project will appear. Regardless, you will still have access to all the standard palettes, which can be accessed by pressing the Tool Palette Properties icon at the lower left of the Tool Palette.

Hands-On

Creating Constructs and Elements in the Project Navigator

This project will have three floors with a basement. The second and third floors will each have two apartments, and the apartments will have bathrooms.

1. In the **Project** tab, select the **Edit Levels** icon in the top right corner of the levels information to bring up the **Levels** dialog box (see Figure 16–8).

Figure 16–8

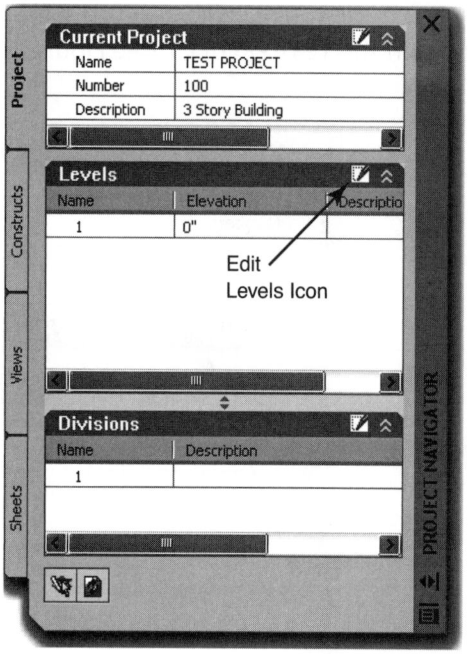

Edit Levels Icon

2. In the **Levels** dialog box, press the **Add Level,** create four levels, and enter the information as shown in Figure Figure 16–9. Be sure to check the **Auto-Adjust** check box so that the **Floor Elevation** adjusts when you enter the **Floor to Floor Height.**

3. In the **Levels** dialog box, press **OK** to return to the **Project Navigator** palette.

4. In the **Project Navigator** palette, select the **Constructs** tab.

Figure 16–9

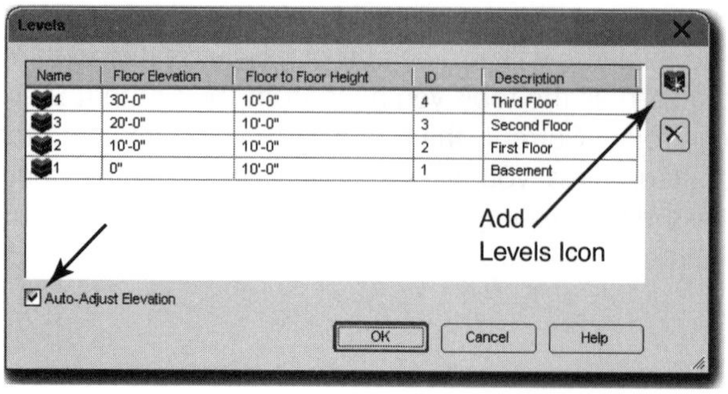

Add Levels Icon

The **Constructs** tab contains the **Constructs** and **Elements** folders, plus preview and detail screens to view their contents (see Figure 16–10).

5. In the **Constructs** tab, select the **Constructs** folder, **RMB,** and select **New** > **Construct** from the contextual menu that appears to bring up the **Add Construct** dialog box.

Figure 16–10

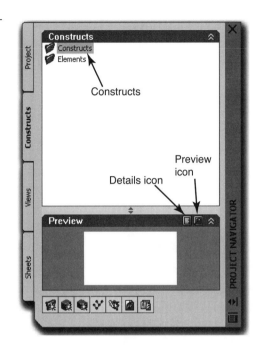

6. Enter **BASEMENT WALLS** in the **Name** field.
7. Check the **Basement** check box and press **OK** (see Figure 16–11).
8. In the **Constructs** tab, select the **Elements** folder, **RMB,** and select **New** > **Element** from the contextual menu that appears to bring up the **Add Element** dialog box.

Figure 16–11

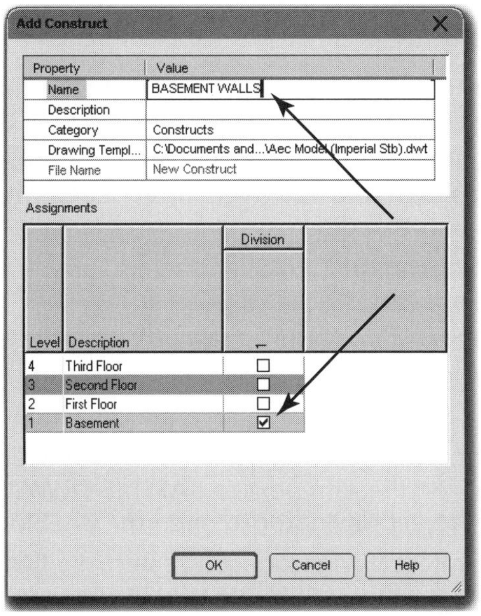

9. Enter **COLUMN GRID** in the **Name** field and press **OK**.

10. Create new elements, and name them **APARTMENT WALLS** and **BATH ROOM** (see Figure 16–12).

Save this file.

Figure 16–12

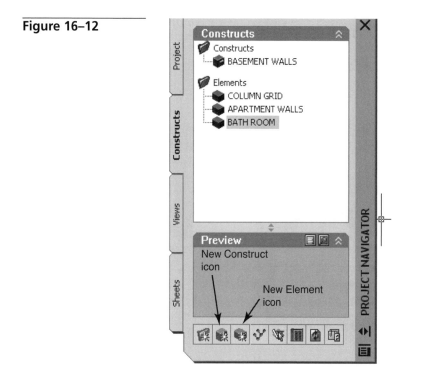

Hands-On

Working with Constructs and Elements in the Project Navigator

1. After the constructs and elements have been labeled, double-click on the **Column Grid** icon to bring up the **COLUMN GRID** drawing.

2. In the **COLUMN GRID** drawing, change to the **Top View**, and place a structural column grid 120′ wide by 60′ deep with 20′-0″ bays in both directions, and 10′ columns.

3. Select the column grid, **RMB**, and select **Label** from the contextual menu that appears.

4. Label the bottom and right of the grid with letters and numbers, respectively (see Figure 16–13).

5. Press **Ctrl + S** (File > Save) to save the drawing.

6. Move your cursor over the **Project Navigator** palette (to open it) and double-click on the icon next to **BASEMENT WALLS** in the Constructs tab of the Project Navigator to open the **BASEMENT WALLS** drawing.

7. Open the **Project Navigator** again, select the **COLUMN GRID drawing,** and drag it into the **BASEMENT WALLS** drawing.

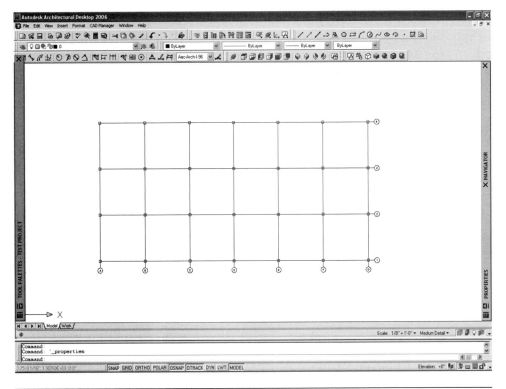

Figure 16–13

The grid you made previously will now be XREFed into the **BASEMENT WALLS** drawing.

9.   Turn the **Node** Object Snap on.

10.   Using the **Node** snap, place Standard 12″-wide, 10′-high walls as shown in Figure 16–14.

Figure 16–14

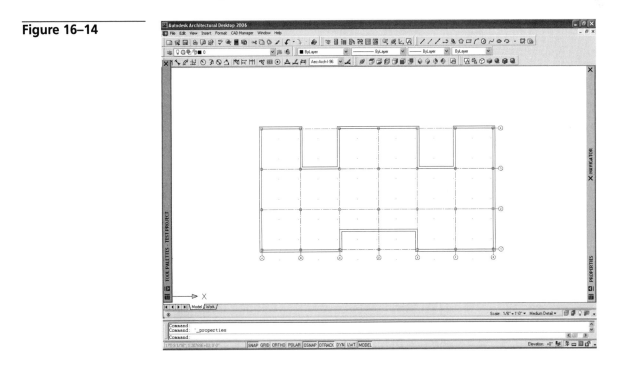

11. Delete the **COLUMN GRID** XREF and save the **BASEMENT WALLS** drawing.

12. Move your cursor over the **Project Navigator** palette to open it, select the **BASEMENT WALLS** construct, **RMB,** and select **Copy Construct to Levels** from the contextual menu that appears to bring up the **Copy Construct to Levels** dialog box.

13. Check the **First Floor, Second Floor,** and **Third Floor** check boxes, and then press **OK.**

The **Project Navigator Constructs** tab now contains three copies of the basement walls labeled **BASEMENT WALLS (2), (3), and (4)** (see Figure 16–15).

Figure 16–15

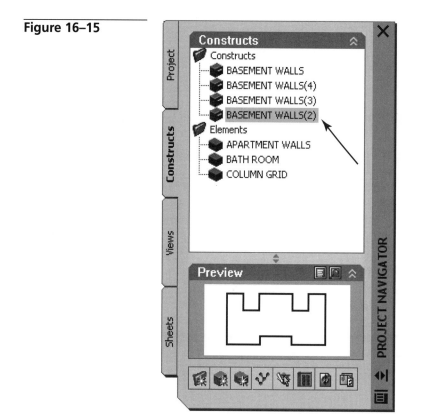

14. Select the **BASEMENT WALLS (2), (3),** and **(4),** and rename them **FIRST FLOOR WALLS, SECOND FLOOR WALLS,** and **THIRD FLOOR WALLS,** respectively.

15. Change to the **Views** tab in the **Project Navigator.**

16. Press the **Add View** icon to bring up the **Add View** dialog box.

17. Select the **General View** radio button (see Figure 16–16).

18. Press **OK** to bring up the **Add General View** dialog box.

19. Enter **TOTAL PERSPECTIVE** in the **Name** field and press **Next.**

20. In the next dialog box, check all **Level** check boxes and press **Next** again.

21. In the next dialog box, make sure that all the check boxes are checked, and press **Finish** to return to the Drawing Editor.

Figure 16–16

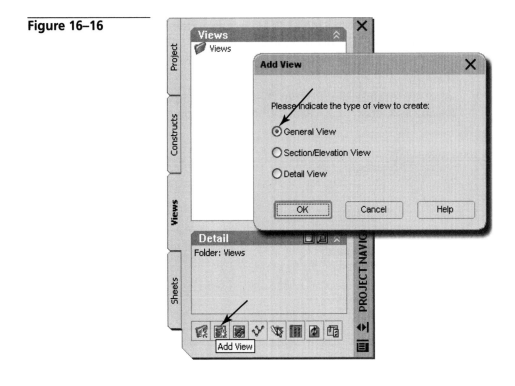

A new view called **TOTAL PERSPECTIVE** will now appear in the **Views** tab of the **Project Navigator.**

22. Double-click on **TOTAL PERSPECTIVE** in the **Views** tab to open it in the Drawing Editor.
23. Select the **Hidden** icon on the **Shading** toolbar, change to the **SW Isometric View,** and save the drawing (see Figure 16–17).
24. Change back to the **Constructs** tab in the **Project Navigator.**

Figure 16–17

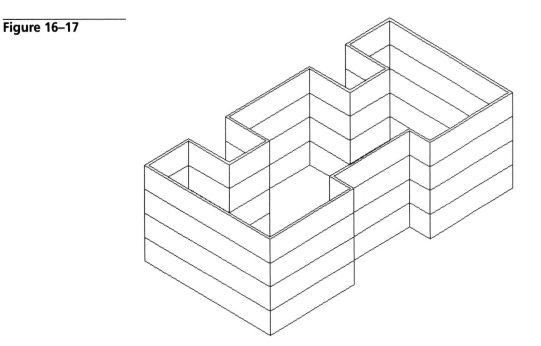

25. Double-click on **APARTMENT WALLS** under **Elements** to bring up the **APARTMENT WALLS** drawing in the Drawing Editor.

26. Drag the **SECOND FLOOR WALLS** construct into the **APARTMENT WALLS** drawing.

27. Select the **Standard** wall from the **Design** tool palette, and place 4″-wide × 8′-high walls and 3′-0″ doors as shown in Figure 16–18.

Figure 16–18

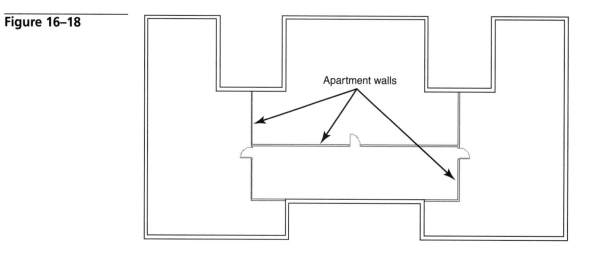

Apartment walls

28. In the **APARTMENT WALLS** drawing, delete the **SECOND FLOOR WALLS** Xref and save the **APARTMENT WALLS** drawing.

29. In the **Constructs** tab of the **Project Navigator,** create two new elements called **COLUMNS** and **FLOORS**.

30. In the **Constructs** tab, double-click **COLUMN GRID** to bring up the **COLUMN GRID** drawing in the Drawing Editor.

31. In the **COLUMN GRID** drawing, select all the columns, **RMB,** and select **Node Anchor** > **Release** from the contextual menu that appears.

32. Again, select all the columns, and select **Edit** > **Cut** from the **Main** menu, and then close and save the **COLUMN GRID** drawing.

33. In the **Constructs** tab of the **Project Navigator,** double-click on **COLUMNS** to open the **COLUMNS** drawing in the Drawing Editor.

34. Select **Edit** > **Paste to Original Coordinates** from the **Main** menu, and save the **COLUMNS** drawing.

35. Double-click on the **FLOORS** element to bring it up in the Drawing Editor.

36. Drag the **BASEMENT** construct into the **FLOORS** element drawing in the Drawing Editor.

37. Enter **BPOLY** in the command line and press **Enter.**

38. Click in the middle of the **BASEMENT WALLS** that have been Xrefed into the **FLOORS** construct to create a polyline.

39. Delete the **BASEMENT WALLS** Xref from the **FLOORS** element drawing leaving only the polyline.

40. RMB the **Slab** tool in the **Design** tool palette, and select **Apply Tool Properties to** > **Linework and Walls** from the contextual menu that appears.

41. Select the polyline you just created and press **Enter.**
42. Enter **Y** (Yes) in the command line and press **Enter.**
43. Enter **D** (Direct) in the command line and press **Enter.**
44. Enter **B** (Bottom) in the command line and press **Enter.**

You have now created the floor slab.

45. While the slab is still selected, change its Thickness to **4"** in the **Properties** palette.
46. Save the **FLOORS** element drawing.
47. Open the **Project Navigator** again, and double-click on the **BATH ROOM** icon under the **Elements** folder to bring up the **BATHROOM** drawing in the Drawing Editor.
48. In the **BATHROOM** drawing, create a 10'-0" square enclosure using Standard 4"-wide × 8'-0"-high walls.
49. Select one wall, **RMB**, and insert a Standard door 2'-6" wide by 6'-8" high.
50. Place a vanity, toilet, and spa tub from the **Design Tool Catalog – Imperial > Mechanical > Plumbing Fixtures** catalog.
51. Select the **Ceiling Grid** icon from the **Design** tool palette, center a 2'-0" × 2'-0" ceiling grid at 7'-6" elevation, and save the file (see Figure 16–19).

You have now created all the parts for your building.

Figure 16–19

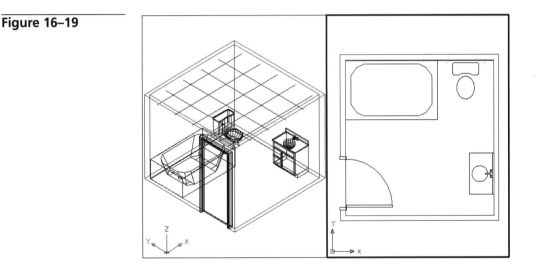

Hands-On

Putting the Elements and Constructs Together

1. In the **Constructs** tab of the **Project Manager,** double-click on the **BASEMENT WALLS** construct to open it in the Drawing Editor.
2. Drag the **FLOORS** and **COLUMNS** elements into the **BASEMENT WALLS** construct, and save the **BASEMENT WALLS** construct file.
3. In the **Constructs** tab of the **Project Manager,** double-click on the **FIRST FLOOR WALLS** construct to open it in the Drawing Editor.

4. Drag the **FLOORS** and **COLUMNS** elements into the **FIRST FLOOR WALLS** construct, and save the **FIRST FLOOR WALLS** construct file.

5. In the **Constructs** tab of the **Project Manager,** double-click on the **SECOND FLOOR WALLS** construct to open it in the Drawing Editor.

6. Drag the **FLOORS, COLUMNS, APARTMENT WALLS,** and **BATH ROOM** elements into the **SECOND FLOOR WALLS** construct.

7. In the **SECOND FLOOR WALLS** construct, copy the **BATHROOM** element twice, arrange as shown in Figure 16–20, and save the file.

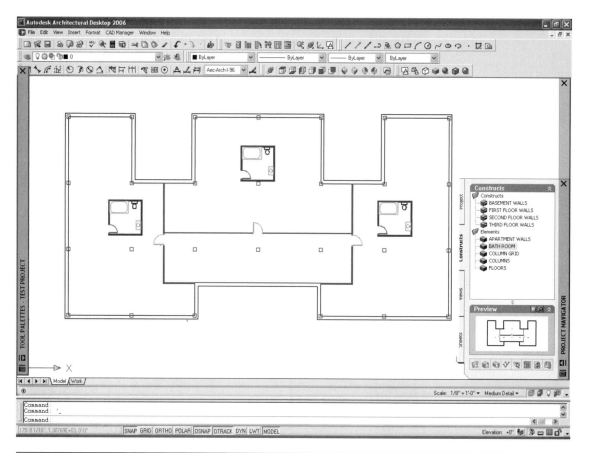

Figure 16–20

8. Select the apartment walls and bathrooms you just dragged into the **SECOND FLOOR WALLS** drawing.

9. While selected, open the **Properties** palette and set the Insertion point Z to **4"** (this places these elements on top of the 4"-thick FLOORS).

10. Repeat Steps 5 to 9 of this for the third floor walls, and save that file.

11. In the **Views** tab of the **Project Navigator,** double-click on **TOTAL VIEW** to open it in the Drawing Editor.

      Note: If the **TOTAL VIEW** drawing is already in the Drawing Editor and changes have been made to any of the xrefs that comprise this view, you will get a yellow message reminding you to reload. To do this, **RMB** on the icon shown in Figure 16–21, and select **Reload Xref** from the contextual menu that appears to create the updated **TOTAL VIEW** drawing (see Figure 16–22).

Figure 16–21

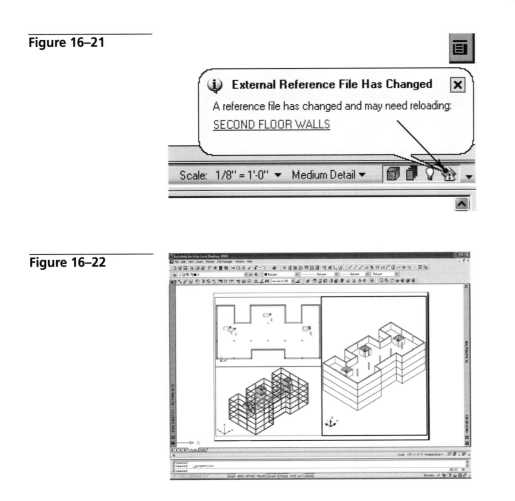

Figure 16–22

Hands-On

Modifying the Constructs and Their Effects on the Views

1. In the Constructs tab of the **Project Navigator,** double-click on the **FIRST FLOOR WALLS** construct to open it in the Drawing Editor.

2. **RMB** the **Curtain Wall** tool in the **Design** menu, select **Apply Tool Properties to > Walls,** and select the indented front wall of the **FIRST FLOOR WALLS** construct.

3. For the curtain wall alignment, choose **Baseline**, and choose **Y** (Yes) to erase the layout geometry.

4. Drag the new curtain wall to a height of 35'.

5. Change to **Front View.**

6. Select the curtain wall, press the **Edit Grid** button, click the left edge of the curtain wall, **RMB**, and select **Convert To Manual** from the contextual menu that appears.

7. Adjust the curtain wall as shown in Figure 16–23 and save its in-place edit changes.

The curtain wall needs to span the first, second, and third floors. To coordinate these, do the following:

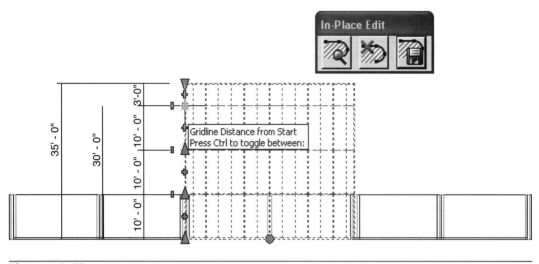

Figure 16–23

8. In the **Constructs** tab of the **Project Navigator, RMB** on the **FIRST FLOOR WALLS** construct, and select **Properties** from the contextual menu that appears to bring up the **Modify Construct** dialog box.

9. Select the **First Floor, Second Floor,** and **Third Floor** check boxes. This will allow the curtain wall to span all three floors (see Figure 16–24).

Figure 16–24

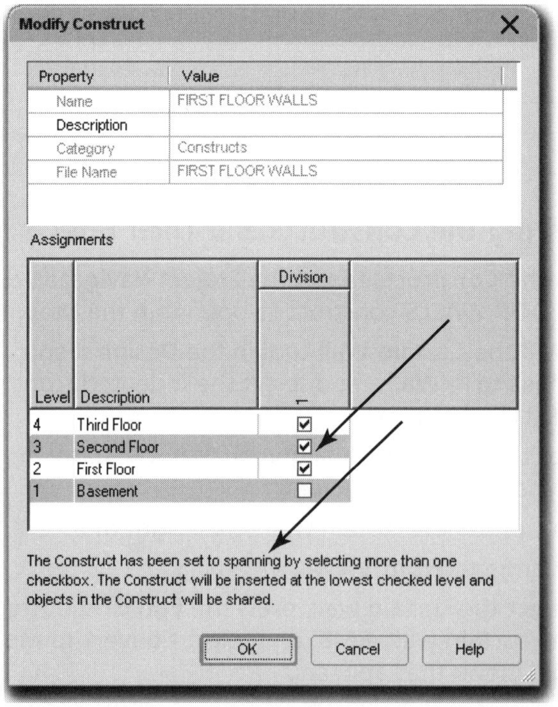

Property	Value
Name	FIRST FLOOR WALLS
Description	
Category	Constructs
File Name	FIRST FLOOR WALLS

Assignments

Level	Description	Division
4	Third Floor	☑
3	Second Floor	☑
2	First Floor	☑
1	Basement	☐

The Construct has been set to spanning by selecting more than one checkbox. The Construct will be inserted at the lowest checked level and objects in the Construct will be shared.

[OK]   [Cancel]   [Help]

10. Save the **FIRST FLOOR WALLS** construct.

11. Open the **SECOND FLOOR WALLS** and **THIRD FLOOR WALLS** constructs, delete their front indented walls, and save those files.

12. In the **Views** tab of the **Project Navigator,** double-click on the **Total View** to bring it up in the Drawing Editor (see Figure 16–25, shown in three views for clarity).

Figure 16–25

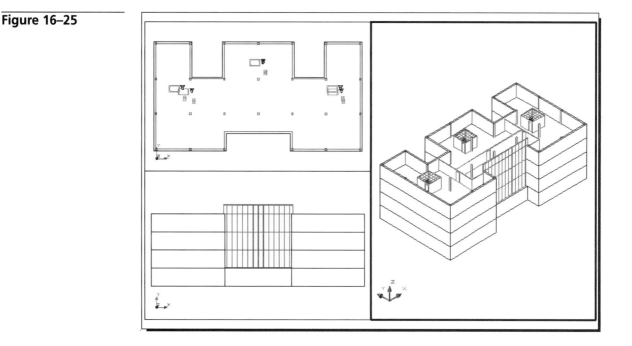

> **!** **Note:** If the **Total View** is already in the Drawing Editor and changes have been made to any of the xrefs that comprise this view, you will get a yellow message reminding you to reload.

Hands-On

Creating Named Views and Plotting Sheets

1. In the **Views** tab of the **Project Navigator,** double-click on the **TOTAL VIEW** to open it in the Drawing Editor.
2. Change to the **SW Isometric View,** and set the scale to 1/8" = 1'-0" from the **Scale** drop-down list at the bottom right of the Drawing Editor.
3. Select **View > Named Views** from the **Main** menu to bring up the **View** dialog box.
4. Select the **New** button to bring up the **New View** dialog box.
5. Enter **SW PERSPECTIVE** in the **View Name** field, select the **Define Window** radio button, select the building with a window selection, and click the mouse to return to the **New View** dialog box, and press **OK** and close the dialog boxes to return to the Drawing Editor.
6. Change to the **Front View,** and repeat the previous process naming the view **FRONT VIEW.**

7. Change to the **Top View,** and again repeat the process naming the view **TOP VIEW.**

8. Save the **Total View.**

Notice that in the **Views** tab of the **Project Navigator,** the **TOTAL VIEW** drawing contains your new named views (see Figure 16–26).

9. In the **Sheets** tab of the **Project Navigator, RMB** on **Plans** and select **New > Sheet** from the contextual menu that appears (see Figure 16–27).

Figure 16–26

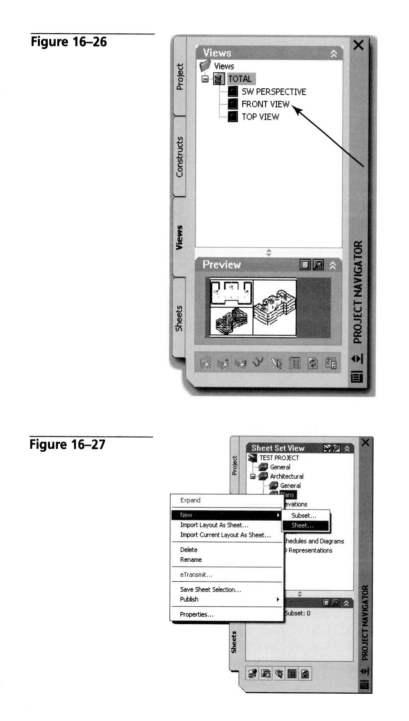

Figure 16–27

10. Enter **A-001** in the **Number** field, enter **TEST PROJECT** in the **Sheet title** field, and press **OK** to add the sheet to the **Plans** folder in the **Sheet** tab.

11. Double-click on **TEST PROJECT** to bring it up in the Drawing Editor (see Figure 16–28).

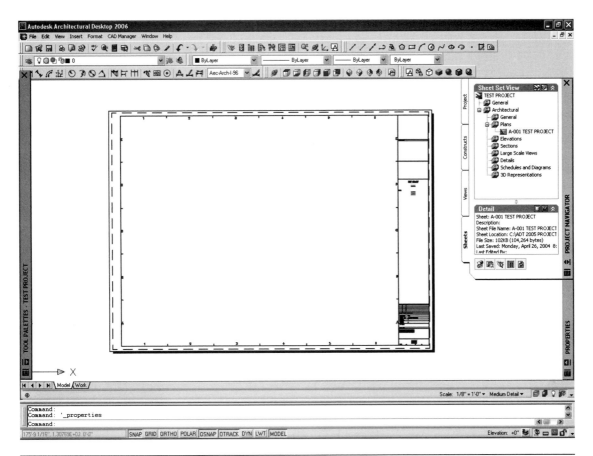

Figure 16–28

12. While the **TEST PROJECT** drawing is showing in the Drawing Editor, change to the **Views** tab in the **Project Navigator** and drag the **SW ISOMETRIC, FRONT,** and **TOP Views** into the **TEST PROJECT** drawing.

While dragging, you can **RMB** and select a scale for the view from a drop-down list (see Figure 16–29).

You have now completed your plot sheet (see Figure 16–30). You will learn more ways to insert views into sheets in the Callouts section.

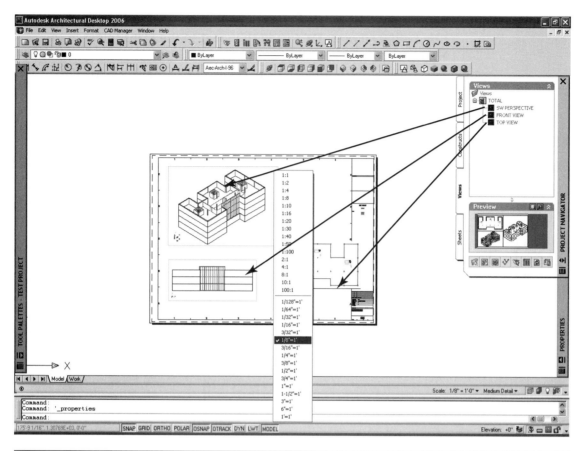

Figure 16–29

Figure 16–30

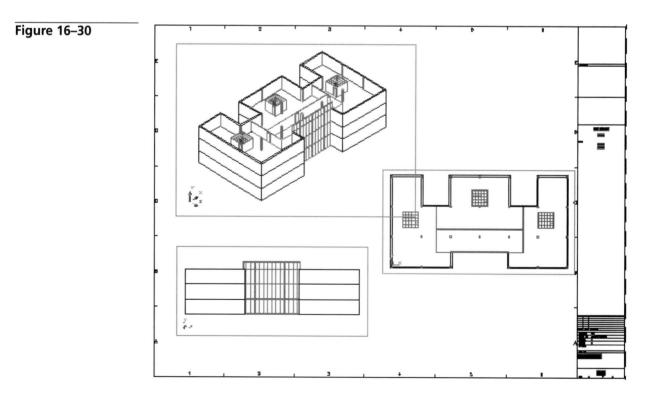

Callouts

When you finish this section, you should understand the following:

✔ How to create plotting sheets in the **Project Navigator.**

✔ How to create a new project with the **Project Browser.**

✔ How to creating a new construct in the **Project Navigator.**

✔ How to create elevations with the **MARK A3 Elevation** callout.

✔ How to create details with the **Detail Boundary** callout.

✔ How to place elevations in an **ELEVATION SHEET.**

✔ How to place details into a **DETAIL SHEET.**

✔ How to place floor plans in a **PLAN SHEET.**

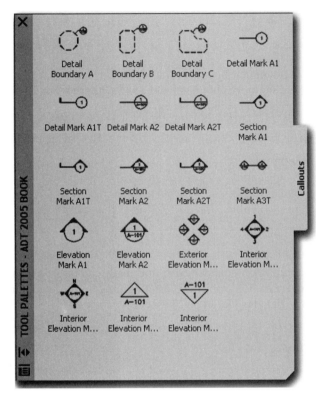

In the last two sections you learned about elevations and sections as well as elevation and section objects. In those exercises, you placed the elevation or section with a callout. In this section, you will learn the new advanced coordination capabilities of the callouts

With Autodesk Architectural Desktop 2006, details, elevations, and sections are views of the building model and part of the construction documentation. They can be created with callouts. Callouts tools create a callout that is referenced to a model space view containing a user-defined part of the building model, such as a section, an elevation, or a detail. They are coordinated across the complete construction document set with the help of projects and sheet sets.

Because callouts operate in conjunction with project management and the sheet sets, it is a good idea to review those sections before doing these exercises.

The following callout tools are provided with Autodesk Architectural Desktop 2006.

A detail callout tool with a circular boundary that optionally can insert a title mark. The callout symbol has field placeholders for the sheet number and a detail number, which are resolved when the detail is placed on the sheet.

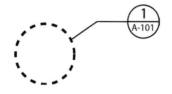

A detail callout tool with a rectangular boundary that optionally can insert a title mark. The callout symbol has field placeholders for the sheet number and a detail number, which are resolved when the detail is placed on the sheet.

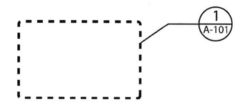

A detail callout tool with a free-form boundary that optionally can insert a title mark. The callout symbol has field placeholders for the sheet number and a detail number, which are resolved when the detail is placed on the sheet.

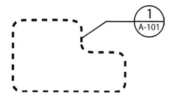

A detail tool with a leader line. The callout symbol has a field placeholder for the detail number that gets resolved when the detail is placed on the sheet.

A detail tool with a leader line and tail. The callout symbol has a field placeholder for the detail number that gets resolved when the detail is placed on the sheet.

A detail tool with a leader line. The callout symbol has field placeholders for the detail number and the sheet number, which are resolved when the detail is placed on the sheet.

A detail tool with a leader line and tail. The callout symbol has field placeholders for the detail number and the sheet number, which are resolved when the detail is placed on a sheet.

A single elevation mark tool. The elevation mark has a field placeholder for the elevation number that gets resolved when the elevation is placed on the sheet.

A single elevation mark tool. The elevation mark has field placeholders for the elevation number and the sheet number, which are resolved when the elevation is placed on the sheet.

A four-way interior elevation mark tool in the format 1/2/3/4. The elevation mark's callout symbol has a field placeholder for the sheet number that gets resolved when the elevations are placed on the sheet.

A four-way interior elevation mark tool in the format N/E/S/W. The elevation mark's callout symbol has a field placeholder for the sheet number that gets resolved when the elevations are placed on the sheet.

A four-way exterior elevation mark tool in the format 1/2/3/4. The elevation mark's callout symbol has field placeholders for the detail number and the sheet number that gets resolved when the elevations are placed on the sheet.

A single interior elevation mark tool. The elevation mark contains field placeholders for the sheet number and the elevation number, which are resolved when the elevation is placed on the sheet.

A single interior elevation mark tool with inverted text. The elevation mark contains field placeholders for the sheet number and the elevation number, which are resolved when the elevation is placed on the sheet.

A single section mark tool with a leader line. The section mark contains a field placeholder for the section number that gets resolved when the section is placed on the sheet.

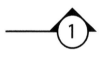

A single section mark tool with a leader line and a tail. The section mark contains a field placeholder for the section number that gets resolved when the section is placed on the sheet.

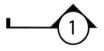

A single section mark tool with a leader line. The section mark contains field placeholders for the section number and the sheet number, which are resolved when the section is placed on the sheet.

A section mark tool with a leader line in a tail. The section mark contains field placeholders for the section number and the sheet number, which are resolved when the section is placed on the sheet.

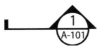

A double section mark tool with a section line. The section marks contain field placeholders for the section number and the sheet number, which are resolved when the section is placed on the sheet.

The Callout Methodology

Callouts are meant to work within the Autodesk Architectural Desktop Drawing Management System. They automatically will reference the drawings in which they are placed. This automatic referencing system is said to be "resolved" when a view is placed on a plotting sheet. *Callouts are meant to work only with 2D details and 2D elevations.*

Hands-On

Creating a New Project with the Project Browser

1. Using the **Windows Explorer** or **My Computer,** create a new folder called **CALLOUTS.**
2. Select **File > Project Browser** from the **Main** menu to bring up the **Project Browser.**
3. Locate the **CALLOUTS** folder from the drop-down list and select the **New Project** icon to bring up the **Add Project** dialog box.
4. Enter the number **001** in the **Number** field, **CALLOUTTEST** in the **Name** field, and press **OK** to return to the **Project Browser** (see Figure 17–1).

Figure 17–1

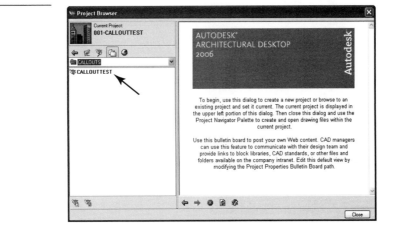

5. In the **Project Browser, RMB** on **CALLOUTTEST,** select **Set Project Current** from the contextual menu that appears, and press the **Close** button to close the **Project Manager** and bring in the **Project Navigator.**

In order for the Drawing Manager system to work, you must have a drawing file in the Drawing Editor. This file is a dummy file and will not be used. The term dummy file refers to the fact that a file must be in the Drawing Editor for the menu bars to appear.

Hands-On

Creating Plotting Sheets in the Project Navigator

1. In the **Project Navigator,** change to the **Sheets** tab.
2. In the **Sheets** tab of the **Project Navigator,** select the **Plans** icon, and then press the **Add Sheet** icon to bring up the **New Sheet** dialog box.
3. Enter **A-101** in the **Number** field, **PLAN SHEET** in the **Sheet title** field, and press **OK.**
4. In the **Sheets** tab of the **Project Navigator,** select the **Elevations** icon, and then press the **Add Sheet** icon to bring up the **New Sheet** dialog box.
5. Enter **A-201** in the **Number** field, **ELEVATION SHEET** in the **Sheet title** field, and press **OK.**
6. In the **Sheets** tab of the **Project Navigator,** select the **Details** icon, and then press the **Add Sheet** icon to bring up the **New Sheet** dialog box.
7. Enter **A-401** in the **Number** field, **DETAILS SHEET** in the **Sheet title** field, and press **OK** (see Figure 17–2).

Figure 17–2

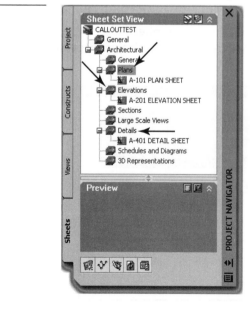

Hands-On

Creating a New Construct in the Project Navigator

1. In the **Project Navigator**, change to the **Constructs** tab.
2. Select the **Add Construct** icon to bring up the **Add Construct** dialog box.
3. Enter **STAIR** in the **Name** field, and press **OK** to return to the Drawing Editor.
4. In the **Constructs** tab of the **Project Navigator,** double-click on the STAIR drawing you created in the previous step to bring that drawing into the Drawing Editor.
5. In the Drawing Editor place a wall with windows, a door, and a stair similar to that shown in Figure 17–3.

Figure 17–3

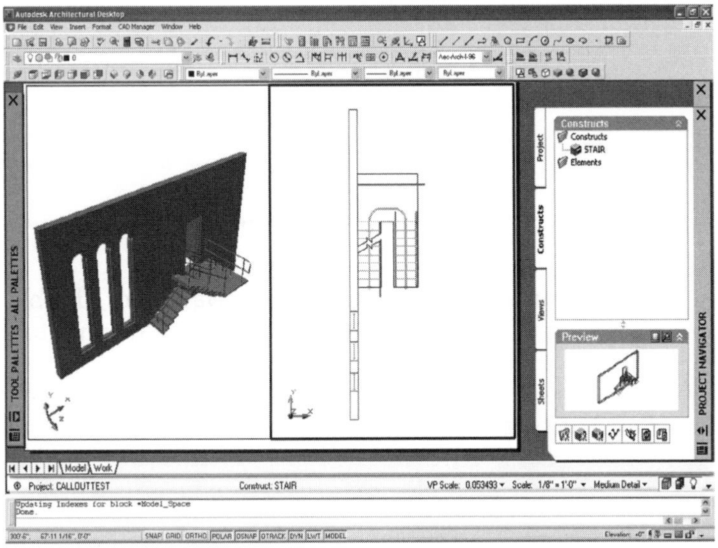

Hands-On

Creating a New Plan View Drawing in the Project Navigator

1. In the **Project Navigator,** change to the **Views** tab.
2. Select the **Add View** icon to bring up the **Add View** dialog box.
3. Select the **General** radio button, and press **OK** to open the **Add View** dialog box.
4. Enter **STAIR PLAN,** and press the **Next** button to bring up the **Context** screen.
5. Check the **Level** check box, and press the **Next** button to bring up the **Content** screen.
6. Make sure the **STAIR CONSTRUCT** check box is checked—this will add the stair construct to your STAIR PLAN drawing. Finally press the **Finish** button in the **Content** screen to return to the Drawing Editor, and create the STAIR PLAN drawing (see Figure 17–4).

Figure 17–4

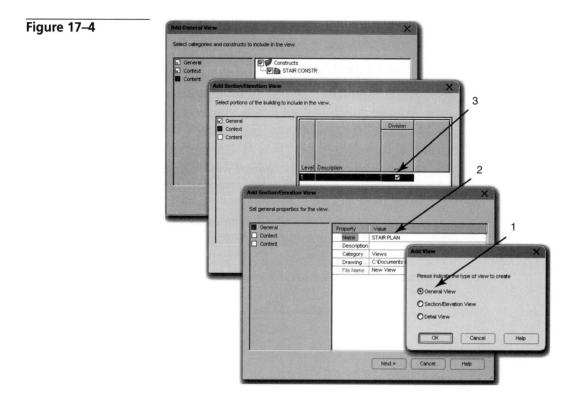

7.   In the **Views** tab of the **Project Navigator**, double-click on the **STAIR Plan** icon to bring the **STAIR PLAN view** drawing into the Drawing Editor.

> **Note:** The STAIR PLAN drawing will contain the stair created in **STAIR** in the **Constructs** tab (it has been XREFed into the STAIR PLAN drawing automatically).

Hands-On

Creating Elevations with the MARK A3 Elevation Callout

1.   Select **Elevation Mark Elevation Mark A3** from the **Callouts** tool palette (see Figure 17–5).

Figure 17–5

2.   In the STAIR PLAN drawing in the **Top View,** place a window selection around the stair construct and click to bring up the **Place Callout** dialog box.

3.   Check the **Generate Section/Elevation** check box, select **1/2″** from the **Scale** drop-down list, and press the **New View** drawing icon to bring up the **Add Section/Elevation View** dialog box (see Figure 17–6).

4.   Enter **ELEVATION VIEWS** in the **Name** field, (this will appear as the drawing file name in the **Project Navigator**) and press the **Next** button to bring up the **Context** screen

Figure 17–6

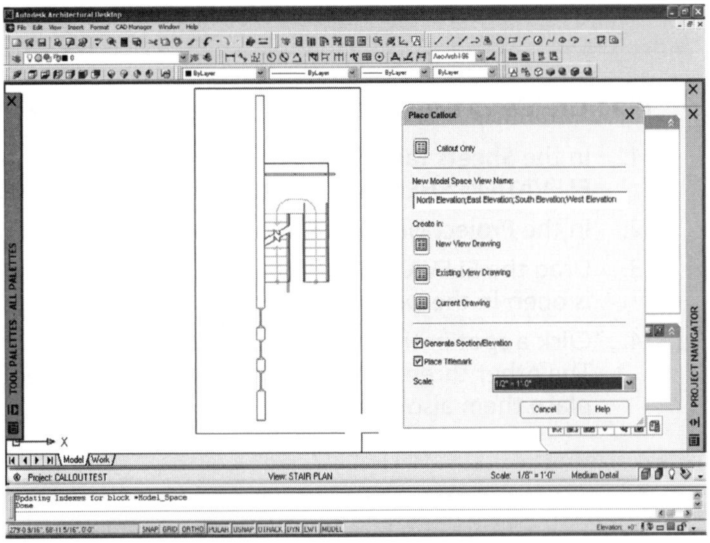

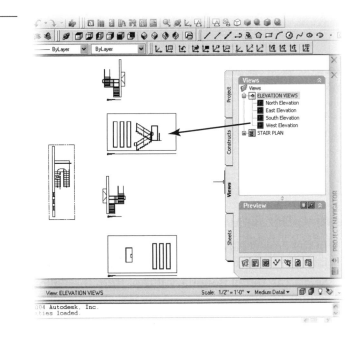

5. Check the **Level** check box, and press the **Next** button to bring up the **Content** screen.

6. Make sure the **STAIR CONSTRUCT** check box is checked, and press the **Finish** button to return to the Drawing Editor.

7. In the Drawing Editor, click to the right of stair (where you click doesn't matter because you are creating the elevations in the new drawing file).

8. Move your cursor down 10' vertically again (this will dictate the distance between the four elevations) and click your mouse button. The **Generate Elevation Progress** dialog screen will appear telling you when the elevations have been created in a new file.

Notice that the **ELEVATION VIEWS** file appears in the **Views** tab of the **Project Navigator.**

9. In the **Views** tab of the **Project Navigator,** double-click on the **ELEVATIONS VIEWS** file to bring that file up in the Drawing Editor (see Figure 17–7).

Figure 17–7

Hands-On

Placing Elevation Views in the A-201 ELEVATION SHEET

1. In the **Sheets** tab of the **Project Navigator,** double-click the **A-201 ELEVATION SHEET** icon, to bring it up in the Drawing Editor.
2. In the **Project Navigator,** change to the **Views** tab.
3. Drag the **ELEVATION VIEWS** icon into the **A-201 ELEVATION SHEET** that is open in the Drawing Editor.
4. Click a spot in the A-201 ELEVATION SHEET to place the first elevation. The other three elevations will appear in sequence automatically—place them also (see Figure 17–8).

Figure 17–8

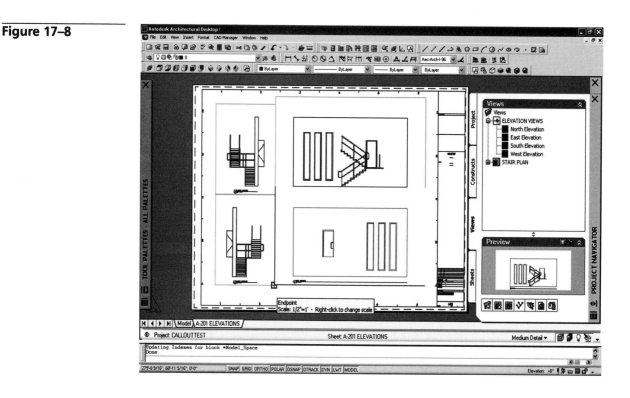

Note: You can place single elevations by dragging the individual elevations from the Views tab into a plotting sheet.

5. Press **Ctrl + S** on your keyboard or select **File > Save** from the **Main** menu to save the A-201 ELEVATION SHEET.

Hands-On

Creating Details with the Detail Boundary Callout

1. In the **Project Navigator,** change to the **Views** tab and double-click the **East Elevation** to bring it up in the Drawing Editor.
2. Select the **Detail Boundary B** tool from the **Callouts** tool palette (see Figure 17–9).

Figure 17–9

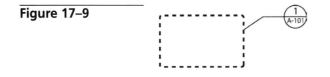

3. Click in the EAST ELEVATION drawing, and select with a window selection the area for your detail (see Figure 17–10).

Figure 17–10

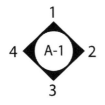

4. Move the leader line location and click to bring up the **Place Callout** dialog box.

5. Enter **DETAIL 1** in the **New Model Space View Name** field, uncheck the **Generate Section/Elevation** check box, select **1″ = 1′-0″** from the **Scale** drop-down list, and press the **New View** drawing icon to bring up the **Add Detail View** dialog box.

6. Enter **DETAILS** in the **Name** field (this will appear as the drawing file name in the **Project Navigator**) and press the **Next** button to bring up the **Context** screen.

7. Check the **Level** check box, and press the **Next** button to bring up the **Content** screen.

8. Make sure the **STAIR CONSTRUCT** check box is checked, and press the **Finish** button to return to the Drawing Editor.

9. In the Drawing Editor, click in the drawing to create the new detail view drawing.

10. In the **Views** tab, expand the DETAILS drawing that you just created to see the **DETAIL 1 View** (see Figure 17–11).

11. Repeat the previous process to create a new detail called **DETAIL 2.**

12. Press **Ctrl + S** on your keyboard or select **File > Save** from the **Main** menu to save the **ELEVATION VIEWS** drawing.

Figure 17–11

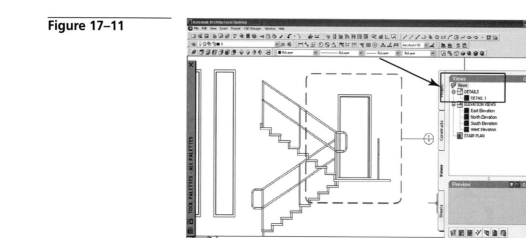

Hands-On

Placing Details into the A-401 DETAIL SHEET

1. In the **Project Navigator,** change to the **Sheets** tab and double-click **A-401 DETAIL SHEET** to bring the A-401 DETAIL SHEET drawing into the Drawing Editor.

2. In the **Project Navigator,** change to the **Views** tab.

3. Drag the **DETAILS** icon into the A-401 ELEVATION SHEET that is open in the Drawing Editor.

4. Click a spot in the A-401 DETAIL SHEET to place the first detail. The other details will appear in sequence automatically—place them as well (see Figure 17–12).

Figure 17–12

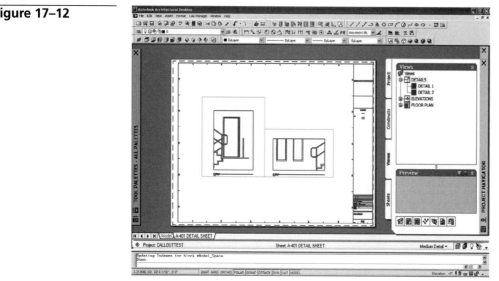

! ***Note:*** You can place single details by dragging the individual details from the Views tab into a potting sheet.

5. Press **Ctrl + S** on your keyboard or select **File > Save** from the Main menu to save the A-401 DETAIL SHEET.

Hands-On

Placing the Floor Plan into the A-101 PLAN SHEET

1. In the **Project Navigator,** change to the **Sheets** tab and double-click **A-101 PLAN SHEET** to bring the A-101 PLAN SHEET drawing into the Drawing Editor.
2. In the **Project Navigator,** change to the **Views** tab.
3. Drag the **FLOOR PLAN** into the A-101 PLAN SHEET that is open in the Drawing Editor (see Figure 17–13).
4. Press **Ctrl + S** on your keyboard or select **File > Save** from the **Main** menu to save the A-101 PLAN SHEET.

Figure 17–13

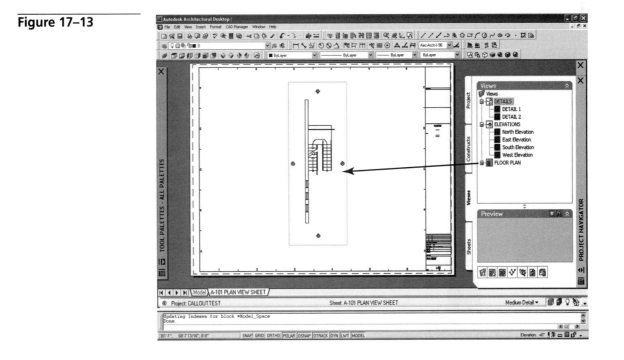

Close all the drawings.

In the **Sheets** tab, double-click on **A-101, A-201,** and **A-401,** and look at the callouts. The callout numbers have been coordinated automatically to the sheet, plan, elevation, and detail numbers (see Figures 17–14 through 17–17).

Figure 17–14

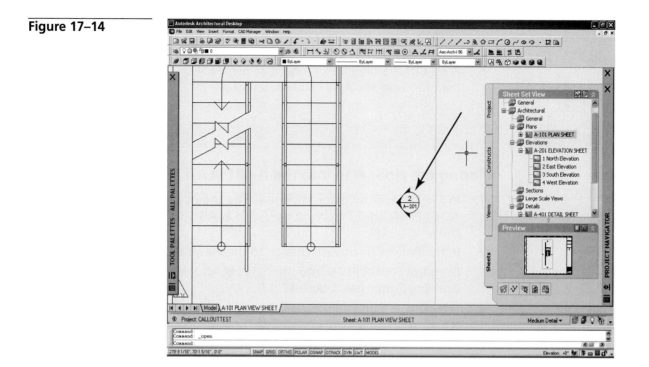

Figure 17–15

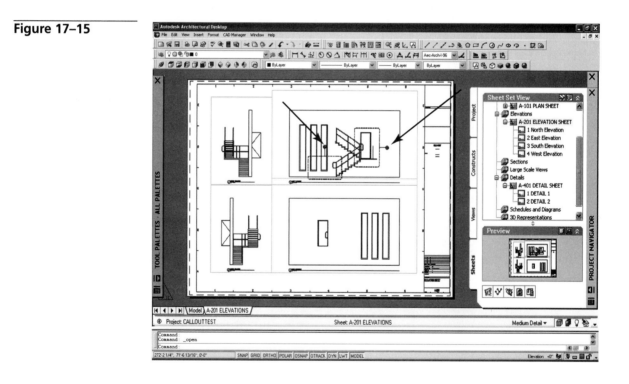

Figure 17–16

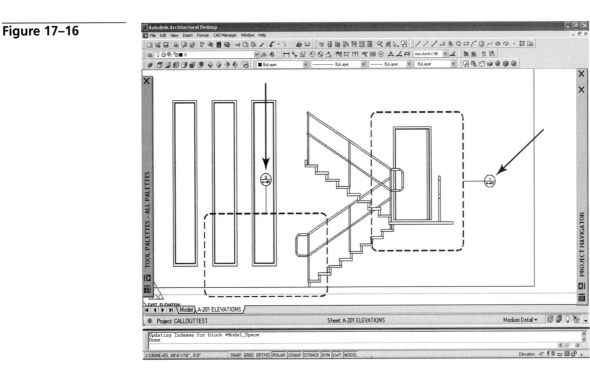

Figure 17–17

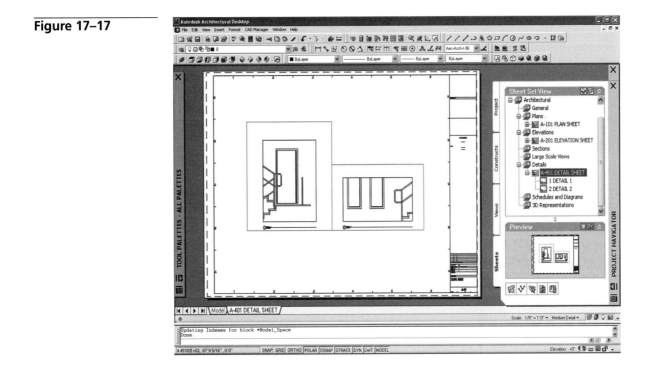

18

Detail Components and the Detail Component Manager

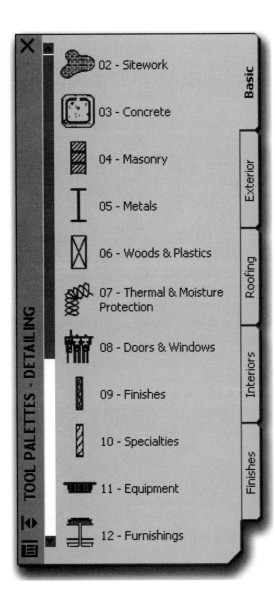

When you finish this section, you should understand the following:

- ✔ The **Detail Component** concept.
- ✔ How to create a wall detail using **Detail Components.**
- ✔ How to place **Detail Components.**
- ✔ How to place **Keynotes.**
- ✔ How to use the **Detail Component Manager.**
- ✔ How to create new custom **Detail Components.**
- ✔ How to use the new **Keynote Editor.**

The Detailer has been around since the beginnings of Autodesk Architectural Desktop. In Autodesk Architectural Desktop 2006, the Detail Component Manager has again been revamped. New components and a Component Editor have been added

Detail components represent specific building materials and products and are made up of simple two-dimensional line work entities such as lines, polylines, arcs, circles, and hatches. In most cases, the detail component is a collection of such entities grouped as a block, which can be easily copied or moved as a single entity. The following are examples of detail components that are inserted as blocks:

- Bolt heads
- Fixed-length nails
- Section reviews of beams and columns
- Most selection views of framing members
- Units such as CMUs, bricks, and pavers
- Connectors
- Materials with reviews generated from interrelating parameters, for example, trusses, precast concrete, and hollow metal frames.

Hands-On

Inserting Detail Components

All detail components are inserted into drawings using the same basic tool, which performs the insertion routine associated with a selected component. Each detail component tool provided on the sample tool palettes represents a different configuration of the basic tool. You can activate the tool insertion tool in five different ways:

1. Click a detail component tool icon on a tool palette.
2. Click on the **Detail Component** icon on the **Navigation** tool bar (see Figure 18–1), and select a component from the **Detail Component Manager** (see Figure 18–2).
3. Drag and drop a detail component that has been placed in a drawing from that drawing into a tool palette (see Figure 18–3).

Figure 18–1

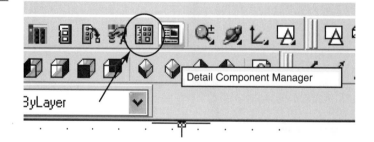

Figure 18–2

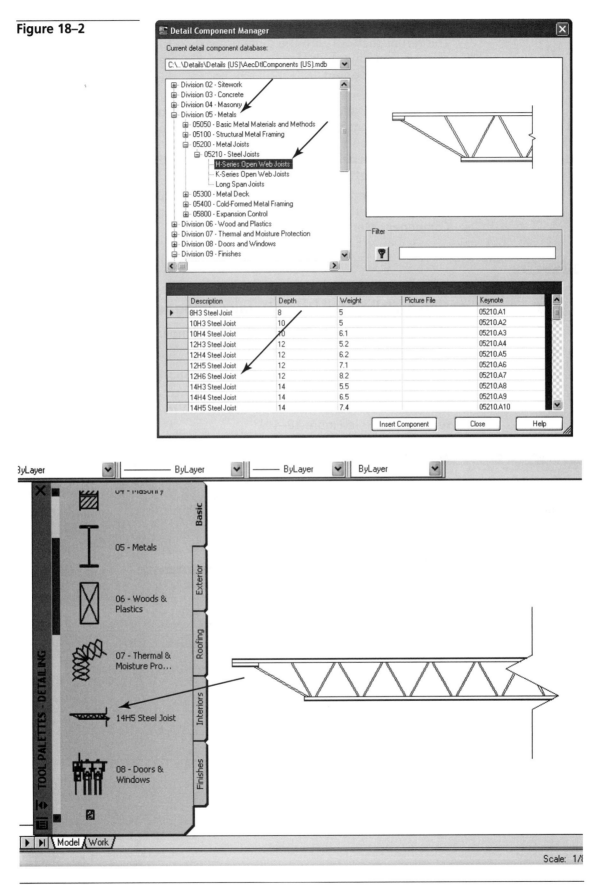

Figure 18–3

4. Select a component in a drawing, right-click, and click **Add selected.**
This reruns the tool with the same property settings used to insert the existing component, so that one can quickly insert additional copies of the same component.

5. Select a component in a drawing, right-click, and click **Replace selected.**
This erases the selected component and reruns the tool with the same property settings used to insert the erased component. However, you can modify the tool to insert a different component by changing the component properties (**Category, Type, Description,** or **View**) on the **Properties** palette.

6. **RMB** on any **Detail Component** tool, and select **Detail Component Manager** from the contextual menu that appears to bring up the **Detail Component Manager.**

Hands-On

Creating a Wall Detail Using Detail Components

1. Start a new drawing using the Aec Model (Imperial Stb) template.

2. Change to the **Top View.**

3. Click on the **03-Concrete** tool in the **Basic** tool palette of the **DETAILING** tool palettes.

4. Move your cursor over the **Properties** palette to open it, and set the settings shown in Figure 18–4.

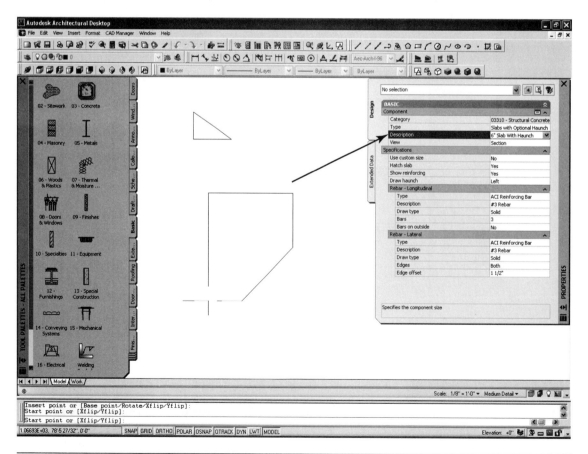

Figure 18–4

5. In the **Description** field of the **Properties** palette, select the **6″ SLAB WITH HAUNCH** option, and return to the Drawing Editor.
6. In the Drawing Editor, click and drag to the right, and then click again to establish the end of the slab.
7. Press **Enter** to complete the command (see Figure 18–5).

Figure 18–5

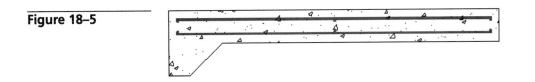

Tip	**Alternative Selection Method**
	a. Select the **Detail Component Manager** from the **Navigation** toolbar to bring up the Detail Component Manager.
	b. In the Detail Component Manager, select **Division 03-Concrete > 03310-Structural Concrete > Slabs with Optional haunch.**
	c. Press the **Insert Component** button to return to the Drawing Editor and begin to place the component.
	d. Before placing the component, move your cursor over the **Properties** palette to open it allowing you to modify all the options of your component (see Figure 18–6).

Figure 18–6

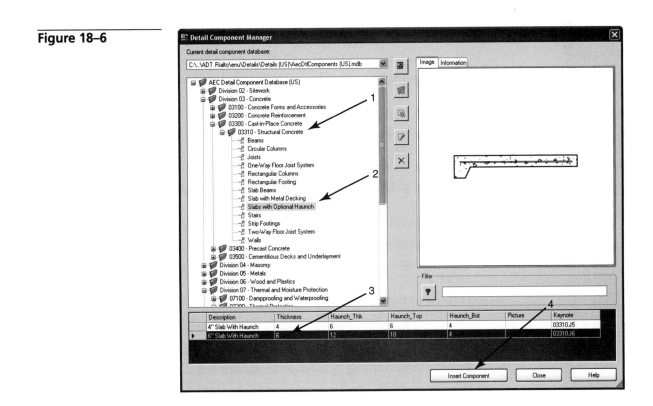

8. Click on the **04-Masonry** tool in the **Basic** tool palette of the **DETAILING** tool palettes.

9. Move your cursor over the **Properties** palette to open it, and set the settings shown in Figure 18–7.

Figure 18–7

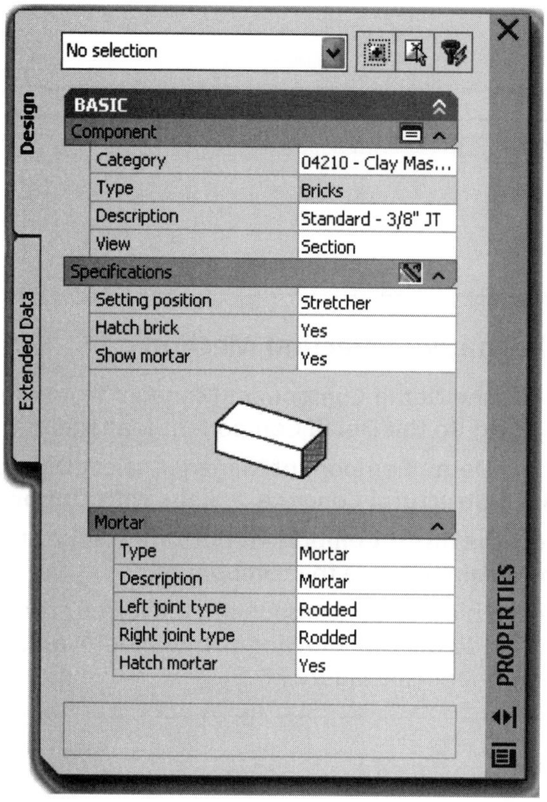

10. Click at the left edge of the slab you just placed, drag vertically, enter **2'** in the **Command line** and press **Enter.** This will make a 2'-high masonry wall.

11. Select the **Detail Component Manager** from the **Navigation** toolbar to bring up the **Detail Component Manager.**

12. Select **Division 09110 - Non-Load Bearing Wall framing > Interior Metal Studs.**

13. Select **3-5/8" Metal Stud,** and press the **Insert Component** button to return to the Drawing Editor.

14. In the **Properties** palette, set the **View** to **Elevation.**

15. Enter **L** (Left) in the **Command line** and press **Enter.**

16. With **Osnap** set to **Endpoint,** enter **fro** in the **Command line** and press **Enter.**

17. Enter **1"** in the **Command line** for the airspace, drag to the right, click again, drag vertically, enter **22-1/2",** and press **Enter** to complete the command (see Figure 18–8).

18. In the **Detail Component Manager,** again select **Division 09110 - Non-Load Bearing Wall framing > Interior Metal Runner Channels,** and rotate and place runners at the top and base of the steel stud.

Figure 18–8

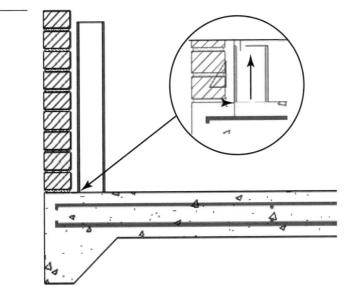

19. Click on the **06-Woods & Plastics** tool in the **Basic** tool palette of the **DETAILING** tool palettes.

20. Move your cursor over the **Properties** palette to open it, set the **Description** drop-down list to **2 × 4,** and **View** to **Section.**

21. Enter **R** (Rotate) in the **Command line** and press **Enter.**

22. Enter **90** in the **Command line** and press **Enter.**

23. Place the bottom right edge of the 2 × 4 with the top right edge of metal stud and runner you placed previously.

24. Select the **Detail Component Manager** from the **Navigation** toolbar to bring up the **Detail Component Manager.**

25. Select **Division 08410 - Metal-Framed Storefronts > Front Double Glazed.**

26. Select **Storefront sill at Finish,** and press the **Insert Component** button to return to the Drawing Editor.

27. Enter **B** (Base point) in the **Command line** and press **Enter.**

28. With **Osnap** set to **Endpoint,** click on the lower right corner of the storefront component.

29. Click on the top right of the 2 × 4 you previously placed (see Figure 18–9).

Figure 18–9

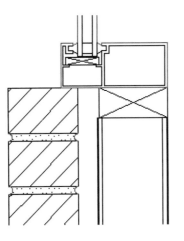

30. Click on the **09-Finishes** tool in the **Basic** tool palette of the **DETAILING** tool palettes.

31. Move your cursor over the **Properties** palette to open it, and select **1/2"Gypsum Wallboard** from the **Description** field

32. Enter **L** (Left) in the **Command line** and press **Enter.**

33. Click at the bottom right of the metal stud, and drag upwards to the midpoint of the right side of the storefront sill component.

34. Select the gypsum board you already placed, **RMB,** and select **Add Selected** from the contextual menu that appears.

35. Place a copy of 1/2" gypsum wallboard on the left side of the metal stud.

You now need to cap the gypsum wallboard at the storefront component.

36. Select the **Detail Component Manager** from the **Navigation** toolbar to bring up the **Detail Component Manager.**

37. Select **Division 09270 - Gypsum Wall Board Accessories.**

38. Select **1/2" J Casing Bead,** and press the **Insert Component** button to return to the Drawing Editor.

39. Enter **B** (Base point) in the **Command line** and press **Enter.**

40. With the **Endpoint Osnap** on, relocate the base point.

41. Enter **R** (Rotate) in the **Command line** and press **Enter.**

42. Enter **270** in the **Command line** and press **Enter.**

43. Place the casing bead as shown in Figure 18–10.

Figure 18–10

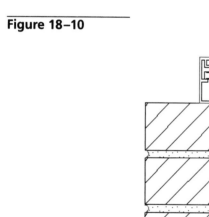

44. Click on the **07-Thermal & Moisture Protection** tool in the **Basic** tool palette of the **DETAILING** tool palettes.

45. Move your cursor over the **Properties** palette to open it. Select **Batt Insulation** from the **Type** field, **3-1/2" R-11 Fiberglass Batt Insulation** from the **Description** field, **Section** from the **View** field, and **Normal** from the **Density** field.

46. Click at the bottom center of the metal stud, drag upwards, and click again to place the insulation (see Figure 18–11).

Figure 18–11

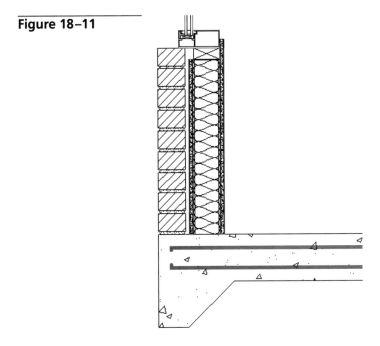

Chamfer the Brick Sill

47. Select the brick directly below the storefront, **RMB,** and select **AEC Modify Tools > Trim** from the contextual menu that appears.

48. Select two points for a trim plane and then select the side to trim (see Figure 18–12).

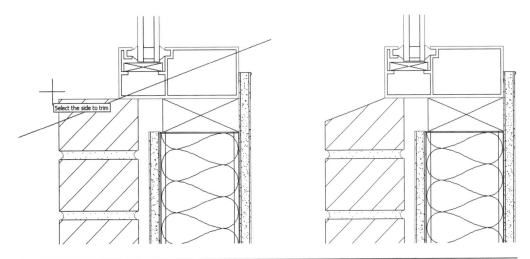

Figure 18–12

Create Sill Flashing

49. Select the **Polyline** icon from the **Draw** toolbar, and create the flashing shown in Figure 18–13.

50. Select the **Detail Component Manager** from the **Navigation** toolbar to bring up the **Detail Component Manager.**

51. Select **Division 07620 - Sheet Metal Flashing.**

Figure 18–13

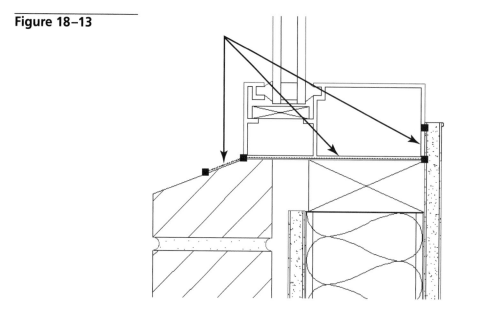

52. Select **Aluminum Flashing** from the list, and press the **Insert Component** button.

53. Select the polyline you just created and press **Enter** twice to complete the command. You have now applied aluminum flashing component information to the polyline that will control the keynote.

Hands-On

Keynoting

Keynoting is Architectural Desktop 2006's automated system for labeling detail components.

First you need to set your text style. This author prefers the Stylus BT text style because it looks like hand printing.

1. Select **Format > Text Style** from the **Main** menu to bring up the **Text Style** dialog box.

2. Select **Arch-Dim** from the **Style Name** drop-down list.

3. Select **Stylus BT** from the **Font Name** drop-down list, and close the **Text Style** dialog box.

4. Set the **Scale** drop-down list below the Drawing Editor to **1″ = 1′-0″**.

5. Change to the **Document** tool palettes.

6. Select the **Reference Keynote** tool from the **Annotation** palette, **RMB,** and select **Properties** from the contextual menu that appears to bring up the **Tool Properties** dialog box.

7. Set the settings shown in Figure 18–14 and press the **OK** button.

8. Click on the storefront, select a point to start the keynote arrow, and then click a second point to place the keynote. The correct keynote for that particular detail component will appear on the drawing.

9. After placing the first keynote, press the space bar on your computer to repeat the keynote command for the next component.

Figure 18-14

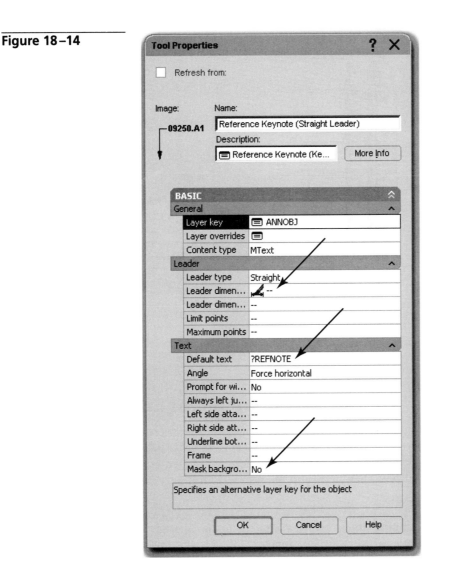

10.   Place all the keynotes (see Figure 18–15).

! *Note:* By changing the **Default** text to **?REFNOTE,** only the name of the material will be placed and not its CSI number.

! *Note:* By setting the **Mask** background to **NO,** you will not see a grey background behind the keynote text.

Figure 18–15

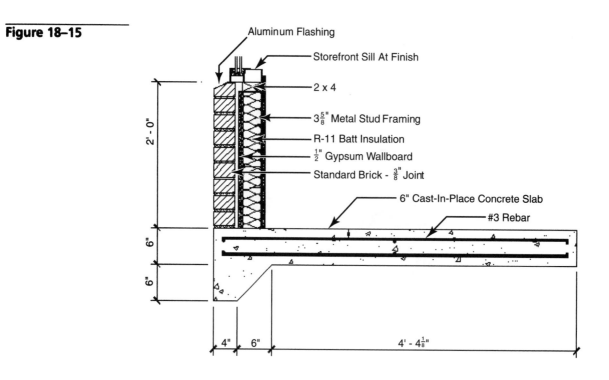

The New Component Editor

In Architectural Desktop 2006, a Component Editor has been added to enable you to create your own automated detail components. In order to automate these detail components you create a "recipe" of instructions using a worksheet called a *jig*. There are six jigs available. They are Stamp, Bookends, Linear Array, Surface, Surface Linetype, and Surface Top.

Stamp Components jig creates components that may need to be depicted multiple times at a particular orientation, such as nails or screws.

Bookends Components jig creates components, such as louvers and vents, that consist of a pattern repeated as a linear array but bounded by unique items at each end.

Linear Array Components jig creates components that consist of a pattern repeated as a linear array, such as shingles or corrugated sheet metal.

Surface Components jig creates components of a specific depth that have a hatch, such as base courses.

Surface Linetype Components jig creates components similar to surface components in that they have a specified depth and a rectangular boundary with user-specified start points and endpoints. Instead of a hatch-filled boundary, however, the surface linetype jig fills the boundary with a wide polyline of a specified linetype.

Surface Top Components jig creates components similar to surface components; however, they are components such as concrete topping, which is poured onto or bounded by another entity, which provides the bottom edge of the rectangle. Thus, the surface top jig draws only the top and side edges of the rectangle. Refer to the following table if you are adding a new detail component (or editing one that was created using the New Component option) and you want to define a recipe that uses a surface top jig to insert the component in the specified view.

Figure 18-16 shows a typical Detail Component jig, located in the Parameters tab of the Components properties.

Figure 18–16

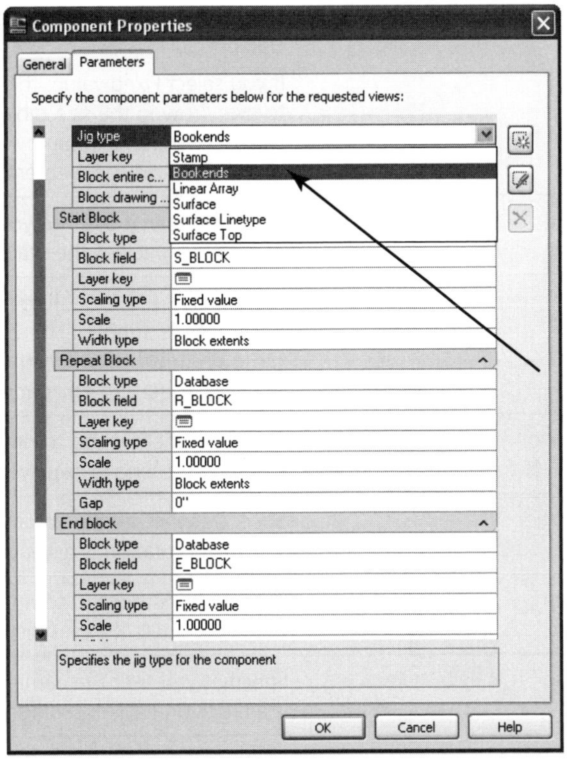

Listed below, from the Architectural Desktop 2006 User Guide located on the first disk of the program, are the parameter names and descriptions for the six available Detail Component jigs.

Parameters for Recipes Using Stamp Jigs

Stamp jigs are used to insert components that consist of a single block.

Parameter Name	Description/Instructions
Layer key	Specifies the layer key for the layer to which the component will be assigned in the specified view.
Block drawing location	The name of the drawing file (a DWG, DWT or DWS file) containing the blocks for the component table.
Block type	A drop-down list lets you specify either Fixed value or Database. If you select Fixed value, the value you enter will apply to every row in the size table for this component. If you select Database, a column will be added to the table allowing values to be entered for individual sizes.
Block	Displayed only if Block type is Fixed value, this parameter specifies the block definition to be inserted for this component.
Block field	Displayed only if Block type is Database, this parameter specifies the name of the component table column in which the block to be inserted is specified for each size

Scaling type	A drop-down list lets you specify either Fixed value or Database. If you select Fixed value, the value you supply will apply to every row in the size table for this component. If you select Database, a column will be added to the table allowing values to be entered for individual sizes.
Scale	Displayed only if Scaling type is Fixed value, this parameter specifies the scaling value for the block.
Scale field	Displayed only if Scaling type is Database, this parameter specifies the name of the component table column in which the scaling value for the block is specified for each size.
Allow scaling	Specifies whether the command-line option for specifying scaling is displayed for this component.
Allow Rotation	Specifies whether the command-line option for specifying rotation is displayed for this component.
Allow X flip	Specifies whether the command-line option for flipping the block on its X axis is displayed for this component
Allow Y flip	Specifies whether the command-line option for flipping the block on its Y axis is displayed for this component.
Allow Base point	Specifies whether the command-line option for specifying an alternate base point is displayed for this component.

Parameters for Recipes Using Bookends Jigs

Bookends jigs are used to insert components that consist of a pattern repeated as a linear array but bounded by unique items at each end. Thus, the recipe must define a start block, a repeat block, and an end block.

Parameter Name	**Description/Instructions**
Layer key	Specifies the layer key for the layer to which the component will be assigned in the specified view.
Block entire component	Specifies whether the blocks comprising the component are inserted as a single block.
Block drawing location	Specifies the drawing file (a DWG, DWT, or DWS file) containing the blocks for the component table.
*Block type	Displayed only if Block type is Fixed value, this parameter specifies the block definition to be used for all sizes.
*Block field	Displayed only if Block type is Database, this parameter specifies the name of the component table column in which the block definition is specified for each size.
*Layer key	A drop-down list lets you specify either Fixed value or Database. If you select Fixed value, the value you enter for the corresponding

	Scale parameter will apply to every row in this component's size table. If you select Database, a column (with the name specified for the corresponding Scale field parameter) will be added to the component table, allowing values to be entered for individual sizes.
*Scaling type	Specifies whether the command-line option for specifying scaling is displayed for this component.
*Scale	Displayed only if Scaling type is Fixed value, this parameter specifies the scaling value for the block.
*Scale field	Displayed only if Scaling type is Database, this parameter specifies the name of the component table column in which the scaling value for the block is specified for each size.
*Width type	A drop-down list lets you specify Fixed value, Database, or Block extents. If you select Fixed value, the value you enter for the corresponding Width parameter will apply to every row in the size table for this component. If you select Database, a column (with the name specified for the corresponding Width field parameter) will be added to the component table, allowing values to be entered for individual sizes. If you select Block extents, then block width is calculated dynamically as the block is inserted.
*Width	Displayed only if Width type is Fixed value, this parameter specifies the width for the block.
*Width field	Displayed only if Width type is Database, this parameter specifies the name of the component table column in which the block width is specified for each size.
Gap	Specifies the distance between repeat blocks. A negative value causes blocks to overlap.
Start prompt	Specifies the string to display for the start point prompt.
End prompt	Specifies the string to display for the endpoint prompt.
Block orientation	Specifies whether the block is oriented along the X axis or the Y axis.
Jig orientation	Specifies whether the jig is oriented along the X axis or the Y axis.
Allow X flip	Specifies whether the command-line option for flipping the block on its X axis is displayed for this component.
Allow Y flip	Specifies whether the command-line option for flipping the block on its Y axis is displayed for this component.

Parameters for Recipes Using Linear Array Jigs

Linear Array jigs are used to insert multiple copies of a block in a line along the X or Y axis.

Parameter Name	Description/Instructions
Layer key	Specifies the layer key for the layer to which the component will be assigned in the specified view.
Block entire component	Specifies whether the blocks comprising the component are inserted as a single block.
Block drawing location	Specifies the drawing file (a DWG, DWT, or DWS file) containing the blocks for the component table.
Block type	A drop-down list lets you specify either Fixed value or Database. If you select Fixed value, the value you enter for the corresponding Block parameter will apply to every row in this component's size table. If you select Database, a column (with the name specified for the corresponding Block field parameter) will be added to the component table, allowing different block definitions to be specified for individual sizes.
Block	Displayed only if Block type is Fixed value, this parameter specifies the block definition to be used for all sizes
Block field	Displayed only if Block type is Database, this parameter specifies the name of the component table column in which the block definition is specified for each size.
Scaling type	A drop-down list lets you specify either Fixed value or Database. If you select Fixed value, the value you enter for the corresponding Scale parameter will apply to every row in this component's size table. If you select Database, a column (with the name specified for the corresponding Scale field parameter) will be added to the component table, allowing values to be entered for individual sizes.
Scale	Displayed only if Scaling type is Fixed value, this parameter specifies the scaling value for the block for all sizes.
Scale field	Displayed only if Scaling type is Database, this parameter specifies the name of the component table column in which the scaling value for the block is specified for each size.
Width type	A drop-down list lets you specify Fixed value, Database, or Block extents. If you select Fixed value, the value you enter for the corresponding Width parameter will apply to every row in the size table for this component. If you select Database, a column (with the name specified for the corresponding Width field parameter) will be added to the component table, allowing values to be entered

	for individual sizes. If you select Block extents, then block width is calculated dynamically as the block is inserted.
Width	Displayed only if Width type is Fixed value, this parameter specifies the width for the block for all sizes.
Width field	Displayed only if Width type is Database, this parameter specifies the name of the component table column in which the block width is specified for each size.
Gap	Specifies the distance between repeat blocks. A negative value causes blocks to overlap.
Display count option	Specifies whether the command-line options for specifying a count are displayed.
Start prompt	Specifies the string to display for the start point prompt.
End prompt	Specifies the string to display for the endpoint prompt.
Count prompt	Displayed only if the Display count option parameter is Yes, this parameter specifies the command-line prompt to be displayed.
Block orientation	Specifies whether the block is oriented along the X axis or the Y axis.
Jig orientation	Specifies whether the jig is oriented along the X axis or the Y axis.
Allow X flip	Specifies whether the command-line option for flipping the block on its X axis is displayed for this component.
Allow Y flip	Specifies whether the command-line option for flipping the block on its Y axis is displayed for this component.

Parameters for Recipes Using Surface Jigs

Surface jigs are used to insert components that have a specified depth and a hatch-filled rectangular boundary with user-specified start points and endpoints.

Parameter Name	Description/Instructions
Layer key	Specifies the layer key for the layer to which the component boundary will be assigned in the specified view.
Layer key (for hatching)	Specifies the layer key for the layer to which the component hatch infill will be assigned in the specified view.
Hatching type	A drop-down list lets you specify either Fixed value or Database.
	If you select Fixed value, the value you enter for the corresponding Hatch alias parameter will apply to every row in this component's size table. If you select Database, a column (with the name specified for the corresponding Hatching parameter) will be added to the component table, allowing values to be entered for individual sizes.

Hatch alias	Displayed only if Hatching type is Fixed value, this parameter specifies the hatch alias (from the Hatches table for this database) for all sizes of the component.
Hatching	Displayed only if Hatching type is Database, this parameter specifies the name of the component table column in which the hatch is specified for each size.
Start prompt	Specifies the string to display for the start point prompt.
End prompt	Specifies the string to display for the endpoint prompt.
Allow X flip	Specifies whether the command-line option for flipping the block on its X axis is displayed for this component.
Allow Y flip	Specifies whether the command-line option for flipping the block on its Y axis is displayed for this component.

Parameters for Recipes Using Surface Linetype Jigs

Surface linetype jigs are similar to surface jigs in that they are used to insert components that have a specified depth and a rectangular boundary with user-specified start points and endpoints. Instead of a hatch-filled boundary, however, the surface linetype jig fills the boundary with a wide polyline of a specified linetype.

Parameter Name	Description/Instructions
Layer key	Specifies the layer key for the layer to which the component boundary will be assigned in the specified view.
Linetype/Layer key	Specifies the layer key for the layer to which the component infill will be assigned in the specified view.
Linetype type	A drop-down list lets you specify either Fixed value or Database. If you select Fixed value, the value you enter for the corresponding Linetype parameter will apply to every row in this component's size table. If you select Database, a column (with the name specified for the corresponding Linetype field parameter) will be added to the component table, allowing values to be entered for individual sizes.
Linetype	Displayed only if Linetype type is Fixed value, this parameter specifies the linetype alias for all sizes of the component.
Linetype field	Displayed only if Linetype type is Database, this parameter specifies the name of the component table column in which the linetype is specified for each size.
Start prompt	Specifies the string to display for the start point prompt.
End prompt	Specifies the string to display for the endpoint prompt.
Allow X flip	Specifies whether the command-line option for flipping the block on its X axis is displayed for this component.
Allow Y flip	Specifies whether the command-line option for flipping the block on its Y axis is displayed for this component.

Parameters for Recipes Using Surface-Top Jigs

Surface-top jigs are similar to surface jigs in that they are used to insert components with a specified depth and a hatch-filled rectangular boundary. However, the surface top jig is designed for components such as concrete topping that is poured onto or bounded by another entity, which provides the bottom edge of the rectangle. Thus, the surface top jig draws only the top and side edges of the rectangle. Refer to the following table if you are adding a new detail component (or editing one that was created using the New Component option) and you want to define a recipe that uses a surface top jig to insert the component in the specified view.

Parameter Name	Description/Instructions
Layer key	Specifies the layer key for the layer to which the component boundary will be assigned in the specified view.
Layer key (for hatching)	Specifies the layer key for the layer to which the component hatch infill will be assigned in the specified view.
Hatching type	A drop-down list lets you specify either Fixed value or Database. If you select Fixed value, the value you enter for the corresponding Hatch alias parameter will apply to every row in this component's size table. If you select Database, a column (with the name specified for the corresponding Hatching parameter) will be added to the component table, allowing values to be entered for individual sizes.
Hatch alias	Displayed only if Hatching type is Fixed value, this parameter specifies the hatch alias (from the Hatches table for this database) for all sizes of the component.
Hatching	Displayed only if Hatching type is Database, this parameter specifies the name of the component table column in which the hatch is specified for each size.
Start prompt	Specifies the string to display for the start point prompt.
End prompt	Specifies the string to display for the endpoint prompt.
Allow X flip	Specifies whether the command-line option for flipping the block on its X axis is displayed for this component.
Allow Y flip	Specifies whether the command-line option for flipping the block on its Y axis is displayed for this component.

Hands-On

Creating the New Custom Detail Component Block

1. Start a new drawing using the Aec Model (Imperial Stb) template.
2. Change to the **Top View.**
3. Select the line icon from the Draw menu, and create the detail of siding shown in (Figure 18–17) (do not include dimensions)

Figure 18–17

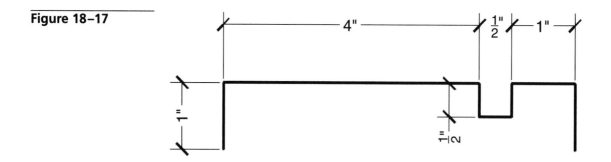

4. Select **Format > Blocks > Block Definition** from the **Main** menu to bring up the **Block Definition** dialog box.
5. In the **Block Definition** dialog box, enter **TEST** in the **Name** field, and press the **Select objects** icon, to return to the Drawing Editor.
6. In the Drawing Editor, select the detail you just drew, and press the **Enter** key on the keyboard to return to the **Block Definition** dialog box.
7. In the **Block Definition** dialog box, select the **Convert to block** radio button, and press the **Pick point** icon to return to the Drawing Editor.
8. In the Drawing Editor, select the lower left corner of the detail you drew to return to the **Block Definition** dialog box.
9. In the **Block Definition** dialog box, press the **OK** button to complete the command.
10. Save the drawing as **SIDING,** and close the drawing.

Hands-On

Editing the Detail Component Database and Creating a Recipe Using the Linear Array Jig

1. Start a new drawing using the Aec Model (Imperial Stb) template.
2. Change to the **Top** view.
3. Select the **Detail Component Manager** icon from the **Main** menu to bring up the **Detail Component Manager** dialog box.
4. In the **Detail Component Manager** dialog box, select the **Edit Database** icon (see Figure 18–18).

This will now light up the four lower icons.

Figure 18–18

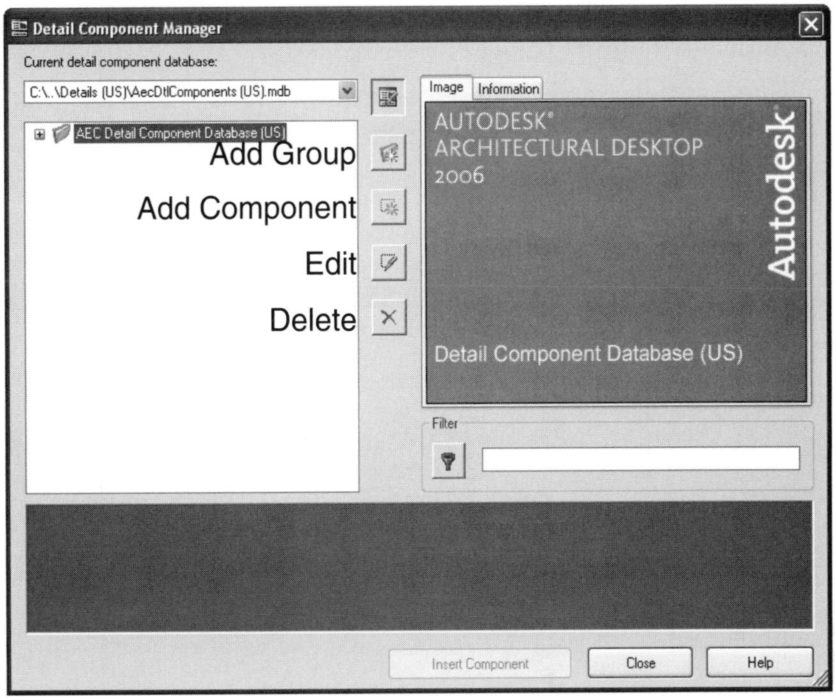

5. In the **Detail Component Manager** dialog box, expand the database, expand **Division 07 - Thermal and Moisture protection,** expand **07400 - Roofing and Siding Panels**, and finally expand **07460 - Siding.**

6. With 07460 - Siding selected, press the Add Component icon to bring up the **New Component** dialog box.

7. In the **New Component** dialog box, change to the **General** tab.

8. Enter **TEST SIDING** in the **Display Name** field; enter **TEST SIDING** in the **Table Name,** and **TESTComponent.xml** in the **Recipe** field.

9. Change to the Parameters tab, and enter the parameters shown in (Figure 18–19).

Refer to the description of the **Parameters for Recipes Using Linear Array Jigs** described at the beginning of this section. Notice that the Jig type was set to **Linear Array**, the **Block drawing** is the drawing you created, and **TEST** is the name of the block you created in that drawing.

10. After you have entered the instructions to create the "recipe" in the Jig, press the OK button to close the **New Component** dialog box, and return to the **Detail Component Manager.**

11. At the bottom of the **Detail Component Manager,** enter **SIDING in** the **Description** column.

12. Press the **Close** button to close the **Detail Component Manager,** and return to the Drawing Editor.

Figure 18–19

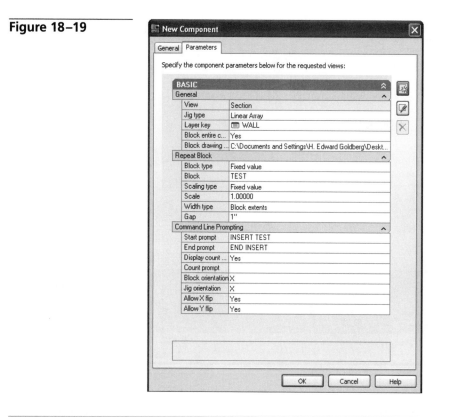

Hands-On

Testing the New Detail Component

1. Start a new drawing using the Aec Model (Imperial Stb) template.

2. Change to the **Top** view.

3. Select the **Detail Component Manager** icon from the Main menu to bring up the **Detail Component Manager** dialog box.

4. In the **Detail Component Manager**, expand the database, and select the **TEST SIDING** component you just created.

5. At the bottom of the **Detail Component Manager,** select the field to the left of **SIDING in** the **Description** column.

6. Select the Insert Component button at the bottom of the **Detail Component Manager** to return to the Drawing Manager.

7. With **Ortho** (on), click to start to place the **SIDING** component.

8. Enter **C** (Count) in the Command line, and press the **Enter** key on your keyboard.

9. Enter 6 in the Command line, and press the **Enter** key on your keyboard.

10. Click the mouse again to place the siding, and then press the **Esc** key to end the command.

You will have now placed six arrayed copies of your new SIDING detail component (see Figure 18–20).

Figure 18–20

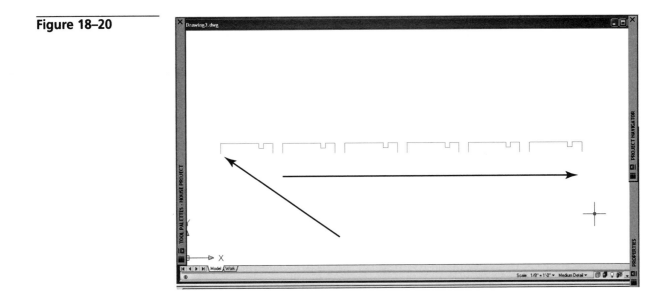

Creating Detail Components is not difficult, but it does take some practice and patience. Remember to create the blocks first, and be sure to read the descriptions for all the different instructions in the Jigs.
    Save this drawing.

The New Keynote Editor

! **Note:** The new Keynote Editor is located under the **CAD Manager** drop-down list. If it is not loaded, please refer to **Loading the CAD Manager** in the second exercise of Section 25.

Hands-On

Creating a New Keynote and Linking It to a Detail Component

1. Use the drawing from the previous exercise that contains the siding.
2. Change to the **Top** view.
3. Select **CAD Manager > Keynote Editor** from the **Main** menu to bring up the **Keynote Editor** dialog box.
4. In the **Keynote Editor,** browse for **C:\Documents and Settings\All Users\Application Data\Autodesk\ADT 2006\enu\Details\Details (US)\AecKeynotes (US).mdb** in the **Keynote Database** drop-down list at the top of the dialog box.
5. In the **Keynote Editor** dialog box, expand **Division 07 - Thermal and Moisture protection,** expand **07400 - Roofing and Siding Panels,** and finally expand **07460 - Siding.**
6. **RMB** on **07460 - Siding,** and select **New Keynote** from the contextual menu that appears to bring up the **Add Keynote** dialog box.

7. In the **Add Keynote** dialog box, enter **07460.A10** (for the Key) and **1″ Corrugated Steel 24 Ga** (for the Note), and press the **Ok** button to return to the **Keynote Editor.**

8. In the **Keynote Editor,** press the **Save** button, and then press the **Close** button to return to the Drawing Editor.

9. Select the **Detail Component Manager** icon from the **Main** menu to bring up the **Detail Component Manager** dialog box.

10. In the **Detail Component Manager** dialog box, select the **Edit Database** icon.

11. Expand the database until you get to the **TEST SIDING** detail component that you created.

12. Double-click on **TEST SIDING** to bring up the **Component Properties** dialog box.

13. In the **Component Properties** dialog box, press the **Select Keynote** button to bring up the **Select Keynote** dialog box.

14. In the **Select Keynote** dialog box, expand the keynotes until you get to the new keynote you just created.

15. Select the **07460.A10 - 1″ Corrugated Steel 24 Ga** keynote, and press the **OK** button to return to the **Component Properties** dialog box.

16. In the **Component Properties** dialog box, press the **OK** button to return to the **Detail Component Manager** dialog box.

17. In the **Detail Component Manager** dialog box, press the **Close** button to return to the Drawing Manager.

Testing the New Keynote

18. Click the scale at the bottom right of the Drawing Editor, and select 1 1/2″ = 1'-0″ (see Figure 18–21).

19. Select the **Reference Keynote (Straight leader)** tool from the **Annotation** tool palette.

Figure 18–21

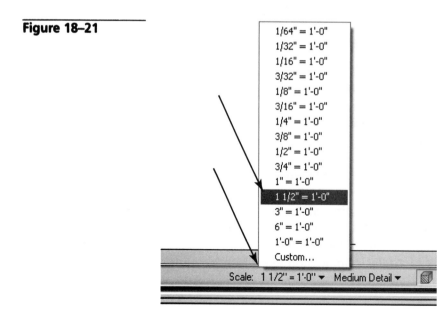

20. Select one of the Siding components that you previously placed, click again on that component, move your cursor up in the direction of 90 degrees, and click again; then move your cursor in the 0 degree direction and click.

21. Press the **Enter** key to complete the tool and place the keynote. (see Figure 18–22).

Figure 18–22

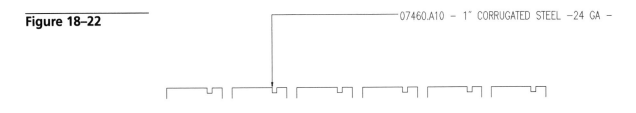

07460.A10 – 1″ CORRUGATED STEEL –24 GA –

When you finish this section, you should understand the
following:

✔ How to create a property set definition.
✔ How to create and use an automatic property.
✔ How to create and use a manual property.
✔ How to create and use a formula property definition.
✔ How to create and use the property data format.

Autodesk Architectural Desktop 2006 uses property set definitions and property
sets as means of codifying information concerning objects in the virtual building
model.

Property Set Definition

A property set definition specifies the characteristics of a group of properties that can be tracked with an object. Each property has a name, description, data type, data format, and default value.

Property Sets and Property Data

A property set is an object created from a property set definition. It contains a user-definable group of related object properties. When you attach a property set to an object or style, the property set becomes the container for the property data associated with the object. Property Data is similar to Block Attributes in AutoCAD

Automatic Properties

Automatic properties are built into objects and styles when they are created. Examples are width, length, height, etc. They consist primarily of the physical properties of an object.

Manual Properties

Manual properties are properties that are entered manually, such as manufacturer, price, etc.

Hands-On

Adding the Automatic Properties

1. Start a new drawing using the Aec Model (Imperial Stb) template.
2. Select **Format** > **Style Manager** from the **Main** menu to bring up the **Style Manager.**
3. Expand the **Documentation Objects** folder.
4. **RMB** on **Property Set Definition,** to create a **New Style Property Set Definition.**
5. Name the new style **WALLPROPERTYSETDEFINITION** (see Figure 19–1).
6. Select the **Applies To** tab.
7. Select the **Objects** radio button and press the **Select All** button. (Use this procedure to list the default auto properties only.)
8. Change to the **Definition** tab.
9. Select the **Add Automatic Property Definition** icon (see Figure 19–2).

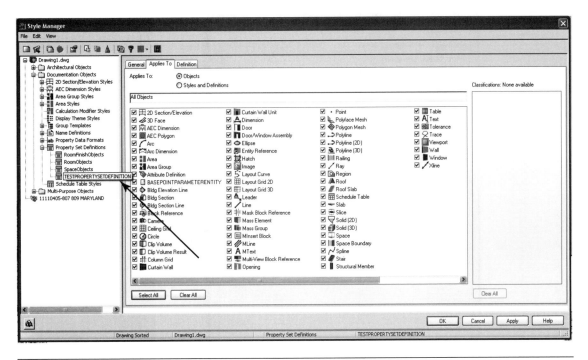

Figure 19–1

Because you have selected all the objects in the **Applies To** tab, you will get a warning message telling you that it will take some time to compile the list of data sources. Press the **Yes** button to proceed.

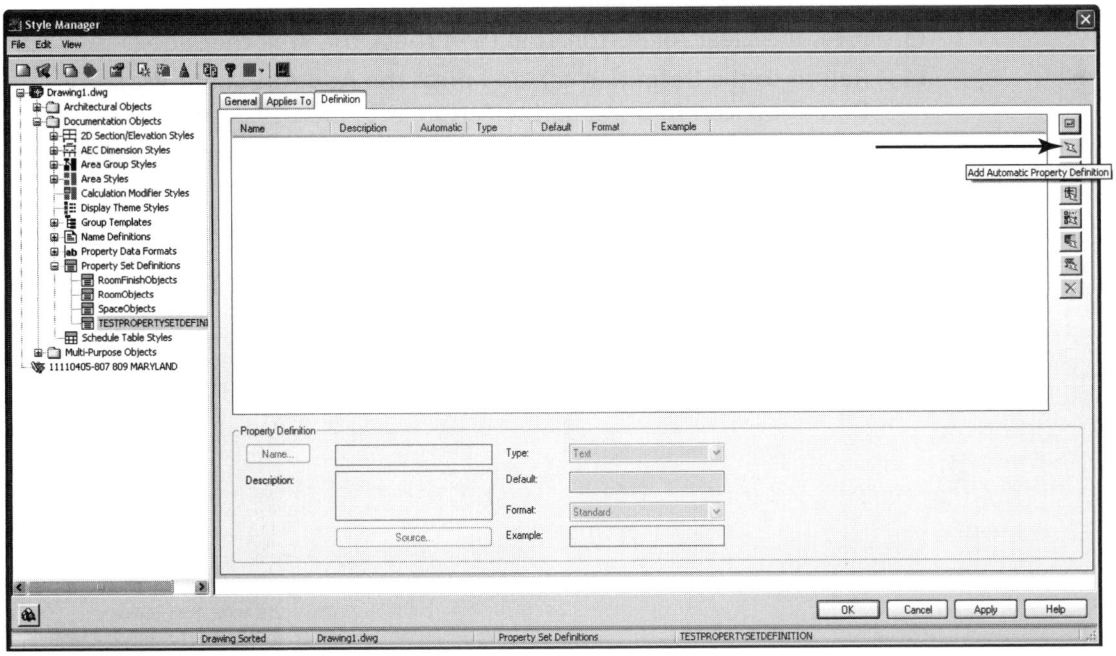

Figure 19–2

10. When the **Automatic Property Source** dialog appears, scroll through it to see all the properties available for all the objects (see Figure 19–3).

11. Press **Cancel** to return to the **Property Set Definition Properties** dialog box.

Figure 19–3

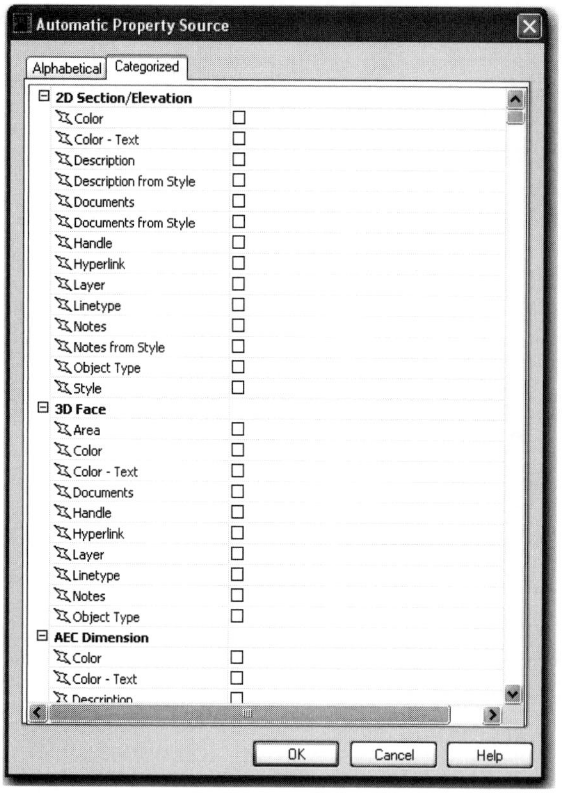

12. Change back to the **Applies To** tab.

13. Press the **Clear All** button, and then check the **Wall** check box.

14. Return to the **Definition** tab and press the **Add Automatic Property Definition** icon to bring up the **Automatic Property Source** dialog box.

15. Check the **Height** check box, and press **OK** to return to the **Property Set Definition Properties** dialog box.

16. Select **Length-Nominal** from the **Format** drop-down list. This will format the height in feet and inches (see Figure 19–4).

Figure 19–4

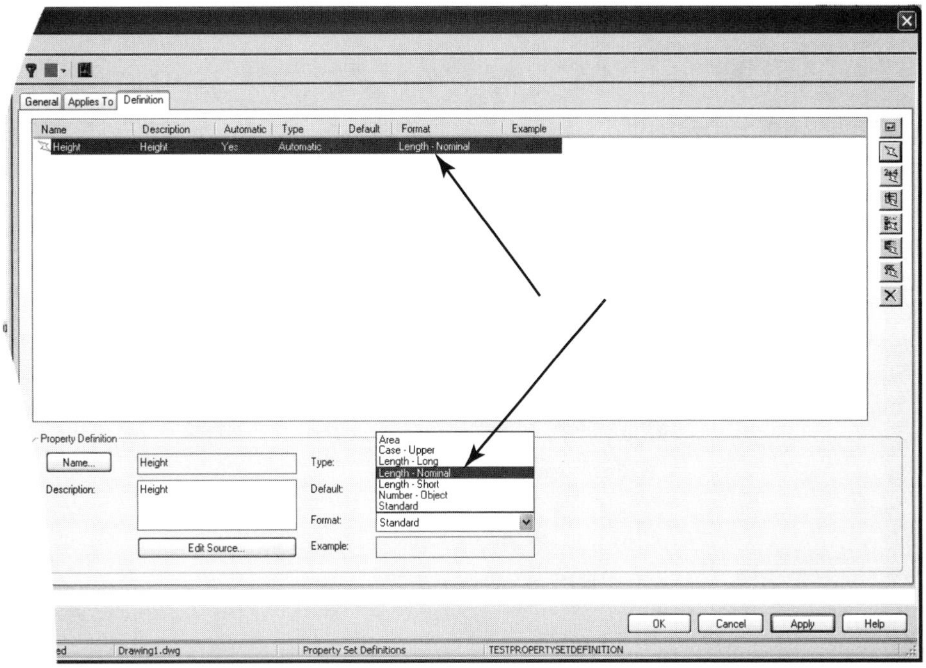

17.   Repeat Steps 15 through 17, but this time hold down the **Shift** key and select **Area-Left Gross, Area-Left Net, Length,** and **Object Type.**

18.   In the **Property Set Definition Properties** dialog box, for **Area-Left Gross** to **Standard** from the **Format** drop-down list. For **Area-Left Net,** select **Area** from the **Format** drop-down list.

Note: We are going to use the **Area-Left Gross** for a formula. If you use any property in a formula you must set its **Format** to **Standard.**

19.   In the **Property Set Definition Properties,** for **Length,** select **Length-Nominal** from the **Format** drop-down list This will format the length in feet and inches. Press the **OK** button to return to the Drawing Editor.

20.   In the Drawing Editor place a 15'-long wall (the style doesn't matter).

21.   Double-click the wall you placed to open the **Properties** palette.

22.   Change to the **Extended Data** tab.

23.   Select the **Add Property Sets** icon to bring up the **Add Property Sets** dialog box (see Figure 19–5).

24.   Press the **Select All** button.

25.   Double-click the wall again to open the **Properties** palette again.

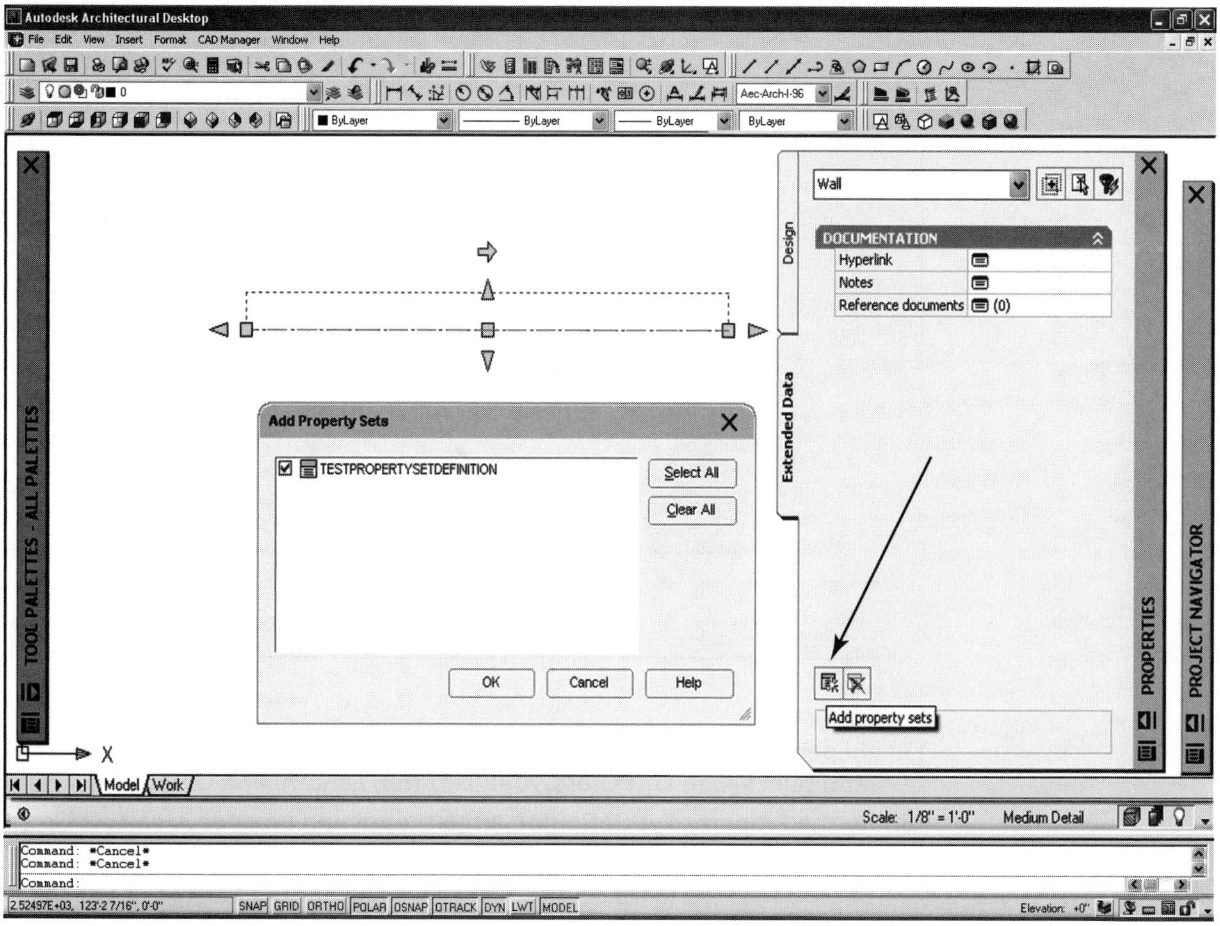

Figure 19–5

26. Again change to the **Extended Data** tab and notice that the height, length, and gross and net areas as well as object type are shown.

You will now be able to read any changes in the length, height, and gross and net areas of that wall in the **Extended Data** tab of the **Properties** palette (see Figure 19–6).

You can add as many automatic properties as you wish, and they will all appear in the **Properties** palette. Later you will be able to pull this data into a schedule object.

27. Select the wall, **RMB,** and insert a door in the wall.
28. Double-click on the wall to open the **Properties** palette. Notice that the **Area-Left Net** field shows how much area has been subtracted by the door (see Figure 19–7).

Figure 19–6

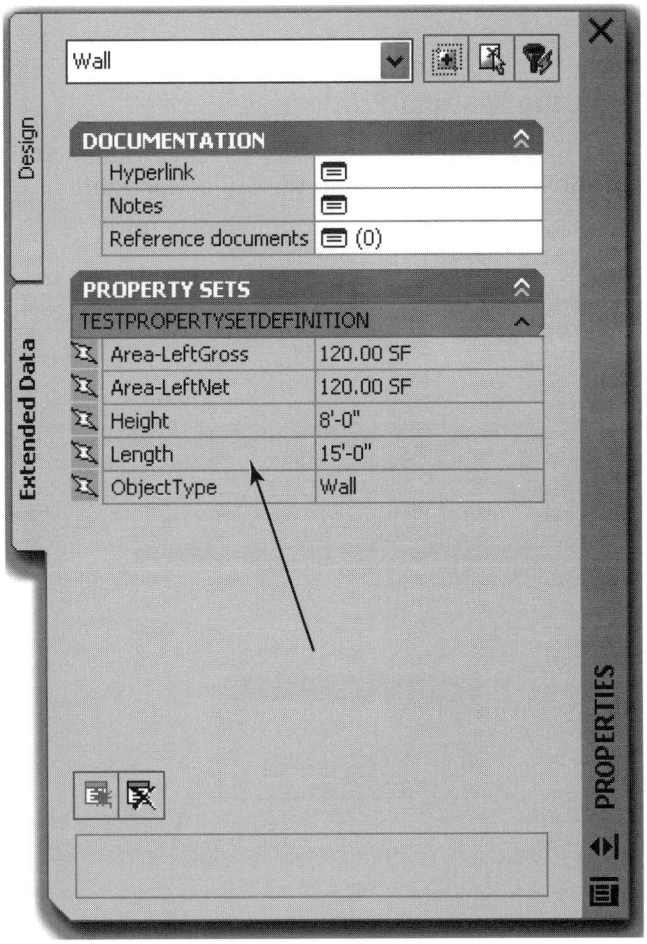

Figure 19–7

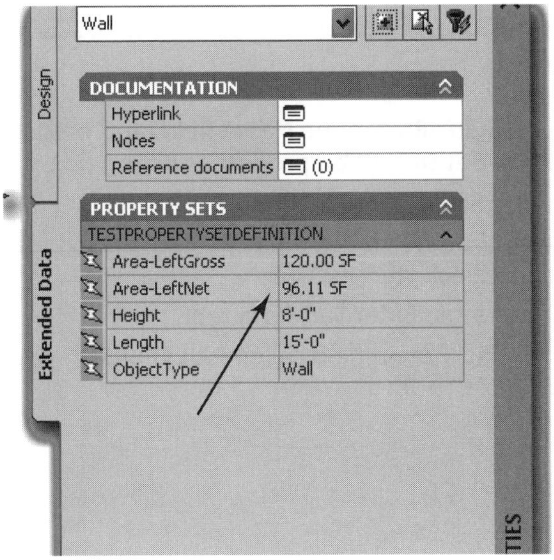

Hands-On

Using the Manual Properties

1. Using the previous exercise, select **Format** > **Style Manager** from the **Main** menu to bring up the **Style Manager.**

2. Expand the **Documentation Objects** folder, and click on **WALLPROPERTYSETDEFINITION.**

3. Select the **Add Manual Property Definition** icon to bring up the **New Property** dialog box (see Figure 19–8).

Figure 19–8

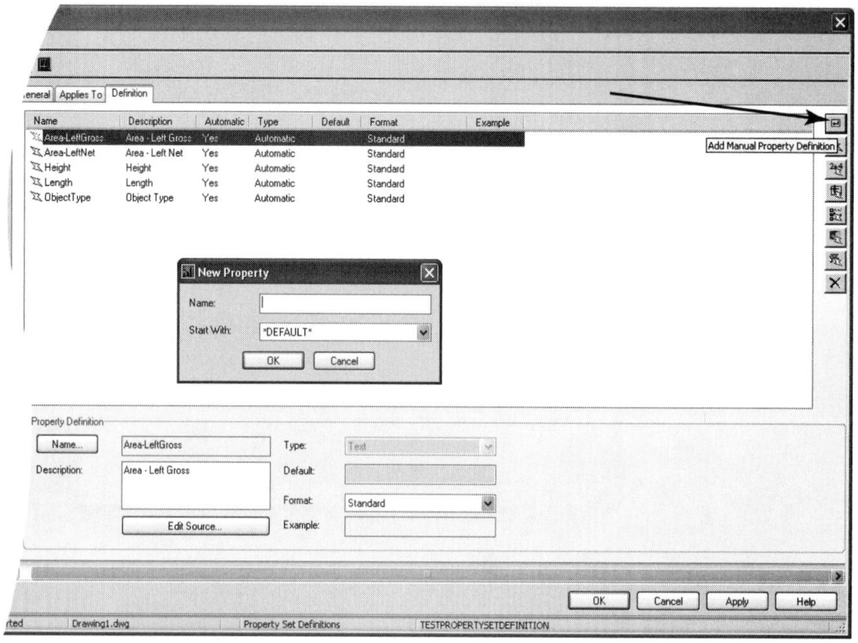

4. Enter **PRICEPERSQ** in the **Name** field, and press **OK** to return to the **Property Set Definition** properties dialog box.

5. Set PRICEPERSQ's **Type** to **Real.**

6. Double-click the wall you placed in the previous exercise to open the Properties palette.

7. Change to the **Extended Data** tab.

8. You will now see a field called **PRICEPERSQ;** enter **2.5** in the field (see Figure 19–9).

Figure 19-9

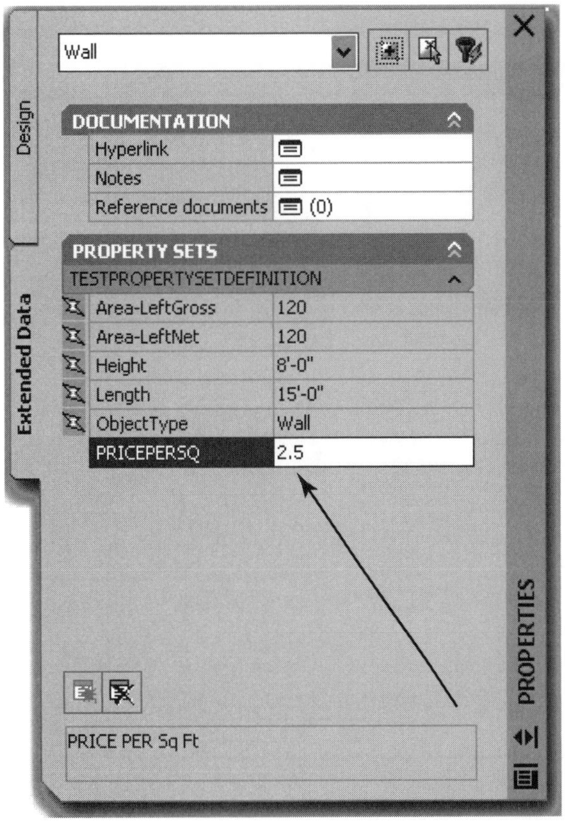

Hands-On

Using the Formula Property Definitions

1. Using the previous exercise, select **Format > Style Manager** from the **Main** menu to bring up the **Style Manager.**

2. Expand the **Documentation Objects** folder, and click on **WALLPROPERTYSETDEFINITION** to again bring up the **Property Set Definition Properties** dialog box.

3. Select the **Add Formula Property Definition** icon to bring up the **Formula Property Definition** dialog box (see Figure 19–10).

4. Enter **WALLCOST** in the **Name** field.

5. Double-click **Area-LeftGross** under **Insert Property Definitions;** then open **Operators > Arithmetic >** under **Insert VBScript** code and double-click the **x** (times) above. Finally, double-click **PRICEPERSQ** under Insert **Property Definitions.**

You have now created a formula that multiplies the area of the wall by the entered price per square foot (see Figure 19–11).

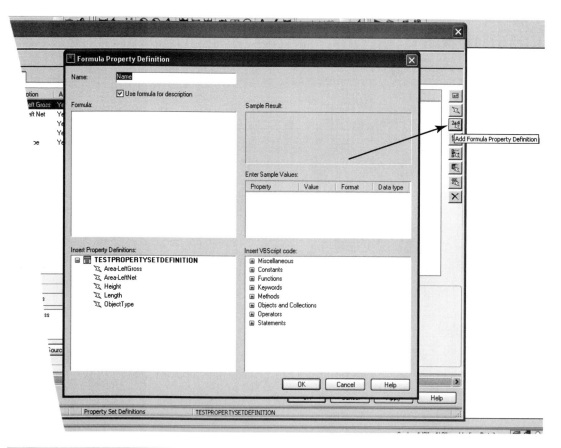

Figure 19–10

Figure 19–11

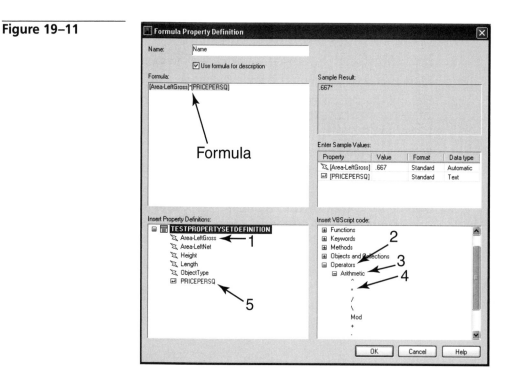

6. Press the **OK** buttons to close the dialog boxes.

7. Double-click on the wall in the Drawing Editor to open the **Properties** palette; notice that **WALLCOST** has been calculated, but it is not in dollars (see Figure 19–12).

Figure 19–12

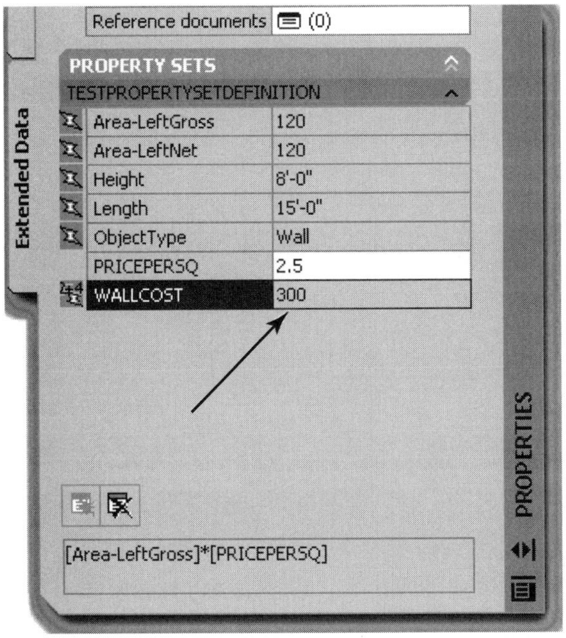

To format **WALLCOST** in dollars, you will need a new property data format.

8. In the **Style Manager,** expand the **Documentation Objects** folder, **RMB** on **Property Data Formats,** and select **New** from the contextual menu that appears.

9. Name the new Property Data Format style to **DOLLARS.**

10. Double-click on **DOLLARS** to bring up the **Property Data Format Properties** dialog box.

11. Change to the **Formatting** tab.

12. Enter **$** in the **Prefix** field, **Decimal** in **Unit Format,** and **0.00** in **Precision** (see Figure 19–13).

13. Press **OK** to return to the **Style Manager.**

14. Open up **WALLPROPERTYSETDEFINITION** again, and select **DOLLARS** (that will now be available) from the **Format** drop-down list for **WALLCOST.**

15. Now press the **OK** buttons to close all the dialog boxes and return to the Drawing Editor.

Figure 19–13

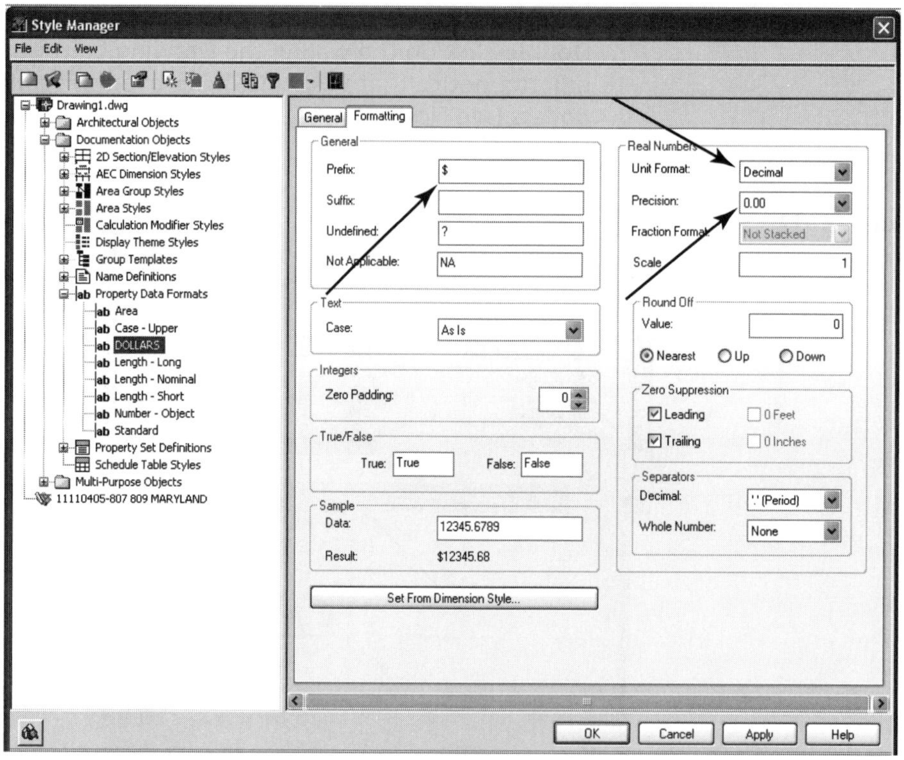

16. Again double-click on the wall to open the **Properties** palette.
17. Again change to the **Extended Data** tab.

WALLCOST will now read **$300.00.** If you change the value in **PRICEPERSQ,** **WALLCOST** will change. If you change the length or height of the wall, **WALLCOST** will also reflect that change.

The best way to learn is to practice. Add different properties, and see their results in the **Properties** palette.

Save this drawing file as **WALLPROPERTYSETDEFINITION** to use with the schedule and schedule tags exercises in the following section.

Schedules and Schedule Tags

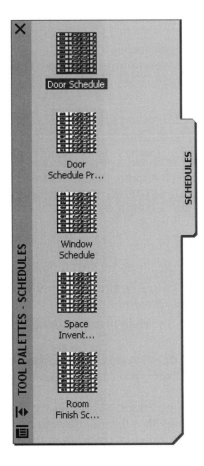

When you finish this section, you should understand the following:

✔ How to create schedule tags and a **Schedules** tool palette.
✔ How to create a schedule.
✔ How to test a schedule.
✔ How to modify a schedule.
✔ How to schedule across drawings.
✔ How to place door and window tags.
✔ How to place schedules.
✔ How to use schedules to locate objects.
✔ How to create and use custom schedules.
✔ How to use the new **Architectural Desktop 2006 Define Schedule Tag routine.**
✔ How to use the new **Architectural Desktop 2006 Tool Catalog Generator.**

Drawing created in this section: **TESTWALLSCHEDULE.dwg**
Reference drawing: **WALLPROPERTYSETDEFINITION.dwg**

Hands-On

Creating a Schedule Tool Palette and Copying Tools from the Content Browser

1. Create a new tool palette and name it **Schedules.**
2. Select the **Content Browser** icon from the **Main** tool bar to launch the **Content Browser.**

3. In the **Documentation Tool Catalog - Imperial,** locate the **Schedule Tables** folder.

4. Drag the **Door** and **Window** schedules and tags into the new tool palette you created.

5. In the **Autodesk Architectural Desktop Documentation Tool Catalog - Imperial,** locate the **Schedule Tags** folders.

6. Drag the **Door Tag** and **Window Tag** tags into the new tool palette you created.

7. Click and hold on the tab of your new tool palette and drag a copy to **My Tool Catalog** in the Content Browser.

This procedure backs up your custom tool palette.

Schedules work in concert with property set definitions, property data formats, and schedule tags.

Hands-On

In order to create a new schedule, you will first have to create a Property Set Definition that can be tracked by a schedule. In Chapter 19, you created a property set definition called **WALLPROPERTYSETDEFINITION.** For these exercises you will use that property set definition as a basis for your new schedule.

Creating a Wall Schedule

1. Start a new file based on the Aec Model (Imperial Stb) template.

2. Save the file as **TESTWALLSCHEDULE**.dwg (the finished schedule should be stored in a template or a **Standards** drawing file).

3. Select **Format > Style Manager** from the **Main** menu to bring up the **Style Manager.**

4. In the **Style Manager,** select the Open Drawing icon, and browse and open the **WALLPROPERTYSETDEFINITION** drawing you created in Chapter 19.

This will not open the drawing in the Drawing Editor, but rather it brings it into the Style Manager. To close this drawing, RMB on the drawing name in the left window, and select Close from the contextual menu that appears.

5. Expand the **Documentation Objects** folder of the **WALLPROPERTYSET- DEFINITION**.dwg.

6. Expand the **Property Set Definitions** folder.

7. Drag **WALLPROPERTYSET** into the **Documentation Objects** folder of the **TESTWALLSCHEDULE**.dwg.

8. Expand the **Property Data Formats** folder.

9. Drag **DOLLARS** into the **Property Data Formats** folder of the **TEST- WALLSCHEDULE**.dwg

10. Expand the **Documentation Objects** folder of the **TESTWALLSCHEDULE**.dwg.

11. **RMB** on **Schedule Table Styles,** and select **New** from the contextual menu that appears.

12. Name the new style **TESTWALLSCHEDULE.**

13. In the right screen of **TESTWALLSCHEDULE,** change to the **Applies To** tab.

14. Press the **Clear All** button, and then check the **Wall** check box (see Figure 20–1).

15. Change to the **Columns** tab.

Figure 20–1

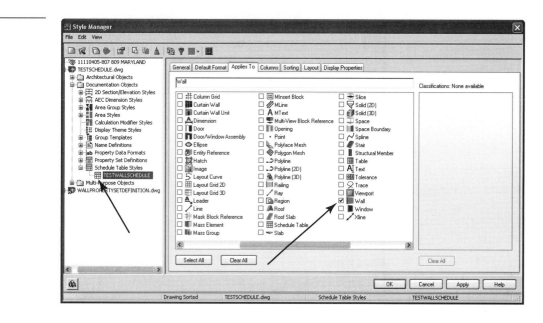

16. Press the **Add Column** button to bring up the **Add Column** dialog box.

17. Change to the **Categorized** tab, and notice that it contains the properties that you set in the exercise on property set definitions in the previous section.

18. Select **WALLCOST**, enter **Cost of Walls** in the **Heading** field, select **DOLLARS** from the **Data Format** drop-down list, check the **Total** check box, and press **OK** (see Figure 20–2).

19. You will now return to the **Columns** tab **TESTWALLSCHEDULE**.

Figure 20–2

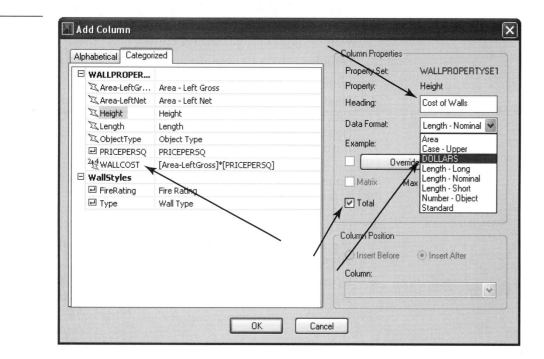

20. In the **Columns** tab, check the **Include Quantity Column** check box to add a **Quantity** column (see Figure 20–3).

Figure 20–3

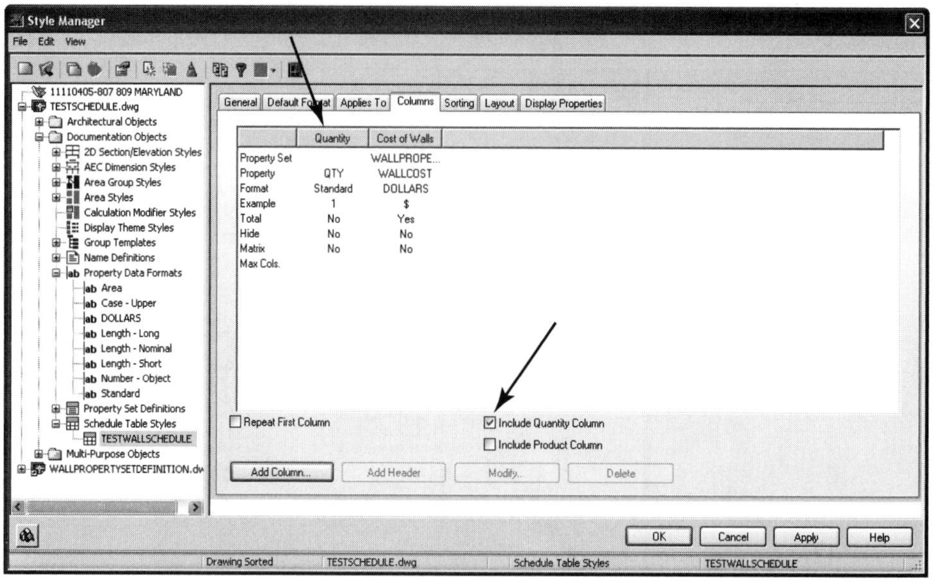

21. Press **OK,** and close all the dialog boxes to return to the Drawing Editor. Save this file as **TESTWALLSCHEDULE**.dwg.

Hands-On

Testing the New Schedule

1. Open the **TESTWALLSCHEDULE**.dwg from the previous exercise, select the **Brick-4 Brick-4 wall** from the **Walls** tool palette, and place a 15′-long wall 10′ high in the Drawing Editor.
2. Double-click on the wall to open the **Properties** palette.
3. Change to the **Extended Data** tab.
4. Press the **Add Property Sets** icon at the lower left of the **Extended Data** tab, make sure the **WALLPROPERTYSETDEFINITION** check box is checked (see Section 19 for directions on doing this operation), and press the **OK** button to return to the Drawing editor.

The property set information will now appear in the **Extended Data** tab of the properties palette when the wall is selected.

5. With the wall selected, in the **Extended Data** tab, enter **2.5** ($2.50) in the **PRICEPERSQ** field and the **WALLCOST** will read **$375** (see Figure 20–4).
6. Open the **Schedules** tool palette you created in the first exercise of Section 20, and set **Auto-hide** to keep the palette open.

Figure 20–4

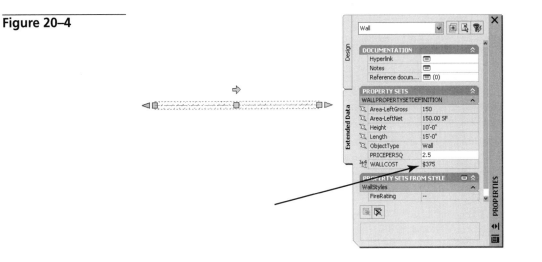

7. Select **Format** > **Style Manager** from the **Main** menu to bring up the **Style Manager.**

8. Expand the **Documentation Objects** folder >**Schedule Table** Style.

9. Drag **TESTSCHEDULE** from the **Style Manager** into the **Schedules** tool palette.

10. Select the **TESTSCHEDULE** tool you just placed in the tool palette, select the **Brick-4 Brick-4 wall** you placed previously in the Drawing Editor, and press the **Enter** key on your keyboard.

11. In the **Top View,** click a placement point below the wall, and then press **Enter** again to place the schedule (see Figure 20–5).

Figure 20–5

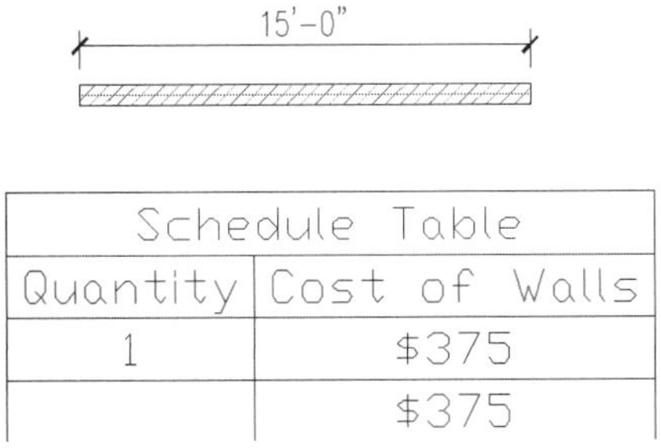

| 15'-0" |

Schedule Table	
Quantity	Cost of Walls
1	$375
	$375

Notice the size of the type in the schedule in relation to the size of the wall. This is because the default **Scale** button of the model layout is 1/8" = 1'-0", and **Plot Size** is 1/8". Refer to **Format** > **Drawing Setup** > **Scale** tab.

12. Delete the schedule you just placed, change the **Scale** at the bottom of the Drawing Editor to **1/4" = 1'–10",** and insert **TESTSCHEDULE** again.

Notice the size of the type in the schedule in relation to the size of the wall. This is because the scale of the model layout is now 1/4" = 1'-0" (see Figure 20–6).

Figure 20–6

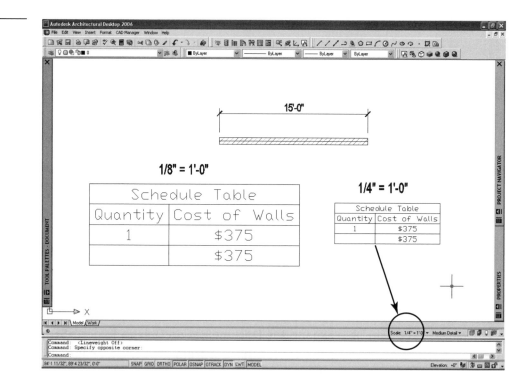

13. Erase the first schedule you placed, leaving only the 1/4"-scale schedule.

14. Double-click the schedule to open the **Properties** palette.

15. In the **Design** tab, under **Update automatically,** select **Yes.** Under **Add new objects automatically,** also select **Yes.** Press the **Enter** key on your keyboard to ensure that the settings are set (see Figure 20–7).

!   *Note:* Although Auto Updating is functional, projects with a large quantity of objects may experience a reduction in performance.

Figure 20–7

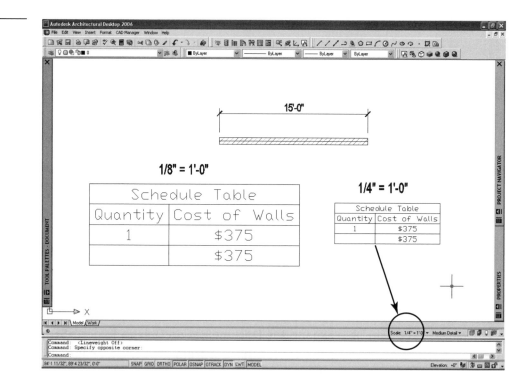

The schedule will now reflect automatically any additional walls having the same property set definition.

16. Press the **Esc** key to clear any selections in the Drawing Editor.

17. Select the wall, **RMB,** and select **Add Selected** from the contextual menu that appears.

Add more walls; the schedule automatically updates (see Figure 20–8). Save this file.

Figure 20–8

Hands-On

Modifying the Schedule—Text Appearance

1. Using the previous file **(TESTWALLSCHEDULE.dwg),** select **Format > Text Style** from the **Main** menu to bring up the **Text Style** dialog box.

2. Press the **New** button, and name the style **TESTTEXT.**

3. Select **Arial** from the **Font Name** drop-down list and **Bold** from the **Font Style** drop-down list.

4. Select **Standard** from the **Style Name** drop-down list, select **Arial** from the **Font Name** drop-down list, select **Regular** from the **Font Style** drop-down list, press the **Apply** button, and then press the **Close** button.

5. Select the schedule you placed in the Drawing editor, **RMB,** and select **Edit Schedule Table Style** from the contextual menu that appears to bring up the **Schedule Table Style Properties** dialog box.

6. Select the **Layout** tab.

7. Enter **WALL Schedule** in the **Table Title** field, and press the **Title Override Cell Format** button to bring up the **Cell Format Override** dialog box.

8. Select **TESTTEXT** from the **Style** drop-down list (see Figure 20–9).

9. Press the **Column Headers Override Cell Format** button, select **TESTTEXT** from the **Style** drop-down list, and press the **OK** buttons to close all the dialog boxes and return to the Drawing Editor (see Figure 20–10).

10. **RMB** on the **TESTSCHEDULE** in the Drawing Editor and select **Edit Schedule Table Style** from the contextual menu that appears to bring up the **Schedule Table Style Properties** dialog box.

Figure 20–9

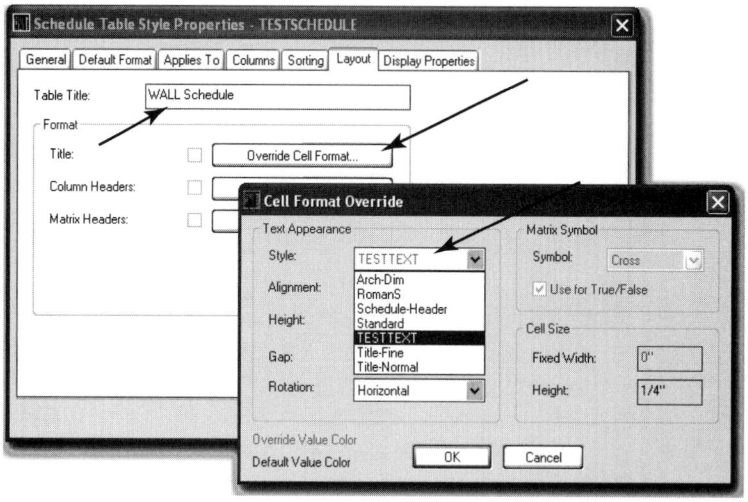

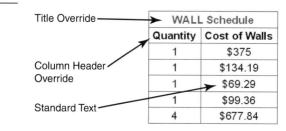

Figure 20–10

Title Override

Column Header Override

Standard Text

WALL Schedule	
Quantity	**Cost of Walls**
1	$375
1	$134.19
1	$69.29
1	$99.36
4	$677.84

Adding a Column to the Schedule

11.   Change to the **Columns** tab.

12.   Press the **Add Column** button to bring up the **Add Column** dialog box.

13.   Select **Wall Type** for **Type,** enter **WALL CODE** in the **Heading** field, press the **Insert Before** radio button, select **QTY** from the **Column** drop-down list, and press the **OK** buttons to return to the Drawing Editor (see Figure 20–11).

Figure 20–11

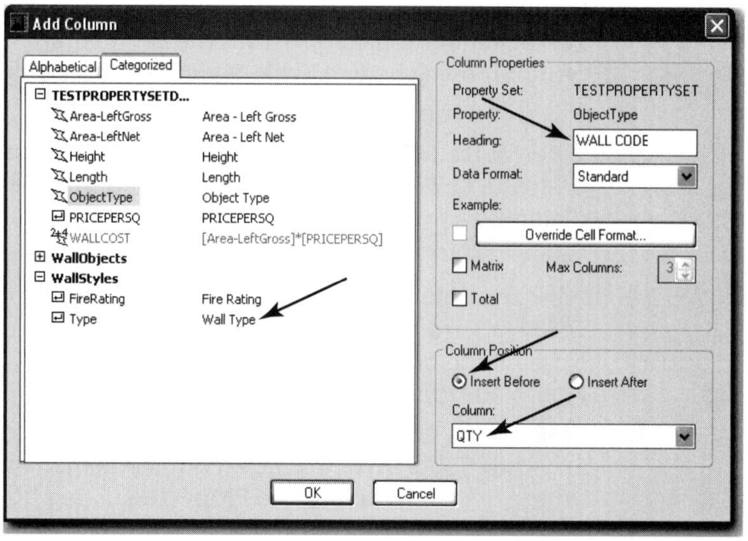

14. The **WALL** Schedule will now include a **WALL CODE** column, but it will not have codes. Because the types are a **Style**-based property, they are usually not predefined in the **Wall** styles out of the box (see Figure 20–12).

To label a wall, do the following (using CMU-8 as an example):

Figure 20–12

WALL Schedule

WALL CODE	Quantity	Cost of Walls
--	1	$375
--	1	$98.34
--	1	$162.31
--	1	$123.15
	4	$758.8

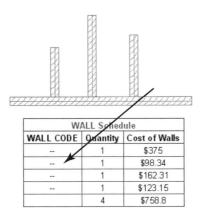

Method 1

a. **RMB** on the **CMU-8** wall in the **Walls** tool palette and select **Re-import** or **Import CMU-8 Wall Style** from the contextual menu that appears.

b. Again **RMB** on the **CMU-8** wall in the **Walls** tool palette and this time select **Wall Styles** from the contextual menu to bring up the **Style Manager.**

c. Double-click the **CMU-8** wall to bring up the **Wall Style Properties** dialog box.

d. Change to the **General** tab.

e. Select the **Property Sets** button to bring up the **Edit Property Set Data** dialog box.

f. Enter **A** in the **Type** field, and press the **OK** buttons to return to the Drawing Editor (see Figure 20–13).

Figure 20–13

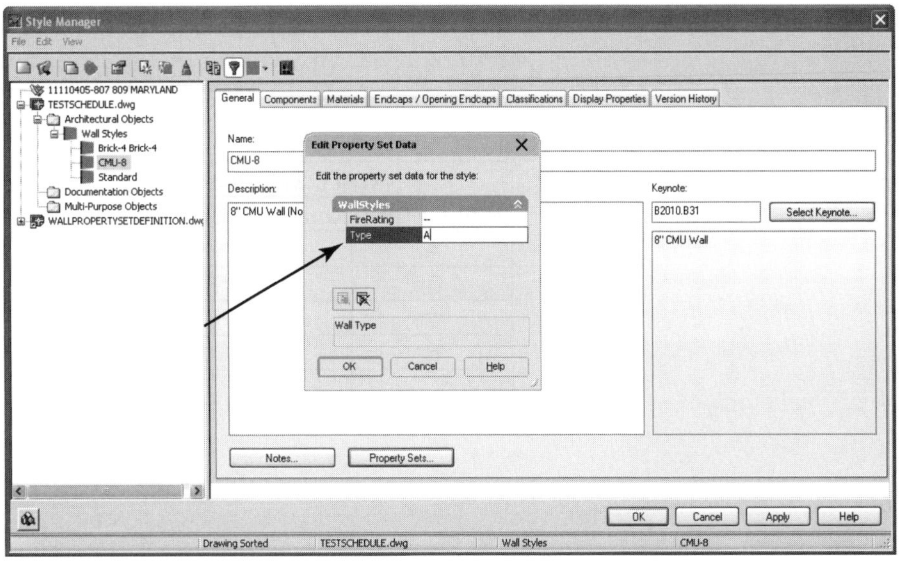

g.   Repeat Steps a through f for some of the other walls types. Once you have labeled walls, place the walls.

Method 2

This method allows data to be pushed from the schedule to intelligent AEC objects.

a.   Select schedule table in the drawing, **RMB,** and select **Edit Table Cell.**

b.   Click on the cell to be edited, input a value, and click the **OK** button

c.   Press the **Enter** key to exit the **Edit Table Cell** command.

15.   After placing some walls, select all the walls and double-click on one to open the **Properties** palette.

16.   With all the walls still selected, select the **Extended Data** tab in the **Properties** palette.

17.   Press the **Add property sets** icon and attach the **WALLPROPERTYSET DEFINITION** property set.

18.   Enter **2.5** in the **PRICEPERSQ** field. Press the **Esc** key to clear the grips.

Your wall schedule is now complete (see Figure 20–14). Save this file as **TESTWALLSCHEDULE.**

Figure 20–14

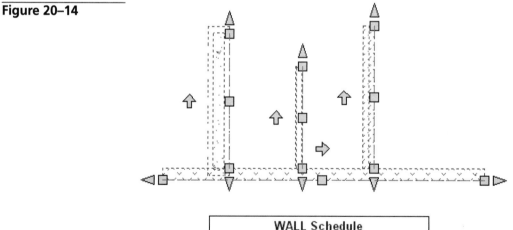

WALL Schedule		
WALL CODE	**Quantity**	**Cost of Walls**
A	1	$486.29
D	1	$215.7
C	1	$147.83
B	1	$206.58
	4	$1056.4

Hands-On

Scheduling across Drawings—Scheduling Xrefs

Because schedules are not necessarily placed on the same page as the objects they are scheduling, Architectural Desktop's scheduling object has an option to schedule "across" drawings.

1. Using the previous file **(TESTWALLSCHEDULE),** select **Edit > Cut** from the **Main** menu. Select all the walls and press **OK.** Your walls should disappear, and the schedule should clear.

2. Start a drawing using the Aec Model (Imperial Stb) template, and save it as **WALLS.** dwg.

3. In the WALLS drawing, select **Edit > Paste to Original Coordinates** from the **Main** menu to paste the walls that you previously cut from the **TESTWALLSCHEDULE** drawing into the WALLS drawing.

4. Press **Ctrl + S** to save the WALLS drawing. *This is essential.*

5. Double-click the schedule object in the **TESTWALLSCHEDULE** drawing to open its **Properties** palette.

6. In the **Properties** palette, select **Yes** from the **Schedule external drawing** field in the **ADVANCED** section. This will then show an **External drawing** field.

7. In the Select **External drawing** field, select **Browse** from the drop-down list, and locate the WALLS drawing (see Figure 20–15).

8. The schedule object in the **SCHEDULE** drawing will show a line across its surface telling you to update the schedule.

Figure 20–15

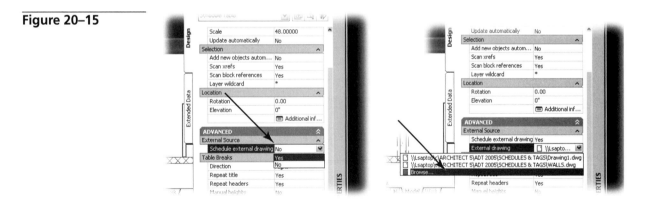

9. **RMB** on the schedule object and select **Update Schedule Table** from the contextual menu that appears. The schedule will now reflect the information from the **WALLS** drawing.

Note: If you change any wall in the **WALLS** drawing and save that drawing, the **SCHEDULE** drawing will be able to show those changes upon updating. In Architectural Desktop 2006, updating can be done automatically through the sheet set (see Figure 20–16).

Figure 20–16

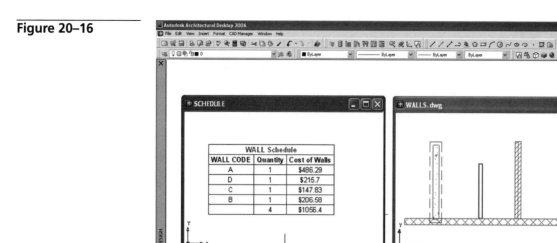

Schedule Tags

In order to compile data into a schedule, objects must be tagged. Autodesk Architectural Desktop 2006 contains tags for the following objects:

- Doors
- Windows
- Room numbers
- Room finishes
- Spaces
- Beams, braces, and columns
- Equipment
- Furniture
- Walls

Hands-On

Placing Door and Window Tags

1. Using the previous **TESTWALLSCHEDULE** drawing, erase everything, select the **Wall** icon in the **Design** tool palette, and create a 30'-0" × 20'-0"-wide enclosure. Make the walls Standard 6" wide, 8' high.

2. Select a wall, **RMB,** and select **Insert > Door** from the contextual menu.

3. Place a 3'-0"-wide Standard door in each wall.

4. Repeat Steps 2 and 3, placing 3' × 5' windows along side the doors (see Figure 20-17).

Figure 20–17

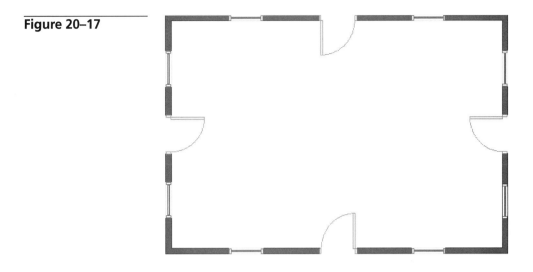

5. Set the **Scale** button for the correct scale that you want the drawing to be in the plot sheets. This will control the tag and annotation size.

6. Select the **Door Tag** icon from the **Schedules** tool palette you created, select the bottom most door, and place the tag in the middle of the door opening.

The **Edit Property Set Data** dialog box will now appear. You can now change data such as **Fire Rating** (see Figure 20–18).

Figure 20–18

Edit Property Set Data	✕

Edit the property set data for the object:

DoorObjects	
Data source	Drawing1.dwg
🗲 DoorSize	3'-0" x 6'-8"
FireRating	--
🗲 FrameDepth	5"
FrameMaterial	--
🗲 FrameWidth	2"
Glazing	--
HeadDetail	--
🗲 HeadHeight	6'-8"
🗲 Height	80
🗲 HeightUnform...	80

OK	Cancel	Help

7. When you are finished, press **OK** in the dialog box to place the schedule tag.

! **Note:** If you do not want to see this dialog box every time you place a tag, do the following:

a. Select **Format > Options** to bring up the **Options** dialog box.

b. Select the **AEC Content** tab.

c. Uncheck the **Display Edit Property Data Dialog During Tag Insertion** check box (see Figure 20–19).

8. Place door tags for the other doors.

9. Zoom close to the doors.

Notice that they are numbered incrementally automatically. To change the settings of the tag, do the following:

Figure 20–19

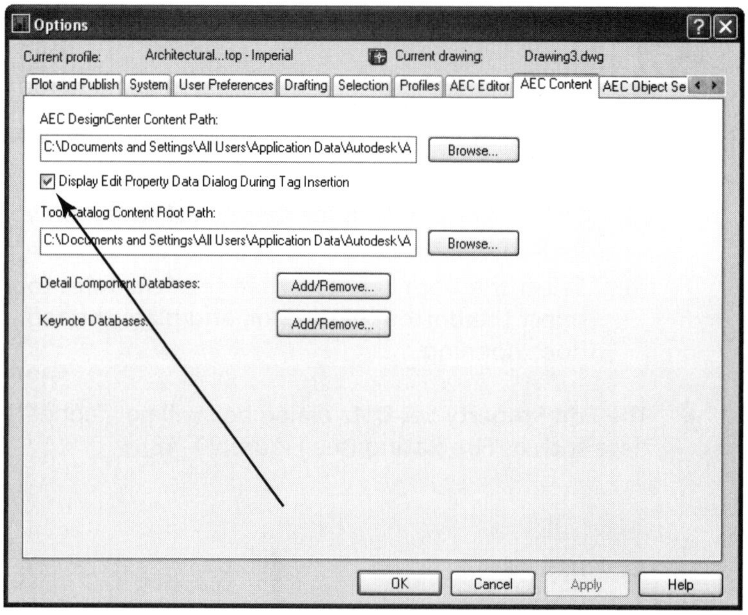

10. Select **Format > Style Manager** from the **Main** toolbar to bring up the **Style Manager** dialog box.

11. Select **Documentation Objects > Property Set Definitions > Door Objects.**

Property set definitions are groups of properties for particular objects that you want to manage in schedules. They can be automatic, deriving their values from the properties of objects, or user-defined.

12. In the Style Manager, Select the **Definition** tab.

If you want to increment the objects number system automatically, select **Number,** change its **Type** to **Auto Increment - Integer,** and set the start number as **Default**. The tags can also be created or modified to display the information defined in the property definition (see Figure 20–20).

13. Place window tags for the windows. If the tags don't increment automatically, change their setting in the property definition set for window objects. Save this file.

Figure 20–20

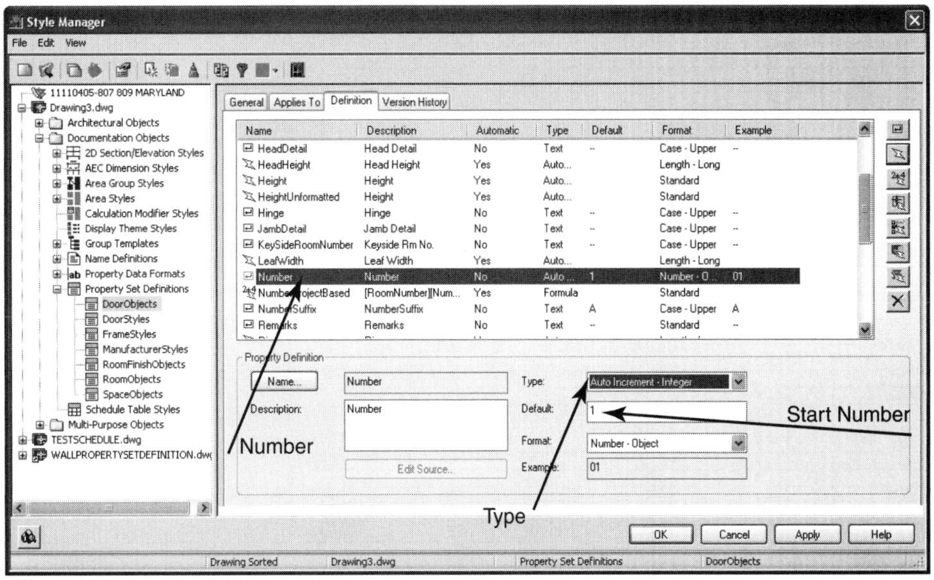

Hands-On

Placing Schedules

1. Using the previous **TESTWALLSCHEDULE** drawing, select the **Door Schedule** icon from the **Schedules** tool palette you created.

2. Move your cursor over the **Properties** palette to open it.

3. Set the following:

   a. Update automatically = **No** (for next exercise)

   b. Add new objects = **No** (for next exercise)

   c. Scan xrefs = **Yes**

   d. Scan block references = **Yes**

4. Select all the doors (this can be done with a selection window).

5. Click in a spot in the drawing to start the upper-left corner of the schedule.

6. Press the space bar or **Enter** key when requested for the lower right corner.

Pressing **Enter** (Architectural Desktop calls it **Return** in the command line) causes the schedule to be scaled automatically at the size set by the drawing scale you set earlier.

7. Select all the doors and their tags, and press **Enter**.

8. Repeat Steps 1–5 for the **window schedule** (see Figure 20–21). Save this file.

DOOR AND FRAME SCHEDULE

| MARK | DOOR | | | | | | | FRAME | | | | | | FIRE RATING LABEL | HARDWARE | | NOTES |
| | SIZE | | | MATL | GLAZING | LOUVER | | MATL | EL | DETAIL | | | | SET NO | KEYSIDE RM NO | |
	WD	HGT	THK			WD	HGT			HEAD	JAMB	SILL				
1	3'-0"	6'-8"	2"	--	--	0"	0"	--	--	--	--	--	--	--	--	--
2	3'-0"	6'-8"	2"	--	--	0"	0"	--	--	--	--	--	--	--	--	--
3	3'-0"	6'-8"	2"	--	--	0"	0"	--	--	--	--	--	--	--	--	--
4	3'-0"	6'-8"	2"	--	--	0"	0"	--	--	--	--	--	--	--	--	--

WINDOW SCHEDULE

| MARK | SIZE | | TYPE | MATERIAL | NOTES |
	WIDTH	HEIGHT			
1	3'-0"	5'-0"	--	--	--
2	3'-0"	5'-0"	--	--	--
3	3'-0"	5'-0"	--	--	--
4	3'-0"	5'-0"	--	--	--
5	3'-0"	5'-0"	--	--	--
6	3'-0"	5'-0"	--	--	--
7	3'-0"	5'-0"	--	--	--
8	3'-0"	5'-0"	--	--	--

Figure 20–21

Hands-On

Updating Schedules

1. Using the previous file, remove two of the doors.

Notice that a line appears across the schedule.

2. Select the door schedule, **RMB,** and select **Update Schedule Table** from the contextual menu.

The schedule will update, removing or changing object data.

3. Add more doors and door tags.

The schedule does not indicate the additions.

4. Select the door schedule, **RMB,** and select **Selection > Add** from the contextual menu.
5. Select all the doors and tags.

The door schedule updates, showing the new doors.

Hands-On

Using Schedules to Locate Objects

If you need to quickly locate an object listed in the schedule, do the following:

1. Select the door schedule, **RMB,** and select **Selection > Show** from the contextual menu.

2. Hold down the **Ctrl** key on the keyboard, and pick any number in a field.

The screen will zoom to the object in that field.
   This feature will work across Xrefs. This feature does *not* work with **Schedule external drawing.**

Hands-On

Exporting Schedules to Databases

If you have Microsoft Excel or a text editor such as Microsoft Word or even Windows Notepad software, you can export your schedules to these formats.

1. Select the door schedule, **RMB,** and select **Export** the contextual menu to bring up the **Export Schedule Table** dialog box.
2. Select **Microsoft [Tab delimited] [*.xls]** from the **Output - Save As Type** drop-down list.
3. Browse to a convenient folder, and press **OK.**

You will be able to open the file in Microsoft Excel 95 and later.

4. If you set the **Output - Save As Type to Text [Tab delimited] [*.txt],** you will be able to open the file in any text editor (see Figures 20–22 and 20–23).

Figure 20–22

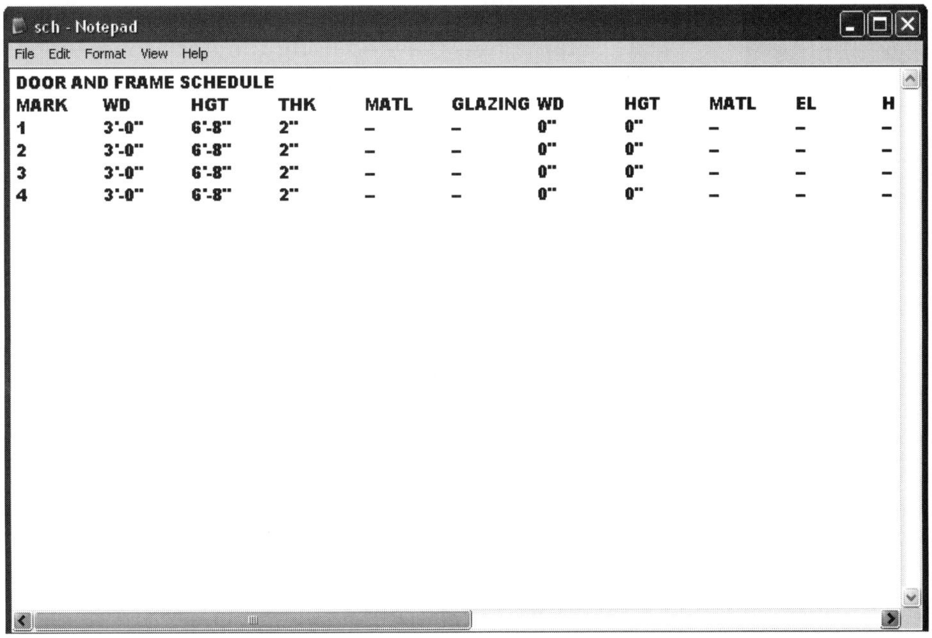

```
sch - Notepad
File  Edit  Format  View  Help
DOOR AND FRAME SCHEDULE
MARK    WD      HGT     THK     MATL    GLAZING WD      HGT     MATL    EL      H
1       3'-0"   6'-8"   2"      –       –       0"      0"      –       –       –
2       3'-0"   6'-8"   2"      –       –       0"      0"      –       –       –
3       3'-0"   6'-8"   2"      –       –       0"      0"      –       –       –
4       3'-0"   6'-8"   2"      –       –       0"      0"      –       –       –
```

Figure 20–23

	DOOR AND FRAME SCHEDULE																
MARK	WD	HGT	THK	MATL	GLAZING	WD	HGT	MATL	EL	HEAD	JAMB	SILL	FIRE RATING LABEL	SET NO	KEYSIDE RM NO	NOTES
1	36.	80.	2.	--	--	0.	0.	--	--	--	--	--	--	--	--	--
2	36.	80.	2.	--	--	0.	0.	--	--	--	--	--	--	--	--	--
3	36.	80.	2.	--	--	0.	0.	--	--	--	--	--	--	--	--	--
4	36.	80.	2.	--	--	0.	0.	--	--	--	--	--	--	--	--	--

Hands-On

Creating and Using Custom Schedules

Schedules in ADT are robust enough to permit scheduling normal AutoCAD entities such as circles in this exercise. This ability can often help keep track of objects while creating drawings.

The Drawing

1. Start a new drawing using the Aec Model (Imperial Stb) template.
2. Place three circles in the drawing with radii of 2′, 4′, and 6′.

You are going to create a schedule that records information about the circles in your drawing. In order to make a schedule you will need to create a property set definition.

The Property Set Definition

3. Select **Format** > **Style Manager** from the **Main** toolbar to bring up the **Style Manager** dialog box from the **Main** toolbar.
4. Expand the **Documentation Objects** > **Property Set Definitions.**
5. **RMB** on **Property Set Definitions,** and select **New** from the contextual menu to create a new property set definition.
6. Rename the new property set definition **CIRCLEPROPERTYSET**
7. In the right pane of the **Style Manager,** select the **Applies To** tab.
8. Select the **Objects** radio button, and then select the **Clear All** button at the lower left of the dialog box. Check the **Circle** check box (see Figure 20–24).
9. In the right pane of the **Style Manager,** change to the **Definition** tab.

Figure 20–24

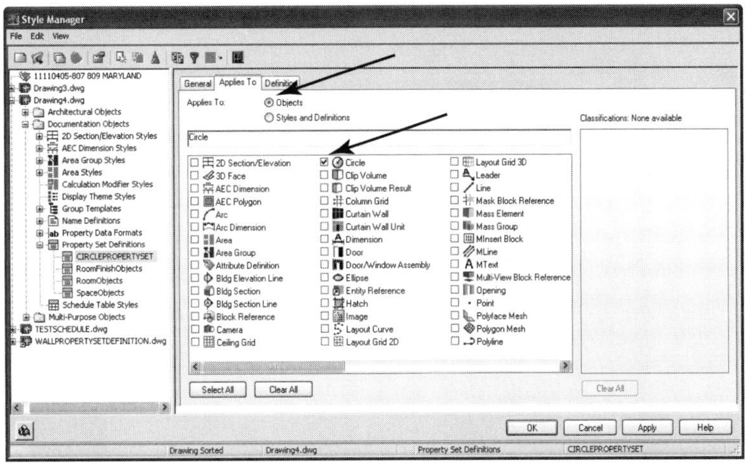

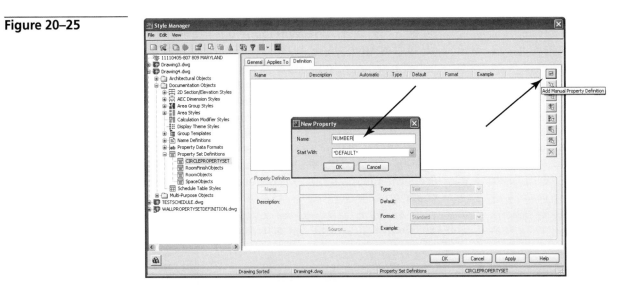

10. Press the **Add Manual Property Definition** icon button at the top right side of the dialog box, to bring up the **New Property** dialog box.

11. Enter the word **NUMBER** in the **Name** section, and press **OK** (see Figure 20-25).

12. In the **Definition** tab, also set the **Type** to **Auto Increment - Integer** and **Default** to **1**, and **Format** to **Number - Object**.

Figure 20–25

13. Next, press the **Add Automatic Property Definition** icon button at the top right side of the **Style Manager** dialog box to bring up the **Automatic Property Source** dialog box.

The **Automatic Property Source** dialog box shows all the properties of a circle.

14. Check the **Area** check box, and press **OK** to return to the **Property Set Definition Properties** dialog box (see Figure 20–26).

15. Add two more automatic property definitions called **radius** and **circumference**, and check their **Automatic Property Sources** check boxes for **radius** and **circumference**, respectively.

16. Press the **Apply** button to apply all this to the **CIRCLEPROPERTYSET** property set definition.

Figure 20–26

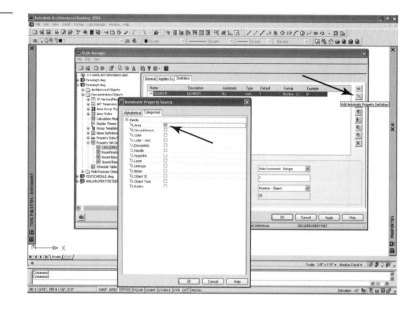

You have now defined all the properties of circles that you wish to be recorded in a schedule.

Creating the Table Style

17. Select **Format** > **Style Manager** from the **Main** menu to bring up the **Style Manager** dialog box.

18. Select **Document Objects** > **Schedule Table Styles.**

19. **RMB** on **Schedule Table Styles,** and select **New** from the contextual menu.

20. Name the new style **CIRCLESCHEDULE,** and press the **Apply** and **OK** buttons.

21. Change to the **Applies To** tab.

22. Press the **Clear All** button to clear the list, and then check the **Circle** check box.

This tells the program that the schedule applies to circles and their properties.

23. Change to the **Columns** tab and press the **Add Column** button at the lower left to bring up the **Add Column** dialog box.

You should now see the property definition set you created in Steps 3–23.

24. Select the **NUMBER** property and press **OK** to return to the **Style Manager** dialog box (see Figure 20–27).

25. Returning to the Style **Manager** dialog box, again press the **Add Column** button.

26. Repeat the steps, adding columns named **RADIUS, CIRCUMFERENCE,** and **AREA** (see Figure 20–28).

27. Hold down the **Ctrl** key and select the **RADIUS** and **CIRCUMFERENCE** headers.

Figure 20–27

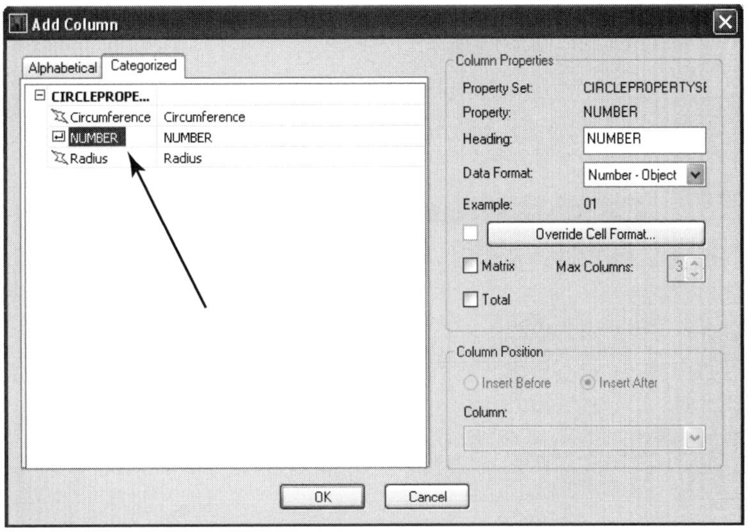

Figure 20–28

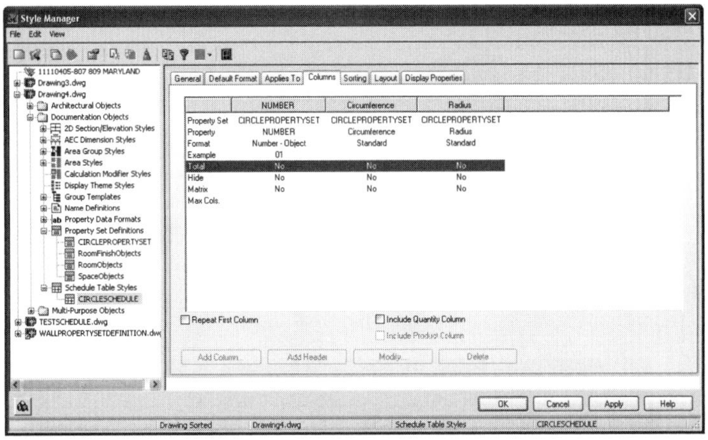

28.   Press the **Add Header** button.

29.   Enter a header name of **CIRCLE DATA** (see Figure 20–29).

30.   Change to the **Sorting** tab.

31.   Press the **Add** button at the top left to bring up the **Select Property** dialog box.

Figure 20–29

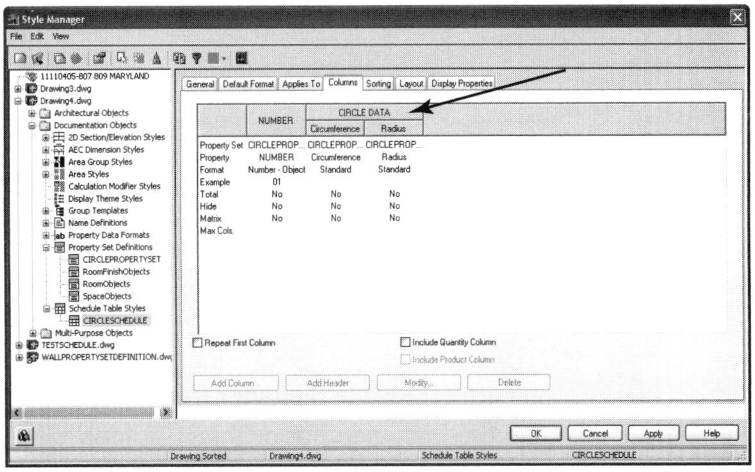

32. Select **CIRCLEPROPERTYSET: NUMBER,** and press **OK** (see Figure 20–30).

33. Repeat for all the other properties.

34. Change to the **Layout** tab.

Figure 20–30

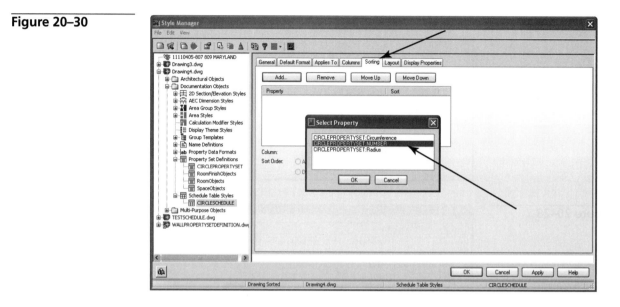

35. Enter a **Table Title** of **CIRCLE SCHEDULE**, and press **OK** to return to the Drawing Editor (see Figure 20–31). IMPORTANT: save this drawing now.

Figure 20–31

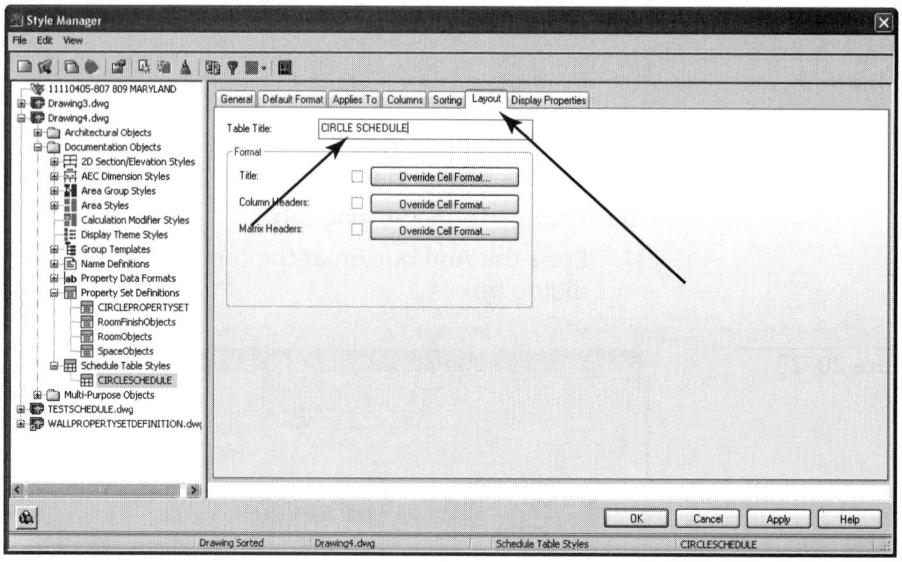

Using the Custom Schedule

36. Open the **Schedules** tool palette you created in the first exercise, and lock it open.

37. Select **Format > Style Manager** from the **Main** menu.

38. Expand the **Documentation Objects** folder.

39. Expand the **Schedule Table Styles.**

40. From the **Schedule Table Styles,** drag the **CIRCLESCHEDULE** table style you created into your Schedules tool palette.

41. In the Style manager, press the **OK** button to return to the Drawing Editor.

42. Select the **CIRCLESCHEDULE** from the **Schedules** tool palette.

43. Move your cursor over the **Properties** palette to open it.

44. Select the following:

   a. Style = **CIRCLESCHEDULE**

   b. Add new objects automatically = **Yes**

45. Select all the circles in your drawing, and press **Enter.**

46. Place the upper left corner of the table, and press **Enter.**

! **Note:** Remember, pressing **Enter** after placing the upper-left corner of a schedule table automatically places the table according to your annotation scale settings.

47. Select the schedule table you placed, **RMB,** and select **Add All Property Sets** from the contextual menu that appears.

48. The schedule table now reads the circumference and radius of each of the circles (see Figure 20–32).

Figure 20–32

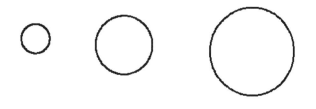

CIRCLE SCHEDULE		
NUMBER	CIRCLE DATA	
	Circumference	Radius
01	150.796	24
02	301.593	48
03	452.389	72

49. Select one of the circles, and use grips to change its size.

Note that a line now appears across the schedule telling you that something has changed.

50. Select the schedule table, **RMB,** and select **Update Schedule Table** from the contextual menu that appears (see Figure 20–33).

51. In the Drawing Editor, add another circle.

Figure 20–33

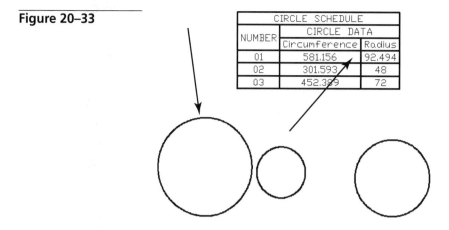

Again a line appears across the schedule table. Update the schedule table, and note that the new circle shows up in the table, but its size is represented by question marks.

52.   Select the schedule, **RMB,** and select **Add All Property Sets** from the contextual menu.

53.   The new circle is now listed in the schedule.

Hands-On

Using the New Architectural Desktop 2006 Define Schedule Tag Routine to Create Custom Schedule Tags

Before Architectural Desktop 2006, the creation of custom schedule tags was quite tedious. With this new version, the programmers have developed the **Define Schedule Tag** routine to aid the user in the creation of these automated tags. Since **Tags** are **Multi-View Blocks,** the **Define Schedule Tag** routine is really an automated **Multi-View Block and Property Set Definition** integrator.

For this exercise, we are going to use the **Project Browser** and project management. If you have problems following the material, please review Chapter 16.

Setting up in preparation for creating a new tag

1.   Select **File > New** from the **Main** menu and create a new drawing using the Aec Model (Imperial Stb) template, and save it as **CUSTOMTAG.dwg.**

2.   Using the **NEW ADT 2006 PROJECTS** folder you created in Chapter 16.

3.   Select **File > Project Browser** from the **Main** menu, browse and locate the **NEW ADT 2006 PROJECTS** folder and then create a new project named **CUSTOM SCHEDULE TAGS.**

4.   While still in the **Project Browser,** set the **CUSTOM SCHEDULE TAGS** project you just created, **current,** and close the **Project Browser** to bring

up the **Project Navigator** and create the **SCHEDULE TAGS** tool palette (see Figure 20–34).

Figure 20–34

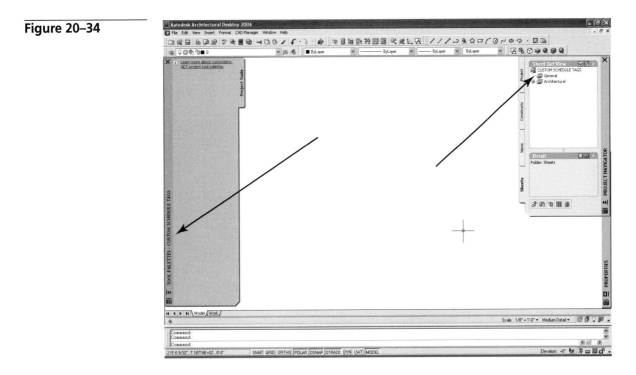

> **Note:** In Architectural Desktop 2006, whenever you create a new project, you automatically create a new, empty, tool palette specifically tied to that new project. Make sure that the tool palette is locked open. If you open the new Content Browser icon (new for ADT 2006) at the bottom of the Project navigator, you will find a Project Catalog also tied to the new project you just created (see Figure 20–35).

Figure 20–35

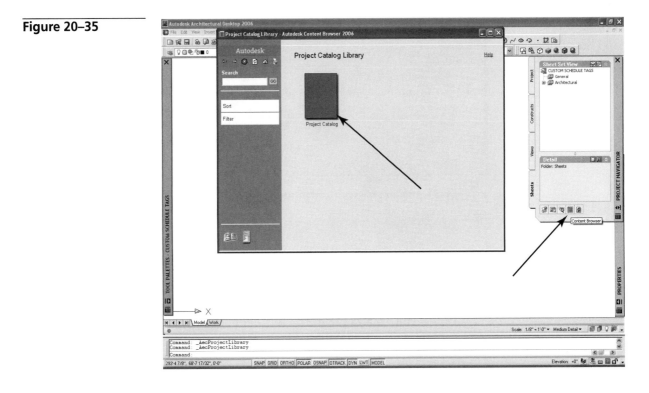

> *Note:* This new **Content Browser** icon located in the **Project Navigator** is in addition to the **standard Content Browser** icon located in the **Main** menu or activated by Ctrl + 4. The **standard Content Browser** will bring down all the catalogs.

We are going to make a custom Door tag, so we will need to have a Door Object property set definition.

5. Select **Format > Style Manager** to bring up the Style manager dialog box.

6. Expand the **Documentation Objects folder**, and then locate the **Property Set Definitions.**

7. **RMB** the **Property Set Definitions,** and select **New** from the contextual menu that appears.

8. Name the new **Property Set Definition - DOOROBJECT** (no spaces).

9. In the right pane of the **Style Manager,** change to the **Applies** tag.

10. In the **Applies** tab, select the **Objects** radio buttons, press the **Clear All** button, and then check the **Door** check box.

11. Change to the **Definition** tab, and select the **Add Manual Property Definition** icon to bring up the **New Property** dialog box.

12. In the **New Property** dialog box, Enter **NUMBER,** and select **RoomObjects:Number** from the **Start With** drop-down list, and press the **OK** button to return to the **Style Manager** (see Figure 20–36).

Figure 20–36

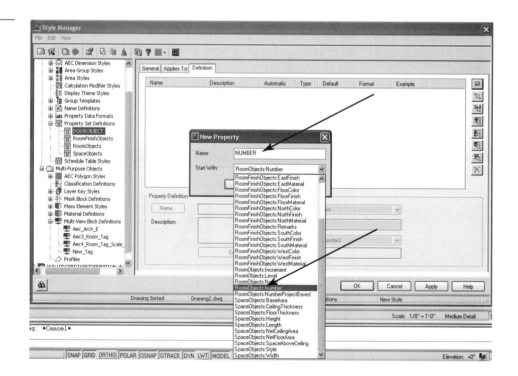

13. In the Style Manager, in the right pane, select **Auto Increment - Integer** from the **Type** drop-down list, enter **100** in the **Default** field, and **Number-Object** in the **Format** field.

14. In the **Style Manager,** in the left pane, expand the **Multi-Purpose** folder, and select the **Multi-View Block Definitions.**

15. Under **Multi-View Block Definitions,** select each of the existing multi-view block definitions, **RMB,** select Purge to delete the definitions, and press the **OK** button to return to the Drawing Editor.

! **Note:** We are removing the existing multi-view block definitions because the new Architectural Desktop 2006 Tool Catalog Generator that we will use in the next exercise will generate all the multi-view block definitions that will exist in this drawing as tags. For clarity in that exercise, we are removing those multi-view block definitions so that the only the new tag that we will create in this exercise will show up in the catalog generated by the next exercise (see Figure 20–37).

Figure 20–37

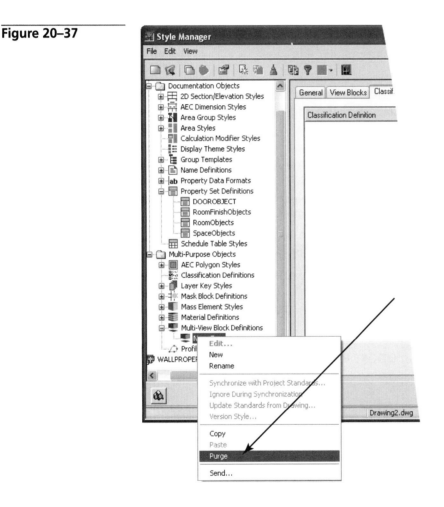

Creating the new tag design

1. Refer to the previous drawing file.

2. Select the **Rectangle** icon from the **Draw** menu, and place a **2-1/2″ × 2-1/2″** rectangle in the Drawing Editor.

3. Using the **Line** command from the Draw menu and the **Mtext** command, create the tag shown in (Figure 20–38). **Save this file**—this is important!

This design is arbitrary; you can make any design you wish. The "A" is just a locator for the door number.

Figure 20–38

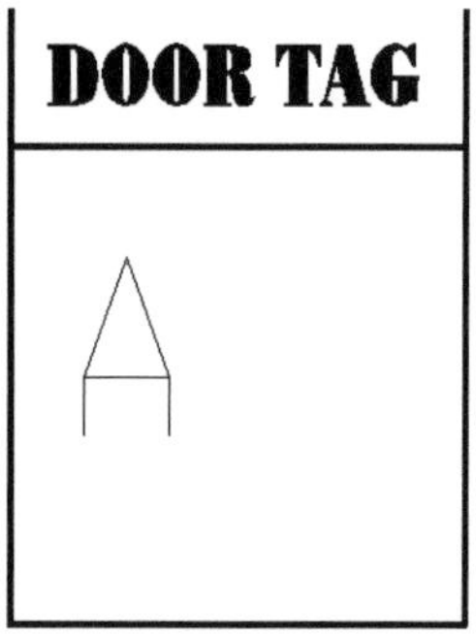

Defining (creating) the Tag using the New Define Schedule Tag routine

1. Select **Format** > **Define Schedule Tag** from the **Main** menu, and with a window marquee, select the tag design you just created.

2. With the tag design selected, press the **Enter** key on your keyboard to bring up the **Define Schedule Tag** dialog box.

3. In the **Define Schedule Tag** dialog box, Name the tag TEST_DOOR_TAG.

4. In the "A" field select Property from the **Type** drop-down list.

5. In the "A" field select **DOOROBJECT** from the **Property Set** drop-down list.

6. In the "A" field select **NUMBER** from the **Property Definition** drop-down list.

Notice that **DOOROBJECT** is the Property Set Definition we created at the start of this exercise, and **NUMBER** is its Property (see Figure 20–39).

7. In the **Define Schedule Tag** dialog box, leave the **DOOR TAG** label as Text in the **Type** column. This is because the word **DOOR TAG** is just part of the design and will not pick up information from the door as we will do with the "A" when we use the tag.

Figure 20–39

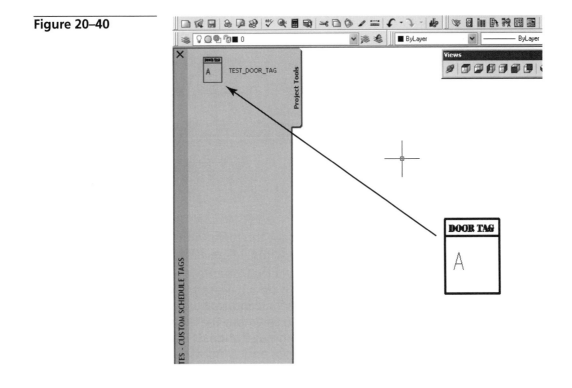

8. In the **Define Schedule Tag** dialog box, press the **OK** button, and select a point at the center of the tag design to define an insertion point, and return to the Drawing Editor.

9. Save the drawing—location doesn't matter.

10. Select the tag design, and notice that it is no longer made of separate parts, but is one object and has become a tag.

11. Move your cursor to the top of the tag, click, and while holding down the left mouse button, drag the tag into your empty Project Tools tool palette (see Figure 20–40).

Figure 20–40

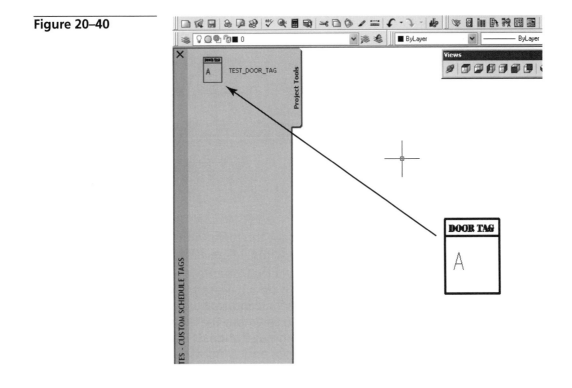

Testing the New Tag

12. Select **Format >Style Manager** from the **Main** menu to bring up the **Style Manager.**

13. In the **Style Manager,** expand the **Multi-Purpose Objects folder,** and then locate the **Multi-View Block Definitions.** Notice that it now contains the **TEST_DOOR_TAG.**

14. Select the Door tool from the **Design** tool palette, and place a Standard door in your drawing Editor.

15. With the door selected, move your cursor over the **Properties** palette to open it.

16. In the **Properties** palette, change to the **Extended Data** tab.

17. At the bottom left of the **Extended Data** tab, select the **Add property sets** icon to bring up the **Add Property Sets** dialog box.

18. In the **Add Property Sets** dialog box, make sure the **DOOROBJECT** check box is checked, and then press the **OK** button to return to the Drawing Editor (see Figure 20–41).

Figure 20–41

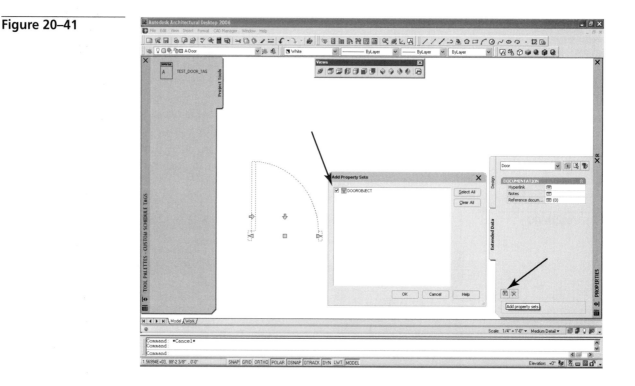

19. Copy the door four times.

20. Select the Scale drop-down list at the lower right of the Drawing editor, and set the scale to drawing scale to 1/4″ = 1′-0″.

21. Select the **TEST_DOOR_TAG** tool that you placed in the **Project Tools** tool palette, and select the first door. Locate the tag at the middle of the door opening, and click the left mouse button to open the **Edit Property Set Data dialog** box (remember that this will appear each time because it has been set to do this in **Options > AEC Content.** See the note after Step 7 of Placing Door and Window Tags).

22. In the **Edit Property Set Data dialog** box, press the **OK** button to return to the Drawing Editor, and place the first tag.

23. Enter M (Multiple) in the Command line, and press the **Enter** key on the keyboard.

24. Select the remaining doors, and again press the **Enter** key on the keyboard to bring up the **Edit Property Set Data dialog** box.

25. In the **Edit Property Set Data dialog** box, press the **OK** button to return to the Drawing Editor, and automatically label all the doors.

Notice that all the doors are incrementally numbered with your custom tag (see Figure 20–42).

Save this drawing file.

Figure 20–42

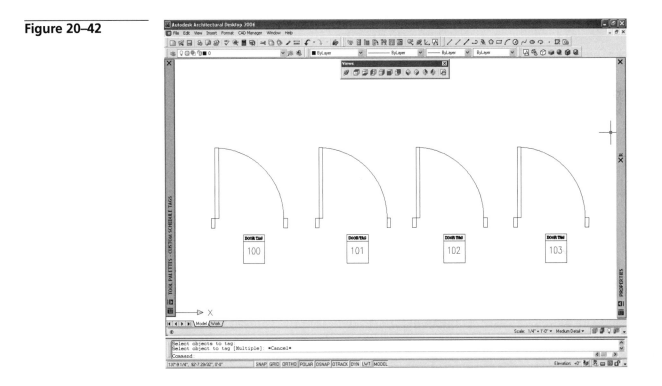

Hands-On

The New Architectural Desktop 2006 Tool Catalog Generator

Catalogs are where we keep our Architectural Desktop tools. For the 2006 version, the developers have created a new tool that creates tool catalogs from **Styles, Mask Block Definitions, Multi-block Definitions,** and **Material Definitions.** The Tool Catalog Generator gets these Styles and Definitions from the Style Manager of selected drawings. If you are using a **Standards** drawing, you might want to generate your a catalog from that drawing. Changing that drawing would allow you to change the tools in the existing catalogs.

The Architectural Desktop 2006 Tool Catalog Generator is located in the **CAD Manager Pulldown** on the **Main** menu. If it is not there, you will need to load it.

1. To load the **CAD Manager** Select **Window > Pulldowns > CAD Manager,** and click **CAD Manager Pulldown** to load it. If it is already loaded, and you Select **Window > Pulldowns > CAD Manager Pulldown,** you will see a check next to it. If you now click on **CAD Manager Pulldown,** you will remove the pulldown from the **Main** menu.

2. Select **File > Open,** and open the drawing you saved from the previous exercise.

Remember that we created this drawing on purpose, having only one **Multi-View Block Definition.**

3. Select **CAD Manager > Tool Catalog Generator** from the **Main** menu to bring up the **Populate Tool Catalog from Content Drawings** dialog box.

4. In the **Populate Tool Catalog from Content Drawings** dialog box, under **Catalog,** select the **Create a new catalog radio button,** and name the Catalog **CUSTOM SCHEDULE TAGS.** Directly below this, press the **Browse** button, to bring up the **Browse For Folder** dialog box and locate the **NEW ADT 2006 PROJECTS > CUSTOM SCHEDULE TAGS** folder that you created at the start of the **Define Schedule Tag** routine exercise.

5. After you have located the folder, press the OK button in the **Browse For Folder** dialog box to return to the **Populate Tool Catalog from Content Drawings** dialog box.

6. In the **Populate Tool Catalog from Content Drawings** dialog box, press the **Clear All** button, and then check the **Multi-View Block Definitions** check box.

7. In the **Populate Tool Catalog from Content Drawings** dialog box, under **Content Source,** select the **Create from drawing** radio button. This tells the generator to generate the catalog from a drawing file.

8. Directly below the **Create from drawing** radio button, press the browse button, and locate the drawing that you have been saving in the exercise on the **Define Schedule Tag** routine.

Finally, under **Tool Organization,** Check the **Group tools by object type** check box, select the **Create tools in Categories** radio button, and then press the **OK** button at the bottom of the dialog box (see Figure 20–43).

The Tool Catalog Generator will now create the catalog file and return you to the Drawing Editor.

Loading the Catalog in the Project Content Browser

1. Open the **Project Navigator,** and press the **Content Browser** at the bottom of the **Project Navigator** to bring up the **Content Browser** for the **CUSTOM SCHEDULE TAGS** project.

2. **RMB** in this **Content Browser,** and select **Add Catalog** from the **contextual** menu that appears to bring up the **Add Catalog** dialog box (see Figure 20–44).

Figure 20–43

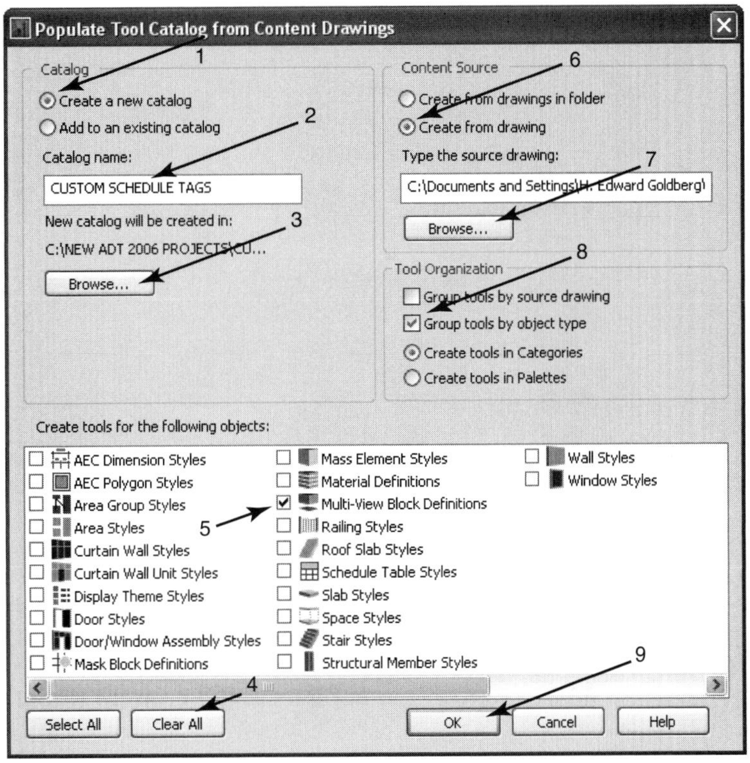

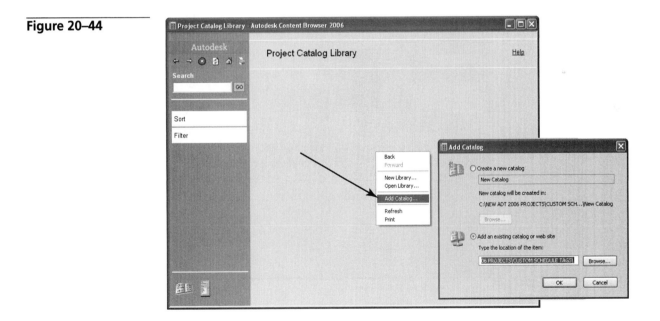

Figure 20–44

3. In the **Add Catalog** dialog box, select the **Add an existing catalog or web site** radio button, and press the **Browse** button to open the **Browse for Catalog Files** dialog box.

4. In the **Browse for Catalog Files** dialog box, select the **CUSTOM SCHEDULE TAGS** catalog file **in the NEW ADT 2006 PROJECTS > CUSTOM SCHEDULE TAGS** folder, and press the **Open** button (see Figure 20–45).

Figure 20–45

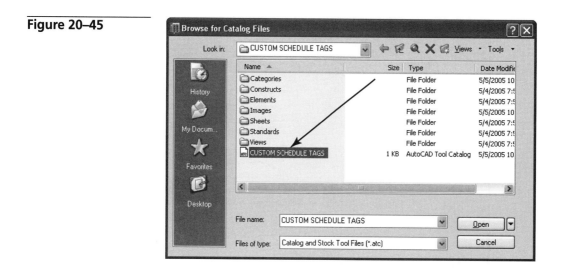

5. Again, open the **Project Navigator,** and press the **Content Browser** at the bottom of the **Project Navigator** to bring up the **Content Browser** for the **CUSTOM SCHEDULE TAGS** project. The **CUSTOM SCHEDULE TAGS** catalog now appears in the **Content Browser** (see Figure 20–46).

Figure 20–46

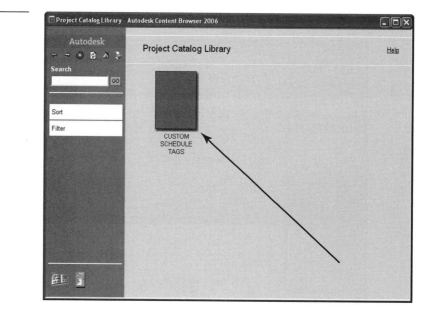

6. Click on the **CUSTOM SCHEDULE TAGS** catalog in the **Content Browser** to see the **Multi-View Block Definitions folder** (see Figure 20–47).

7. Finally, double-click on the **Multi-View Block Definitions folder** to see the TEST_DOOR_ TAG (see Figure 20–48).

Figure 20–47

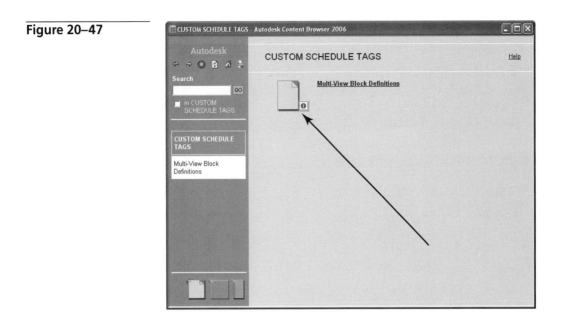

Figure 20–48

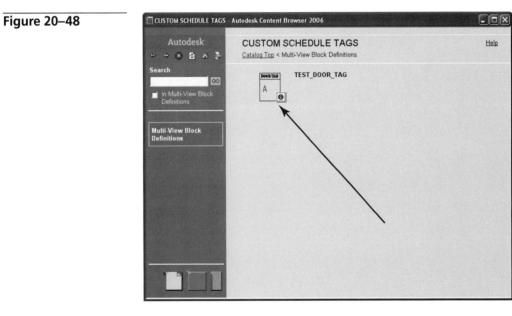

The **Content Browser** that is activated from the **Project Navigator** is always related to the project made current in the **Project Browser**. If you create catalogs with tools and connect them to the **Project Navigator Content Browser,** every time you change a project, the correct catalogs and tools for that project will be in the **Project Navigator Content Browser**. Besides this, the **Tool Palettes** are also automatically connected to the current project.

21

Sheet Sets

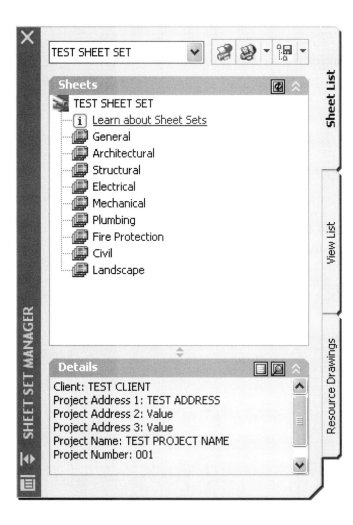

When you finish this section, you should understand the following:

- ✔ How to create a **Sheet Set.**
- ✔ How to modify a **Sheet Set.**
- ✔ How to test a new **Sheet Set.**

A sheet set is an ordered collection of sheets derived from several drawing files. You can manage, transmit, publish, and archive sheet sets as a unit.

Hands-On

Creating a New Sheet Set

1. Start a new drawing using the AEC Model (Imperial Stb) template.
2. Type **sheetset** in the **Command line** to bring up the **Sheet Set Manager.**
3. Select the drop-down list shown in Figure 21–1, and select **New Sheet Set** to bring up the **Begin** dialog box.

Figure 21–1

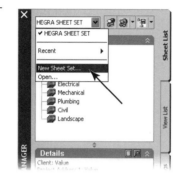

4. Select the **An example sheet set** radio button, and then press the **Next** button to bring up the **Sheet Set Example** dialog box.
5. Select the **Select a sheet set to use as an example** radio button, select **Architectural Imperial Sheet Set,** and then press the **Next** button to go to the **Sheet Set Details** dialog box (see Figure 21–2).

Figure 21–2

Create Sheet Set - Sheet Set Example

Begin
▶ Sheet Set Example
Sheet Set Details
Confirm

Autodesk

◉ Select a sheet set to use as an example

Architectural Imperial Sheet Set
Architectural Metric Sheet Set
Civil Imperial Sheet Set
Civil Metric Sheet Set
Manufacturing Imperial Sheet Set
Manufacturing Metric Sheet Set

◯ Browse to another sheet set to use as an example

nu\Template\AutoCAD Templates\Architectural Imperial Sheet Set.dst

Title: Architectural Imperial Sheet Set

Description: Use the Architectural Imperial Sheet Set to create a new sheet set with a default sheet size of 24 x 36 inches.

[< Back] [Next >]   [Cancel]

6. Name the sheet set **TEST SHEET SET.**
7. Press the **Sheet Set Properties** button at the bottom of the dialog box to bring up the **Sheet Set Properties** dialog box. In this dialog box, you can control the location of a custom drawing template, sheet storage, client and project, etc. (see Figure 21–3).

Figure 21–3

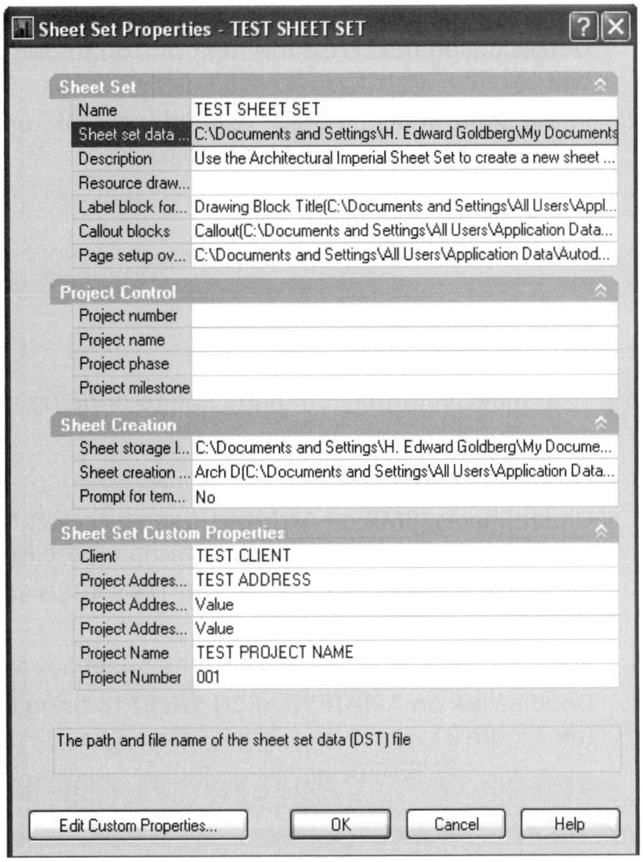

8. Press the **Edit Custom Properties** button to open the **Custom Properties** dialog box. Here you can also edit information on the client, address, etc.

9. Press the **Add** button to bring up the **Add Custom Property** dialog box. Here you can add new places or make changes for information to be added automatically to the drawings

10. In the **Custom Properties** dialog box change the Project Address 1 and 2 to **TEST STREET** and **TEST CITY,** respectively (see Figure 21–4).

Figure 21–4

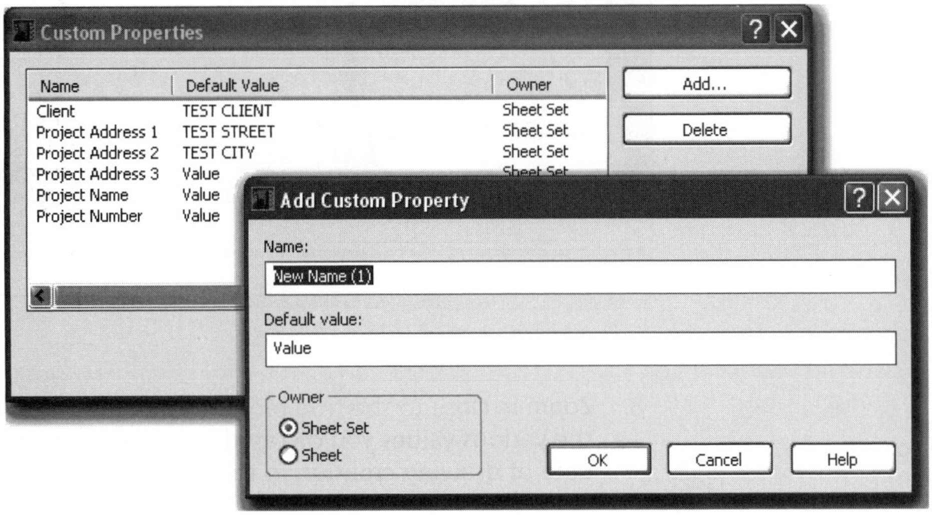

11. When you are finished, press the **OK** buttons to return to the Sheet **Set Details** dialog box. Press the **Next** button to go to the **Confirm** dialog box.

12. In the **Confirm** dialog box, if everything is OK, press the **Finish** button to create the sheet set. Save this file.

Hands-On

Testing the New Sheet Set

1. Type **sheetset** in the **Command line** to bring up the **Sheet Set Manager**.

2. Select **Open** from the drop-down list.

3. Locate **TEST SHEET SET.**

4. Under **Sheets**, **RMB** on **Architectural,** and select **New Sheet** from the contextual menu that appears to bring up the **New Sheet** dialog box.

5. Enter **A-1** in the **Number** field, and **TEST ARCH SHEET** in the **Sheet title** field.

6. Press the **OK** button to return to the **Sheet Set Manager**.

7. Double-click on **A-1- TEST ARCH SHEET** to bring up the new drawing (see Figure 21–5).

Figure 21–5

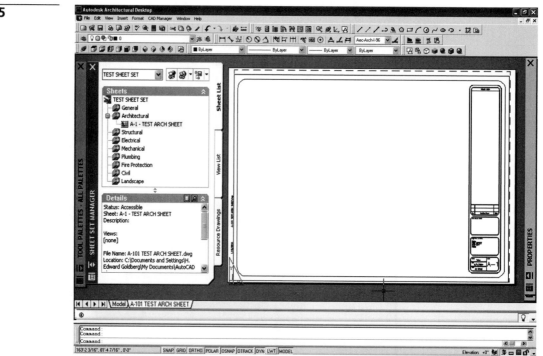

8. Zoom in close to the title block. Notice that it automatically contains the various values you dictated in the set. Notice that it also places the date of drawing creation in the date field (see Figure 21-6).

Figure 21–6

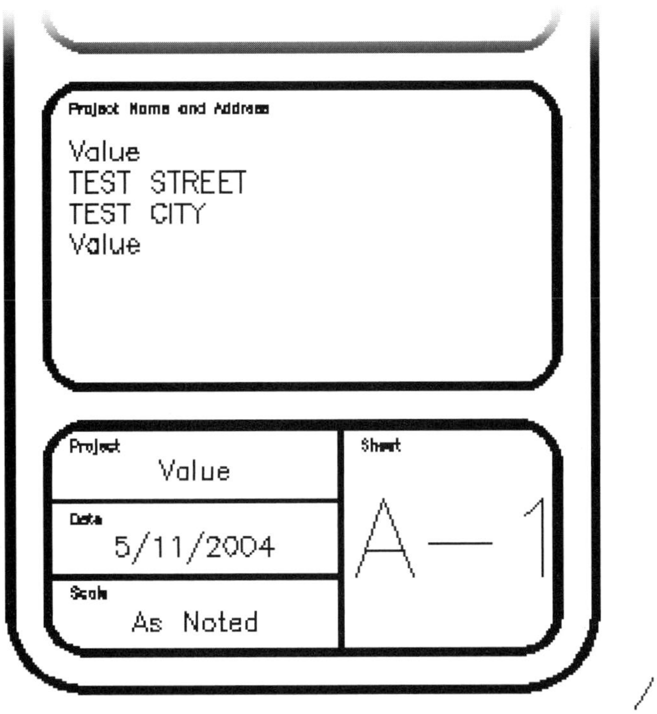

Project Name and Address

Value
TEST STREET
TEST CITY
Value

Project
Value

Sheet

Date
5/11/2004

A — 1

Scale
As Noted

Although the sheet set command is included in AutoCAD 2006, it has been seamlessly integrated in Architectural Desktop 2006 in the **Project Navigator.** Adding a sheet and double-clicking on it to bring it up in the Drawing Editor is performed in the identical manner in the **Project Navigator** as was demonstrated in the Drawing Management section.

Mask Blocks

When you finish this section, you should understand the following:

✔ The purpose of **Mask Blocks.**
✔ How to create, modify, and use **Mask Blocks.**

Mask blocks are two-dimensional blocks that mask the graphic display of AEC Objects in Plan View.

Mask blocks are often combined with AutoCAD objects such as lay-in fluorescent fixtures to mask the AEC ceiling grid. With a thorough understanding of mask blocks, you will probably find a myriad of uses for these objects.

Hands-On

Creating a Custom Fluorescent Fixture Called New Fixture

1. Start a new drawing using the AEC Model (Imperial Stb) template.
2. Change to the **Model Layout.**
3. Change to the **Top View.**
4. Using the standard AutoCAD drawing commands, draw the ceiling fixture shown in Figure 22–1.
5. Enter **Pedit** in the **Command line,** select the outline, and join the outline into a closed polyline.

! **Note:** If you don't know how to convert and join a line into a polyline, consult the AutoCAD 2006 help for **Polyline Edit (Pedit).**

6. **RMB** anywhere in the Drawing Editor and select **Basic Modify Tools > Offset** from the contextual menu that appears.
7. Enter **2″** in the **Command line,** and press **Enter** to create the 2″ outline shown in Figure 22–1.
8. Select **Format > Style Manager** from the **Main** toolbar to bring up the **Style Manager** dialog box.
9. Open the **Multi-Purpose** folder and double-click on the **Mask Block Definitions** icon.

465

Figure 22–1

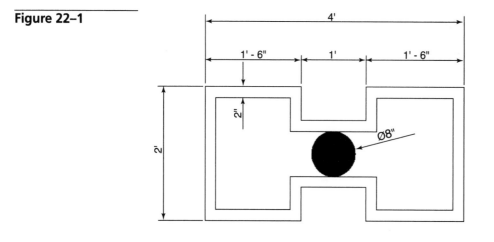

10. Select the **New Style** icon from the **Main Style Manager** toolbar.

11. Rename the new style to **NEW LIGHT FIXTURE**.

12. Select the **NEW LIGHT FIXTURE** icon, and select the **Set From** icon from the **Main Style Manager** toolbar.

13. Select the outline when asked to **"Select a close polyline"** at the **Command line.**

14. Accept **N** when asked to **"Add another ring?"** at the **Command line.**

15. Make the insertion point for the mask the center point of the outline.

16. Select everything except the outline when asked to **"Select additional graphics"** at the **Command line.**

17. In the **Style Manager** dialog box, press the **Apply** button, and then press **OK**.

The outline will become the mask block, and the interior objects of the drawing will become the fixture graphics.

Hands-On

Testing the New Light Fixture Mask Block

1. Erase everything.

2. Create a 30′ × 30′ standard wall enclosure 10′ high.

For this exercise you will need to add the **Mask Block** tool to your **Design** tool palette, so do the following:

  a. Select the **Content Browser** icon from the **Main** toolbar to launch the Content Browser.

  b. Locate the **Stock Tool Catalog.**

  c. Locate the **Drafting Tools** folder.

  d. From the **Drafting Tools** folder, drag the **Mask Block** tool into your **Design** tool palette.

3. Select the **Rectangle** icon from the **Draw** toolbar, and place a rectangle inside the 30′ × 30′ enclosure you created (see Figure 22–2).

Figure 22–2

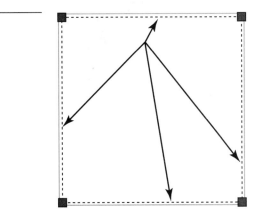

4. Change the **Display Configuration** to **Reflected.**
5. Select the **Ceiling Grid** icon from the **Design** tool palette, and enter **S** (Set boundary) in the **Command line,** and press **Enter.**
6. Select the rectangle you placed in Step 3 of this exercise.
7. Move your cursor over the **Properties** palette to open it.
8. Set the following:

   a. Specify on screen = **No**
   b. X-Width = **40′**
   c. Y-Depth = **40′**
   d. XAxis Layout type = **Repeat**
   e. XAxis Bay size = **2′-0″**
   f. YAxis Layout type = **Repeat**
   g. YAxis Bay size = **4′-0″**

9. Enter **SN** (Snap to center) in the **Command line,** press **Enter** twice, and then press the **Esc** key to complete the command.

You have now placed a centered ceiling grid, but it is located at elevation 0″.

10. Select the ceiling grid again, and move your cursor over the **Properties** palette to open it.
11. Set the **Elevation** to **8′-0″** (see Figure 22–3).

Figure 22–3

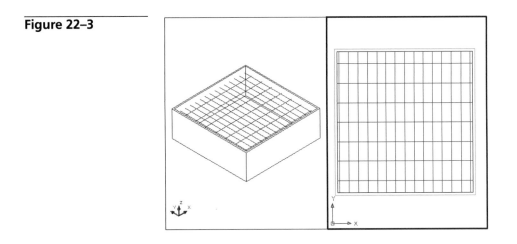

12. Select the **Mask Block** tool icon that you placed in the **Design** palette.
13. Move your cursor over the **Properties** palette to open it.
14. Enter **R** (Rotation) in the **Command line,** enter **90,** and press **Enter.**
15. Insert 12 copies of the mask block vertically.
16. Insert two more copies horizontally (see Figure 22–4).

Notice that the horizontal mask blocks cross over a grid (see Figure 22–5).

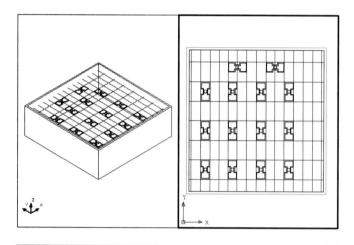

Figure 22–4

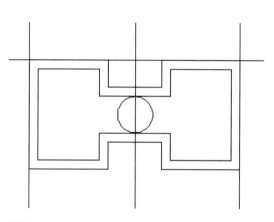

Figure 22–5

To correct this do the following:

17. Select the horizontal mass blocks you placed, **RMB,** and select **Attach Object** from the contextual menu that appears.
18. Select the ceiling grid to bring up the **Select Display Representation** dialog box.
19. Press **OK** to return to the Drawing Editor.

The grid is now masked by the NEW LIGHT FIXTURE mask block (see Figure 22–6). Save this file.

Figure 22–6

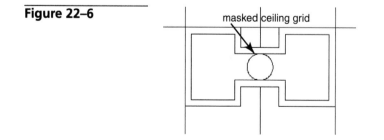

masked ceiling grid

Hands-On

Using Create AEC Content to Place the New Light Fixture in the DesignCenter

1. Erase everything but one NEW LIGHT FIXTURE in the **Top View.**

The icon that will be used in the **DesignCenter** will be taken from the current view.

2. Select the **Format > AEC Content Wizard** from the **Main** toolbar to bring up the **Create AEC Content Wizard** dialog box.
3. Select the **Masking Block** radio button, press the **Add** button to add the **NEW LIGHT FIXTURE** mask block to the **Content File,** and press the **Next** button (see Figure 22–7).

Figure 22–7

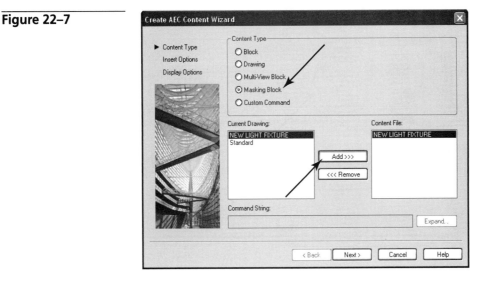

4. **Insert Options,** press the **Select Layer Key** button to bring up the **Select Layer Key** dialog box.
5. Select the **LIGHTCLG** under **Layer Key,** and press **OK** (see Figure 22–8).

Figure 22–8

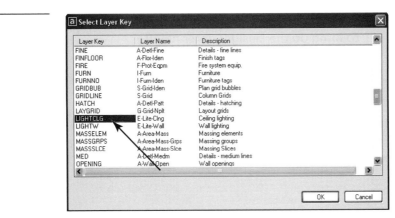

Selecting the **LIGHTCLG** layer key assures you that when you insert the content it will be placed on that layer.

6. Select the **Next** button in the **Create AEC Content Wizard** dialog box.
7. In **Display Options** press the **Browse** button.
8. At the **Save Content File** dialog box, locate the **Program Files\Autodesk Architectural Desktop 2005\Sample\Design Center** folder, name the file **CEILING FIXTURES,** and press the **Save** button to return to the **Create AEC Content Wizard** dialog box.
9. Type in a description for the masking block in the **Detailed Description** space, and press the **Finish** button (see Figure 22–9).

Note that the current viewport drawing is shown as an icon.

Figure 22–9

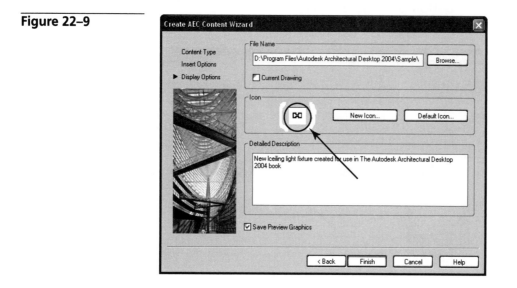

Hands-On

Testing the New Light Fixture Mask Block from the DesignCenter

1. Erase everything in the previous drawing.
2. Select the **DesignCenter** icon from the **Main** toolbar or press **CTRL + 2** to bring up the **DesignCenter** palette.
3. Click on the CEILING FIXTURES drawing that you saved.
4. Select and drag the **NEW LIGHT FIXTURE** icon into a new drawing, and zoom extents (see Figure 22–10).

The **Create AEC Content Wizard** will place blocks, drawings, masking blocks, and custom command strings in the **DesignCenter.** The process is essentially the same for all these different forms of content.

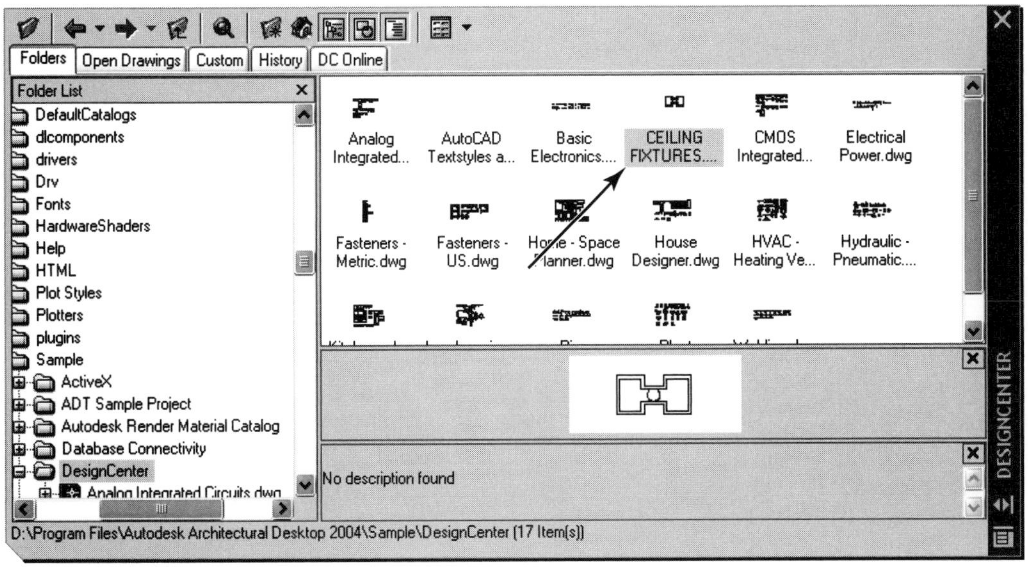
Folders
Open Drawings
Custom
History
DC Online
Folder List
DefaultCatalogs
dlcomponents
drivers
Drv
Fonts
HardwareShaders
Help
HTML
Plot Styles
Plotters
plugins
Sample
ActiveX
ADT Sample Project
Autodesk Render Material Catalog
Database Connectivity
DesignCenter
Analog Integrated...
AutoCAD Textstyles a...
Basic Electronics....
CEILING FIXTURES....
CMOS Integrated...
Electrical Power.dwg
Fasteners - Metric.dwg
Fasteners - US.dwg
Home - Space Planner.dwg
House Designer.dwg
HVAC - Heating Ve...
Hydraulic - Pneumatic....
No description found
DESIGNCENTER
D:\Program Files\Autodesk Architectural Desktop 2004\Sample\DesignCenter (17 Item(s))

Figure 22–10

Multi-View Blocks

When you finish this section, you should understand the following:

✔ How to create the **Autodesk Website** icon.
✔ How to get content from a website.
✔ How to create content from a 3D **Mesh.**
✔ How to create the **Multi-View Block.**
✔ How to test the **Multi-View Block.**

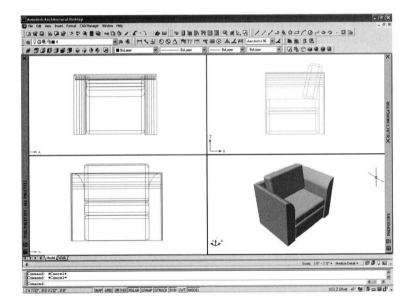

In combination with Autodesk Architectural Desktop's display system, the program uses a multi-view block system. This system allows you to place content in one view, and have the appropriate view appear in the other viewports. Although the program comes with a great deal of content, it includes controls that enable you to create your own custom content.

The following exercise illustrates the creation of a custom multi-view block.

The Chair

For this exercise you will need to use the Web to get content. You can go directly to the Web from inside Autodesk Architectural Desktop 2006 by activating the **Autodesk Website** icon from the **Main** toolbar.

Hands-On

Creating the Autodesk Website Icon

If you do not have this icon on any toolbar, do the following:

1. **RMB** on any toolbar icon, and select **Customize** from the contextual menu that appears to bring up the **Customize User Interface** dialog box.
2. Change to the **Customize** tab.
3. Follow the directions in Figure 23–1, and drag the **Autodesk Website** icon to the **Standard** toolbar.
4. Press the OK button in the **Customize User Interface** dialog box to close it.

The **Autodesk Website** icon will now appear in the **Standard** toolbar above the Drawing Editor.

Figure 23–1

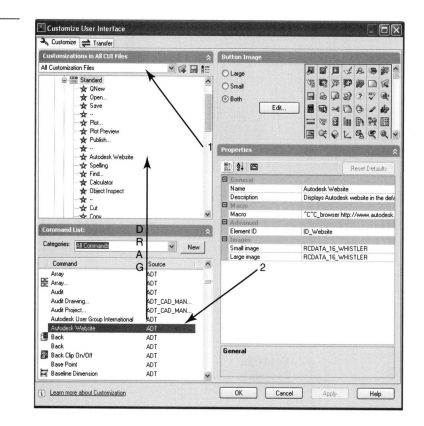

Hands-On

Going to the Chair at the 3D Cafe Website

! **Note:** Sometimes websites change addresses or just close down. At the time of publishing, the site for this exercise was active. If the site is unavailable, you can search the Web for 3D content in 3DS (3D Studio, VIZ or MAX content).

1. Go to http://www.3dcafe.com/asp/househld.asp.
2. Download the **Chair11.zip** under **Furniture,** unzip it, and place it in a folder on your computer (see Figures 23–2 and 23–3).

Figure 23–2

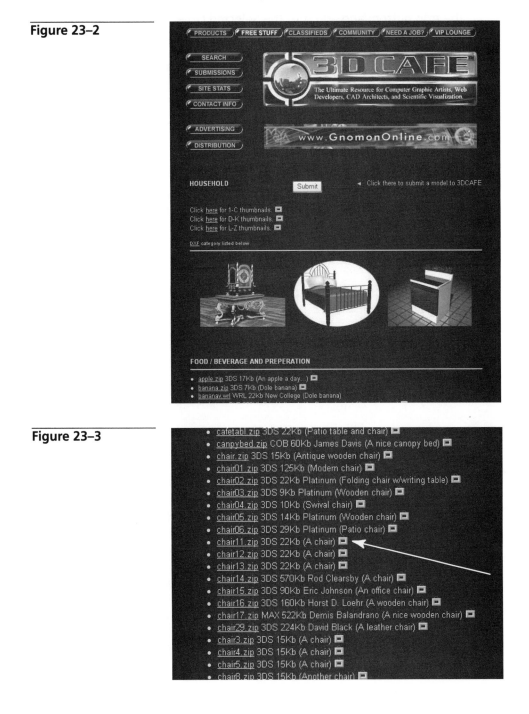

Figure 23–3

Creating Content from a 3D Mesh

1. Start a new drawing using the Aec Model (Imperial Stb) template.
2. Change to the **Model Layout.**
3. Change to the **SW Isometric View.**
4. Select **Insert > 3D Studio** from the **Main** toolbar, and import the file that was downloaded and unzipped from the Web.
5. At the **3D Studio File Import** dialog box select the Sofa1B mesh from the **Available Objects,** select the **Don't Assign a Material** radio button, press the **Add** button, and add it to the **Selected Objects** (see Figure 23–4).

Figure 23–4

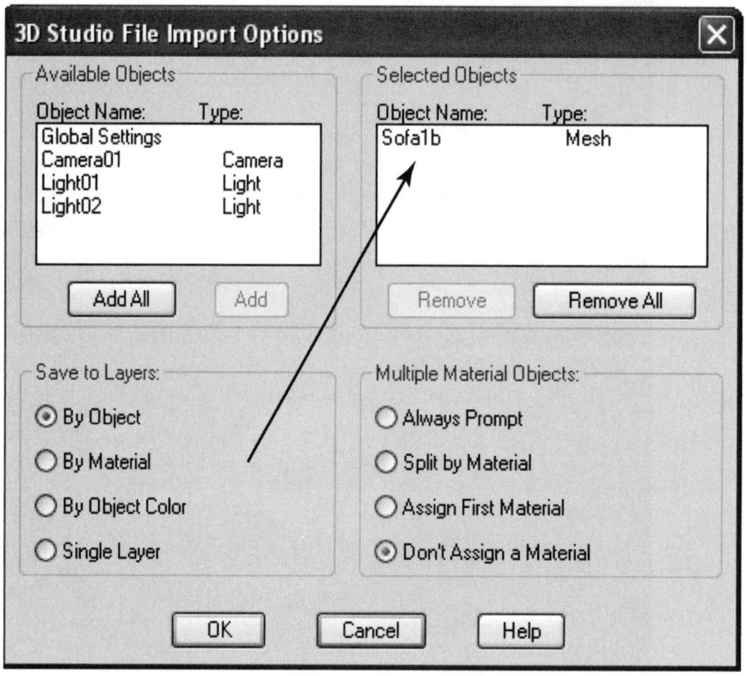

6. Change to the **Work Layout.**
7. Erase all the viewports.
8. Select **View > Viewports > 4 Viewports** from the **Main** menu.
9. Change all the views in each viewport to **Top, Front, Left,** and **SW Isometric,** respectively, and zoom extents in all viewports.

You have now imported a 3D mesh model of a chair (see Figure 23–5).

10. Select the **Content Bowser** icon from the **Main** toolbar to open the Contact Browser.
11. Select the **Autodesk Architectural Desktop Stock Tool Catalog.**

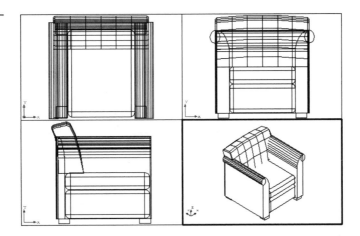

12.   Select the **Helper Tools** folder.

13.   From the **Helper Tools** folder drag the **Hidden Line Projection** to the **Design** tool palette.

14.   Select the **Hidden Line Projection** icon, select the chair, and press **Enter.**

15.   Select any block insertion point, and type **Y** in the **Command line** to insert in **Plan View.**

16.   Return to a **SW Isometric View** to see the chair and its new 2D hidden line projection.

You have now created a 2D hidden line projection of the left view of your model (see Figure 23–6).

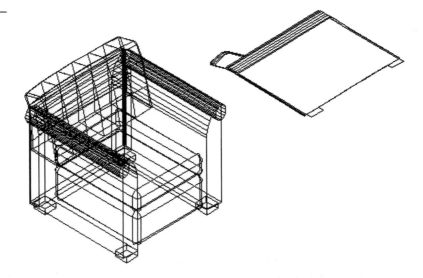

17.   Repeat this process for the **Top** and **Front Views** (see Figure 23–7).

18.   Select an empty place in the viewport, **RMB,** and select **Basic Modify Tools > 3D Operations > 3D Rotate** from the contextual menu that appears. Rotate the front and side views, and place them as shown in Figure 23–8. Create insertion points that align all the views and the model.

Figure 23–7

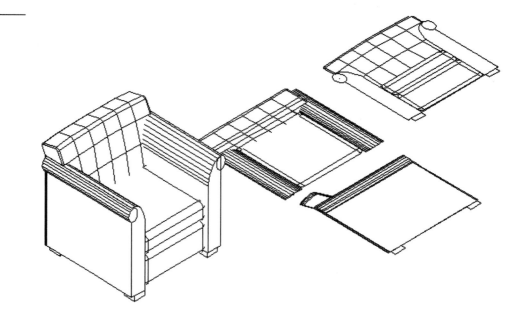

19.   Select **Format > Blocks > Block Definition,** and save each view as a block, naming them **CHAIR FRONT, CHAIR SIDE, CHAIR TOP,** and **CHAIR MODEL,** respectively, using the insertion points also shown in Figure 23–8.

Figure 23–8

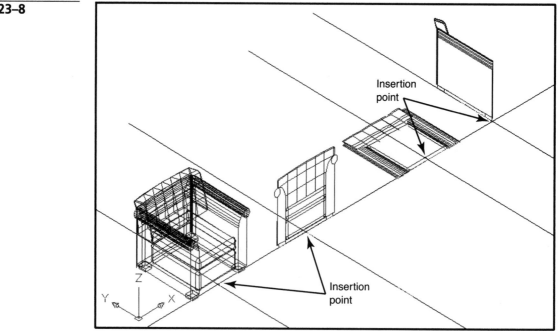

Hands-On

Creating a Multi-View Block

1. Select **Format** > **Multi-View Block** > **Multi-View Block Definitions** from the **Main** toolbar to bring up the **Style Manager** dialog box.
2. Select the **New Style** icon and create a new style; name it **CHAIR.**
3. Select **Chair Style, RMB,** and select **Edit** from the contextual menu that appears to bring up the **Multi-View Block Definition Properties** dialog box.
4. Select the **View Blocks** tab.
5. Select **General,** press the **Add** button, and select the **CHAIR FRONT** block.
6. After adding the **CHAIR FRONT** block, check the **Front** and **Back** check boxes under **View Directions** (see Figure 23–9).

Figure 23–9

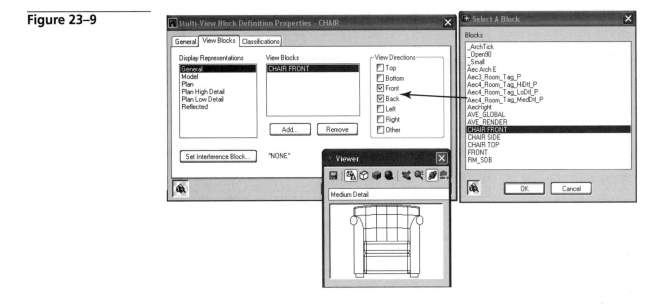

7. Repeat this process for the **CHAIR SIDE,** and **CHAIR TOP** blocks selecting the check boxes as shown (see Figures 23–10 and 23–11).

Figure 23–10

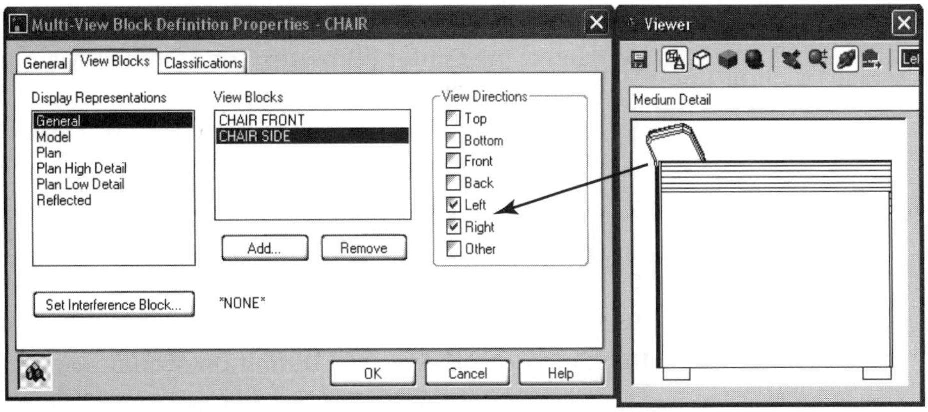

Figure 23–11

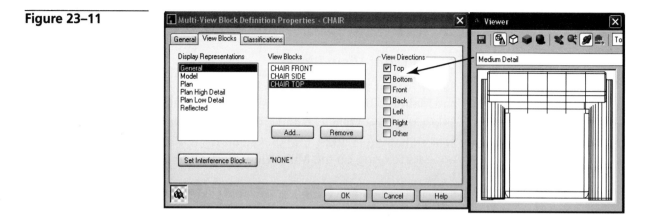

8. Select **Model** from the **Display Representations,** add the **Model** block, and check the **Other** check box (see Figure 23–12).

Figure 23–12

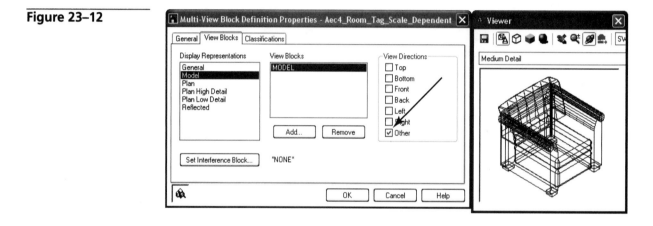

You have now created the multi-view block.

Hands-On

Testing a Multi-View Block

1. Erase everything in the drawing.
2. Change to the **Work Layout.**
3. Activate the **Top View** viewport.
4. Select the **Content Browser** icon from the **Main** toolbar to open the Contact Browser.
5. Select the **Autodesk Architectural Desktop Stock Tool Catalog.**
6. Select the **Helper Tools** folder.
7. From the **Helper Tools** folder drag the **Multi-View Block Reference** icon to the **Design** tool palette.
8. Select **Multi-View Block Reference** icon from the **Design** tool palette.
9. Move your cursor over the **Properties** palette to open it.
10. Select **CHAIR** from the **Definition** drop-down list.
11. Click in the **Top** viewport, and press **Enter** to complete the command.

The correct view of the chair appears in all the different viewports. Zoom extents in each viewport (see Figure 23–13). Save this exercise.

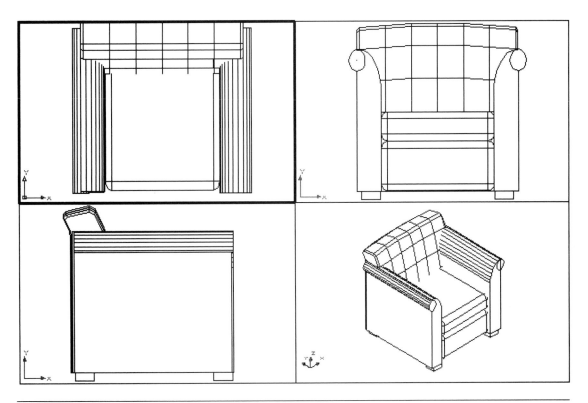

Figure 23–13

There are many ways to make 3D content. You can use AutoCAD's 3D modeling capability, 3D Studio Viz, or search the Web for free content. With multi-view blocks, the sky is the limit.

The DesignCenter

When you finish this section, you should understand the following:

✔ How to use the **DesignCenter** to create a kitchen.
✔ How to add appliances.
✔ How to create the counter.
✔ How to place the sink.
✔ How to generate a kitchen secton/elevation.

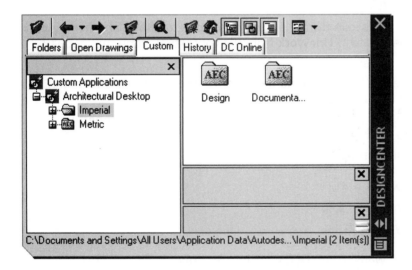

! **Note:** Everything shown in this section can also be gotten from the Content Browser Catalogs; the DesignCenter is another method.

In order to understand architectural construction documents, designers include symbols of equipment such as bathroom fixtures, beds, chair, and kitchen cabinets. Autodesk Architectural Desktop 2006 includes a very comprehensive set of generic content symbols in both 2D and 3D. Much of the content is created utilizing Architectural Desktop's multi-view block representation system. (See "Using **Create AEC Content** to Place the New Light Fixture in the **DesignCenter**," page 469 in Section 22, and Section 23, "Multi-View Blocks"). Multi-view blocks allow the Display System to place the representation of the object in the appropriate view (for example, 3D in Model View, plan representation in Plan View, etc.)

Content

All the symbols and as well as schedules, documentation symbols, and styles are contained in a folder called **Aec Content** in **C:\Documents and Settings\All Users\Application Data\Autodesk\ADT 2006\enu\AEC Content\Imperial\ (C:\Documents and Settings\All Users\Application Data\Autodesk\ADT 2006\enu\AEC Content\ Imperial\Design**—if you are using **Metric**). This content is placed in this location by default. Be sure you have sufficient space on your C drive regardless if you assign the Architectural Desktop 2006 program to a different drive than the C drive.

All content is held in standard AutoCAD drawings (DWG) and can be modified using standard AutoCAD commands.

Hands-On

Using the DesignCenter to Create a Kitchen

Creating the Kitchen

1. Start a new drawing using the Aec Model (Imperial Stb) template.
2. Change to the **Model Layout.**
3. Change to the **Top View.**
4. Place a 15'-0" × 10'-0" rectangle.
5. Select the **Walls** icon from the **Design** tool palette, **RMB,** and select **Apply Tool Properties to > Linework** from the contextual menu that appears.
6. Select the rectangle.
7. Type **Y** (Yes) in the **Command line** to erase the geometry (rectangle), and press **Enter** to create walls.
8. With the walls still selected, move your cursor over the **Properties** palette to open it.
9. Set the following parameters:

   a. Wall width = **4"**
   b. Base height = **8'-0"**
   c. Justify = **Right**

10. Modify the walls to create the enclosure shown in Figure 24–1.

Figure 24–1

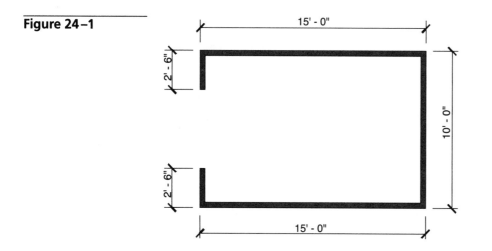

Adding the Appliances

11.   Select the **DesignCenter** icon from the **Main** toolbar (or press **Ctrl + 2**) to bring up the DesignCenter.

12.   Select the **AEC Content** tab.

13.   Select **Custom Applications > Architectural Desktop > Imperial > Design > Equipment > Food Service > Refrigerator** (Figure 24–2).

Figure 24–2

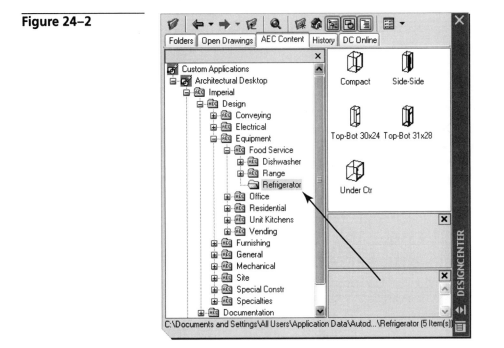

14.   Double-click the **Refrigerator** folder to open it.

15.   Select the **Side-Side** refrigerator, and drag it into the Drawing Editor.

The refrigerator will come into the drawing with the insertion point at its rear center.

16.   Type R in the Command line, and press the **Enter** key on your keyboard.

17.   Enter **270,** and press the **Enter** key on your keyboard.

18.   Enter **B** (Base point) in the **Command line,** and press the space bar or **Enter** key on your keyboard.

This will allow you to relocate the insertion point of the refrigerator. Select the upper-left corner of the refrigerator in the plan.

19.   With the **End point** Object Snap set, place the refrigerator as shown in Figure 24–3.

20.   Return to the **DesignCenter** and select **Architectural Desktop > Imperial > Design > Furnishing > Casework.**

Figure 24-3

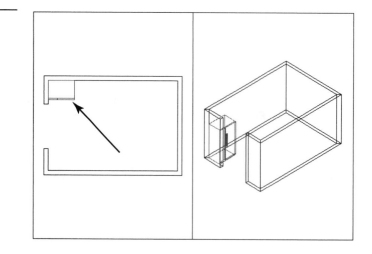

21. Double-click the **Base with Drawers** folder to open it.

22. Continue to place base cabinets, a stove, and a tall cabinet until you create a kitchen layout similar to the one in Figure 24-4. Save this drawing as **Kitchen.**

Figure 24-4

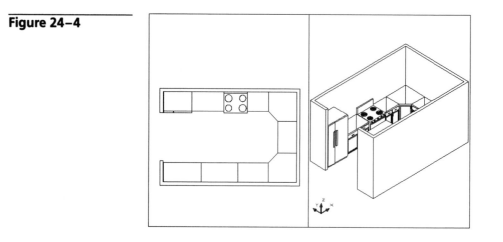

The Counter: The Splash Edge Style

1. Using the previous drawing.

2. Select the **Rectangle** icon from the **Draw** toolbar, and create a **1″ × 4″**-high rectangle.

3. Select the rectangle, **RMB,** and select **Convert To > Profile Definition** from the contextual menu that appears.

4. Pick the lower-right corner of the rectangle to bring up the **New Profile Definition** dialog box.

5. Enter **SPLASH PROFILE** in the **New Name** field, and press **OK** to create the profile.

6. Select **Format > Style Manager** to bring up the Style Manager.

7. Select **Architectural Objects > Slab Edge Styles.**

8. Select the **Slab Edge Styles** icon, **RMB,** and select **New** from the contextual menu that appears.

9. Rename the new slab edge style **SPLASH EDGE.**

10. Select **SPLASH EDGE, RMB,** and select **Edit** from the contextual menu to bring up the **Slab Edge Styles - SPLASH EDGE** dialog box.

11. Select the **Design Rules** tab.

12. Check the **Fascia** check box, and select **Splash Profile** from the drop-down list (see Figure 24–5).

13. Press **OK,** and close all the dialog boxes.

Figure 24–5

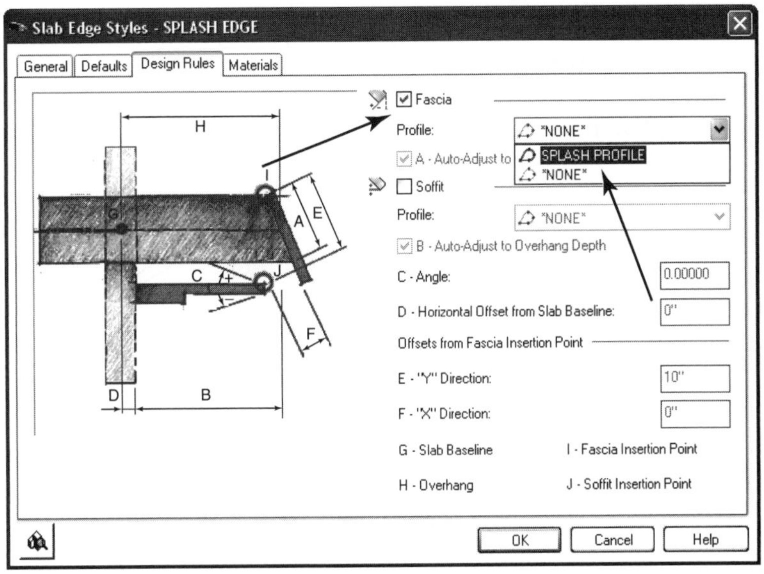

![Slab Edge Styles - SPLASH EDGE dialog box showing the Design Rules tab with the Fascia check box checked and the Splash Profile selected from the drop-down list]

You have now created the splash edge style. You can keep this style for any future use.

Now it's time to place the counter.

1. In the **Top View,** place polylines where you want counters (make sure the polylines are on the 0 layer), and that 0 is the active layer.

2. Using the **Layer Manager,** turn off visibility for everything but the 0 layer (see Figure 24–6).

Figure 24–6

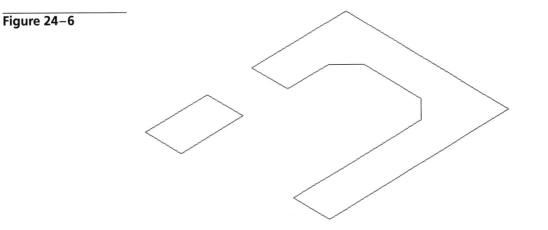

3. Select the **Slab** icon from the **Design** tool palette, **RMB,** and select **Apply Tool Properties to > Linework and Walls** from the contextual menu that appears.

4. Select the two polylines you just created.

5. Enter **Y** (Yes) in the **Command line** and press **Enter.**

6. Enter **P** (Projected) in the **Command line** and press **Enter.**

7. Enter **36″** in the **Command line,** and press **Enter.**

8. Enter **T** (Top) in the **Command line** and press **Enter** to create the counter.

9. Turn the visibility of everything back on in the **Layer Manager,** and regenerate the drawing.

You have now created the counter over the base cabinets (see Figure 24–7).

Figure 24–7

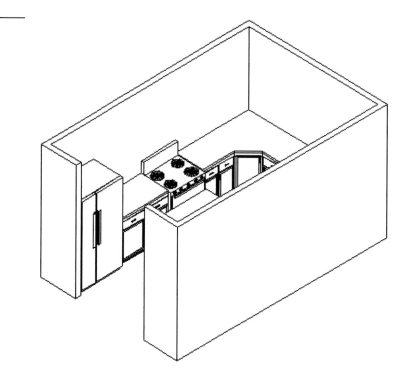

10. Select a counter you created, and move your cursor over the **Properties** palette to open it.

11. Set the Thickness to **2″,** and press the **Edges** icon to bring up the **Slab Edges** dialog box.

12. Select all the edges, and then select **SPLASH EDGE** from the **Edge Style** drop-down list, and then press **OK.**

13. Repeat Steps 11 and 12 for the other counter.

You have now added a splash edge to all the edges of the counter. You need to remove the splash from the front edges. Do the following:

a. Select a counter, **RMB,** and select **Edit Slab Edges** from the contextual menu that appears.

b. Select the slab edge you wish to remove, and press **Enter** to bring up the **Edit Slab Edges** dialog box.

c. Select **Standard** from the **Edge Style** drop-down list and press **OK.**

d. Repeat Steps b and c for the other counter.

You have now completed the counters (see Figure 24–8).

Figure 24–8

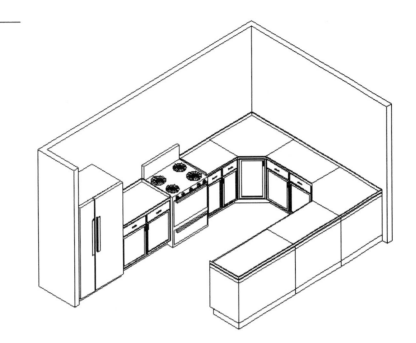

Placing the Sink

1. Change the **UCS** (User Coordinate System) to a **Z height** equal to the top of the counter.

This will allow the sink to be brought in at counter height.

2. Select the **Architectural Desktop > Imperial > Design > Mechanical > Plumbing Fixtures > Sink** from the **DesignCenter.**

3. Double-click the **Sink** folder to open it.

4. Select the **Kitchen-Double B** sink, **RMB,** and drag it into your drawing.

5. Place the sink in the center of the counter.

Turning on **Gouraud** shading shows that the counter cuts through the sink (see Figure 24–9).

Figure 24–9

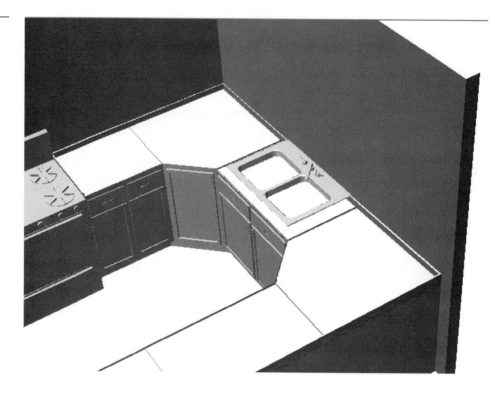

Real counters need cutouts for sinks.

6.   Select the **Rectangle** icon from the **Draw** menu and place a rectangle as shown in Figure 24–10.

Figure 24–10

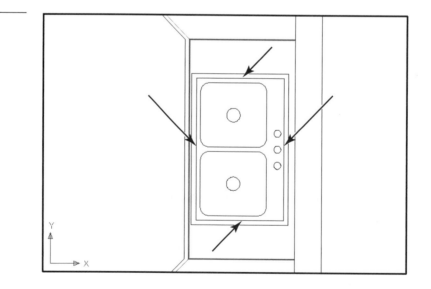

7.   Select the **Slab, RMB,** and select **Hole Add** icon from the contextual menu that appears.
8.   Select the rectangle and press **Enter.**
9.   Enter **Y** (Yes) in the **Command line** and press **Enter.**

The sink and counter are shaded correctly (see Figure 24–11).

Figure 24–11

10. Place the upper cabinets and a window, and complete the kitchen (see Figure 24–12).

Figure 24–12

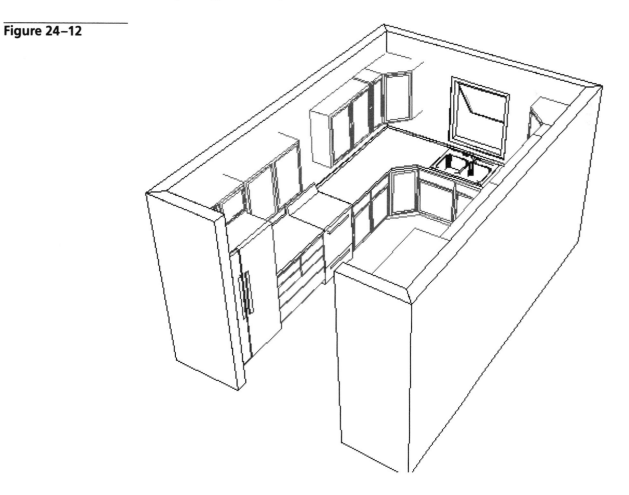

Kitchen Section/Elevation

11. Select the **Elevation Line** icon from the **Design** tool palette.
12. Place an elevation line through the kitchen as shown in Figure 24–13.

Figure 24–13

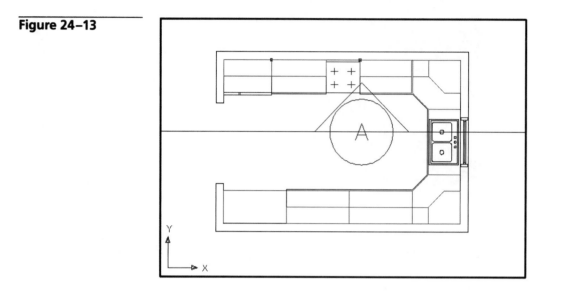

13. Select the elevation line, **RMB,** and select **Generate Elevation** from the contextual menu, and generate an elevation of your finished kitchen (see Figure 24–14).

Figure 24–14

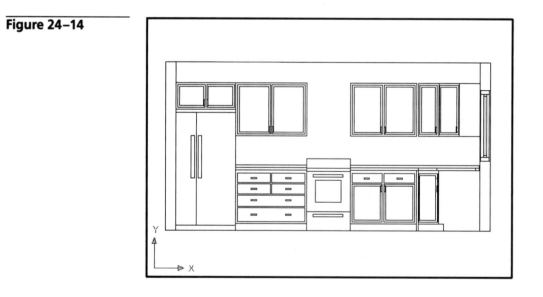

AEC Project Standards

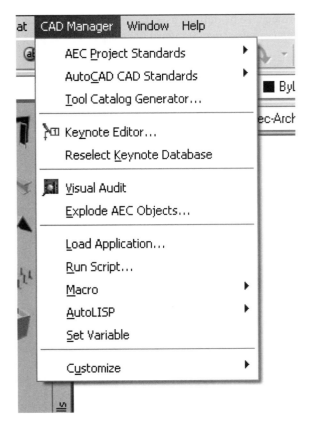

When you finish this section, you should understand the following:

✓ How to use the **AEC Project Standards**
✓ How to create and locate the **Standards Drawing.**
✓ How to load the **CAD Manager** and configure the **Standards Drawing.**
✓ How to change a project drawing(s) by synchronizing the project with the **Standards Drawing.**
✓ How to replace an AEC object in a project drawing by synchronizing it with the **Standards Drawing.**

The Project Standards feature is new to Architectural Desktop 2006. It lets you establish, maintain, and synchronize standards across all drawings in a project. Project standards include standard styles, display settings, and AutoCAD standards that are used across all project drawings. AutoCAD blocks and the new Dynamic blocks are *not* managed by Project Standards. Standard styles and display settings are specified in one or more standards drawings associated with the project. Project drawings can then be synchronized with these standards throughout the project life cycle, either automatically, or on demand. In addition, you can designate tool palettes and a Content Browser library that are associated with the project.

Project Standards is optional; however, the advantages of making changes across multiple files without opening them individually is very compelling.

Project Standards Terminology

Project drawing: A drawing file belonging to an Autodesk® Architectural Desktop project. A drawing must be part of a project to access and be synchronized with project standards.

Standards drawing: A file (DWG, DWT, DWS) that contains standard styles and display settings associated with the project. Standards drawings can be placed in a folder within the project folder, if they contain project-specific standards, or outside the project folder if they contain department-specific or companywide standards.

Standard style or display setting: A style or display setting that has been defined as a standard for a certain project. To be defined as a standard style or display setting, *it needs to be contained in a standards drawing.* Standard style types and display settings include the following:

- Object styles (for example, wall styles, door styles, and so on)
- Property set definitions
- Property data formats
- Schedule table styles
- Classification definitions
- Display theme styles
- Layer key styles
- Mask block definitions
- Material definitions
- Multi-view block definitions
- Profile definitions
- Display properties
- Display sets
- Display configurations

Synchronization: The process of checking a drawing or project against its associated standards to identify and remove version discrepancies between the standards and the project. Synchronization can be set up to run invisibly in the background, can run automatically with user prompting, or can be manually initiated by the user.

Standards Drawing Location

When standards drawings, catalogs, and libraries are located within the project folder, they are treated as project-specific. For example, if the project is used as a template for a new project, all files from the standards folder are copied to the new project to enable changing and overwriting them in the new project. Standards files that are located outside the project folder are not copied when creating a new project; they are only referenced from their original location in both the existing and the new project. This would be appropriate for files containing company standards that should not be changed from project to project.

Specify AutoCAD Standards files containing dimension, layer, linetype, and text styles. Project drawings may be checked against these standards using the **Check-Standards** command or the **Batch Standards Checker.**

Project standards can be accessed from a variety of AutoCAD file formats. They can be saved in one or more drawing files (DWG), drawing templates (DWT), or

AutoCAD standards drawings (DWS). Each of these file types can be associated with a project as standards drawings.

Hands-On

Creating and Locating the Standards Drawing

1. Before opening Architectural Desktop 2006, use the **Windows "My Computer"** to create a new directory called **TEST PROJECT STANDARDS DIRECTORY.**

2. From the standard Windows desktop, start Architectural Desktop 2006 or maximize it if it is already loaded.

3. In Architectural Desktop **Select File > Project Browser** from the **Main** menu to open the **Project Browser** dialog box.

4. In the **Project Browser** dialog box, double-click on the **TEST PROJECT STANDARDS DIRECTORY** to make it the current directory (see Figure 25–1).

Figure 25–1

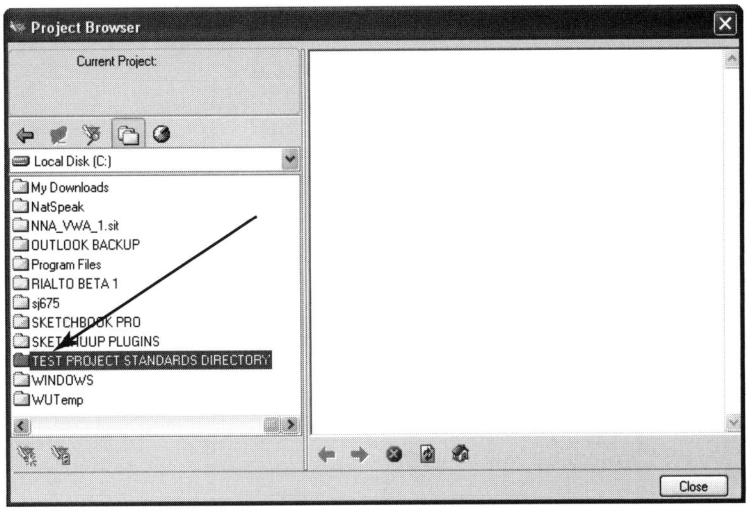

5. Click the **New Project** icon at the bottom left of the **Project Browser** dialog box to bring up the **Add Project** dialog box.

6. In the **Add Project** dialog box enter **001** as the **Project Number,** and **PROJECTS STANDARDS EXERCISE** as the **Project Name,** and press the OK button (see Figure 25–2).

7. Press the **Close** button at the bottom-right corner of the Project Browser to bring up the Project Navigator.

You have now automatically created all the project folders and subfiles that make the Project Navigator work for this new project. If you minimize Architectural desktop and again use the **Windows "My Computer"** to go into the **TEST PROJECT STANDARDS DIRECTORY,** you will see the files and folders that have been created (see Figure 25–3).

Figure 25–2

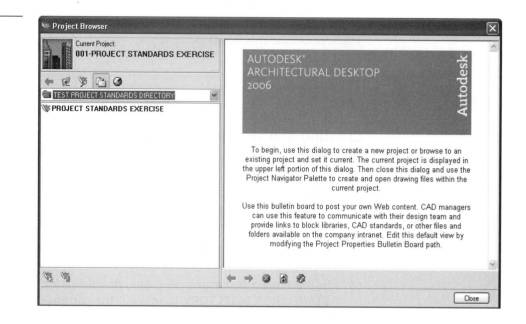

Figure 25–3

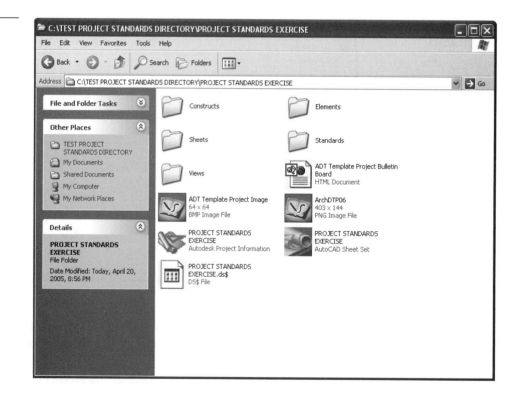

8. Maximize Architectural Desktop, and notice that you now have an empty Project Tools tool palette labeled **PROJECTS STANDARDS EXERCISE** and that the drawing in the Drawing Editor is labeled (Drawing1.dwg).

9. Select **File > Save As** from the **Main** menu, and save this drawing as **WINDOW and DOOR STANDARDS in the TEST PROJECT DIRECTORY > PROJECTS STANDARDS EXERCISE** folder (see Figure 25–4).

Figure 25–4

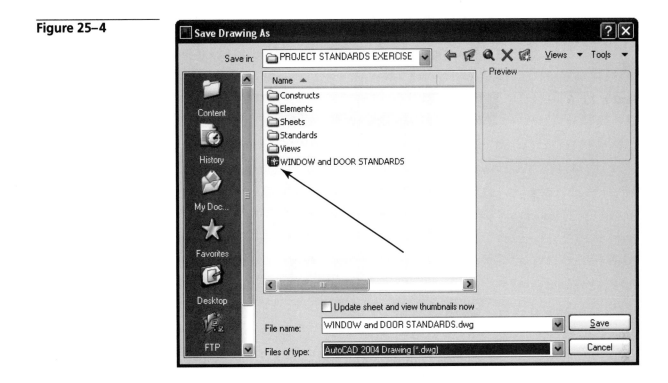

Hands-On

Loading the CAD Manager and Configuring the Standards Drawing

1.   Select **Window > Pulldowns > CAD Manager** to load the **CAD Manager** into the **Main** menu (see Figure 25–5).

Figure 25–5

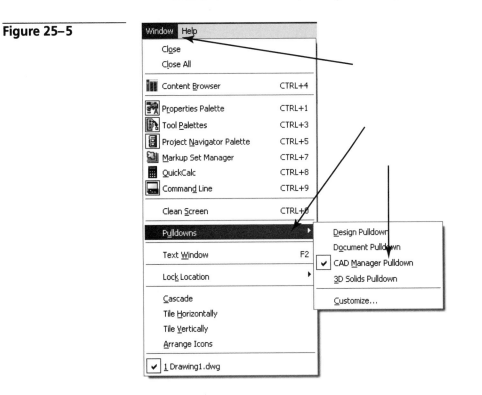

2. After the CAD Manager pulldown is loaded, select **CAD Manager** > **AEC Project Standards** > **Configure** from the **Main** menu to bring up the **Configure AEC Project Standards** dialog box (see Figure 25–6).

Figure 25–6

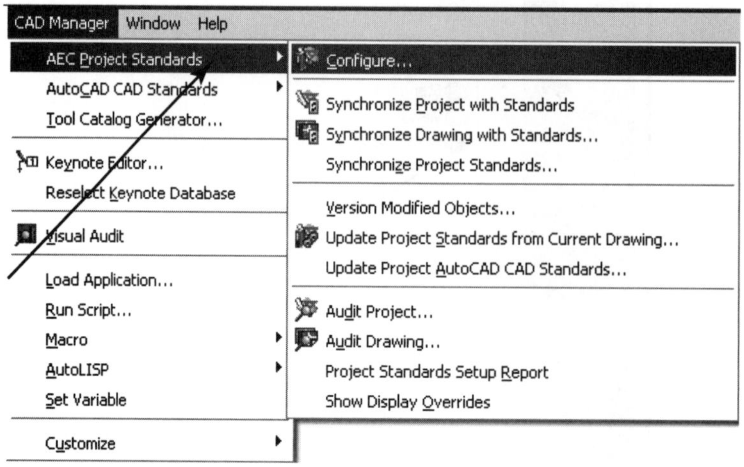

3. In the **Configure AEC Project Standards** dialog box, select the **Standards** tab, and make sure **All Objects** is showing in the object display drop-down list.

4. Press the **Add** icon to the right of the **Configure AEC Project Standards** dialog box, and select the **WINDOW and DOOR STANDARDS** drawing in the **TEST PROJECT DIRECTORY** > **PROJECTS STANDARDS EXERCISE** folder.

5. Press the **Open** button to return to the **Configure AEC Project Standards** dialog box.

You have now set the **WINDOW and DOOR STANDARDS** drawing to be a **Standards** drawing. Next you will tell the program which objects that drawing controls.

6. Under the Objects list, check the Wall Styles and Window Styles check boxes that are in line with the vertical name of the **WINDOW and DOOR STANDARDS** drawing, and press the **OK** button (see Figure 25–7).

This purpose is to set the relationship between the **Standards** file and the objects to be managed.

7. Under the Objects list, check the Door Styles and Window Styles check boxes that are in line with the vertical name of the **WINDOW and DOOR STANDARDS** drawing, and press the **OK** button (see Figure 25–7).

8. The **Version Comment** dialog will appear. Enter **FIRST WINDOW and DOOR STANDARDS** in the comment field and press the **OK** button to return to the Drawing Editor (see Figure 25–8).

You will now place doors and windows into your Project Tools tool palette labeled **PROJECTS STANDARDS EXERCISE,** which was automatically created when you created this project. This tool palette will automatically appear every time you bring up this project.

Figure 25–7

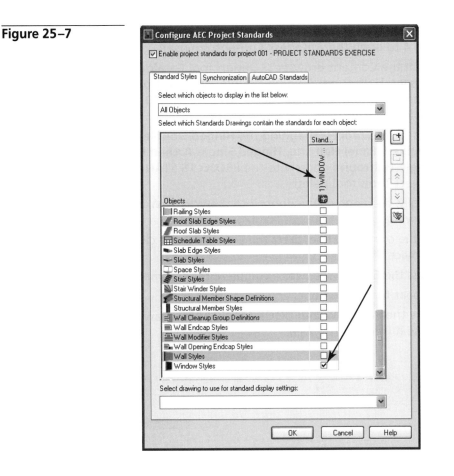

Figure 25–8

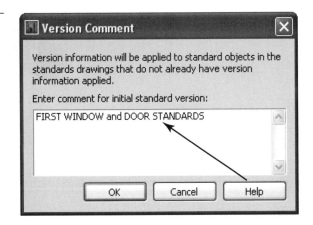

9. In the **Configure AEC Project Standards** dialog box, change to the **Synchronization** tab.

10. In the **Synchronization** tab, select the **Manual** radio button, and press the OK button to return to the Drawing Editor.

Note: It would be a good idea to read in the **Synchronization** tab the explanation of the Manual standards synchronization behavior. If you select the other **radio** buttons, you can read their behavior.

11. Select the **Content Browser** icon from the **Navigation** tool bar or select **Ctrl 4** to open the Autodesk **Content Browser.**

12. From the Content Browser > Design Tool Catalog- Imperial, drag the **Awning Halfround, Awning-Double, Awning-Double Octagon,** and **Bay** windows into the locked open **PROJECTS STANDARDS EXERCISE** Project Tools tool palette.

13. Repeat this process dragging the **Hinged-Double-6 panel, Hinged-Double-6 Panel Half Lite, Hinged-Single-Arched Full Lite,** and **Hinged-Single-Halfround** doors into the **PROJECTS STANDARDS EXERCISE** Project Tools tool palette.

14. Finally, drag one of the doors into the **WINDOW and DOOR STANDARDS** drawing.

15. At the command line, press the **Enter** key, and click the mouse button to place the door.

16. Press the **Enter** key twice to complete the command, and place the door.

17. Repeat for all the doors and windows.

18. Save the **WINDOW and DOOR STANDARDS** drawing again, and then close it (see Figure 25–9).

Figure 25–9

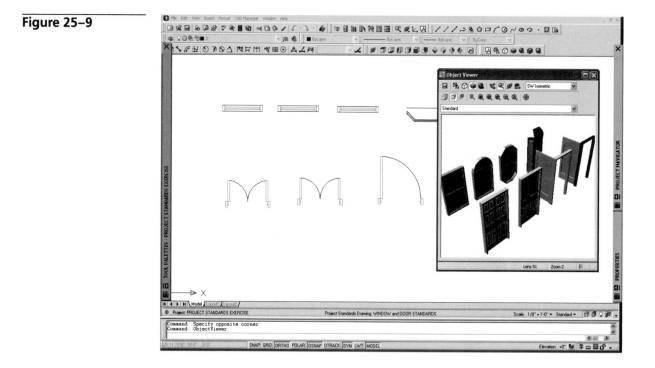

Hands-On

Changing a Project Drawing by Synchronizing It with the Standards Drawing

1. In the **PROJECT STANDARDS EXERCISE,** open the **Project Navigator** and change to the Constructs tab.

2. In the **Constructs** tab click the **Add Construct** icon to bring up the **Add Construct** dialog box.

This is a good opportunity to check what you learned in Section 16, "Drawing Management."

3. In the **Add Construct** dialog box, enter **WINDOW and DOOR CONSTRUCT** in the name field, and press the **OK** button to return to the Drawing Editor.

4. Open the Project Navigator again, select the Constructs tab, and double-click on **WINDOW and DOOR CONSTRUCT** to bring it up in the Drawing Editor.

5. From the Design tool palette, select and place a **Standard** 6″ wide wall with a base height of 8′-0″ and 15′ long into the **WINDOW and DOOR CONSTRUCT** drawing.

6. From the **PROJECT STANDARDS EXERCISE** > **Project tools** tool palette place a Hinged- Single- Halfround door, an Awning Double, and an Awning Halfround window in the wall you previously placed.

7. Change to the SW Isometric view (see Figure 25–10).

Figure 25–10

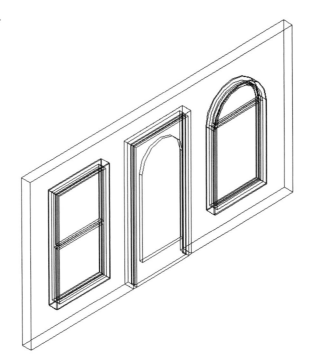

8. Select **Format** > **Style Manager** from the **Main** menu to bring up the **Style Manager.**

9. Click the + next to **001 PROJECT STANDARDS EXERCISE** at the top left pane to expose the **WINDOW and DOOR STANDARDS.dwg.**

10. Click the + next to **WINDOW and DOOR STANDARDS.dwg** to expose the **Architectural Objects** in that drawing.

11. Click the + next to **Architectural Objects** to expose the **Door Styles** and **Window styles.**

12. Click the + next to **Door Styles** and **Window styles** to expose their different doors and windows (see Figure 25–11).

Figure 25–11

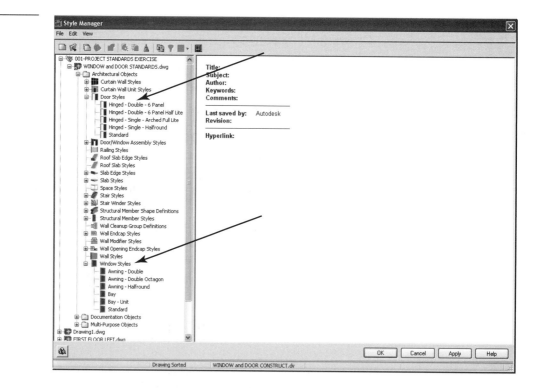

13. Click on the **Awning-Double** window style to bring up its properties in the right pane of the Style Manager.

14. Change to the **Dimensions** tab.

15. In the Dimensions tab, change the **B-Depth** to **24"**.

16. Change to the **Version History** tab.

17. In the **Version History** tab, press the **Version** button to bring up the **Version Object** dialog box.

18. In the **Version Object** dialog box, enter **24" B-Depth** (see Figure 25–12).

Figure 25–12

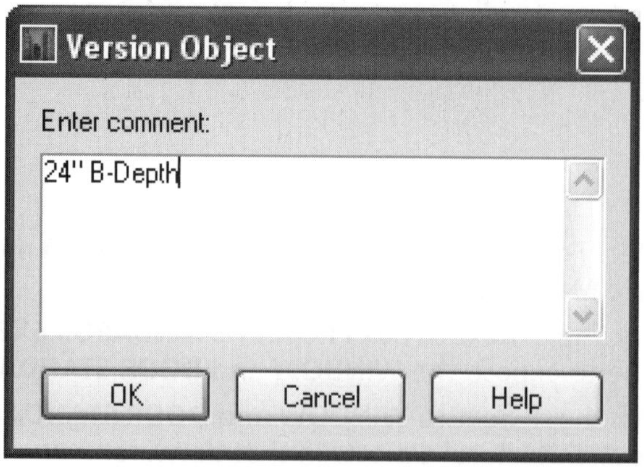

19. In the **Version Object** dialog box, press the **OK** button to return to the **Style Manager** dialog box, and press the **OK** button in the **Style Manager** dialog box to close it.

An **AutoCAD** information dialog box will now appear telling you that you have changed the **Standards** drawing, and asking if you wish to save the changes. Press the **Yes** button to save the changes and return to the Drawing Editor (see Figure 25–13).

Figure 25–13

To synchronize the Awning-Double window in the **WINDOW and DOOR CONSTRUCT** drawing with the changed Awning-Double window in the **Standards** drawing, do the following:

20.   Be sure the **WINDOW and DOOR CONSTRUCT** drawing is in the Drawing Editor.

21.   Select **CAD Manager** > **AEC Project Standards** > **Synchronize Project with Standards** to bring up the > **Synchronize Project with Standards** dialog box.

22.   In the **Synchronize Project with Standards** dialog box, select the Window Style, select **update from Standard** from the **Action** drop-down list, and press the **OK** button to return to the Drawing editor (see Figure 25–14).

Figure 25–14

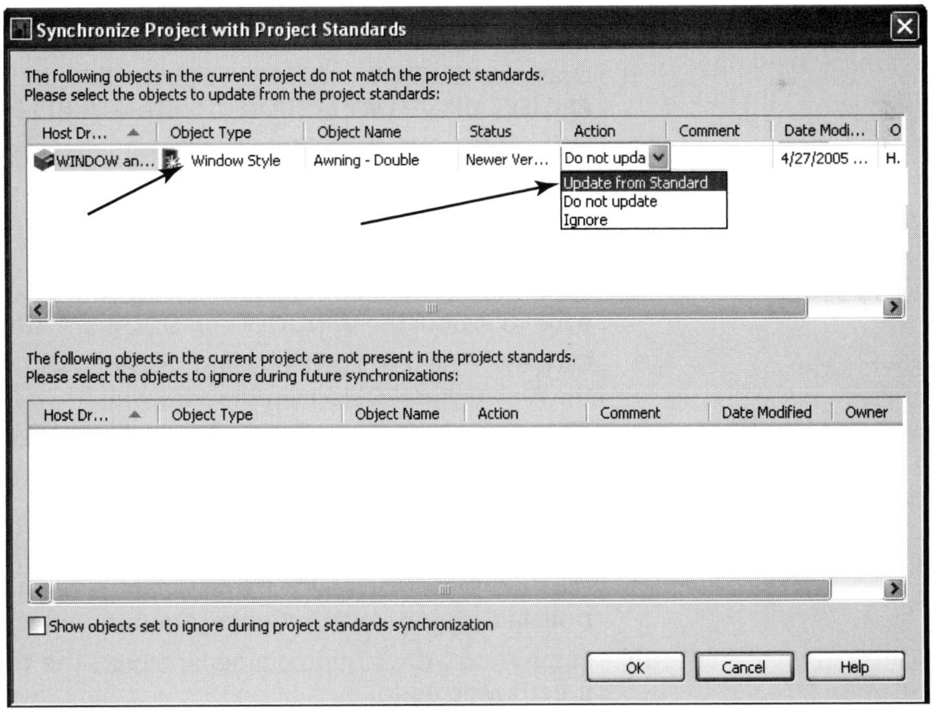

23.   Select Flat Shaded, Edges On from the Shading tool bar, and notice that the Awning window in the **WINDOW and DOOR CONSTRUCT** drawing has changed (see Figure 25–15).

Figure 25–15

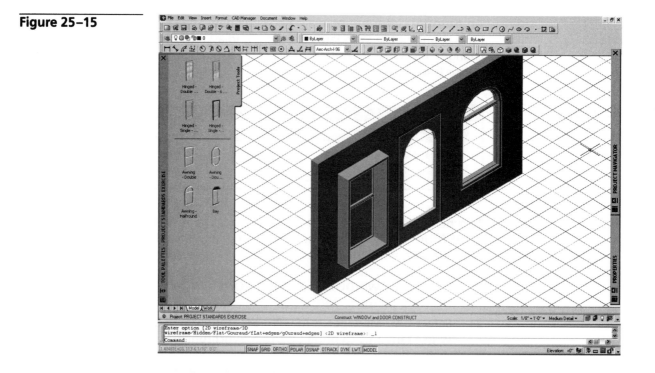

Hands-On

Replacing an AEC Object in a Project Drawing by Synchronizing It with the Standards Drawing

1. Open the **WINDOW and DOOR STANDARDS** drawing from the **TEST PROJECT DIRECTORY > PROJECTS STANDARDS EXERCISE folder.**

2. In the **WINDOW and DOOR STANDARDS** drawing, delete the **Awning-Double** window, and save the file.

3. Select **Format > Style Manager** from the **Main** menu to bring up the **Style Manager.**

4. Click the + next to **001 PROJECT STANDARDS EXERCISE** at the top left pane to expose the **WINDOW and DOOR STANDARDS.dwg.**

5. Click the + next to **WINDOW and DOOR STANDARDS.dwg** to expose the **Architectural Objects** in that drawing.

6. Click the + next to **Architectural Objects** to expose the **Window styles.**

7. Click the + next to **Window styles** to expose its windows.

8. Select the **Awning-Double** window style, **RMB,** and select **Purge** to purge the **Awning-Double** window style from the **Style Manager.**

9. With the **Style Manager** still open, change the name of the **Awning Double Octagon** style to **Awning-Double,** and press the **OK** button.

10. In the AutoCAD warning dialog box, press the **Yes** button to return to the Drawing editor.

Since the left window in your WINDOW and DOOR CONSTRUCT drawing was originally named **Awning–Double,** the renamed Awning-Window Octagon window will replace it. Do the following:

11. Be sure the **WINDOW and DOOR CONSTRUCT** drawing is in the Drawing Editor.

12. Select **CAD Manager** > **AEC Project Standards** > **Synchronize Project with Standards** to bring up the > **Synchronize Project with Standards** dialog box.

13. In the **Synchronize Project with Standards** dialog box, select the **Awning-Double** Window Style, select **update from Standard** from the **Action** drop-down list, and press the **OK** button to return to the Drawing editor.

14. Select Flat Shaded, Edges On from the Shading tool bar, and notice that the Awning window in the **WINDOW and DOOR CONSTRUCT** drawing has changed to the Awning-Double Octagon window (see Figure 25–16).

Figure 25–16

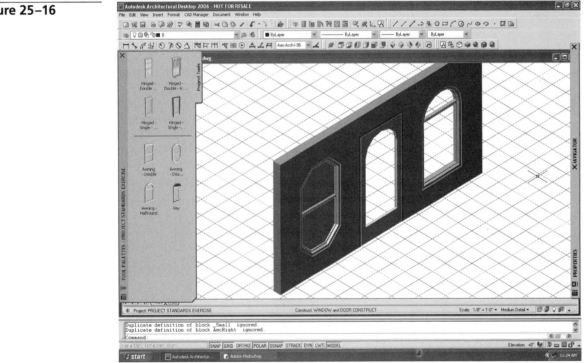

Experiment with changing different doors and windows until the operation becomes natural. Door widths and heights cannot be changed and synchronized unless you substitute different styles as shown in the above exercise.

The following points need to be taken into consideration to work efficiently with the project standards feature:

■ Project standards can be used only with projects. A drawing must be part of a project to be synchronized with project standards. Project standards cannot be applied to standalone drawings. You can copy standard styles and display settings into stand-alone drawings, but they will not be synchronized when the standards change.

- Project standards can be distributed among multiple standards drawings, if desired. However, there can be only one drawing that is designated for the display settings in a project.
- Project standards can be stored in DWG, DWT, and DWS files.
- AutoCAD standards for layers, text styles, linetypes, and AutoCAD dimension styles must be placed in DWS files.
- Demand loading needs to be enabled for working with project standards. The XLOADCTL system variable must be set to 2 (default value).
- There is no auto-updating between Project Standards and Project-based catalogs and Project-based tool palettes in the workspace.

26

Display Themes

When you finish this section, you should understand the following:

- ✔ How to use set up an AEC object for **Display Themes.**
- ✔ How to coordinate an AEC object with the **Display Themes Style.**
- ✔ How to place a **Display Theme Schedule** object.

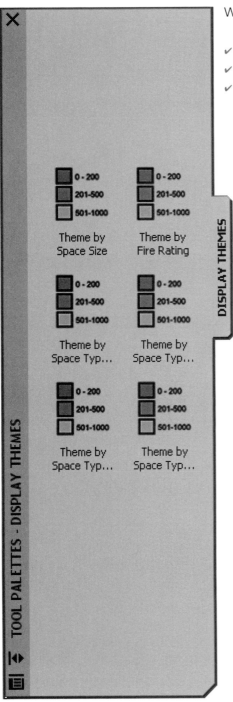

Hands-On

Creating a Test Floor

1. Using the **Wall** tool from the **Design** tool palette, create the floor and walls shown in Figure 26–1.

Figure 26–1

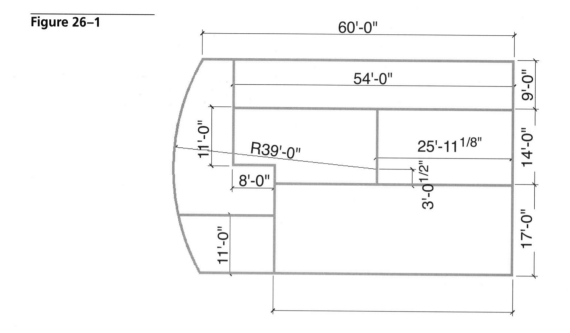

2. Select the **Space Auto Generate** tool from the **Design** tool palette, and place spaces (see Figure 26–2).

Figure 26–2

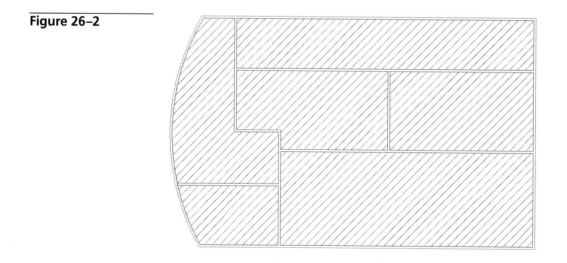

3. Select one of the spaces, **RMB,** and select **Edit Space Style** from the contextual menu that appears to bring up the **Space Style Properties** dialog box.

4. In the **Space Style Properties** dialog box, press the **Property Sets** button to open the **Edit Property Set Data** dialog box.

5. In the **Edit Property Set Data** dialog box, select the **Add Property sets** icon to open the **Add Property sets** dialog box.

6. In the **Add Property sets** dialog box, make sure the **SpaceStyles** check box is checked, and press the **OK** buttons to return to the drawing editor (see Figure 26–3).

Figure 26–3

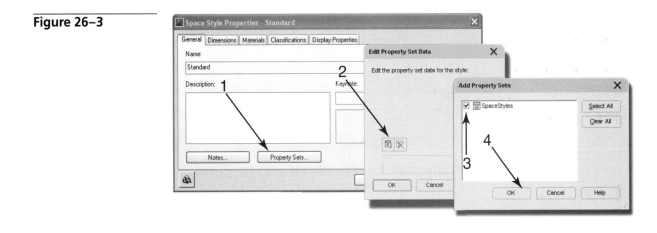

7. Select the **Theme by Space Size** tool from the **Scheduling** tool palette.

8. Click in the **Drawing Editor,** and then press the **Enter** key to complete the command. The spaces now change color according to size as dictated in the **Display Theme** schedule (see Figure 26–4).

Figure 26–4

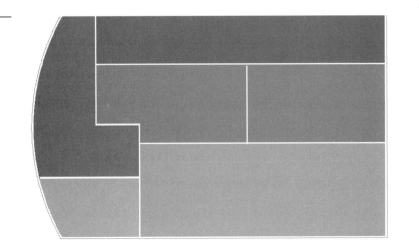

Space Size Legend
0–50
51–100
101–150
151–200
201–250
251–300
301–350
351–400
401–450
451–500
501–550
551–600
601–650
651–700
701–750
751–800
801–850
851–900
901–950
951–1000
1001–

To understand what is happening, select the **Display Theme** schedule you just placed, **RMB,** and select **Edit Display Theme** Style from the contextual menu that appears to bring up the **Display Theme Style Properties** dialog box. In the **Theme Rules for selected Theme Setting** panel you will find the drop-down lists for the **Property Set Definitions, Property,** and **Condition** that connect AEC objects to Theme Display schedules (see Figure 26–5).

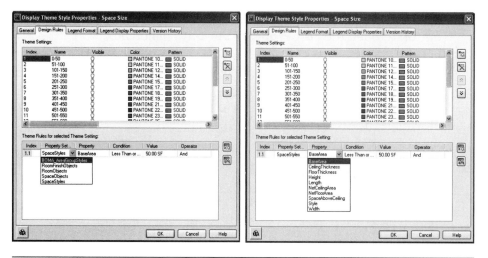

Figure 26–5

Try experimenting with different property set definitions for different AEC objects and different configurations for Display Theme schedules. It is really quite easy.

Section **27**

VIZ Render

When you finish this section, you should understand the following:

- ✔ How best to learn to operate **VIZ Render.**
- ✔ Making a simple scene.
- ✔ Using **VIZ Render.**
- ✔ Creating and modifying **Materials.**
- ✔ Placing **Materials** in ADT.
- ✔ People and trees.
- ✔ Using **ArchVision RPS content plug-in.**
- ✔ Using the **Bionatics EASYnat plug-in.**

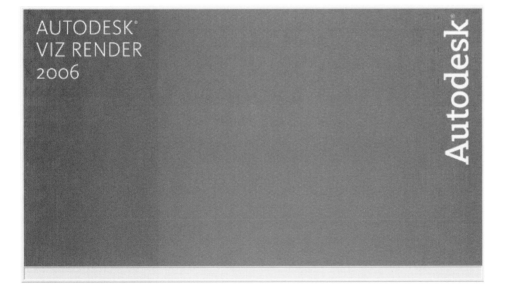

AUTODESK®
VIZ RENDER
2006

Autodesk

VIZ Render brings much of the power of Autodesk VIZ 6 to the program. Although the VIZ Render engine is a separate module, it should be activated from within ADT directly. Selecting VIZ Render from within ADT links the two programs together. While the original ADT drawing has to be saved, once saved, any changes to the ADT drawing can be updated within VIZ Render.

Besides the ability to create and place materials, and to render (color wireframe models), VIZ Render brings radiosity and animation to ADT. Radiosity is a system that accurately and easily represents lighting. In this system, one places a sun, lightbulbs, light fixtures, and so on, and the render engine calculates the effects of these light sources on the scene. Rendered output can be a bitmap (JPG, TIF, TGA, GIF), a movie file (MOV, AVI, FLI), or other formats for the Web (PGN) and for 2½ D programs such as Piranesi (RLA). Professional high-resolution movies can be made from numbered TGA, AVI, or MOV files but can be played back best from the hard drive when used in conjunction with hardware compression devices such as Pinnacle's Pro-One video board. The movies can also be compressed as MP2 files and burned to CDs or DVDs giving excellent results.

Besides VIZ Render, ADT 2006 also comes with plug-ins from ArchVision and Bionatics. Using its RPC concept, ArchVision has become the de facto standard for architectural 3D digital content. Bionatics provides an excellent 3D vegetation solution, which can be modified by season. Its trees, flowers, bushes, and so on can be animated to show wind.

How Best to Learn to Operate Viz Render

The best way to learn the VIZ Render techniques is to start out with a very simple structure. Once you have learned the techniques, you can easily apply those techniques to more complex structures. Keep your experimentation simple, make one change at a time, and observe the changes.

Hands-On

Making a Simple Scene

1. Start a new drawing using the Aec Model (Imperial Stb) template.
2. Change to the **Model Layout.**
3. Change to the **Top View.**
4. Using Standard 6″ × 8″-high walls, create a 20′-long by 10′-wide enclosure.
5. Place a roof on the structure with the following parameters:

   a. Thickness = **10″**

   b. Edge cut = **Plumb**

   c. Overhang = **1′-0″**

   d. Plate height = **8′-0″**

   e. Slope = **45.00**

6. Select the roof to activate its grips, and pull the center end grips to create gable ends (see Figure 27–1).
7. Enter **roofline** in the **Command line,** and press **Enter.**
8. Enter **A** (Auto project) in the **Command line,** and press **Enter.**
9. Select the two end walls, and press **Enter.**

Figure 27–1

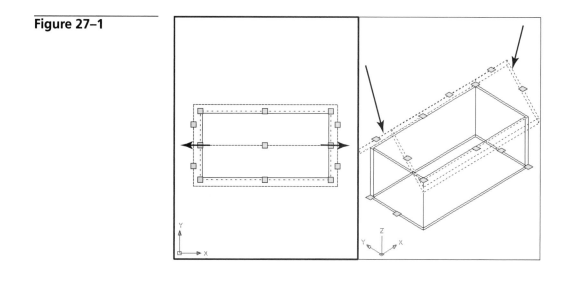

10. Select the roof and press **Enter** twice to make the walls meet the roof peak, and finish the command (see Figure 27–2).

Figure 27–2

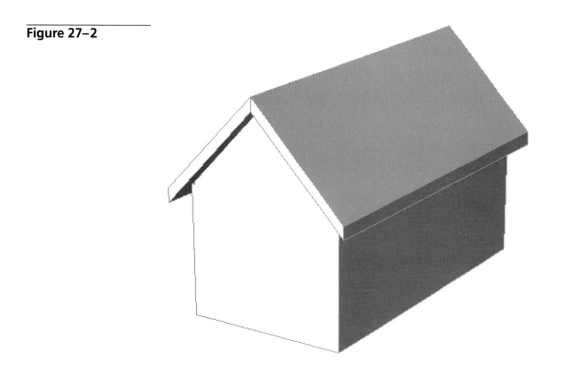

11. Add windows and doors as shown in Figure 27–3. The glass in the windows has been turned off; the doors have been opened to 90°.
12. Change to the **Front View.**

Figure 27–3

13. Place a rectangle as shown in Figure 27–4.
14. Select the rectangle, **RMB,** and select **Polyline Edit** from the contextual menu that appears.
15. Enter **E** (Edit vertex) in the **Command line** and press **Enter.**

Figure 27–4

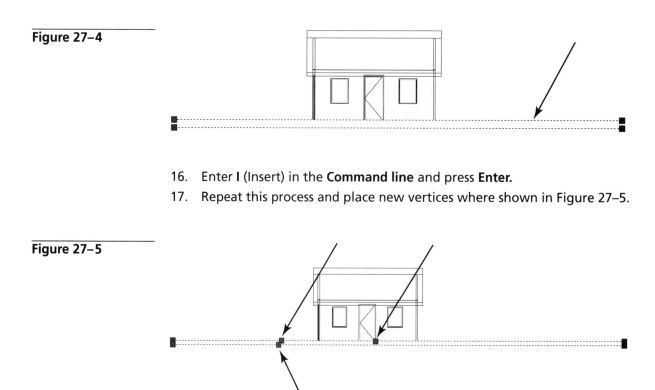

16. Enter **I** (Insert) in the **Command line** and press **Enter.**
17. Repeat this process and place new vertices where shown in Figure 27–5.

Figure 27–5

18. Move the vertices until you achieve a result similar to that in Figure 27–6.

19. Select the modified rectangle you created, **RMB,** and select **Convert To >
     Mass Element** from the contextual menu that appears.

Figure 27–6

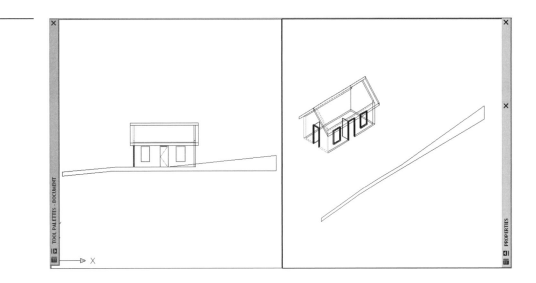

20. Enter **Y** (Yes) in the Command line to erase the selected linework, and
     press the **Enter** key on your keyboard.

21. Enter **-50'-0"** in the **Command line** and press the **Enter** key to finish
     the command. If you did not create the mass object under the
     building, just move the finished mass object into position. (See
     Figure 27–7.)

Figure 27–7

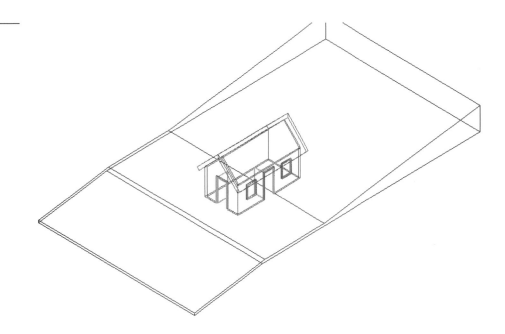

22. Change to the SW Isometric view.

23. Using the Layer Manager, create a new layer, and name it **GRADE.**

24. Select the mass object you created, and assign it the new layer **GRADE**.
25. Save the file as **ADTVIZ RENDER PROJECT.**

You have now created a scene with a simple building and a base (see Figure 27–8).

Figure 27–8

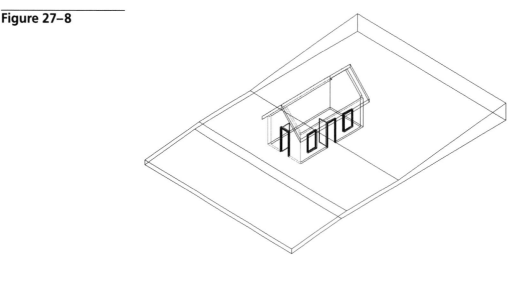

Hands-On

Using VIZ Render

VIZ Render is very complex and requires some study to use it effectively. This tutorial is meant only as a simple introduction.

For this tutorial and to get the real benefit from VIZ Render, it is very helpful if you have a basic knowledge of how to move, scale, and Pan objects in Max or Autodesk VIZ—any version. It is also recommended that you get a third-party book on VIZ or MAX. Although VIZ Render is excellent, once you have the model and scene (which is really a mesh with instructions), MAX and VIZ can twist and manipulate the model and scene much more effectively than ADT. Unfortunately, the change in the model in VIZ and MAX cannot be sent back to ADT.

1. Open the **ADTVIZ RENDER PROJECT.**
2. Select the **Open drawing menu** icon, and then select **Link to VIZ Render** (see Figure 27–9).
3. After about 15 seconds, the VIZ Render interface will appear with your scene (see Figure 25–10).

Figure 27–9

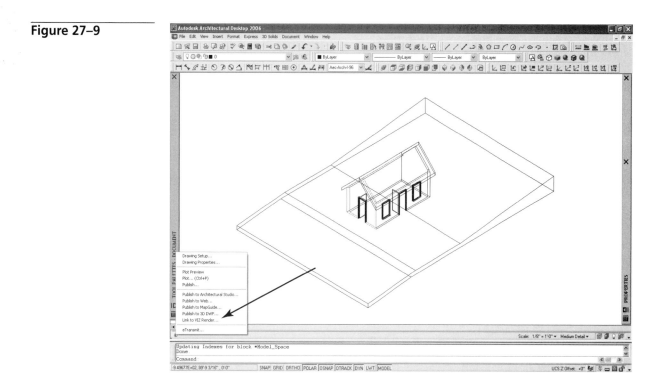

Figure 27–10

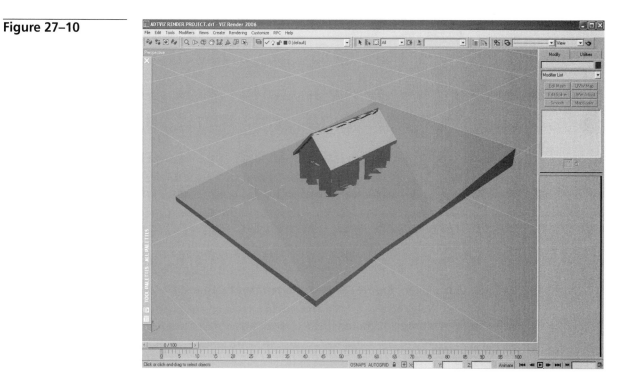

4.   Select the VIZ **Minimize Viewport** icon to change the interface into four viewports (see Figure 25–11).

Figure 27–11

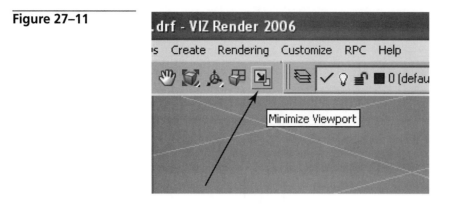

5. Select the **Zoom Extents All** icon to fill each viewport view (see Figure 25–12).

Figure 27–12

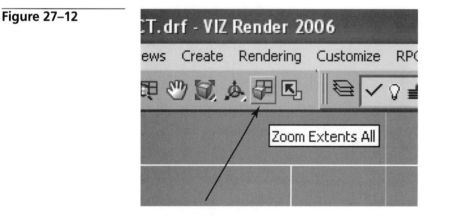

6. Select **Create > Daylight System** from the **Main** toolbar to bring up the **Daylight Object Creation** dialog box.

7. Press the **Yes** button in the **Daylight Object Creation** dialog box.

8. Click in the **Top** viewport in the middle of the structure.

9. Move your cursor to the **Front View**, move the cursor vertically, and click again to place the sun object (see Figure 25–13).

10. Select **Create > Cameras > Target Camera** from the **Main** toolbar.

11. Click to the left of the enclosure in the **Top** viewport, click again in the center of the enclosure, and move your cursor over the **Front** viewport; move the cursor vertically, and click again to set the camera (see Figure 27–14).

12. Click in the **Perspective** viewport, and press the letter **C** on the keyboard to change the **Perspective** viewport to a **Camera** viewport. (The **Camera** viewport shows what the camera sees.)

13. Change to the **Top** viewport, select the camera, **RMB**, and select **Move** from the contextual menu that appears.

Figure 27–13

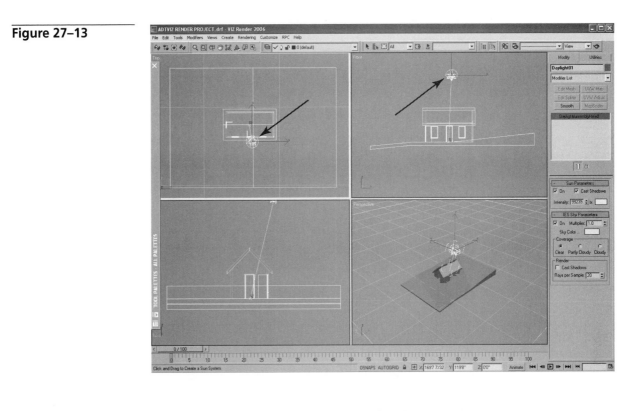

Figure 27–14

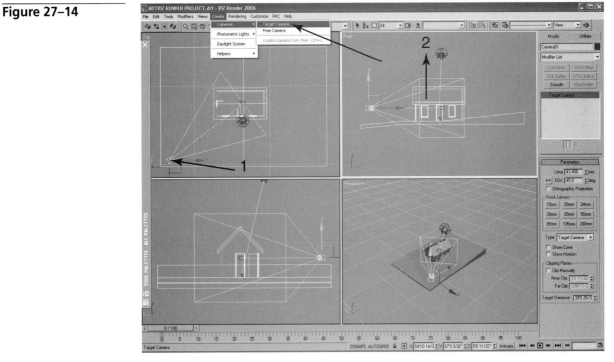

14. Move the camera in the **Top** viewport while watching the camera viewport. You can adjust the height of the camera by moving it in the **Front View** (see Figure 25–15).

15. Select the sun object to open the Sun's parameter panel on the right side of the screen.

Figure 27–15

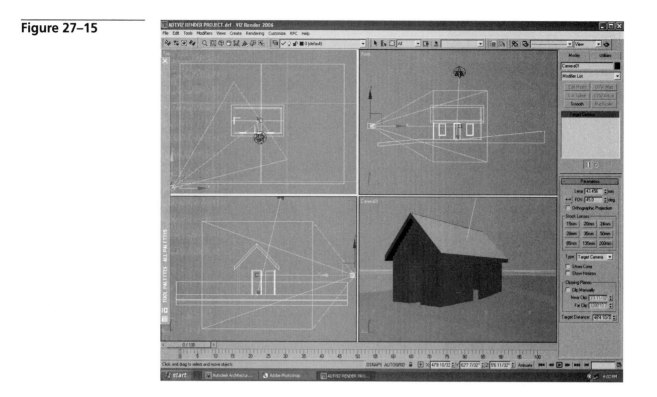

16. In the **Sun Parameters** panel, check the **On** and **Cast Shadows** check boxes.

17. In the **IES Parameters** section, check the **Cast Shadows** check box, and leave all the other parameters as defaults (see Figure 27–16).

Figure 27–16

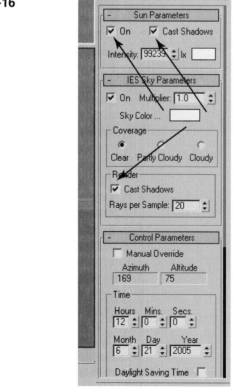

18. Select **Rendering** > **Render** from the **Main** menu to bring up the **Render Scene: Photorealistic render** dialog box.

19. Select the **Radiosity** tab.

20. At the bottom of the **Radiosity** tab, select **Draft** from the **Preset** drop-down list.

21. This will bring up the **Select Preset Categories** dialog box.

22. In the **Select Preset Categories** dialog box, select **Radiosity**, and then press the **Load** button (see Figure 27–17).

Figure 27–17

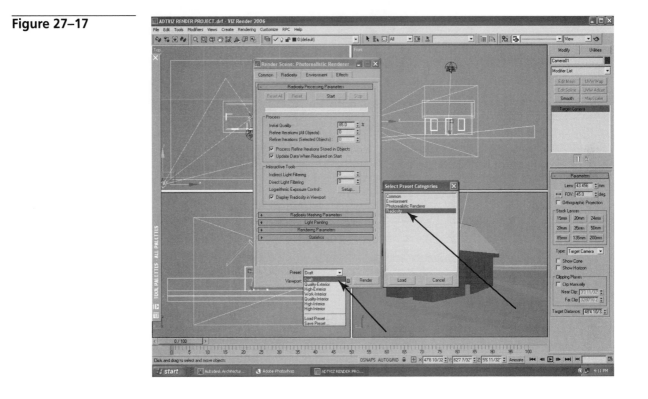

23. At the bottom of the **Radiosity** tab, select **Camera 01** (the right bottom viewport) from the **Viewport** drop-down list.

24. In the **Radiosity** tab, press the **Start** button to start creating the radiosity solution.

What Is the Radiosity Solution?

In order for the VIZ Render engine to create realistic lighting, a Radiosity solution is generated as a mesh throughout your scene. Each part of the mesh tells the render engine what shade of color and shadow to use for each area. If you move an object or change the number of light fixtures, you must reset the solution and start it again before rendering.

25. When the **Continue** button appears at the top of the **Radiosity** tab, press the **Render** button at the bottom right of the tab.

A new window will now appear with the rendering; this may take 15 or more seconds to render depending on computer speed (see Figure 27–18).

Figure 27–18

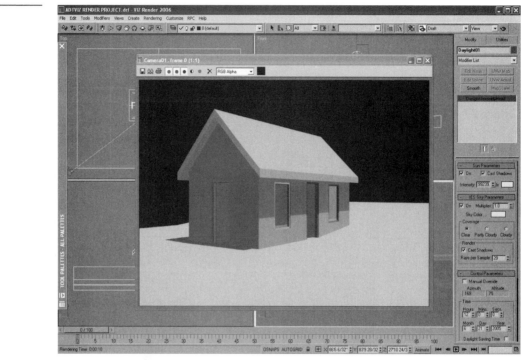

26.   Close the rendering.

27.   In the Select the **Render Scene: Photorealistic render** dialog box, under Common Parameters, select the **Single** radio button, and press the **800 × 600** button for the **Output Size.**

28.   Make sure that the **Antialias Geometry, Mapping,** and **Shadows** check boxes are checked.

29.   Again, change to the Radiosity tab, and this time, select **Quality-Exterior** from the **Preset** drop-down list.

30.   Again, **load** the **Radiosity** solution.

31.   Again, start a radiosity solution.

32.   After the radiosity solution has been made, again, select **Camera 01** from the **Viewport** drop-down list, and render the scene.

The render engine will now create an 800 × 600 higher-quality image with shading and shadows. The best practice is to use only the higher-quality presets when you are near the finished project because the radiosity solution and rendering can take a great deal of time. Increase the image size to give higher clarity when using it for large images.

33.   Select **File > Save Copy As** from the VIZ Render **Main** menu, and save the file as **ADTVIZ RENDER PROJECT.drf.**

Hands-On

Placing Materials in ADT

1. Return to Architectural Desktop.

2. Select the **Material** tool from the **Design** tool palette, and select the roof object in the Drawing Editor to bring up the **Apply Material to Components** dialog box.

3. In the **Apply Material to Components** dialog box, select **Thermal & Moisture.Shingles.Asphalt Shingles.3-Tab.black** and then select **Object** from the **Apply to** column. Press the **OK** button to return to the Drawing Editor (see Figure 27–19).

Figure 27–19

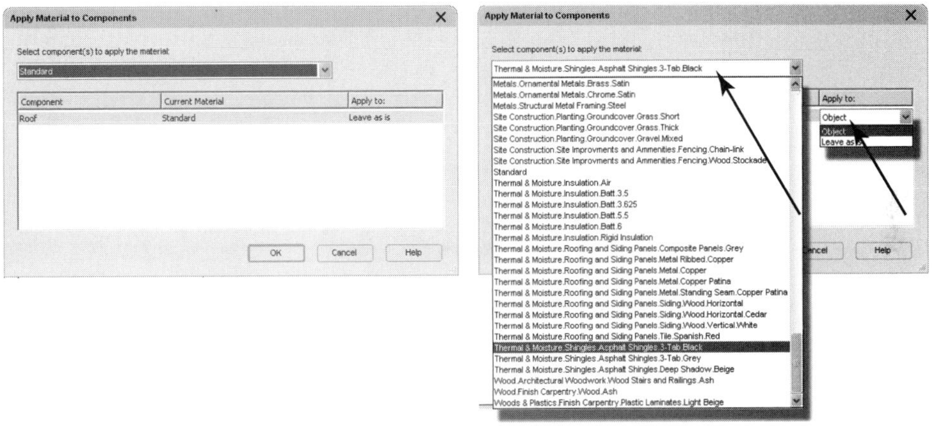

4. Again select the **Material** tool from the **Design** tool palette, and select the front wall of the building to bring up the **Apply Material to Components** dialog box.

5. This time, select **Masonry Unit Masonry. Brick.Modular,** and **Style** from the **Apply to** drop-down list for The **Unnamed** field.

Because all the walls are the same style, they will all have the material applied to them.

6. Press **Ctrl + S** to save the ADT drawing.

7. Again, select the **Open drawing menu** icon, and then select **Link to VIZ Render.**

8. When you return to VIZ Render, the **File Link Settings** dialog box will appear; press the **OK** button in this dialog box.

The building in VIZ render now shows material on the roof and walls.

9. Select **Rendering > Render** from the **Main** menu to bring up the **Render Scene: Photorealistic render** dialog box.

10. Again, change to the Radiosity tab, and this time, select **Draft** from the **Preset** drop-down list.

11. Again, **load** the **Radiosity** solution.

12. Again, start a radiosity solution.

13. After the radiosity solution has been made, again, select **Camera 01** from the **Viewport** drop-down list, and render the scene (see Figure 27–20).

Figure 27–20

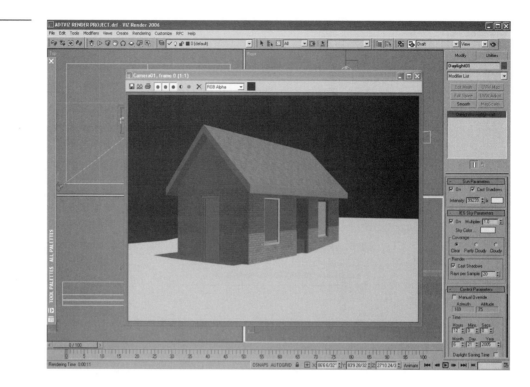

Notice that the roof edges have no applied material. To apply a new material to the roof, do the following:

14. Change to the **Scene-Unused** tab in the **Tool Palettes**.

15. In the **Scene-Unused** tab in the **Tool Palettes,** select the **Create New** icon, **RMB,** and select User-Defined from the contextual menu that appears to create a new material.

16. Select the **User-Defined** icon, **RMB,** and select **Properties** from the contextual menu that appears to bring up the **Material Editor** for the **User-Defined** material.

17. In the **Material Editor,** enter **ROOF EDGE, Shininess:** to 74%, select the **Diffuse Color** button, and change the color to white (see Figure 27–21).

18. Close the **Material Editor,** and return to the **Scene-Unused** tab.

Figure 27–21

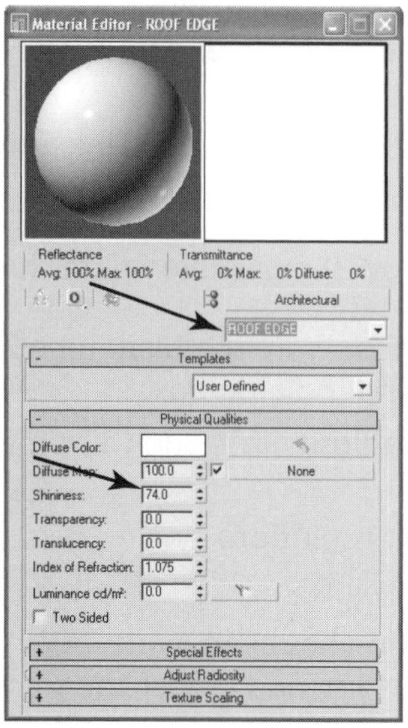

19.   Select the roof of the building, and press the **Edit Mesh** button in the **Modify** tab at the top right of your modeling area (see Figure 27–22).

20.   The **Edit Mesh** tool controls will now appear.

Figure 27–22

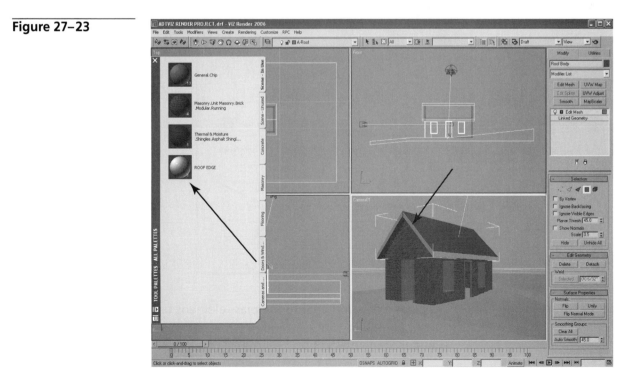

21.   Press the **Polygon** icon (it will select full faces of a mesh), and select a roof edge. The roof edge will turn red when selected.

22.   Hold down the **Ctrl key**, and select the other roof edges.

23.   Select the **ROOF EDGE** material in the **Scene-Unused** tab, **RMB**, and select **Apply To Selected** from the contextual menu that appears.

24.   Deselect the edges by clicking in an empty area of the screen.

25.   Select the **Scene - In Use tab**, and notice that the **ROOF EDGE** icon now appears there (see Figure 27–23).

Figure 27–23

26. In the **Scene - In Use tab,** select the **ROOF EDGE** icon, **RMB** and select **Copy** from the contextual menu that appears.

27. Maximize Architectural Desktop, and open the **Project Tools** tab.

28. In the Project Tools tab, **RMB,** and select **Paste** from the contextual menu that appears.

The new **ROOF EDGE** material is now available from the Architectural Desktop interface. To be able to apply it from within Architectural Desktop, you must first convert it to an AEC Material. To do this, **RMB** on the icon, and select Convert to AEC Material from the contextual menu that appears. Then press the **OK** button in the **Create AEC Material** dialog box. Save the drawing to ensure the tool works correctly.

29. Return to VIZ Render, and create a new material named **GRASS.**

30. Select the **GRASS** icon, **RMB,** and select **Properties** from the contextual menu that appears to bring up the **Material Editor** for the **GRASS** material.

31. In the **Material Editor,** press the **Diffuse Color** button, enter a dark green color, **Shininess:** to **30%,** and press the **None** button opposite **Bump** in the **Special Effects** section.

32. In the **Special Effects** section, select change Color 1 to green and Color 2 to light grey (see Figure 27–24).

Figure 27–24

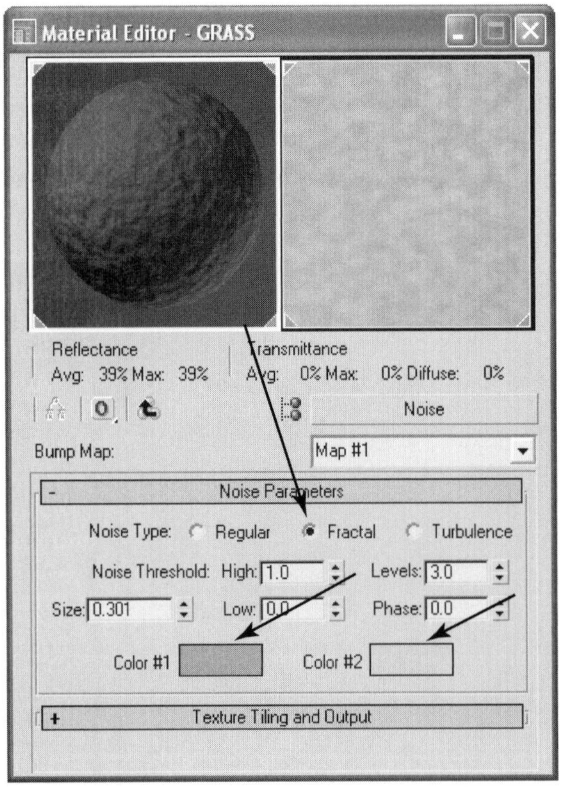

33. Apply the new material to the mass element base object you created.

34. Select **Rendering > Environment** from the **Main** menu to bring up the **Render Scene** dialog box.

35. In the **Render Scene** dialog, under **Background,** check the **Use Map** check box, press the map button, and browse for a background bitmap.

! *Note:* This author had sky maps available from 3D MAX, but you can use any bit map source available from the Internet or take pictures with a digital camera.

36. Render the Scene (see Figure 27–25).

Figure 27–25

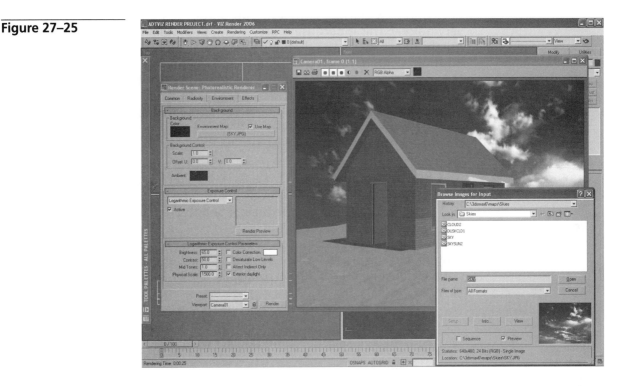

Hands-On

People and Trees

VIZ Render comes with content from two developers, ArchVision and Bionatics.

ArchVision is the developer of the RPC people, foliage, and automobiles that have become the industry standard and are available in most of the leading visualization and CAD packages. A sample demo person is included with VIZ Render, and more libraries are available by download at http://www.archvision.com.

Bionatics's EASYnat software brings highly customizable trees and plants to VIZ Render. Three trees and a plant are included, and more libraries are available online at http://www.bionatics.com. EASYnat trees can be made to wave in the wind and can be modified automatically according to season.

To load the Archvision RPC plug-in do the following:

1. Select the **Content Browser icon** in the **Tools** menu to bring up the Content Browser.

2. Select the **Architectural Desktop & VIZ Render Plug-ins** catalog.

3. Double-click on the **Architectural Desktop/VIZ Render–Plug-ins** catalog to open it. Inside the catalog are eight folders—one is labeled **RPC** and the other labeled **Bionatics.**

4. Double-click the **RPC** folder and follow the directions to go to the RPC website and download the RPC plug-in and Tina, the sample person. (You can also browse the dozens of RPC content libraries that include people, trees, cars, and even furniture.)

RPC content is unusual in that it is absolutely photorealistic but renders very quickly. This is because it uses a unique system of compiled photographs of actual objects that appear correctly in relation to camera position. Content is being upgraded and improved constantly. RPC's Moving People content creates the most realistic architectural visualization animations available.

Once installed, the RPC content will become available as a menu choice on the **Main** menu bar.

To use ArchVision RPC content, do the following:

5. Activate the **Top** viewport and press **W** on the keyboard again to maximize the **Top** viewport.

6. Select **RPC > RPC** from the **Main** menu to bring up the RPC tools.

The author has more content than you will have if you use only the demo content, but the process will be the same. The demo person (Tina) does not have the highest resolution available.

7. Select the name of the person (**Tina** if only demo content) in the **RPC Selection** tree.

8. Push the **RPC Selection** tools upward to expose the **RPC Parameters** tools.

9. Set the following:

   a. Height = **5.6666**

If this is preset in meters, select **Customize > Units Setup** from the **Main** menu, and set the units to **feet and inches.**

   b. Check the **Cast Reflections** check box if you intend to reflect your RPC content in windows or mirrors.

   c. Uncheck the **Jitter** check box. Jitter is used when animating; it makes smoother animated content.

   d. Uncheck the **Billboard** checkbox. Billboard is used when you want to concentrate several pieces of content into one quick rendering object, such as trees into a tree line.

   e. Check the **Cast Shadows** check box.

   f. Uncheck the **Apply Filter Effect** check box. This allows you to use Photoshop filter effects on the content. The effects must be loaded into the RPC directory (see Figure 27–26).

10. Move your cursor into your scene.

11. Click and hold the left mouse button to place and rotate Tina into position.

Figure 27–26

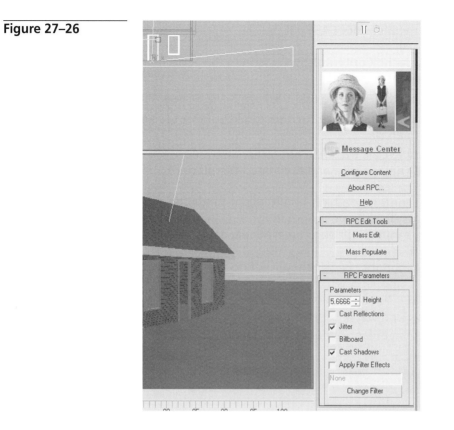

12. Add more people if you have them, or just add more copies of Tina.

13. Because you have placed new content, it is a good idea to reset and start a new radiosity solution.

14. After finishing the radiosity solution, render the **Camera View** (see Figure 27–27).

Figure 27–27

To load the **Bionatics EASYnat** plug-in, do the following:

1. Select the **Content Browser** icon in the **Tools** menu to bring up the Content Browser.
2. Select the **Architectural Desktop & VIZ Render Plug-ins** catalog.
3. Double-click on the **Architectural Desktop/VIZ Render Plug-ins** catalog to open it.
4. Double-click the **EASYnat** folder and follow the directions to go to the EASYnat website and download the plug-in.

EASYnat content is a high-quality plant-modeling program featuring virtual plants that can be modified for age and season. Once installed, the EASYnat content will become available as a menu choice on the **Main menu** bar.

To use Bionatics EASYnat content do the following:

5. Delete the Archvision content you placed in the previous exercise.
6. Select **EASYnat > Create** from the **Main** menu to bring up the **Create EASYnat Plant** dialog box (see Figure 27–28).

Figure 27–28

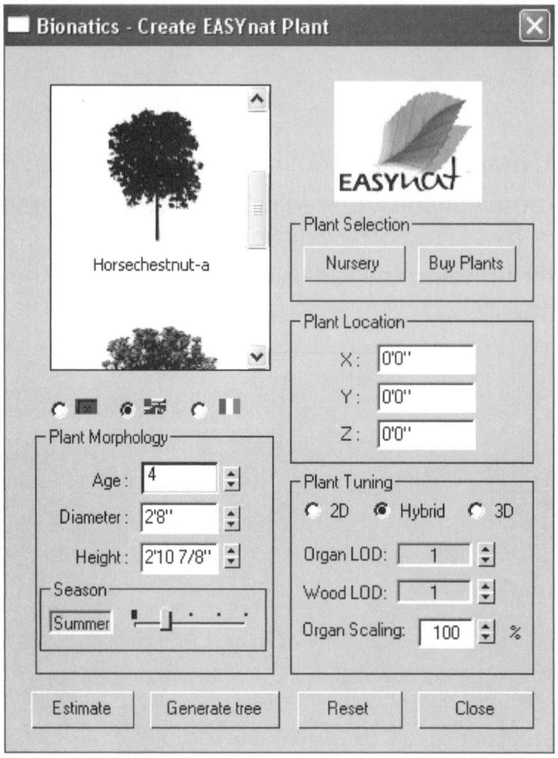

7. Select the tree desired from the main screen or press the **Nursery** button to open the **EASYnat Nursery** dialog box.
8. Double-click on **Horsechestnut**, and return to the **Create EASYnat Plant** dialog box.
9. Select the **Plant Tuning Hybrid** radio button, and set the **Age** of the tree to **12.**

10. Set the **Season** to **Summer**, and press the **Generate tree** button to generate the tree.

The **Tree Generation** timer will appear. After it closes, your tree will be in the scene.

11. Move your tree into position, and repeat the generation and placement of another tree, but set the **Age** to **9** for this tree.

12. Reset, start a new radiosity solution, and then render the scene (see Figure 27–29).

Figure 27–29

Select the different radio buttons for 2D and 3D trees, and then press the **Estimate** button to see the difference in triangles. The more triangles and the more they are realistic, the more time they take to render.

Section

28

Tutorial Project

For the tutorial project, this author has chosen a small country house. The project progresses through the design process to the construction documentation stage.

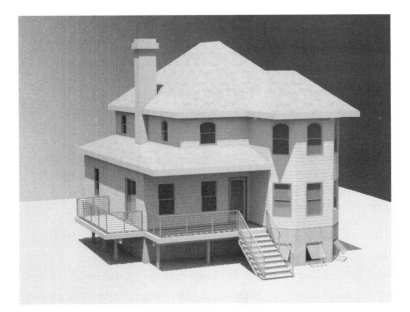

Before starting the project, it will be necessary to create a customized plotting sheet that includes the company logo. Using Adobe Illustrator, Adobe Photoshop, Corel Draw, Paint Shop Pro, Macromedia FreeHand, Canvas, or even Windows Paint, create a JPG of your logo. The logo the author created looks like Figure 28–1.

The author started with an Adobe Illustrator file and exported it as an RGB JPG.

/   **Note:** The jpg must be in RGB mode; CMYK mode won't work in AutoCAD.

Figure 28–1

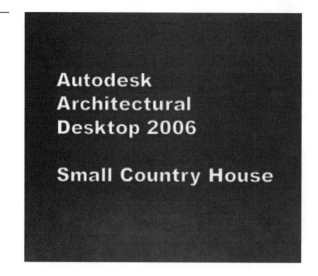

Hands-On

Placing the Logo in the Template File

1. Select **File > Open** from the **Main** menu to bring up the **Select File** dialog box.
2. In the **Look in** drop-down list, browse to the C drive.
3. Browse to **Documents and Settings > All Users > Application Data > Autodesk >ADT 2006 > Enu > Template**.
4. In the **File** dialog box, select **Drawing Template (*.dwt)** from the drop-down list.

The default template files will appear. This author suggests that novice users modify a predefined template file; seasoned AutoCAD users should be able to create template files from scratch and add blocks with attributes. Template files are ordinary AutoCAD files with a .dwt file extension.

5. Select the Aec Sheet (Imperial Stb).dwt template.
6. Change to the preset Arch D (24 × 36) Layout (see Figure 28–2).
7. Select **Insert > Image** from the **Main** menu to bring up the **Select Image File** dialog box (see Figure 28–3).
8. Select the logo you created, and press **Open** to bring up the **Image** dialog box.

Figure 28–2

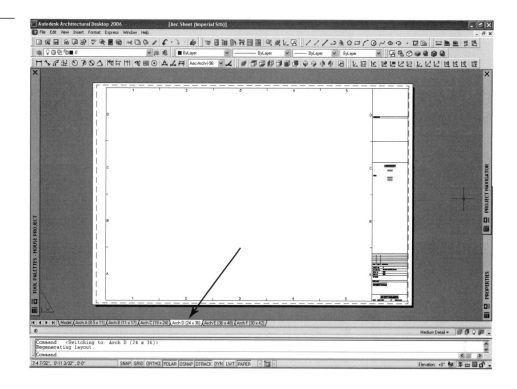

Figure 28–3

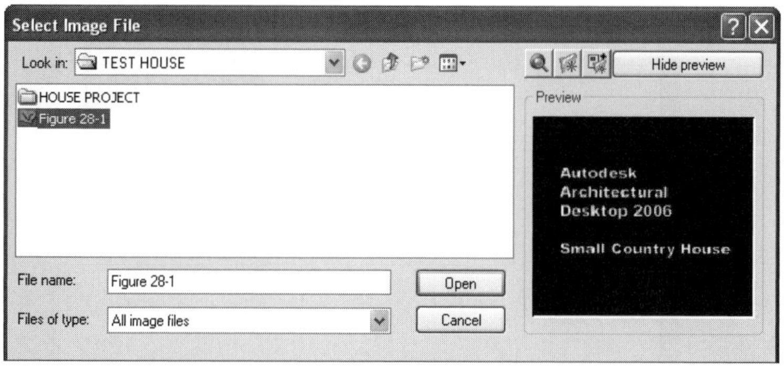

9. Check the **Insertion** and **Scale Specify on-screen** check boxes, and press **OK** to return to the Drawing Editor (see Figure 28–4).

10. Place the logo JPG in the Aec Model (Imperial Stb) template (see Figure 28–5).

11. Save the template drawing as **TEST HOUSE PROJECT,** and be sure the **Files of type** drop-down list is set to **AutoCAD drawing Template (*.dwt).** Press the **Save** button.

12. The **Template Description** dialog box will appear; enter a description of the template and press **OK** (see Figure 28–6).

You have now created a custom plotting sheet.

Figure 28–4

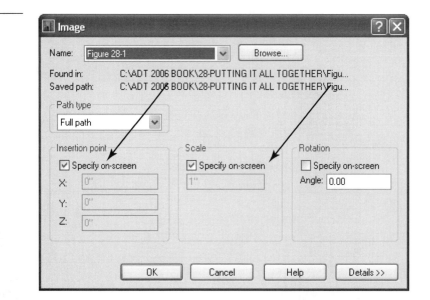

Figure 28–5

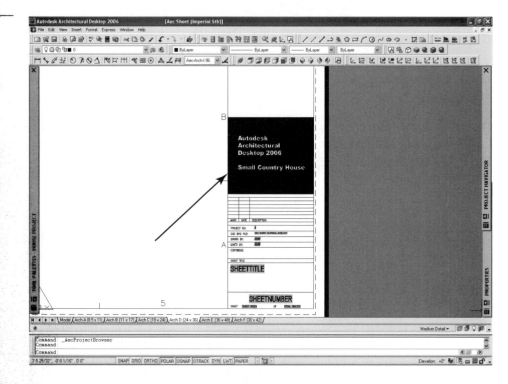

Figure 28–6

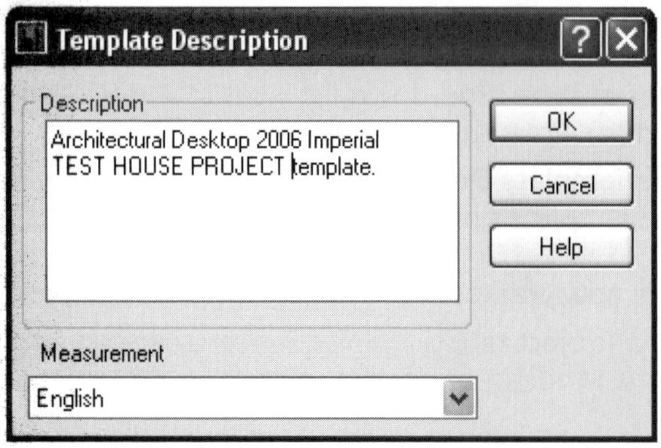

Setting Up the Project

1. Select the **My Computer** icon on your desktop or from the **Start** menu, select **All Programs** > **Accessories** > **Windows Explorer** to bring up the **My Computer** or **My Documents** dialog box.

2. Create a new folder and name it **TEST HOUSE.**

3. Select **File** > **Project Browser** from the **Main** menu to bring up the **Project Browser** dialog box.

4. Locate the **TEST HOUSE** folder, and press the **New Project** icon to bring up the **Add Project** dialog box.

5. Enter the following:

   a. Number = **2006**

   b. Name = **SMALL COUNTRY HOUSE**

   c. Description = **SMALL COUNTRY HOUSE CREATED IN AUTODESK ARCHITECTURAL DESKTOP 2006**

   e. Check the **Create from template project** check box and press the **OK** button to return to the **Project Browser** (see Figure 28–7).

Figure 28–7

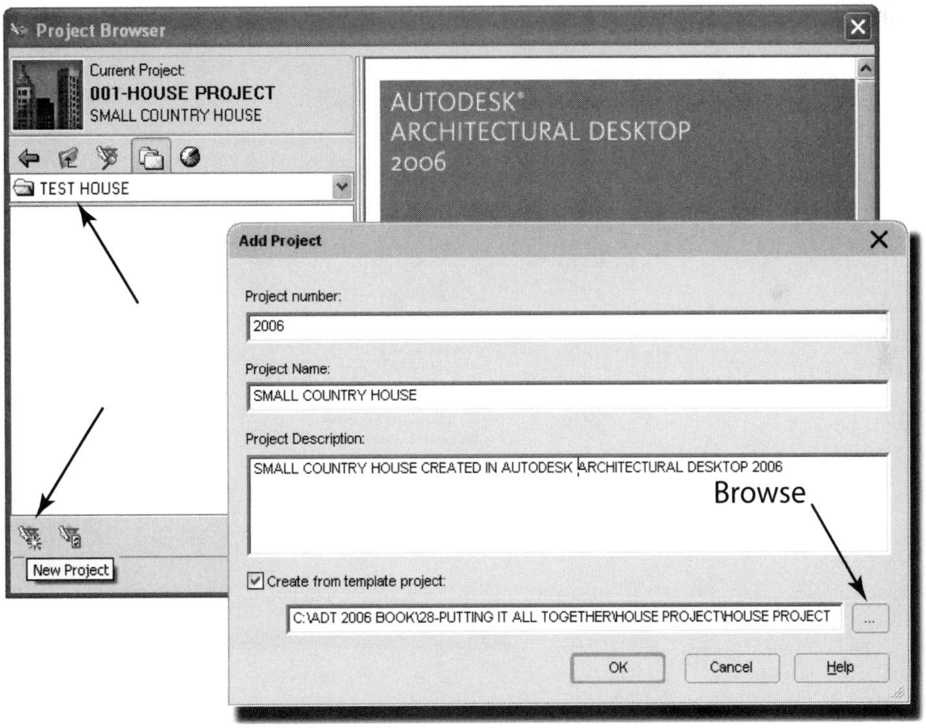

6. In the **Project Browser,** press the Close button to load the **Project Navigator,** and create the blank **SMALL COUNTRY HOUSE** tool palette.

7. Open the **Project Navigator,** and select the **Project** tab.

8. In the **Project** tab, select the Edit project icon (see Figure 28–8) to bring up the **Modify Project** dialog box.

Figure 28–8

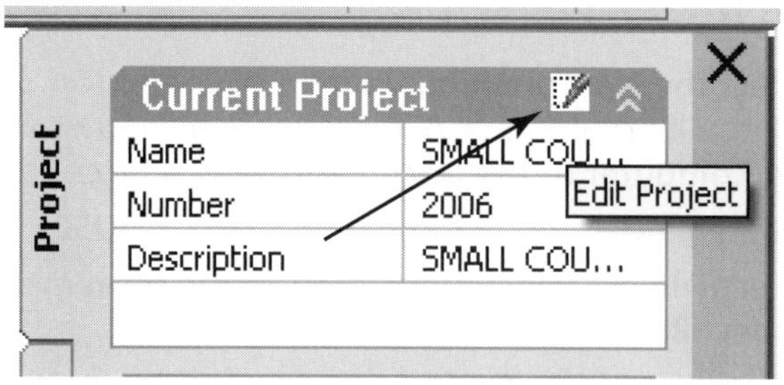

9. In the **Modify Project** dialog box, select **Yes** from the Prefix Filenames with Project Number drop-down list.

10. Press the **Edit** button to bring up the **Project Details** dialog box.

11. In the **Project Details** dialog box, enter **TEST STREET, TEST CITY, and TEST STATE** in the **Project Address** fields. You can add any other information you wish in the remaining fields, or you can add fields. Press the **OK** buttons to return to the **Project Browser** (see Figure 28–9).

Figure 28–9

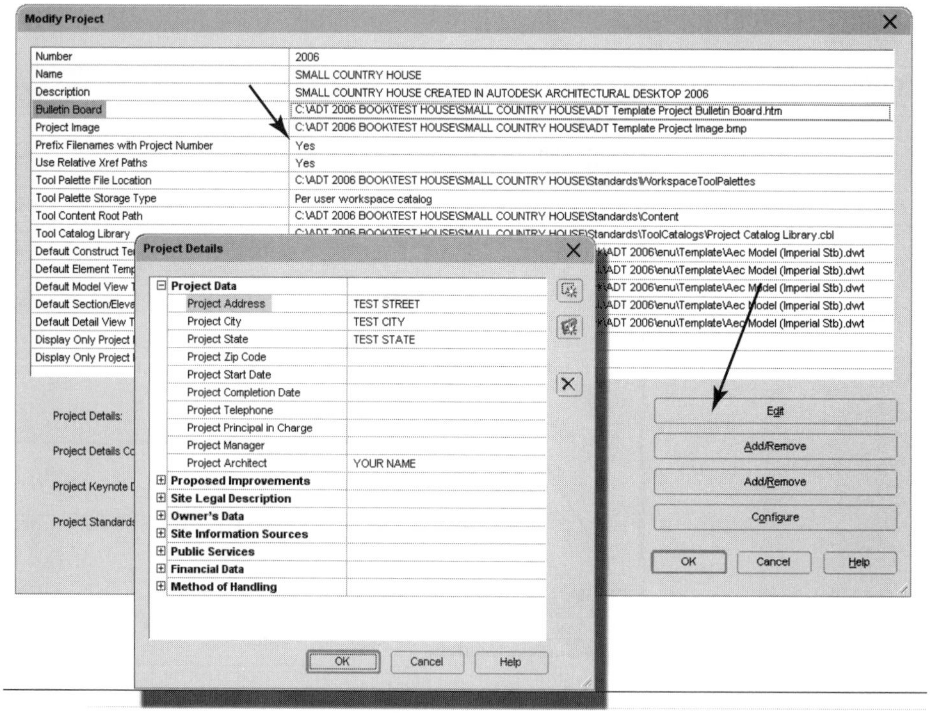

Assigning the Custom Sheet Template

1. Open the **Project Navigator.**

2. Change to the **Sheets** tab.

3. **RMB** on **SMALL COUNTRY HOUSE** to bring up the **Sheet Set Properties** dialog box.

4. Click on the **Sheet creation template** for the browser to bring up the **Select Layout as Sheet Template** dialog box.

5. Select the **Arch D (24 × 36)** layout from the **Select a layout to create new sheets** list, click the **Drawing template file name** browser, and

select the **TEST HOUSE PROJECT.dwt,** the template you created in the
previous exercise (see Figure 28–10).

Figure 28–10

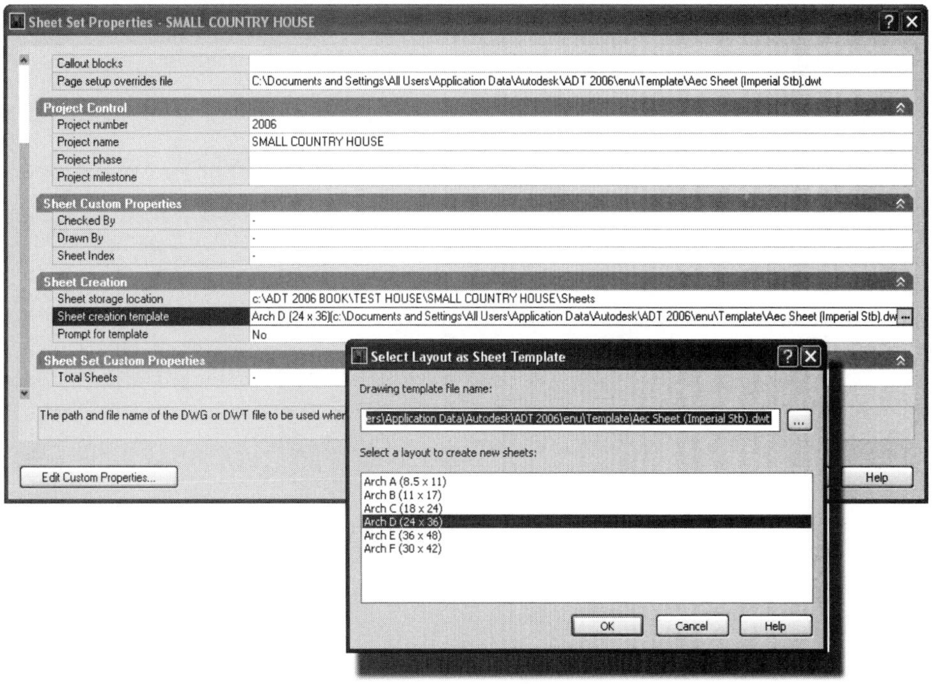

6. Press the **OK** buttons to close the dialog boxes and bring up the
    Confirm Changes dialog box (see Figure 28–11).

7. Press the **Yes** button to apply the changes you just made to all the
    nested subsets.

Figure 28–11

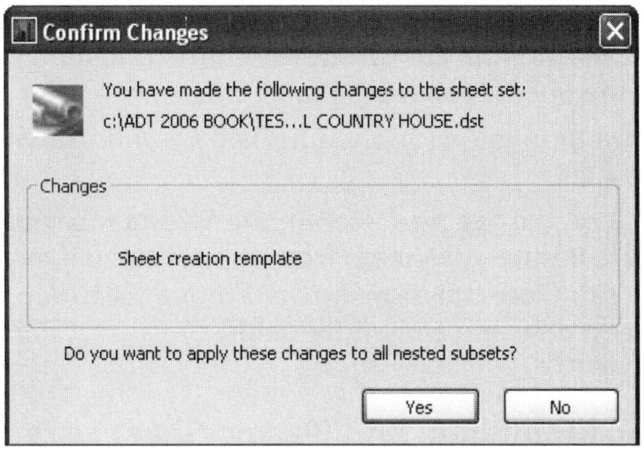

Testing and Modifying the Custom Sheet

1. In the **Sheets** tab of the **Project Navigator,** select **Plans,** and select
    the **Add Sheet** icon to bring up the **New Sheet** dialog box (see
    Figure 28–12).

2. In the **New Sheet** dialog box, enter **A-101** in the **Number** field, **SHEET
    TEST** in the **Sheet title** field, and press **OK** to return to the Drawing
    Editor.

3. In the **Sheets** tab of **Project Navigator**, double-click on **A-101 SHEET
    TEST** to bring that drawing up in the Drawing Editor.

4. Zoom in to examine the drawing, and notice that the title block contains the custom logo, project name, owner's name and address, project number, Cad dwg file name, sheet title, and drawing number (see Figure 28–13).

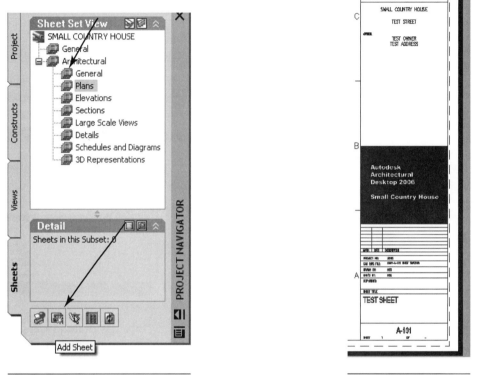

Figure 28–12   **Figure 28–13**

5. In the **Project Navigator, RMB** on **A-101 TEST SHEET** in the **Sheets** tab, and select **Properties** from the contextual menu that appears to bring up the **Sheet Properties** dialog box.

6. Put your in initials in the **Checked By** and **Drawn By** fields and then press **OK.**

7. **RMB** on the top most icon in the **Sheets** tab (the project name) and select **Resave All Sheets** from the contextual menu that appears to save the set. Close the drawing, and reopen it to see your initials in the **Checked By** and **Drawn By** fields.

Making, Modifying, and Placing Sheet Lists

Autodesk Architectural Desktop 2006 features a sheet list option. This creates an automated table of all your drawings that can be added to a cover page.

1. Using what you just learned in the previous exercises of this section, create several new plan drawings labeled **A-101** to **A-104.** Give each drawing a different name.

2. Select the **General** icon at the top of the **Sheets** tab, select the **Add Sheet** icon at the bottom of the tab, and name the sheet **TITLE SHEET.**

3. Double-click **TITLE SHEET** in the **Project Navigator** to bring it up in the Drawing Editor.

4.   **RMB** on **SMALL COUNTRY HOUSE** (under **Sheet Set View**)at the top of the **Sheets** tab, and select **Insert Sheet List** from the contextual menu that appears to bring up the **Insert Sheet list Table** dialog box.

5.   In the **Insert Sheet list Table** dialog box, select the **Standard Table Style**.

6.   Under **Column Settings**, select **Drawn By** from the third drop-down list, and press the **OK** button to return to the Drawing Editor (see Figure 28–14).

7.   Place the sheet list in the **TITLE SHEET** (see Figure 28–15).

Figure 28–14

Figure 28–15

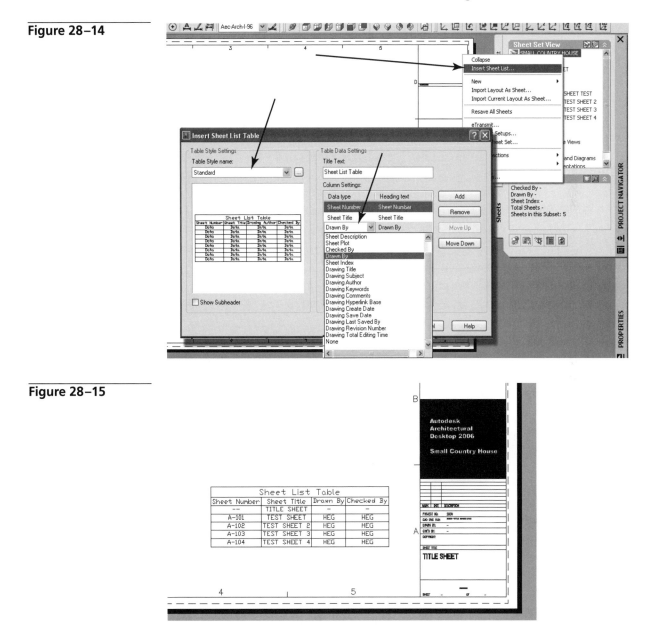

The SMALL COUNTRY HOUSE Project

There are many methodologies for creating a virtual model in Autodesk Architectural Desktop 2006. This project uses one method. As you become more familiar with the program, you will discover the methods and tools that best suit the way you work.

Creating the TITLE SHEET

1. Make sure that you have the **SMALL COUNTRY HOUSE** set as the current project in the **Project Browser.**
2. Close the **Project Browser** to bring up the **SMALL COUNTRY HOUSE.**
3. In the **Sheets** tab of the **Project Navigator,** create a sheet named **TITLE SHEET.**
4. In the **TITLE SHEET,** insert a sheet list as explained in the previous exercise.
5. Save and close the **TITLE SHEET.**

The Current Project Settings

1. Change to the **Project** tab.
2. Select the **Add Levels** icon to bring up the **Levels** dialog box.
3. Un-check the Auto-Adjust Elevation check box.
4. Set the settings shown in Figure 28–16 and press **OK.**

Figure 28–16

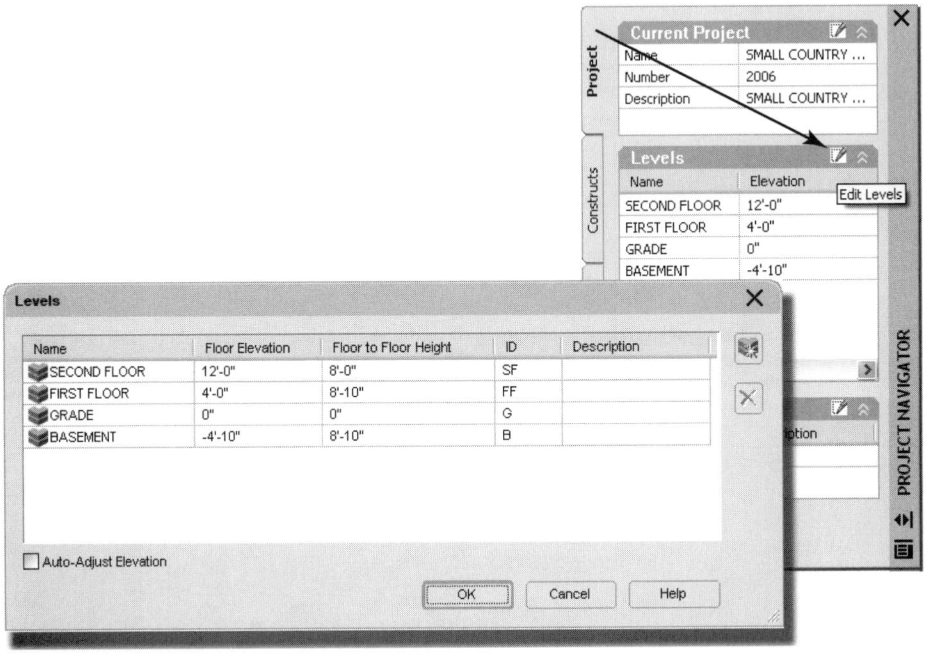

The BASEMENT Construct

Creating the walls

1. Change to the **Constructs** tab.
2. Press the **Add Construct** icon and create a new construct called **BASEMENT,** check the **BASEMENT division** check box, and press **OK.**
3. In the **Constructs** tab, double-click on **BASEMENT** to bring up the BASEMENT construct in the Drawing Editor.
4. Set the **Scale** to **1/4″ = 1′-0″.**
5. Change to the **Top** view.
6. Using the **Line** tools from the **Draw** menu, create the line drawing shown in Figure 28–17.

Figure 28–17

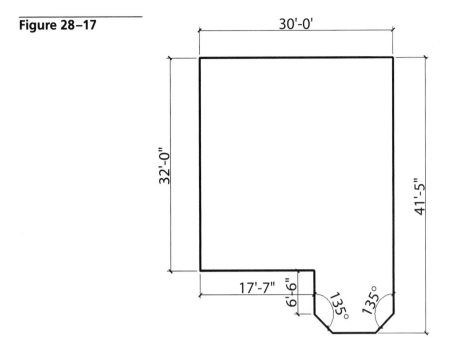

7. RMB on the **Concrete-8 Concrete-16 × 8** footing wall tool from the **Walls** tool palette, and select **Apply Tool Properties to > Linework** from the contextual menu that appears.

8. Select all the lines you created, and press the **Enter** key.

9. Enter **Y** (Yes) in the **Command line** to erase the linework, and press the **Enter** key to create the walls.

10. Select all the walls you created, and move your cursor over the **Properties** palette to open it.

11. In the **Properties palette,** set **Base height** to 8'-10" and **Justify** to **Baseline.**

The baseline of the walls may not be oriented correctly to the lines you drew. To check and repair this, do the following:

12. Select one of the lines you created, **RMB,** and select **Select Similar** from the contextual menu. Check the lines to see where the wall is oriented incorrectly.

13. Select the walls shown in Figure 28–18, **RMB** and select **Reverse >In Place** from the contextual menu.

All the walls are now placed correctly.

14. Select the **Quick Select** icons at the top right of the Properties palette, select the lines, and delete them.

15. Press **Ctrl + S** on the keyboard to save the construct.

Figure 28–18

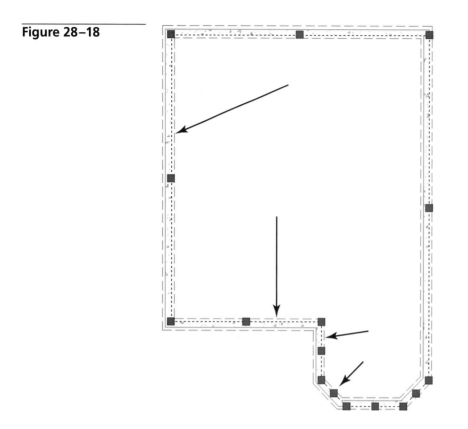

Creating the Basement Floor Slab and Ceiling Component

16. Select the **Space Auto Generate** tool from the **Design** tool palette.

17. In the **Top** view, click inside the walls to place a space object.

18. Double-click the space object to open the **Properties** palette.

19. In the **Properties** palette, set the **Space height** to **8'-9", Floor boundary thickness** to **4",** and **Ceiling boundary thickness** to **1",** and **Height above Ceiling** to **0.** After finishing, press the **Esc** key to de-select the space object.

20. Select the Slab tool from the **Design** tool palette, **RMB,** and select **Apply Tool Properties to** > **Space** from the contextual menu that appears.

21. Select the space object you just created, and press the **Enter** key on your keyboard to bring up the **Convert Space to Slab** dialog box.

22. In the **Convert Space to Slab** dialog box, check all the check boxes, and press the **OK** button to create the basement slab, and first floor component. Press the **Esc** key to deselect the objects you just created.

Creating the Basement Ceiling Framing

23. Select a wall, **RMB,** and choose **Select Similar** from the contextual menu to select all the walls.

24. With all the walls selected, **RMB** and select **Isolate Objects** > **Hide Objects** from the contextual menu to hide the walls.

25. Change to the **SW Isometric** view.

26. Select **Format** > **Structural members** > **Catalog** from the **Main** menu to bring up the **Structural Member Catalog.**

27. In the **Structural Member Catalog,** expand the **Imperial > Timber >
    Plywood Web Wood Joists.**

28. In the right pane, double-click on **10in Plywood Web Wood Joist** to
    bring up the **Structural member Style** dialog box.

29. In the **Structural member Style** dialog box, press the **OK** button, and
    close the **Structural Member Catalog** and return to the Drawing
    editor.

30. Select the **Structural Beam** tool, and move your cursor over the
    Properties palette to open it.

31. In the **Properties** palette, select the following:

    Style = **10in Plywood Web Wood Joist**
    Layout type = **Fill**
    Justify = **Top Left**
    Array = **Yes**
    Layout Method = **Repeat**
    Bay size = **2'-0"**

32. Move your cursor over the left side of the ceiling component, and
    click to place the joists. Repeat to fill the ceiling component with
    joists. Change the **Properties** palette to Layout Type = Edge, and
    complete applying joists. The author added the joists in the bay by
    using Copy and then selecting the bay joists, **RMB,** selecting **Trim
    Planes > Add Trim Plane,** and trimming the bay joists (see
    Figures 28–19 and 28–20).

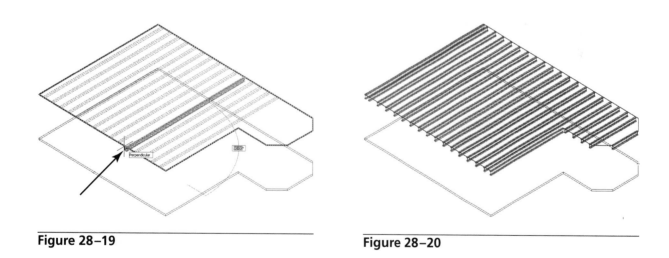

Figure 28–19   **Figure 28–20**

33. In the Drawing Editor, **RMB,** and select **Isolate Objects > End Object
    Isolation** from the contextual menu to unhide the walls.

34. Press **Ctrl + S** on the keyboard to save the construct (see
    Figure 28–21).

Figure 28–21

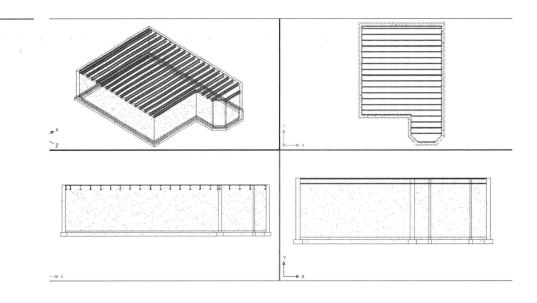

The FIRST FLOOR Construct

1. Change to the **Top** view.

2. Change to the **Constructs** tab.

3. Press the **Add Construct** icon and create a new construct called **FIRST FLOOR,** check the **FIRST FLOOR** check box, and press **OK.**

4. Double-click on the **FIRST FLOOR** to bring up the **FIRST FLOOR** construct in the Drawing Editor.

5. Set the **Scale** to **1/4″ = 1′-0″.**

6. From the **Constructs** tab, drag the **BASEMENT** construct into the **FIRST FLOOR** construct.

7. Select the **Replace Z value with current elevation** icon; this will maintain the **0″** elevation while you trace over the **BASEMENT** with the **End** Osnap on (see Figure 28–22).

Figure 28–22

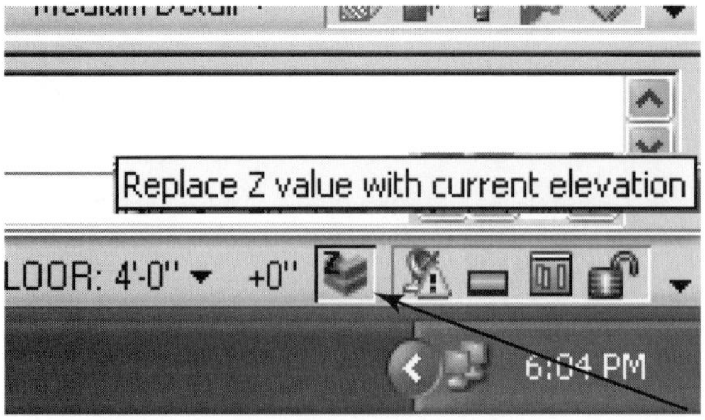

Replace Z value with current elevation

LOOR: 4'-0" ▼   +0"

6:04 PM

8. Select the **Wall** tool from the **Design** tool palette.

9. With the Wall tool selected, move your cursor over the **Properties** palette to open it.

10. Set **Base height** to **8′-10″**, **Width** to **4-1/2″**, and **Justify** to **Left.**

11. Set **OSNAP** to **Endpoint.**

12. In the **Top View,** using the BASEMENT construct as a guide, snap the walls in place on top of the lower level exterior walls (see Figure 28–23).

Figure 28–23

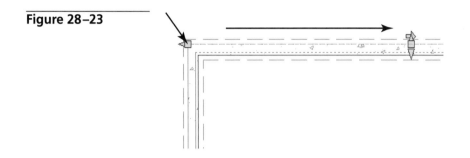

13. Change to the **SW Isometric** view (see Figure 28–24).

14. Click on the **Manage Xrefs** icon at the bottom right of the Drawing Editor to bring up the **Xref Manager.**

Figure 28–24

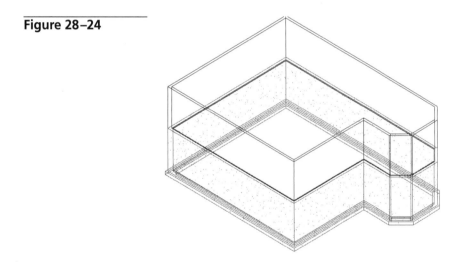

15. In the **Xref Manager,** select **BASEMENT,** and press the **Detach** button, and then press the **OK** button to return to the Drawing Editor, and remove **BASEMENT** construct from **FIRST FLOOR** construct.

16. Press **Ctrl + S** on the keyboard to save the **FIRST FLOOR** construct.

The SECOND FLOOR Construct

1. Change to the **Constructs** tab.

2. **RMB** on **FIRST FLOOR,** and select **Copy Construct to Levels** from the contextual menu that appears to bring up the **Copy Construct** to Levels dialog box.

3. Check the **SECOND FLOOR** check box and press **OK**.

4. **FIRST FLOOR (SECOND FLOOR)** will now appear in the **Constructs** tab. To change the construct's name to **SECOND FLOOR,** do the following:

5. **RMB** on **FIRST FLOOR (SECOND FLOOR)** and select **Rename** from the contextual menu that appears.

6. Change the **Name** to **SECOND FLOOR,** and press **OK** to return to the Drawing Editor.

7. Press **Ctrl + S** on the keyboard to save the **SECOND FLOOR** construct.

The GRADE Construct

There are several ways to create the ground plane. If you have a topographical map, you can create a 3D mass element using the **Mass Element "Drape"** tool. This project uses a simpler method, but it does not have the accuracy that a topographical map permits.

1. Change to the **Constructs** tab.

2. Press the **Add** Construct icon and create a new construct called **GRADE,** check the **GRADE** check box, and press **OK**.

3. In the **Constructs** tab, double-click on **GRADE** to bring up the **GRADE** construct in the Drawing Editor.

4. Set the **Scale** to **1/4" = 1'-0"**.

5. From the **Constructs** tab, drag the **BASEMENT** construct into the **GRADE** construct.

6. Change to the **Left** view.

7. Using the PLINE command, create the polyline shown in Figure 28–25.

Figure 28–25

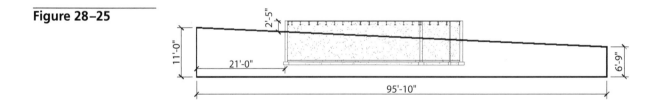

8. Select the polyline you just created, **RMB,** and select **Convert To > Mass Element** from the contextual menu that appears.

9. Enter **Y** (Yes) in the Command line, and press the **Enter** key.

10. Enter **100'** in the Command line, and press the **Enter** key to create the mass element.

11. Change to the **Top** view, and move the mass element so that the basement is centered on it (Figure 28–26).

12. Press **Ctrl + S** on the keyboard to save the **GRADE** construct.

Figure 28–26

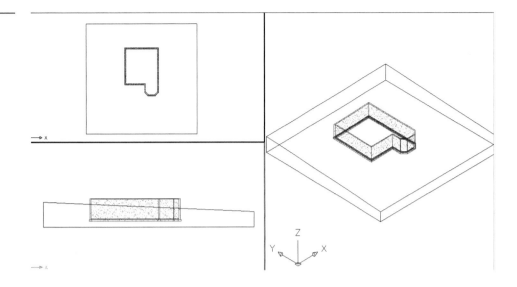

EXCAVATING the GRADE Construct

You will need to remove material from the **GRADE** equal to the exterior side of the **BASEMENT** in order for the **SECTIONS** to work appropriately.

1. With the **GRADE** construct open, **RMB** in the Drawing Editor, select **Isolate Objects > Hide Objects,** and hide the grade, leaving only the **BASEMENT.**
2. Using the **PLINE** command, trace the outline of the exterior footing. Double-click the polyline to open the **Properties** palette. In the **Properties** palette, change the **Elevation** to **-1'-0".**
3. Select the Polyline, **RMB,** and select **Convert To > Mass Element** from the contextual menu.
4. Enter **Y** (Yes) in the Command line, and press the **Enter** key.
5. Enter **8"** in the Command line to extrude the mass element **8",** and then press the **Enter** key (Figure 28–27).

Figure 28–27

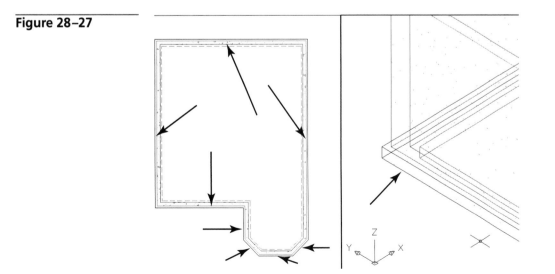

6. Using the **PLINE** command again, trace the outline of the exterior foundation. Double-click the polyline to open the **Properties** palette. In the **Properties** palette, change the **Elevation** to **-4″.**

7. Select the Polyline, **RMB,** and select **Convert To > Mass Element** from the contextual menu.

8. Enter **Y** (Yes) in the Command line, and press the **Enter** key.

9. Enter **15′-0″** in the Command line to extrude the mass element **15″-0″,** and then press the **Enter** key.

10. Click on the **Manage Xrefs** icon at the bottom right of the Drawing Editor to bring up the **Xref Manager.**

11. In the **Xref Manager, Detach** all the Xrefs, and then press the **OK** button to return to the Drawing Editor.

12. Select one of the mass elements that you have created, **RMB,** and select **Boolean > Union** from the contextual menu.

13. Select the other mass element, enter **Y** (Yes) in the Command line, and press the **Enter** key.

14. **RMB** in the Drawing Editor, and select **Isolate Objects > End Object Isolation,** and unhide the grade.

15. Change to the **SW Isometric** view.

16. Select the grade mass element that you have created, **RMB,** and select **Boolean > Subtract** from the contextual menu.

17. Pick the basement mass element that you have created, and press the **Enter** key.

18. Enter **Y** (Yes) in the Command line, and press the **Enter** key.

You have now created the grade with the basement excavated. Save the file (Figure 28–28).

Figure 28–28

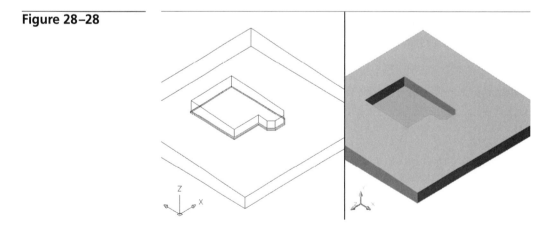

The COMPOSITE VIEW

1. Change to the **Views** tab.
2. Select the **Add View** icon at the bottom of the **Views** tab to bring up the **Add View** dialog box.
3. In the **Add View** dialog box, select the **General View** radio button and press **OK.**
4. Name the new view **COMPOSITE VIEW,** and press the **Next** button.
5. Check all the check boxes, and press the **Next** button.
6. Press the **Finish** button to return to the Drawing Editor.
7. Change to the **SW Isometric View.**
8. Select the **3D Orbit** tool from the **Navigation** toolbar.
9. **RMB** in the Drawing Editor, and select **Projection > Perspective** from the contextual menu that appears.
10. Enter **V** in the **Command line,** and press **Enter** to bring up the **View** dialog box.
11. Press the **New** button to bring up the **New View** dialog box.
12. Enter **PERSPECTIVE** in the **View name** field, select the **Define Window** radio button, and press **OK** to return to the Drawing Editor.
13. Select the view with a selection window, and press the **OK** buttons to close all the dialog boxes and return to the Drawing Editor.
14. Select the **Views** tab in the Project Navigator, and expand the **COMPOSITE VIEW.** Notice that the **COMPOSITE VIEW** drawing now contains the **PERSPECTIVE** view (see Figure 28–29).

Figure 28–29

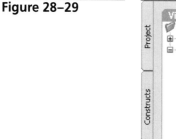

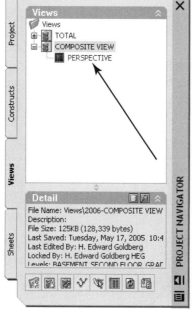

15. Press **Ctrl + S** on the keyboard to save the file (see Figure 28–30).

Figure 28–30

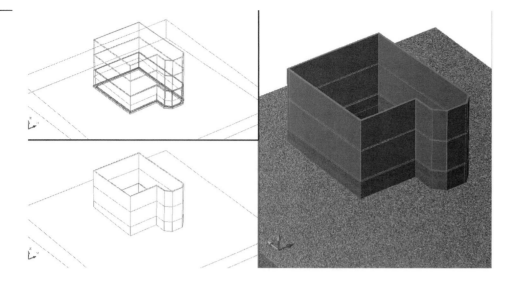

The ELEVATIONS

1. In the **Views** tab, double-click the **COMPOSITE VIEW** to bring it up in the Drawing Editor.

2. Change to the Top View. Select **Basement** from the **Elevation** drop-down list, set the **Elevation relative to selected level** to **-6'-0",** and select the **Replace Z value with current elevation** button at the bottom right of the Drawing Editor.

3. Select the Properties icon at the bottom left of the Tool Palettes, and choose **Documentation.** Then click and select **Exterior Elevation Mark A3** from the **Callouts** palette.

This will cause your sections and Elevations to extend below the grade and building.

4. In the **COMPOSITE VIEW** drawing in the **Top View,** place a selection window around the building and grade, and click to bring up the **Place Callout** dialog box (see Figure 28–31).

Figure 28–31

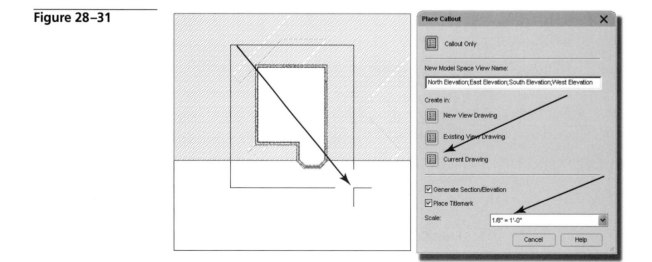

5. In the **Place Callout** dialog box, check the **Generate Section/Elevation** check box, select **1/8"** from the **Scale** drop-down list, and select the **Current Drawing** icon (see Figure 28–31).

6. Click to the right of the building.

7. Move your cursor down 5′ vertically (this will dictate the distance between the four elevations) and click your mouse button. The **Generate Elevation progress** dialog screen will appear telling you when the elevations have been created in a new file.

8. Press **Ctrl + S** on the keyboard to save this drawing (see Figure 28–32).

Figure 28–32

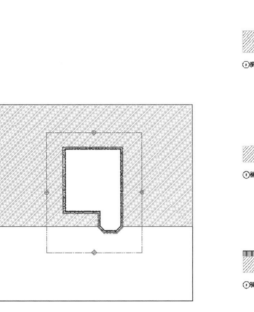
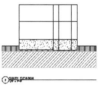
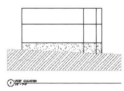

The SECTIONS

1. In the **COMPOSITE VIEW** that you saved in the previous exercises, do the following.

2. Select **Section Mark A2T** from the **Callouts** tab.

3. In the **COMPOSITE VIEW** drawing in the **Top View,** click and place the section mark through the building from top to bottom, click again, and press the **Enter** key.

4. In the **COMPOSITE VIEW** drag your cursor past the left-hand extents of the building, and click again to bring up the **Place Callout** dialog box.

5. In the **Place Callout** dialog box, enter **SECTION AA** in the **New Model Space View Name** field, check the **Generate Section/Elevation** check box, select **1/4"** from the **Scale** drop-down list, and select the **Current Drawing** icon (see Figure 28–33).

Figure 28–33

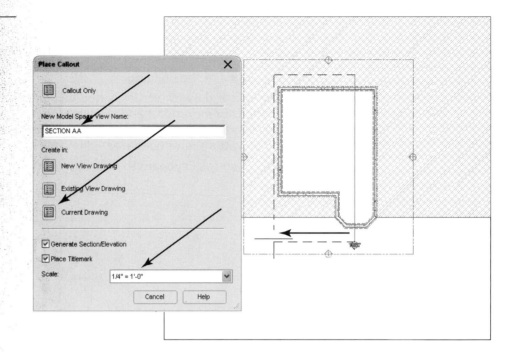

6.   Click to the left of the building (where you click doesn't matter because you are creating the elevations in the new drawing file).

7.   Press **Ctrl + S** on the keyboard to save this drawing (see Figure 28–34).

Figure 28–34

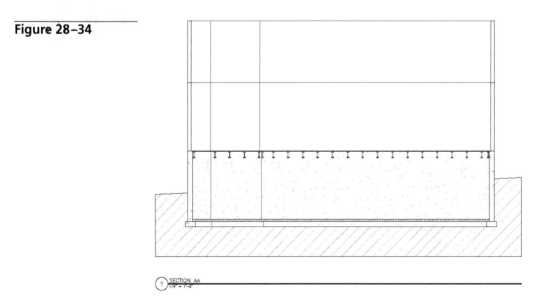

Repeat the process shown in the last seven steps to create a longitudinal section labeled **SECTION BB** (see Figure 28–35).

Note: If you enter **V** (View) in the **Command** line and press **Enter,** you will get the **View** dialog box, listing all the views you have created. When you create a section or elevation in Architectural Desktop, you are automatically creating views.

Figure 28–35

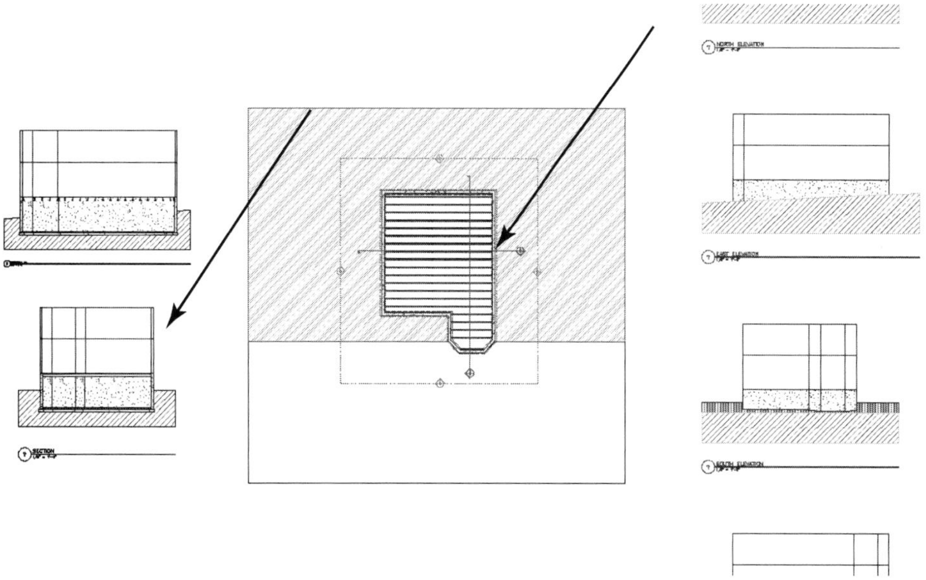

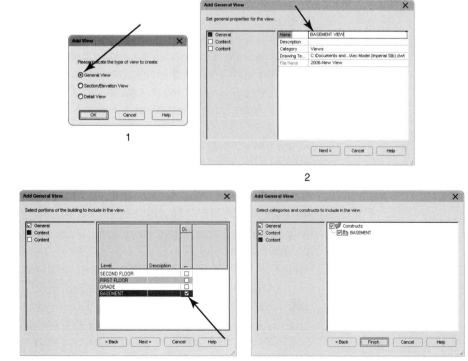

The Floor Views

1. In the **Views** tab of the **Project Navigator** tab, click the **Add View** icon at the bottom of the tab to bring up the **Add View** dialog box. In the **Add View** dialog box, select the **General View** radio button, and press the **OK** button to bring up the **Add General View** dialog box.

2. In the **Add General View** dialog box, enter **BASEMENT VIEW** in the **Name** field, and press the **Next** button to bring up the next dialog box. In this dialog box, check the **BASEMENT** check box, and press the **Next** button to bring up the next dialog box. In this dialog box, check the Basement check box, and press the **Finish** button to create the view (see Figure 28–36).

3. Repeat the previous steps, checking the appropriate levels and constructs to create **FIRST FLOOR VIEW** and **SECOND FLOOR VIEW** drawings.

Figure 28–36

Figure 28–37

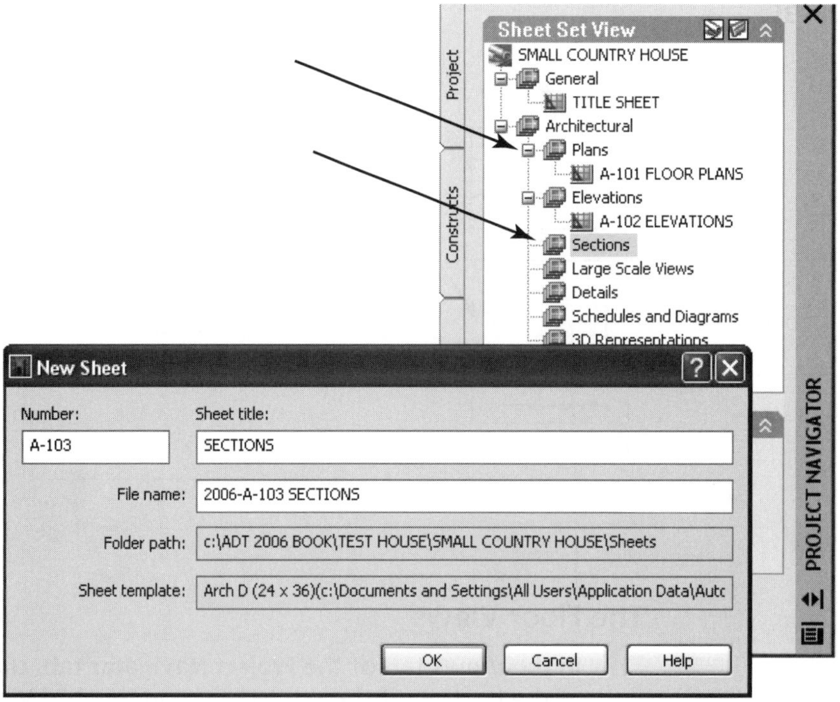

Creating the SHEETS

1. In the **Sheets** tab of the **Project Navigator** tab, create sheets called **A-101 FLOOR PLANS, A-102 ELEVATIONS,** and **A-103 SECTIONS** under the **Plans, Elevations** and **Sections** icons (see Figure 28–37).

2. In the **Sheets** tab of the **Project Navigator** tab, double-click on **A-101 FLOOR PLANS** to bring it up in the Drawing Editor.

3. Change to the **Views** tab of the **Project Navigator.**

4. Drag the **BASEMENT VIEW** from the views tab into the **A-101 FLOOR PLANS** drawing in the Drawing Editor.

5. If it comes in too small, before you click to set the **BASEMENT VIEW** drawing, **RMB** to open the scale drop-down list.

6. From the scale drop-down list, select **1/4″ =1′-0″,** and then click to place the **BASEMENT VIEW** drawing (see Figure 28–38).

7. Repeat this process until the **BASEMENT, FIRST FLOOR,** and **SECOND FLOOR** views have been placed in the **A-101 FLOOR PLANS** sheet. Press **Ctrl + S** on the keyboard to save the sheet (see Figure 28–39).

8. In the **Sheets** tab of the **Project Navigator** tab, double-click on **A-102 ELEVATIONS** sheet to bring it up in the Drawing Editor.

9. Change to the **Views** tab, expand the **COMPOSITE VIEW,** and drag the **North Elevation, East Elevation, South Elevation,** and **West Elevation** into the **A-102 ELEVATIONS** sheet.

10. As you begin to place the elevations, **RMB,** and set the scale to **1/8″** before placing.

11. Press **Ctrl + S** on the keyboard to save the sheet.

12. In the **Sheets** tab of the **Project Navigator** tab, double click on **A-103 SECTIONS** sheet to bring it up in the Drawing Editor.

13. Change to the **Views** tab, expand the **COMPOSITE VIEW,** and drag the **SECTION AA and SECTION BB** views into the **A-103 SECTIONS** sheet. Set their scale to **1/4″ = 1′-0″** when inserting.

Figure 28–38

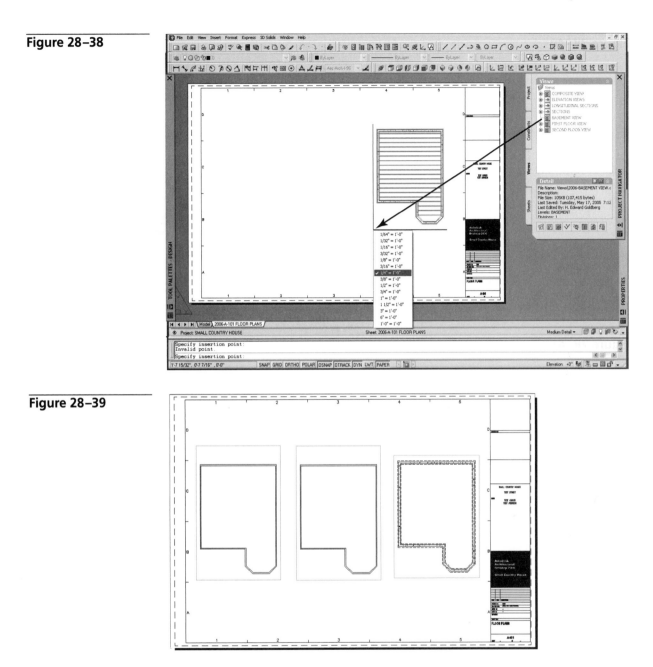

Figure 28–39

14. Press **Ctrl + S** on the keyboard to save the sheet.

You have now created the basic sheets (see Figures 28–40, 28–41, 28–42, and 28–43).

! **Note:** If your sections insert with the grade and walls filled in black, do the following to make them appear as shown in Figure 28–43:

1. Open the **Composite** view drawing.
2. Select one of the sections, **RMB**, and select **Edit 2D Elevation/Section Style** from the contextual menu to bring up the **2D Section/Elevation Style Properties** dialog box.
3. In the **2D Section/Elevation Style Properties** dialog box, select the **Display Properties** tab.

Figure 28–40

Figure 28–41

Figure 28–42

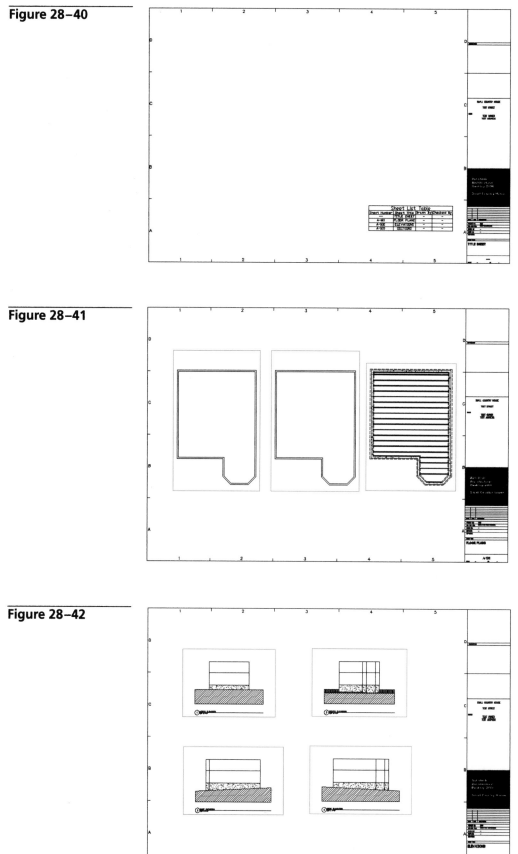

Figure 28-43

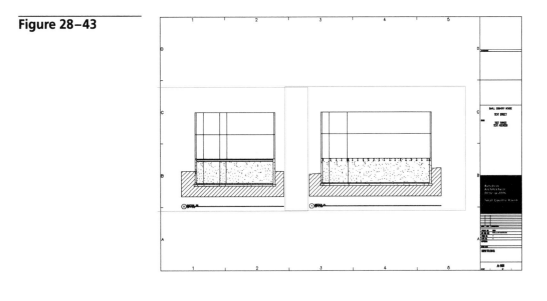

4. In the **Display Properties** tab, click on the **Edit Display Properties** icon at the top right of the tab to open the **Display properties** dialog box.

5. In the **Display properties** dialog box, turn off the **Shrinkwrap Hatch** visibility, and press the **OK** button to close the dialog box.

6. Press **Ctrl + S** on the keyboard to save the sheet (see Figure 28–44).

Now that you have created the sheets, you can return to modifying the building model, and all your changes will be updated on the sheets.

Figure 28-44

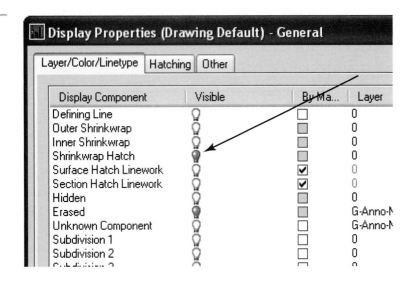

Modifying the 3D Model: Adding the Upper Roof

1. Change to the **Constructs** tab.

2. In the **Constructs** tab, double-click on the **SECOND FLOOR** construct to bring it up in the Drawing Editor.

3. In the **SECOND FLOOR** construct, select the left wall, and drag it to the right 6'-0" (see Figure 28–45). (*Hint*: Stretch the wall from the middle box grip.)

Figure 28–45

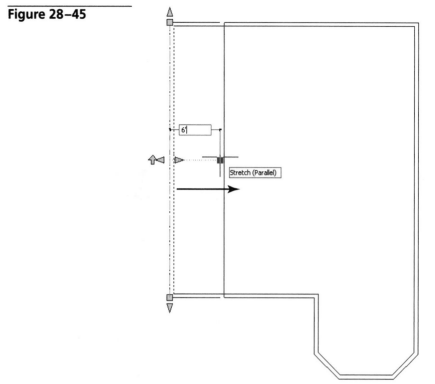

4.   Using the **PLINE** command, create the outline shown in Figure 28–46.
5.   Select the **Roof** tool from the **Design** tool palette, **RMB**, and select **Apply Tool Properties to > Linework and Walls** from the contextual menu that appears.

Figure 28–46

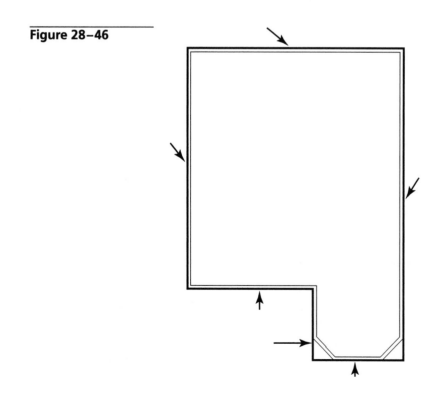

6. Select the Polyline you just created, enter **Y** (Yes) in the Command line, and press the **Enter** key to create the roof.

7. With the new roof still selected, move your cursor over the **Properties** palette to open it.

8. In the **Properties** palette change the **Edge cut** to **Plumb, Plate height** to **8'-0"**, and **Rise** to **9"**. Press the **Enter** key on the keyboard.

9. Press the **Esc** key to deselect the roof.

10. Press **Ctrl + S** on the keyboard to save the **SECOND FLOOR** construct.

11. Select **View > Refresh Sections/Elevations** from the **Main** menu to bring up the **Batch Refresh 2D Sections/Elevations** dialog box.

12. In the **Batch Refresh 2D Sections/Elevations** dialog box, select the **Current Project radio** button, and then press the **Start** button (see Figure 28–47).

Figure 28–47

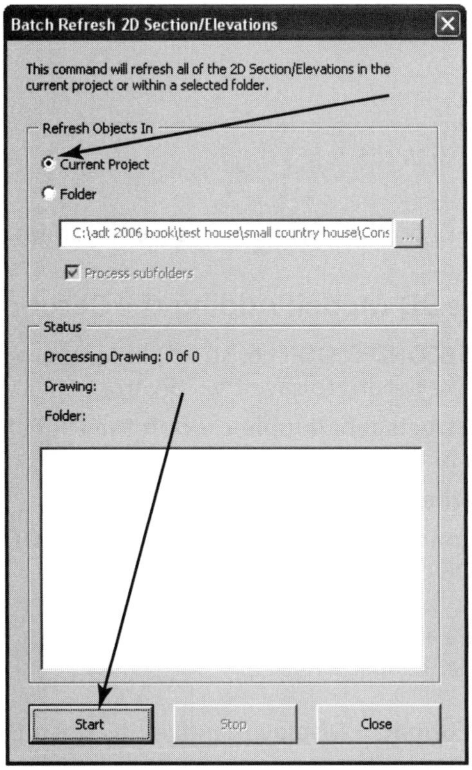

13. After the **Batch Refresh 2D Sections/Elevations** has processed the files, the **Close** button will be active; press it to close the dialog box.

14. Change to the **Sheets** tab, and double-click on the **A-102 ELEVATIONS** sheet to bring it up in the Drawing Editor.

Notice that the Roof that you placed on the **SECOND FLOOR** construct now appears on the **A-102 ELEVATIONS** sheet. Also note that the roof has been cut off. This is because the elevation views that you placed on the sheet did not anticipate the future roof. To fix this, select the blue frame around each elevation, and drag the top upward until the roof is exposed as shown in Figure 28–48.

Figure 28–48

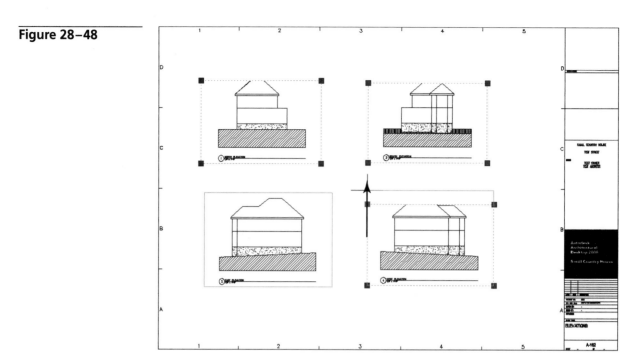

15.   Press **Ctrl + S** on the keyboard to save the sheet.

Modifying the 3D Model: Adding the Second Floor Roof

16.   Open the **SECOND FLOOR** construct, hide the roof, and then press **Ctrl + S** on the keyboard to save the construct.

17.   In the **Constructs** tab, double-click on the **FIRST FLOOR** construct to bring it up in the Drawing Editor.

18.   Change to the **Top** view.

19.   From the **Constructs** tab, drag the **SECOND FLOOR** construct into the **FIRST FLOOR** construct.

Note: Because you are on the first floor, you will not be able to see the second floor. To fix this, do the following:

    a.   Select **Format > Display Manager,** to open the **Display Manager** dialog box.

    b.   In the **Display Manager** dialog box, expand **FIRST FLOOR.dwg > Configurations > Medium Detail,** open the **Cut Plane** tab, and set the **Cut Height** to **25'-0".** (When you are through working on this drawing, change the Cut height back to 3'-6"). Press the **OK** button to return to the Drawing Editor (Figure 28–49).

20.   Using the **PLINE** command, create the outline shown in Figure 28–50.

21.   Select the **Roof** tool from the **Design** tool palette, **RMB,** and select **Apply Tool Properties to > Linework and Walls** from the contextual menu that appears.

22.   Select the Polyline you just created, enter **Y** (Yes) in the Command line, and press the **Enter** key to create the roof.

Figure 28–49

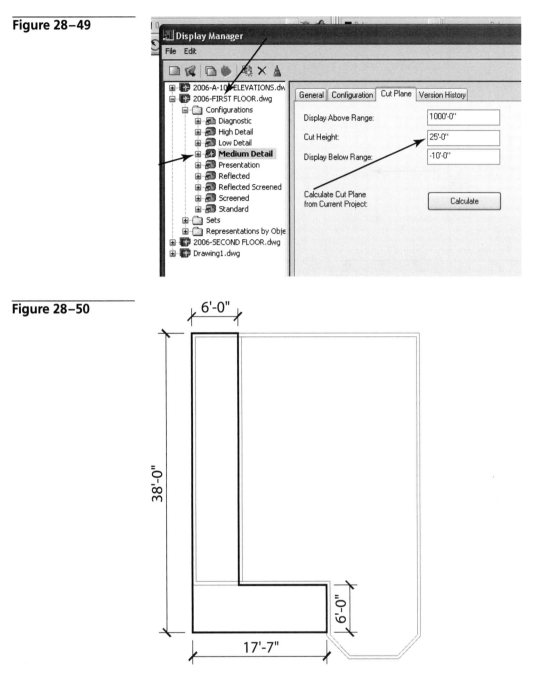

Figure 28–50

23. With the new roof still selected, move your cursor over the **Properties** palette to open it.

24. In the **Properties** palette change the **Edge cut** to **Plumb**, **Plate height** to **8'-10"**, and **Rise** to **9"**. Press the **Enter** key on the keyboard to create the roof object.

The roof object has been created as a Four-Wall roof; you will change it into a Two-Wall, Two-Way Shed roof.

25. Select the roof and drag the vertices as shown in the four steps in Figure 28–51.

26. Select the roof, **RMB,** and select **Edit Edges/Faces** from the contextual menu.

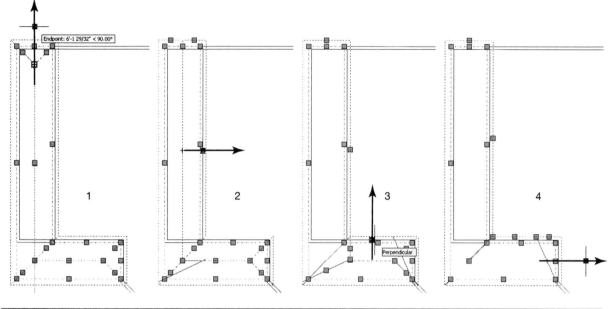

Figure 28–51

27. Select the roof edge shown in Figure 28–52, and press the **Enter** key to bring up the **Roof Edges and Faces** dialog box. In the **Roof Edges and Faces** dialog box, enter **0″** in the **Overhang** field, and press the **Enter** key.

Figure 28–52

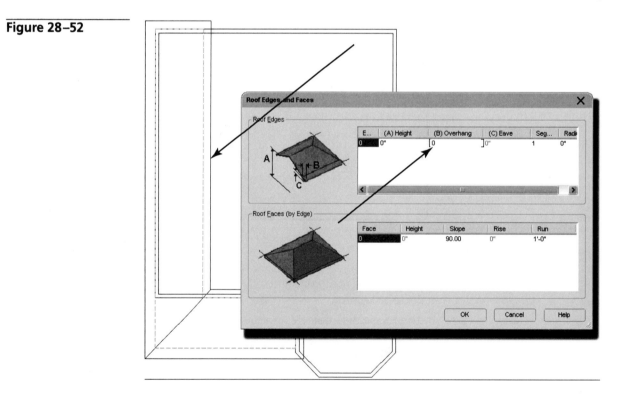

28. Repeat Step 27 for all the remaining edges that meet the second floor.
29. Press **Ctrl + S** on the keyboard to save this drawing.
30. Open the **SECOND FLOOR** construct.
31. In the **SECOND FLOOR** construct, unhide the roof and save the drawing.

Save all the Sheets: **RMB** on SMALL COUNTRY HOUSE at the top of the
Sheets tab and select **Resave All Sheets** from the contextual menu. This
refreshes all the links (see Figure 28–53).

Figure 28–53

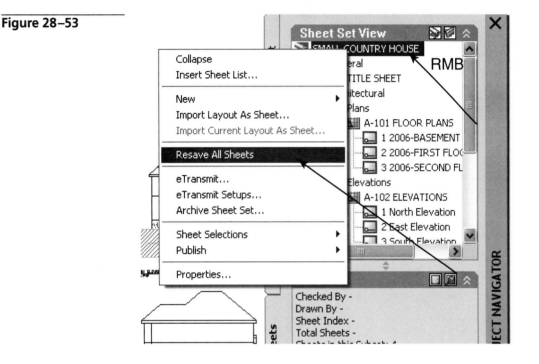

Modifying the 3D Model: Adding Windows

1. In the **Constructs** tab, double-click the **BASEMENT** to bring it up in the
   Drawing Editor.
2. Change to the **Top** view.
3. From the Design tool palette, place a 3′ × 3′ Awning window in the
   center of each from wall as shown in Figure 28–54. Select all the placed
   windows, and change their **Sill height** to **3′-8″** in the **Properties** palette.

Figure 28–54

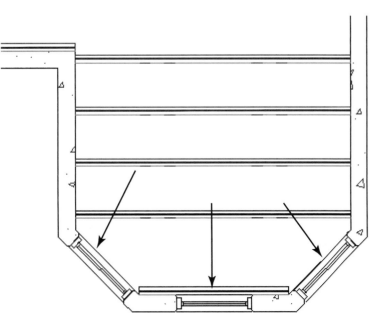

! **Note:** Can't see the windows in plan view? If you don't see the windows, the **Cut Plane** for the wall is too low. To fix this, select a typical wall, **RMB,** and select **Edit Wall Style** from the contextual menu to bring up the **Wall Style Properties** dialog box. In the **Wall Style Properties** dialog box, change to the **Display Properties** tab. In the **Display Properties** tab, double-click on **plan** to bring up the **Display Properties** dialog box. Here, set the **Cut Plane Height** to **6'-0"** then press the **OK** buttons to close the dialog boxes.

4. Press **Ctrl + S** on the keyboard to save the **BASEMENT** construct.
5. In the **Constructs** tab, double-click the **FIRST FLOOR construct** to bring it up in the Drawing Editor.
6. Place doors and windows as shown in Figure 28–55.

Figure 28–55

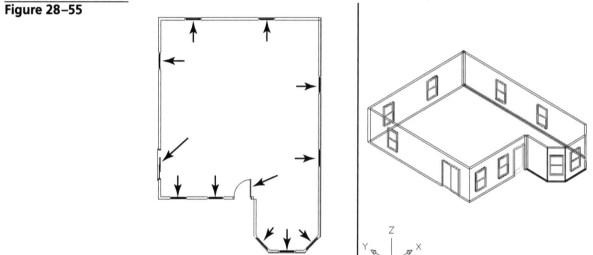

7. Press **Ctrl + S** on the keyboard to save the **FIRST FLOOR** construct.
8. In the **Constructs** tab, double-click the **SECOND FLOOR construct** to bring it up in the Drawing Editor.
9. Place doors and windows as shown in Figure 28–56. Make the windows in the three angled walls in the right front 3' × 5'-high double-hung windows.

Figure 28–56

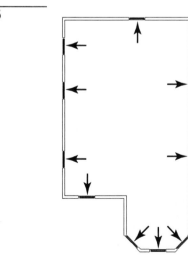
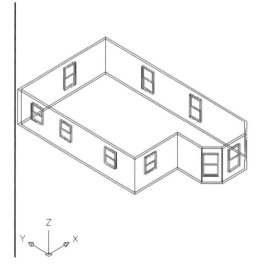

10. Be sure you are in the **Top** view, Select the three angled walls in the right front of the **SECOND FLOOR** construct, **RMB,** and select **Isolate Objects > Edit in Elevation** from the contextual menu that appears.

11. Click to place a reference line, drag your cursor upward to enclose the three windows, and then click again to bring the windows into elevation view (see Figure 28–57).

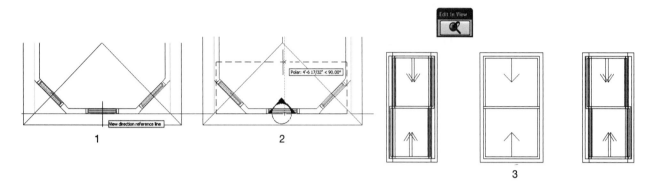

Figure 28–57

12. Click the center window, **RMB,** and select **Add Profile** from the contextual menu to bring up the **Add Window Profile** dialog box.

13. In the **Add Window Profile** dialog box, leave the **Profile Definition** as **Start from scratch,** enter **CURVED TOP WINDOW** as the **New Profile Name,** and press the **OK** button.

The blue hatch will now appear on the window.

14. Drag the top center vertice of the blue hatch upward, press the **Ctrl** key on your keyboard twice to create an arc, enter **9** on the keyboard, and press the **Enter** key (see Figure 28–58).

15. Press the **Save All Changes** icon in the **In-Place Edit** dialog box to finish the routine and modify the window.

Figure 28–58

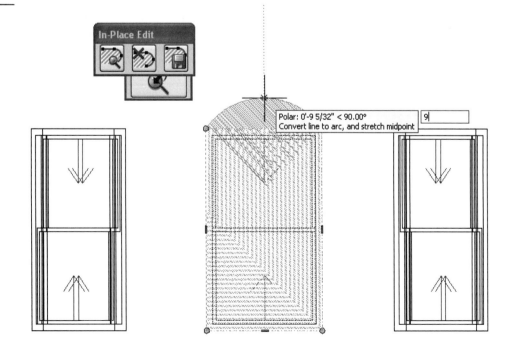

The other windows will change but will not be as high. To fix this:

16. Select all three windows, and move your cursor over the **Properties** palette to open it.

17. In the **Properties** palette enter **5'-0"** in the **Height** field, set **Vertical alignment** to **Sill** and **Sill height** to **1'-8",** and then press the **Enter** key to change all the windows.

18. Click the **Edit In View** icon to return to the **Top** view.

19. From the **Constructs** tab, drag the **FIRST FLOOR construct** into the **SECOND FLOOR** construct.

20. Again, using **Isolate Objects > Edit In Elevation**, elevate the left side of the house.

21. Select the side windows, and move your cursor over the **Properties** palette to open it.

22. In the **Properties** palette enter **3'-8"** in the **Height** field, set **Vertical alignment** to **Sill** and **Sill height** to **3'-0",** and then press the **Enter** key to change all the windows (see Figure 28–59).

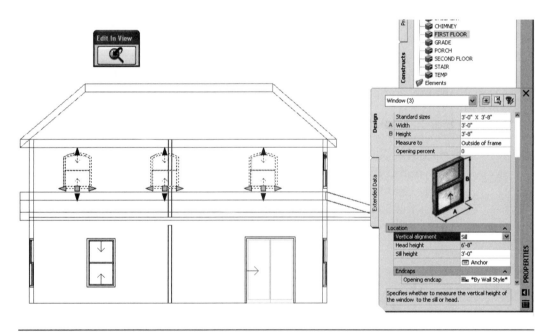

Figure 28–59

23. Click the **Edit In View** icon to return to the Top view.

24. Detach the **FIRST FLOOR** construct, and press **Ctrl + S** on the keyboard to save the **SECOND FLOOR** construct.

Modifying the 3D Model: Creating the Porches, Exterior Steps, and Railings

1. In the **Constructs** tab, create a new construct named **PORCH,** and set its level to **FIRST FLOOR.**

2. Double-click on the **PORCH** construct to bring it up in the Drawing Editor.

3. Change to the **Top** view

4. From the **Constructs** tab, drag the **FIRST FLOOR construct** into the **PORCH** construct.

5. Using the **Rectangle** command, place the two rectangles shown in Figure 28–60.

Figure 28–60

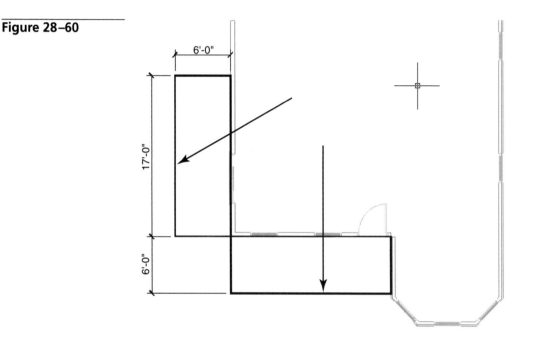

6. Select the rectangles, and move your cursor over the **Properties** palette to open it.

7. In the **Properties** palette enter **-5"** in the **Elevation** field, press the **Enter** key, and then press the **Esc** key to deselect the rectangles.

8. Select the Slab tool from the **Design** tool palette, RMB, and select **Apply Tool Properties to > Linework and Walls** from the contextual menu that appears.

9. Select the polylines you just created, enter **Y** (Yes) in the **Command** line, and press the **Enter** key.

10. Enter **D** (Direct) in the **Command** line, and press the **Enter** key.

11. Enter **B** (Bottom) in the **Command** line, and press the **Enter** key to create the new slab.

12. Select the new slabs you just created, and move your cursor over the **Properties** palette to open it.

13. In the **Properties** palette enter **-1"** in the **Thickness** field, press the **Enter** key, and then press the **Esc** key to deselect the rectangles.

14. Detach the **FIRST FLOOR** construct.

15. Select **Format > Structural members > Catalog** from the **Main** menu to bring up the **Structural Member Catalog**.

16. In the **Structural Member Catalog,** expand the **Imperial > Timber > Lumber > Nominal cut Lumber.**

17. In the right pane, double-click on **2 × 8** to bring up the **Structural member Style dialog** box.

18. In the **Structural member Style dialog** box, press the **OK** button, and close the **Structural Member Catalog** and return to the Drawing editor.

19. Select the **Structural Beam** tool from the **Design** tool palette, and move your cursor over the **Properties** palette to open it.

20. In the **Properties** palette, select the following:

   a. Style = **10in Plywood Web Wood Joist**
   b. Layout type = **Fill**
   c. Justify = **Top Left**
   d. Array = **Yes**
   e. Layout Method = **Repeat**
   f. Bay size = **2'-0"**

21. Change to the **SW** Isometric view.

22. With the **MID** Osnap on, click on the midpoint of the front edge of the left slab; repeat on the right slab (see Figure 28–61).

Figure 28–61

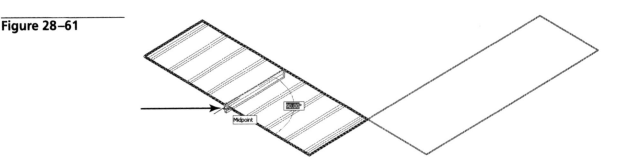

23. Select the **Structural Beam** tool, and move your cursor over the **Properties** palette to open it.

24. In the **Properties** palette, set **Layout type = Edge.**

25. Click on the all four edges of each slab to edge each slab with a **2 × 8.**

26. Change to the **Top** view.

27. Select the left front edge **2 × 8, RMB,** and select **Trim Planes > Miter** from the contextual menu that appears.

28. Select the adjacent **2 × 8** to miter the two members. Repeat for all edge members.

29. Select all the left fill members, **RMB,** and select **Trim Planes > Add Trim Plane** from the contextual menu that appears, move to the trim point (a light blue line will appear), and click to trim the fill members to the edge member. Repeat for all slabs, where fill members meet edge members (see Figure 28–62).

30. Select the **Stair** tool from the **Design** tool palette and move your cursor over the **Properties** palette to open it.

31. In the **Properties** palette, select the following:

   a. Style = **Standard**
   b. Shape = **Straight**
   c. Vertical Orientation = **Down**

Figure 28–62

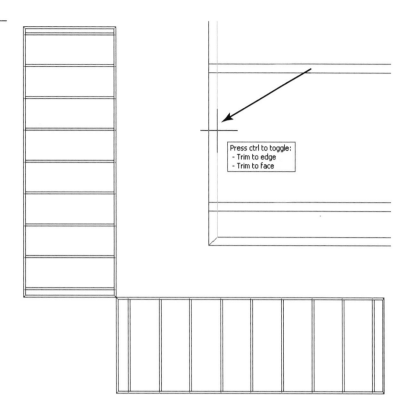

Press ctrl to toggle:
- Trim to edge
- Trim to face

    d. Width = **5′-0″**

    e. Height = **5′7**

    f. Justify = **Left**

    g. Elevation = **-4″**

32. Place a stair.

33. Select the **Replace Z value with current elevation** icon at the bottom of the screen, and set the **Elevation relative to selected level** to **-4″**

34. Select the **Content Browser** icon in the **Navigation** toolbar (or **Ctrl +4**) to open the **Content browser.**

35. From the **Design Tool catalog –Imperial > Stairs and Railings > Railings,** drag the **Guardrail-Pipe +Rod Horiz.** railing into your **Design** tool palette.

36. Select the **Railing** tool you just placed in the **Design** tool palette, and move your cursor over the **Properties** palette to open it.

37. In the **Properties** palette, select ***NONE*** from the **Attached to** drop-down list.

38. Place Railings on the two slabs.

39. Select the **Railing** tool again, and move your cursor over the **Properties** palette to open it.

40. In the **Properties** palette, select **Stair flight** from the **Attached to** drop-down list.

41. Click on both sides of the stair to place the rails.

Press **Ctrl + S** on the keyboard to save the **PORCH** construct. Figure 28–63 shows the completed porch on the COMPOSITE VIEW.

Figure 28–63

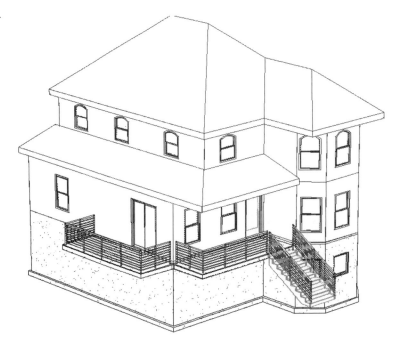

Modifying the 3D Model: Creating the Chimney

1. In the **Constructs** tab, create a new construct named **CHIMNEY,** and set its level to **BASEMENT.**
2. Double-click on the **CHIMNEY** construct to bring it up in the Drawing Editor.
3. Change to the **Top** view.
4. From the **Constructs** tab, drag the **FIRST FLOOR construct** into the **CHIMNEY** construct.

! **Note:** Because you are working in the **BASEMENT LEVEL,** you must change the **Display Configuration Cut Plane** to be able to see the first-floor walls.

5. Using the **Rectangle** command create a **2'-6 × 6'-0"** rectangle and place it as shown in Figure 28–64.
6. Select the rectangle, move your cursor over the **Properties** palette to open it, and set the **Elevation** to **0".**
7. Select the rectangle, **RMB,** and select **Convert To > Mass Element** from the contextual menu that appears.
8. Enter **Y** (Yes) in the Command line, and press the **Enter** key on your keyboard.
9. Enter **36'-10"** in the Command line (for the extrusion height), and press the **Enter** key on your keyboard.
10. Detach the **FIRST FLOOR** construct, and change to the **Front** view.
11. On the mass element you just created, create the closed polylines shown in Figure 28–65.
12. On the mass element you just created, create the closed polylines shown in Figure 28–65.

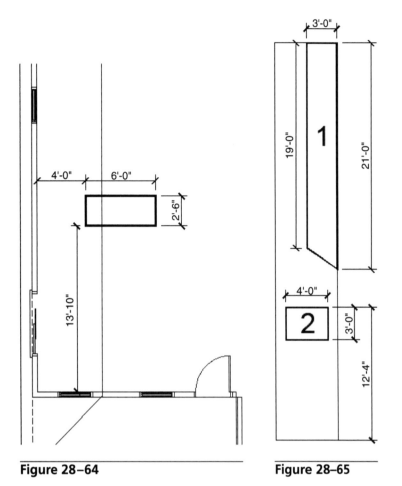

Figure 28–64   **Figure 28–65**

13. Convert the closed polygons you just created to mass elements. Make the extrusion height for polyline 1 **(-2'-6")**, and polyline 2 **(-1'- 6). This will extrude the mass elements in the negative direction.**

14. Select the first mass element you created in Step 7, **RMB,** and select **Boolean > Subtract** from the contextual menu that appears.

15. Select the new mass elements you created in Step 12, and press the **Enter** key on your keyboard.

16. Enter **Y** (Yes) in the command line, and press the **Enter** key on your keyboard (see Figure 28–66).

17. Refer back to Section 1 on Mass Elements.

18. Select the mass element you have created, **RMB,** and select **Split Face** from the contextual menu that appears.

19. Following the commands, pick points on all the faces 1'-8" below the top to split the mass element.

20. Click on a face, to show the edit dots. Select the dot, drag outwards, press the **Ctrl** key twice, enter **4"** in the Command line, and press the **Enter** key on your keyboard.

21. Repeat for all the faces, and then repeat Steps 18–20, dragging inward to complete the chimney cap (see Figure 28–67).

Press **Ctrl + S** on the keyboard to save the **CHIMNEY** construct.

Figure 28–66

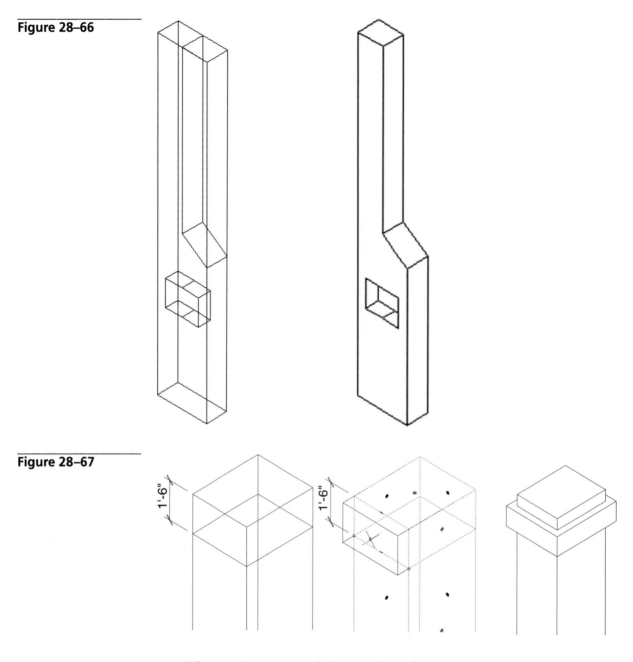

Figure 28–67

Modifying the 3D Model: Creating the Interior Stairs

1.   In the **Constructs** tab, create a new construct named **BASEMENT STAIR,** and set its level to **BASEMENT.**
2.   Double-click on the **BASEMENT STAIR** construct to bring it up in the Drawing Editor.
3.   Drag the **BASEMENT** construct into the **BASEMENT STAIR** construct.
4.   Select the **Stair** tool from the **Design** tool palette and move your cursor over the **Properties** palette to open it.
5.   In the **Properties** palette, select the following:

        Style = **Standard**
        Shape = **Straight**

Vertical Orientation = **Up**
Width = **3'-0"**
Height = **8'-10"**
Justify = **Left**
Elevation = 0"

6. Place the stair as shown in Figure 28–68.
7. Detach the **BASEMENT** construct.

Figure 28–68

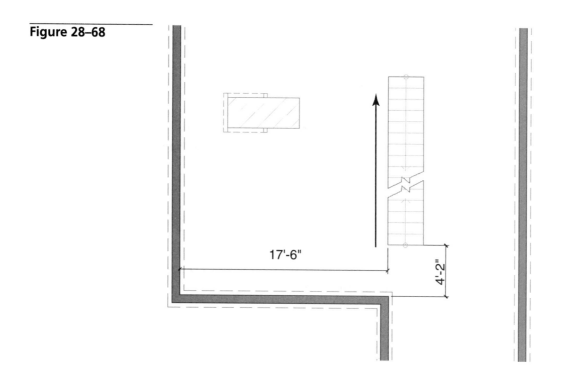

17'-6"

4'-2"

The basement stair should show that the stair goes up only. Do the following:

8. Select the stair, **RMB,** and select **Edit Object Display** from the contextual menu to bring up the **Object Display** dialog box.
9. In the **Object Display** dialog box, check the **Object Override** check box for the **Plan Display Representation** to bring up the **Display Properties** dialog box.
10. In the **Display Properties** dialog box, select the **Other** tab.
11. In the **Other** tab, set the **Cut Plane Elevation** to 3'-6", and then change to the **Layer/Color/Linetype** tab.
12. In the **Layer/Color/Linetype** tab, turn off the visibility of the **Riser down, Nosing down, Path down,** and **Outline down.** Finally, press the **OK** buttons to return to the Drawing Editor.
13. Press **Ctrl + S** on the keyboard to save the **BASEMENT STAIR** construct (see Figure 28–69).
14. In the **Constructs** tab, select the **BASEMENT STAIR** construct, **RMB,** and select **Copy Construct to Levels** to bring up the **Copy Construct to Levels** dialog box.

Figure 28–69

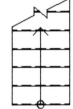

15. In the **Copy Construct to Levels** dialog box, check the **FIRST FLOOR** check box to create a new stair construct, and press the **OK** button to return to the Drawing Editor.

16. In the **Constructs** tab, rename the new construct you just created to **STAIR (FIRST FLOOR).**

17. Double-click on the **STAIR (FIRST FLOOR)** construct to bring it up in the Drawing Editor.

18. Select the stair, **RMB,** and select **Edit Object Display** from the contextual menu to bring up the **Object Display** dialog box.

19. In the **Object Display** dialog box, double-click **Plan** to bring up the **Display Properties** dialog box.

20. In the **Display Properties** dialog box, select the **layer/Color/Linetype** tab.

21. In the **Layer/Color/Linetype** tab, turn on the visibility of the **Riser down, Nosing down, Path down,** and **Outline down.** Finally, press the **OK** buttons to return to the Drawing Editor.

22. Press **Ctrl + S** on the keyboard to save the **STAIR (FIRST FLOOR)** construct (see Figure 28–70).

Figure 28–70

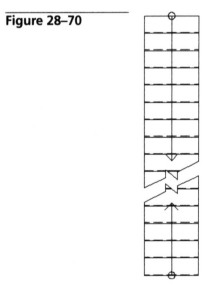

23. In the **Constructs** tab, select the **STAIR (FIRST FLOOR)** construct, **RMB,** and select **Copy Construct to Levels** to bring up the **Copy Construct to Levels** dialog box.

24. In the **Copy Construct to Levels** dialog box, check the **SECOND FLOOR** check box to create a new stair construct, and press the **OK** button to return to the Drawing Editor.

25. In the **Constructs** tab, rename the new construct you just created to **STAIR (SECOND FLOOR).**

26. Select the stair, **RMB,** and select **Edit Object Display** from the contextual menu to bring up the **Object Display** dialog box.

27. In the **Object Display** dialog box, double-click **Plan** to bring up the **Display Properties** dialog box.

28. In the **Display Properties** dialog box, select the **Other** tab.

29. In the **Other** tab, set the **Cut Plane Elevation** to 10′-6″, and then change to the **Layer/Color/Linetype** tab.

30. In the **Layer/Color/Linetype** tab, turn on only the visibility of the **Riser up, Nosing up,** and **Outline up.** Finally, press the **OK** button to return to the **Object Display** dialog box.

> **!** **Note:** Although you will want the stair to show in the second-floor plan view, you will not want it to show in the model view.

31. In the **Object Display** dialog box, double-click **Model** to bring up the **Display Properties** dialog box.

32. In the **Display Properties** dialog box, turn off the visibility of the **Stringer, Tread, landing,** and **Riser,** and then press the **OK** buttons to return to the Drawing Editor.

33. Press **Ctrl + S** on the keyboard to save the **STAIR (SECOND FLOOR)** construct (see Figure 28–71).

Figure 28–71

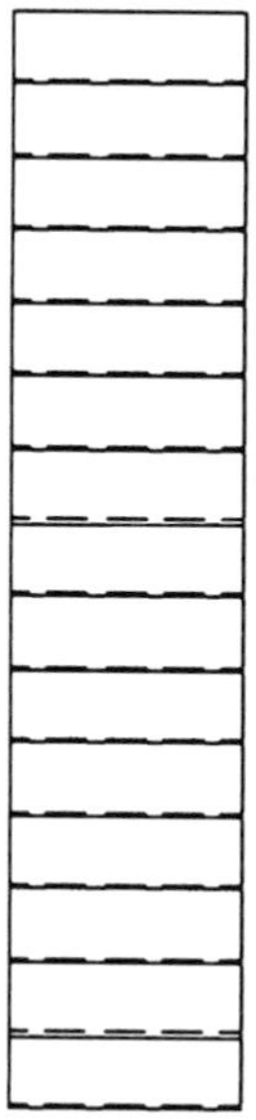

Modifying the 3D Model: Creating the Bathrooms

The bathroom is an element so that it can be placed on both floors.

1. In the **Constructs** tab, select the **Add Element** icon at the bottom of the tab, and create a new element called **BATHROOM.**

2. In the **Constructs** tab, double-click on the **BATHROOM** element you just created to bring it up in the Drawing Editor.

3. Using the **Wall** tool from the **Design** tool palette create an **8′-8″ × 5′-9″** enclosure **8′-0″** high with **4-1/2″**-thick walls.

4. Select the **Content Browser** icon or press **Ctrl + 4** on the keyboard to bring up the **Content Browser.**

5. In the Content browser, select **Design Tool Catalog - Imperial** > **Mechanical** > **Plumbing Fixtures** > **Toilet**, and drag the **Tank 2** toilet into your enclosure.

6. In the **Design Tool Catalog - Imperial** > **Mechanical** > **Plumbing Fixtures** > **Lavatory** > **Page 3;** drag the **Vanity** into your enclosure. (When you drag the lavatory into the Drawing Editor, notice that there are options on the **Command line.** By pressing **choosing B** (Base point) and pressing the **Enter** key, you can cycle through placement points on the object).

7. In the **Design Tool Catalog - Imperial** > **Mechanical** > **Plumbing Fixtures** > **Lavatory** > **Page 3;** drag the **Tub 30x60** into your enclosure.

8. Press **Ctrl + S** on the keyboard to save the **BATHROOM** element (see Figure 28–72).

Figure 28–72

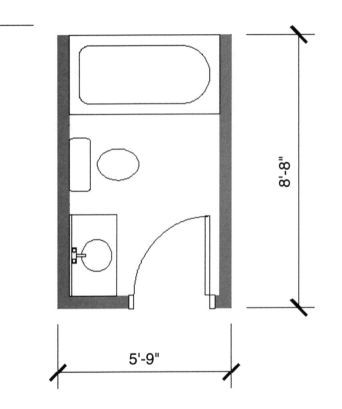

9. In the **Constructs** tab double-click on the **FIRST FLOOR** construct to bring it up in the Drawing Editor.

10. From the **Constructs** tab, drag the **BATHROOM** element into the **FIRST FLOOR** construct.

! **Note:** You may have to **Zoom Extents** after dragging the **BATHROOM** element into the **FIRST FLOOR** construct to locate it because the **BATHROOM** element may not yet be located inside the building.

11. Repeat, placing the **BATHROOM** element in the **SECOND FLOOR** construct, and then save the **FIRST FLOOR** and **SECOND FLOOR** constructs (see Figure 28–73).

Figure 28–73

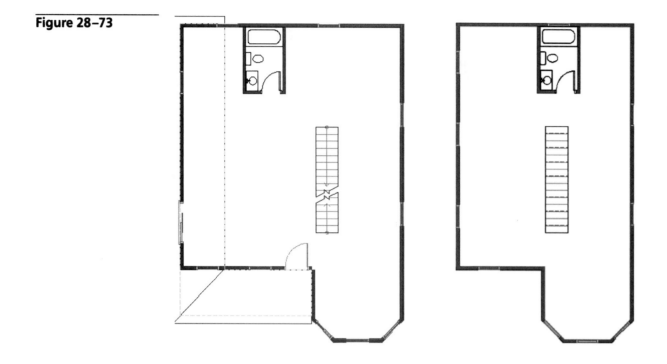

! **Note:** Walls can clean up across **Xrefs.** This is a property of wall cleanup group definitions. Go to **Format > Style Manager > Architectural Objects > Wall Cleanup Group Definition.** In the **Design Rules** tab, there is a check box to allow cleanups between a **Host** and an **XREF.**

Modifying the 3D Model: Placing Materials on the Exterior

1. In the **Constructs** tab double-click on the **FIRST FLOOR** construct to bring it up in the Drawing Editor.
2. Change to the **SW Isometric** view.
3. Select the **Content Browser** icon or press **Ctrl + 4** on the keyboard to bring up the **Content Browser.**
4. In the Content browser, select **Render Material Catalog > Thermal & Moisture.Roofing & Siding Panels** and drag the **Panels.Wood. Horizontal.White** material into your **Project Tools** tool palette (see Figure 28–74).
5. In the **Project Tools** tool palette, select the **Panels.Wood.horizontal. White material** icon, **RMB,** and select **Convert to AEC Material** from the contextual menu to bring up the **Create AEC Material** dialog box.
6. In the **Create AEC Material** dialog box, enter **WOOD SIDING** in the **New AEC Material Name** field, and press the **OK** button (see Figure 28–75).

! **Note:** You will now get an AutoCAD warning to save the drawing. Press the **OK** button and save the drawing.

7. Select the **Panels.Wood.Horizontal.White material** icon, **RMB,** and select **Apply Tool Properties to Object** from the contextual menu that appears.

Figure 28-74

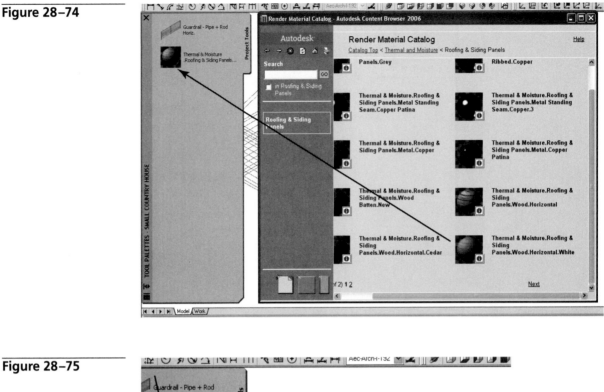

Figure 28-75

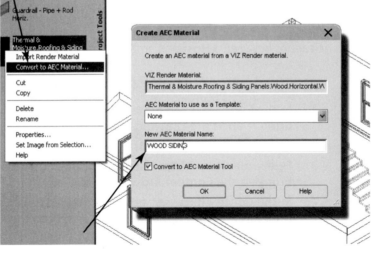

8. Pick one of the exterior walls to bring up the **Apply Material to Components** dialog box.

9. In the **Apply Material to Components** dialog box, select **Object Override** as shown in Figure 28-76, and press the **OK** button to return to the Drawing Editor.

10. Pick the left exterior wall to apply the material.

! **Note:** Because we used the Standard style for the exterior walls as well as the **BATHROOM** walls, applying this material to a Style would apply it to the **BATHROOM** as well as the exterior walls. If you had created a custom wall with components, you would have been able to assign this material to just the exterior component.

Figure 28-76

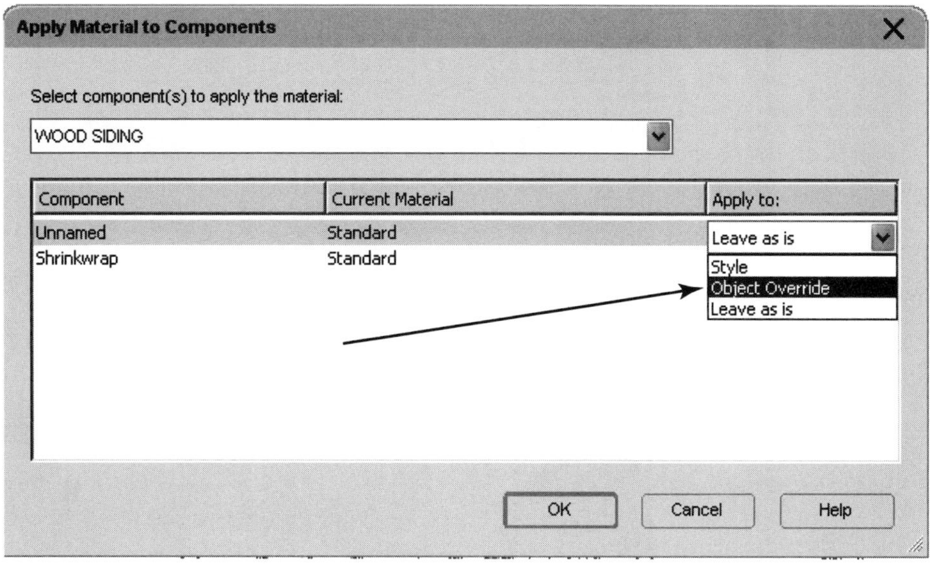

11. Repeat applying the SIDING material to all the exterior walls.
12. Return to the **Spanish.Red.1** material in your **Project Tools** tool palette.
13. Convert the **Spanish.Red.1** material to an AEC material, and place it on the Porch Roof.
14. Press **Ctrl + S** on the keyboard to save the **FIRST FLOOR** construct.
15. Select the **SECOND FLOOR** construct, and apply materials to its walls and roof.
16. Press **Ctrl + S** on the keyboard to save the **SECOND FLOOR** construct.

Rendering the Model

1. Change to the **Views** tab in the **Project Navigator.**
2. Double-click the **COMPOSITE** view to bring it up in the Drawing Editor.
3. In the **COMPOSITE** view, **Isolate > hide** all the sections and elevations, and all the section and elevation marks.
4. Select the **Open Menu** icon at the lower left of the Drawing Editor, and select **Link to VIZ Render** from the contextual menu that appears.

VIZ Render will now start, and the complete building will appear in that program.

5. In **VIZ Render**, press the **Minimize Viewport** icon to divide the screen into four viewports.
6. In **VIZ Render**, select **Create > Daylight System** from the **Main** menu.
7. Click in the **Top** viewport to place the daylight symbol, move to the **Front** viewport, click and drag upward to place the daylight object in the sky above the house, and then click again to complete the command (see Figure 28-77).
7. Select the Perspective viewport, and press **C** on your keyboard to bring up the **Select Camera** dialog box.
8. In the **Select Camera** dialog box, select **Camera: Perspective**, and press the **OK** button to change the Perspective viewport to the **Camera: Perspective** viewport.

Figure 28–77

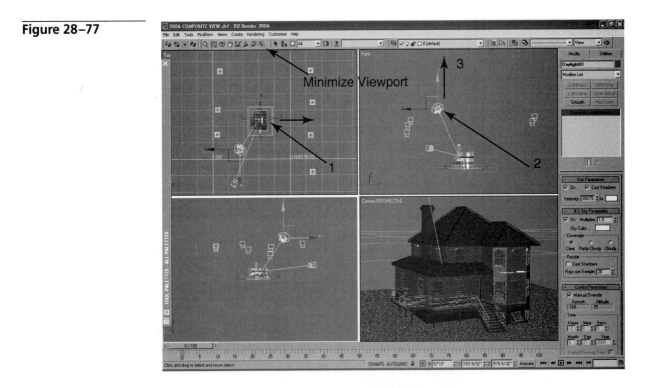

9. Use the **Orbit Camera, Truck Mode, and Dolly Camera** icons from the **Viewport navigation Tools** toolbar, to adjust the scene (see Figure 28–78).

10. Select **Rendering > Radiosity** from the **Main** menu to bring up the **Render Scene: Photorealistic Renderer** dialog box.

Figure 28–78

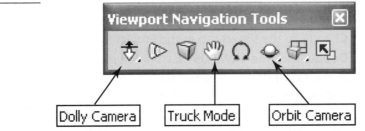

11. In the **Render Scene: Photorealistic Renderer** dialog box, select **Quality-Exterior** from the **Preset** drop-down list to bring up the **Select Preset Categories** dialog box.

12. In the **Select Preset Categories** dialog box, select Radiosity, and press the Load button. If the **Change Advanced Lighting Plug-in** warning appears, press the **Yes** button.

13. Make sure the **Camera: Perspective** viewport is selected, and press the **Start** button at the top of the **Render Scene: Photorealistic Renderer** dialog box (see Figure 28–79).

This will cause **VIZ Render** to calculate a Radiosity solution. When it is finished, the **Start** button will be replaced by a **Continue** button. For **Quality-Exterior,** this may take 20 minutes on a fast computer. When the solution has been created, press the **Render** button at the bottom right of the **Render Scene: Photorealistic Renderer** dialog box to create the final rendering.

Figure 28-79

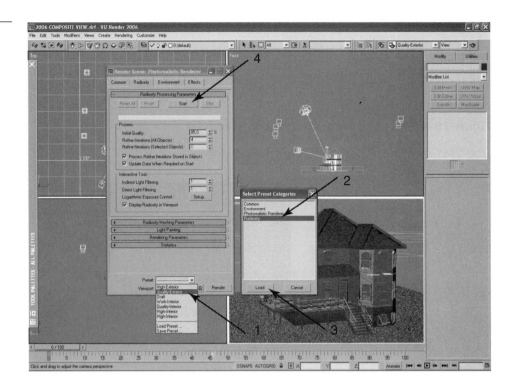

14. After the rendering has been created, press the **Save Bitmap** icon to bring up the **Browse Images for Output** dialog box. In this dialog box, name and save your rendering as **HOUSE JPG,** and select **JPEG** from the **Type** drop-down list (see Figure 28–80).

Figure 28-80

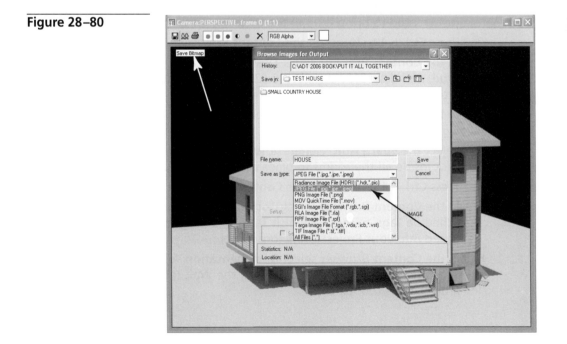

15. Finally, open your **TITLE** sheet, select **Insert** > **Image** from the **Main** menu, and browse and get the rendering you just made.

16. Click in the Drawing Editor, and place the image (see Figure 28–81).

Figure 28–81

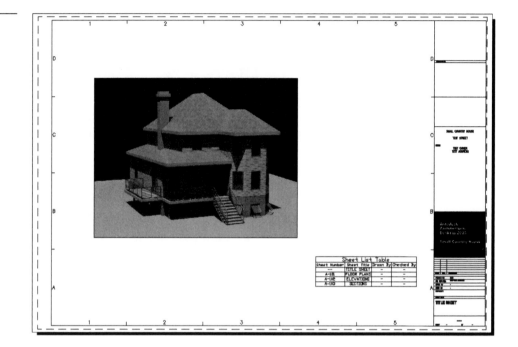

Placing Room Numbers, Interior Doors, and Door Numbers

1. In the **Constructs** tab, double-click on the **FIRST FLOOR** construct you just created to bring it up in the Drawing Editor.

2. Press **Ctrl + 4** to bring up the **Content Browser.**

3. In the **Content Browser** select **Design Tool Catalog- Imperial** > **Walls** > **Stud,** and drag **Stud-2.5 GWB-0.625 Each Side** and **Stud-2.5 Brick-4** walls into your **Project Tools** tool palette.

4. In the **FIRST FLOOR** construct, insert walls and doors shown in Figure 28–82.

5. Select the **Space Auto Generate Tool** from the **Design** tool palette, and click inside all the rooms to place spaces (see Figure 28–83).

6. Press **Ctrl + 4** to bring up the **Content Browser.**

7. In the **Content Browser** select **Documentation Tool Catalog- Imperial** > **Schedule Tags** > **Room & Finish Tags,** and drag the **Room Tag - Project Based** into your **Project Tools** tool palette.

8. In the **Content Browser** select **Documentation Tool Catalog- Imperial** > **Schedule Tags** > **Wall Tags,** and drag the **Wall Tag (Leader)** into your **Project Tools** tool palette.

Figure 28–82

Figure 28–83

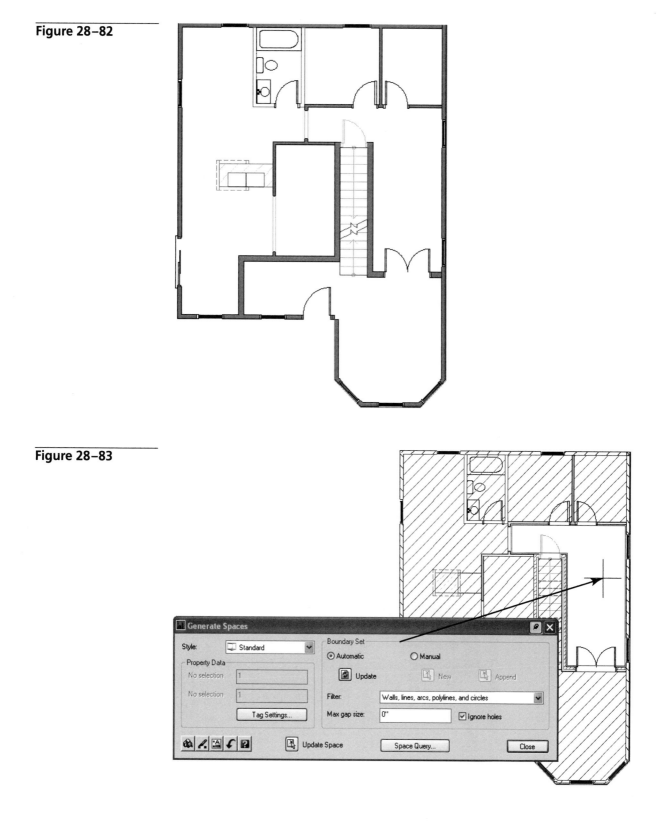

9. In the **Content Browser** select **Documentation Tool Catalog- Imperial >
    Schedule Tags > Door & Window Tags**, and drag the **Door Tag - Project
    Based**, and **Window Tag** into your **Project Tools** tool palette (see
    Figure 28–84).

Figure 28–84

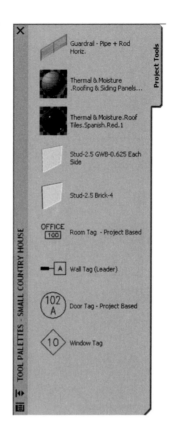

10. Select the room tag you just placed in the **Project Tools** tool palette, and click on the lower-right space to bring up the **Edit Property Set Data** dialog box.

11. Expand the **Edit Property Set Data** dialog box, and notice all the information about that space.

12. In the **Edit Property Set Data** dialog box, press the **OK** button to place the room tag (see Figure 28–85).

Figure 28–85

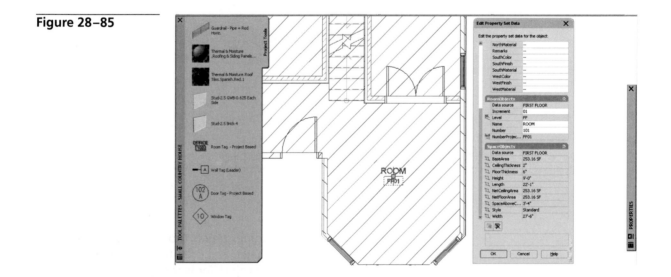

Notice that the room number includes an **FF.** That stands for **FIRST FLOOR,** and corresponds to the **ID** that you placed in the **Levels** dialog box at the beginning of this project (see Figure 28–86).

Figure 28–86

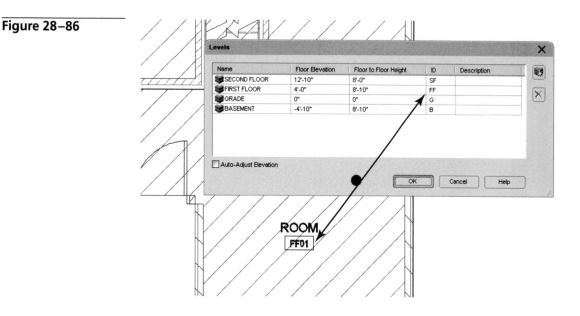

13. Continue to tag the other rooms, giving them each a different name when the **Edit Property Set Data** dialog box appears. (You can also use the **Multiple** option to speed up this procedure.)

14. Now place the door tags. Notice that the door tags include the number of the space adjacent to that door.

15. In the **Layer Manager,** turn off the visibility of the **A-Area-Space** layer.

16. Tag the windows with the window tag.

17. Tag the walls, and notice that they contain two dashes in the tag field. This is because a type has not been set for those walls.

18. To set a type, select **Format > Style Manager** to bring up the **Style Manager.**

19. In the **Style Manager,** select **FIRST FLOOR.dwg > Architectural Objects > Wall Styles > Stud-2.5 GWB- 0.625 Each Side.**

20. In the **Stud-2.5 Brick-4** wall style, select the **General** tab.

21. In the **General** tab, press the **Property Sets** button to bring up the **Edit Property Set Data** dialog box.

22. In the **Edit Property Set Data** dialog box, enter **A** in the **Type** field, and press the **OK** buttons to return to the Drawing Editor.

23. Repeat the previous steps for the **Stud-2.5 GWB- 0.625 Each Side** wall style, enter **B** in the **Type** field, and press the **OK** buttons to return to the Drawing Editor (see Figure 28–87).

24. Press **Ctrl + S** on the keyboard to save the **FIRST FLOOR** construct.

25. Install walls and doors and annotation to complete the **BASEMENT** and **SECOND FLOOR** constructs.

Figure 28–87

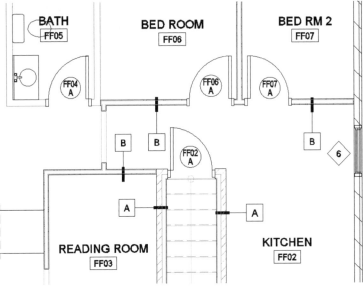

Creating the Door Schedules

1. In the **Sheets** tab, double-click on the **TITLE SHEET** sheet.

2. Change to the **Document** tool palettes, and select the **Scheduling** tab.

3. In the **Scheduling** tab, select the **Door Schedule Project Based** icon, **RMB**, and select Schedule Table Styles from the contextual menu to bring up the **Style Manager.**

4. In the **Style Manager**, select the **Door Schedule Project Based** style, **RMB,** and copy and paste a copy of the **Door Schedule Project Based** style. This will create **Door Schedule Project Based (2).**

5. Select **Schedule Project Based (2),** and change to the **Columns** tab.

6. Delete all the columns except those shown in Figure 28–88.

Figure 28–88

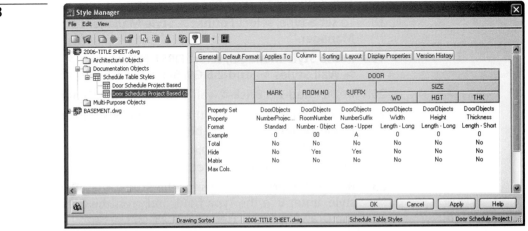

7. Press the **OK** button to return to the Drawing Editor.

8. In the **Scheduling** tab, select the **Door Schedule Project Based** icon, and move your cursor over the **Properties** palette to open it.

9. In the **Properties** palette, select **Door Schedule Project Based (2)** from the Style drop-down list.

10. Click in the **TITLE** sheet, and press the **Enter** key on your keyboard.

11. Double-click on the door schedule you just placed, to open the **Properties** palette.

12. In the **Properties** palette, under **ADVANCED**, select **Yes** from the **Schedule external drawing** drop-down list, and browse for the **FIRST FLOOR VIEW.dwg** in the **External drawing** drop-down list (see Figure 28–89).

Figure 28–89

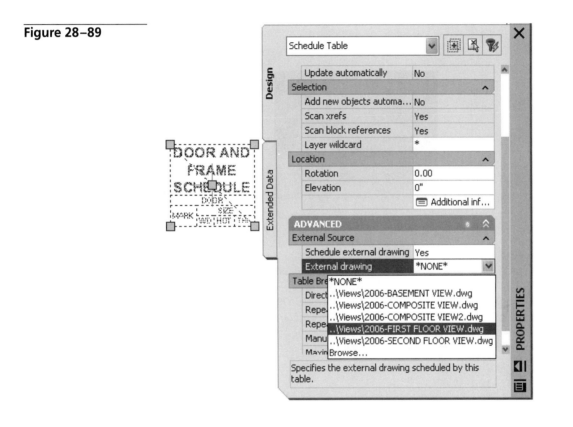

13. Select the door schedule you placed, RMB, and select Update Schedule table from the contextual menu that appears. The table will now contain the marks, and sizes for all the doors on the **FIRST FLOOR VIEW** (see Figure 28–90).

Note: You will have to have a separate door schedule for each floor, so be sure to change the title of the schedule to reflect the floor it is referencing.

This is as far as we go; the rest is up to you. Remember to make new Constructs, Views, and Sheets. Once you have the methodology down, the system is really quite straightforward (see Figures 28–91 through 28–95).

Figure 28–90

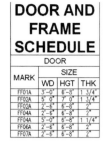

DOOR AND FRAME SCHEDULE			
DOOR			
MARK	SIZE		
	WD	HGT	THK
FF01A	3'–0"	6'–8"	1 3/4"
FF02A	5' 0"	7' 0"	1 3/4"
FF02A	2'–6"	6'–8"	2"
FF04A	2'–6"	6'–8"	2"
FF04A	5'–0"	6'–8"	1 1/4"
FF06A	2'–6"	6'–8"	2"
FF07A	2'–6"	6'–8"	2"

Figure 28–91

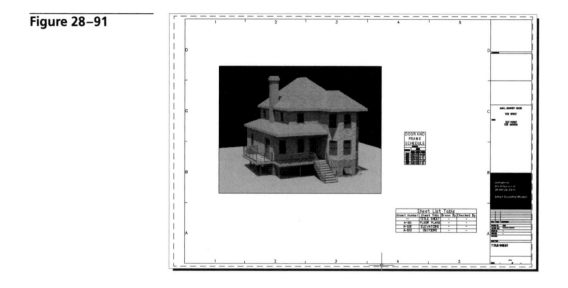

Figure 28–92

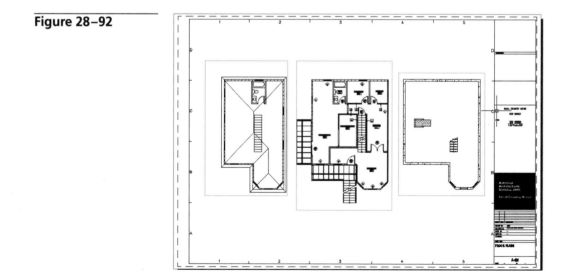

Figure 28-93

Figure 28-94

Figure 28-95

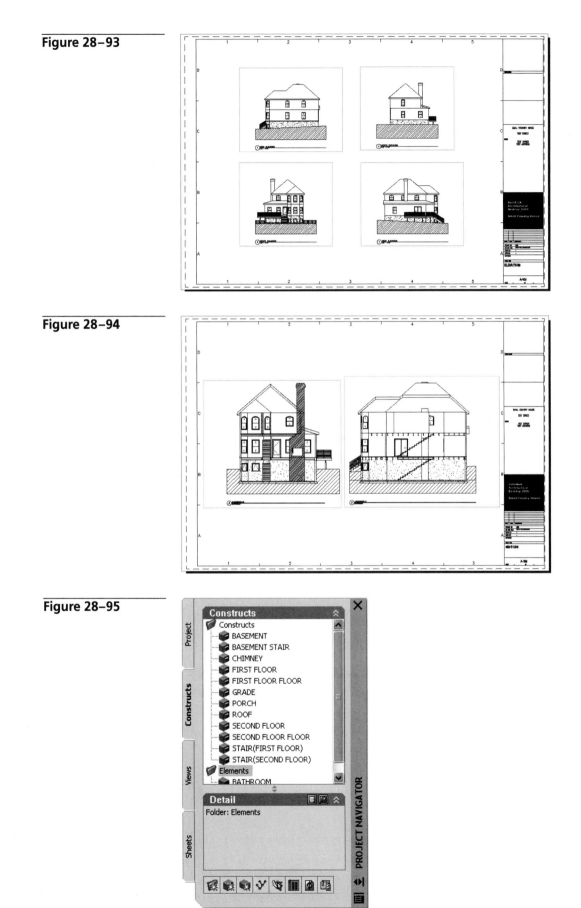

Index

Page numbers followed by f indicate figure.